Filming Modernity and Islam in Colonial Egypt

To the joy makers on the Nile

Many thanks,
Heba Arafa Abdelfattah

Filming Modernity and Islam in Colonial Egypt

Heba Arafa Abdelfattah

EDINBURGH
University Press

Edinburgh University Press is one of the leading university presses in the UK. We publish academic books and journals in our selected subject areas across the humanities and social sciences, combining cutting-edge scholarship with high editorial and production values to produce academic works of lasting importance. For more information visit our website: edinburghuniversitypress.com

© Heba Arafa Abdelfattah, 2023, 2025

Edinburgh University Press Ltd
13 Infirmary Street,
Edinburgh, EH1 1LT

First published in hardback by Edinburgh University Press 2023

Typeset in 11/1pt5 EB Garamond by
Cheshire Typesetting Ltd, Cuddington, Cheshire

A CIP record for this book is available from the British Library

ISBN 978 1 3995 2075 1 (hardback)
ISBN 978 1 3995 2076 8 (paperback)
ISBN 978 1 3995 2077 5 (webready PDF)
ISBN 978 1 3995 2078 2 (epub)

The right of Heba Arafa Abdelfattah to be identified as author of this work has been asserted in accordance with the Copyright, Designs and Patents Act 1988 and the Copyright and Related Rights Regulations 2003 (SI No. 2498).

Contents

List of Figures	vi
Acknowledgments	xi
Note on Transliteration	xiii
Preface	xiv
1 Introduction: Basic Concepts	1
2 Regulating the Amour-propre of the Colonized	80
3 Protecting the Amour-propre of Islam	147
4 Caricaturing Dominant Modernity (*Tafarnug*)	198
5 Lampooning Residual Modernity (*Ta'ssul*)	274
6 Celebrating Emergent Modernity (*Asala*)	346
Bibliography	436
Index	454

Figures

1.1	Actress 'Aziza Amir dressed as a car mechanic	4
1.2	A still from the film *Malik al-Bitrul*	4
1.3	Solidarity between the *khawagat* and *awlad al-balad*	6
1.4	A collage of Muhammad Karim as a young actor	15
1.5	Muhammad Karim in *al-Ithnayn* magazine	16
1.6	The alliance between autocratic rule and religious despotism	33
1.7	The subjugation of the peasant by state autocracy	35
1.8	Gazing at the peasant's body as a commodity	36
1.9	Religion as an inspiration to subaltern resistance (1)	36
1.10	Religion as an inspiration to subaltern resistance (2)	37
1.11	Folk art as resistance	37
1.12	Raqiya Ibrahim as Zaynab performing ablution	41
1.13	Raqiya Ibrahim as Zaynab supplicating after prayer	42
1.14	Poster of Zaynab remake in *al-Ithnayn*	43
2.1	Censorship meeting with the Minister of Social Affairs (1)	117
2.2	Censorship meeting with the Minister of Social Affairs (2)	118
2.3	Censorship meeting with the Minister of Social Affairs (3)	118
2.4	Inauguration of Nihas Studio	124
2.5	Aerial view of Nihas Studio	125
2.6	Sound recording machine in Nihas Studio	125
2.7	The camera dolly in Nihas Studio	126
2.8	Shooting in Nihas Studio	127
2.9	Actors' rooms in Nihas Studio	127
2.10	A makeup room in Nihas Studio	128
3.1	Wahbi's publicity photographs as published in *al-Masrah*	149
3.2	'Abd al-Majid Wafi adding the final strokes to his painting	155

3.3	Students of al-Azhar on stage with director Mahmud 'Uthman	170
3.4	Students from al-Azhar during rehearsals	171
3.5	A student from al-Azhar reminds actors of their lines	171
3.6	Students getting ready to appear on stage	172
3.7	Teachers at al-Azhar University attending rehearsal	172
3.8	Students acting in the play *Khalid Ibn al-Walid*	173
3.9	An Azhari student trying the piano during rehearsal	173
3.10	Poster showing the actor Ahmad Mazhar in *Zuhur al-Islam*	181
3.11	A scene from *Fath Misr*	184
4.1	Staging *tafarnug* (1)	201
4.2	Staging *tafarnug* (2)	202
4.3	*Tafarnug* blocks Isma'il's conscience	206
4.4	Trapped in *tafarnug*	206
4.5	Dad's favourite doll	209
4.6	Creating psychological distance	210
4.7	The marble-like rigidity of *tafarnug*	210
4.8	What went wrong?	213
4.9	Fatima Rushdi as Fatima	218
4.10	Fatima after changing her apparel	218
4.11	Mizrahi's deep shot	223
4.12	Inferiority gaze at the peasant woman's hairstyle	223
4.13	Transferring the inferiority gaze to the subaltern	225
4.14	Subaltern internalization of the inferiority gaze	225
4.15	Subaltern realization of the inferiority gaze	226
4.16	Mastering *tafarnug* (1)	227
4.17	Mastering *tafarnug* (2)	227
4.18	Mastering *tafarnug* (3)	228
4.19	The body of the peasant as a commodity	230
4.20	Metaphors of Islam ridiculed	232
4.21	Arrival of the peasants at the banquet	234
4.22	The Orientalist gaze; the gaze of the *Khawagat*	235
4.23	*Tafarnug* and the ridicule of Islamic festivities	237
4.24	Confronting *tafarnug*	243
4.25	Yusuf Wahbi as Satan before metamorphosing	246
4.26	The arrival of American *tafarnug*	246

4.27	Correlating American *tafarnug* with demise	248
4.28	Correlating American *tafarnug* with the utilitarian use of technology	248
4.29	American *tafarnug* and the spread of weapons of mass destruction	249
4.30	Introducing the subaltern to American *tafarnug*	249
4.31	American *tafarnug* and the false notion of choice	250
4.32	Correlating American *tafarnug* with loss of integrity	252
4.33	*Tafarnug* appropriating Islamic personal law	255
4.34	Mary Quini and Muhammad Fawzi	257
4.35	*Tafarnug* abusing Islamic personal law	258
4.36	Poster for *Mughamarat Khadra* in *al-Ithnayn*	260
4.37	Human–animal bond	262
4.38	Transferring the inferiority gaze	263
4.39	Gazing at the unfamiliar	264
4.40	Unknown actors as a subject of the peasant gaze	265
4.41	Counter-modernity and the condemnation of *tafarnug*	270
4.42	The female body as a battlefield	270
5.1	Confronting *effendiness* (1)	279
5.2	The hypocrisy of the *effendi* unfolds	280
5.3	Condemning egocentrism as the driving force of the *effendi*'s *ta'ssul*	280
5.4	Breaking up with *ta'ssul*	283
5.5	*Ta'ssul* rejected by *awlad al-balad*	286
5.6	Amin Wahba as 'Azzuz reciting his poetry among his drunk friends	287
5.7	Raqiya Ibrahim plays Samira disguised as a maid	289
5.8	Ibrahim Husayn as Badawiyya	289
5.9	*Ta'ssul* as a mythical construct	293
5.10	Poster of *Man al-Gani* in *Akhir Sa'a*	295
5.11	Historicization of bureaucratic corruption in Egypt	307
5.12	Advertisement for *Ma'alihshi Ya Zahr*	310
5.13	Poster of *Ma'alihshi Ya Zahr*	311
5.14	The idolization of *effendiness*	313
5.15	Externalization of *effendiness*	314

5.16	Accommodating *effendiness*	319
5.17	Confronting *effendiness* (2)	325
5.18	Modernity trapped between *tafarnug* and *ta'ssul*	326
5.19	Al-Shaykh Hasan, promotional photograph (1)	328
5.20	Al-Shaykh Hasan, promotional photograph (2)	329
5.21	Ridiculing Muslim prayer	333
5.22	Islam as a faith.	341
6.1	Caged modernity.	347
6.2	Resisting harassment.	351
6.3	Modern woman subjected to the gaze of patriarchy	352
6.4	The mission of subjugation accomplished	352
6.5	Working women and the male gaze	354
6.6	Choosing vulnerability	356
6.7	Enforcement of the patriarchal gaze	357
6.8	Patriarchy and the restoration of sovereignty	358
6.9	Celebrating the Egyptian countryside and its environs	364
6.10	The depiction of folk-dancing scenes	364
6.11	Celebration of peasant aesthetics	365
6.12	Folk music tools	365
6.13	The religious domain as a host domain for art.	367
6.14	Beyond literalist interpretation of *qawama*	368
6.15	Fu'ad Shafiq as Shaykh Mustafa listening to his angry wife	368
6.16	Celebration of Azhari dress	369
6.17	Azharis attending Kamal's wedding	369
6.18	Externalization of the artist's conscience	370
6.19	Celebration of *asala*	373
6.20	Resisting *tafarnug*	376
6.21	Celebrating the aesthetics of peasant women: main roles	383
6.22	Celebrating the aesthetics of peasant women: minor roles	384
6.23	Mizrahi's empowerment of the village woman through a character's positioning	386
6.24	Mizrahi's subaltern speaking	386
6.25	*Awlad al-balad* practicing *a'da* in the coffee shop	395
6.26	Emergent modernity resisting local monopoly	398
6.27	Advertisement for *Dunya* in *Ruza al-Yusuf*	405

6.28 Advertisement for *al-Bayt* al-Kabir in *al-Ithnayn* (1) 407
6.29 Advertisement for *al-Bayt al-Kabir* in *al-Ithnayn* (2) 408
6.30 Contesting polygamy 413
6.31 Asserting female sexual desire 418
6.32 Advertisement for *Bayumi Afandi* 422
6.33 Report on *Bayumi Afandi* in *al-Ithnayn* 423
6.34 Yusuf Wahbi greeting the audience 423
6.35 Externalizing Bayumi's conscience 427
6.36 Qur'an used to transition between scenes (1) 428
6.37 Qur'an used to transition between scenes (2) 428

Acknowledgments

While writing this book, I have accumulated many debts of gratitude. I wish to thank my mentors who read early drafts and made numerous suggestions: Felicitas Opwis and Nathan Hensley at Georgetown University and Joel Gordon at the University of Arkansas. Felicitas's expertise, patience, and confidence as my thought processes were developing, and her constant encouragement and interest in my intellectual curiosity, have tremendously empowered me as a graduate student. Joel's inspiring comments and suggestions on various chapters, his dedicated reading and comments on the data presented in this book, and his many questions improved the research. Nathan's mentorship, gracious advice, solidarity, and guidance on managing the book publishing process have made this book possible. I also wish to thank my mentor at Yale University, Frank Griffel, whose advice brought this project to light. My advisors and colleagues at Yale Institute of Sacred Music(ISM) generously shared their experiences, moments of joy, jiggling laughs, and very delicious meals. I am incredibly grateful to Martin Jean and Eben Graves for making my time at ISM fruitful. As an ISM fellow, I had the privilege of meeting weekly with a diverse cohort of fellows, exceptional scholars, and artists. I thank them all for our weekly gatherings, which supported me during the lockdown caused by the COVID-19 pandemic and as I was working on rewriting some chapters.

My family in Egypt lent me assistance and counsel in personal matters. I thank all my family members, especially my maternal uncle, Muhsin, whose concise and compact advice helped me remain focused in moments of distraction and confusion. My deepest gratitude is for all the memories that my late maternal grandfather, al-Sayyid al-Isawi, gave me as a child. The way he celebrated my presence in his life and his passion for knowledge and education have always motivated me to keep calm and carry on. Much of this book describes a milieu that shaped the Egypt in which my grandfather lived and which he cherished. To him, I dedicate this book, and to all the affection with which he showered me, I shall always remain indebted.

Many thanks to all the friends who inspired me along the journey of researching and writing this book. I especially thank my Dehradunian best friend and philosopher, Batta, whose insights on many aspects of the philosophy of humanities were illuminating. To all the great moments, long conversations, and disputes, I shall remain eternally grateful.

Penelope Woolley, my landlady, friend, and art instructor in Washington, DC, was gracious enough to share her house, food, and knowledge. Our weekly Friday painting sessions were liberating and, in many ways, helped me unpack the numerous entangled thoughts in my mind. As I painted, meanings got polished, and ideas started to shine. Our conversations on life, spirituality, politics, and occasional trips to watch movies and dine whenever time and budget allowed us, helped a lot during the initial steps taken to write this book.

I want to thank the EUP editorial team who worked diligently with me on this manuscript, namely Nicola Ramsey, Emma House, Louise Hutton, Isobel Birks, and Eddie Clark. Special gratitude is due to Michael Ayton for meticulously editing the manuscript and for his queries that helped me unpack and clarify my ideas.

Last but not least, I thank Shashi Kapoor and his Prithvi Theatre for all the love and joy that helped me survive very painful moments as I was finalizing the proofs of this book. The Prithvi Café's mango cheesecake and its love-shaped cappuccino cup never failed to rejuvenate and uplift my spirit.

Note on Transliteration

Standard Arabic words have been transcribed according to a simplified system based on the *International Journal of Middle East Studies* (IJMES). All diacritical marks have been omitted except for the *'ayn* (') and the *hamza* ('). For colloquial expressions, texts, songs, names of popular actors, and film dialogues, I have slightly modified the transliteration system based on IJMES. Instead of *jim* (j), I use *gim* (g), for example writing Miligi instead of Miliji. Also, the definite article (al-) in the Standard is transliterated as (il-) in Egyptian Colloquial. The name Nasir is kept as Nasser; King Faruq is referred to as Farouk. The names of Egyptian authors writing in French or English have not been changed.

Preface

This book accounts for Egyptian cinema's ability as an art and public culture to critique rigid social realities and imagine modern social experiences, despite overt and covert censorship regimes, thereby pushing boundaries towards social change. I want to draw attention to Egyptian cinema—often dismissed as less artistic or at best studied as an emblem of failed modernity projects—as a vernacular artistic experience, a public culture, a significant element in an emerging public sphere, and an exemplar of the continuity of the public use of reason during the first half of the twentieth century. I am not suggesting that cinema was a substitute for a physical public sphere such as public houses (i.e. coffee shops, social clubs, playhouses, theatres, etc.). I aim to complement the study of modernity in Egypt through the lens of cinema as a vernacular cultural production of the educated middle class and the uneducated without the framework of nationalism. Perhaps cinema is relevant even now, as suggested by Egyptian cinema's visible presence in the region with the advance of specialized satellite channels that broadcast Egyptian classics 24/7. The significance of Egyptian cinema is significantly heightened if we consider that it is a majority Muslim film industry that occupies a central place in the Arabic popular culture of the vernacular, given the limitations of print capitalism in the context of low literacy rates at the turn of the twentieth century. Cinemas and theatres supplemented—and perhaps even offered a counter-discourse to—public meeting places where ordinary Egyptians gathered to discuss issues concerning the common good.

When I started the early drafts of this manuscript, I visited the archives right after Muhammad Morsi had won the presidential election. It was a time when the religious right with its fifty shades of gray seized every opportunity to express a sense of fulfillment by displaying power and dominance in the public sphere. Being mostly on the wide-ranging and divided political left, the Egyptian film industry voiced its worries about suppression and censorship. Regardless of whether they actually had factual bases, these worries were intensified on Friday, May 11, 2012, when a group of protestors set a fire near the statue of pioneer film director Muhammad Karim standing inside the High Institute of Cinema. According to one faculty member, the statue was vandalized by Islamist protestors who installed a turban on the statue's head, a gesture taken as condemning Karim's legacy as "westernization" that should no longer exist in Egypt, now led by an Islamist administration. Thus, it is not surprising that many filmmakers, despite their fear of military dictatorship scenarios, were the biggest supporters of the June 30 military-led protest that toppled Morsi and restored the status quo.

Standing at a distance from competing parties and cultural wars, this book attempts to answer the seeming contradiction: if Islam prohibits modern innovations like cinema and considers it harmful, how is it possible that Egypt, a country with a majority Muslim population, has simultaneously hosted and celebrated the most extensive Arabic film industry, and al-Azhar, the most significant and oldest institution of Islamic theology? I examine the formative years of Egyptian cinema, 1919–1952—a culturally progressive and inter-revolutionary moment in Egypt's history before the beginning of state intervention in the film industry in 1952—to understand the contexts in which a product of modernity like film is proscribed or sanctioned in a majority Muslim society. To this end, I engage with a number of scholarly approaches to the study of Egyptian cinema, the study of modernity, the study of modernity in Egypt, and the study of Islam. I investigate the reception of the film medium by three centers of power: the British colonial authorities, the Muslim theologians (*'ulama'*), and the Cairene-bourgeoisie. I inquire about representations of modernity in more than thirty feature films. Simultaneously, I trace how filmmakers have employed metaphors respresenting Islam while constructing modernity on the screen. The data is multidisciplinary, covering over thirty feature films, Arabic and English archival material including records of the British Foreign Office, records of the Egyptian National Archive, diaries of filmmakers and film censors, variety magazines and newspapers, religious magazines and newspapers, and Islamic legal opinions on theater and cinema. While I borrow interdisciplinary analytical frameworks from literary and film critics, cultural historians, art historians, postcolonial theorists, Islamicists, and linguists, my analysis remains loyal to the close reading of texts.

The narrative unfolds with the emergence of film as a powerful communication medium in Egypt, like elsewhere. The new medium's rising popularity attracted many young artists who had a passion for photography or theater. Simultaneously, film was one of the apparatuses most sought-after by the British colonial authorities, the Cairene-bourgeoisie, and the 'ulama', who sought to use film to essentialize their different understandings of modernity as the only ideal path to becoming modern. The British colonial authorities used film to propagate an amour-propre (i.e. self-presentation aimed at cultivating a certain style of being in the eyes of others) of modernity rooted in the superiority of the "White" man as ultra-rational, disciplined and hence civilized. I invite the reader here to think beyond the confines of race, skin color, and complexion, to consider "White" as a colonialist discourse of modernity in which the will of European supremacies to exercise dominant control over the world's wealth and resources, which led to the growth of empires, was accompanied by the capacity to confirm European notions of utility, rationality, and discipline as absolute truth. This supremacist discourse was exercised across the empire in the periphery and the center, leading to people's dehumanization on both fronts by making them superhuman or less human. By adopting a similar path, the Cairene-bourgeoisie aspired to have a local film industry only in order to advocate the amour-propre of Egypt (reduced to Cairo) as a country that was no less modern and civilized than Western European countries. The ulama, who were carving a space for themselves in the predominantly colonialist and nationalist secular efforts at modernization, used the Islamic concept of public welfare (*maslaha*) to sanction film and regulate Islam's amour-propre as a rational and civilized religion capable of accommodating modern innovations. But Hollywood's dominance over the film market, in addition to the mobility and novelty of film as a platform for freedom of expression and creativity, made it difficult to control its production and distribution. The censorship of film seemed a more efficient and less expensive instrument capable of serving the same ends. Thus, the colonial authorities favored film censorship over film production; this strategy better suited a long-standing negative British cultural policy in Egypt. The reliance of the ulama on *maslaha* to sanction film appeared to be a new alternative; it allowed the medium to exist as a permissible practice among Muslims. However, *maslaha* placed many limitations on the content depicted and on Muslim women's participation in acting. The novelty of film as a platform for freedom of expression and creativity, both of which are core values of modernity, was absent from public Islamic legal debates on the lawfulness of cinema's two roots, namely photography and acting. By the same token, the Cairene-bourgeoisie censored critical films and considered their makers a threat to Egypt's amour-propre as a modern country. In response, pioneer filmmakers used the screen to construct an inclusive public sphere where subaltern social groups—such as uneducated working-class Egyptians, peasants, women, and performing artists—occupied a central position. A secularizing (but not anti-religion) society, in which people enjoyed surprising levels of social liberty and social justice for the period, was the marker of that cinematic public sphere. Ethical intuitions of Islam featured as a substratum of the everyday life practices of subaltern film characters, who adopted and adapted Islam for their common good. In this, early Egyptian cinema amplified the unheard voices of the marginalized within the public sphere. Simultaneously, cinema critiqued the root causes—not the symptomatic policies—of the modernity discourses shaping the overt and covert censorship of film.

By shedding light on the contexts of censorship and resistance in which pioneer filmmakers operated, this book advances the dialectical study of suppression and resistance while studying forms of knowledge to underscore the continuity of the public use of reason, despite censorship. To this end, the book makes a twofold argument. At one level, I contend that the deep-seated problem of censorship in Egypt, and perhaps even elsewhere, is not a by-product of a fundamental clash of civilization or of Islam and Muslims' incompatibility in adopting and adapting to products or values of modernity. Overt and covert censorship regimes are both symptoms of multiple performances and re-performances of the false consciousness of modernity, which is reduced to sustaining an amour-propre of a modern civilizational image without the internalization of modern notions of equity and social justice. In the case of Egypt, this false consciousness of modernity drove a set of passive colonialist cultural policies and anti-colonialist reactions, which reduced a product of modernity like film to an instrument of cultural hegemony. At another level, the book shows how, contrary to the common nationalist myth that Egyptian cinema emerged as a state-sponsored art, and hence a by-product of colonialist and nationalist projects of modernization, it actually emerged on the margin among amateur theater actors and photographers who belonged to different religions, ethnicities, nationalities, and genders. Those pioneers operated under overt and covert censorship regimes shaped by exclusionist colonialist, nationalist, and Islamist modernization projects. They negotiated by constructing and critiquing the discourses of modernity, shaping the overt and covert censorship of their art and profession. Their films, when studied without the Orientalist formalist approach that subjects subaltern cinema to the Hollywood standards of film language, and without the post-1952 nationalist discourses of national authenticity, offers an example of a world cinema that presented an inclusive secular public sphere, which is not anti-religion. Early films served as a supplemental public sphere that accentuated the crucial difference between "Islam as a faith," "Islam as ideology," and "Islam as a body of legal knowledge" that has the vital semantic potential to be translated into secular idioms and in a universally accessible language. In doing so, these films underscored the importance of decoding the ethical intuitions of religious traditions, which could be incorporated into a post-secular stance that finds an ally in religious sources of meaning in challenging the forces of global capitalism, something that has only been fairly recently acknowledged by Habermas. More importantly, early films show us that such a task falls not only to experts (these here being the ulama) and religious citizens, but also to all citizens—both religious and secular—engaged in the public use of reason. This should not be mistaken for an attempt to prorogate an Islamist ideology. Instead, pioneer filmmakers were—to use Charles Taylor's words—early internal critics of Islam; they attempted to create a space for religion to exist among predominantly secular efforts of modernization while simultaneously safeguarding the screen as a secular domain that primarily aims at revealing the ideology of the powerful. During the formative period, Egyptian cinema functioned as a zone of cultural debate about discourses of modernity, which was depicted, as Michel Foucault describes it, as an attitude of risk-taking and as relating to contemporary reality. This attitude was not merely a constant act of revolt (to which Habermas often objected); it was not a replica, or even, as Timothy Mitchel suggests, "a restaging," of European forms of modernity. Instead, it could be best described through Raymond Williams' concept of a structure of feeling; it was a practical consciousness that was depicted as being continuously in conflict with dominant and residual cultures of modernity; it was continuously negotiating for an interdependent humanist experience of coexistence rooted in social justice and, more importantly, freedom of conscience, which remain core values of liberal political philosophy and functioning democracies, as Saba Mahmood once emphasized. That is why Egyptian classics continue to be celebrated in a majority Muslim society like Egypt. They continue to have an evident presence in today's Arabic and Islamic popular culture.

Thanks are due to everyone who helped to make the writing of this monograph possible. All errors in and shortcomings of the book are mine.

1

Introduction: Basic Concepts

1. On the Roots of Cinema in Egypt

To speak of Egyptian cinema¹ is to face the persisting question of origins. Does cinema as an art and popular culture of modernity in Egypt² owe its origin to Muslims or to non-Muslims? Was it introduced by the *khawagat*, foreigners of European descent whose first language was not Arabic, or by the local population or by the Levantine immigrants? While I find the question of origins compelling, it seems less fruitful to study it in relation to constructed polarizations resulting from identity politics that are often marked by religion, ethnicity, race, gender, or national origin. Instead, I want to explore the question of origin vis-à-vis more pertinent variables of cultural modernity like the notion of citizenship and the two modern professions which are the backbone of any film industry, namely, photography and theater. Despite tight circles of censorship in colonial Egypt, both photography and theater emerged as public cultures (i.e. zones of debate about discourses of modernity).³ Both were shaped by interdependent human experiences and molded by the mobility of people and objects across empires before the formation of the Egyptian nation-state.

According to director and scholar Muhammad Kamil al-Qalyubi, when the Lumière Brothers screened their first film in Toussoun Bourse in Alexandria in 1896, there was nothing known as Egyptian citizenship, despite the prevalence of a collective national identity, as Ziyad Fahmy suggested in his seminal work *Ordinary Egyptians*. Being an Ottoman subject was the dominant status. Foreigners, who came to Egypt from the time of Khedive Isma'il (r. 1863–79) up until 1929, were either citizens of other countries or subjects of foreign powers, and significantly benefited from the Capitulations until it was abolished in 1937. The idea of Egyptian citizenship dominated the nationalist elite's agenda in 1900 when the Ottoman Porte issued a decree that gave Egypt more power in administering its internal affairs as an autonomous province of the Ottoman Empire. The association between Egypt and the Ottoman Empire did not end until 1914 when the British Empire declared Egypt a protectorate, which the new Turkish government acknowledged at the Lausanne conference in 1923. Egypt became a separate "supreme" state on February 28, 1922. This "supremacy," however, was disparaged by the four reservations which allowed the British government to announce, unanimously, its right to secure the British empire's transportation via Egypt, the right to defend Egypt against any other non-British aggression, the right to protect minority rights, and the right to protect interests of foreign nationals.

When the Egyptian citizenship law came into being on February 28, 1929, it had twenty-seven articles. The first five dealt with the Ottoman subjects, who became Egyptians. Article 6 defined who the Egyptians were. Articles 7, 8, and 11 dealt with foreigners who wished to obtain Egyptian citizenship. Article 7, in particular, stated that every person who was born in Egypt to alien parents and who continued to reside in Egypt when they reached adulthood had the right to apply for Egyptian citizenship within a year, given that they would give up their original citizenship. Article 8 gave citizenship rights to every foreigner who lived in Egypt for ten years. This article was restricted by maintaining proper conduct, having a profession, and gaining knowledge of the Arabic language. Article 11 gave the Egyptian government the right to withdraw citizenship from foreigners involved in fraudulent activity or convicted in a criminal case that required incarceration for two years. The state can revoke citizenship because of disturbing the peace and stability of the Egyptian state and society by acting on or publishing, outside or inside Egypt, revolutionary ideas contradictory to the Egyptian constitution.

Therefore, a distinction needs to be made between the *khawaga*, who was an Egyptian of Greek, Italian, Armenian, or any other European origin, and the *Khawaga*, who was a European colonizer. This distinction appears in the legacy of many filmmakers and in early 1930s and 1940s films. One example is the legacy of the actor Istifan Rusti (1891–1964), known as the *khawaga*, who was a working-class Egyptian (sig. *ibn al-balad*, pl. *awlad al-balad*).[4]

The expression *ibn al-balad* translates literally as the son of the country. It is inclusive because it has a feminine equivalent, namely, the daughter of the country (*bint al-balad*). Sawsan al-Misiri describes the various uses of the term since the Mamluk era and up until the 1950s. I use the term in reference to a group of Egyptians who spoke in colloquial and who, during the inter-revolutionary period of 1919 and 1952, included uneducated (they could be literate or illiterate) local traditional merchants, craftsmen, and the masses of the urban working classes. As a group, *awlad al-balad* used to be identified by clothing and locality. Their apparel used to consist of a galabiya and headdress (which could be a tarbush or a turban).[5] But fashion cannot be a reliable defining marker, because *ibn al-balad* might occasionally dress in a suit. For *ibn al-balad*, quality and comfort are what matters in dress, which must reflect his character as that of an honorable/generous (*nazih*) person who treats himself and his family members generously. It is a mistake to think of *awlad al-balad* from a centralized point of view as a Cairene group only. *Awlad al-balad* resided in different folk quarters across the main cities in Egypt. They, unlike the white-collar bureaucrats known as *effendis*, worked independently, had a day-to-day income, and lacked degree-level education. While religion existed as a substratum of their everyday life, it is not "the" marker of the group. *Ibn al-balad* could be Muslim, Christian or Jew.[6] Under British occupation, *awlad al-balad* defined themselves against colonizers, nationalist elite, *effendis*, and peasants.[7] Their financial status suffered from economic marginalization caused by the absorption of the Egyptian economy into the colonial economic system. By contrast, *effendis* succumbed in varying degrees to what they believed to be the modern good life.[8]

It was among *awlad al-balad* that Rusti's mother sought refuge after separating from her husband, an Austrian baron, whose family disapproved of their marriage. The wife took her son to Alexandria before settling in the densely populated working-class neighborhood of Shubra in Cairo, where Rusti attended a public high school. During the interwar period, Rusti traveled to Europe and met with pioneer director Muhammad Karim, studying film in Berlin. In his diaries, the latter mentioned how he convinced Rusti to return to Egypt and work in filmmaking in Cairo. Rusti then joined the theater troupe of 'Aziz 'Id and participated in the Nagib al-Rihani troupe's performance of the famous anti-colonialist operetta *al-'Ashara al-Tayyiba*—initially composed by the famed musician and singer

Figure 1.1 The actress 'Aziza Amir dressed as a car mechanic in Istifan Rusti's film *al-Warsha*, 1940.

Figure 1.2 A still from the film *Malik al-Bitrul*, 1962 showing the actor Istifan Rusti.

Shaykh Sayyid Darwish. Rusti co-directed early silent features like *Layla*/Leila, 1927 after a conflict arose between its producer, 'Aziza Amir, and its Turkish director Widad Urfi. One of Rusti's most famous films that dealt with working women's social status in Egypt is *al-Warsha*/The Workshop, 1940. It is not surprising to find Rusti acting the role of a *Khawaga* during the 1956 war in *Sajin Abu Za'bal*/Prisoner of Abu Za'bal, 1957, directed by Niyazi Mustafa.

In one interview, Rusti recalled how as a young boy he could deceive the anti-colonialist nationalist leader Sa'd Zaghlul. The latter was a minister of education at the time. Rusti was completing his primary education at Ra's al-Tin School in Alexandria when he violated the school's rules by eating sardines during class while Zaghlul was passing by to inspect the school. Noticing the smell, Zaghlul requested Rusti to inform him about the session in which the rules were violated. Rusti, who did not like his English teacher, lied to Zaghlul and said it had occurred during the English class. The English teacher was suspended, something that Rusti was not so proud of, but the matter that he cherished the most about this incident was his ability, as *ibn balad*, to challenge authority figures and caricature them. When Rusti died in 1964, he had acted in 122 films, most of which became canons of Egyptian cinema.[9] He built his star aura by mastering the European code of dress and etiquette while simultaneously using the slang metaphors of working-class Egyptians, thereby creating a correlation between his star aura and critique of the European code's superiority in dress and etiquette. This caricature was not so much a dehumanization as a humanization of the Other. To dismiss Rusti from the history of Egyptian cinema because he was not born to Egyptian parents who fit the definition of "the Egyptian" in the 1923 constitution is to dismiss iconic movies that shaped the culture of acting and filmmaking in Egypt. It is to ignore the modern local experience of coexistence that shaped an anti-colonialist humanist stance taken by a generation of filmmakers, be they *khawagat* or locals, against the *Khawaga*.

Similarly, early films marked the distinction between the *khawaga* and the *Khawaga*, especially before the 1956 Suez Crisis/the Tripartite Aggression. The *khawaga* was depicted as a normal and integral member of society. This is quite evident in movies starring the notorious comedian Nagib al-Rihani. In *Salama fi Khayr*/Salama is Safe, 1937, the director Niyazi Mustafa depicts the working-class *khawaga* Kustin[10] who lives in the same apartment complex as *awlad al-balad* and the *effendis*. Kustin's wife (Madam Grapes) is given the title Umm Yanni, after the name of the eldest son, a common practice among working-class Egyptians. Umm Yanni is depicted as an empathetic neighbor who supports Salama's wife, Sattuta (Fardus Muhammad), when her husband disappears. Umm Yanni goes with Sattuta to the police station and comforts her while they all look for Salama. Umm Yanni speaks colloquial Egyptian and uses *awlad al-balad* idioms in her speech. She even pays respect to Imam al-Husayn by saying in broken Arabic: "shay' lilah ya sayyiduna al-Husayn" in hope that they will find Salama. There is also the upper-middle-class merchant *khawaga* Hindawi (Fu'ad Shafiq), who appears as the owner of a textile business. Hindawi insists on naming his long-awaited baby boy after the ancient Egyptian king Menkaure. Simultaneously, the *khawaga*'s wife wants to name the baby "Joseph" instead of "Yusuf," which is Arabic for Joseph. Here, Niyazi Mustafa sends up Hindawi's secular, nationalist, and anti-religious sentiments, emphasizing the secular nationalist project's centrality in the bourgeoisie

Figure 1.3 Solidarity between the *khawagat* and *awlad al-balad*. *Salama fi Khayr*, 1939.

culture. It is imperative to note that the word *khawaga* indeed signifies non-Muslims. But not every non-Muslim was called a *khawaga*. European origin was undoubtedly a defining marker.

Inasmuch as the new concept of citizenship redefined filmmaking in Egypt, so did the rise of theater. Contrary to André Bazin's argument, which sees cinema as an extension of photography and plastic art without theater, Egypt's filmmaking is deeply rooted in theater. Most of the film industry's infrastructure came from theater. Theater giants like Nagib al-Rihani, 'Ali al-Kassar, and Yusuf Wahbi were the early film stars. Many theater troupes formed early studio systems. Yet the question of origin again persists in the case of theater. Some scholars trace theater in Egypt back to shadow, passion, and mimicry plays, common across the Ottoman Empire,[11] while others attribute it to the ninth-century Arab Fatimid Caliphate.

For example, Li Guo dates the first confirmed documentation of shadow plays to the time of the father of scientific method, Ibn al-Haytham (d. 1039). The latter describes a play's performance in which the presenter (*mukhayyil*) moves figures behind a screen so that their shadows appear on the screen and the wall behind the screen. Saladin reportedly brought in a shadow play performer. Various aspects of shadow play were used as metaphors in Arabic theological, philosophical, and literary discourse. The Andalusian jurisprudent Ibn Hazm (d. 1064), for instance, likened life in this world to a shadow play on account of its temporality. Muhammad al-Sharif al-Jurjani (d. 1078), the literary theorist, who laid the foundation for classical Arabic discourse on metaphor, cited a popular saying, "The world is a vanishing shadow,"[12] to drive home his observation of the aesthetic and psychological impact of the metaphorical message. Al-Ghazali illustrated Aristotle's concept of a Prime Mover by using the example of a puppet master working behind the screen. A similar metaphor was used by 'Umar Khayyam (d. 1131), the Persian astrologer and poet, in declaring that, as in a shadow play, "we are the puppets, and the firmament is the puppet master."[13] Ibn al-'Arabi (d. 1240), the Sufi thinker, drew a sophisticated analogy between the imagery of a shadow play and his vision of reality through the negation of borders between the actual and the hypothetical. By the time of the Egyptian Sufi poet Ibn al-Farid (d. 1235), the shadow play had developed into something more sophisticated, like the shadow plays by Ibn Daniyal (1248–1310). The Arabic shadow play continued to be performed in Cairo during the fifteenth and sixteenth centuries. The poet Ibn Sudun (d. 1464) compared his fleeting pleasure-seeking life with a shadow play that comes and goes. The historian Ibn Iyas (d. 1523) described a shadow play depicting the hanging of Tuman Bay (d. 1517), the last Mamluk sultan. It was staged for the Ottoman sultan Salim (r. 1512–20). Ibn Iyas reported that shadow plays were prohibited in the year 1518 out of public safety concerns. The ban was introduced by the same Ottoman sultan Salim who had earlier taken a liking to the shadow play. The shadow theater continued throughout nineteenth- and twentieth-century Egypt. Edward William Lane observed some shadow plays. Although shadow theaters existed in Cairo up until 1903, they did not survive after that. Some were closed by "order of the authorities, possibly as a measure intended to prevent the spreading of infectious diseases [during the summer of 1903]."[14]

At the turn of the twentieth century, cultural historian and novelist Jurji Zaydan (1861–1914) argued that the art form known as modern/contemporary Arabic acting (*al-tamthil al-'Arabi al-hadith/mu'asir*) was a product of the late seventeenth-century European Enlightenment.[15] Zaydan made a distinction between modern and pre-modern acting. He argued that pre-modern acting was tied to rituals long before the emergence of Greek civilization. In India, for example, acting could be traced back to the story of Brahma, who communicated it to the wise Bharata, to whom the *Natya Shastra*, the ancient Indian treatise on the performing arts, was attributed. The art of acting was put into the service of rituals in Ancient Egypt and Greece.[16] The Greeks, however, classified acting into tragedy and comedy; they introduced stage performance, singing, and the use of costumes. By the late seventeenth century in Europe, there were serious efforts to revive, restore, and develop Greek art.[17] French gazettes from the time of the French campaign in Egypt tell us that French plays were performed in Egypt as early as 1800 and were attended by the Egyptian elites.[18] At the end of Muhammad Ali's reign, around 1846, Syrian travelers such as Marun al-Naqqash and Salim al-Naqqash founded early Arabic theater troupes performing in standard Arabic. In 1869, Isma'il inaugurated The Cairo Opera House, which hosted different foreign theater troupes. Initially, only French troupes were allowed to perform in the Opera. In 1870, Ya'qub Sannu', supported by Khedive Isma'il, established Egypt's first Arabic theater company.[19] However, all of Sannu's plays were performed in colloquial Egyptian and contained subtle nationalistic themes and a significant amount of social criticism:

> For instance, *al-Duratayn* (The co-wives) openly criticized polygamy. In *al-Amira al-Iskandaraniyya* (The Alexandrian princess), Sannuʿ warned middle-class Egyptians against blindly imitating European customs and habits, a cause championed later by ʿAbdallah Nadim and other nationalists. In *al-ʿAlil* (The sick man), Sannuʿ expressed the theme by supporting modern medicine against [the appropriation] of traditional medicine, stereotypically represented by a Moroccan religious quack who summons spirits.[20]

As the subject matter of Sannuʾs plays became more critical of elite society, his theatrical activities were banned by the government in 1872.[21] In 1878, the Syrian actor Yusuf al-Khayyat moved to Cairo and performed the play *al-Zalum* (The Oppressor), which Ismaʿil found insulting as it hints at the injustice of the ruler in the play. He ordered the deportation of al-Khayyat and his troupe. When the British arrived and forced Ismaʿil to leave Egypt in 1882, another Syrian, Sulayman al-Qirdahi, founded a theater troupe whose members included the—today more popular—Shaykh Salama Higazi. However, modern theater acting remained underdeveloped due to a lack of state support until, in 1910, Khedive Abbas sent the Lebanese actor George Abyad to study acting in Paris. The theater of Abyad at that time attracted the educated, who were able to understand standard Arabic.[22] As Ziad Fahmy noted, it was Sayyid Darwish who professionally developed acting in Egyptian colloquial. But Darwish's anti-colonialist plays further intensified state mistrust of theater because the performances often critiqued the alliance between the Turkish ruling elite and the British colonizer. By the 1920s and 1930s, Cairo and Alexandria had hosted a vibrant theatrical scene expanding to rural centers, especially in the Nile Delta. For example, the director Hasan al-Imam recalled in a radio interview how he had grown up watching his father, a factory owner in the delta city of Mansoura, inviting theater troupes to perform for his factory workers every month during the 1930s.

Many pioneer filmmakers emerged from this theatrical scene, and they were strongly influenced by the anti-colonialist stances expressed in theater. The names are numerous in this regard, and it suffices here to mention some of the popular names which will recur in this book: Yusuf Wahbi, Muhammad

Karim, Anwar Wagdi, Husayn Sidqi, Istifan Rusti, Mary Munib, Fardus Muhammad, Amina Rizq, 'Ulwiyya Gamil,[23] Fu'ad Shafiq, Sirag Munir, Sulayman Nagib, Ahmad 'Allam, Nigma Ibrahim, Husayn Riyad, Mimi Shakib, Zuzu Shakib, Nagib al-Rihani, 'Ali al-Kassar, Isma'il Yasin, 'Abd al-Warith 'Asar. Most of these actors started their film careers in theater.

While theater actors provided cinema with the necessary labor force, cinema's second root, namely, photographers, produced early silent reels. Muhammad Bayumi, Aziz Bender Lee, Umberto Doris, and Elvisi Orfanelli, unlike Lumière's touristic and somehow Orientalist themes, expressed an anti-colonialist stance by focusing on local sights and points of attraction to the lay public in early silent films. For example, Bender Lee and Doris shot their first film on June 11, 1907.[24] The film documented the Ottoman Porte's visit to the mosque of the Sufi saint al-Morsi Abu al-'Abbas (1219–86). Doris, supported by Bank De Rome, established an Italian–Egyptian film company and a studio in the neighborhood of al-Hadara in Alexandria. The company produced short silent features like *Sharf al-Badawi*/The Honor of The Bedouin, 1918, and *al-Zuhur al-Qatila*/The Deadly Roses, 1918. The latter was the first silent feature in which an Egyptian actor, Muhammad Karim, participated. Up until then, he had not shifted direction.[25] Lee, Doris, and Bayumi used four cameras to shoot the inauguration of the Parliament in 1924 by King Fu'ad I, thereby eternalizing the emergence of constitutional rights in Egypt.[26]

Sources are limited and, when found, are silent on the legacy of the *khawagat* photographers. Yet Muhammad Kamil al-Qalyubi's rediscovery of Muhammad Bayumi's legacy shows how an anti-colonialist stance shaped Egypt's early years of filmmaking. This stance, however, did not turn into an exclusionary nationalism. Bayumi began his early career as a military officer. He graduated from the Egyptian military academy in 1912 in the same class as the first Egyptian president, Muhammad Najib (1953–4). He served in Khartoum and in Jaffa. While in Jaffa, Bayumi refused to pardon a British soldier, who declined to salute him as a senior officer because Bayumi was not a British officer. Bayumi's decision angered his superior British officers, who suspended him. This experience inspired Bayumi to learn more about Europe. Giving up on his military career, he traveled to study cinema in Austria, where he met and married his Austrian wife. He came back to Egypt after World War I and opened a studio in the neighborhood of Shubra in Cairo, where his first model was his daughter, Dawlat. In 1922, Bayumi traveled again, but this time to Germany, where he met the German director Wilhelm Carol and the German cinematographer Boehringer. Bayumi acted in minor roles in German films such as *Die Grüne Manuela*, released in 1923.[27] Most of his films focused on anti-colonialist themes. His first film documented the return of Sa'd Zaghlul from exile on September 18, 1923. Other films focused on local events such as the opening of the tomb of Tut Ankh Amun and the release of the anti-colonialist nationalist General 'Abd al-Rahman Fahmi from jail in January 1924. Bayumi also filmed the funeral of Sir Lee Stack, governor of Egypt and Sudan. He shot the funeral of Yusuf Wahbi's brother-in-law, 'Ali Fahmi, who was murdered by his wife, Margret Fahmi. The case caused public controversy by reminding the public of foreigners' legal privileges in Egypt due to the Capitulations. As much as Bayumi's anti-colonialist humanist stance distinguished between the *khawaga* and the *Khawaga*, he was simultaneously disappointed with the dominance of exclusionist nationalism in Egypt. For example, Bayumi's studio was the nucleus for the first big film studio, Studio Misr.[28] The establishment of this studio is often credited to the nationalist banker Tal'at Harb. The latter had bought the machines of Bayumi's studio, but never acknowledged Bayumi's efforts in establishing it. In a letter to Harb, Bayumi complained about the schemes and intrigues of the Egypt Company for Acting and Cinema that had led him to resign. Similar echoes of Bayumi's complaints came in Karim's diaries, in which he described the lack of effective management in the company that had had five managers in less than seventeen months.[29]

2. The Pioneers, and Accounts of Exclusion

Despite the prevalence of theater and photography as professions, the idea of becoming a filmmaker was not publicly well-received in the first half of twentieth-century Egypt, especially among the Cairene-bourgeoisie networks. In Egypt, as elsewhere at this time, an actress was perceived as a "whore." The Egyptian government associated acting with prostitution. For example, the Government issued legislation in 1929 requiring any woman who wished to pursue a career in the performing arts to obtain a professional license. The legislation also required every theater house to register all its actresses' names by reporting their names to local authorities.[30] Thus, pursuing a career as an actress was a precarious decision and sometimes a life-threatening one, especially for those who belonged to feudal families. But censorship is not absolute. A countless number of Muslim and non-Muslim actresses operated in theater and cinema. Their names included Rusa or Fatima al-Yusuf, Fatima Rushdi, Layla Murad, Raqiya Ibrahim, Amina Rizq, Amina Muhammad, Ihsan al-Gazayrli, 'Aqila Ratib, Biba 'Izz al-Din, Mimi Shakib, Zuzu Shakib, Layla Fawzi, Ilham Husayn, Samiha Samih, Najat, Madiha Yusri, Umm Kulthum, Tahiyya Kariyuka, Rawhiya Khalid, Amal Zayid, Samira Khulusi, Dawlat Abyad, Raga' 'Abduh, Thuraya Fakhri, Zinat Sidqi, 'Aziza Fakhri, 'Ulwiyya Gamil, and Kuka, among many others.

Each actress experienced some level or other of marginalization, and each story deserves a book. Still, it suffices here to mention one account of Bahiga Hafiz (1901–83), who played the role of Zaynab in Karim's *Zaynab*, 1930, the first silent feature to depict village life in Egypt. Bahiga Hafiz came from an aristocratic family. Her father was Isma'il Muhammad Hafiz pasha, and her cousin was Isma'il Sidqi, the Prime Minister of Egypt (1930–3). She married an Iranian royal, whose name was not mentioned in the sources, but was soon divorced. Hafiz often expressed her disappointment at the false consciousness of modernity that dominated Cairene-bourgeoisie families and their exclusionist nationalism. In one interview she said:

> I expected support from my family and my country. I failed to convince them that my music is not less than Western music. They refused to listen to me, claiming that I belonged to the *Khawagat* and my music was an imitation of their music. My family saw my music as devoid of Eastern sensibilities. They failed to understand the universality and inclusiveness of my music. I strived to appeal to a universal audience. I was keen to mix my music to appeal to the tango audience and the local audience. Had the Ministry of Education encouraged me as it did with the *Khawagat*, I would have been able to develop my music.[31]

Hafiz condemned the censorship of her movie *Layla Bint al-Sahara'* / Leila, Daughter of the Desert, 1937, the first Arabic film to be screened at the Berlin Film Festival. It was a time when the royal marriage between Princess Fawziyya Fu'ad and the Shah of Iran, Muhammad Rida Bahlawi, was about to take place. That the movie depicted Chosroes, King of Persia, as a tyrant who mistreated women was seen as an insult to the Egyptian royal family's new in-laws.[32]

Even for a male actor, acting was a stigma; to become an actor was to be singled out as an unemployed clown (*qaraquz*), and in Egypt, under colonization, an actor was also seen as an agent of the colonizers and their efforts at westernization. For those who belonged to marginalized social groups, becoming an actor meant a threat to the family's income because the income of an actor at that time was not stable. For those who belonged to aristocratic families, becoming an actor did not just mean the loss of an income, loss of social status, public shaming, and disgrace to the entire family. It also meant possessing the will and perseverance to succeed, understanding the position of the governed, and appealing to the vast majority of the uneducated working class. This process necessitated first escaping the hegemony of aristocracy and developing an anti-colonialist, humanist stance against the norms of the Cairene-bourgeoisie exclusionist nationalist milieu in which pioneer filmmakers grew up.

Experiencing marginalization made many filmmakers aware of "Otherness," which shaped their anti-colonialist humanist stance. I aim to shed light in the following pages by discussing accounts narrated by Muhammad Karim and Yusuf Wahbi in their diaries. I focus on these two filmmakers because Karim and Wahbi made many of the films studied in this book. Karim's diary is also unique because it fills the knowledge gap regarding the two decades leading to the rise of cinema in Egypt. It provides significant insights into questions of the supremacy of the *Khawaga*'s forms of modernity, "Otherness," and exclusionist nationalism. As I hope to show below, Karim makes a clear distinction between the *khawaga* and the *Khawaga*. More importantly, his memoirs also reveal his awareness of cinema's potential as a public sphere where marginalized social groups could come together and communicate about issues of the common good. In later chapters, as much as possible and is relevant to the analysis, I address the legacies of other pioneers, including Tugu Mizrahi, Ahmad Badrkhan, Anwar Wagdi, Kamal Salim, and Husayn Sidqi, among others.

Muhammad Karim's interest in cinema started when he befriended his neighbor Yusuf Wahbi. They both grew up in 'Abidin, by then an upper-class neighborhood near the famous 'Abidin Palace (now a presidential palace). Karim's father died when he was young, and he was raised by his brother, a law graduate who worked for the Ministry of Foreign Affairs. Wahbi was a son of 'Abdullah bey Wahbi, a close friend of the nationalist leader Sa'd Zaghlul. The two young boys' fascination with cinema started at the age of seven when they accompanied Karim's brother Hasan to watch short silent features like *Bout-de-Zan Vole un Elephant*/Tiny Tim and the Adventures of His Elephant, 1913 directed by Louis Feuillade. As Karim puts it in his memoir, Italian films appealed to them more than French films, since Italian movies had in them actors like Francesca Bettini (1892–1995), Lida Borelli (1884–1959), and Maria Jacobini (1890–1944). The Italian films they watched were also adaptations of William Shakespeare's plays, such as *Antony and Cleopatra*, or Alexandre Dumas' works like *The Lady of the Camellias*, or Henryk Sienkiewicz's *Quo Vadis*.[33] American movies did not attract them, since most of the screenings which they came across were Western genera starring William Hart (1870–1946), Tom Mix (1880–1940), and Eddie Polo (1875–1961).[34] Soon, Karim and Wahbi started performing scenes at home by imitating the movies they watched. They acted in scenes from *Les Vampires*/The Vampire, 1915, and *Fantômas*, 1913, directed by Louis Feuillade. The character of Fantômas intrigued them to the extent that Karim made a black costume similar to that of Fantômas and roamed the streets of Cairo at night, imagining he was Fantômas. Wahbi used to act the character of a police officer chasing Fantômas. Their performance, however, was not a mere imitation; it showed their early awareness of and interest in adapting the film medium to their local aesthetics. On one occasion, Wahbi is disguised in a female costume known as a black wrap (*milaya*) to help Fantômas escape the police.[35] This reveals how Wahbi and Karim were grappling with the possibility of using film to express local sensibilities. These early amateur performances and efforts to make the film medium their own continued all through their years as teenagers. They befriended an Olympia Cinema employee and used to rent a ten-minute movie for three days for ten piasters.[36] Initially, they re-performed film scenes in the courtyard of Karim's house. Still, when Wahbi's family moved to the neighborhood of al-Munira, the performances transferred to Wahbi's bigger house, and they started to attract an audience. Most of their audience came from door attendants, servants, cooks, and laundry workers in the neighborhood. Wahbi often used a white bed sheet as a projector board. They used dozens of cups, plates, forks, water buckets, and knives, along with fireworks, to create sound effects for silent movies. They offered souvenirs (perfume, chocolate, biscuits, and handkerchiefs) to attract more audiences.[37] In a way, their efforts to make these performances succeed reveal their growing awareness of cinema as a public sphere in which marginalized social groups could come together. More importantly, these amateur performances alerted Wahbi and Karim at a very young age to censorship and the false consciousness of modernity among their Cairene-bourgeoisie families. It also drew their attention to how marginalized social groups were more capable of engendering social change. For example, during one of the screenings that Karim and Wahbi used to hold at Wahbi's palace, Wahbi's father showed up unexpectedly. He was angry at the scene of the servants gathering in one room to watch a movie, which he considered a shameful practice. As Karim put it, Wahbi's father arrived while the screen showed a kissing scene. Simultaneously, Karim was standing behind

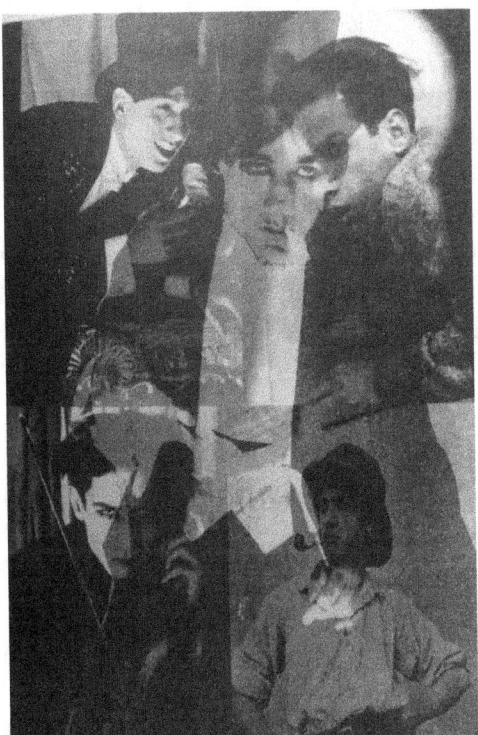

Figure 1.4 A collage of Muhammad Karim as a young actor. Image adapted from Karim's memoir.

Figure 1.5 Muhammad Karim in *al-Ithnayn* magazine in 1951.

the screen and kissing his hand to create a sound effect and amplify the silent scene's impact. Faced with Wahbi's father's anger, the audience took off, while Wahbi ducked, hiding under a table. Karim recalled how Wahbi's dad pulled Karim's ear and reproached him. Wahbi had his share of slapping later. The father then confiscated their projector machine.[38] For Wahbi's father, who was an active nationalist and participant in the anti-British nationalist al-Wafd party's meetings at the house of Sa'd Zaghlul,[39] Wahbi faced a lost future. He had wanted his son to be a doctor or an engineer, professions representing societal modernization and progress. Disappointed by his son's interest in cinema, the father withdrew all financial support from Wahbi and used to call him *Khawaga* Yusuf.

This early incident of censorship motivated Karim and Wahbi, instead of giving up on acting, to find room for their hobby outside the walls of the Wahbi palace, which symbolized the rigid Cairene-bourgeoisie norms. They joined the Association of Reviving the Art of Acting, where they started to act professionally in supporting roles. However, their childhood memory of censorship left them with a question that continued all through their lives: how could Wahbi's father claim to be a supporter of an independent modern

Egypt and oppose the idea of having an Egyptian theatrical tradition and a film industry?[40] This conflict also shows in Karim's life through his brother Hasan, who was a political activist. Hasan encouraged Karim and appreciated his interest in acting. However, Hasan could not face his family with his younger brother's interest in studying film. As Karim put it, Hasan was an employee in the Ministry of Foreign Affairs, and acting created a stigma that could affect his career.[41] When Karim decided to travel to Italy and later to Germany to study cinema in the early 1920s, Hasan lied to their relatives, telling them that Karim was traveling to study engineering. This conflict was resolved gradually, as both Wahbi and Karim became conscious of class struggle. However, a premature answer came early in their lives from Wahbi's nanny, the only family member who dared to break the tight circles of censorship and the norms in Wahbi palace. When Wahbi wanted to travel to Milan to study acting, his nanny loaned him her golden bracelet to sell. The nanny's stance drew Karim's and Wahbi's attention to the idea that marginalized social groups are more capable of change than the bourgeoisie.[42]

While early experiences of covert censorship and marginalization sharpened Karim's awareness of the double consciousness of the Cairene-bourgeoisie, his early attempts to carve a space for himself in the emerging film industry reveal his awareness of the difference between the *Khawagat* and the *khawagat*, as well as the Orientalist discourse propagated by the *Khawagat*. When Karim left theater to start a film career there were not many film companies in Egypt. He had hoped to join an Italian company owned by Bank De Rome. However, working in a new and foreign company required a great deal of fluency in Italian, which Karim lacked. He started hanging out at Ventura Café on 'Imad al-Din Street, where many theaters and nightclubs existed at that time. There, he mingled with *khawagat* of Italian origin. In particular, he befriended a *khawaga* by the name of Enrico Cristopher, who introduced him to artists like Enrico Caruso (1873–1921), Tullio Carminati (1894–1971), and Gustavo Serena (1881–1970).[43] Through this connection, Karim secured some roles with the Italian Film Company. But since the film crew were mostly Italians, Karmi's poor Italian proficiency continued to be challenging.[44] He spent days lost in the studio until he met the art manager, Francesco,[45] whom Karim described as "the *khawaga* who mastered Egyptian colloquial like any working-class Egyptian (*ibn balad*)."[46] From Francesco, Karim learned that a professional actor should act in any role regardless of how short or long the role might be.⁴⁷ Although Karim's income reached twenty Egyptian pounds, a large sum of money at that time, he was not content with the small roles he played through the Italian Film Company. He viewed himself as equal to Charlie Chaplin, who had started only four years before him.⁴⁸ With that ambition, Karim began corresponding with studios in the United States of America. He sent his photographs to Paramount Studios. They replied with a note of rejection without examining his pictures: his envelope was returned unopened.

Given that many actors in the United States at that time came from outside, Karim found it difficult to believe the claim of the company that the American audience was not interested in foreign actors. In the frustration of the moment, Karim saw the incident as an act of discrimination.⁴⁹ He then tried to study through distance learning at Victoria Cinema College in London. However, he received a rejection letter stating that owing to his "Oriental features" he did not have a chance of success at that time. To Karim, "that time" referred to the 1919 anti-British revolution, which he saw as reason enough for rejection.⁵⁰ As much as *Khawaga*'s Orientalist discourse increased Karim's awareness of the monopoly of *Khawaga* over his dream art and profession, it did not lead him to develop a reactionary exclusionist nationalist stance. This seems to have resulted from his awareness during his childhood of the false consciousness of modernity in the nationalist discourse. And it also seems due to his interest in resisting "Otherness."

The rejection made Karim, like Muhammad Bayumi, invest more in encountering Europe, of which he did not construct a monotone image in his memoirs. Instead, he presented a self-reflective account that took into consideration his emotional status in response to reality. And we know from his diaries that he developed an early awareness of the difference between reality and the representation of reality during childhood. For example, he mentioned that he used to read a column in the *al-Hal* newspaper in his teenage years. The column focused on everyday conversations on public transport. Karim described his excitement when he took the tram for the first time. He thought he would jump into the rich political and cultural discussions he used to read and enjoy. But he was surprised that people were silent most of the time. When they talked, the conversations were not always as attractive as they had sounded in the column. This anecdote underscores Karim's early awareness of how authors use their imagination to represent and sometimes amplify reality. Karim's memories of his experience in Europe show how he writes about his initial impression and gradual change of view. Through this shift in tone, his awareness of "Otherness" and his resistance to it is revealed to the reader. For example, Brindisi and Rome scenes were shocking to Karim because World War I had just ended when he arrived in 1920. The miseries of the war were highly visible on buildings. He confessed that he had a romanticized image of Rome and did not expect scenes of poverty in its streets. Contrary to the stereotypes he held of Italians, he learned that artichoke with olives was a favorite Italian food, like spaghetti, if not more so. His host family asked about urbanization in Egypt; they wondered whether Egyptians knew anything about silverware and dining tables.[51] He described how he struggled to convince them, for example, that his pictures in Cairo were not taken in Paris or London.[52]

Similarly, awareness of and resistance to "Otherness" shaped Karim's first day at Cesar Film Studio. In the beginning, his fellow actors did not take him seriously; they laughed when they knew he was an Egyptian coming to study film in Italy.[53] Karim wrote, "They used to look at me with no interest. Rather they were indifferent to me, as if I were not a human. I thought to myself, what could I do to convince them that I am as human as they are, that I also have the artist's ambition and perseverance to make a name for myself?"[54] The solution came from a packet of cigarettes that he had carried with him from Egypt. Within twenty minutes of sharing cigarettes with the crew, he became the most famous person in the studio.[55] This incident's significance lies in how it shows Karim's awareness of "Otherness" as being a social construct, not as an innate behavior in humans. He had faced a similar situation while working with an Italian company in Egypt. He had also initially met with indifference until he figured out that one has to share the group's worries and concerns to be a part of it or to be considered an insider. At that time, the Italian Film Company's crew members welcomed him after he had participated with them in their search for a lost diamond in the studio. After the diamond was found, he recalled that everybody became friendlier, and the crew members started calling him "Senior Muhammad." To Karim, it seemed that being called "Senior Muhammad" was not necessarily a question of identity, that is, being more of an Italian or less of an Egyptian. Instead, his account indicates his awareness of the markers of inclusion and exclusion in everyday life practices. It is not surprising that Karim commented in his diaries on how he gradually restored his fascination with Rome; how he regained his joy at the sights of the fountains and churches on every corner.[56] But after he had spent a year in Italy, most of the studios where Karim worked ceased their activities, and he headed to Berlin.[57]

Likewise, Karim's description of his experience in Berlin reveals his awareness of class struggle, which further developed his anti-colonialist humanist stance. For example, when he compared Berlin to Rome he noted that Berlin, unlike Rome, matched the dreamy picture that he had constructed from his friends' stories of how clean and organized Berlin was. But he soon reassessed his initial fascination with Berlin. He attributed this to two primary reasons, which had to do with his experience of leading the life of two social classes in Berlin. When he arrived, he saw Berlin from the viewpoint of a monied adventurer. The value of sterling, which was the currency Egyptians used abroad, was on the rise when he arrived. Initially, his money was more than sufficient for room and board expenses and for learning German. He lived in the best neighborhoods like Kurfürstendamm Avenue, and he spent nights at the most expensive nightclubs like Beckershof. While Wilhelm II's surrender saved Berlin from the war's atrocities, it changed Karim's social class. When a new German currency was issued in 1924, and one pound sterling became equal to twenty marks, Karim's pounds were not enough to meet the cost of living, and Berlin would have become for him an isolating place shaped by poverty were it not that there he met his wife, who was German. But his marriage, also, was not free from "Otherness." He mentioned, for example, how his in-laws welcomed the wedding, all except his wife's aunt. The latter accused her niece of treason for getting married to a Briton, since Egypt was under British rule. This anti-colonialist humanist stance of Karim's developed further in the German motion picture production company known as Universum Film-Aktien Gesellschaft (UFA Studios) in Berlin, where Karim attended the shooting of Fritz Lang's masterpiece, *Metropolis*.

At UFA, Karim faced the question of the place of religion in his anti-colonialist humanist stance. For example, he recalled that the two UFA studios in Babelsberg and Tempelhof used to produce movies in the East. On one occasion, an actor was performing the Muslim prayers, and he completed the steps incorrectly. Karim interfered and pointed out that the actor had made a mistake. Had Karim wanted to cite this incident in his diaries as an incident of pure Orientalist discourse, he would have stopped there. However, he added that some of the film crew took him to meet a researcher in the studio library. The latter explained to Karim, with what Karim described as "unprecedented simplicity,"[58] that Islamic sources recorded variations in the steps of Muslim prayers.[59] In a way, this incident reveals Karim's keenness to create an accurate representation of religion in film. At the same time, it shows his awareness of the interpretations of religion as a social construct. However, this awareness does not mean that Karim denied the Orientalist discourse in films at the time. For example, he mentioned how he had noted that, in some scenes, Qur'anic verses appeared upside down on the walls and how the staff fixed the mistake when he pointed it out. However, Karim also noted that he still felt the crew's carelessness was the product of an Orientalist discourse that cared for the exotic depiction of the calligraphy more than its relevance to the scene.[60] These details, which appear minor in Karim's description of his experience of Orientalism, are of significant value. They reveal his awareness of the difference between Orientalism as an imperialist agenda and the study of civilizations, which Said noted later when he distinguished between British and French Orientalism, on the one hand, and German Orientalism on the other. Thus it is not surprising that Karim related that his best experience in Berlin came when UFA recommended him for a role with an American Film Company. He described the best part of that experience as its humanitarian aspects, which allowed actors from different national origins to work in harmony together. This anti-colonialist humanist stance did not cease to exist when Karim returned to Egypt in 1926, despite the lack of state support and the entrenched monopoly of the *Khawagat* over cinematograph halls and the importing of equipment.

By 1926, when Karim returned to Egypt, cinema had become more recognized, especially in Alexandria. Some short silent features were shot, including *Barsum Yabhath 'an Wazifa*/Barsum Looks for Employment, 1923, directed by Muhammad Bayumi. Universal Pictures Cooperation of Egypt had its office in Alexandria, and films were distributed by the American Union Film Society, the Jozy Film Society, the American Cosmography Society, and the United Film Service. In 1927, the Egyptian production company Sawsan

Film was established, owned by Ihsan Sabri; it produced films like *al-Hubb al-Khalid*/Eternal Love, 1927, and *al-Dahaya*/The Victims, 1928, directed by Ihsan Sabri and Widad 'Urfi and written by Ihsan Sabri. In 1928, the Egyptian Film Society was founded by the Italian Amando Puccini and the Frenchman Jacques Schultz to produce Egyptian films starring Egyptian actors. Its first film was *Su'ad al-Ghajariyya*/Su'ad the Gypsy, 1928, written and directed by Jacques Schultz. Popular names participated in it, including Fardus Hassan, 'Abd al-'Aziz Khalil, Amina Rizq, and Muhammad Kamal al-Masri. In 1933, Behna Film started importing films by Charlie Chaplin and Laurel Hardy films; Behna made its fame by subtitling and/or dubbing. One of Behna Film's first productions consisted of Frankles cartoons presented by the Frankles, two Alexandrians with a Jewish background; they created the animated Egyptian hero Mech Mech.[61] In the same year, the Alexandria Cinema Institute was established by Muhammad Bayumi in Alexandria. It produced documentary films and a fifty-minute-long feature entitled *al-Khatib Nimra 13*/Fiancé Number 13, directed by Bayumi. Tugu Mizrahi, who earned his doctoral degree in economics from Italy, returned to Egypt around the same time Karim returned from Berlin and started a series of silent features. Mizrahi made in his Studio in Alexandria before moving to Cairo. These included movies like *Cocaine*, 1930, *5001*, 1932, *Awlad Masr*/Sons of Egypt, 1933, and al-*Manduban*/The Two Delegates, among many other films.[62] Three major newspapers reported on cinema at the time, *al-Balagh al-Usbu'i*, *al-Musawwar*, and *al-Lata'if al-Musawwara*.[63] In Karim's words, Cecil B. DeMille's *The Ten Commandments* occupied the Cairo media for weeks.

Despite the rising interest in film, state support was almost non-existent. Karim blamed this on the Cairene-bourgeoisie and the nationalist elite, whom he repeatedly accused of failing their country. Even when some of them showed an interest in the Egyptian film industry, they had a very utilitarian vision of what cinema could present to Egypt.[64] For example, while in Berlin, Karim had heard news of the establishment of the Egypt Company for Acting and Cinema. The *al-Waqai'* newspaper published a royal decree allowing Ahmad Midhat Yakan pasha, Fu'ad Sultan bey, 'Abd al-Hamid Suyufi bey, Ahmad Shafiq pasha, Zakariyya Mahran pasha, Ahmad Hegazi bey, Ibrahim al-Zahiri bey, and Tal'at Harb pasha to establish a film company with a capital of 15000 Egyptian pounds divided into 350 stocks. Each stock sold for four pounds.

Bank Misr owned the majority of the stocks.⁶⁵ Karim expressed his disappointment at the company's unrealistic and insufficient budget when he met Talʻat Harb in Berlin. Karim was further disappointed by Harb's utilitarian views of film. Harb told Karim that the company did not intend to produce any feature films and would only shoot short films depicting natural sights.⁶⁶ Later, Karim was surprised to find himself accused of westernization and reluctance to help his country. The *al-Ittihad* newspaper, which was government-owned, blamed Karim for not returning to Egypt and for working abroad.⁶⁷ Similar complaints about lack of state support appeared the same year in *Ruza al-Yusuf* magazine. The leading feminist and journalist Ruza al-Yusuf complained that the government had no clear vision in supporting the performing arts. It had done nothing since it had sent the theater actor Zaki Tulaymat to Paris to study acting.⁶⁸ Al-Yusuf questioned the Ministry of Education's plan regarding allocating insufficient funds (10000 Egyptian pounds), which had been approved by the parliament to revive the performing arts. She further wondered about the financial aid promised by the Ministry of Public Works to playwrights.⁶⁹ It should not be surprising that when Karim met Talʻat Harb again in Egypt in 1927, the latter offered Karim a job with no salary.⁷⁰ The lack of state support continued all through the 1930s and 1940s. For example, in *Lastu Malak/I Am No Angel*, 1946, directed by Muhammad Karim, the latter presented a scene between the actor Bishara Wakim and Muhammad ʻAbd al-Wahhab; they were complaining about the futility of the government art study missions (*baʻathat al-funun*), after which students came back to Egypt and continued to be unemployed.

At the time, the nascent industry was also challenged by the monopoly of the *Khawagat* over the film exhibition halls. This monopoly resulted from the Société Artistique de' l'Egypte's power in 1897 in constructing theaters and nightclubs. The Société's power came from its partners' control over major infrastructure companies such as real estate, water, and electricity companies like the Light and Electricity Company, established to supply power to the Azzbakiyya neighborhood. This neighborhood became dense with theaters and movie theaters.⁷¹ Many major movie theaters were owned by *Khawagat*, including American Cosmograph, Empire, Radium, Coliseum, Metropole, Caliper, and Ideal. There were a few locals, such as the Coptic Maqar family who owned al-Ahli Movie Theater. Most screenings included foreign films distributed according to a quota system that gave American movies the highest distribution rate. The British empire failed to challenge this system either at home or in the colonies. For example, a confidential report on the distribution of films in Egypt noted that American films constituted 68 percent of movies screened in Egypt. French movies constituted 21 percent, while Britain and Egypt combined had 4 percent and other countries 7 percent.[72]

These exclusion accounts, which could have dissuaded Karim and many other pioneers from pursuing film as an art and profession, were further complicated by overt censorship. For instance, Karim accepted Tal'at Harb's offer to work without salary at the Egypt Company for Acting and Cinema. His early production was *al-Ta'awun* (Cooperation), a development film similar to those made after the Great Depression of 1929. It was produced by the Cooperation Division, a subdivision of the Ministry of Agriculture. Ahmad Hasanayn, a public official with the rank of investigator in the Ministry of Agriculture, invited Karim to direct a silent cartoon film. The aim was to raise awareness among farmers of the dangers of taking loans with high interest rates. The movie was meant to publicize the new project intended to help farmers establish a cooperation fund.[73] The scenario included the flag and international slogan of the Cooperation Division, pictures of the employees as well as the headquarters of the project, and a picture of 'Umar Lutfi bey, the founder of the Cooperation project. Scenes also included Qur'anic verses on the virtues/benefits of cooperation and a map showing the project's statistics.[74] Karim did not receive any initial funding for the movie. He produced it despite being out of pocket. He traveled to rural centers such as al-Hawamidiyya, Zagazig, and Faqqus, where the project had already started. He listened to the speeches given by the Ministry of Agriculture officials to promote the project. These tours raised his awareness of the need for cinema to speak to the majority of Egyptians, namely, the peasants, in Egyptian colloquial. During these tours, Karim noticed that the public officials' speeches were ineffective since the farmers did not understand standard Arabic.[75] His experience with this movie also brought Karim face to face with overt censorship. Before the scheduled time of the film premiere, supposedly Friday, March 6, 1931 at 4:00 p.m., the Ministry of Agriculture requested a special screening of the film at the Ministry's headquarters. Karim refused and insisted on screening the movie premiere in the movie theater. After a series of negotiations, the Ministry of Agriculture agreed to rent cinema Jose Palace for a special screening in front of the Minister of Agriculture, Hafiz Hasan pasha, Mr. Yeller,[76] a Dr. Rashad of the British Economic Committee,[77] and the manager of the project, among others. Many newspapers wrote about the film. For example, the *al-Wadi* newspaper wrote, on March 9, 1931: "cinema was used as a means for propaganda by many developed modern nations. We are pleased that the Egyptian government paid attention to the importance of films for promoting Egypt and its products."[78] The movie was screened multiple times in agricultural and industrial exhibitions. Its success disturbed a foreign chancellor, whose name is not mentioned in Karim's diaries. The chancellor presented a petition to the Egyptian government condemning Karim's film. A state committee invited Karim for investigation, and the subsequent interrogation took place:

> *Interrogator:* What do you mean by the *Khawaga* who ate spaghetti and loaned money through an excessive interest system (*riba fahish*) to the farmers?
> *Karim:* I meant any *Khawaga* who practices that manipulative profession.
> *I:* Is not your depiction of spaghetti an explicit reference to a particular group of foreign nationals?
> *K:* Of course not. The spaghetti scene in movies was more of a technical issue. Spaghetti was more photogenic than rice, for example.
> *I:* Did you not know that nobody ate spaghetti except a particular group of foreign nationals?
> *Karim*: I eat spaghetti, and undoubtedly so do many Egyptians and many foreigners living in Egypt.

While Karim's movie was eventually released for public exhibition, he received 215 pounds (almost a third of the overall cost of 600 pounds). Karim's experience with censorship in this short film was not necessarily unusual. These instances of censorship and the exclusionary nationalist discourse that Karim faced at the Egypt Company for Acting and Cinema seem to have pushed him to work independently. He was reunited with his childhood friend Yusuf Wahbi, and they made Karim's first silent feature *Zaynab*, which was shot in Wahbi's Ramsis Studio, built on the infrastructure of Wahbi's Ramsis Theater.[79]

But the freedom that Karim gained by working with Wahbi brought more overt and covert censorship. Karim's memories of making *Zaynab* reveal how his anti-colonialist humanist stance was challenged by hegemonic Islamic legal discourses that proscribed the performing arts and figural representation. To film *Zaynab*, Karim traveled to Kafr Ghannam, the village where the real events of Haykal's novel took place. The presence of filmmakers and machines in the village caused a scene. While some peasants welcomed the experience and served as extras, others were suspicious. It was a challenge to convince some of them that cinema was not prohibited (*haram*) from a religious point of view. On one occasion, Karim happened to be driving near a field, where he saw a peasant with his ox struggling to plow the field. It occurred to Karim that he could shoot a scene for the hero (Zaki Rustum) in the same location. He stopped the car and walked toward the field to initiate a conversation with the farmer, whom he greeted saying, "Peace be upon you" (*salamu 'alayikum*). The farmer looked at Karim and did not return the expected greeting, which would typically be "And peace be upon you too" (*wa-'alayikum al-salam*). Instead, the farmer replied, "Hope you had a nice day so far" (*sa'ida*). Surprised by the farmer's unexpected greeting, Karim asked him, "Why are you not greeting me back as usual?" (*lih ma bitruddish al-salam*). The farmer said, "You look like a foreigner" (*shaklak Khawaga*). Karim smiled and replied, "I am a Muslim, for the Prophet's sake, and my name is Muhammad" (*la wi-l-nabi ana Muslim wi-ismi* Muhammad). The encounter does not just show how Karim emphasized a religious affiliation or a group identity. Rather, it shows how being a Muslim was, at the time, sometimes defined against being a *Khawaga*, especially in peasant communities. The farmer had reacted to the hat which Karim used to wear while shooting to protect him from sunburn. To the farmer, the hat was a marker of the *Khawaga*. What seems like a side note in Karim's memoir is an attempt on Karim's part to reiterate Muhammad 'Abudu's Islamic legal opinion, which stated that Muslims are free to wear a hat so long as they do not intend by that choice to declare themselves as non-Muslims.[80] While the farmer eventually agreed to rent his field and ox, he repeatedly interrupted shooting; he was concerned that God would punish him for renting his land and ox to filmmakers.[81]

Similarly, censorship intensified when shooting *Awlad al-Dhawat/ The Children of the Nobles*, 1932. This was the first Arabic talkie. It was based on 'Ali Fahmi, the son of 'Ali pasha Fahmi, the Grand Chamberlain to King Fu'ad I. He was also Wahbi's brother-in-law, since Wahbi was by then married to 'Aisha Fahmi. The Italian architect Antonio Lashak designed a palace for him, still standing today at the entrance of Zamalek (which now is a museum of art). 'Ali Fahmy lived there with his wife, Margert, before 'Aisha Fahmi bought the palace and lived there with Yusuf Wahbi, who later divorced her as he could not stand her jealousy regarding his star aura. While recalling the murder of 'Ali Fahmi, Wahbi mentions how Margret Fahmi's lawyer, Sir Edward Marshall Hall, convinced the jurors that Mrs. Margert Fahmi was not guilty by building a defense on the barbaric behavior typical of an Arab man, who advanced on his wife in a threatening manner that made her shoot her husband in self-defense. The jurors all but ignored the fact that Margret Fahmi had shot her husband at point-blank range. Given the movie's controversial topic, foreign film distributors encouraged French magazines in Egypt to attack the film. *LA Pors* magazine was the first to accuse the film of promoting fanaticism. The magazine mocked the direction techniques and described them as archaic and funny. It claimed the movie was Russian communist propaganda targeting foreigners in Egypt and European women, especially French women, who were depicted as immoral. The magazine added that the movie presented all evils in one character to frame French women as a symbol of "Western vice." It further stated that if a French film depicted a young Egyptian man seducing a French woman, a European audience would find such a film boring.[82] *Muqattam* magazine, known for its loyalty to British authorities, published the news that some *Khawagat* had written a petition to the Ministry of Interior claiming that the film included defamation and hate speech (*asbab lil-nufur*). The Minister of Interior sent a committee, chaired by Mr. Griffith, to investigate similar incidents.[83] The committee decided that the movie did not include any defamation and lifted the ban. However, the Interior Minister enforced the ban, despite demand for the film in Cairo, Alexandria, and other cities. Therefore, looking at *Awlad al-Dhawat* today as a didactic film aimed at warning "young vulnerable Egyptian men" against "the immoralities of the West" gravely overlooks its historical context and how it presented a harsh critique of the supremacy of the *Khawaga*.

A more in-depth investigation into the life of the makers of *Awlad al-Dhawat*, Wahbi, and Karim reveals their awareness of the distinction between the *khawaga* and the *Khawaga*. Karim's wife was of German origin; she migrated with him to Egypt and became a Muslim, taking the Arabic name Ni'matallah. Wahbi's first wife was an American opera singer whom Wahbi married while studying in Italy. Both Wahbi and Karim speak very positively about the experience of marrying women of European origin. In one interview, Wahbi attributes his separation from his first wife to professional ambitions. He explained that it was unfair that her talent should have been wasted by her moving back with him to Egypt, where opera was not flourishing as it was in the United States or Europe. Seen through this lens, Wahbi's condemnation of Margert Fahmy needs to be understood as a condemnation of her actions, not her identity. This view is missing from the reaction of the Arabic newspapers that supported the film at the time. For example, *al-Sabah*, a local Arabic magazine, made the film look like anti-foreign propaganda when it published an article titled "Foreigners and cinema in Egypt: the campaign of hate against Egyptian Arab film." The newspaper criticized the *Khawagat* and their lack of interest in Arabic cultural production. They lacked interest in Arabic, the majority language, yet appeared only on a side-screen during foreign film screenings. The captions used to be pale and incorrect, and their expressions never matched the scenes.[84] Despite the controversy, *Awlad al-Dhawat* was eventually screened at Royal Cinema. Many prominent nationalists and public figures such as Mustafa al-Nahhas and Safiyya Zaghlul took the time to attend the first show.[85]

While shooting his third film, *Dumu' al-Hub*/Tears of Love, 1935, Karim wanted to film students inside a school. The headmaster refused and claimed that cinema was immoral. Three years later, when the movie was screened in Lebanon in 1938, the French colonial authorities objected to 'Abd al-Wahhab's song *Ahib 'ishit il-hurriya* (I Love the Life of Freedom), and they licensed the film after cutting the song.[86]

Despite censorship, Karim's anti-colonialist nationalism did not shift to exclusionary nationalism, which dominated the public sphere in late 1952. Nothing, perhaps, describes this social milieu more than Karim's comments on the shooting of *Yawm Sa'id*/Happy Day, 1939. The movie was supposed to be shot in Paris, but the interruption caused by World War II forced the film crew to shoot in Cairo. Karim heard the war news while shooting one of the film songs, namely *Ya ward min yishtirik* (Flowers for Sale). He recalled that it was a moment when the plateau had three hundred female actors from different nationalities, and could never forget the scene of the French film crew comforting the German and vice versa.

This awareness of the human condition under colonization and war was, as I hope to show, a driving force behind the making of early films in Egypt. Early filmmakers were amateurs whose art and profession emerged on the margins of the state's efforts at modernization. Cinema emerged before the nation-state formation; its makers came from different cultural, religious, and national backgrounds; the industry catered to audiences and dealt with humanitarian themes that resonated with human experience beyond Egypt's national borders. Therefore, a study dealing with the formative years of filmmaking in Egypt necessitates a step outside the national cinema framework and the consumption approaches that study cinema as nationalist mass culture or a superstructure necessitated by the industrial and economic base.[87] Instead, I want to draw attention to early films made by Muhammad Karim, Yusuf Wahbi, Tugu Mizrahi, Kamal Salim, Ahmad Kamil Mursi, Ibrahim 'Imara, al-Sayyid Ziyada, Ahmad Badrkhan, Husayn Sidqi, Anwar Wagdi, Fatin 'Abd al-Wahhab, and Henry Barakat as *critical realisms* that unmasked and combated hegemonic images and hence have continued to enjoy a higher level of recognition inside Egypt and in many Arab and Muslim countries.

3. Egyptian Cinema as Critical Realism

This book complements the study of narrative structure in Egyptian cinema by reading early films as critiques of both the colonialist narrative and the limits of the Cairo-centric elitist categories embedded within that nationalist narrative. I examine rhetorical aspects of the film, such as authorship and adaptations, thereby acknowledging that many early films were adapted from successful theatrical performances. I do not intend to focus only on the ideological effects produced through montage and perspective. While the creation of meaning is traced in aspects of film language such as *mise-en-scène*, movement, and montage, I pay more attention to screenwriting tools in order to scrutinize the metaphors used to represent modernity and Islam in basic storytelling techniques. These include the world of the story, dialogue, characterization, externalization of the internal, the power of uncertainty, main tension, culmination, and resolution. In doing this, the book aims, first, to step outside the Orientalist formalist approach, which subjects Egyptian cinema to the standards of film language, thereby reducing it to the works of Youssef Chahine or Shadi 'Abd al-Sallam. Second, it elucidates how early films did not achieve space–time continuity through montage, but through dialogue used to carry the artist's plan.

When it comes to image, the book focuses more on analyzing the construction of meaning through the delimitation of the image, the distance from the object, the pictured space, and the edge that cuts off what lies behind it. The cinematic text is read here as art that begins "where mechanical reproduction leaves off, where the conditions of representation serve in some way to mold the object." Again, cinema is an heir to a long-standing theatrical tradition that artistically combines staging and speech. The mouth, in early Egyptian cinema, speaks to the ear more than it speaks to the eye. This is partly because early film stars were singers. But more importantly, human sound, as opposed to melody, remains the primary entertainment source in theater and cinema. It remains a fact still today that the actor who creates a style of enunciation through mastery of diction is the most successful in the long run. Egyptian filmmakers were alert to this fact, which is why early books on acting, chief of which is 'Abd al-Warith 'Asar's *Fann al-Ilqa'* (The Art of Diction), focused mainly on diction which was seen as the most important training to be received by an actor.

Representation and framing are central to the analysis of films as social critique in this book. That is to say, I hope to show how early filmmakers did not create sociological systems to be innocently consumed. Instead, they used film to reveal the nature of the ideologies of the powerful; they showed how these ideologies were perpetuated through the generalized and final assigning of values to real or imaginary differences, to the accuser's benefit and his victim's disbenefit, to justify the former's privilege or aggression. Explicit depiction of inferiority thus is read as a critique of racism. This is evident in the dominant presence of film characters representing historical subjects of racism and inferiority. Early filmmakers were least interested in creating an elaborate fabric of fantasy in films. Their films employed comprehensive mediations that intervened between reality and representation. This is evident in their political positioning in ruling out possibilities of sympathy with the oppressor or with social injustices. It is also evident in codes and counterstrategies, which present a more comprehensive analysis of character status as a speaking subject. It is evident in image scale and duration in relation to questions of respect, audience sympathy, understanding, and identification.

Star power receives limited attention in this book, which focuses more on film *directors*, who often receive marginal attention in scholarship on the formative period of Egyptian cinema. By focusing on pioneer film directors, I avoid perpetuating elitist post-1952 nationalist discourse, which saw early films as mediocre art and as mere propaganda projects for the Egyptian music industry. Thus, early musicals starring the singer 'Abd al-Wahhab are studied here from the point of view of their director, namely, Muhammad Karim. Similarly, early musicals for Layla Murad are studied from the point of view of directors like Tugu Mizrahi and Anwar Wagdi. Comedies starring Nagib al-Rihani are examined from the point of view of their director, Niyazi Mustafa. Some early studies on theater and cinema's history claimed that pioneer directors had little training. The screen lovers and frontrunner pioneers whose passion for film caused them to be renounced by their aristocratic families, those who crossed the Mediterranean under colonization and war to study theatre and cinema in Italy, Germany, and France, those who sold the furniture in their houses for a few seconds of shaky images, to use André Bazin's words, were neither industrialists nor pundits. They were artists who believed in the power of their imagination to embody social experience and communicate with the majority of the uneducated masses, who were free to assess, accept, or reject that communication.

Early films were not merely didactic films. Pioneer directors did not see cinema's function as preserving or creating an ideal world, but rather in revealing the discourses shaping Egypt's harsh social realities during the first half of the twentieth century. This does not necessarily mean that this book reads Egyptian cinema as a third cinema, because the tight circles of censorship under which the industry operated during the formative period made it difficult to explicitly express anti-imperialist stances in films. But when it comes to local films facing competition from foreign capitals over local markets, the book does see Egyptian cinema as a third cinema.

This book reads early Egyptian films through the lens of *critical realism*.[88] To speak of critical realism in Egyptian cinema is to talk about realism that differs from socialist realism, which emerged from Marxist criticism. Socialist realism taught that it was the duty of the filmmaker, as an artist, to provide an accurate historico-concrete portrayal of reality in its revolutionary development considering ideological transformation and the education of the workers in the spirit of socialism. Art had to be party-minded, optimistic, and heroic; it had to be infused with revolutionary Romanticism portraying Soviet heroes and prefiguring the future. According to Terry Eagleton, Trotsky departed from socialist realism's narrowly genetic sense of art. He saw art as a "secularist 'realist' experience [in which] ... realism itself is intrinsically neither revolutionary nor reactionary. It is, instead, a philosophy of life [that simultaneously represents reality and critiques it]."[89] Critical realism extends beyond the mechanistic view of film as the passive reflex or the superstructure necessitated by the economic base, to a Romantic belief in film as projecting ideals and stirring people to new values. Critical realism escapes partisanship and the ideologization of art by encouraging the filmmaker to move beyond both the photographically observable and the imposed rhetoric of a political solution. However, it does this via what Marxist criticism describes as objective partisanship. Partisanship is inherent in reality itself; it emerges as a method of treating social reality rather than as a subjective attitude toward it. That is to say, filmmakers do not impose their political views on the work. They reveal the real and potential forces objectively at work in a situation. And thus it is that a film can reveal the nature of ideology, and helps the audience communicate. The filmmaker thus brings on new, or embodies existing, modern social experiences that push boundaries toward social change.

Examples of Egyptian critical realist cinema are countless. The master here, of course, is the director Salah Abu Sayf. For instance, Abu Sayf's critically acclaimed film *al-Zawja al-Thaniya* /The Second Wife, 1967 can easily be reduced to a clichéd folk story about an oppressive patriarchal society, and an impotent village mayor who takes a second wife to secure a male heir.[90] However, if read without the Orientalist scrutiny that subjugates Egyptian cinema to Hollywood standards of film language, the film can be read as a black comedy that comments critically on the failure of the Nasir [Nasser] regime. Following the sweeping and unexpected national defeat (*naksa*) of June 1967, the film was released in October of the same year. It critiques social injustices among peasant communities (*fellahin*), the vast majority of the Egyptian population whom the 1952 Officers Movement promised social justice rooted in citizenship rights. Abu Sayf metaphorizes Egypt as a village suffering from high taxation rates, forced conscription, and epidemics, all of which are perpetuated by an unjust alliance between religious despotism and autocratic rule. He lampoons the alliance in a scene showing the village mayor (Salah Mansur), the clergy (including Hasan al-Barudi), and the police chief (Ibrahim al-Shami) dining together. A reaction shot is used to employ the character of an uneducated soldier ('Abd al-Mun'im Ibrahim), who lives in servitude at the mayor's house, as a witness to the injustices resulting from such an alliance. The soldier's physical presence in the scene and his gaze at the food convey the ill-gotten nature of the food (*suht*) and the alliance. The dialogue elaborates on the injustice by revealing how the mayor forced the peasant Abu al-'Ila (Shukri Sarhan) to divorce his wife, Fatima (Su'ad Husni), so that he could marry her and produce the long-awaited heir. The clergy legalizes the divorce by appropriating the meanings in the Qur'anic verse Q4: 59 and argue that the divorce is in accord with the Islamic ruling that summons believers to obey God, his Prophet, and the ruler.[91] When Abu al-'Ila and his family decide to flee the village, the mayor and the police chief fabricate robbery charges

Figure 1.6 The alliance between autocratic rule and religious despotism. 'Abd al-Mun'im Ibrahim, as the uneducated soldier, stands on the right. *Al-Zawja al-Thaniya*, 1967.

against Abu al-'Ila and detain him. Under the threat of imprisonment, Abu al-'Ila divorces his wife, who is forced to marry the mayor.

The director's camera blames the displacement of the peasant on an oppressive bourgeoisie ideology that commodifies the peasant's body, here a metaphor for the vast majority of Egyptians. To reveal the nature of ideology, the director presents a dark comic scene where the mayor and his wife, Hafiza (Sana' Gamil), appear gazing at a group of village girls dancing. They try to spot the most vulnerable peasant girl, who is beautiful enough to accord with the mayor's taste but weak enough to be under the thumb of the mayor's wife. The scene also reveals the power dynamics between the two bourgeoisie characters, who do not want to spend much money on securing an heir. They agree on Fatima as a potential bride. She and most of her family's female members are known for giving birth to baby boys. But Fatima also lacks any power and wealth and could easily be controlled by the mayor's wife.

As presented by Abu Sayf in *al-Zawja al-Thaniya*, critical realism is a secular critique that is not anti-religion. Abu Sayf seems to suggest that equitable change is possible if an alliance takes place between the uneducated soldier, the unarmed civilian, and liberating interpretations of religion. Thus, the movie takes a sharp turn when Fatima visits a mosque in Cairo. She meets a member of the 'ulama', who explains that any forced marriage or divorce is void because Islamic legal tradition dictates that any action is invalid if taken against the person's will (*karaha*). Abu Sayf thus does not employ religion in and by itself as a liberation. He employs religion to inspire the subaltern to resist social injustice and liberate themselves. This is evident in his equal emphasis on folk art (*al-fann al-sha'bi*) as a central tactic in subaltern resistance. For example, Fatima is depicted overhearing a puppet show (*qaraquz*) that motivates her to resist her subjugation at the mayor and his wife's hands. She pays attention to a line of dialogue that reads, "No one can defeat a smart and determined woman." This line inspires her to create excuses to prevent the consummation of her forced marriage to the mayor.

The alliance among different subaltern groups becomes the driving force against social injustice in *al-Zawja al-Thaniya*. For example, Fatima creates a network of interests with other subaltern characters, such as the uneducated soldier whom the mayor assigns to police her. She empathizes with the soldier and acknowledges his misery in the mayor's house. Her attitude helps her create contexts for resistance. For example, she could visit her expelled family and bear a child with her first husband, Abu al-'Ila. As the mayor's impotence becomes confirmed, the news of Fatima's pregnancy shocks the mayor, who dies after a short struggle with paralysis. Fatima takes over his wealth, and the movie ends with her returning all the property which the mayor had earlier confiscated by force to the peasants. By depicting the subaltern as a female protagonist regaining her share in power and wealth through her own willpower, Abu Sayf avoids foisting political solutions on the viewer in his film. Thus, Abu Sayf's critical realism reveals the nature of coercion and empowers the subaltern to resist coercive ideologies. In doing this, Abu Sayf simultaneously represents reality and critiques it. Therefore, it is not surprising to see this scene widely circulating on social media in order to comment on political transformations and social injustices in today's Egypt.

The formative years of Egyptian cinema are no exception regarding critical realism. Muhammad Bayumi's *Barsum Yabhath 'An Wazifa*/Barsum Looks for a Job, 1923, critiques unemployment among the educated middle class. Karim's first silent feature, *Zaynab*/Zeinab, 1930, and its 1952 talkie version are not merely sentimental stories of forced marriage. In an interview in 1929,

Figure 1.7 The subjugation of the peasant by state autocracy. On the right, Shukri Sarhan as the peasant Abu al-'Ila. *Al-Zawja al-Thaniya*, 1967.

Figure 1.8 Gazing at the peasant's body as a commodity. Salah Mansur as the mayor, gazing at peasant women. *Al-Zawja al-Thaniya*, 1967.

Figure 1.9 Religion as an inspiration to subaltern resistance (1). Su'ad Husni as Fatima visiting a maqam of a member of Prophet Muhammad's household. *Al-Zawja al-Thaniya*, 1967.

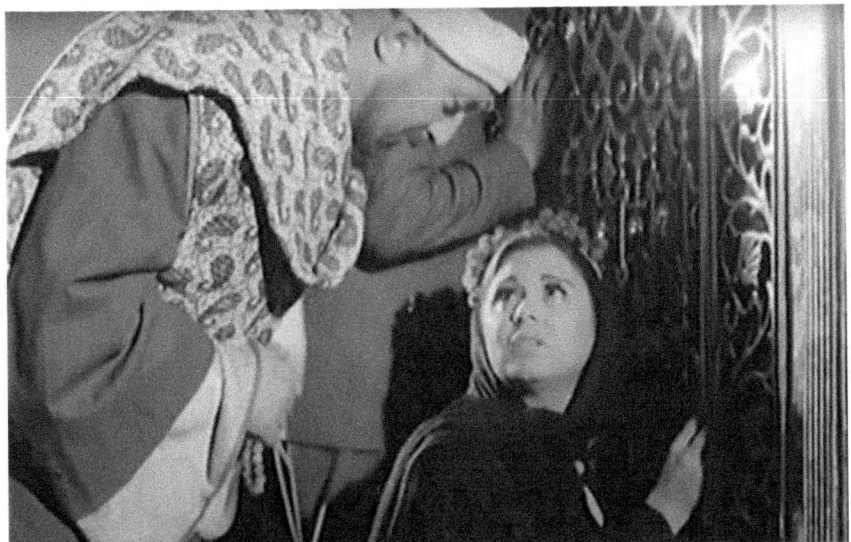

Figure 1.10 Religion as an inspiration to subaltern resistance (2). On the right, Suʿad Husni appears as Fatima. On the left, ʿAbd al-ʿAzim Kamil as a member of the 'ulama'. *Al-Zawja al-Thaniya*, 1967.

Figure 1.11 Folk art as resistance. *Al-Zawja al-Thaniya*, 1967.

Karim referred to *Zaynab* as representative of a critical realist trend that he defined as the representation and critique of harsh social realities:

> When I directed *Zaynab*, I did not intend to succeed only inside Egypt. I was hoping the movie would gain the same level of success in Europe and the USA so that it engraves Egypt's name among the nations occupied with making film industries. Nowadays, there is a persistent question, among filmmakers around the world, about what kind of cinema is worth producing. *Zaynab* is Egypt's answer to this issue. The cinema that is worthy of production is the one that depicts life as it is. That is to say; cinema has to represent bitter realities without sugar coating. No matter how harsh the realities are, we must face them. The west has minimal knowledge of today's Egypt. I am sure that *Zaynab* will show western nations a kind of cinema that they will appreciate. The film market is open to competition now. If the Egyptian government seizes this opportunity, Egypt can produce more movies like *Zaynab*.[92]

Zaynab is a nascent attempt to present a critical realist cinema that mirrors the unjust social conditions under which most peasants lived at the tail-end of the nineteenth century. Karim adapted Muhammad Husayn Hakayl's novel *Zaynab* twice. The first was a silent feature released in 1930, and the second was a talkie released in 1952. The silent version is considered a landmark in the history of Egyptian cinema for various reasons, chief of which is the fact that it is one of the earliest (if not the first) screen representations of Egyptian peasant life. Yet the true merit of Karim's two adaptations of *Zaynab* (1930 and 1952) lies in his critique of the commodification of women's labor in an Egyptian rural community where women are perceived as a source of income to be transferred from father to husband. In his memoirs, Karim laments the loss of the silent version's negative, for Yusuf Wahbi, the producer, sold it to a party contractor. Karim's 1952 talkie does not seem to differ significantly from the silent version. Some characters, however, do not exist in Haykal's story and were added to the talkie. The actor 'Abd al-Warith 'Asar, who wrote the screenplay, met with Haykal and consulted with him on characterization to ensure that the additional characters would not affect the story. In the absence of the silent version, one can only speculate that the 1952 remake, being a *talki*, provided a more crystalized depiction of the injustice caused by the commodification of the village woman's labor. While the 1952 version has a more optimistic ending, the plotline and the misfortunes of the protagonist remain similar in both versions. I rely here on the talkie to show how Karim presents *Zayanb* as critical realism.

Zaynab is not merely a story of a rural woman (Raqiya Ibrahim) trapped between her suitor, Hasan (Farid Shawqi), and her lover, Ibrahim (Yahya Shahin). It is a story of a peasant woman, who tries to "become modern," not only through "believing in love as the foundation of marriage," but by achieving sovereignty over her body and mind so as to control the fruits of her labor. To this end, Karim creates sympathy for Zaynab (Raqiya Ibrahim) through the character of a feudal bey, played by Sulayman Nagib, the landlord of the estate where both Zaynab and Ibrahim work, who encourages them to marry. When Zaynab's family rejects her marriage to Ibrahim, the bey offers to help Ibrahim financially so that he can secure Zaynab's dowry. His character is a metaphor for hope and the possibility of change. However, hope remains arrested. When Ibrahim proposes to Zaynab, and her family turns down his offer, Ibrahim and Zaynab decide they cannot live as individuals in the village. Escaping the rural for the urban, namely Cairo, becomes an exit strategy for the two lovers. They agree to meet at dawn to elope. Haunted by her family's worry about the shame that will befall them if she elopes, Zaynab convinces Ibrahim that their plan is selfish. Failure here is not merely the failure of a modern social experience rooted in love as the foundation for marriage. Rather, it is the failure of an uneducated peasant woman's quest for social justice that allows her to control the fruits of her labor. Zaynab's attitude is suppressed due to the grand strategy of shame, rendering her unable to regard her own interest as a priority in a society shaped by interest, even though it strives to project itself otherwise. Karim further reveals the nature of the ideology suppressing Zaynab's attitude by underscoring the discourses used by her community to manipulate her labor. For example, when the news spreads in the village that Zaynab is receiving marriage proposals, her mother says, "I am not quite sure I want to marry her off. Her siblings are still young. And she is a great help in running the household." To Zaynab's mother, the marriage of Zaynab to a wealthy farmer like Hasan will save Zaynab from poverty. The mother fancies the luxury that her daughter will enjoy if she agrees to marry into a wealthy family. Trying to convince Zaynab, she says,

"You will become a lady (*titsattiti*), you will be veiled (*tithaggibi*), you will sit on sofas (*tiglisi ʿala al-kanab*), and you will sleep in a bed (*wi-tinami fi il-sirir*). These forms of luxury are available only for the rural bourgeoisie class that owns the land, not for the permanent field peasants (*tamalli*) whose daily income comes from working in the fields of the rural bourgeoisie. For Zaynab's father, the marriage of Zaynab means he can rent two acres from Hasan's father and become a land tenant (*ugari*), which means he will be his own boss. When Hasan's friends ask him about the identity of his bride, he says, "It does not matter; any girl will do." And when they blame him and ask "How is it possible to marry blindly?," he says "It does not matter; Zaynab will know how to take care of the house and serve us." When Hasan's father discusses his son's marriage plans with his wife, the former states that the purpose of getting his son married is to bring somebody in to help the mother in the household. For Hasan's father, Zaynab is a suitable wife because she is poor and will not be as outspoken as other rural bourgeoisie girls. Therefore, when Zaynab contracts tuberculosis, her body loses its worth as a commodity in the eyes of her father-in-law, who controls the family wealth and is not ready to fund her treatment. Karim depicts the father-in-law character (Yusuf Maʿluf) calculating the cost of Zaynab's treatment, which comes to three hundred pounds. To the father-in-law, this sum of money could purchase him two acres of land. And Zaynab's life is not worth it. Karim critiques the father-in-law's unjust stance by depicting him refusing to let Zaynab go to the local health clinic because he is concerned his social image will be disparaged in the village. He does not want his bourgeoisie class to stigmatize him as a poor man unable to fund his daughter-in-law's treatment. Zaynab is also depicted as aware of the commodification of her body and labor. When Zaynab's mother tells her daughter about Hasan's proposal, Zaynab refuses the proposal and says, "I do not want that marriage. Let me stay with you. I shall work in the field and bring you money every day." By depicting Zaynab as aware of the value of her labor, Karim reveals the suppressive ideology dominating the village while simultaneously giving voice to a peasant woman (*fallaha*), a marginalized member of a marginalized community, and, more importantly, her quest to gain control over her body and mind by resisting the commodification of her labor. Therefore, Zaynab's death in the novel and the silent film represents a powerful protest of the peasant woman's body against its labor commodification. The different ending in the talkie, in which Zaynab leaves the house alone to get treatment at the newly established village clinic, is another protest by the body that sees hope in the 1952 Officers Movement symbolized by Ibrahim's new job in the military.

Karim's critical realism assigns a central place to religion. For example, in *Zaynab*, the Muslim call for prayer serves as a marker of time; the five calls for prayer regulate the sense of time and everyday life practices. To Zaynab's family, the day starts after her father comes from dawn prayer. In the opening scene, Karim uses a narrator to tell viewers that the dawn call to prayer breaks the silence of darkness to announce the day's beginning in the village. Zaynab dates Ibrahim under a fig tree right after the afternoon call to prayer. On the day Zaynab plans to flee with Ibrahim to Cairo, their meeting time is marked by the dawn call to prayer. As she listens to the call, she starts imagining the shame which would befall her family if she were to flee.

Figure 1.12 Raqiya Ibrahim as Zaynab performing ablution. *Zaynab*, 1952.

Figure 1.13 Raqiya Ibrahim as Zaynab supplicating after prayer. *Zaynab*, 1952.

In this context, the call to prayer is a marker of tormented conscience. Karim uses it as a soundtrack to depict Zaynab rethinking the consequences of her plans for her family's ability to survive in the village. Zaynab is often depicted praying. The scenes of Zaynab performing ablution and supplicating are rare instances of an Egyptian Jewish actress acting as a practicing Muslim in a movie.

It is imperative here to note that Karim does not idealize Islam in his movie. His movies often condemn the appropriation of Islam. For example, Zaynab's marriage-party scene presents a critique of the Islamic legal opinions that consider a woman's silence a sign of consent to her marriage. As the village men ask Zaynab whether she agrees to marry Hasan or not so that the marriage contract can be signed, everybody is depicted laughing and taking her silence

Figure 1.14 Poster of Zaynab remake in *al-Ithnayn*, 1951.

to be a sign of shyness. Simultaneously, Karim's camera zooms in on her face to show her torment and refusal of the marriage.

By the same token, movies like *Awlad al-Dhawat* /Children of the Nobles, 1932 by Muhammad Karim and *Yaqut*/Yaqout, 1934, co-directed by Willy Rosé and Ahmad Badrkhan, presented, long before Edward Said talked about Orientalism, a harsh humanist critique of Orientalism by highlighting when "Otherness" enters the discourse.[93] These movies depict Orientalism as an injustice that dehumanizes both the colonizers by making them superhuman and the colonized by making them less human. The master of critical realism, Salah Abu Sayf, is a student of Niyazi Mustafa, who directed Nagib al-Rihani's most successful comedies, namely *Salama fi Khayr*/ Salama is Safe, 1937, and *Si 'Umar*/Mr. Omar, 1941. Both movies, which will be discussed later in the book, are harsh critiques of institutional corruption and bureaucracy in feudal Egypt.

Because of critical realism, Egyptian cinema has always been subject to censorship regimes. Censorship is not only overt enforcement of policies and laws. Exclusion, marginalization, and public shaming of filmmakers are also covert forms of censorship. While both overt and covert censorship of film exist in Egypt today, their roots, as I hope to show in this book, extend deep into the colonial era. Examples are countless in this regard. It suffices here to mention a few popular cases that occurred in colonial and post-colonial times. In 1926, the pioneer filmmaker Yusuf Wahbi was publicly shamed and accused of being a renegade (*mariq*) for accepting the role of Prophet Muhammad in a German production movie called *al-Nabi Muhammad*/Prophet Muhammad, 1926, to be directed by Widad 'Urfi. When Karim released *Zaynab* in 1930, media controversies arose over his depiction of scenes of poverty in the countryside. He was blamed for disparaging Egypt's modern civilizational image (*al-shakl al-hadari al-'asri*) in his movies.[94] The journalist, novelist, screenplay writer, and feminist Ihsan 'Abd al-Quddus expressed non-conformist political stances that cost him his liberty during the reign of King Farouk and the rule of Nasser. His entire literary oeuvre continues to suffer the consequences of his stances. His novels, most of which were adapted for the screen, continue to be considered sentimental stories unworthy of scholarly investigation.[95] During the Mubarak era, the composer, singer, and film star Muhammad 'Abd al-Wahhab (1902–91) faced legal accusations of apostasy (*ilhad*) via the claim that his song *Min ghayr lih* (Without Why) suggested the absurdity of God's Creation. Some critics said that the legal case aimed to threaten 'Abd al-Wahhab, who had revealed to his close circle of friends that he had wished to revive the idea of singing the Qur'an. He would have started with Chapter 39. The novelist Ihsan 'Abd al-Quddus welcomed the idea, which 'Abd a-Wahhab dismissed when news of the legal case reached him in Paris.[96] And censorship continues in today's Egypt. Following January 25, 2011, many artists faced prosecution, including Rami 'Isam, an emerging rock singer, and the graffiti artist Hisham Rizq. The latter's paintings on the walls of the street leading to Tahrir challenged the state's erasure of the memory of the protest.[97] The novelist Ahmad Naji was sentenced to two years' imprisonment after being accused of intentionally disparaging public decency (*khadsh al-haya' al-'am*) in his novel *Istikhdam al-haya* (Using Life).[98] Members of the emerging street theater troupe Atfal al-Shawari' were jailed after using an iPhone to shoot a standup comedy video that criticized the government's lack of transparency in the negotiations over redefining national borders between Egypt and the Kingdom of Saudi Arabia.[99] The filmmaker Muhammad Diyab faced accusations of disparaging Egypt's modern civilizational image in his movies *Cairo 678* and *2010*, which dealt with sexual harassment. It was the same with his film *Ishtibak*/Clash, 2016, dealing with human rights violations post-January 25.[100] The emergent satirist and theater director Ahmad al-Jarhi [al-Garhi] and his theater troupe were sentenced to two months in prison for performing a play on the story of the controversial death of the Egyptian soldier Sulayman Khatir. In one of his last interviews, the film star Nur al-Sharif said that if people wanted to understand why people took to the streets on January 25, 2011, they should check the records of censorship of his movies during the Mubarak era.[101] All these instances of censorship are examples of suppression of the public use of reason, which left its scars on the project of modernity in Egypt. Still, this does not necessarily render the project of modernity in Egypt a failure. Critical realism in Egyptian cinema provides a rich archive enabling us to understand how the construction of modern social experience continues and will continue, as everywhere else, to take place, despite censorship regimes and shrinking public spheres.[102] One way of understanding this continuity is to understand the relationship between film as art and the construction of modern social experience.

As art, film serves at the very center of modern society and its public culture. It embodies the shared meanings of society. The filmmaker is not a lonely artist, who is a front-runner and explorer, but rather is at the center of society; the artist is the voice of her community. While creating art, the filmmaker is in a continuous process of communication, in which both the artist and the spectator participate. When art communicates, human experience is actively offered and actively received. The artist shares with other people what Raymond Williams describes as the creative imagination, that is, the capacity not only to find and organize new descriptions of experience but also to embody known experiences.[103] The creative filmmaker observes to convey new information to others about matters that were not a topic of discussion before. Creativity here is not merely a matter of inspiration; "it is not a question of 'inspired' or 'uninspired' transmission to a passive audience. It is, at every level, an offering of experience, which may then be accepted, rejected, or ignored."[104] In other words, creativity, which starts as an act of mimesis, is an improvement and learned skill like other ways of describing and communicating,

> which must be known and practiced in a community before their great power in conveying experience can be used and developed. Human community grows by the discovery of common meanings and common means of communication. Over an active range, the patterns created by the brain and the patterns materialized by a community continually interact. The individual creative description is part of the general process, which creates conventions and institutions, through which the meanings that are valued by the community are shared and made active.[105]

This experimental and community-based process of film as art, and the avant-garde filmmaker's presence in the public sphere, increase the possibilities for constructing emergent social experiences and alternatives to the dominant culture in society. Accordingly, film constitutes a threat to the status quo that resorts to either appropriation or censorship.

Censorship, however, is not absolute. For example, Michel De Certeau accounts for the agency of the common person, who is often treated as a passive recipient of dominant ideas. Due to the silent nature of agency, it often passes unnoticed in everyday life practices. De Certeau explains the silent nature of agency by revising the subordinate relation between strategy and tactics in military terminology. He argues that tactics are equal to strategies for guerrilla war; tactics are the deciding factors in winning battles. Despite lacking strategy, the common person exercises agency through tactics, which serve as techniques of adaptation to the environment enforced by the strategies of the powerful. For example, a city's urban planning division can have a strategy for streets, but the inhabitants of the city figure out how best to navigate the lived reality of those streets. Similarly, the act of reading or watching a movie might seem passive and silent, but the reader or the viewer is continuously engaged in tactics of reassessment, interpretation, correction, and observation. And agency as a silent act, it seems to me, is not a sweeping wave; it is a fragmented, gradual, and continuing process of independent deliberation that takes place within the self until it reaches its peak and communicates in different forms, driven sometimes by interest and at other times by ideology. A critical realist filmmaker thus capitalizes on the potential agency of audiences and their ability to communicate. While censorship policies often restrict the explicit critique of political reality in Egypt, critical realism becomes a double-entendre, through which filmmakers comment critically on strategies of marginalization and exclusion, thereby carving out a space for the public use of reason to assess dominant, residual, and emergent experiences, despite censorship.

4. Dominant, Residual, and Emergent Modernities

Scholarship that attempts to define modernity does not follow one accepted definition of modernity. Two major conceptual frameworks dominate the research in this regard. On the one hand, modernity is conceptualized as a process of societal modernization that emerged in and outside the West, accompanied by a set of liberal values regulated by the state's acknowledgment of the entitlement of the laity as citizens to participate in the affairs of the state, with the main goal of improving the human condition. Alternatively, modernity is studied as a colonialist discourse that leads to the accumulation of wealth and power in the West, causing displacement and further deterioration in the human condition. Post-colonial nation-states continue to adhere to and exalt forms of knowledge produced in colonial times and continue to suffer from incomplete[106] or failed projects of modernity.

In this book, I speak neither of an alternative to European modernity[107] nor of a "restaging of European modernity."[108] Perhaps Foucault was right when he tried to understand modernity vis-à-vis Kant's question "What is Enlightenment?" Like Baudelaire, Foucault argues that the modern person is not the one who goes off to discover self, secrets, and hidden truth, but the one who tries to invent themselves. This modernity is not in itself liberating, Foucault notes. It only compels the person to face the task of producing oneself. Thus, Foucault finds Baudelairean modernity an exercise of liberty that simultaneously respects reality and violates it. While Baudelaire argues that modernity is an experience that is possible only in art, Foucault finds it possible in society itself if modernity is separated from understanding Enlightenment as an epoch (1715–89)[109] and is seen, instead, as an "attitude." By "attitude," Foucault refers to "a mode of relating to contemporary reality; a voluntary choice made by certain people; in the end, a way of thinking and feeling; a way, too, of acting and behaving that at one and the same time marks a relation of belonging and presents itself as a task. A bit, no doubt, like what the Greeks called an ethos."[110] As an attitude, modernity involves a breakup with the tradition that shapes the present. However, the break does not mean a radical and clean discontinuity with the entire knowledge of the past, but rather a consideration of what is "no longer indispensable"[111] for the constitution of ourselves as autonomous subjects in the present. Foucault does not provide a clear statement of what exactly is "no longer indispensable." However, he suggests seeking to treat the instances of discourse in that past to understand how they articulate what we think, say, and do as historical events. Social change occurs through experimentation, that is, testing for pushing boundaries.

Contrary to what Habermas suggests, Foucault does not argue for the enforcement of global or radical experimentation. He speaks of experimentation that engenders partial social transformation.[112] In other words, in using Foucault's epistemology, I do not undertake a postmodern or post-Enlightenment project that reduces "cultural modernity"[113] to a process of exalting the present that lives on the experience of rebelling against all that is normative. I agree with Habermas's critique of Foucault that understanding modernity as an "attitude" should not lead to understanding modernity as a constant state of revolt. It is true that such an understanding discloses a longing for the unpolluted, perfect, and stable present that risked neutralizing history, thereby lifting the blame from all historical actors and blurring the difference between problems caused by social modernization and those resulting from cultural modernity.[114] While I refuse to study modernity as one package of Enlightenment, I lean toward acknowledging a fundamental change that Enlightenment brought. That is the awareness on the part of the "laity,"[115] not just the middle class, of their legal entitlement as citizens—as opposed to subjects—to participate in the affairs of their state, which is run by a "governmentality"[116] that *is not pastoral*. Therefore, I rely on the work of the Egyptian intellectual Mahmud Amin al-'Alim to highlight what seems to me to be a missing dimension in Foucault's Eurocentric epistemology. That is to draw a line between consciousness and false consciousness of modernity and to underscore the place of religion in modernity as an "attitude." Early films saw the importance of incorporating a post-secular stance that allows the vital potential semantics of religious traditions to emerge.[117]

As I bring Foucault and Habermas into my conversation, I am careful not to reduce modernity to a process that emerged only in Europe. I talk neither of singular modernity that defines all other histories in its terms, nor of the easy pluralism of alternative modernities. I acknowledge imperialism as the most powerful expression of universal modernity, steered by a crony capitalist project of modernization that survived by displacing, subordinating, and marginalizing all elements that appear incompatible with the modern, Western, or capitalist.[118] However, I agree with Timothy Mitchel that in the very process of their subordination and exclusion, marginalized elements infiltrate and influence history. These elements continually redirect, divert, and mutate the modernity they help constitute,[119] and eventually they come up with their own representation of modernity. Charles Taylor describes this process as "divergence within convergence," that is, the act of divergence in modernity as massive convergence. Taylor's cultural theory of modernity accounts for understanding modernity not as specifically Western, even though it may have started in the West. It acknowledges modernity as those forms of life toward which all cultures converge as they go through, one after another, substantially the same changes in both outlook and institutional arrangements. Nevertheless, since the historical trajectories of people differ, new differences will always emerge from the old. Institutions and practices (emergence of the market-industrial economy, a bureaucratically organized state, modes of popular rule) converge while cultures diverge.[120] One way of understanding this process is to study the pull to sameness and the forces causing divergence.[121] In Taylor's view, a functional project of modernity involves people finding resources in their traditional culture, which, modified and transposed, will enable them to take on the new practices. "There is never an atomistic and neutral understanding of modernity; there are only constellations with different imaginations."[122]

However, I break with the scholarly polarization of colonialist versus nationalist modernity or modernity inside the West versus alternative modernity outside the West. In other words, provincializing Europe is not my focus here. Instead, I want to explore the possibility of studying modernity as a structure of feeling, as, that is, a practical consciousness that is often in conflict with dominant and residual cultures of modernity. That is to say, when I speak of the emergence of alternative modernities, I speak of an "alternative" to dominant cultures of modernity (be it colonialist, nationalist, or any other dominant culture) as an attempt to restore the voice of the subaltern in its modernity.

Accordingly, I do not study modernity in Egypt through the more common scholarly statist and *acultural* approaches that understand modernity as creative destruction, emphasizing discontinuity with the tradition of the past as means of clearing the ground for more rational forms of society.[123] My goal is not to scrutinize the formation of the nation-state, arguing that competing nationalist ideologies (Pharaonic, Islamic, and Arabic) led to a crisis in national identity, hence the failure of modernity in Egypt.[124] I do not intend to tell the story of modernity in Egypt as a partial success of constitutional democracy as experienced in Egyptian political life between 1922 and 1936 and the consequent efforts of modernization marked by industrialization, the emancipation of women, and the spread of education and the Anglo-Egyptian Treaty of Alliance of 1936. One can hardly overlook reading the modern nation-state and nationalism as colonial constructs shaped by colonial policies and technologies of rule developed under Muhammad Ali and British occupation.[125] However, this book hopes to provincialize the state and foreground the voice of filmmakers as artists and public intellectuals in Egypt's story of modernity. I focus instead on a more *cultural* approach that studies modernity within the dialectics of censorship and resistance. Likewise, I am not invested in the study of modernity in Egypt through the formation of the educated middle class represented through the *effendi*, a subject formed between the empire and the nation.[126] The book is not concerned with the *effendi* as a class or a social position.¹²⁷ I aim to provincialize the *effendis* and their cultural production in what constitutes middle-class culture in Egypt, given the higher rates of illiteracy at the time. I present pioneer filmmakers' alternative reading of the *effendi* as a caricature of modernity, a failed quest for individualism, and false consciousness of modernity. In doing so, I capitalize on recent attempts to bring the vernacular culture of the uneducated urban masses more fully into the historical narrative of modern Egypt without the framework of nationalism. This approach aims to decentralize the study of modernity and emphasize the heterogeneity of the vernacular forms of modernity in the public sphere in order to draw a line between vernacular modernity that cheers totalitarianism and vernacular modernity which is primarily occupied with questions of social justice for all citizens.

In doing this, the book revises popular culture approaches that frame modernity in Egypt as a failure due to a hegemonic discourse of authenticity (*asala*)—the desire to embrace modern social values without losing connection with the past—as a marker of an authentic culture of the past. Instead, I differentiate between *asala* and the nationalist "hegemonic discourse of authenticity," which is actually nothing but *an appropriation of asala*. The Arabic word *asala* is a verbal noun derived from the Arabic root *a-s-l*, which corresponds to the English word "origin" or "root." It is not clear when and how *asala* started to signify "tradition" or "cultural heritage" (*turath*). The meaning of *asala* gets further complicated when it is framed in the expression *al-asala wa-l-muʿasara* as an antonym to the word *muʿasara*, which connotes "contemporaneity," or "adaptation to"/"coping with" contemporary life changes. The two meanings of *asala* are apparently not synonymous. Exclusive nationalist discourse uses the two significations interchangeably to legitimize its dominance. That is to say; exclusive nationalism seeks to legitimatize its dominance by establishing a historical specificity (*khususiyya*),¹²⁸ often reduced to the continuity of an "abstract"¹²⁹ centralized power as the only path via which formerly colonized societies can carry out a functioning project of modernity. For example, Egypt's historical specificity is reduced to Ahmose, Muhammad Ali, and Nasser. The exclusive nationalist quest for its forged historical specificity requires a search for *asala* (here being the roots), which is seen in terms of the victorious historical moments of patriotism or patriots. Due to their interest in appearing consistent and inclusive to the public, exclusive nationalist discourses often sweep under the rug contradictions in the cultural heritage produced by those patriotic moments. To exclusive nationalism, authenticity means "nationalist authenticity," and it is achieved by a submissive return to the roots or retrieval of the roots in a frozen form in the present; or by casting a modern frame on the roots so as to argue for their ability to function withstanding the passage of time and the factors of change. What gets suppressed is the idea that *asala* (the roots) are actually the people; their cultural heritage is produced by their quest for free movement in the public sphere and free use of public reason to create an equitable local and colloquial alternative to dominant exclusive nationalist discourse. To study people and their cultural heritage through a historical specificity of retrenched nationalist projects of "Enlightenment" and its dramas of nationhood is to do a favor to exclusive nationalism, and allow it to use a forged historical specificity to localize injustice in the name of *asala*. It also means to miss the difference between the hegemonic subaltern, who allies with the centralized power, and the subaltern, who rebels against it. A distinction needs to be made between *asala* and its appropriation by exclusive nationalism to avoid mistaking *asala* for "hegemonic discourses of authenticity," which I refer to here as dominant modernity (*tafarnug*) and residual modernity (*ta'ssul*).

In using the term *tafarnug*, I do not refer to the words *afranji* and *firanji*, often used to signify a foreigner of European origin, especially of French descent. I also do not use *tafarnug* to refer simply to the attempt to imitate or blindly mimic Western social practices. Blind imitation is an achievement when compared to *tafarnug*. The word "*tafarnug*", dictionaries tell us, is a pattern five verbal noun. However, its foreign origin makes it quite difficult to guess its pattern. (I wish it could be spelled with double "rr" to better reflect how I use it here.) To speak of *tafarnug* in early Egyptian cinema is to speak of the cinematic critique of reducing modernity to a social practice that gives priority to cultivating an amour-propre of a modern civilizational form (*al-shakl al-hadari al-'asri*) which projects itself as the guardian of the local culture of the past.[130] *Tafarnug* involves the imposition of European and later American everyday life practices in local dining habits, dress code, house decor, workspaces, and leisure-time activities without the internalization of modern notions of equity and social justice. The end of *tafarnug* is to exercise patronization so as to regulate attempts to imagine "the modern" and reinterpret the cultures of the past, only to sustain *tafarnug* as a dominant culture of modernity. Egyptian cinema depicts *tafarnug* as both an end and a means. The purpose is not to mimic to learn, but to counterfeit in order to accumulate and centralize power and wealth. Any local alternative that did not lead to *tafarnug* needed to be suppressed or appropriated. *Tafarnug*, thus, is a delusive amour-propre and a discourse of modernity which the Cairene-bourgeoisie used to construct their social and political power. Ironically, this delusive amour-propre is a colonialist discourse that was used to construct centralized Cairene social and political power during the colonial period. Egyptian film classics presented several patterns of how *tafarnug* appropriated, suppressed, and ridiculed colloquial cultures. Often, films showed how metaphors representing Islam among adherents of *tafarnug* appeared as marginalized, appropriated, or ridiculed. In this, early filmmakers presented their critique of *tafarnug* as a means of contesting the modernity discourses shaping the overt censorship of their art and profession.

As a dominant culture, *tafarnug* tolerates the presence of another false consciousness of modernity and another delusive amour-propre. I call this the "as if becoming modern" or residual modernity (*ta'ssul*), by which I refer to the practice of establishing continuity between the past and the present by means of denying conflicts and suppressing the difference between the new experiences and the experiences of the past. Adherents of *ta'ssul* are portrayed as Cairene-bourgeoisie keen on disseminating their views across different social classes. The adherents of *ta'ssul* follow the adherents of *tafarnug* in the imposition of contemporary foreign everyday life practices in daily dining habits, dress code, house decor, workspaces, and leisure-time activities as a condition for being modern. At the same time, the adherents of *ta'ssul* condemn *tafarnug* and stigmatize it as a blind imitation of European practices. Between 1919 and 1952, filmmakers followed two patterns in depicting *ta'ssul*. Some film characters were depicted practicing *ta'ssul* by resurrecting an imagined ideal tradition in a modern frame. Alternatively, they appeared to project a traditional frame onto modern ideas, which were claimed to have existed as part of an imagined ideal past. Early films lampooned both patterns as a delusive amour-propre and a false consciousness of modernity that strived to present itself as an innovation, while being a travesty that presented nothing new and appropriated metaphors representing Islam. While *ta'ssul* was tolerated by the Cairene-bourgeoisie, it was dismissed by working-class Egyptians.

In discussing the cinematic depiction of *ta'ssul*, I pay close attention to its masters, namely, the *effendis*, the white-collar bureaucrats whose colonial education and bureaucracy shaped their habits, education, and training during the interwar period. The characteristics of the *effendis*, be they a class, a community, or a mere bureaucratic rank, have for long occupied a central position in the study of modernity in Egypt. The word *effendi* itself is of Turkish origin; it signifies some of the government employees who did not hold nobility titles like bey or pasha. The signification of the word, however, can be confusing. Used by someone of higher social status, the word can be used to emphasize the *effendi*'s inferior status. Depending on the context, an uneducated working-class Egyptian may use it to imply respect or mediocrity. The popular colloquial Egyptian statement "Don't you dare think I'm an *effendi*" (*inta fakirni effendi*) implies that the speaker is street-savvy and cannot easily be fooled. The term also signifies the apparel of a male dressed in a suit or a shirt and trousers versus a galabiya. The social character of the *effendi* seems more complex than his characteristics. Considering the emergence of the *effendi* under colonial rule, Wilson Jacob reads him as a subject whose formation, on the nonmetropolitan side, yet between the empire and the nation, produced him as a mythical figure "emerging into history as questionably Egyptian and less certainly modern and debatably masculine."[131] In the process of forming the *effendi* as a modern subject, local forms of masculinity were suppressed. Walter Armbrust attributes the rise of the *effendis* to print capitalism, which accelerated cultural production in the high linguistic register of Modern Standard Arabic, whose masters, the *effendis*, functioned as mediators between modern progressive social values and the vast majority of *awlad al-balad* who spoke in the low, illogical, colloquial register. Armbrust acknowledges the difficulty of studying the *effendis* as a group due to their contingency and situational performance, which makes it difficult to locate them as a class.[132] Luci Ryzova also finds the class approach limited, due to the impossibility of fitting the *effendi* into the Egyptian middle class with its blurry markers. Surely, education marks the middle class. But the high illiteracy rates in Egypt during the first half of the twentieth century place a question mark on whether the educated *effendis* were a representative pool of the middle class at the time. Therefore, Ryzova suggests studying the *effendi* as a social category, a social position, and a worldview, marked by some socially recognized signs of Western education and the famous apparel of suit and tarbush. She sees the *effendis* as makers and primary consumers of modern Egyptian political life, social institutions, and cultural production; they are major actors of modern Egyptian nationalism and "the first self-consciously modern generation in Egyptian history."[133] By considering the semi-educated in her definition of the *effendis*, she avoids replicating the state's claim to modernize people through state institutions.

For my purposes in this book, I read the *effendi* through the pre-1952 cinematic critique of the *effendi* (of the interwar and post-World War II periods) in terms of a suppressed quest for individualism. In doing so, I do not intend to present a generalized view of the *effendis*. Instead, I underscore the distinction made in early films between the *effendis* who *adhere to* the social practices of *tafarnug* or *ta'ssul* and the *effendis* who *condemn* both practices as byproducts of colonial education, which reduces modernity to an egocentric view of individualism. A revealing example is found in the movie *Ibn al-Fallah*/Son of the Peasant, 1948, directed by 'Abd al-Fattah Hasan. In a bar scene, the dialogue of the film's hero, played by Muhammad al-Kahlawi, explicitly condemns the *effendi*'s egocentric view of modernity and simultaneously denies the generalization. My discussion here focuses on the *effendi* who belongs to the first group. This *effendi* goes through a struggle to differentiate himself from his social group of origin and become part of a state-controlled system that regulates availability in time and space as well as rights and responsibilities in society. Under colonization, being an individual is more complicated for the *effendi*, who has to differentiate himself culturally from the colonial powers that introduced him to the cult of individualism. Because of the contexts of war, colonization, and liberation struggle, the colonial state, and its bureaucratic institutions, fail to present to the individual in Egypt as a periphery what it presents (if it does) in the metropole (e.g. London or Paris). The *effendi* struggles to construct boundaries between himself and those below as well as those above. Failing to achieve individualism, the *effendi* "acts as if he is individual;" he mingles in different domains according to need. The *effendi*'s mobility and shifting loyalties make it difficult to pinpoint him in a social class. He appears as an agent while associating himself with different classes, but remains a hegemonic subject in his relationship with the institution. Within the *effendi*'s suppressed quest for individualism, modernity becomes *ta'ssul*, a utilitarian worldview that prioritizes the formal manifestation of modernity at the expense of its core foundations of social justice among citizens (not subjects) of the state. This egocentric view of individualism functioned as the sword of the corrupt feudal institution and did not shy away from appropriating metaphors representing Islam to serve its interests.

In response to *tafarnug* and *ta'asul*, early filmmakers depicted *asala* as a structure of feeling a positive, that is an active, equity-based, alternative. *Asala* is a dynamic, practical consciousness, a voluntary choice to relate to contemporary reality by contesting the correlation between becoming modern and the imposition of European, and later American, everyday life practices in local dining, work, and leisure habits. Here *asala* does not emerge as a stance against the foreign; it is a stance against the claims of superiority of the foreign; it questions the idolizing of the *Khawaga*'s social practices while simultaneously stigmatizing local social practices as vulgar, backward, primitive, and incompatible with modernity. Filmmakers often tied a character's attitude of *asala* to vulnerability, which was not depicted as a sign of the character's weaknesses. Rather, a character's vulnerability was depicted as a sign of courage that enabled the character to overcome a myth of shame associated with breaking a dominant societal norm. This process often involved challenging the delusive amour-propre of *tafarnug* or *ta'ssul* or introducing an unprecedented practice (in its context). Early movies presented diverse depictions of *asala* as an emergent culture of modernity, which used to be a topic for discussion in the social practice of *a'da* among marginalized social groups such as peasants, workers, women, and performing artists. *A'da* is quite similar to the social practice of *adda* from the city of Calcutta in the first half of the twentieth century as an example of the emergence of the public sphere outside Europe.[134] As Dipesh Chakrabarty points out, "the men of Calcutta—in the matter of their devotion to *adda*—come second only to the men of Cairo."[135] Chakrabarty questions the etymology of the word *adda*, stating:

> I am not a pundit; I do not know the etymology of the word [*adda*]. It sounds non-Sanskritic [and] Muslim. If we Hinduize it and call it *sabha*, it loses everything. If we Anglicize it and call it "party," we kill its spirit . . .

Does *adda* have an exact synonym in any other language of the world? Even without being a linguist, I can say no.[136]

A similar practice with an etymological resemblance to *adda* evolved in Egypt by the late nineteenth century. Perhaps Chakrabarty was right in guessing that the word sounds Muslim (or perhaps he meant Arabic), as it could be traced to the standard Arabic noun *qaʿda*, which relates to the English "sitting" and is partially used in the Arabic expression *qaʿdat ʿarab*, signifying a common social practice of gathering among tribal chiefs. In this sense, *qaʿda* resembles what Chakrabarty describes as *majlis*, where the gathering has a goal, here, conflict resolution, unlike the freer casual atmosphere of *adda*. Remarkably, the Egyptian colloquial pronunciation of the standard Arabic *qaʿda* as *aʿda* sounds very similar to the pronunciation of *adda*. The Egyptian colloquial word *aʿda* with the initial *q* dropped and replaced with the famous Egyptian glottal stop is used to refer to "a setting" for a social gathering that echoes the practice of *adda*. I am not sure if the Arabic complex middle sound /ʿayn/ in *aʿda* underwent a variation and was replaced with a /d/, turning *aʿda* into *adda*, or if it was the other way round, in the same way as the famous Indian dish Kishri reached Egypt and became known as Kushari Masri. Like having *adda*, having *aʿda* meant the social practice of intellectuals, musicians, poets, singers, students, and workers gathering at a friend's house or a coffee house or a social club or a barber's shop to merely chat and talk about life, its ways, events, and conditions (*ahwal al-dunya*). Apart from the fact that cinema and theater evolved to be public spheres and a form of *aʿda*, Egyptian cinema provides a rich archive for understanding *aʿda*. Early depictions of *aʿda* appear in Kamal Salim's *al-ʿAzima*/Perseverance, 1939 and *al-Mazahir*/Appearances, 1945, which will be analyzed in later chapters. Topics discussed in *aʿda* include but are not limited to politics, the narration of personal experiences, and discussions of sport and news. It is not uncommon to discuss *tafarnug*, *taʾssul*, and *asala* in *aʿda*. When singing takes place in *aʿda*, it becomes called *sahba*, and the participants are called *sahbagiyya*. The practice of *aʿda* existed in both urban and rural Egypt, where men gathered in *al-mandara*, a large room similar to Chakrabarty's *rwak*. Folk singing and colloquial poetry recitation become a marker of *aʿda* in the countryside, known in Egyptian as to debate with me to outsmart me (*tikhushili afiya*). Karim's 1952 remake of

Zaynab presents an explicit depiction of *a'da* in the countryside. Women also had a visible presence in *a'da*, where genders mixed, especially during extended family gatherings.

It is important here to note that the cinematic depictions of *tafarnug*, *ta'ssul*, and *asala* are not static. And they are not easily detectable by applying fixed categories of analysis such as fashion, gender, and film language. Again, when cinema flourished in Egypt, cinema had already started talking worldwide. Filmmakers, who came from theater, where the dialogue was the driving force of the performance, produced most early talkies, which spoke in colloquial Egyptian that Nagib al-Rihani described as the language of the box office. Thus, extending beyond the cinematic form to a serious consideration of the tools of screenwriting and context is necessary to understand how early films motivated the marginalized, who did not read or write in standard Arabic, and who made up the bulk of the population, providing them with clues as to what better social conditions of life might be. Early films created a massive growth in imaginativeness about alternative lifeways and a simultaneous interest in finding institutional means for handling these lifeways.[137] This should not be mistaken for suggesting that Egyptians should learn to admire and consume precisely the same things as people in Europe. What filmmakers suggested is that before any enduring public transformation can bear fruit in Egypt, people there will have to, autonomously and without government supervision, learn about the lifeways that evolved in other contemporary societies. What they subsequently accept, adapt, or reject is a matter which each citizen will decide for themselves in due course.[138]

Metaphors representing Islam featured significantly in the depiction of *tafarnug*, *ta'ssul*, and *asala*. While these metaphors are marginalized, appropriated, or ridiculed by adherents of *tafarnug* and *ta'ssul*, they are emphasized as a substratum of the everyday life practices of film characters adhering to *asala* in which ethical intuitions of Islam were negotiated and communicated in ways that presented Islam as a lived experience, thereby underscoring the place of religion in modernity and the place of cinema in the public cultures produced among Muslims.[139]

5. On Film Metaphors Symbolizing Islam

This book breaks with existing approaches to the study of Islam, which have fallen short of capturing the coherence (i.e. diversity and breadth) of Islam by focusing either on particular aspects of Islam or on contradictions in the previous systematization of it.[140] The late Shahab Ahmad tried to create a space for accepting the word "Islamic" as a conceptualization of Islam that is not based on the elimination of difference but on the inclusion of difference. To that end, he seems to treat Islam as a message (i.e. as a human and historical phenomenon characterized and constituted not merely by immense variety and diversity, but by the prodigious presence of outright contradiction). This message has three stages: pre-text (i.e. revelation), text (i.e. Qur'an-anchoring of the meaning), and context (i.e. the standardization of text, its interpretations, and the discourses that shaped its meanings). The three stages interact with each other in history to account for both Islam-making Muslims and Muslims-making Islam. To study this message today is to acknowledge how our research is limited by the fragmentation of the pre-text state, leaving one thus at the context stage (i.e. one can only study the parts of the discourses that have surrounded the message and may throw light on its meanings). Yet the limitations of the context stage and its fragmentation have resulted in a scholarly polarization that drives the ways in which the message is framed, presented, and received both historically and in various media outlets available today.

On the one hand, there are the Salafist discourses, the puritans who dominate twenty-first-century Islamic discourse and champion the Prophet Muhammad as the founder of a pristine, uniform faith that every Muslim should aspire to replicate. Reductionist and decontextualized understandings of the writings of Ibn Taymiyya inspire these discourses, which flood the internet with websites describing how to get "the true" knowledge about Islam, how to lead an Islamic "lifestyle" which is the only path to salvation in this world and in the afterlife. What gets swept under the rug here is how the status of human knowledge about the message that the Prophet bequeathed remains fragmented and confused. Muslims themselves have not rediscovered the bulk of the knowledge produced in the Islamic golden age; they are still grappling with questions about the founders of Islam, the necessities of its laws, and how Islam expanded by absorbing the traditions of the peoples who fell under its rule and whether these traditions shaped Islam as we know it today or not. These questions, which were indeed shaped by the scares of colonization, continue to persist in the post-colonial nation-states, primarily because the puritanist quest for structured, absolute, and certain knowledge about the message overlooks the fact that skepticism and confusion are natural stages when it comes to the pursuit of knowledge. Skepticism is a founding principle of Abraham's monotheism, at least as expressed in the Qur'an.[141]

The second discourse is the Orientalist/Islamicist discourse that studies the context stage, despite fragmentation, and underscores the contributions of Islam to the growth of human civilization. This camp hails the production of philosophy and sciences through figures like Ibn al-Hayathm, al-Farabi, Ibn Sina, al-Kindi, Ibn 'Arabi, Rumi, al-Zahrawi, al-Idrisi, al-Khawarizmi, Hunyan Ibn Ishaq, Ibn Rushd, Ibn Tufayl, Abu Bakr al-Razi, and Ibn al-Nafis, and the list can go on. Adherents of this discourse see that the tightening grip of orthodoxy and the triumph of the Asha'rite position is the main reason that led to Islam's supposed inexorable civilizational decline. Here, one is reminded of those asserting the primacy of reason over revelation. An archetypal example is a hypothetical debate between Ibn Rushd and al-Ghazali. The Orientalist/Islamicist camp also reminds us that the philosophers' defense that reason was a gift of God is what spares them from charges of blasphemy. While the second approach revives the social milieu in which Islam produced institutions that facilitated the production of knowledge and hence shaped human civilization in the Middle Ages, it remains less influential in the public sphere today. The vast majority of Muslims today lack access to such knowledge; it is uncommon to find a school textbook detailing how the father of the scientific method, Ibn al-Haytham, contested Aristotle's notion of vision, how his doubt about Greek knowledge led to the human discovery of how vision actually occurs. And even when these figures are celebrated, the celebration appears to be a mere appropriation of their legacy by dictatorships, who are happy to inaugurate a statue for Ibn al-Haytham as "the Muslim" scientist and are more invested in suppressing his struggle with the rulers of his time, his prosecution and imprisonment, and even his scholarly legacy that started with skepticism. After all, Ibn a-Haytham's legacy of perseverance might encourage Muslims to exercise the public use of reason and hence engender a social change that is rooted in citizenship rights and social justice. At least, this is the case in many Arabic-speaking countries today.

I contend, however, that there is a third discourse that was part of Islam's popular culture and continues to be part of it, and that is the popular culture discourse that often gets marginalized in the study of Islam. It is lived Islam. This popular culture discourse remains suppressed because of the dominance of the "Salafist" discourse, which will continue to be at the forefront so long as Islamicist/Orientalist scholarship continues to invest its resources in engaging more with the "Salafist" discourse as the more dominant and hence more representative, while ignoring the popular culture discourse. I argue thus that the popular culture discourse reveals how Islam as a message in its three stages produced dominant, residual, and emergent cultures, which need to be studied correspondingly to understand the contexts and the forms in which the message originates, gets disseminated, received, and expressed or suppressed in everyday life practices in different zeitgeists. This lived Islam is expressed in poetry, in travelogue literature, in literary texts like the *One Thousand and One Nights* and Ibn Tufayl's *Hayy Ibn Yaqzan*, in Ibn Danyal's shadow plays, and in the music treatise by al-Kindi, Abu al-Faraj al-Isfhani, al-Farabi, and in some of the works by al-Ghazali. It is expressed in figural representation (which is often taken for granted to be prohibited in Islam). It exists even in sex manuals such as al-Nafzawi's *The Perfumed Garden of Sensual Delight*. And it continues to exist in modern Arabic theater and in cinema, which is a majority Muslim film industry, even though its artists are often stigmatized as less Muslim, and their art is often studied as a mere westernization, or a predominantly secular domain that is anti-Islamic. The formative years of Egyptian cinema present an example of popular culture shaped by ethical intuitions of Islam, especially those relating to modern social experiences of women as citizens. Recognizing how early films referenced Islamic concepts is profoundly significant to understanding modernity in Egypt, and Egyptian cinema as an Islamic popular culture invested in the public use of reason, despite the harsh realities of colonization and war during the first half of the twentieth century. My reference to "Islamic" popular culture here refers to a conceptualization of Islam not based on the elimination of difference but rather on the inclusion of difference; Islam as a human and historical phenomenon characterized and constituted not merely by immense variety and diversity, but by the remarkable presence of outright contradictions, which interact with each other in history to account for Islam making Muslims and non-Muslims, while both also make Islam.

While the book acknowledges the fact that Egyptian cinema is a majority Muslim film industry (in its labor force, its target audience, and its themes), just as the Bombay film industry is a majority Hindu film industry despite the visible presence of Muslim actresses like Wahida Rahman and Nargis, the book, again, underscores Egyptian cinema as an Islamic popular culture shaped by both Muslims and non-Muslims. Many Muslim filmmakers operated before 1952. Directors include, but are not limited to, Yusuf Wahbi, Muhammad Karim, Kamal Salim, Ahmad Kamil Mursi, Waliyy al-Din Samih, Ibrahim 'Imara, Ahmad Badrkhan, Husayn Sidqi, Anwar Wagdi, 'Izz al-Din Dhu al-Faqqar, Ahmad Galal, Mahmud Dhu al-Faqqar, Fu'ad al-Gazayrli, and al-Sayyid Ziyada. There were also countless Muslim film stars before 1952. Five out of seven female pioneer filmmakers who started their careers in the 1920s are Muslims: Bahiga Hafiz, 'Aziza Amir, Amina Rizq, Amina Muhammad, and Fatima Rushdi. Other Muslim women who played leading roles in some of the most popular classics include names like Samira Khulusi, Ihlam Husyan, Madiha Yusri, Layla Fawzi, Fardus Muhammad, Umm Kulthum, Mimi Shakib, Zuzu Shakib, Fardus Muhammad, Zinat Sidqi, and Raga' 'Abduh. Male leads were more numerous than female leads. Names included Zaki Rustum, 'Abd al-Wahhab, Sirag Munir, Sulyamn Nagib, Husayn Riyad, Yusuf Wahbi, Ahmad Salim, Fakhir Fakhir, Husayn Sidqi, Muhsin Sarhan, Muhammad Fawzi, 'Imad Hamdi, Kamal al-Shinnawi, Yahaya Shahin, Mahmud Dhu al-Faqqar, and Izz al-Din Dhu al-Faqqar, among many others. Many non-Muslims were also early film stars during the formative period. At least six out of fifty outstanding filmmakers who operated before 1952 were non-Muslim. Three of them share a Jewish background, namely the director Tugu Mizrahi, the actress Raqiya Ibrahim, and the singer and actress Layla Murad. The latter married two Muslim filmmakers; her first husband was the actor and director Anwar Wagdi, and the second the director Fatin 'Abd al-Wahhab. Layla Murad converted to Islam during her first marriage; she died in Egypt and was buried in a Muslim cemetery. Shaykh Mahmud Abu al-'Uyun, whose views on acting and cinema are discussed in Chapter 6, witnessed her conversion. In addition, the actor Istifan Rusti, the actress Mary Munib, and the actor Nagib al-Rihani were from Christian backgrounds. Like Layla Murad, Mary Munib also converted to Islam. Both Rusti and Munib mastered supporting roles, unlike al-Rihani, who was a theater and film star. But we ought not to forget that without the second pillar of al-Rihani theater, namely Badi' Khayri, a Muslim playwright and screenplay writer, there could not have been a Rihani theater troupe that trained many actors, including Rusti and Munib. Of the many directors whose films are covered in this book, Tugu Mizrahi stands out as the only outstanding Egyptian Jewish filmmaker in the history of Egyptian cinema. The surviving legacy of Tugu Mizrahi consists of around thirty-three films. His most remembered and popular films are seventeen films made between 1939 and 1946. The leading stars in all of these films are Muslims, including Yusuf Wahbi, 'Ali al-Kassar, Sulyamn Nagib, Amina Rizq, Ahmad al-Haddad, Fu'ad and his sister Ihasan al-Gazayyrli, 'Aqila Ratib, Fatima Rushdi, Biba 'Izz al-Din, Mimi Shakib, Layla Fawzi, Husayn Sidqi, Anwar Wagdi, Muhammad Amin, Madiha Yusri, Umm Kulthum, and Karim Mahmud. It remains unfortunate, however, that the popularity of Tugu Mizrahi's films in Egyptian popular culture is rarely credited to him. Most of his films are credited to their Muslim stars, namely, Layla Murad, Yusuf Wahbi, and 'Ali al-Kassar. I hope this book underscores the role of Mizrahi in his own films, a role that is often suppressed by nationalist propaganda against Mizrahi after 1952. While Mizrahi worked with Layla Murad and Yusuf Wahbi in a series of films capitalizing on the success of Layla Murad as a singer, he did not cooperate with other famous actresses of Jewish backgrounds like Raqiya Ibrahim, who mostly appeared in films written, produced, and directed by Muslim directors like Muhammad Karim, Yusuf Wahbi, and Niyazi Mustafa. Their choice of Raqiya Ibrahim was not so much related to her talent as to her availability and her astonishing looks. Muhammad Karim, for example, used to struggle with his female leads about their diet. This was not a problem he had to face with Raqiya Ibrahim. It is also imperative to note here that Raqiya Ibrahim married a Muslim sound engineer at Studio Misr, namely Mustafa Wali. This was a time when sound recording used to be made in Paris, and Studio Misr had the only sound machine in the Middle East. This marriage positioned Raqiya Ibrahim at the center of the film industry in Egypt and gave her access to the tight network of filmmaking. This is, of course, not to undermine Raqiya Ibrahim's talent, but to draw attention to the fact that her talent and stardom were not as compelling as that of Layla Murad or another Egyptian Jewish actress, Nigma Ibrahim, who was Raqiya's sister and who made her name at a fairly advanced age, and after 1952. If Alfred Hitchcock had ever met Nigma Ibrahim, the world could have seen some of the best thrillers, but, unfortunately or fortunately, they did not meet.

It remains imperative here to remind the reader that the main criteria used for selecting films to be studied in this book had to do with whether the film engages with questions of modernity and Islam regardless of the background of the directors, whose points of view drive the analysis of films in Chapters 4, 5, and 6. Thus, supporting roles, which often carry the director's message, are extensively studied in the book. The goal is to show how the making of films during the formative period endured despite colonialist, nationalist, and Islamist overt and covert censorship rulings. This grip of censorship left its scars on the physical public sphere as well as on theater and cinema as supplemental public spheres. But early filmmakers still succeeded in offering an account of modernity in Egypt as a non-Eurocentric, decolonial secular notion of history that does not exclude religious sources of meaning.

Chapter One examines the place of film in British cultural policies in Egypt vis-à-vis two historical moments, the Anglo-Egyptian 1936 Treaty, which was a significant step toward Egypt's political independence, and the outbreak of World War II. I draw on records of the British Foreign Office, News Department, and Embassy in Egypt, and a collection of newspapers and magazines, in addition to the memoir of the first Egyptian female film censor, I'tidal Mumtaz. Initially, British cultural interest in Egypt was shaped by a negative policy, that is, an indirect cultural strategy that focused on limiting other European cultural expansion in Egypt more than on promoting British cultural hegemony. After the Treaty, a shift to a positive cultural policy (i.e. a direct one) aimed to sustain the amour-propre of the "White" man, hence the soldier of the British Empire, as the ultramodern civilized man. With the shadow of World War II looming, it was hoped that the new positive policy would ensure stability in Egypt during the war. It was also hoped that the post-Treaty amour-propre of the Egyptian ruling elite as modern sovereign rulers of a modern and civilized Egypt could be regulated. Film, being a new powerful medium of communication, was anticipated as contributing to these ends. But the entrenched French cultural hegemony in Egypt, and Hollywood dominance over the film market, proved that the shift came too late to bear the expected fruit. A more affordable solution was film censorship. Censorship better suited the long-standing British negative cultural policy; plus, film censorship had practical roots in post-1919 censorship of public media, which first included the printing press and theater. Most of the censorship rulings were orally executed by the Egyptian Ministry of the Interior, which was under the thumb of British colonial authorities. After World War II, a transition to written censorship rules culminated in the formation of the 1947 Egyptian Code of Film Censors, which echoed the code of the British Board of Film Censors. It codified pre-war oral policies into written rules, which ironically served the colonial ends even more efficiently. The Egyptian code censored the depiction of the lifestyle, the everyday practices, and the colloquialism of the peasants and working-class Egyptians who, despite being the majority of Egyptians, were seen by the code as disparaging Egypt's amour-propre as a modern and civilized country. This continuity does not just reveal how the colonized's forms of knowledge blindly follow the colonizer's. Rather, it shows how the colonized's reactionary forms of knowledge could lead to far more repression and marginalization of the colonized people.

British cultural hegemony in Egypt thus was promoted through oral and written rules of censorship, which before and after the Anglo-Egyptian Treaty and World War II were driven by a consciousness of modernity that was more invested in privileging White supremacy, and least interested in the public and in freedom of expression. Not surprisingly, the first threat to British business in Egypt after the war came from the attempt of local film producers to gain control over film exhibition halls owned by British film tycoon J. Arthur Rank around the same time as the famous Cairo Riots.

Chapter Two traces the covert censorship of film in early Islamic public discourses and legal opinions on the lawfulness of the two primary components of movie production: photography and acting. It draws on a collection of legal opinions published in *al-Manar* and *al-Azhar*, the two major religious journals of the time. I discuss the legal opinions issued by diverse channels through which Islamic legal discourses on photography and acting were disseminated during the first half of the twentieth century. For many Muslim 'ulama' who were carving a space for themselves in predominantly secular efforts to modernize Egypt, the lawfulness of film, like other modern innovations, posed a challenge. I want to examine here mainstream and non-mainstream legal opinions (*fatawa*)[142] issued by several jurisprudents, including Rashid Rida (1865–1935), Hasanayn Makhluf (1890–1990), 'Abdullah al-Ghumari (1910–93), and Ahmad al-Sharabasi (1918–80). Some of these opinions are published in the popular religious journals *al-Manar* and *al-Azhar*. Others are published in a private collection of legal opinions. The widespread popularity of film made it necessary for the 'ulama' to reopen a set of classical legal disputes over violating the Islamic doctrine of the oneness of God (*tawhid*), regulating the conduct of Muslim women, and forging Hadith. A major key to these disputes was the permissibility of creating images and of making images of the Prophets and Companions, in particular. Another major issue was the lawfulness of acting as a profession for Muslim women. By invoking the legal concept of public welfare (*maslaha*), some of the 'ulama' were able to sanction photography positively, thereby paving the way for the permissibility of acting in theater and cinema. However, these *maslaha* rulings also placed limitations on the scope of acting, limiting its use to cases of necessity and need. This use of *maslaha* did not provide room for the innovation that is crucial to maintaining the status of film as art and as a domain for experimentation, freedom of expression, and creativity. The use of *maslaha* by these scholars was further limited by the legal principle of blocking the legal means that could lead to sin (*sadd al-dhara'i'*), which overrules the use of *maslaha* even in cases of necessity and need.[143]

Chapter Three examines the cinematic critique of dominant modernity (*tafarnug*) as a screen resistance to the modernity discourses driving overt censorship. I show how filmmakers employed supporting roles to lampoon *tafarnug* as a false consciousness of modernity, which marginalized or ridiculed metaphors representing Islam. Each film presents a different contextualization of *tafarnug*, reveals the expansion of its dominance, and how eventually reducing modernity to *tafarnug* produced a reactionary counter-modernity stance that framed modernity as a fundamentally anti-Islamic project. While Muhammad Karim's *al-Warda al-Bayda'/ The White Rose*, 1933 acknowledges *tafarnug* as a false consciousness of modernity, Karim's *Yawm Sa'id/ Happy Day*, 1939, contests reducing the freedom of women to *tafarnug*. Kamal Salim's *al-'Azima*/Perseverance, 1939, critiques *tafarnug* as a hegemonic practice among working-class Egyptians. Tugu Mizrahi's *Layla Bint al-Rif*/Leila, Daughter of the Countryside, 1941 reveals how *tafarnug* perpetuates an inferiority gaze at peasants. Yusuf Wahbi's *Bint Dhawat*/Daughter of the Nobles, 1942, blames *tafarnug* for the systematic dehumanization of peasants. In *Ibn al-Haddad*/Son of the Blacksmith, 1944, Wahbi condemns *tafarnug* as a radical stance that objectifies women in the name of modernity. Salim's *al-Mazahir*/Appearances, 1945 records the enforcement of *tafarnug* and early signs of resistance among working-class women (*banat al-balad*). Wahbi's *Safir Gahannam*/Ambassador of Hell, 1945 announces the arrival of American *tafarnug* and the dire consequences of its neo-liberalization on art and education. In *Talaq Su'ad Hanim*/The Divorce of Su'ad Hanim, 1948 and *al-Zawja al-Sabi'a* /The Seventh Wife, 1950, Anwar Wagdi and Ibrahim 'Imara share a critique of the false ways in which modernity materializes and lead to the appropriation of Islamic legal tradition in order to sustain a class hierarchy that thrives on colonization and war. Al-Sayyid Ziyada's *Mughamarat Khadra*, 1950 and *Khadra wa-l-Sindibad al-Qibli*, 1951 show how reducing modernity to *tafarnug* produces a reactionary counter-modernity stance that framed modernity as a fundamentally anti-Islamic project.

Chapter Four examines the cinematic critique of residual modernity (*ta'ssul*) as a contestation of the modernity discourses shaping covert censorship. As a false consciousness of modernity, *ta'ssul* seems to have been first depicted in Niyazi Mustaf'a *Salama fi Khayr*/Salama Is Safe, 1937, which lampoons how the *effendi* reduces modernity to an egocentric view of individualism and does not shy away from appropriating metaphors representing Islam to serve his interests. Muhammad Karim's *Yahya al-Hub*/Long Live Love, 1938 and *Yawm Sa'id*/Happy Day, 1939 underscore the falsity of *ta'ssul* and its claims to support the modern social roles of women as citizens. In *'Aris Min Istanbul*/A Groom from Istanbul, 1941, Yusuf Wahbi takes the critique of *ta'ssul* a step further by depicting it as deformed modernity (*maskh*) in both form and content; he shows how *ta'ssul* appropriates Islamic trust fund law (*waqf*) and how it eventually produces *tafarnug*, thereby sustaining the cycle of injustice, an idea further explored by Ahmad Badrkhan in *Man al-Gani*/ Who Is the Criminal?, 1944. In *Abu Halmus*/Father of Halmus, 1947, Ibrahim Hilmy correlates *effendiness* and institutional corruption. In *Ma'alihshi Ya Zahr*/Never Mind, 1950, Henry Barakat caricatures the *effendi*'s obsession with *effendiness*. Fatin 'Abd al-Wahhab, in *al-Ustadha Fatima*/Attorney

Fatima, 1952, interrogates the *effendi*'s position on women's education. Husayn Sidqi's *al-Shaykh Hasan*/Sheikh Hasan, 1951 shows how *effendiness*'s obsession with rationality threatens social peace and order. Here, Sidqi makes a clear distinction between religion as faith and spirituality and religion as an ideology that assumes moral supremacy.

Chapter Five analyzes diverse depictions of emergent modernity (*asala*). I trace the ways in which filmmakers depict their characters, attempting to make a seemingly impossible condition possible, and how these attempts are depicted as suppressed, tolerated, or emergent. Karim's *al-Warda al-Bayda'*/The White Rose, 1933 constructs *asala* through the female protagonist's awareness of how patriarchy commodifies the female body (as a source either of income or class superiority). Karim's *Yawm Sa'id*/Happy Day, 1939 depicts *asala* forcing patriarchy to reconsider its injustices. Here the notion of *tawakkul* appears as the driving force behind the empowerment of women and local artists. In Salim's *al-'Azima*/Perseverance, 1939, rebellion against *effendiness*, along with the collective agency of working-class Egyptians (*awlad al-balad*), bring about social change. In *Layla Bint al-Rif*/Daughter of the Countryside, 1941, Tugu Mizrahi unprecedentedly depicts *asala* resisting the inferiority gaze at the peasant by positioning the uneducated peasant woman at the center of Egypt's modern renaissance. Here, Mizrahi's female protagonist is as iconic as the female figure in Mahmud Mukhtar's famous post-1919 statue, which used to decorate Cairo station square (now Ramses station) before it was replaced with Ramses' statue. However, Mizrahi's peasant woman, unlike Mukhtar's, needs no sphinx; she is far more empowered; she speaks and condemns *tafarnug* as a false consciousness of modernity by evaluating it against the perspective of human rights and social justice. Wahbi's *Ibn al-Haddad*/Son of the Blacksmith, 1944 and Salim's *al-Mazahir*/Appearances, 1945 show the collective agency of working-class Egyptians (*awlad al-balad*) and suggest that for *asala* to be a collective emergent culture it has to break the myth of shame constructed around "the origin" without reactionary stances that idolize it. Again, the Islamic notion of *tawakkul* motivates these discussions. Karim's *Dunya*/Dunya 1946 uses the theme of revenge to interrogate a number of questions with regard to 1940s public discussions on civil liberties for women in relation to sexual harassment and retribution-based versus rehabilitation-based justice. In *al-Bayt al-Kabir* /The Foremost House, 1949, Ahmad Kamil

Mursi presents *asala* as an exercise in the public use of reason among students of Islamic law who question orthodox interpretations of Islamic law with regard to the question of polygamy. In *Bayumi Afandi*/Mr. Bayumi, 1949, Yusuf Wahbi correlates between *tafarnug* and the Qur'anic concept of *kufr* reinterpreted as "ingratitude," as opposed to the popular interpretation of the concept as "infidelity."

Notes

1. On the history of Egyptian cinema, see Viola Shafik, *Popular Egyptian Cinema: Gender, Class, and Nation* (Cairo: American University in Cairo Press, 2007), Sherif Boraïe, Mustafa Darwish, Rafik al-Saban, and Yasser Alwan, *The Golden Years of Egyptian Cinema* (Cairo: The American University in Cairo Press, 2008), and the new three-volume edition of Ahmad al-Hadari, *Mawsu'at Tarikh al-Sinima fi Misr* (Cairo: al-Hay'a al-'Ama al-Misriyya lil-Kitab), 2019.
2. On the history of modernity in Egypt, see Afaf Lutfil Sayyid-Marsot, *Egypt's Liberal Experiment: 1922-1936* (Berkeley: University of California Press, 1977), Selma Botman, *Egypt from Independence to Revolution 1919-1952* (Syracuse, NY: Syracuse University Press, 1991), Israel Gershoni and James Jankowski, *Egypt, Islam, and the Arabs: The Search for Egyptian Nationhood, 1900-1930* (New York: Oxford University Press, 1986), Elliott Colla, *Conflicted Antiquities: Egyptology, Egyptomania, Egyptian Modernity* (Durham, NC: Duke University Press, 2007), Timothy Mitchell, *Colonizing Egypt* (New York: New York University Press, 1991), Khaled Fahmy, *All the Pasha's Men: Mehmed Ali, His Army, and the Making of Modern Egypt* (Cambridge: Cambridge University Press, 1997), Ziad Fahmy, *Ordinary Egyptians: Creating the Modern Nation through Popular Culture* (Stanford, CA: Stanford University Press, 2011), and Jessica Winegar, *Creative Reckonings: The Politics of Art and Culture in Contemporary Egypt* (Stanford, CA: Stanford University Press, 2006).
3. Arjun Appadurai and Carol A. Breckenridge, "Why Public Culture?," *Public Culture* 1, no. 1 (1988): 5–9
4. Sawsan Messiri, *Ibn al-Balad: A Concept of Egyptian Identity* (Leiden: Brill, 1978), 44.
5. Ibid.
6. Deborah A. Starr, "Chalom and 'Abdu Get Married: Jewishness and Egyptianness in the Films of Togo Mizrahi," *Jewish Quarterly Review* 107, no. 2 (2017), 209–30.
7. Messiri, *Ibn al-Balad*, 85.

8. Ibid., 6.
9. Ashraf Baydas, *Abyad wa-Aswad* (Cairo: Sama, 2013), 43–50.
10. The name of the actor who played the role of *khawaga* Kustin is not mentioned in the credits of the film. This is unusual, but is probably because he appeared in fewer scenes than his wife, for example.
11. See Jacob Landau, *Studies in the Arab Theater and Cinema* (Philadelphia: University of Pennsylvania Press, 1958), 1. See also Afif Arabi, *The History of Lebanese Cinema, 1929–1979: An Analytical Study of the Evolution and the Development of Lebanese Cinema* (Ohio State University, 1996).
12. See Li Guo, *The Performing Arts in Medieval Islam: Shadow Plays and Popular Poetry in Ibn Daniyal's Mamluk Cairo* (Leiden: Brill, 2012), 105–6.
13. Ibid.
14. Ibid.
15. Jurji Zaydan, "Al-Tamthil al-'Arabi wa-Nahdatuhu al-Akhira 'ala Yadd al-Janab al-'Ali," *al-Hilal* 18 (1910): 464–72.
16. See Kurt Sethe, *Die Alta Egyptischen Pyramidentexte* (Leipzig: Hinrichs, 1908).
17. Zaydan, "Al-Tamthil al-'Arabi," 464–72.
18. Sayyid 'Ali Isma 'il, *al-Raqaba wa-l-Masrah al-Marfud* (Cairo: al-Haya's al-'Ama al-Misriyya lil-Kitab, 1996), 14.
19. Fahmy, *Ordinary Egyptians*, 45.
20. Ibid., 46.
21. Ibid. See also Landau, *Arab Theater*, 65–7.
22. Zaydan, "Al-Tamthil al-'Arabi," 464–72.
23. The pronunciation of her first name is disputed. She pronounces her name 'Ulwiyya while some of her peers say 'Alawiyya. Transliteration of her name here follows the actress's choice.
24. Ibrahim al-Dusuqi, Sami Hilmi and Muhammad al-Qalyubi, *Al-Sinima al-Misriyya al-Samita al-Watha'iqiyya al-Tasjiliyya, 1897–1930* (Cairo: al-Majlis al-A'la lil-Thaqafa, 2010), 68.
25. Ibid., 74.
26. Al-Dasuqi, *Al-Sinima al-Misriyya*, 87.
27. Ibid., 91.
28. *Al-Ithnayn*, no. 863, 25 December 1950. Between 1934 and 1948, seven major studios were operating in Egypt: Studio Misr (1934), Studio Nasiban (1935), Studio Tugu Mizrahi (1936), Studio Shubra (1944), Studio Galal (1944), Studio al-Ahram (1945), and Studio Nihas (1948). It is important here also to note that Nihas Film Company was operating through Ramsis Theater Company, both owned by Yusuf Wahbi.

29. Muhammad Karim, *Mudhakkirat Muhammad Karim*, ed. Madkur Thabit (Cairo: Akadimiyyat al-Funun, 2006), 109.
30. *Majallat al-Dunya al-Musawwara*, no. 7, July 24, 1929, 18.
31. Baydas, *Abyad wa Aswad*, 177.
32. Ibid., 181.
33. Karim, *Mudhakkirat*, 40.
34. Ibid.
35. Ibid., 37.
36. Wahbi, *'Ishtu Alf 'Am*, 1: 38.
37. Karim, *Mudhakkirat*, 38.
38. Wahbi, *'Ishtu Alf 'Am*, 1: 38.
39. Ibid., 1: 67.
40. Ibid., 1: 103.
41. Karim, *Mudhakkirat*, 48–59.
42. Wahbi, *'Ishtu Alf 'Am*, 1: 109.
43. Karim, *Mudhakkirat*, 34–44.
44. Ibid.
45. The last name is not mentioned in the sources.
46. Karim, *Mudhakkirat*, 51.
47. Ibid., 51.
48. Ibid., 53.
49. Ibid., 55.
50. Karim, *Mudhakkirat*, 57.
51. Ibid., 61.
52. Ibid., 64.
53. Ibid.
54. Ibid., 65.
55. This could be an exaggeration on Karim's part, but it is not uncommon for smoking to create social bonding.
56. Karim, *Mudhakkirat*, 62.
57. Ibid., 69
58. Ibid., 82.
59. Ibid.
60. Ibid. 83.
61. Mohamed Awad and Sahar Hamouda, "Mediterranean Voices: Oral History and Cultural Practice in the Mediterranean," *Voices of Cosmopolitan Alexandria* (Alexandria: Bibliotheca Alexandrina, 2006).
62. Deborah A. Starr, "Chalom and 'Abdu Get Married: Jewishness and

Egyptianness in the Films of Togo Mizrahi," *Jewish Quarterly Review* 107, no. 2 (2017): 209–30.
63. Ibid.
64. Karim, *Mudhakkirat*, 83.
65. See *al-Waqai' al-Misriyya*, July 21, 1925.
66. Ibid., 98.
67. Ibid.
68. See Ruza al-Yusuf, *Majallat Ruza al-Yusuf Magazine* (3), Monday November 9, 1925.
69. Ibid.
70. Karim, *Mudhakkirat*, 109.
71. Ahmad Ra'fat Bahgat, *Al-Yahud wa-l-Sinima fi Misr* (Cairo: Sharikat al-Qasr, 2005), 13.
72. "Report on the Distribution of Films in Egypt, a Copy Submitted to His Majesty's Embassy at Cairo for Observations," Great Britain, Public Records Office, 12 June 1939, P News 2388/143/150.
73. Karim, *Mudhakkirat*, 156.
74. Ibid., 157.
75. Ibid., 58.
76. Full name is not mentioned in the sources.
77. Full name is not mentioned in the source.
78. Karim, *Mudhakkirat*, 159–61.
79. Ibid.
80. Muhammad 'Abdu, *Fatawa al-Imam Muhammad 'Abdu*, ed. 'Ali Gum'a. Cairo: al-Jam'iyya al-Khayriyya al-Islamiyya, 2006, 251.
81. Karim, *Mudhakkirat*, 130.
82. Ibid., 186–7.
83. Last name is not mentioned in the sources.
84. Karim, *Mudhakkirat*, 187.
85. Ibid., 233.
86. Ibid., 259. Ironically, even today the Lebanese singer Nancy 'Ajram has commented, on her Twitter account, on the Lebanese authorities being alert enough to censor and request the omission of the word "revolution" (*thawra*) from one of her songs, while not paying enough attention to the tons of ammonium nitrate that caused the sweeping explosion that hit Beirut in August 2020.
87. See Theodor Adorno and Max Horkheimer, "The Culture Industry: Enlightenment as Mass Deception," in Gunzelin Schmid Noerr (eds), *Dialectic*

of Enlightenment, trans. Edmund Jephcott (Stanford, CA: Stanford University Press, 2002), 94–137. See also Fredric Jameson, "Reification and Utopia in Mass Culture," *Social Text*, no. 1 (1979), 130–48, and Walter Armbrust, *Mass Culture and Modernism in Egypt* (Cambridge, NY: Cambridge University Press, 1996), 8–9.

88. Critical realism is a movement in philosophy and the human sciences and cognate practices most closely identified with or emanating from—though by no means restricted to—the work of Roy Bhaskar. Since the initial publication of Bhaskar's *A Realist Theory of Science* in 1975 critical realism has gained new meanings. I use the term here in reference to pre-1975 contexts and, more specifically, in reference to how Egyptian pioneer filmmakers expressed it in their filmic production between 1930 and 1952. Terry Eagleton's attempt to explain the term in his seminal work *Marxism and Literary Criticism* is the closest description to how I employ the term in this book.

89. Terry Eagleton, *Marxism and Literary Criticism* (Berkeley, CA: University of California Press, 1976), 40.

90. See 'Ali Shalash and Ahmad Yusuf, *Salah Abu Sayf wa-l-Nuqqad*, Cairo: Apollo, 1992, 231–3.

91. Seyyed Hossein Nasr, Caner K Dagli, Maria Massi Dakake, Joseph E. B. Lumbard, and Mohammed Rustom, *The Study Quran* (Sydney: HarperOne, 2015), 553. Kindle edition.

92. Muhammad Karim, "Laqad Akhrajtu Zaynab wa Kunt Radiyan Tamaman 'Anha," *al-Dunya al-Musawwara Magazine*, September 25, 1929 to October 9, 1929, 19–21: 20.

93. See Edward Said, *Humanism and Democratic Criticism* (Columbia: Columbia University Press, 2004).

94. Karim, "*Laqad Akhrajtu Zaynab*," 20.

95. See Joel Gordon, *Nasser's Blessed Movement: Egypt's Free Officers and the July Revolution* (New York: Oxford University Press, 1992). See also Mahmud Sa'd, "Al-Liqa' al-Kamil ma'a al-Muhandis Ahmad Ihsan 'Abd al-Quddus," *Barnamj Bab al-Khalq*, al-Nahar TV, November 10, 2019, https://www.youtube.com/watch?v=2z5jTIE4x9M (last accessed December 12, 2020).

96. See Ayman al-Hakim, *Al-Fann al-Haram: Tarikh al-Ishtibak Bayn al-Salafiyyin wa-l-Mubdi'in* (Cairo: Dar Kitabat, 2012), 28–38.

97. See Ahdaf Soueif, *Cairo: My City, Our Revolution* (New York: Pantheon, 2013), 147. See also Ahmad al-Shaykh, "Ba'i' al-Basata," June 29, 2015, https://www.youtube.com/watch?v=__dvlfB_MHw (last accessed December 12, 2020); Ala'

Sa'd, "Bi-l-Suwar: Rahala Hisham Rizq Rassam Graffiti Muhammad Mahmud Wala'allahu Yakun Dhalik al-Rajul al-Muntazar," *Bawwabat al-Shuruq*, January 28, 2016, http://www.shorouknews.com/news/view.aspx?cdate=03072014&id=efd2d99f-9d01-4a38-930c-21f487f24cf1 (last accessed December 12, 2020).

98. Mona Karim, "An Interview with LARB: The Persecuted Novelist of Dystopian Cairo" *Los Angeles Review of Books*, January 11, 2016, https://lareviewofbooks.org/interview/the-persecuted-novelist-of-dystopian-cairo (last accessed December 12, 2020).

99. Mohamad Hamama and Shady Zalat, "Atfal al-Shawarea: A Fatherly Fear of Sarcasm and the Street," *Mada Masr*, 13 May 2016, http://www.madamasr.com/sections/culture/atfal-al-shawarea-fatherly-fear-sarcasm-and-street (last accessed December 12, 2020).

100. [Mada Masr,] "A Report on Mohamed Diab's Clash: How State TV Deals with Art," trans. Amira El-Masry, *Mada Masr*, May 27, 2016, http://www.madamasr.com/opinion/report-mohamed-diabs-clash-how-state-tv-deals-art (last accessed December 12, 2020).

101. Midhat al-'Adl and Nur al-Sharif, *Anta Hurr*, CBC Egypt, August 12, 2015, https://www.youtube.com/watch?v=1Ur8hRpqEgM (last accessed December 12, 2020).

102. Khaled Fahmy, "Limadha Sanantasir: al-Thawara Mustamira," *al-Shuruq*, January 26, 2015, http://www.shorouknews.com/columns/view.aspx?cdate=26012015&id=c62319b0-6d99-4418-865a-f460a6991399 (last accessed December 12, 2020).

103. Raymond Williams, *The Long Revolution* (New York: Parthian Books, 2013), 16–60.

104. Ibid., 49.

105. Ibid., 58.

106. See Jürgen Habermas, "Modernity—An Incomplete Project," *The Anti-Aesthetic: Essays on Postmodern Culture*, ed. Hal Foster (Port Townsend, WA: Bay Press, 1983), 3–15.

107. Dilip Gaonkar, "On Alternative Modernities," *Alternative Modernities*, ed. Dilip Goanker (Durham, NC: Duke University Press, 2001), 1–23.

108. Timothy Mitchell, "The Stage of Modernity," *Questions of Modernity*, ed. Timothy Mitchell (Minneapolis: University of Minnesota Press, 2000), 1–34.

109. Broadly speaking, Enlightenment is conceived as a European philosophy from the late seventeenth century through most of the eighteenth century. When speaking of the philosophers of Enlightenment, attention is usually given to

Newton and Locke because of their influence on Enlightenment elsewhere. Wales produced Richard Price. Ireland produced Berkeley and Burke. The Scots influenced *Aufklärung* in Germany, not least the thought of Kant. The avant-garde of Enlightenment commonly used the metaphor of spreading light to refer to the kind of intellectual and cultural progress they believed in. During the nineteenth century, Enlightenment began to be used in retrospect for the period as a whole. The early English Enlightenment is marked by vigorous controversy between two extremes—the anti-authoritarian "deists" and the High Church defenders of hierarchy and orthodoxy. The philosophical scene came to be dominated by moderate opinion. The leading figures included moderate Anglican clergymen such as Joseph Butler and William Paley. When deism declined radicalism re-emerged, and was represented by scientists and Unitarian ministers such as Joseph Priestley. During the mid-eighteenth century, English philosophy, unlike French, commonly lacked the anti-clerical, anti-Establishment materialism common amongst the French philosophes. See Stuart Brown, *Routledge History of Philosophy Volume V: British Empiricism and the Enlightenment*. London: Routledge, 1995), 1–12.
110. Michel Foucault, "What Is Enlightenment?" *The Foucault Reader* (New York: Pantheon, 1984), 32–50.
111. Ibid.
112. Ibid.
113. Cultural modernity, Habermas argues, is an optimistic project formulated in the eighteenth century by the philosophers of Enlightenment, primarily Condorcet (1734–94), who aimed to develop some sort of coherence among objective science, universal morality law, and autonomous art. Condorcet hoped to utilize the accumulation of specialized culture to enrich everyday life. He thought that the arts and sciences would promote the control of natural forces, understanding of the world and the self, moral progress, the justice of institutions, and even the happiness of human beings. See Jürgen Habermas, "Modernity—An Incomplete Project," *The Anti-Aesthetic: Essays on Postmodern Culture*, ed. Hal Foster (Port Townsend, WA: Bay Press, 1983) 3–15.
114. While the first relied more on instrumental rationality and even on the punitive use of reason, the second relied more on rationality as a humanistic reason.
115. See Brown, *Routledge History of Philosophy Volume V*, 1–12. The laity included all who were not clergymen, including lay philosophers—those who were not trained in a university. Enlightenment marks the involvement of the laity in philosophy. The Catholic tradition had its Latin Bible and a clerical hierarchy,

who laid down how it was to be understood. The Protestant Reformation committed itself to a vernacular Bible. While most Protestant groups retained clergy and attached importance to their mission as teachers, they encouraged the laity, in varying degree, to learn to read and to understand the Bible. Descartes wrote in French and used it as a vehicle, not just for popular works but to express and argue for a difficult and demanding set of doctrines. By writing in his native language, he was able to win for his philosophy the support and patronage of influential lay people, and this helped Cartesianism to survive despite it being banned from the French universities.

116. Michel Foucault, "Governmentality," *The Foucault Effect: Studies in Governmentality*, ed. Graham Burchell and Colin Gordon (Chicago, IL: University of Chicago Press, 1991), 87–105.

117. Critics of Habermas have pointed out that he paid insufficient attention to religion in this early work. Craig Calhoun noted not only his relative "neglect of religion" but also his "antireligious assumptions." Yet, and in recognition of the fact that religion has not shrunken away under the pressures of modernization, Habermas has turned increasingly to questions of religion, as in his recent investment in the mechanisms through which myth is preserved in rituals. See Mendieta and Vanantwerpen, *The Power of Religion in the Public Sphere* (New York: Columbia University Press) 2011, 3–6.

118. See Diana K. Davis, *Resurrecting the Granary of Rome: Environmental History and French Colonial Expansion in North Africa* (Athens, OH: Ohio University Press, 2007). See also James C. Scott, *Seeing Like a State: How Certain Schemes to Improve the Human Condition Have Failed* (New Haven, CT: Yale University Press, 1998). See also Abi-Mershed, Osama, *Apostles of Modernity: Saint-Simonians and the Civilizing Mission in Algeria* (Stanford, CA: Stanford University Press, 2010).

119. See Timothy Mitchell, "The Stage of Modernity," 1–34.

120. The underlying premise here is to understand one's culture as agent among many other cultures that might be dominant, but that dominance is not absolute.

121. See Charles Taylor, "Two Modernities," *Alternative Modernities*, ed. Dilip Gaonkar (Durham, NC: Duke University Press, 2001), 172–96. He explains that these are irresistible and that whoever fails to take them or some good functional equivalent will fall so far behind in the power stakes as to be taken over and forced to undergo these changes anyway; original cultures are destroyed, people die or are forced to assimilate.

122. Ibid.

123. See Charles Taylor, "Two Modernities," 172–96. See also Timothy Mitchell, *Questions of Modernity* (Minneapolis: University of Minnesota Press, 2000), xiii–xiv. *Acultural* approaches present modernity as a sweeping wave; a theory of convergence put in place through culture-neutral operations that cause transition from tradition to modernity. Transition is treated as a loss of traditional beliefs and allegiances violated by mobility and urbanization. Transition also involves eroding rural society that is perceived as static. The limitations to the acultural approach lie in how it overlooks the fact that modernity in the West is a culture sustained by its own original moral spiritual vision, that is, not one generated simply and inevitably by transition. Moreover, acultural theory imposes a false uniformity on the diverse and multiple encounters of the non-Western with the allegedly cultural neutral processes (science, and technology, secularization, bureaucratization, and so on) characteristic of societal modernization. All cultures thus emerge into a single, homogeneous world culture.
124. See Gershoni and Jankowski, *Egypt, Islam, and the Arabs: The Search for Egyptian Nationhood, 1900-1930*, 3. Gershoni and Jankowski classified three competing intellectual loyalties: (a) religious nationalism, (b) territorial patriotism, and (c) ethnic or linguistic nationalism. See also Elliott Colla, *Conflicted Antiquities: Egyptology, Egyptomania, Egyptian Modernity* (Durham, NC: Duke University Press, 2007). Here Colla makes a distinction between the modernity presented by Naguib Mahfouz and that of Sayyid Qutb, with the latter's modernity gaining more popularity.
125. See Khaled Fahmy, *All the Pasha's Men: Mehmed Ali, His Army, and the Making of Modern Egypt* (Cambridge: Cambridge University Press, 1997).
126. Jacob Wilson, *Working Out Egypt: Effendi Masculinity and Subject Formation in Colonial Modernity, 1870-1940* (Durham, NC: Duke University Press, 2011), 5.
127. Lucie Ryzova, *The Age of the Efendiyya: Passages to Modernity in National-Colonial Egypt* (Oxford: Oxford University Press 2014), 8.
128. By historical specificity, Marx refers to the study of society in a specific historical epoch to show the nature of its socio-economic construction within its dialectical interaction (taking into account internal as well as external conditions and contexts) in that specific epoch. Thus, the historical specificity of Egypt during the nineteenth century is different from its historical specificity in the second half of the twentieth century. Historicity in Marx thought does not refer to the continuity of time so much as to specific social function in a specific period. It is true that Marx talked about Oriental despotism when he talked about the

Asian mode of production in river valley civilizations. So did Engels and Lenin, but they did not refer to the issue as a historically continuous attribute. They presented it as a symptom revealing specific socio-economic contexts.

129. That is to say, it overlooks that different social conflicts drove the centralized power in Egypt across history. Within that centralized power, military personnel and 'ulama', in addition to other social groups, shared the ownership of the land. Sometimes the ownership of the land was a matter of formality without actual control. Thereby, it concealed a beneficiary ownership and the struggle between the owners and the beneficiaries within that centralized power. Those struggles stood behind the fall of one centralized power and the rise of another.

130. See Hani Shukrallah, "'Iyal al-Nafura wa al-Shakl al-Hadari," *Al-Ahram*, August 4, 2014.

131. Jacob, *Working Out Egypt*, 5.

132. Walter Armbrust, "The Formation of National Culture in Egypt in the Interwar Period: Cultural Trajectories," *History Compass* 7, no. 1 (2009), 155–80.

133. Lucie Ryzova, *The Age of the Efendiyya: Passages to Modernity in National-Colonial Egypt* (Oxford: Oxford University Press 2014), 8.

134. Dipesh Chakrabarty, "Add, Calcutta: Dwelling in Modernity," *Alternative Modernities*, ed. Dilip Gaonkar (Durham, NC: Duke University Press, 2001), 123.

135. Dipesh Chakrabarty, "Add, Calcutta: Dwelling in Modernity," 130.

136. Ibid.

137. Daniel Lerner, *The Passing of Traditional Society: Modernizing the Middle* East (New York: Free Press, 1964), 41.

138. Lerner, *The Passing of Traditional Society*, 41.

139. See Mendieta and Vanantwerpen, *The Power of Religion in the Public Sphere* (New York: Columbia University Press) 2011, 3–6.

140. Shahab Ahmed, *What Is Islam: The Importance of Being Islamic* (Princeton, NJ: Princeton University Press, 2017), 542.

141. Paul Heck, *Skepticism in Classical Islam: Moments of Confusion* (London: Routledge, 2014), 4.

142. On *fatawa*, see Wael Hallaq, "From *Fatawa* to *Furu'*: Growth and Change in Islamic Substantive Law," *Islamic Law and Society* 1, no. 1 (1994): 29–65.

143. Noel J. Coulson, *A History of Islamic Law* (Edinburgh: Edinburgh University Press, 1964), p. 141. See also *EI2*, s.v., "Sadd al- dhara'i'" and Opwis, "Islamic Law and Legal Change," p. 68. The phrase *sadd al-dhara'i'* is made up of the verbal noun *sadd* ("to close") and a broken plural *dhara'i'* (sg. *dhari'a*)

("excuses/reasons"). As a legal concept and a derivative of *maslaha*, it is not clear if *sadd al-dhara'i'* is a source of law (*asl*)—*asl* refers to a textual source of law, such as the Qur'an or Sunna; it refers to "the base" of an analogy or to a legal principle based on necessity—a legal indicator (*dalil*), or an established legal principle (*qa'ida*). Some jurisprudents treat it as a continuation of "unattested benefit" (*maslaha mursala*). This view is based on its application as a part of the overarching purpose of the law, the prevention of harm (*dar' al-mafasid*), and on the legal maxim that preventing harm has preference over achieving benefits (*jalb al-masalih*). A major difference between *maslaha* and *sadd al-dhara'i'* is that the latter does not target what is "beneficial"; it targets what is "harmful" or may lead to harm (*darar*). While using *sadd al-dhara'i'*, jurisprudents differentiate between three levels (*darajat*) of harm: recurrent, infrequent or rare, and imminent. The third category is based on the person's intention rather than the possible outcome. Due to the different methodologies used in establishing a person's intention, jurisprudents from the four Sunni legal schools differ in how often they refer to *sadd al-dhara'i'*, with the Hanbali and Maliki schools referring to it most frequently. The Hanafis, Malikis, and Hanbalis refer to the circumstances to find proof of intention. Al-Shafi'is, on the other hand, was reluctant to formulate a ruling based on showing how circumstances prove the intention of a person.

2

Regulating the Amour-propre of the Colonized

1. From Negative to Positive Cultural Policies

In 1896, almost two decades after British troops bombarded Alexandria in 1882 and suppressed the local 'Urabi uprising, London's Polytechnic Institute and Alexandria's Toussoun Bourse hosted the first screenings of the Lumière Brothers' new moving pictures device, the Cinématographe. Film, thus, is a medium that simultaneously reached the center and the periphery; it developed under and despite the reality of colonization.[1] As this powerful new medium grew in popularity, the British colonial authority sought to use film to advance its plans of cultural expansion across the empire. In Egypt, however, film production did not top the colonial officials' priority list. Instead, it was film censorship that played a crucial role in promoting British cultural hegemony. To understand this milieu, one must recognize how the colonialist cultural policies followed the same negative–positive dichotomy that shaped the empire's political interest in Egypt vis-à-vis the signing of the 1936 Anglo-Egyptian Treaty and World War II.

British political interest in Egypt began in the late eighteenth century before the first British military expedition was sent to Alexandria in 1807.[2] Initially, it was a negative interest, that is, it was shaped by a passive or indirect interest that aimed to prevent the colonization of Egypt by other European powers as part of emphasizing British naval supremacy in the Mediterranean. After 1807, the need to use the short overland route through Egypt to expedite mail and passengers between England and India generated a positive interest (i.e. having direct control over Egypt). By 1840, a regular mail service between England and India via Egypt was in operation.[3] Soon, various British capitalists started thinking of "constructing a railway across Egypt, between Alexandria and Suez via Cairo, as means of both increasing the speed and efficiency of transit and of exporting British capital foods at the height of what was then the Railway Age."[4] However, there was a more ambitious French-sponsored scheme for constructing a ship canal through Suez linking the Mediterranean with the Red Sea. Neither of these plans made any progress during the lifetime of Muhammad Ali (r. 1805–48), who died in 1849. However, the British railway plan found its way during the reign of ʿAbbas I (r. 1848–54), and the French project was passed during the reign of Muhammad Saʿid (r. 1854–63), despite British efforts to prevent it. The Canal operated in 1869 and, within a few years, revolutionized the pattern of mercantile traffic. Despite its being a French plan, the British benefited tremendously from the Canal. They were major users of the Canal "from the beginning, and they used it both for naval and military communication East of Suez, and for their rapidly increasing mercantile traffic with India, East Africa, Australia, and the Far East."[5] The actual occupation in 1882 thus was not the beginning, but rather the apogee of a long journey of pursuing Britain's positive political interest in Egypt.

Between the actual occupation in 1882 and the signing of the 1936 Anglo-Egyptian Treaty of Alliance, power dynamics fluctuated due to the outbreak of World War I, the 1919 anti-British revolution, and the 1935 uprising. The war ended Ottoman political control over Egypt, which became a British protectorate. After the war, the anti-colonialist nationalist movements led by the famous al-Wafd delegation officially demanded independence. They presented themselves with Saʿd Zaghlul as their representative to Reginald Wingate, the British governor in Egypt, and requested that they should represent Egypt at the Paris Peace Conference. The Wafd was denied its request to go to London and speak with the British home government; it was not allowed to attend the Paris Peace Conference. Zaghlul succeeded in creating popular discontent with Egypt's status as a British protectorate. British authorities arrested Zaghlul and his fellows, namely Muhammad Mahmud, Ismaʿil Sidqi, and Hamad al-Basil, and exiled them to Malta in 1919. This move accelerated the 1919 revolution, after which Zaghlul and his fellows were released. Egypt was declared a sovereign state when the British government issued the famous February 28, 1922 declaration. But its four reservations proved that the British government was selling the Egyptian elite an amour-propre of sovereignty, not actual sovereignty. The same applied to the first Egyptian constitution in 1923, which, despite marking the beginning of the parliamentary political system in Egypt, remained heavily constrained by British interference in its draft and in the further rights given to the King. Not surprisingly, the first constitutional Prime Minister, Sa'd Zaghlul, was terminated on November 19, 1924, after the assassination of Major-General Sir Lee Oliver Fitzmaurice Stack, the Governor-General of the Anglo-Egyptian Sudan, and Sir George Lloyd succeeded him.[6]

The pro-British Ahmad Ziwar pasha became Prime Minister; he suspended the parliament and called for new elections. The majority party, al-Wafd, won the election and its leader, Zaghlul, became speaker of the house. But the newly elected parliament survived only for nine hours, because Ziwar tendered his resignation, which King Fu'ad rejected. Ziwar continued to serve, again dissolved parliament and postponed the new elections because drafting new rules to govern the electoral process needed time. This move was taken by the al-Wafd party as a maneuver to ensure that al-Wafd would lose the election. In September 1925, the Liberal-Constitutionalist party withdrew from Ziwar's government following the crisis over Ali 'Abd al-Raziq's famous book *al-Islam wa Usul al-Hukm* (Islam and the Foundations of Political Power). The cabinet was re-formed, mainly from the al-Ittihad pro-palace party. By relying on constitution article no. 96, the Wafd formed a coalition and suggested that the parliament had the right to meet independently without being invited by the King. Police forces tried to but could not prevent the meeting in the Intercontinental Hotel instead of the parliament. The attendees criticized Ziwar's government for violating the constitution and attacking liberties through its new legislation that subjugated civil society originations to government supervision. They then withdrew trust from the cabinet according to article 65 of the constitution. Popular and partisan opposition to Ziwar intensified when his government succumbed to Italian demands in Jaghbub on December 6, 1925, by giving away Egyptian land. This step was seen as a matter of high treason for which Ziwar deserved to be put on trial. His position was also complicated by the new election law, issued on December 8, 1925, which gave voting rights only to men above thirty years old and conditionally for men above twenty-five. When the political parties threatened to boycott the election, the government canceled the legislation. This election again brought al-Wafd to power. The British authorities did not like the results and threatened to use force. Zaghlul gave up on his constitutional right to form a government, pleading his deteriorating health condition. The Ziwar government resigned on June 7, 1926.

A coalition government was formed from the Liberal-Constitutionalist party led by 'Adli Yakan, who was both a friend of and a rival to Zaghlul due to Yakan having played the middleman between Lord Millner and al-Wafd before the 1922 declaration.[7] On the same day, Zaghlul was elected the house speaker, with Mustafa al-Nahhas and Wisa Wasif as vice-speakers. The parliament canceled all legislation made since December 1924 and deposited large sums of government funds in the rising Bank Misr to support the local economy. Political prisoners arrested between 1924 and 1926 were released. On April 19, 1927, another constitutional crisis arose when 'Adli Yakan's cabinet resigned unexpectedly because the parliament rejected a proposal to thank the cabinet for its policy of supporting Bank Misr and because of criticism of the budget. The crisis ended when the government was re-formed, with 'Abd al-Khaliq Tharawt leading a coalition government instead of Yakan, on April 25, 1927. But this cabinet also soon resigned in March 1928 because the parliament rejected the Chamberlain–Tharwat draft treaty over the terms of occupation.

A new cabinet led by the Liberal-Constitutionalist Muhammad Mahmud was appointed after the British authorities helped King Fu'ad oust al-Wafd from the coalition on June 27, 1928. Muhammad Mahmud suspended the parliament for a month and soon dissolved it, on July 19, 1928. While the police attempted to prevent parliament meetings, its members met and declared that the royal decree to suspend the parliament was anti-constitutional. Muhammad Mahmud's cabinet was not popular, and was weakened by the transfer of its supporter Lord George Lloyd, after the Labour Party took control in Britain in May 1929. This was followed by the failure of the treaty negotiations between Muhammad Mahmud and the Labour Foreign Secretary Arthur Henderson. The al-Wafd party led demonstrations against the government of Muhammad Mahmud, who resigned in October 1929.

'Adli Yakan's third cabinet was formed on October 3, 1929, and called for elections on December 31, 1929. The Wafd won the majority of seats, as usual. On December 31, 1929, 'Adli Yakan resigned, since he thought his cabinet's job was to restore constitutional life, not govern.

King Fu'ad invited the al-Wafd leader, by then al-Nahhas, to form a government in January 1930, given that the latter was the leader of the majority in the house. The parliament met on January 11, 1930. But this government also resigned, due to the failure of negotiations with Henderson and the King's reluctance to sign legislation that aimed to prevent the cabinet from putting on trial its members who had violated the constitution. Al-Nahhas's cabinet resigned on June 19, 1930, because it could not carry out its constitutional duties.

In order to form a government, King Fu'ad called upon the hugely unpopular Isma'il Sidqi, the Minister of the Interior in Ziwar's government and opponent of the Wafd party (despite his having been banished with Zaghlul to Malta). Sidqi suspended the parliament before it had had a chance to approve the budget. Parliament members saw this as anti-constitutional, since articles 140 and 96 required parliament to be in session for at least six months. They then ignored Sidqi's decision and met on July 26, 1930 to condemn Sidqi's violations of the constitution; they further threatened to withdraw trust from the government. Supported by King Fu'ad, Sidqi suspended the constitution of 1923 on October 22, 1930 and dissolved parliament. A new election law was issued to prevent men under twenty-five from voting and prevent any non-government employee residing outside Cairo from running for election. The year 1931 was foreshadowed by bloody confrontations between al-Wafd demonstrations and the government. The elections were held, and Sidqi's newly formed party, al-Sha'b, won. Sidqi governed via the 1930 new constitution for three years until he resigned on September 27, 1933.

The King summoned 'Abd al-Fattah Yaha, who was pro-palace, to form a government. The pro-palace Tawfiq Nasim soon replaced him. Nasim's government issued a royal decree on November 30, 1934, to cancel the 1923 and 1930 constitutions so that a new one could be written. This step placed both legislative and executive powers with the King. The British authorities endorsed Nasim and announced their lack of interest in entering into any negotiations. By September 1935, demonstrations had erupted inside and outside Cairo, leading to the 1935 social uprising, which demanded that the 1923 constitution be restored, new elections be held, and the British High Commissioner in Egypt accept the terms of the al-Nahhas–Henderson treaty negotiations.

It was not until January 30, 1936, that King Fu'ad issued a royal decree to form a government led by the pro-palace 'Ali Mahir, who restored the 1923 constitution and called for new elections that brought the Wafd back to power. Simultaneously, the British authorities accepted the demands to resume negotiations, on condition that it did not have to abide by the al-Nahhas–Henderson treaty negotiations. A royal decree appointed the official delegation to negotiate the 1936 Treaty. While some considered the Treaty a plan that mainly benefited the British and allowed them to regulate occupation before World War II, others saw it as a document that set a seal on the people's efforts and sacrifices in 1919 and 1935 by blocking British political, economic, and cultural interest from turning Egypt into another French Algeria or British India.

Amidst this fluctuating political scene, and up until 1936, British efforts at cultural expansion focused on English language instruction, which was a vehicle of cultural hegemony in public schools.[8] The majority of subjects were taught in English. Egyptian officials used to serve under an English chief. This policy was not only intended to maintain Egyptian officials' familiarity with the English language. The hope was, also, *"to some extent [to make them] acquire English habits of thoughts and mind* [a matter that] perhaps [applied] more to Egyptian Public Works and Irrigation officials,"[9] who, as will be discussed later in this chapter, played a crucial role in licensing films.

After the 1936 Treaty, British officials found that their focus on the English language as a vehicle for British cultural hegemony in Egypt was not as fruitful as expected. They discovered that they had already lost the battle for cultural hegemony in Egypt to France and Italy. For example, the British ambassador to Egypt, Sir Miles Lampson, evaluated the British cultural expansion plan as follows: "It is humiliating that after fifty-five years of British political predominance in Egypt, we are not sufficiently firmly entrenched to meet any [French and] Italian advances of this kind."[10] According to Lampson, the primary cultural influence in Egypt and the Eastern Mediterranean was French. It had been so since the days of the Crusades, and it further grew after French schemes secured the Capitulations. French missionaries, of course, played a significant role. The French mission schools led the efforts to offer modern education throughout the old Turkish Empire.[11] In 1937, Egypt had 157 French schools with over 32000 pupils.[12] By the same token, the Italian government relied in its propaganda efforts on the large number of Italians residing in Egypt. "No Italian lacked an excellent education, which was given to him in modern schools, which could not fail to impress Egyptians and other foreigners in Egypt."[13] The Italian government was more willing to spend money on propaganda. It dedicated 9000 lire per year to schools and hospitals. By World War I, there were 2000 Egyptians among the 12000 pupils in Italian schools.[14] The Italian government also provided educational facilities for Egyptian students in Italy, either in grants or on reduced terms. There were also plans to encourage Egyptians to spend holidays in Italy. Italy provided the finest shipping service connecting Egypt with Europe. The very numerous Italian colonies were also knit together by their schools and by the efforts of the fascist organizations, which were subsidized extensively and indulged in military training.[15] Besides, the huge number of Italians residing in Egypt had a significant influence on commercial life. For example, the international crisis of the winter of 1933–6 revealed that Egypt depended heavily on the Italian workforce. Italian clerks occupied critical positions in British business. Their services could be dispensed with neither at the national bank nor at the British telecommunications company Marconi. The greater proportion of telephone operators and shipping clerks were Italians, and "had the crisis developed to the extent of making it necessary to intern Italians in Egypt, those vital services would have been completely disorganized."[16] In response to the crisis, British firms realized that they had to train more Maltese and Cypriots to replace Italians in the British and Egyptian organizations.[17]

Still, Lampson viewed French and Italian cultural schemes as non-threatening if the British government were to shift to a more positive cultural strategy. This view is primarily driven by the overall British colonial model, which focused on controlling the elites. It was very rare among Lampson's contemporary ruling Turco-Egyptian elite to send their children to Italian schools, even though two rulers of Egypt, namely Isma'il and his son Fu'ad, had been educated in Italy. For example, Prince Muhammad Ali objected to his sister's wish to send her son to an Italian school because he would get an affordable education, one preparing him for a commercial, rather than a diplomatic, occupation in Egypt.

The shift to a positive cultural policy came after the 1936 Treaty through a proposal to establish a British university in Cairo in 1937. The main goal was to compete with French and Italian cultural hegemony and challenge nationalist education at the Egyptian University. In January 1937, Lord de La Warr, Parliamentary Under-Secretary of State for the Colonies, passed through Egypt on his way to investigating schools in British East Africa and Sudan.[18] He had a project for opening a British university, but the location was yet to be decided. Three sites were suggested for Warr's project, Jerusalem, Cyprus, and Cairo. Jerusalem was considered out of the question because of the 1936 Palestinian uprising demanding independence from British colonial rule and opposing massive Jewish immigration to Palestine. Cyprus was thought to be "too much of a backwater to attract Egyptians bred in Cairo's lively atmosphere."[19] Warr and his advisors felt it was hardly possible under post-Treaty conditions to start a British university in Cairo, despite it being an apparent cultural center in the Near East. Therefore, the plan to open a British University in Cairo was canceled. Instead, a new agenda was prepared for discussion with Lord George Lloyd, who became president of the British Council and was tasked with improving Britain's image in Portugal, Greece, Turkey, Yugoslavia, Romania, Poland, and the Middle East, especially Egypt.[20] Most of the items on the agenda leaned toward capitalizing on what had already been done in the field of cultural expansion. For example, items discussed included the grant of 2000 pounds to the Anglo-Egyptian Union, a proposed school in Port Said, and an additional grant of 10,000 pounds to the British Girl's school in Alexandria.

Why did the British government change the agenda and give up on new cultural expansion domains in Egypt? The answer was well crafted in a letter from Sir Robert Greg[21] on May 31, 1937, to the British Foreign Office. On the one hand, the letter was written to justify the extension of Greg's career. The assertive testimonial tone of the letter repeatedly described how Sir Robert Greg was the only hope regarding keeping the British cultural flag flying. On the other hand, the letter served as a cultural memorandum on the weakness of the British cultural position in Egypt; it described the reasons behind that weakness and made suggestions for improvement. For example, it contested the British government's plan to replace French with British culture in Egypt, finding that the plan was part of the same negative political interest. Greg objected to the replacement plan; he found it ambitious and challenging, if possible at all given that the target was to install British heads at all higher cultural domains such as archeology, *Beaux-Arts*, the Arab Museum, and *Amis de l'Art*. Lack of adequate financial support was key and required a change in London's financial policy. Moreover, Greg recognized challenges caused by French cultural supremacy, the shadow of World War II, and lack of interest in British culture and civilization among the Egyptian ruling elite.

French cultural supremacy came primarily from French control over the Department of Antiquities and the Egyptian Museum. The French government sent out "first-rate men from France, and if one departed, another good man immediately replaced him."[22] So the Department of Antiquities was left in French hands even when French direction did not meet the post-war standards of administration.[23] The British government, on the contrary, was almost entirely lacking in men. Sir Robert Greg was the sole British member of the *Comité d'Egyptologie* attached to the Egyptian Museum. The only two other outstanding British figures were Captain Creswell in Islamic Art and Mr. Emery in Egyptology. However, apart from those three, "the land was barren indeed."[24] The shadows of World War II made it clear that it was not in Britain's interest to irritate the French government and weaken the position of the *Khawagat* in Egypt by what would be considered a dog-in-the-manger attitude. Moreover, the revived *Entente Cordiale* with France, while it might help to lessen the sharpness of French cultural jealousy, might make it more difficult for the British to oppose, at any rate in the open, French cultural propaganda and what the French government imagined to be its acquired rights in that field. Not surprisingly, Greg's suggestions about facing French cultural supremacy were in line with the British policies since the Canal project, and that was to let the French do the job and then become its primary beneficiary. Greg suggested, instead, that it was more worthy of consideration to "work with the French up to a point."[25] He saw French culture as the best ally for preventing the rapid introduction of Italian or German institutions, which would be politically far more dangerous. It was true that the Germans were prevented from doing their excavation work after the unfortunate incident of the bust of Queen Nefertiti.[26] However, the threat still existed, because of an exception made for Hermann Junker and because "Germans seemed to have been liked in Egypt and seemed to have a way of getting on with the Egyptians."[27]

The Egyptian ruling elite, according to Greg, lacked interest in British culture and civilization. Greg divided the Egyptian ruling elites into four categories: the Palace, the land-owning Turco-Egyptian governing class, leaders of the majority party (i.e. the Wafd Party), and Egyptian intellectuals, especially members of the Faculty of Arts at the Egyptian University. Seeking support from the Egyptian elite to strengthen the British cultural position in Egypt was described by Greg as useless and rather hopeless. King Fu'ad lacked respect for British culture and civilization. In general, the old Turco-Egyptian governing class in which Fu'ad had been brought up was "French-speaking, Latin culturally and anti-British sentimentally, even when, in the case of King Fu'ad, a community of political interests was admitted on both sides."[28] The Palace Clique and the Queen Mother were only expected, as in the past, to advertise their independence and detachment from the British connection by maintaining acquaintance with all foreigners other than the British and by employing the French language with ostentation. Similarly, al-Nahhas pasha, the head of the Wafd party and the Prime Minister of Egypt, was found by Greg to "be fundamentally ignorant of the realities of British civilization and culture,"[29] for al-Nahhas only spoke French. The Minister of Foreign Affairs not only did not know English, but also "resided largely in France and was married to a French lady, who in *the trouble of 1919* [i.e. the 1919 anti-British revolt], openly ostentatiously and indeed forcefully espoused the Nationalist cause."[30] French also became the exclusive language of the Ministry of Foreign Affairs. The Minister of Public Works, Zaki 'Urabi pasha, spoke English, but he was "such a backboneless nonentity that it was impossible to count on him even when he had pledged himself to a line of action."[31] The only Wafdist minister who could have given hope to Greg was Mahmud Fahmi al-Nuqrashi, because of his English educational background, but he was not in charge of the Ministry of Public Works, which was overseeing cultural matters in Egypt, including theater and film. Yet Greg doubted that "al-Nuqrashi's narrow doctrinaire outlook"[32] would have gradually yielded to his earlier English cultural training, supposedly more liberal. As for the members of the Faculty of Arts, Greg seemed to have been ill-acquainted with them, for he misspelled the name of the Dean as "Taher" instead of "Taha" Husayn bey, from whom Greg expected no support as he was French-speaking and married to a French wife. Therefore, Greg left the burden of reporting on the position of the Faculty of Arts from British culture to Mr. Purness, Professor of English Literature at the Egyptian University. Greg's efforts to gain the interest of the Egyptian ruling elite in British culture, as he put it, were either ignored or were not met with enthusiasm. For example, the brother of the Queen Mother, Sharif pasha Sabri, Madam 'Ali pasha Sharwal, Prince Yusuf Kamal, and Mahmud bey Khalil, who possessed an outstanding collection of nineteenth-century paintings, often sponsored the annual Cairo salon and many fine arts exhibitions. A group of amateurs, largely French or with French education, however, organized the salon. When the British members of the salon, namely Sir John Home, Mr. Robert Rolo, Mr. Ralph Marari, and Greg, suggested an exhibition of British art, other members did not receive the idea enthusiastically.

To advance British cultural hegemony, Greg suggested three strategies that echoed the British cultural agenda discussed between Warr and Lloyd. Greg endorsed the plan to capitalize on what had already been done. That is to say, he recommended increasing the scholastic facilities that the British had already offered in Egypt and made British cultural hegemony in the lower and middle spheres of culture as strong as the French position in the higher branches. For that purpose, Greg stressed the importance of firmly resisting any attempt to lessen the hours of English in public schools or to weaken the position of English teachers. He found it equally important to make English as much a second or indeed an alternative language as it was in the Far East and as it was tending to become in the late years in Egypt before the 1936 Treaty. He urged the British government to make every effort to get good English staff at the Egyptian University and support such men as Captain Creswell, who, however difficult they might be, were real authorities in their subjects. He requested financial aid for the Anglo-Egyptian Union, an idea that was brought to the attention of Greg by Dr. Muhammad Sharif, who found the union the best way to celebrate the signature of the 1936 Treaty. Another strategy was to focus on the newly emerging Egyptian class with less interest in French culture and more interest in English. Greg saw "the old aristocracy on the wane and the native Egyptian middle class,"[33] which was replacing it, was English rather than French-speaking by temperament"[34] and "apparently genuinely friendly to Great Britain despite 18 years of political controversy."[35] Ironically, Greg attributed the reasons for the emergence of a new Egyptian middle class to "the decency and influence of the majority of the British officials in Egypt for fifty years. [It was also] partly due to the insincerity and absence of any real convictions among Egyptian politicians, whether they are pro or anti-British, as it happens at that moment to suit their political game. Also, the Treaty and British assistance over the capitulations further helped create something of a setback."[36] A third strategy was to rely on the Crown Prince, Farouk, and his rich knowledge of English since he had visited England to study at a young age, despite the fact that his father's death had suspended British plans for him to pursue higher education in London.

It seems that Greg was very optimistic when he thought that even if Farouk's British education did not make him pro-British, it would compel him to come into contact with many leading British personalities, and he would eventually acquire British habits and sensibilities.[37] For example, On September 3, 1937, a letter from Sir Charles Dalton to the British Embassy in Egypt revealed how the British government perceived the personal interest of Farouk in the opera *The Diadem of Stars* as a compliment to British culture in Egypt.[38] Farouk expressed his wish that *The Diadem of Stars* should be performed in Cairo in winter as part of his accession celebrations. Mr. Dalton found that he deserved full official interest and support, for the opera powerfully expressed motives of peace and idealism, which were of higher significance to the world at that moment of unrest. And it was the first time first-class British opera singers would have a chance to be heard in Cairo, a territory hitherto exclusively Italian. Moreover, *The Diadem of Stars* introduced local Egyptian instruments such as the *darabukka*.[39] To Dalton's disappointment, the British Embassy in Cairo followed its negative cultural policy wholeheartedly and did not show the expected interest in *The Diadem of Stars*. Regardless of the Embassy's reaction, this incident proved that the British hopes for an alliance with Farouq were false. After all, the Opera was not focused on British culture and civilization, and it was its Egyptian aspects that attracted him, not British production.

With all these unsuccessful efforts to advance British cultural interest in Egypt, many calls for action proposed the utilization of film as an instrument of British cultural hegemony. This plan, however, was far more complicated. It was not that the British colonial authority did not know how to use film for cultural propaganda. As Burns put it, each portion of the British empire reflected a different relationship with film. Zimbabwe/Rhodesia was home to two of the most ambitious state-sponsored film production units in Africa, the Central African Film Unit (CAFU) and the Rhodesian Information Services' Film Unit (RIS). Those units served as instruments of cultural hegemony.[40]

While it is true, as Burns suggested, that Egypt had developed a film industry at the time, the British did not lack interest in using film as an instrument of cultural hegemony in Egypt. The major difference was in the target audience. While, in Zimbabwe, the audience came from the majority of the illiterate lay public, the target audience in Egypt was the educated Egyptians or the *effendis*—the white-collar bureaucrats whose colonial education and bureaucracy shaped their habits, education, and training during the interwar period.[41]

2. Film and the Shy Efforts of British Propaganda

The use of film to advance British cultural expansion plans in Egypt aimed at impressing the few educated Egyptians with the ideal modern civilizational image of London as the center of the empire. Such an ideal image was a result of harmonization between a tradition of romance and grandiose history and societal modernization and industrial progress. For example, the Foreign Office sent a letter, received in August 1937, to the British Embassy in Cairo regarding the possibility of exhibiting short British silent and sound films in Egypt to university students.[42]

Sound films alluded to London's "salient features and arresting contrasts, her romantic past, and bustling present."[43] The green and floral view of London's administrative area from the angle of St. James's Park was emphasized. Themes also covered tradition, as reflected in England's cathedrals that "endeavored to show their significance in English history as well as their essential beauty in the English landscape."[44] The English village was presented as the backbone of English life with its ancient churches and its ancient farms. British peasants were depicted as "decent men and women,"[45] providing an example of citizens in the public sphere, this here being the inn where "tankards of ale assist the wise discussion of world's affairs."[46] Aspects of societal modernization were introduced by tracing the progress of the county of Lancashire from the days of water power to those of electrically-driven machinery.[47] Examples of sound films included *So This Is London, The Heart of an Empire, For All Eternity, Around the Village Green*, and *So This Is Lancashire*.

Silent films covered aspects of urbanization; economic and cultural milieus in London as seen in the daily parade of traffic; a parade of businessmen and typists to their offices in the city; markets and shops; a parade of fashion, theaters, and cinemas; and electric signs in Piccadilly Circus and the fall of night.

Some movies contrasted the more primitive types of transport, like the donkey that was still used in Britain, with the modern. The ideal British justice was celebrated by representing judiciary life through a judges' procession and the opening of the Parliament. The state and its power were displayed by showing buildings of state and statues of famous men. Buckingham Palace and scenes of Horse Guards Parade were also depicted. Edinburgh Castle was shown as the fortress guarding the road to the South, and the sea route to England was introduced to emphasize the connection between the castle and the church. Industrialization was shown as a paradise for city workers on the seaside, enjoying the varied attractions of the South coast, "which caters to every type of visitor."[48] Examples of films included *Pageantry of Parade, St. James's Park, Edinburgh, Cathedral of England, Britain's Countryside, South Coast of England, Lancashire at Work,* and *Transport in Britain.* None of these films referenced the harsh realities of the Great Depression and the rise of unemployment in London.[49]

As for the use of feature films to serve British cultural hegemony in Egypt, the supply was restrained. On the one hand, the Egyptian film industry was on the rise; filmmakers had been operating in Egypt since 1898, and by 1936 hundreds of features were produced. Theater actors started shifting to filmmaking, and there were at least thirty known directors and producers operating, including Istifan Rusti, Tugu Mizrahi, Ibrahim Lama, Muhammad Karim, Yusuf Wahbi, Mario Folbi, Shukri Madi, Manual Fihmann, Bahiga Hafiz, Mahmud Khalil Rashid, 'Aziza Amir, Mustafa Wali, Fatima Rushdi, Ahmad Galal, Muhammad Bayumi, Willy Rozier, Shalum, Alexander Farkash, Fritz Krampe, Alphizi Orphanili, Ahmad Badrkhan, Amina Muhammad, 'Abd al-Fattah Hasan, Niyazi Mustafa, Fu'ad al-Gazayrli, Kamal Salim, Ahmad Salim, Husayn Fawzi, Ahmad Kamil Mursi, and Tawfiq al-'Aqqad. Other film industries also had a market in Egypt. Almost 65 percent of films exhibited in Egypt were Hollywood productions. British movies constituted less than 4 percent.[50] The British government could not break the Hollywood quota system in London,[51] let alone in the colonies.[52] On the other hand, "the ambivalent status of [British] film—as an industry, entertainment and, in some cases, 'art'—has also been evident in the application of film policy in London. Unlike the traditional arts, the cultural value or aesthetic worth of cinema . . . [was] not a given, and the film . . . [did] therefore not automatically fall within the domain of 'arts policy' (or, following its establishment, the Arts Council)."[53] According to Geoffrey Macnab in his seminal work *J. Arthur Rank and the British Film Industry*, it was not until 1936 that the British General Cinema Finance Corporation was established. It resembled the Cinema Finance Corporation set up in 1921 by a group of Los Angeles bankers who knew little about film but were keen to invest in the new medium because they were lured by the glamour of cinema and, more pertinently, the chance of making some easy money.[54]

Supplying feature films to serve British cultural hegemony in Egypt was further restrained by the cost of shipping and import duties. For example, in July 1939, a project of a film library for the use of the Anglo-Egyptian Union and the Egyptian Ministry of Education was proposed by the British Embassy in Cairo.[55] The proposal was to supply the library with sufficient films for eight hours of projection and with a 35 mm projector renewable each year. The Foreign Office was not enthusiastic, for its broad strategy was to avoid mobilizing a large number of films in any one country. It thus found the Embassy's request unjustifiable since seven 16 mm silent films had previously been sent to the Egyptian Ministry of Education, and eight 35 mm sound films to the Anglo-Egyptian Union. The Foreign Office found it difficult to justify spending five hundred pounds sterling on a new projector on loan, since the item required would be a 35 mm sound projector.[56] Also, import duty on developed film positives was around two pounds sterling per kilo (450) plus 10 percent representing customs dues and other auxiliary charges, bringing the total to approximately six pounds sterling a reel.[57] Besides, there were difficulties with 35 mm projectors owing to fire regulations, even if non-flammable films were used. Therefore, the Foreign Office suggested a less ambitious plan, which included sending films lasting for an hour or two hours, and when those films were returned, a fresh supply could be sent out.[58]

Lack of funding persisted even when film was used for British military propaganda purposes. On 21 January 1939, the Air Ministry sent a letter in which it expressed concerns about the acquisition of photographs, at the cost of fifty to a hundred pounds a year, for publicity in Egyptian newspapers and films. The purpose was to exhibit in Cairo short films like *Raising Air Fighters*,[59] which depicted the training of pilots for permanent and short service commissions in the Royal Air Force. While *Raising Air Fighters* was approved for exhibition in Egypt, another, comedy feature entitled *It's In the Air*, in which British comedian and songwriter George Formby took the leading role, was not found suitable for exhibition in Egypt. Ironically, the films were part of a general effort to assure the Egyptian Government and the public that air attacks would not be as terrible as they feared. Giving publicity to the frightfulness of airstrikes was perceived as essential in order to create enthusiasm for the Air Force and to obtain the necessary funds.[60] Up until June 7, 1939, no progress occurred with regard to the supply of movies for exhibition in Egypt.

Nevertheless, the lack of funding, the cost of shipping, and the modest interest in producing British feature films, as well as the cost of shipping, were not the only reasons why British officials were reluctant to see film production as a practical means of advancing British cultural hegemony. One root cause of this reluctance was the presence of a more practical and affordable solution that served the same purposes and was even better. This was film censorship. To understand the roots of this development, one must zoom out of the Egyptian scene to recognize the grandiose colonial administrative challenge caused by the many parties involved in licensing films across the British empire. Producers had to deal with the British Board of Film Censors, the Colonial Office, the Federation of British Film Industries, and the Cinematograph Trade, which held the actual licensing authority. For example, two British movies, *Tommy Atkin*, directed by Norman Walker, and *Show Life*, were banned in Malaya in 1925 because the portrayal of a young Chinese girl living with and being brutally treated by a White man was seen as a sordid subject and unfair for exhibition before mixed audiences. Another scene, a fight between British troops and Arab tribesmen, was likely to offend Muslim susceptibilities. When the issue was not resolved through the British Board of Film Censors, the producers communicated directly with the Colonial Office, to which they sent a letter of complaint in which they expressed their astonishment that the Board had banned a British picture like *Show Life* in a British colony and passed two American films dealing with the activities of the French Foreign Legion, *Beau Geste* and *Beau Sabreur*, the heroes of which were Englishmen. They complained that *Tommy Atkins* had been passed by censors all over the world and was shown in India, where problems on the score of offending racial susceptibilities should be somewhat similar to those in the Straits Settlements. The producers made the further criticism that the foreign managers at UFA of Berlin had no difficulties with censorship of their films in that territory, despite the fact that their production was frequently of a controversial nature that should have made them liable to the censor's knife. It was only two years after the first constitution of the British Board of Film Censors came into being in 1927 that the Federation of British Film Industries replied to the Secretary of the Colonies, urging the Colonial Office to lift the ban on the two movies as they were of the greatest importance in opening the overseas markets for British films as wide as possible, since the home market was not sufficient to pay for a production that was significant enough to compete with the American and German films.[61]

3. Censorship and British Cultural Hegemony

The British Board of Film Censors, an unofficial body financially independent of the Cinematograph Trade, which held the licensing authority, started to regulate the process of licensing films as early as 1927. The initial constitution of the Board classified six categories of prohibited incidents that required the intervention of the censors. The category of religion banned the depiction of the materialized figure of Christ, and religious rites and ceremonies treated with irreverence, or in a way calculated to bring religion into contempt (even when the treatment was reverent). The irreverent introduction of quotations from the Bible or church services to produce comic effects, and, equally, the comic introduction of biblical characters, angels, gates of Heaven, etc., which were offensive to a vast majority of the audience in England, were subject to censorship. Topics that could wound the susceptibilities of foreign peoples, and especially of fellow-subjects of the British empire, were not allowed. And the same rule applied to stories and scenes which were calculated and possibly intended to provoke social unrest and discontent.[62] The social incidents category banned nudity, both in actuality and shadowgraph, and swearing or language in the nature of swearing, in titles or subtitles. Incidents that broke class hierarchy by bringing into contempt public characters acting in their capacity as such were not tolerated. That is to say, officers and men wearing a military uniform, ministers of religion, ministers of the crown, ambassadors and representatives of foreign nations, administrators of the law, and medical men could not be criticized. Any scenes of embrace that "over-stepped" the limits of affection or passion, and became lascivious, were cut. Excessive drunkenness, even when treated in a comic vein, was considered offensive vulgarity not suitable for public screening. The same rule applied in the case of suggestive and indecorous dancing. Scenes connected with childbirth, such as puerperal pains, were considered too intimate for public exhibition. Subjects dealing with venereal disease or any other matters suitable only for the hospital or medical lecture were banned. It was not permitted to depict any stories showing antagonistic relations between White men and the colored population of the British Empire, particularly with respect to the question of sexual intercourse, moral or immoral, between individuals of different races.[63] Issues of sex were covered under a separate category that censored scenes of rape and intentions to commit rape; stories about immoral women; scenes of street soliciting; White slave traffic; and procurement. Scenes of a father making love to his unknown daughter or a brother to his unknown sister were classed as repugnant.[64] The crime category discouraged the depiction of crime, especially scenes demonstrating the methods of crime, which might lend themselves to imitation. As regards subjects dealing with a drug habit, the Board classified it as a vice with its insidious allurements that involved the danger of spreading the pernicious habit. The Board objected to prolonged scenes of extreme violence and brutality, hanging scenes, and the depiction of actual executions treated either seriously or in a comic spirit. Stories in which the sole interest was that of crime and the criminal life, without any counterbalancing element such as love or adventure, were also censored. Organized fights and themes calculated to give an air of romance and heroism to criminal characters were cut. Also, the story should not be told in such a way as to enlist the sympathies of the audience with the criminals, whilst the constituted authorities and administrators of the law were held up contempt as being either unjust or harsh, incompetent or ridiculous.[65] Another category covered cruelty, which included scenes of cruelty to children, and incidents which appeared to involve the infliction of cruelty on animals.[66]

The constitution was amended in 1929 to shorten the religious category. The objection to the depiction of the materialized figure of Christ was omitted; censoring only included scenes relating to the consecration and administering of the Eucharist; travesty and mockery of biblical characters; and the comic treatment of incidents connected with death. The political category grew into a more detailed one. The Board censored any reference to the Prince of Wales, libelous reflections on Royal dynasties, or any parts of British possessions, which could not be represented as "lawless sinks of iniquity."[67] Some rules remained the same, especially those applying to themes that were likely to wound the just susceptibilities of friendly nations, the depiction of White men in a state of degradation amid Far Eastern and Native surroundings, and equivocal situations between White girls and men of other races. The social category had two new objectionable depictions, namely, the reference to well-known and public characters and the depiction of painful scenes of lunacy. The sex category was modified to include themes indicative of habitual immorality, crude immorality, women in alluring and provocative attitudes, street scenes of accosting, lives of prostitutes, procurement, incidents intended to show how clearly an outrage had been perpetrated, scenes depicting white slave traffic, indecorous bathroom scenes, vamping, men and women in bed together, and indecent inscriptions.[68] The crime category was modified to include the banning of scenes depicting the breaking of a bottle on a man's head. The cruelty category included new items like bullfights, fight scenes involving girls and women, torture scenes, carnage scenes, and scenes of martyrdom exploiting the agony of the victim. Three new categories were added, namely military, the administration of justice, and titling. The new military category banned the depiction of officers in British uniform shown in a disgraceful light, the depiction of conflicts between the armed forces of a state and the populace, and reflection on wives of responsible British officials stationed in the East. Under the administration of justice category, the Board censored any scenes referring directly or indirectly to police firing on the defenseless populace, fights between police and organized criminal gangs, and incidents that conveyed false and derogatory impressions of the police forces in Britain, in addition to prison scenes, and persecution of ex-convicts by detectives. The category of titling was added to ban offensive main movie titles, irreverent quotations of biblical texts, irreverent and blasphemous subtitles, inflammatory subtitles, subtitles in the nature of political propaganda, subtitles in the nature of swearing, expressions regarded as objectionable in Britain, equivocal and suggestive subtitles, and objectionable innuendo.

But how did these censorship rulings materialize in Egypt while Egypt did not have a film censorship code until 1947? The question of censorship and its archives inside Egypt has never been an easy task for the researcher due to the shifting censorship responsibility between the Ministries of Public Works, Social Affairs, and the Interior, with the final word going always to the latter. For the researcher today, it is almost impossible to access the archives of The Ministry of the Interior.[69] Apart from the difficulty of locating a policy for information access in Egypt, every new regime destroyed the previous records, either by neglecting documentation in daily routines or by hiding information from the new staff.[70] Besides, the Public Security Administration, which was in charge of the Printing Press Administration, which oversaw film censorship, had undergone many changes, which caused the loss of most records, including those of administrations dealing with cinema. The most important of these administrations was the European Administration, which supervised everything that concerned foreigners since 1922, and used to participate, with the head of the Printing Press Administration, in licensing films and appointing staff. While some documents are available in the Egyptian National Archives, there seem to be no records of the silent era, as the records started in 1933 and even those early documents are difficult to reach owing to (claimed) long-continuing renovation work.

Nevertheless, film censorship in Egypt could be understood by stepping back in time to examine the relationship between public media (which first included the printing press and theater before film was added) and local authorities. The Egyptian Ministry of the Interior, which was under the thumb of the British colonial authorities, executed oral censorship policies that aimed to essentialize the supremacy of the colonizer and suppress the public use of reason in theater and film halls, which were a threat to the public order.

4. Suppressing the Public Use of Reason in Theater

Available sources on censorship in Egypt tell us that the first censor that Egypt knew was General Diageo, during the French Campaign.[71] Under Muhammad ʿAli, Antoine Barthelemy Clot bey, a French physician (1793–1868), addressed consulates of foreign countries and foreign theater troupes to regulate the relationship between actors and the audience for the protection of public order.[72] Under Ismaʿil, the latter appointed Paulino Dranit pasha, the first chair of the Opera House, to be the censor in January 1879.[73] The first censorship law for the printing press was issued on

November 26, 1881.[74] It came in response to the revolutionary narrative in newspapers during the 'Urabi revolt. After the British occupation, a constitution that regulated the work of public houses was issued on June 13, 1891. The first article stated that Acting Houses (*dur al-tamthil*), be they in the form of a circus, a *teatro* or theater or horse clubs, or any shop to which the expression circle club (*mahallat al-tashkhis*) applied, should obtain a license. Article 7 exempted religious public festivals, known in Arabic as *mawalid*, from getting a permit. However, article 19 gave police absolute authority to enter any public house to protect public order. A new constitution known as the Teatri Bylaw (*la'ihat al-tiyatrat*) was issued in June 1896 to regulate the work of the Teatri Company in Egypt and Cairo, that being the major Theater Company in Egypt between 1897 and 1899. The constitution dealt with public houses that could cause civil unrest and that were harmful to health. The available version of that constitution was the version amended in 1904. The Alexandria Comisión issued the amendment to regulate the relationship between the city council and theater halls. It included general rules on safety measures, fire prevention rules, and fines for violating safety measures. In 1909, the cinematograph halls were added to the 1904 bylaw and were listed as dangerous public houses that could cause civil turmoil. The task of censorship between 1882 and 1909 fell to the head of the local police authorities, which were under the control of the British colonial authorities since Egypt was, during that time, an occupied territory, even though the Khediviate of Egypt remained an autonomous province of the Ottoman Empire. There were no written rules to guide censorship at that point. The overall strategy, however, was to exercise absolute control over public spaces in order to suppress any anti-colonialist stances. Media reports on police censorship of theater performances clearly reflect this strategy.

As early as 1900, the police censored a play called *'Urabi pasha* ('Urabi) performed by the al-Qabbani theater troupe.[75] In 1906, the play *Dinshuway* was censored since it commemorated the unjust execution of Egyptian peasants by British colonial authorities. Attempting to resist censorship, the author of *Dinshuway* Hasan Mar'i[76] printed the text of the play and published it under a different title, *Sayyad al-Hamam* (Pigeon Hunter). While the published text was initially not censored, the police confiscated many copies in 1908.[77] The author, Hasan Mar'i, contested the decision of the Ministry of the Interior and complained that the censorship decision had been delivered to him orally, not in a written legal form that allowed him to contest the censorship decision legally. He wrote, "There is no law nor a regime that can prevent me from performing a play, which is based on a true story that was authored and performed in every brutal manner by the same authorities that is trying to censor the play now."[78] The stance of Hasan Mar'i, according to Samir Farid, was the first time in which an Egyptian author called for a law to regulate the censorship of performing arts. In the same year, the 'Aziz 'Id troupe presented a play called *Fi Sabil al-Istiqlal* (Independence), which was censored after the first day of performance since it represented Muhammad Ali as "a heartless monster"[79] who did not hesitate to kill even during the time of the Muslim call to prayer (*adhan*).[80]

The mechanisms by which the police forces implemented censorship in theaters show that theaters were public spaces that constituted a major threat to the colonial authorities and the local government, which gave the police absolute power, often directed by the chief commissioner of the police, who used to be a British officer. One example is the dynamics of censoring the play *Dahaya al-Jahl* (Victims of ignorance), performed on the stage of the Arabic Acting House by the troupe of the Egyptian Teatro run by Iskandar Farah. In July 1910, Ibrahim Rizq, the chief of the Muski police station, led a force of twenty policemen and cracked down on the Arabic Acting House during the performance of *Dahaya al-Jahl*.[81] The main reason was that Imam al-'Abd, a member of the troupe, gave an improvised speech (*khutba irtijaliyya*) between acts three and four. The speech commented on the injustice that befell peasants and the importance of pursuing freedom despite all dangers.[82] The police arrested the speaker, turned off the theater lights, dismissed the audience, and arrested the owner of the theater, Hasan Kamil.[83]

In response to the censorship of the play, the *al-Liwa'* newspaper led a campaign against the government and accused it of testing suppression strategies against theaters as a part of a general plan to suppress and censor freedom of expression and to issue laws in that direction.[84] Since World War I was approaching, the paper considered the incident an attack on freedom of protest, freedom of public gathering, and freedom of expression as a pretext for the absolute enforcement of martial law. The paper warned the government against the futility of policing the thoughts of people, for every person in the land of Egypt became aware that no one possessed control (*sultan*) over a person's thoughts except God. People know that no human authority can control or prevent them from thinking of and believing in what they choose. Any government that tries to police thought and control it acts like a person chasing the air to hold it.[85]

The strategy of suppression, the paper pointed out, was

a mediocre and impossible strategy because, as Spencer put it, tactic (*hila*) is a consequence of injustice and authoritarianism. What he means is that when the ruler's oppression and authoritarianism intensify, the oppressed resort to *hila* to accomplish their goals. That is the nature of things (*sunnatallah*), which the government strives to change, despite the fact that all modern governments that exercised what the Muski police chief exercised ended up realizing it is impossible to control the spirits and thoughts of nations. Those governments resorted to appealing to their people and negotiating to achieve through justice what they could not achieve through authoritarianism and oppression. European and American histories are full of similar examples.[86]

At another level, *al-Liwa'* further questioned the double standards of the police in implementing censorship. While the police chief was shutting down the Arabic Acting House, a foreign troupe was performing a play in which a French girl was killed by a German officer. The girl was serving her country during the Franco-Prussian War. The play had many killing and death scenes and many speeches on freedom. Yet the foreign play was not censored. The newspaper blamed the government "for allowing the police to treat the foreign theater audience humanely while ordering the police to treat its own country's audience inhumanely."[87]

Al-Muqattam newspaper[88] often spoke in the voice of the British colonial authorities, supported the decision of the police, and argued that the play could have disturbed the diplomatic relationship between Egypt and Greece. In support of the police, *al-Muqattam* claimed that it had received a letter from an honorable citizen (*muwatin sharif*) by the name of Ahmad bey Khayri. It is quite ironic, here, that the idea of the "honorable citizen" has its roots in the colonial era. It is well-known that during the January 25, 2011 revolt in Egypt, news channels called upon the "honorable citizens" living in the neighborhood of 'Abbasiyya to save the police from protestors.[89] And the "honorable citizen," who identified himself as "Tamir from Ghamra," phoned many news channels to condemn protestors during the first eighteen days of the protest. More ironically, I still recall how, during the 2015 Baltimore riots in the USA, Charli Rose spent over an hour on-air talking to the "honorable Black American citizen" who did not support the riots and who discouraged the participation of her son and his friends in the protest. More ironically, the CBC channel hosted the same lady to deliver the same message. Going back to Ahmad Khayri bey in Cairo in 1910, the latter complained that the speech given between acts was an interruption to the play. He lamented his loss, for he neither watched the play nor got his money back, a matter that, as he expressed it, did not become the amour-propre of Egypt as a modern country, and could have never happened in any other civilized country. While *al-Muqattam* blamed the police for excessive use of force during its crackdown on the performance of the play *Dahaya al-Jahl*, the newspaper tried at the same time to justify the violence by claiming that it was not a policy but an individual behavior on the part of the police. To justify this further, the newspaper framed the incident in terms of good intentions on the part of the government, which was not attempting to silence or suppress freedom of expression as much as it was pushing for a new firm policy instead of its former lenient one.[90]

The Prime Minister, Muhammad pasha Sa'id, responded to the incident by giving an assurance that he was against the unconditional application of martial law. *Al-Liwa'* criticized his laid-back attitude, for he knew about the incident from newspapers, not from a special report that should have been submitted to him by the Ministry of the Interior. The newspaper further blamed Harvey pasha, the British Commissioner of Cairo police, because he had ordered the Muski police chief to dismiss the audience in an inhuman manner. The newspaper found Harvey pasha's attitude not surprising since it reflected his long-standing policy of suppression, for he used to tell protestors, "'I am the law' (*ana al-qanun*)." *Al-Liwa'* called upon people to express their dissatisfaction at the incident and to organize a non-violent protest. The newspaper further urged the Prime Minister to lift the ban on the theater troupe and to order the police chief to acknowledge his mistake officially, but this never happened.[91]

The government counteracted this by reducing the number of police forces in theater houses to five instead of twenty. They no longer wore uniforms in the theater. Instead, they used to dress as civilians, thereby serving as secret police.[92] In addition, the police established a new division called public moralities (*al-adab*).[93] The division was to appoint three writers/journalists to decide on censorship-related issues, because the police chief did not have the skill to determine the implicit meanings of Arabic sentences and metaphors. In 1911, another constitution, also known as the Teatro Bylaw,[94] was issued to regulate police intervention. Article 10 censored all acting and public gathering that violated public order. The article gave powers to the police to interrupt the performance and shut down the theater. Article 11 allowed the police to suspend performance if the audience was present in passageways, if the audience smoked, or if any noise occurred while acting. Article 12 stated that the police should be assigned a place in the theater to be able to monitor the performance. Article 13 required theater owners to obtain permission from the police to open after midnight. Article 17 instructed that any person who intended to transfer his shop into a theater, a circus, or an acting house had to apply for a new license.[95] In 1915, actors started thinking of forming a syndicate.[96] Three troupes, namely, the Abyad, the Hijazi, and the 'Ukasha, were the nucleus of the syndicate. The basic idea was to have a shared fund: that is, the revenue of the three troupes would be put into a shared fund and would be redistributed among all troupes. This plan, however, did not succeed, and it was not until 1919 that the syndicate was established.[97] But as of 1919, theater started to decline. 'Abd al-Rahman Rushdi broke up his troupe.[98] The Abyad troupe left Egypt, and the 'Ukasha troupe stopped its activities for renovations.[99] By 1920, cinema was starting to attract more of an audience, and the police considered any store that had more than 50 grams of raw celluloid to be rest-disturbing (*muqliq lil-raha*). In 1922, 'Abd al-Khaliq Tharwat pasha, the Minister of Interior, consulted with Ibrahim Fathi, the Vice Minister of Finance,[100] to approve a decree to regulate the import of films that violated public morals (*adab*) and public order.[101] Article 1 banned custom clearance of films without a license being obtained from the Ministry of the Interior. The importer had to pay an extra 4 percent, in addition to customs. On April 15, 1922, the Court of Appeal approved a law to restore and amend the 1904 constitution to ban immoral scenes from entertainment public houses (*malahi*). The same law applied to any public gatherings that were against civility and public order. In 1928, 'Ali Mahir pasha, the Minister of Finance, in consultation with the Minister of the Interior, Muhammad Mahmud pasha, issued Decree no. 42 to regulate the export of films shot in Egypt. The goal was to regulate the amour-propre of Egypt and its inhabitants abroad. Article 1 banned any attempt to export films shot in Egypt without a license being obtained from the Ministry of the Interior.

5. Early Oral Policies of Film Censorship

According to I'tidal Mumtaz, film censorship started as a process of following oral instructions.[102] Censors relied on analogy (i.e. new cases were decided on the basis of older ones). Mumtaz described the process as a settled norm or custom (*'urf*), which was decided by the British head of the English Department at the Faculty of Arts, Cairo University, Mr. Francis,[103] who became the general censor in the Ministry of the Interior in 1938. The chairman of the English Department at Alexandria University, Nur Sharif, used to perform censorship duties on foreign news as assigned by the general censor.[104] Films were reviewed before screening in the basement of the Ministry of the Interior through the Film Censorship Department, which was directed by the Printing Press Administration. The basement had a wide room in which censors were seated. It also had two exhibition halls, a small room reserved for the manager, and another smaller room used as storage for movies or files.[105] Initially, two male censors held a brief review session after watching the film. One censor represented the Ministry of the Interior, and the other the Ministry of Social Affairs, which used to share the task of censorship with the Ministry of the Interior. A more detailed review session administered by five women censors followed.[106] Three of them were *khawagat* and two were locals. As for the *khawagat*, the first was Randa Clementine, the Italian daughter of a police commissioner. She had lived in Egypt since childhood and spoke Arabic very well. She joined the department in 1923 and reviewed Arabic, Italian, French, and English films.[107] The second was Madam Cunneil,[108] who was of Russian origin and had a British husband. She had lived in Egypt with refugee status since the Russian Revolution of 1917. She joined the department in 1922, and supervised English and French movies.[109] The third was of Turkish origin, Zaynab Fu'ad. She used to review Arabic, English, and Turkish films.[110] As for the two female censors of local origin, the first was Nur Sharif, chair of the English Department at Alexandria University, and the second Safiyya Rabi', a professor of English at the Faculty of Arts at Cairo University.[111] I'tidal Mumtaz was the sixth woman censor.[112]

In 1938, the Ministry of Social Affairs administered censorship duties. Nevertheless, the Ministry of the Interior restored duties back that same year, for military reasons, namely, the outbreak of World War II. After the war, tension arose between the two ministries over the control of the Film Censorship Department.[113] One proposal to resolve the issue was to divide censors into two groups to represent the two ministries. The group appointed by the Ministry of the Interior would present reports about public safety and order. The Ministry of Social Affairs supervised the second group, which used to report issues affecting social order, family, public morality, social structure, customs, and traditions. However, the upper hand always used to be with the Ministry of the Interior. Mumtaz, however, objected to the process, for she found it impractical to ask the censor to censor herself while taking notes. Instead, she suggested that all censors take notes, and the burden should be left to the two ministries to decide which censored parts fell under their domain.[114]

Examples of censorship of foreign films included cutting a scene with Gary Cooper holding a gun and aiming at balloons on the stage while nude actresses were coming out of the balloons.[115] Other examples included a scene for Maureen O'Hara sitting in a relaxed posture and saying to the hero, "I am ready." Samuel Goldwyn, the producer of *Roman Scandals*, 1933, directed by Frank Tuttle, objected when the censors cut a scene for 500 dancers wearing only fig leaves. The idea behind the scene was to depict Adam and Eve in paradise, and the company found it impossible to depict the scene in any other fashion. *Notorious*, 1946, directed by Alfred Hitchcock and featuring Ingrid Bergman and Cary Grant, was subject to the censor's knife because of an extended kiss scene in which Bergman touched Grant's hair with her fingers. The censorship found the depiction of the kiss in that fashion too seductive.[116]

It is imperative here to mention that, in the absence of written rules of censorship, authority did not always lie with local censors as colonial authorities influenced the process, especially in the case of British films. One example was the British movie *Four Feathers*, 1939, directed by Zoltan Korda. The governor-general of Sudan wrote a letter on January 22, 1939, to Foreign

Secretary Viscount Halifax. The former expressed reservations about the movie *Four Feathers*, in which a scene portrayed a successful attack by dervishes on a small British force encamped in a thorn *zariba*. The *zariba* was fired on and carried by storm, and, after the massacre of most of the survivors, two British officers were tied up and dragged away behind camels to the Khalifa's camp. An Englishman in disguise was shown under the liberal application of whips in a further incident. Some of the scenes captured British officers driven through the streets of Omdurman; there were prison scenes of varying degrees of brutality, and the character of the Khalifa himself was painted in very dark colors. On February 8, 1939, Viscount Halifax endorsed the view of the governor-general of Sudan in banning *Four Feathers*. Halifax further suggested that it might be of interest that a similar omission was made in a film recently shown in Cairo entitled *Sixty Glorious Years*, in which a column of purely British troops was shown marching into Omdurman after the defeat of the dervishes. The Foreign Office replied to Halifax on March 8, 1939. It advised that while the Foreign Office would forward the concern about *Four Feathers* to the British Board of Film Censors, the Board was not officially concerned with licensing of films outside Britain, and therefore the local censorship authorities should take whatever steps necessary to prevent the exhibition of the film in Egypt. On March 11, 1939, the War Office that had assisted in the production of *Four Feathers* resolved the issue by sending eight representatives, who watched the film on April 4, 1939, at 2:30 p.m. Foreign Office personnel were welcome to attend. Mr. Kelly and Mr. Fraser of the Sudan agency saw the film; they had some objections, which they communicated to the producer. Considering the British amour-propre in Egypt and Sudan, they objected to certain episodes in the treatment of two British officer prisoners, notably them being dragged behind camels, exposed in a cage and pelted with dust, and being manhandled when put into prison. They requested that the producer cut those scenes out, especially the cage scene, which irritated the War Office representative. With regard to the effect on Egyptian amour-propre, the representatives concluded that the script was always careful to refer to the Anglo-Egyptian Army; the Egyptian national anthem was played at an inspection of the British troops in which some Egyptian troops also figured, and they found nothing positively wounding to Egyptian susceptibilities.[117] The representatives suggested that the only way to improve the film would be by introducing further scenes to compensate for the meager appearances of Egyptians and make them appear as partners. Lampson requested the exclusion of Egypt from the exhibition of *Four Feathers*. Kelly perceived Lampson's decision as drastic, and decided to influence the decision of the local authorities in Egypt to override Lampson's view.[118] The records are silent on whether or not *Four Feathers* was screened in Egypt. It could be that Kelly's request projected an indirect exercise of colonial power, thereby ignoring the new political form of the Egyptian state after the 1936 Treaty. Lampson warned that similar situations had culminated in clashes with Egyptian authorities, a matter that the British government was keen to avoid after the 1936 Treaty and during World War II. However, many incidents of intervention occurred during the war. Chief among these was, of course, the siege of the 'Abidin Palace in 1942, which crushed the ruling elite's amour-propre of national sovereignty.

A more convoluted review process was used for Egyptian movies, which were evaluated once on the basis of the scenario, and another time after shooting. An Egyptian company, one day, presented a scenario to the Film Censorship Department. The returned notes implied that the overarching goals of oral censorship were: (a) to protect class hierarchy, (b) to maintain the superiority of the soldiers of the British Empire, and (c) to regulate the amour-propre of Egypt as a modern and civilized country. For example, the censors ordered the omission of a scene in which an upper Egyptian man was calling his wife "mother of Kitchener" in respect of the memory of Lord Kitchener, thereby protecting the amour-propre of the soldiers of the British Empire.[119] Another note reflected the importance of preserving class hierarchy; the note stated that since the hero of the novel was depicted as a villain, he could not be a pasha. Under the fourth category dealing with questions of sex, the British Code regulated what constituted an appropriate depiction of the father–daughter relationship. In addition, the third category covering social incidents suggested that any scenes of embrace that over-stepped the limits of affection or passion and became lascivious were to be cut. It was common for a father to kiss a daughter or hug her in Egypt at that time. It was quite customary for men to kiss women they were not legally eligible to marry, since it was not common for them to kiss women who they were legally eligible to marry. Yet the censor's third note on the returned scenario addressed the same concern as that addressed in the British Code. The note stated that the father should not kiss his daughter twice, for it was enough to kiss her once to keep within the norms of propriety. Under the same category of the British Code, bringing into contempt public characters acting in their capacity as officers in uniform was considered an attempt to break class hierarchy. A note on the returned scenario requested the omission of the phrase "Your eyes are a threat to public order"[120] because it implicitly lampooned the duties of the Public Security Administration. For the same reason, the censor cut the sentence "You are economical, and we will appoint you as the Minister of Supply (*tamwin*) in the house"[121] because it disparaged the Ministry of Supply. By the same token, the remark "I knew you were with him yesterday. I have secret police"[122] was cut, because it hinted at the state security known as the Political Division. Even cruelty-related issues were addressed in the notes. For example, the censors ordered the omission of the slang phrase "I will gouge out your eyes" (*abazzaz 'iyniyyik*),[123] because it was thought to encourage cruelty.

The toughest clash over licensing Egyptian films materialized in the censorship of the movie *Lashin*/Lashin, 1938, directed by Fritz Krampe, assisted by Ahmad Badrkhan. The clash occurred primarily because the film discussed autocratic rule and religious despotism. It was the first movie to depict a revolution that toppled a king. Egypt's Company for Acting and Cinema produced the film. The works of the German novelist Heinrich Mann (1871–1950), whose novels had strong socialist themes, inspired the story.[124] The poet Ahmad Rami (1892–1981), who was a mentor to the Egyptian diva Umm Kulthum, wrote the dialogue. Initially, the Censorship Division approved the movie for public screening; it was supposed to be in movie theaters on March 17, 1938. But the Vice Minister of the Interior, Hasan pasha Rif'at, banned the movie under the claim that it disparaged the royal persona (*al-dhat al-malakiyya*) — a legal rule of British origin — and the political regime at the time.[125] The movie was released on November 14, 1938 after the director changed the ending, making the army leader save the king, whose corrupt advisors had misled him.

Another movie that faced censorship because of its political themes was *Min Fat Qadimuh*/Never Give Up on the Origin, 1943, directed by Farid al-Gindi and produced by Yahya al-Sayyid, son of the Liberalist-Constitutionalist Ahmad Lutfi al-Sayyid. The movie criticized party politics in Egypt and attacked al-Nahhas, the head of the Wafd majority party at that time. Since the film depicted the wife of a party leader interfering in party and government decisions, the film was seen as hinting at Zaynab al-Wakil, the wife of al-Nahhas pasha. Because it was made while al-Wafd was not in power, the movie was not initially censored. When al-Wafd was restored to power on February 4, 1942, the government recommended a cut of 480 feet of the film, which rendered it meaningless. When the movie screened on January 18, 1943, the audience rioted and almost destroyed the movie theater.[126]

By 1945, the Ministry of Social Affairs had regained its shared responsibility for film censorship with the Ministry of the Interior.[127] This continued up until the outbreak of the 1948 war known as the *nakba*, after which responsibility for film censorship shifted back to the Ministry of the Interior. Between 1945 and 1947, the Publicity and Social Instruction Division in the Ministry of Social Affairs created a film censorship code, issued in February 1947, to empower the decisions of the censors against the complaints of production companies.[128]

While it might appear that the Egyptian 1947 code resembles the American Motion Picture Production Code of 1946, the two codes differ significantly. The American code was not legally binding as that would violate the first amendment. It was merely a set of ideas or rules for the producers to take into consideration. The Egyptian 1947 code, however, was the law. It is referred to in Arabic as the law of censorship (*qanun al-raqaba*). The Egyptian code was more detailed than the American code. There is no category for public order under the American code. The category of religion in the American code includes three articles dealing with the ridicule of religion and ministers of religion. In the Egyptian code, the religion category had five detailed articles specifying what constitutes censored religious practices; the articles paid more attention to Islamic practices than those of other religions. Under the crime category, the American code abided by the second amendment; thus, it did not specify the types of weapons banned in films. The crime category in the Egyptian code had a detailed description of banned weapons. The sex category was more detailed in the American code than in the Egyptian one. While examples of obscene expressions were not detailed in the American code, the Egyptian code classified the slang expressions of specific social classes as obscene. The Egyptian code thus emphasized the importance of preserving and sustaining class hierarchy, leaning more toward the British code. This similarity between the British and Egyptian codes essentialized colonialist forms of knowledge and carried out the British negative cultural policy in Egypt more excessively.[129]

6. Codification of Film Censorship

The 1947 Egyptian Code of Film Censorship constituted the most concrete knowledge on the exercise of film censorship in Egypt at that time. Inspired by the constitution of the British Board of Film censors, the Egyptian code had three major goals. The first was to ensure that the soldiers of the Empire would not be misrepresented in films. The second was to avoid any incidents that could offend religious susceptibilities and arouse undesirable racial and political sentiments. The third was to sustain the amour-propre of the Egyptians as equal partners even though, in reality, the power balance subjugated the Egyptian ruling elites to the British ruling elite.[130] The code included seven categories: security, public order, religion, crime, sex, and the amour-propre of Egypt abroad and in neighboring countries.

The religion category banned the representation of the power of God through materialized things such as a body, sound, etc., or the depiction of any of the Abrahamic prophets. Religious ceremonies and rituals, especially Islamic ones, could only be depicted in an appropriate and respectful manner. It was not permitted to depict Quranic recitation taking place on the side of the road (or in an inappropriate place). If the film depicted a reciter, the latter should not be depicted wearing his shoes while reciting. It was not permitted to quote from holy texts, including dialogues from the Qur'an, or quote Prophetic tradition in a comic fashion. Films were expected to respect all religions and avoid disparaging beliefs. All topics and dialogues that could cause religious or national divides had to be avoided.[131]

The security and public order category censored scenes and themes that explicitly or implicitly encouraged disdain for or hurt the feelings of Egyptians or foreigners residing in Egypt. No topics of a communist nature or that included propaganda against royal regimes were allowed. No references to social justice were permitted. Depictions of hostile indifference caused by opinions about the social or political order were banned. The depiction of workers gathering or going on strike or suspending work, or of workers attacking the business owner, was censored. The favorable depiction of crime among workers could not be shown. Films could not depict workers spreading the spirit of rebellion among themselves as a means of fulfilling their demands and their rights. Scenes of revolution, protests, or strikes were considered violations of social order and were censored. Nationalist figures and their legacy had to be represented accurately, especially when stories could cause riots (*shaghab*) or agitate sentiments (*itharat al-khawatir*). Political regimes in Egypt or any other friendly country had to be treated with respect in films. Scenes depicting political speeches or talks that were controversial were not allowed. It was not acceptable to hint at the founding principles of the constitution. It was not permitted to disparage political life in Egypt, or senators or members of parliament. Public officials—judges, police officers, and army personnel—had to be depicted fittingly. It was not permitted to disparage honorary titles, ranks, and medals. No critical depiction of the police or the military was permitted. None of the following locations could be filmed without written permission from the Ministry of Defense:

1. Military constructions, entrenchments, airports, artillery, searchlights, camps.
2. Arsenals, ammunition storage locations or factories in which work took place for national defense purposes.
3. Major telephone/telegraph stations, and water, gas, electricity, fuel, or oil labs.
4. Installations in harbors or in the Suez Canal.
5. Military formations, especially those considered secret in terms of the army and its special operations.

The category of crime banned scenes of criminals depicted as patriots and scenes that gained them sympathy while simultaneously ridiculing police officers as oppressive or inefficient. Law could not be subject to ridicule. Innovative ways of committing crimes were censored, along with scenes conveying criminal tactics that could be replicated. No scenes of severe violence and cruelty or aggression, especially those applied to children or animals, were allowed. Scenes of hanging, whipping, torture, and cruel ways of taking revenge (such as slaughter or cutting body parts) were cut. Films about vendettas were not allowed unless they presented vendetta as a reprehensible custom. Violent murders could be shown briefly to prevent imitation. Exaggerated use of guns and killing scenes had to be cut. The code banned scenes of firing weapons such as machine guns and guns on armored cars used by gangsters or criminals; the same rule applied to every conversation about such weapons, especially conversations suggestive of the use of weapons as a source of pride. Scenes featuring innovative ways of hiding weapons were deleted. Crimes of child kidnapping, unless the story depicted the criminal receiving a deterrent punishment, had to be avoided. The same rule applied to scenes of kidnapping and the depiction of criminal schemes to release the kidnapped person for ransom. Scenes and dialogue that led to events in the movie where crimes were committed were censored. Scenes showing innovative ways of hiding or distributing drugs and drug consumption were deleted.[132]

The sex category banned scenes of men and women in the same bed, and seductive baths. Hugs and kisses that exceeded normal passion via lustful depiction, and extreme positions, which stimulated "mean" desires, had to be avoided. In general, seduction scenes and scenes encouraging young women and men to go astray (*fisq*) or indulge in immoral physical pleasures (*fujur*) were discouraged. Scenes of white slave trafficking, unless it was a historical story, were cut. Films could not mention sexually transmitted diseases or childbirth diseases, and similar medical issues, which were of a private nature—scenes of nudity, whether as photographs or shadows, were censored. Scenes of body movements that violated public civility, such as indecent (*khaliʿ*) seductive dance, were not allowed. The code also banned dance costumes exposing private body parts in the performance of distasteful dance movements. Body parts, which modesty required be covered, had to be depicted covered, especially female body parts (e.g. stomach, chest, and other private body parts). In addition, zooming in on private body parts in a way that could make them appear in violation of public civility or in a way that violated public taste (*al-dhawq al-ʿam*) was not permitted.[133]

The category dealing with the amour-propre of Egypt strived to suppress the life of the peasants and *awlad al-balad* on the screen. For example, the code banned scenes showing the houses of peasants and traditional pieces of furniture in those houses, such as the water storage container (*zir*), especially if the furniture appeared in poor condition, which could reduce Egyptian amour-propre. Exceptions were made in cases of cultural-educational films, which the code described as objective (i.e. showing the good and bad sides of the subject matter). Scenes of working-class women (*banat al-balad*) wearing their black wrap gowns while talking and using "distasteful hand gestures" were banned as they could degrade the amour-propre of Egypt. Only limited depiction of scenes of begging, beggars, and bare-footedness was possible. Interior scenes depicting the Egyptian household needed to pay attention to social status and follow Eastern traditions and customs. In general, Eastern customs and traditions had to be followed. Examples of violations of Eastern customs included scenes of sons attacking parents, scenes of smoking or consumption of wine among young women and men, or scenes of unfamiliar gender mixing. While filming Egyptian social life, the code urged filmmakers to avoid all that could disparage or distort the amour-propre of the Egyptian family. That included any hints of local practices of quackery, magic, or fortune-telling and parties held to dismiss evil spirits (*zar*). These were considered non-modern practices that had to be omitted unless the practice was treated in a way that outweighed its effect and directed the attention of the audience to its falsity and harmful consequences. Scenes of prostitution and parties that exceeded the limits of civility were considered a threat to Egypt's amour-propre. The same rule applied to the depiction of "effeminate" movements among young men (e.g. a man could not be depicted trying a dance that was common only among women). In addition, a man could not be depicted making any gestures or saying any phrase that imitated a woman, especially if she was *bint balad*. Examples included phrases common among *banat al-balad* such as "Oh boy! What a loss!" (*yakhti ya nadamti*). Scenes showing consumption of wine, profligacy, explicit and implicit courting, and going to a *garçonnière* were classified as a source of evil and a threat to Egypt's amour-propre as a modern and civilized country. Cabarets, if depicted, could not be shown if "dirty." The definition of dirty included the depiction of women, wine, profane movements, obscene laughs, and indecent positions.[134]

Under a category that regulated the amour-propre of Egypt in neighboring countries,[135] dirty bars, phrases like bandit nests (*wakr al-'isabat*), scenes of dirty allies, donkey carts, handcarts, street vendors, and coppersmith whitening copper were banned. The category promoted Egypt's soft power in the region by appealing to a rising understanding of Islam, which advocated the suppression of what it perceived to be non-modern Islamic practices. For example, a bier or a stone grave could not be depicted, out of respect for the glory of death. Scenes of women walking in funerals following the dead were also censored. Egyptian customs of mourning tended to follow Shi'i rituals at that time. It was customary to commemorate the dead every Thursday for at least forty days. Groups of women also used to walk in funerals. Women used to follow funerals, involving a professional person known as the mourner (*al-mi'addida*), who used to count the good traits of the dead person. The suppression of mourners aimed to suppress the display of rituals of death as practiced by working-class Egyptians and peasants, thereby silencing the local theatrical display of power that was common in Egypt at that time.[136]

It goes without saying that the Egyptian 1947 censorship code offered a brief snapshot of the deep imprints of the British colonial era, which regulated not only how Egyptians thought of the colonizer but also how they dealt with their amour-propre of modernity; modernity was reduced to the cultivation of a modern civilizational image in the eyes of the Other (this here being the British colonizer or the *Khawaga*) by means of suppressing the voices of the peasants and the working class. These two social groups were treated as a burden and source of shame that threatened and disparaged the amour-propre of Egypt as a modern country. The idea of preventing women from walking in funerals shows a covert interest in regulating the amour-propre of Islam by regulating what it meant to be a modern Muslim woman, by regulating her presence in space and time. Similarly, the idea of banning the depiction of the stone grave was a reaction to a growing rationalist Sunni narrative that prohibited the glorification and visiting of graves, a practice that continues to be common in Egypt today. This discourse served the British colonial strategy of suppressing diversity and relying on standardization, hence suppressing the diversity and breadth of Islamic traditions as a more convenient way to govern.

After 1947, even though film censorship was a shared task between the Ministry of Social Affairs and the Ministry of the Interior, the latter continued to control censorship issues. One example was a meeting with the Minister of Affairs in December 1949 involving a number of filmmakers, including Anwar Wagdi, Farid al-Atrash, Ahmad Kamil Mursi, Yusuf Wahbi, Husayn Sidqi, and Ibrahim 'Izz al-Din, along with Muhammad Salah al-Din bey, the head of a government committee tasked with promoting acting and cinema. The meeting was hosted at the office of the *al-Ithnyan* magazine and moderated by Fikri Abaza. Filmmakers raised concerns about a number of issues, chief of which were the frozen assets of some film companies in neighboring Arab counties, the need to decrease the costs of renting studios, and the entertainment tax (*daribat al-malahi*), which became 37 percent of the ticket price, in addition to the demand that tax money be allocated to promoting cinema and acting in society. Yusuf Wahbi complained that even after actors' payment was cut by half, studios and movie theaters did not lower rent prices. Filmmakers also requested an increase in government subsidy for the publicity of Egyptian films by holding film festivals; they demanded an increase in subsidy allocated to theater troupes so that a new musical theater could emerge. They further demanded ending the absurdity of censorship rules by making it fall within the responsibility of one institution, which should appoint educated censors well-versed in studying the arts.

When Yusuf Wahbi sharpened his criticism of the censors, Anwar Wagdi interrupted and said, "No. Please do us a favor, Yusuf bey, and do not talk about them. May God make our words sweet in their ears. We do not want to upset them." Yusuf Wahbi got the hint and resumed in a positive tone, "Yes. Some of the censors are indeed understanding and reasonable in their comments." Wagdi cheered Wahbi and said: "Yes. This kind of talk is good." Wahbi then went on to share his concerns about the unreasonableness of some censors. For example, he described how one day, a censor had objected to a scene in which a father kissed his daughter twice. Other censors wanted to omit the phrase "secret police," while a third deleted the word "bomb" from the sentence "Boy, slow down, why are you rushing like a bomb." Wahbi recalled the most unreasonable reaction he had received from the censors when he had presented his movie *Yad Allah*/The Hand of God, 1946 for licensing. According to Wahbi, the film had revenge as a central theme. To use Wahbi's sarcastic words, "It seems that I did an excellent job in the script that the censors rejected the film because it was 'scary' and were it not for the interference of Anwar Ahmad, the film would not have been released." Anwar Ahmad, who was present at the meeting, commented sarcastically, "Well, I did not get scared, I guess." When asked about censorship laws, Anwar Ahmad said that although the Ministry of Social Affairs shared the responsibility for censorship with the Ministry of the Interior, the latter had had the upper hand since martial law was enforced.[137] The writer Firki Abaza asked about the legal grounds that drove censorship rulings. The minister again emphasized that the rulings were guided by the authority of the police and changing circumstances. Yusuf Wahbi suggested that a committee be formed to solve disputes between the censor and the producer.

The minister then suggested that censorship disputes could be handled by the Ministry of Education (*wizarat al-ma'arif*). Farid al-Atrash objected to such a move as it could further complicate the issue, because the minister was conservative and might demand that actresses wear scarves and loose clothing. Ibrahim Izz al-Din urged that censorship rulings must change and perhaps follow the American model since no supervision existed for American producers except for their conscience. In the USA, he added, cinema enjoyed all possible liberties; the government did not interfere in the stories or direct it; this freedom was the main reason the USA has a flourishing film industry. He added that he had attended the production of the American film *Pinky*, 1949, directed by Elia Kazan and produced by Darryl F. Zanuck. Its story is based on condemning racism against African Americans, and the film lampoons

Figure 2.1 Censorship meeting with the Minister of Social Affairs (1). In the middle, Anwar Wagdi, sitting next to Fikri Abaza (right) and Anwar Ahmad (left).

الأستاذ محمد عبد الوهاب ، يتحدث والأستاذ إبراهيم عز الدين يستمع بإهتمام

Figure 2.2 Censorship meeting with the Minister of Social Affairs (2). On the right, Muhammad 'Abd al-Wahhab talking to director Ibrahim 'Izz al-Din.

من اليمين : يوسف وهبي بك، ومحمد صلاح الدين بك، والأستاذ حسين صدقي

Figure 2.3 Censorship meeting with the Minister of Social Affairs (3). On the right, Yusuf Wahbi next to Muhammad Salah (middle) and Husayn Sidqi (left).

fanaticism and the rigidity of the mindset of some Americans. Yet, he added, no one interfered by censoring such a film. The meeting ended with the minister promising to look into these grievances and the filmmakers suggesting the inauguration of a film festival and film productions dubbed in English.

Another example that shows the complexity and the varying levels of censorship, and the absolute authority of the Ministry of the Interior over film censorship after 1947, is the case of Paramount Production's *Samson and Delilah*, 1949, directed by Cecil B. DeMille. The company submitted its request for licensing on December 13, 1949. The movie was reviewed by Safiyya Rabi' and Madam Cunneil, who censored the film. They both found the film to be Zionist propaganda unsuitable for screening after 1948. The company refused the censors' decision and filed a complaint with Jamal al-Din al-'Utayfi, the Vice-Minister of the Interior, who was also the general censor at the time. The latter requested a second review, which was undertaken by the head of the censorship department, Muhammad Shawqi, who licensed the film. He stated in his report:

> the story of the film upon review is a well-known historical narrative. It does not refer to anything that could violate Egypt's political position from Zionism. The film did not include any references to a national homeland for the Jews. Many Christian institutions supported the screening of the film. The Egyptian government had recently invited an Italian troupe to perform the same story in the Opera House. The invitation implies the government's absence of objection to the representation of the biblical story of Samson and Delilah.[138]

During that time, 'Abd al-Basit Hajjaji became head of the Printing Press Administration, which supervised film censorship in the Ministry of the Interior. Hajjaji asked 'Abd al-Mun'im Shumays, an employee at the Printing Press Administration, to watch the movie and write a report. The latter endorsed the initial censorship decision since he considered the movie to be Zionist propaganda. Hajjaji sent the report to 'Abd al-Fattah pasha Hasan, the parliamentary representative of the Ministry of the Interior, who licensed the movie under the condition that it could be censored if problems arose. Hajjaji sent the film again for a third round of review by I'tidal Mumtaz, who recommended the deletion of sentences that referred to Egypt. Examples included:

"My silver will open the gates that bar your way," "By nightfall, we will be in the land of the Pharaohs," "In the Valley of the Nile, we will be safe. We will be together," "Hurry, Samson! Egypt has a thousand temples, each more beautiful," "By midday, we can be in the spring of Yumis with Egypt almost in sight," and "the Bible the greatest of all books." While most of the phrases above appeared unobjectionable, Mumtaz explained her reasons for censoring two of the sentences. She recommended cutting the first sentence because it implied that Egypt was a land of corruption and that bribes opened all doors. She objected to the use of the superlative adjective "greatest" to describe the Bible in a majority Muslim country like Egypt. Following Mumtaz's suggestions, the movie underwent a fourth review. The Ministry of the Interior appointed Lieutenant-Colonel Kamal Riyad to investigate all previous reports and write his own. He found the idea that the movie was Zionist propaganda to be farfetched. The cinematography focused mostly on the physical power of Samson, whose people gave him up to their Palestinian enemies, who were depicted as the rulers of the kingdom. Since the dialogue did not include the word "Israel" or the word "Jew," Riyad licensed the movie on January 3, 1951. But the Minister of the Interior banned the film, and shows were canceled in Royal and Muhammad 'Ali movie theaters in Alexandria and the Diana Movie Theater in Cairo. Examples of Egyptian movies that were censored after the 1947 Code include the movie *Mustafa Kamil*/Mustafa Kamil, 1952, directed by Ahmad Badarakhan. While the film was being shot, martial law was announced because of the 1951 Cairo riots.

In January 1951, *al-Fann* magazine published an article summing up a meeting between the head of the Film Censorship Department, 'Abd al-Basit Hajjaji, and filmmakers[139] including Asiya, Mary Quieni, Yusuf Wahbi, Ahmad Badrkhan, and Husayn Sidqi.[140] The main purpose of the meeting was to urge Egyptian filmmakers to give attention to Egypt's amour-propre in films. When filmmakers objected, Wahbi calmed them down and responded to Hajjaji's request as follows:

> A good film story is derived from everyday life events that ought to be depicted without sugar-coating truths. We must record the three social classes in the film story. The first class has to be represented by rich families that monopolize wealth, power, and resources. Those families are full of

problems that cause social problems, which need to be addressed to push boundaries for social reform. The second is the suppressed middle class that strives to achieve social justice. The third is the working class, which includes various professions that require physical labor. As filmmakers, we cannot be expected to overlook depicting rich families or the gap between classes, thereby ignoring social injustice and depriving the working class of learning better lifestyles, which otherwise are inaccessible. If we were to avoid all that, we would be killing the film industry in Egypt.

Wahbi then questioned the censorship regime that denied filmmakers the right to make films on the 1919 revolution and other anti-colonialist national themes. Hajjaji denied that the Censorship Division objected to Wahbi's argument. In response, Husayn Sidqi, whose movie *Yasqut al-Isti'mar*/Down with Imperialism was censored, questioned the censorship of anti-colonialist movies, including *Mustafa Kamil*. Hajjaji claimed that the film was approved. Sidqi objected, pointing out that the Censorship Division had requested the deletion of the *Dinshuway* story. Wahbi interrupted to underscore that deleting the story of *Dinshuway* rendered the film story meaningless. Hajjaji stated that the censorship decision was motivated by the political need to avoid any clashes with the *Khawagat*. Attendants complained that the censorship process embodied double standards, applying the rules more strictly to Egyptian films than to foreign films, especially American ones. While Sidqi's *Yasqut al-Isti'mar* and Badrkhan's *Mustafa Kamil* were released after 1952, Egyptian cinema has up until today continues to shy away from presenting movies with explicit anti-colonialist themes, in which injustices committed primarily due to racial supremacy are discussed.[141]

Example of foreign films that were censored and showed the continuity of the power of the Ministry of the Interior after 1947 included the review of the *Three Musketeers* 1948, directed by George Sidney. The film went through two censorship processes under two different political regimes. In 1949, two women censors, 'Aliyya Farid and Saniyya Mahir, reviewed the film. The first censor licensed the film and suggested cutting three sentences, "It is imperative to destroy the king," "The king's position is critical," and "Your loyalty to the throne will make you fail." She considered the sentences to be a disparagement of the royal persona. She also recommended cutting a scene showing the Prime

Minister kissing the Queen Mother, and a scene of the King appearing weak in front of his Prime Minister. These scenes were considered controversial because of the alleged relationship between the Queen Mother and Ahmad Hasanayn pasha, the mentor of King Farouk and the head of the royal court at that time. At the same time, tensions always existed between al-Nahhas pasha, the head of the majority Wafd party, and King Farouk. The second censor decided to ban the film completely. The head of the Printing Press Administration, Yahya Khashshab, reviewed the film himself on September 3, 1949, and endorsed the ban. The film copy was sent back to Borders and Customs three days later. The production company complained and requested a third review, which was conducted by Madam Cunneil and I'tidal Mumtaz, who recommended cutting all phrases that referred to the weak image of the king. The movie was finally licensed when the 1952 Officer's Movement occurred. The company requested a permit to show a fifth edition of the film. Anwar Habib, the socialist public prosecutor, and Major Muhammad Thabit, the military censor, reviewed the film and licensed the original copy without any cuts.[142] The review process for the *Three Musketeers* revealed not only the absolute power of the Ministry of the Interior when it came to licensing films, but, more importantly, how various regimes and governments burdened the Ministry of the Interior with tasks outside its expertise; it had to carry the burden of evaluating the political context and issuing rules to regulate the relationship between society and political authority. In doing this, the British colonial authorities changed the function of the institution, thereby making it operate as a legislative power instead of an executive power. This outcome seemed to echo Antonio Gramsci's point that the most tragic difficulty for modernity in a majority Muslim society like Egypt was the fact that it was a society in a state of torpor being put into brusque contact with a frenetic civilization already in its phase of dissolution.[143] Accordingly, the roles of modern institutions, like the Ministry of the Interior, continued to be appropriated until today. The phenomenon is often referred to in today's public media as the security solutions (*al-hulul al-amniyya*), which filmmakers were aware of.[144] One example in which this phenomenon materialized very clearly was the dispute over the ownership of the Rivoli cinema after World War II.

7. Rivoli Cinema and the First Attack on British Business

While the year 1947 marked the birth of the first code of film censorship in Egypt, it also saw the beginning of a series of waves of political turmoil shaped by decolonization efforts. A series of post-World War II massacres occupied the public media from August 1947 until May 1948. The first was the India–Pakistan partition and the subsequent horrors, which furnished very rich material in both religious and specialized film magazines. The second was the Arab–Israeli war. The news of Zionist militia attacks on Palestinian villages and the counter-news of patriotism on the side of Egyptian military units led by Brigadier Ahmad Abd al-Aziz flooded the pages of various magazines. At the local Cairene front, the news of the assassination of the Egyptian Prime Minister al-Nuqrashi and the subsequent banning of the Muslim Brotherhood, as well as the growing anti-Jewish sentiments in Egypt, dominated magazine headlines in 1947 and 1948, especially after the sweeping defeat of the Arab armies known in Arabic as the *nakba* and the allegations of corruption within the Egyptian army and ruling elites. This was followed by al-Nahhas's decision to abrogate the 1936 Treaty unilaterally, and the declaration of war against British forces in the Canal.

Amidst all these waves of political turmoil, the 1947 code of film censorship led to a number of compelling developments in the film industry. It placed higher pressure on American films. The British Foreign Office refused to act on behalf of American producers, despite repeated requests by the American Foreign Office and despite the quota system that privileged American films around the world. The code further provided a framework of operation for the government to encourage the establishment of new local production companies like Nihas Film Company, which moved its offices from Alexandria to Cairo in 1941. Nihas Film Company, owned by Jibra'il Nihas and Antuwan Khuri, partnered with Yusuf Wahbi to establish Nihas Studio, which was inaugurated by the Minister of Public Works, who oversaw the Film Censorship Division. On the eve of its grand opening, Nihas Studio was the fifth largest film institution worldwide and the largest in Egypt, which had so far hosted nine major studios, including Misr Studio, al-Ahram Studio, Tugu Studio, Lama Studio, Galal Studio, Nasiban Studio, and Shubra Studio.[145]

Nihas Studio produced some of the finest Egyptian classics, which con-

معالي وزير الشؤون بين أصحاب شركة نحاس فيلم

المنشأة السينمائية الخامسة في العالم ..

Figure 2.4 Inauguration of Nihas Studio. Minister of Social Affairs, second from the right. Yusuf Wahbi is second from the left. They are flanked by Jibra'il Nihas and Antuwan Khuri.

tinue to circulate and screen today. It created a boom in the industry, especially after a 50 percent drop in the production rate in 1946 caused by the withdrawal of a hundred production companies and the foreclosure of three studios. With its newly established Nihas Studio, Nihas Film Company constituted major competition for the Egyptian Company for Acting and Cinema and its famous Misr Studio, the first film studio in Egypt with sound recording. Nihas Studio produced popular classics, including *Rajul La Yanam*/Sleepless Man, 1948; *Bayumi Afandi*/Bayumi Effendi, 1949; *Kursi al-I'tiraf*/Confession Chair, 1949; *Amina*/Amina, 1949; *Ghazal al-Banat*/Girls' Love, 1949 directed by Anwar Wagdi, *al-Avukatu Madiha*/Madiha the Lawyer, 1950, and *Awalad al-Shawari'*/Street Children, 1951. Moreover, the demand for Egyptian films

REGULATING THE AMOUR-PROPRE OF THE COLONIZED | 125

Figure 2.5 Aerial view of Nihas Studio.

Figure 2.6 Sound recording machine in Nihas Studio.

Figure 2.7 The camera dolly in Nihas Studio.

and movie theaters led to the rise of the al-Sharq and Rivoli movie theaters, which became the two main entertainment centers in downtown Cairo.[146]

While Egyptian films started gaining more chances in exhibition halls and movie theaters, conflicts of interest arose between British and Egyptian capitals over movie theater ownership. These conflicts reached their peak in 1951 with the dispute over Rivoli Cinema, owned by J. Arthur Rank, and two Egyptian brothers, Muhammad and Mustafa Ga'far. The British Foreign Office considered the incident to be the first attack on British business in Egypt after the news of the Wafd's intentions with regard to unilateral abrogation of the Anglo-Egyptian Treaty the previous year.

The dispute over Rivoli Cinema dates back to January 3, 1951, when the representative of J. Arthur Rank, Mr. Victory Finney, phoned Sir Pierson Dixon, Deputy Under-Secretary of State at Downing Street in London, to seek help for the British manager of Rivoli Cinema, Mr. Smeedon, who had

REGULATING THE AMOUR-PROPRE OF THE COLONIZED | 127

اثناء تصوير مشهد احد الأفلام

Figure 2.8 Shooting in Nihas Studio. The two actresses in the middle appear to be Fardus Muhammd and Raqiya Ibrahim.

نموذج من غرف الممثلين

Figure 2.9 Actors' rooms in Nihas Studio.

Figure 2.10 A makeup room in Nihas Studio.

been summoned by the Cairo police to appear with his passport, within 24 hours, before the Egyptian Minister of the Interior. Finney feared Smeedon's deportation and the subsequent financial loss that would befall the Rank Organization. From Finney's point of view, the whole issue was orchestrated by Rank's greedy Egyptian partners, Mustafa and Muhammad Ga'far, who had suborned a minor official in the Ministry of the Interior to execute Smeedon's arrest in order to obtain control of the business in Cairo.

The partnership between Rank and the Ga'far brothers started when the Rank Organization and the Egyptian Association, owned by Muhammad and Mustafa Ga'far, signed a principal agreement to establish Odeon (Cairo) Ltd on November 22, 1945. The ordinary shareholding in Odeon (Cairo) Ltd. was £ 30,010. Rank's Overseas Cinematograph Theaters Ltd. held £15,010, and Messrs. Ga'far held £ 15,000. The preference capital of £100,000 was also held equally between Overseas and the Messrs. Ga'far.[147] Under the principal agreement, Odeon (Cairo) Ltd. acquired from Messrs. Ga'far the site and premises known as the Park Cinema for the respective interests of Odeon Theatres Ltd., which was also owned by the Rank Organization since J. Arthur Rank had bought the chain known as Oden from Oscar Deutsch back in 1938.[148] Another supplemental agreement was made on June 20, 1946, under which Odeon (Cairo) Ltd. and all its interests in the principal agreement were assigned to Rank's Overseas Cinematograph Theaters Ltd., with the result that Overseas stood in the position of Odeon (Cairo) Ltd. On 11 December 1947, Odeon (Cairo) Ltd. and the Egyptian Association signed an agreement by which a cinema, the Capitol, on lease to the Ga'fars was to be completed and equipped by the Ga'fars and assigned together with the lease to Odeon (Cairo) Ltd. The Ga'fars were to receive £ 50,000 in payment when the cinema was completed. The agreement was conditional on the consent of the Bank of England, which was obtained in early 1948. Odeon (Cairo) Ltd also owned Rivoli Cinema, of which the Ga'fars' share was 49 percent, and Overseas had 51 percent.

Tensions erupted in the 1950s when Messrs. Ga'far complained about the mismanagement of the Rivoli cinema. The brothers were aggrieved by certain actions of Overseas in relation to the business of the Odeon (Cairo). These included a lack of flexibility with deadlines and blaming the delay in completing the Capitol Theater on the financial difficulties of the Ga'fars, whose 50,000 L.E. worth of preference shares were taken over by the banks in 1947. According to the Ga'fars, the delay was primarily caused by the unfortunate collapse of the roof of the cinema in November 1948, while the Egyptian Association's resources were simultaneously dedicated to the construction and inauguration of Rivoli. Their plans to inaugurate the Capitol were announced in *Akhir Sa'a* in June 1948, long before the collapse of the roof, and this proves their dedication. They thus believed that the arrangements set out in the principal agreement should continue without time-limit. Messrs. Ga'far were also aggrieved by the manner of operation of Odeon (Cairo) Ltd, which had a Board of five directors; three of these were English directors nominated by Overseas, and two were the Messrs. Ga'far, who objected to holding regular board meetings in London at fifteen days' notice. The brothers were offended by the lack of interest in their attendance, which was left to the discretion of the British directors. The brothers Ga'far also disapproved of the exaggerated payments made to Rivoli's British director, whose salary and incurred expenses were much more given to suit his social status than his experience in comparison with those of the Egyptian manager, 'Abdullah Mahmud, whom the Ga'fars had appointed earlier. The fact that the British manager had the final say on administrative questions, such as film selections, times of opening, and remuneration of staff, also unsettled the Ga'fars. The tensions escalated when, on June 23, 1951, the Ga'fars issued a summon claiming from Odeon (Cairo) Ltd. the sum of L.E. 285 000 (more precisely, L.E. 284 871) in the case of the Capitol cinema.[149] The sum was claimed to cover rent, cost of furnishings, loss of profits, etc. And on July 3, 1951, an application was made to the Egyptian Courts for a Writ of Sequestration to be appointed for the Rivoli on the grounds that the cinema had been grossly mismanaged.

In defense of his client J. Arthur Rank, Mr. Finney asserted that Rivoli was most carefully run as an Egyptian and not primarily as a British theatre, and the policy had been to cater to Arab tastes and give encouragement to Arab ideas. The dispute over the theater started as soon as the Anglo-Egyptian Treaty was abrogated, when the Egyptian press attacked the British management of Rivoli. Demonstrations also took place in and outside the cinema. Finney found that there was enough circumstantial evidence to point to the hand of the Ga'fars behind all these troubles. In order to inform the Egyptian public of the true position, that the Ga'fars had a 49 percent interest in the cinema, a banner was displayed outside the cinema to advertise the fact of Egyptian participation without actually mentioning the Ga'fars. The Ga'fars took grave exception to this, and at their request the banner was removed.

On July 19, 1951, the disputes were negotiated through two memoranda of settlements. One was titled "Memorandum of Settlement Rivoli Cinema, Cairo," which was entered into to put an end to all matters in dispute or disagreement between the parties in relation to the Rivoli cinema in Cairo and in relation to the respective interests of parties in Odeon (Cairo) Ltd. The Ga'fars were requested to renounce all their rights in respect of matters stated in the Writ of Sequestration and bring it to an end. Odeon (Cairo) Ltd was to continue to operate as set out in the principal agreement, and if the brothers Ga'far believed from their experience in Cairo that the manager was making wrong decisions, they should communicate their views in writing to the English directors at the office of the company in London for consideration at the next board meeting. Surprisingly, and in a major departure from Mr. Finney's statement, the memorandum urged the Ga'fars to appreciate that, as set out in the principal agreement, one of the objects of Overseas in forming Odeon (Cairo) Ltd, and in financing the acquisition and building of the Rivoli cinema, was to exhibit British films, whether or not other films were available; the Ga'fars thus should agree to continue with that policy. Allegations of mismanagement and impropriety of conduct contained in the Writ had to be withdrawn. As was set out in the supplemental agreement, the monies advance by Overseas to Odeon (Cairo) Ltd. for the acquisition and building of the Rivoli cinema were repayable by Odeon (Cairo) Ltd in priority of any redemption of its preference shares, and it was decreed that until the large sums of money owed to Overseas were substantially reduced, any distribution of profits to shareholders had to be postponed. The Ga'fars were pressed to record their understanding that in the accounts of Odeon (Cairo) Ltd, the trading profits had to be treated as available for writing off the cost of the cinema, which was only held on a short lease. In order to improve the position of Odeon (Cairo) Ltd. in the interests of all the shareholders, the Ga'fars had to confirm that they would take all possible steps to obtain an extension of the lease and to vest the extension so obtained in Odeon (Cairo) Ltd.

A second memorandum, titled "Memorandum of Settlement Capitol Theater 'Imad al-Din," was entered into to bring an end to the claims that the Ga'fars had put forward against Overseas and Odeon (Cairo) Ltd in respect of the agreement under which Odeon agreed to buy from the Messrs. Ga'far the leasehold cinema at 'Imad al-Din Cairo, called the "Capitol" but formerly called the "Printania," given that it was completed on time. After discussions in London between the interested parties, it was agreed to settle the matter upon Messrs. Ga'far renouncing their rights in respect of the matters alleged in the summons and their agreement to withdraw the summons. Overseas, upon being satisfied that the proceedings were brought to an end, would pay the Messrs. Ga'far the sum of L.E. 35000, which would be payable in Cairo at the offices of Messrs. Fanner Perrott and Sims Marshall at 28 'Adli Pasha Street. This done, the agreement with regard to the Capitol would thus be declared at an end, and neither Overseas nor Odeon (Cairo) Ltd. would have any further obligation to the Messrs. Ga'far in respect of the Capitol or any other matter mentioned in the summons, and all claims by the Messrs. Ga'far in respect thereof would thereby absolutely be withdrawn and at an end.

Given that Mustafa Ga'far signed all the above memorandum of settlements, Mr. Finney found the legal position of the Rank Organization to be sound. But he advised that the political circumstances might nevertheless cause the Rank Organization to lose the case if the Ga'fars went to court. The political situation referred to was the failure of the negotiation between the British and the Egyptian governments following the end of World War II, which demanded the modification of the 1936 Treaty to terminate British military presence and allow the annexation of the Anglo-Egyptian Sudan. Following the al-Wafd Party's victory in the boycotted 1950 election, the new al-Wafd government led by al-Nahhas pasha unilaterally abrogated the Treaty in October 1951. This led to the beginning of anti-British military operations in the Canal. The Rank Organization was most reluctant to give way any further. J. Arthur Rank was not certain whether, if he stood firm on his offer, the Egyptian partners would, in the end, accept his price. Since he was convinced that the weakness of his position derived mainly from the political situation, he sought advice or assistance from the Foreign Office.

In support of the Rank Organization, the British Foreign Office communicated with the British Embassy in Cairo, which made enquires through an "influential intermediary," whose name is not mentioned in the sources but who seems to have been a high-ranking official with direct access to the Minister of the Interior, by then the Wafdist Fuad Siraj [Sirag] al-Din, who replied that he had not been consulted about the arrest of Mr. Smeedon. The Minister agreed that the instruction was quite wrong and gave orders for it to be withdrawn. While the order against Mr. Smeedon was withdrawn, his annual work permit was coming up for renewal on February 10, 1952, and his position was still uncertain. The Ga'fars had threatened to take action, either legal or otherwise, with effect from January 31 unless some arrangement for the sale of the Rivoli cinema to the Ga'fars, or letting with complete control in the Ga'fars' hands, was arrived at. According to the Rank Organization, Prince Talal of Saudi Arabia was providing the necessary financial backing to enable the purchase of Rivoli to take place, although, according to the Foreign Office assessment, he possibly was not aware of the pressure that was being brought to bear so as to affect the sale.

On January 18, 1952, the director of Odeon (Cairo) Ltd sent a letter to Mr. Nabi, the representative of the Ga'fars, to inform them that the Rank

Organization was prepared to sell its interest in Rivoli (which was very largely financed by advances from Overseas Cinematograph Theaters Ltd., amounting to a total of £398,427, of which £20,000 was repaid). He set out as a basis that the purchase price in respect of property other than goodwill[150] should be L 250000, with L 40000 payable on the signature of documents, three further quarterly payments of L 40000 each in the first year, and L 90000 in the second year, payable in four equal quarterly installments. As the purchase price of the goodwill, the sum of L 30000 would be payable in monthly installments of L 1000 spread over thirty months, the first becoming payable on the signature of the documents. On signature of the documents, possession of the theatre would be given to the purchaser, and as from such date, all expenses regarding the theatre and the property, no matter of what nature, would be the responsibility of the purchaser. The Rank Organization was prepared to pay the Ga'fars a commission of L 5000 in respect of their service for negotiation of the deal, to be payable upon final payment of the sum of 250000. No commission would be paid to any other party, and in particular not to Mustafa Ga'far. All payments of the purchase price should be payable in sterling in London, and, in the event of failure by the purchaser in making any such payment, the whole balance then remained unpaid should immediately become payable. "On any such failure to pay continuing for more than fourteen days, the purchaser should give up possession of the theatre with its contents in a good state, repair, and condition as the same upon the time of signing the memorandum of settlement, and shall not be entitled to repayment of any monies previously paid." Upon signature of the documents, the purchaser should deliver to the company such promissory notes or notes, or other documents and guarantee, for the said two sums of L 250000 and L 30000 as the company might, on the advice of its lawyers, require to secure the payments as aforesaid, such promissory notes or other documents being guaranteed by endorsement or otherwise by Prince Talal of Saudi Arabia or a bank approved by the Company. The said monies, when received by Odeon (Cairo) Ltd., should forthwith be applied in reduction of the indebtedness from Odeon (Cairo) Ltd to Overseas Cinematograph Theatres Ltd. and should not be applied to any other purpose. The arrangement was set to be terminable by Odeon (Cairo) Ltd. if the documents were not signed, and the first payment of the purchase price was paid on or before February 29, 1952.

The Foreign Office communicated with the Board of Trade and confirmed that the Rank Organization had offered to sell its interest for L.E. 280000 to the brothers Ga'far, who offered L.E. 275000 and intimated that if this offer were not accepted within a week they would take legal action. It was quite puzzling to the Foreign Office that J. Arthur Rank was making such a fuss about so small a sum as 5000 pounds. The Foreign Office also wondered whether there was more to the story than the Rank Organization cared to share. The records are silent in this regard, thereby raising many questions. Why did the Rank Organization decide to sell Rivoli if it was largely financed by advances from Overseas? Why did Finney lie about Rivoli being most carefully run as an Egyptian theater catering to Arab tastes and encouraging Arab ideas, while the terms of the principal agreement, as J. Arthur Rank stated, requested the Ga'fars to agree that one of the objects of Overseas in forming Odeon (Cairo) Ltd. and in financing the acquisition and building of the Rivoli cinema was to exhibit British films? A close look at films screened by Rivoli Cinema in 1948 revealed that most films were British or American, including David Macdonald's *Snowbound*, 1948, Emeric Pressburger's *The Red Shoes*, 1948, David Lean's *Oliver Twist*, 1948, and Charles Barton's *Mexican Hayride*, 1948.[151] And why should J. Arthur Rank make such a fuss about such a sum as 5,000 pounds? Why did the Rank Organization condition the selling of its shares in Rivoli with the statement that, as indicated above, reads "On any such default continuing for more than fourteen days, the purchaser shall give up possession of the theatre with its contents in a good state, repair, and condition as the same upon the time of signing the memorandum of settlement, and shall not be entitled to repayment of any monies previously paid"? The statement sounds normal, except for the mention of the fourteen days and the fact that less than a week from the date on which the Rank Organization made the offer the Cairo riots erupted (January 26, 1952) and the Rivoli was gutted completely. Only the shell of the cinema remained standing. The offices of Fanner Perrott and Sims Marshall in the B.O.A.C. building were destroyed. Whether Rank and the brothers Ga'far would be faced with a total loss, particularly if the cinema was not insured against destruction through rioting and incendiarism, was not clear even to the Foreign Office. Did J. Arthur Rank know about the riots? Is it possible he had a hand in burning down Rivoli and, for that matter, the riots themselves? Why also did the Ga'far brothers give only a week from January

18 to receive an answer to their offer of 275000? Did they burn their most and only celebrated accomplishment, losing 49 percent of the shares? Rivoli was unparalleled, with the exception of its twin sister in New York City. It not only served as a movie theater, but it was also a downtown entrainment center. It had, in addition to the theater, a coffee shop and a ballroom on the second floor. It had a restaurant with specialty food and live music. The theater hosted many of Umm Kulthum's parties, and was a destination for the Egyptian elites at the time. It was the first movie theater to hold parties in honor of King Farouk. In June 1948, Rivoli held a party in the King's honor and donated a sum of L.E. 6000 (its Sunday revenue) to support the Egyptian troops fighting in Palestine.[152] Since the disputes started in late 1948, is it possible that J. Arthur Rank was upset by the Ga'fars' stance? If not, was the sum of L.E. 6000 an issue for Odeon (Cairo) Ltd., at least long before the collapse of the Capitol's roof? It is beyond the scope of this book to find answers to these questions. And while there is very limited information about the Ga'fars, some insights could be gained from J. Arthur Rank's legacy and the real reason could be learnt as to why the Foreign Office was concerned about Rivoli as a sign of the first attack on British business after the abrogation of the Anglo-Egyptian Treaty.

J. Arthur Rank was one of the most famous film tycoons between 1933 and the late 1950s. He entered the British industry in 1933 as a middle-aged Methodist flour-miller; he was politically conservative, and was not especially keen on cinema.[153] Rank was not another Alexander Korda, the great British producer.[154] It was religion that brought Rank into the industry; it was his desire to furnish Methodist halls with projectors and to establish a "Cinema for Christ."[155] He had been drawn to the cinema through his conviction that "pictures would get through to people whereas church would not."[156] He was not countering Hollywood but wanted to use film in a relatively modest way as a vehicle for religious education in Sunday schools and Methodist halls.[157] Some of the most famous films produced by Rank are *The Life and Death of Colonel Blimp*, 1943, *Henry V*, 1944, *A Matter of Life and Death*, 1946, *Black Narcissus*, 1947, and *The Red Shoes*, 1948. It was the first British national film, *The Turn of the Tide*, released in 1935 and directed by Norman Walker, that turned out to be a landmark and was the picture that drew Rank into the mainstream of the British industry.[158] In less than nine years, between 1933 and 1942, Rank laid the basis of his film empire by securing for himself a niche in the Hollywood film industry through his shares in Universal Pictures, Pinewood Studios (of which he became chairman in 1937), and Odeon and Gaumont, which owned more than three hundred cinemas worldwide.[159] The British government had grown concerned in 1944, and the Palache Committee delivered its report, "Tendencies to Monopoly."[160] According to Macnab, Palache's assertion that the industry was under the thumb of one dominating personality was but an oblique way of referring to Rank. It is easy to assume here that the statement is a kind of left-wing absurdity.[161] After all, and according to the Palache Committee's calculations, the 50 percent of available sound stages controlled by the Rank Organization was not a representative figure, when the dozen or so studios were put out of action by the looming threat of Hitler and closed down or commandeered by the government; had they reopened, the holding would have dwindled to 41 percent of the total space. This hardly constitutes a monopoly given that Rank owned only 600 cinemas of the 4000 in the country as a whole. Rank could plausibly argue that his group was no bigger than any of the Hollywood majors, who were, after all, his main competitors.[162] But the Palache Committee's primary concern was that there could not be a sound British cinematograph industry unless independent production was safeguarded:

> The report posits an antinomy, monopoly versus independence, which itself harks back to British realism. A monopoly is associated with big business, inertia, and a lack of creative imagination: it is the force for the bad. Independence, by contrast, is linked with flair, imagination, and integrity. Independent producers are the Davids to Rank's Goliath.[163]

What constituted independence? Again, the report is a little vague. By "independent," one might have in mind both freedom from foreign domination and freedom from the state apparatus. And that is exactly the driving force behind the Ranks–Ga'far's dispute over Rivoli Cinema and Odeon (Cairo) Ltd.

It goes without saying that the grave conditions of the partnership between Rank and the brother Ga'far, albeit legalistically sound, were driven by monopoly and an abuse of power imbalance. The Ga'fars signed the memorandums of settlements because they simply had no other option. Whether they were reliable partners or merely gamblers, the fact remains that they were the biggest losers for Rivoli, which, albeit restored, continues to stand today, and became the property of Prince Talal. The dispute over Rivoli thus was not merely a threat to British business in Egypt; it was, rather, a sign of the fading British dominance and the rising American influence at a time when the Egyptian government was anxious to appease the USA as a new power and potential partners. The arrest of Mr. Smeedon might not necessarily have been a plan on the part of the Gaʿfars so much as a byproduct of the Sequestration Writ, which was an opportunity that could be used by the Egyptian government to test the water regarding the Egyptian cabinet's plan to expel 800 prominent British subjects. The British Foreign Office came to know about this from the American Embassy in Cairo when ʿAbbud Pasha telephoned from al-Nahhas pasha's house and told the American ambassador the news. The latter assured his British colleague that he sought to dissuade the Egyptian government from taking any violent action, and he assured his British colleague that the Egyptian cabinet would not go so far as to break off diplomatic relations or expel British subjects (especially those working in the Canal Zone) as they were considering other alternatives, which unfortunately were not discussed in the declassified archival sources.[164]

Undoubtedly, the expulsion of British nationals could have been excruciating for British amour-propre, especially at the peak of the Egyptian–British armed conflict in al-Ismaʿiliyya, which was a bedrock of anti-British militant resistance after the unilateral abrogation of the 1936 Treaty. The conflict reached its peak on January 25, 1952, when British troops bombarded the police station for an hour with heavy artillery, leading to the death of fifty-five police personnel who had previously been ordered by the Minister of the Interior, Fuʾad Sirag al-Din, to stand their ground and refuse British orders to evacuate. The following day riots erupted, and the greater part of Cairo's business district was set aflame. By evening, when authorities finally acted to restore order, some eight hundred buildings had been burnt, and twenty-five people, Egyptians and non-Egyptians, were dead. Al-Nahhas declared martial law that night, and the King dismissed Egypt's only majority government in the post-World War II period. The parliament was suspended, then dissolved, and elections were postponed indefinitely. Of course, diverse forces working at cross-purposes share responsibility for the Cairo riots. Agent provocateurs provided incendiary devices and directed the mob against specific targets and foreign business establishments. Egyptian intelligence blamed the Socialist Party, formerly Young Egypt, for inciting the riots, although the script of the investigation reads like a joke in which randomly arrested laborers are accused of burning the city. The British accepted this assessment, but were concerned about placing official blame on the Wafd, which blamed the British for orchestrating the affair to outset the Wafd, which, for similar motives, pointed fingers at the King, who might be charged with negligence for not canceling the birthday party for his baby child on the same day. The Wafd was to be blamed for failing to handle the situation and for behaving recklessly in Ismaʻiliyya.

When a new Minister of the Interior took office, he made the usual declaration about offering the fullest security to resident foreigners and examined any complaints against the Passport and Nationality Department of the Ministry of the Interior. The British authorities saw the Passport Department as some sort of "Augean stables" which was at the root of almost all its troubles: the actual ill-treatment of British subjects, and the particular chaotic and obstructive procedure used to handle renewal applications for the residency visas of British subjects working in the Canal Zone.[165]

While the British emerged as the winners and al-Wafd emerged as the political loser, the true losers were those workers and business owners whose livelihoods relied on the downtown Cairo business district and whose businesses, companies, hotels, and cinemas were gutted.

Notes

1. The British government did not claim that it discovered Egypt, nor request British suzerainty over Egypt; nor did it have settlements in Egypt, as was the case with India. It did, howver, have an economic and military interest in Egypt.
2. Robert T. Harrison, "Alexandria, British Occupation of (1807)," James Stuart Olson and Robert Shadle, *Historical Dictionary of the British Empire* (London: Greenwood, 1996), 26.
3. The new route considerably shortened the length of the journey between England and India as compared to the Cape route, and the volume of traffic carried by it steadily increased.
4. John Marlowe, *Cromer in Egypt* (London: Elek, 1970), 6.
5. Ibid., 7.
6. British Pathé, "Sir George Lloyd 1925," April 13, 2014, https://www.youtube.com/watch?v=os733QckDf0 (last accessed December 12, 2020).

7. See Ahmad Zakariyya al-Shalq, *Al-Ahrar al-Dusturiyyin 1922–1952* (Cairo: Dar al-Shuruq, 2010) 13–158.
8. See Shlomit Shraybom-Shivtiel, "Language and Political Change in Modern Egypt," *International Journal for the Sociology of Language* 137 (1999): 131–40. See also Mark Schaub, "English in the Arab Republic of Egypt," *World Englishes* 19, no 2 (2000): 225–38. For an account of nineteenth-century educational missions carried by Protestant missionaries among Copts and their resistance, see Paul Sedra, *From Mission to Modernity Evangelicals, Reformers and Education in Nineteenth Century Egypt* (London: I. B. Tauris, 2011).
9. Sir Miles Lampson, "English Education and Culture Reviews: Relative Position of Italian and French Culture as Rivals to British Cultural Expansion in Egypt," Great Britain, Public Records Office, May 1937, FO141/677/4N1143.
10. Lampson, "English Education and Culture Reviews," FO141/677/4N1143.
11. Lampson's source was an account of French schools in 1914 in Maurice Baine's book *L'Enquête aux Pays du Levant*. In Egypt, French cultural hegemony predominated primarily through education. See Jack Sislian, "Missionary Works in Egypt during the Nineteenth Century," *Educational Policy and the Mission Schools: Case Studies from the British Empire*, ed. Brian Holmes (London: Routledge & Kegan Paul, 1968), 171–236. See also James Heyworth-Dunne, *An Introduction to the History of Education in Modern Egypt* (London: Frank Cass, 1968), 436.
12. Lampson, "English Education and Culture Reviews," FO141/677/4N1143.
13. Ibid.
14. Ibid.
15. Ibid.
16. Ibid.
17. Ibid.
18. Ibid.
19. "British Education and Culture Summary (for Annual Report) of British Cultural Developments in 1936," Great Britain, Public Records Office, January 1936, FO141/677/4N 1143.
20. Louise Atherton, "Lord Lloyd at the British Council and the Balkan Front, 1937–1940," *The International History Review* 16, no. 1, 1994: 25–48.
21. Sir Ropert Greg, "English Education and Culture Memorandum on General Cultural Position in Egypt," Great Britain, Public Records Office, May 31 1937, FO141/677/4N 1143.
22. Ibid.
23. See Donald Reid, Whose *Pharaohs? Archaeology, Museums, and Egyptian*

National Identity from Napoleon to World War I (Berkeley, CA: University of California Press, 2002).

24. Greg, "English Education and Culture Memorandum," FO141/677/4N 1143.
25. Ibid.
26. The sources are not clear as to whether the German archaeologist Ludwig Borchardt discovered the bust or bought it from a local peasant, who found it while plowing his field. More recently, archeologists have suggested that Nefertiti's undiscovered tomb could actually be in a chamber behind King Tut's chamber. It is not clear how the bust of Nefertiti reached the peasant's field. Given that King Tut's tomb was accessed twice before the sands covered it for thousands of years, it thereby remained protected in the Valley of the Kings. It is possible that Nefertiti's tomb could also have been accessed, and this could justify the presence of her bust in a nearby agricultural field. As of now, so far as I know this remains a hypothesis.
27. Greg, "English Education and Culture Memorandum," FO141/677/4N 1143.
28. Ibid.
29. Ibid.
30. Ibid.
31. Ibid.
32. Ibid.
33. Here, Greg refers to government Public Works and Irrigation officials.
34. Greg, "English Education and Culture Memorandum," FO141/677/4N 1143.
35. Ibid.
36. Ibid. See also Salah Abu al-Nar and Muna 'Abd al-'Azim Anis, *Yawamiyat Lord Millner fi Misr wa Watha'iq Ukhra* (Cairo: Dar al-Shuruq, 2019).
37. Here I mark the difference between Farouk as a crown prince, as a young king, and as the corrupt king of 1952. See Joel Gordon, "The Myth of the Savior: Egypt's 'Just Tyrants,' on the Eve of Revolution, January–July 1952," *Journal of the American Research Center in Egypt* 26 (1989): 223–37.
38. Greg, "English Education and Culture Memorandum," FO141/677/4N 1143.
39. On July 10, 1937, in an interview with the composer in the Egyptian *Sphinx* magazine that gave a good deal of publicity to the opera, the American composer Ruth Linda Deyo talked about the introduction of local Egyptian instruments such as the *darabukka* in addition to the piano, as well as the tenor and soprano roles sung by Mr. Frank Sale and Miss Monica Warner; there was free interweaving of Egyptian and Nubian traditional themes in the score.

40. See James Burns, *Flickering Shadows: Cinema and Identity in Colonial Zimbabwe* (Ohio: Ohio University Center for International Studies, 2002).
41. Wilson Jacob, *Working Out Egypt: Effendi Masculinity and Subject Formation in Colonial Modernity, 1870–1940* (Durham, NC: Duke University Press, 2015), 5.
42. "Films/Film Library for Egyptian Ministry of Education," Great Britain, Public Records Office, 12 Jan 1939, FO 395/655/P143/143/150.
43. Ibid.
44. Ibid.
45. Ibid.
46. Ibid.
47. Ibid.
48. Films/Film Library for Egyptian Ministry of Education," Great Britain, Public Records Office, 12 Jan 1939, FO 395/655/P143/143/150.
49. See H. W. Richardson, "The Economic Significance of the Depression in Britain," *Journal of Contemporary History* 4 no. 4 (1969): 3–19.
50. "Report on the distribution of films in Egypt," P News 2388/143/150. See also Vincent Porter, "The Robert Clark Account: Films Released in Britain by Associated British Pictures, British Lion, MGM, and Warner Bros., 1946–1957," *Historical Journal of Film, Radio & Television* 20, no. 4 (October 2000) 469–511. Virtually no written records have survived of the Associated British Picture Corporation (ABPC), which was one of Great Britain's principal exhibition, distribution, and production companies between 1933 and 1969. Most of its surviving records begin in 1942.
51. The American Embassy in London repeatedly interfered in every attempt to raise the quota of British films in England and within the British Empire. See Victoria de Grazia, "Mass Culture and Sovereignty: The American Challenge to European Cinemas, 1920–1960," *The Journal of Modern History* 61, no. 1 (March 1989): 53–87. See Andrew Ali Ibbi, "Hollywood, The American Image and the Global Film Industry," *CINEJ Cinema Journal* 3, no. 1 (2013) 96–106. See also Jens Ulff-Moller, "The Origins of French Quota Policy Controlling the Import of American Films 1920–1939," *Historical Journal of Film Radio and Television* 18, no. 2 (June 1998): 167–82.
52. This continued after 1952. See Robert Vitalis, "Hollywood and Revolution on the Nile," *Mass Mediations: New Approaches to Popular Culture*, ed. Walter Armbrust (Berkeley, CA: University of California Press, 2000), 269–91.
53. John Hill, "UK Film Policy, Cultural Capital and Social Exclusion," *Cultural*

Trends 13.2 no. 50 (2004), 32. It is true that the Cinematograph Films Act of 1927 established quotas that survived in varying forms until the early 1980s. Such measures, however, were primarily protectionist in impulse, intended to provide support for British films in London in the face of competition from Hollywood.

54. One of GCF's more surprising interventions in the business was its bold 1936 swoop for a quarter-share of the ailing Hollywood outfit Universal, which had offloaded most of its theatres in the wake of the Depression, and had grimly fallen into receivership by 1933, but was nonetheless part of the cartel, one of the "big eight" studios that dominated the American film industry.
55. "Films/Film Library for Egyptian Ministry of Education," FO 395/655/P143/143/150.
56. Ibid.
57. "Report on the Distribution of Films in Egypt," P News 2388/143/150.
58. "Films/Film Library for Egyptian Ministry of Education," FO 395/655/P143/143/150.
59. Ironically, it was a Paramount production.
60. "Publicity in Egypt for Her Majesty's Government's Rearmament Programs," Great Britain, Public Records Office, 23 January 1939, FO 371/23358.
61. The ban was lifted on June 20, 1929, "British Cultural Propaganda," Great Britain, Public Records Office, August 1925, CO 323/10145/1
62. "British Cultural Propaganda," CO 323/10145/1.
63. Ibid
64. Ibid.
65. Ibid.
66. Ibid.
67. Ibid.
68. Ibid.
69. See Mahmud 'Ali, "Al-Judhur al-Tarikhiyya lil-Raqaba wa-Masadiriha", *Al-Raqaba 'ala al-Sinima al-Quyud wa-l-Hudud*, ed. Husayn Bayyumi (Cairo: Maktabat al-'Usra, 2012), 117–36.
70. Ibid.
71. See 'Ali, "Al-Judhur," 117–36.
72. I'itidal Mumtaz, *Mudhakkirat Raqibat Sinima* (Cairo: al-Hay'a al-'Ama al-Misriyya lil-Kitab, 1985), 27.
73. See Sayyid Isma'il, "*Paulino Dranit pasha awwal mudir lil-ubira al-khidiwiyya*," *Al-Ahram al-Masa'i*, December 16, 1996.

74. See Samir Farid, *Tarikh al-Raqaba 'ala al-Sinima fi Misr* (Cairo: al-Maktab al-Dawli li-Tawzi' al-Matbu'at, 2001), 6.
75. See Ramsis 'Awad, *Itijahat Siyasiyya fi al-Masrah Qabl 1919* (Cairo: al-Hay'a al-Misriyya lil-Kitab, 1979), 19–20. Available reports on this play are ambivalent. Some sources suggest that it was a critique of the 'Urabi movement while others suggest that the play promoted the movement. Most sources, however, agree that the play was censored.
76. In another source, the last name is Ramzi. I accept Mar'i as the correct name on the basis of a recent interview with the grandson of the author, who confirmed that his grandfather Hasan Mar'i worked as a journalist and playwright. He also opened an acting-costumes shop which was a camouflage for anti-British activism after 1919. See Mahmud Sa'd, "Bab al-Khalq Liqa' ma'a 'Amm Kamal Mar'i," al-Nahar TV, November, 3, 2019, https://www.youtube.com/watch?v=lSIF278LUHc (last accessed December 12, 2020).
77. See 'Awad, *Itijahat*, 22.
78. Ibid., 23.
79. Ibid., 24.
80. Ibid., 27. The play was not, however, censored outside Cairo as it was performed in Mansoura and Tanta in June 1908.
81. *Al-Jarida*, July 3, 1910, 5.
82. *Al-Liwa'*, July 3, 1910, 4.
83. Ibid.
84. Ibid.
85. Ibid.
86. Ibid.
87. Ibid.
88. *Al-Muqattam*, July 8, 1910, 5.
89. Mervat Youssef, Heba Arafa, and Anup Kumar, "Mediating Discourse of Democratic Uprising in Egypt: Militarized Language and the 'Battles' of Abbasiyya and Maspero," *International Journal of Communication* 8 (2014): 871–89.
90. *Al-Liwa'*, July 11, 1910, 1.
91. *Al-Liwa'*, July 18, 1910, 4, and *al-Balagh al-Misri*, July 23, 1910.
92. *Al-Liwa'*, July 30, 1910, 4.
93. *Al-Liwa'*, September 3, 1910, 1.
94. *Al-Jarida*, July 18, 1911, 5.
95. Farid, *Tarikh*, 2001, 9.
96. *Al-Mahrusa*, January 20, 1917, 1.

97. *Al-Basir*, May 1, 1919, 2.
98. *Al-Minbar*, September 7, 1919, 3.
99. *Al-Minbar*, September 30, 1919, 1.
100. The minister was by then Isma'il Sidqi
101. Farid, *Tarikh*, 2001, 19.
102. Ibid., 12.
103. The last name is not mentioned in the sources.
104. I'itidal Mumtaz, *Mudhakkirat Raqibat Sinima* (Cairo: al-Hay'a al-'Ama al-Misriyya lil-Kitab, 1985), 13.
105. Ibid., 12.
106. In another source they were eight.
107. She continued to work in the Department of Film Censorship until she left Egypt for Italy in 1967. Mumtaz, *Mudhakkirat*, 1985, 12.
108. The last name is not mentioned in the sources
109. She continued to work in the Department of Film Censorship until she died in 1951.
110. Mumtaz, *Mudhakkirat*, 13.
111. The names are not mentioned in the sources.
112. Mumtaz, *Mudhakkirat*, 13. She joined in 1945.
113. Ibid., 14.
114. Ibid.
115. The name of the movie is not mentioned in the primary source. Further research is required in this regard.
116. Mumtaz, *Mudhakkirat*, 14.
117. "Concerns about the Representation of British Officers and Depiction of Egyptian Participation in the Re-Conquest of Sudan: Films for Egypt and Sudan," Great Britain, Public Records Office, 20 February 1939, P 553/143/150-P553/205
118. Ibid.
119. *Akhir Sa'a*, no. 658, 1947, 13.
120. Ibid.
121. Ibid.
122. Ibid.
123. Ibid.
124. The name is not clear in the sources. It was written in Arabic. It appears to me that he is Heinrich Mann, whose works were adapted for the screen at that time. Examples include his book *Professor Unrat*, which was freely adapted

into the legendary movie *The Blue Angel* (dir. Josef von Sternberg, 1930). See David Gross, *The Writer and Society: Heinrich Mann and Literary Politics in Germany, 1890–1940* (Atlantic Highlands, NJ: Humanities Press, 1980); Walter Delabar and Walter Fähnders, *Heinrich Mann 1871–1950* (Berlin: Weidler, 2005); Martin Mauthner, *German Writers in French Exile, 1933–1940* (London: Vallentine Mitchell in association with the European Jewish Publication Society, 2007).

125. See Yunan Labib Rizq, *Al-'Ayib fi dhat Afandina* (Cairo: Dar al-Shuruq, 2009), 49–50.
126. Farid, *Tarikh*, 55
127. *Akhir Sa'a*, no. 658, 1947, 13.
128. 'Ali, *Al-Judhur*, 122.
129. See Bernard Cohn, *Colonialism, and Its Forms of Knowledge* (Princeton, NJ: Princeton University Press, 1996).
130. Ibid. For example, a film committee was appointed by the Secretary of State to examine the existing arrangement for the supply and censorship of cinematograph films for public exhibition in the Colonies, Protectorates, and Mandated Territories. On October 22, 1927, the governor-general of Dar al-Salam Tanganyika Territory wrote a letter in which he transmitted a Report of a Select Committee of Legislative Council on film. The Committee saw that it was impracticable to prevent certain classes of people from going to any particular Hall. This meant that if, for example, a film was passed for Europeans, only no other class could be allowed into the hall where it was being exhibited. In this case, the film would go through three processes of censorship and a note had to be placed on the door of the movie theater to announce which class was admitted at what time. Thus, the committee recommended that the films be censored for all classes of the population.
131. 'Ali, *Al-Judhur*, 122–3.
132. Ibid.
133. Ibid.
134. Ibid.
135. Ibid.
136. Cohn, *Colonialism and its Forms of Knowledge*, 3.
137. *Al-Ithnayn*, no. 811, 1949, 28.
138. Mumtaz, *Mudhakkirat*, 1985, 32–6.
139. Farid, *Tarikh*, 60.
140. These were the only names listed.

141. Consider, for example, movies like *Lagan* (dir. Ashutosh Gowariker, 2001) or *Rang De Basanti* (dir. Rakeysh Omprakash Mehra, 2006).
142. Mumtaz, *Mudhakkirat*, 32–6.
143. Antonio Gramsci, *Further Selections from the Prison Notebooks* (Minneapolis, MN: University of Minnesota Press: 1995), 133–4.
144. For example, Sharif 'Arafa explicitly addresses this issue in his famous blockbuster *al-Irhab wa-l-Kabab*/Terrorism and Kabob, 1992, starring 'Adil Imam.
145. *Al-Ithnayn*, 1951, no. 864, 50.
146. *Akhir Sa'a*, no. 693, 1948.
147. Ordinary shares are the main source of finance for the company and they represent ownership in the company, whereas preference shares are held by the lender of capital to the company and do not confer voting rights in the company.
148. The name "Oden," after all, stands for the motto "Oscar Deutsch Entertains our Nation."
149. It is worth mentioning here that in 1951 the exchange rate for sterling was L.E. 97.4 piasters.
150. Goodwill is calculated as a difference between the purchase price and the total value of assets and liabilities of an acquired company.
151. "J. Arthur Rank Theater in Cairo," Great Britain, Public Records Office, January 6, 1951, FO 371 E1611/1
152. *Akhir Sa'a*, 1948, no. 710.
153. Geoffrey Macnab, *J. Arthur Rank and the British Film Industry* (London: Routledge, 1993), 4.
154. Ibid, 5.
155. Ibid.
156. Ibid.
157. Ibid., 13.
158. Ibid., 15.
159. Macnab, *J. Arthur Rank and the British Film Industry*, 30.
160. Ibid., 43.
161. Ibid., 44.
162. Ibid.
163. Macnab, *J. Arthur Rank and the British Film Industry*, 44.
164. "The Egyptian Cabinet May Consider the Expulsion of 800 British Subjects," FO 371, JE 1611/3.
165. J E 1611/5 African Department.

3

Protecting the Amour-propre of Islam

1. Islamic Public Discourse on the Lawfulness of Film

As with other modern innovations, the arrival of film in colonial Egypt posed a challenge for many 'ulama' who were carving a space for themselves in predominantly secular efforts to modernize Egypt. The widespread popularity of the new medium made it necessary for the 'ulama' to reopen a set of classical legal disputes over violation of the Islamic doctrine of the oneness/unity of God (*tawhid*), regulation of the conduct of Muslim women, and the forging of the prophetic tradition known as Hadith literature. A major key to these disputes was the permissibility of creating and making images of the Prophets and Companions in particular. Another major issue was the lawfulness of acting as a profession for Muslim women. By invoking the legal concept of public welfare (*maslaha*), some of the 'ulama' were able to sanction photography positively, thereby paving the way for the permissibility of acting in theater and cinema. However, these *maslaha* rulings also placed limitations on the scope of acting, limiting its use to cases of necessity and need. This use of *maslaha* did not provide room for the innovation that is crucial for maintaining the status of film as art and as a domain for experimentation, freedom of expression, and creativity. The use of *maslaha* by these scholars was further limited by the legal principle of blocking the legal means that could lead to sin (*sadd al-dhara'i'*), which overrules the use of *maslaha* even in cases of necessity and need.

In 1926, a famous public controversy on the lawfulness of film occurred when the pioneer Egyptian theater and film actor Yusuf Wahbi announced his intention of playing the role of the Prophet Muhammad in the Turkish-German movie *The Prophet Muhammad*.[1] *Al-Masrah* (The Theater), a popular variety magazine, campaigned against the film, questioning the company's motives for producing the film and calling upon the 'ulama' of Egypt to protest against it. The magazine claimed that Wahbi's characterization of the Prophet resembled his earlier characterization of the Russian monk and libertine Rasputin and was thus defamatory. The magazine accused Wahbi of committing an act that made him a renegade (*mariq*).[2] The newspaper *al-Ahram* (The Pyramids) published an essay by 'Abd al-Baqi Na'im Surur, whom the paper characterized as a keen (*ghayur*) Muslim. Surur claimed that it was anti-Islamic to produce such a film in a country whose constitution acknowledged Islam as the official religion of the state. He urged the government to prevent Wahbi from traveling to shoot the movie in Europe, where people perceived the Prophet differently from in Egypt. Surur claimed that religion was often subject to ridicule in cities such as Paris, which he characterized as a place of reprehensible leisure and recklessness (*khala'a*).[3] He concluded that if the movie were to be made, it would disparage the reputation of the Prophet and would serve the interests of the enemies of Islam. Such accusations dispirited public officials, who initially supported the film. These included the head of the Royal Court, Ahmad Hasanayn, the former Prime Minister Sa'id Dhu al-Faqqar, Prince Isma'il Shirin, and the Prime Minister Ahmad Ziwar.[4] King Fouad of Egypt (r. 1917–36) threatened to banish Wahbi and revoke his citizenship if he were to carry out his plans to play the Prophet Muhammad in the film.[5]

In response to this media campaign, Wahbi published a letter in *al-Ahram* titled *Khitab maftuh lil-'ulama'* (An Open Address to the Scholars), saying, "I write to you as a Muslim man who loves his religion and his Prophet and as a man who loves his country. I seek your help to decide on a project that, if it happens, might be a major event in the Muslim world."[6] The motivation behind the production, according to Wahbi, was to explain the character of the Prophet Muhammad to Europeans and to correct the Christian misconception of Muslims as idol worshipers. Wahbi hoped that his letter would encourage the 'ulama' to approve his project. He emphasized that if he were to refuse the opportunity, the company would assign the role to a European actor.[7] He also denied accusations that his characterization of the Prophet was comparable to that of his earlier role as Rasputin in a play that carried the same name. Wahbi assured his readers that he was keen not to violate any religious

PROTECTING THE AMOUR-PROPRE OF ISLAM | 149

Figure 3.1 Wahbi's publicity photographs were published in *al-Masrah* magazine. Report adapted from the magazine.

rules while playing the role of the Prophet and offered to share the publicity photographs taken for the film.[8]

Wahbi's letter merely intensified the campaign against the film, with Azhari graduates now taking the lead. For example, Ibrahim Jaballah accused Wahbi of misguidance and deceit. Jaballah questioned the film company's motivation for producing the movie and accused it of using religion for financial gain.⁹ Another Azhari graduate, Ahmad Haridi al-Sari, wrote a response to Wahbi in *al-Ahram* calling upon the 'ulama' participating in the Caliphate Conference, held in Cairo in 1926, to discuss the lawfulness of the movie.¹⁰ Al-Sari claimed that many established legal opinions prohibited the practice of figural representation in general and the depiction of the Prophet in particular. He supported his claim with the argument that the figural representation of the Prophet might lead to the disrespect (*imtihan*) of Muhammad's holy status in the future. Al-Sari suspected that the movie was a conspiracy to ignite sectarianism (*fitna*) in the Muslim world.

On May 27, 1926, *al-Masrah* published al-Azhar's response to the debate and described the institution's intensified efforts to censor the film. These efforts culminated on May 18, when al-Azhar asked the government to contact the German Ambassador in Cairo in order to prevent the Marcos Film Company from producing the film. Al-Azhar also asked the Ministry of the Interior to intervene and prevent Wahbi from traveling abroad to participate in the making of the film. The Ministry called on Wahbi to announce in the newspapers that he had turned down the offer from the Marcos Film Company. On May 30, Wahbi announced that in deference to the 'ulama', he had declined the offer, noting, however, that another company might produce the movie in Algeria or Tunisia. Sarcastically, Wahbi urged the 'ulama' who supported censorship to contact every other country in the world about the film because censorship inside Egypt would not necessarily prevent the film from being produced outside Egypt.

Wahbi saw the film as a lost opportunity for Muslims to represent their religion themselves. He realized, however, that the censorship of his role was the symptom of a deeper Islamic discourse on the adaptability of Islamic law to meet new and changing social conditions. He expressed his views as follows:

> I wonder if it would have been possible for us to have a renaissance in painting (*rasm*) and sculpting (*naht*), among many other forms of art that flourished in our civilized time, if we had continued to hold onto what some people [in the past] thought of as prohibited, impermissible, and a deviation from religious teachings. However, I would rather not delve any further into this controversial issue.¹¹

One way to understand the conflict between Wahbi and those 'ulama' who opposed his film is to recognize the roots of censoring and positively sanctioning figural representation in Islam.

During the formative period of Islam, the noun *taswir* was the principal Arabic term used to signify the representational arts (drawing, sketching, engraving, and sculpture). The practice of *taswir* during the lifetime of the Prophet Muhammad continues to be a subject of dispute among art historians.[12] The Qur'an does not explicitly prohibit painting or other representational arts, and the Arabic root *s-w-r* appears in the Qur'an in several forms.[13] For example, the term *sawwarna* (We fashioned) in the third person verbal form is usually interpreted to refer to God as the Creator and Fashioner of forms. Similarly, the active participle *musawwir* refers to God as the Fashioner of Forms (cf. Q 59:24). Also, the noun *sura*—meaning image, picture, or anything that is formed, fashioned, figured, or shaped—sometimes appears in the Qur'an as referring to the form of a human being well-fashioned by God (cf. Q 64:3).

The first clear evidence for the prohibition of *taswir* as representational art comes from Hadith literature. The six canonical Sunni collections of hadith all include a chapter on *taswir*. Five widely circulated hadiths point to the prohibition of *taswir*. The first hadith promises dire punishment on the Day of Judgment for depictors (*musawwirin*) because their activity is considered an emulation (*mudahat*) of God's creation. The second hadith mentions a curse on the *musawwirin*, whose activities are depicted as being as evil as turning the graves of Prophets into mosques. The same punishment applies to people who commemorate the legacy of the good men of their community by installing images (*suwar*) of them on their graves. The third hadith refers to curtains embroidered with pictures (*tasawir*) that might distract a believer while praying or prevent angels from entering a house. By contrast, a fourth hadith records the Prophet Muhammad's tolerance of images found on cushions or pillows. The fifth hadith orders the obliteration of cross-like images.[14]

Not all of these hadiths have a high degree of validity (i.e. soundness [*sahih*]). Some, however, are well-known (*mashhur*)[15] and serve as textual evidence for the prohibition of *taswir*. In addition, nouns meaning image (*sura*) and picture (*taswira*) are often interpreted in the Hadith corpus as referring to idols that were worshiped in the Arabian Peninsula before the arrival of Islam. Idol worship thus serves as the primary *ratio legis* (*'illa*) for the prohibition of *taswir* in the Hadith. For this reason, many classical jurisprudents regarded the prohibition of images as a precautionary act (*ihtiyat*) required to block the means to unbelief (*shirk*) and protect the Islamic doctrine of the unity of God.[16] This prohibition, however, was not absolute, because not every representational image was made for the purpose of worship.

Jurisprudents from the four Sunni law schools (*madhhab*) developed different legal positions on various types of *taswir*. For example, they distinguished between *taswir* without a shadow (*ma laysa lahu zill*), that is, flat depictions, and *taswir* with a shadow (*ma lahu zill*), that is, installed statues. They also distinguished between the *taswir* of a living being with a soul (*ma lahu ruh*) and of a living being without a soul (*ma laysa lahu ruh*),[17] as well as between complete and incomplete forms of *taswir*. With regard to *taswir* with a shadow, Maliki jurists adopted the view that *taswir* is prohibited only when a living being with a soul (*ma lahu ruh*) is represented as a visible full-form statue and with all the organs necessary for survival. They believed that if a hole were created in the head or in the stomach of the statue, the hole would invalidate the prohibition since no living being with a soul has a hole in its head or stomach. The Hanafis and Hanbalis agreed with the Malikis, but added the stipulation that a permissible statue should possess a visible and significant imperfection (*naqs*), such as a missing head or vital organ.[18] With regard to *taswir* without a shadow (i.e. flat images),[19] some Maliki jurists permitted it, while others found it reprehensible (*makruh*). Hanbalis and Hanafis were in agreement with the Malikis in this regard. However, the Malikis and the Hanbalis maintained that a flat image should not be magnified or treated with respect because the permissibility of this form of *taswir* is conditioned by its disrespect, which ensures that over time the image would not be worshiped and thus would not thereby violate the Islamic doctrine of the unity of God.[20] In a major departure from the other three Sunni legal schools, the Shafi'is distinguished between "making" and "owning" *taswir*. They allowed ownership of all types of *taswir*, so long as they are conditioned by disrespect (i.e. not venerated). They also allowed for making *taswir* of living beings without a soul, such as plants. However, they prohibited making any types of *taswir* of living beings with a soul.

At the turn of the twentieth century, Muhammad 'Abduh drew an analogy (*qiyas*) between *taswir* and poetry, arguing that *taswir* is a silent form of poetry. Both *taswir* and poetry serve as platforms for expressing conceptual images. Moreover, both preserve the cultural heritage of communities. According to 'Abduh, those who advocate the prohibition of *taswir* interpret the relevant hadiths in a stagnant and literal manner. They overlook the possibility that "the direst punishment" applies only to those who create images used as idols. 'Abduh concluded that creating images for the purpose of beauty and entertainment is permissible, so long as it does not serve the purpose of idol worship.[21] 'Abduh's views made it possible for many students at al-Azhar to study and create representational art. Chief among these was 'Abd al-Majid Wafi, a student at al-Azhar and a professional painter for *al-Ahram* from 1949 to 1955.[22] However, 'Abduh's position did not solve the problem of the lawfulness of *taswir* in general. Many jurisprudents[23] considered 'Abduh's argument as a mere opinion (*ra'y*),[24] which rendered it less authoritative as an argument for the permissibility of *taswir*. The emergence of new forms of representational arts, such as photography, further complicated the legal debate.[25] Rashid Rida, a student of 'Abduh's, sanctioned photography by invoking *maslaha* to break the prior consensus (*ijma'*) on prohibited types of *taswir*. Before exploring Rida's activation of *maslaha*, I will first shed light on models of *maslaha* in order to explain the model used by Rida and the limitations causing *maslaha* to function as covert censorship.

Maslaha, literally a source of good or benefit,[26] functions in Islamic legal tradition as a vehicle for finding solutions to unprecedented cases. According to Opwis, the use of *maslaha* to articulate legal opinions was primarily influenced by the debate on the purposes of law (*maqasid al-shari'a*) shaped by the works of Abu Hamid al-Ghazali (1058–1111), who placed these under three categories of interests (*masalih*): (a) necessities (*al-darurat*), (b) needs (*al-hajiyyat*), and (c) improvements (*al-tahsinat*).[27] He defines *maslaha* as the advancing of good (*manfa'a*) and the averting of harm (*madarra*). He activates the use of *maslaha* only in necessities, which have a certain (*qat'i*) *ratio legis* that applies to all believers universally. He excludes the activation of *maslaha* for needs and improvements unless supported by a textual source, consensus, or legal analogy.[28]

While later jurisprudents accepted al-Ghazali's definition of *maslaha*, they disagreed with him on how detectable *maslaha* is without revealed texts and on the inactivation of *maslaha* in needs and improvements. Fakhr al-Din al-Razi (1149–1209) activated *maslaha* in the case of necessities that were not certain and did not apply to all believers. Shihab al-Din al-Qarafi (1228–85) expanded the use of *maslaha* to de-activate existing legal principles, as in the use of legal licenses (*rukhas*) and the principle of blocking the legal means (*sadd al-dhara'i*).[29] Najm al-Din al-Tufi (1276–1316) employed *maslaha* as legal evidence (*dalil*)[30]—"one that was known with certainty, based on an inductive reading of the scriptures and that was perceptible by the human intellect."[31] Al-Tufi gave *maslaha* priority over contradictory textual rulings, but he limited this priority by de-activating *maslaha* in cases associated with acts of worship (*'ibadat*). Yet *maslaha*, for al-Tufi, could not override a legal indicator from the Qur'an, the Sunna, and consensus.[32] Abu Ishaq al-Shatibi (1320–88),[33] like al-Tufi, excluded acts of worship from *maslaha*. In a major departure from his earlier peers, he adopted a theory of law in which he distinguished between the purposes of the verses (*asbab al-nuzul*) revealed to the Prophet in Mecca and those revealed in Medina. The Meccan verses embodied "the general message of Islam in which the universal sources of law [had been laid] down."[34] He considered the Medinan verses, as well as accounts of the Sunna constituents "of the particulars of the law that elucidate, specify, and qualify or complement the Meccan revelation."[35] Al-Shatibi contended that an act was in line with the law based on its outcome. He adopted the view "that attaining *maslaha* and averting harm (*mafsada*) at the level of necessities, needs, and improvements was a universal source of the law and the purpose of the Lawgiver."[36] He gave priority to *maslaha* over any particular ruling from the Qur'an or Sunna. In a sense, al-Shatibi's deliberation on *maslaha* pushed for its activation in the domain of independent legal reasoning (*ijtihad*).[37] Although all these models of *maslaha* continued to influence its use in twentieth-century Egypt, al-Ghazali's model surpassed all other models, thereby limiting the use of *maslaha* to necessities and needs.

The legal principle of *sadd al-dhara'i*, which de-activates the use of *maslaha*, also placed many limitations on the use of *maslaha*. The term *sadd al-dhara'i* consisted of the verbal noun "to close" (*sadd*) and the broken plural "excuses/reasons" (sing. *dhari'a*, pl. *dhara'i*). As a legal concept, it was

Figure 3.2 'Abd al-Majid Wafi adding the final strokes to his painting entitled *al-Wafa'* (Loyalty). Image adapted from *al-Ithnayn* magazine.

not clear whether *sadd al-dhara'i'* was a source of law (*asl*),[38] evidence (*dalil*), or an established legal principle (*qa'ida*). Some jurisprudents saw it as a continuation of unattested benefit (*maslaha mursala*). This view is based on its application as part of the overarching purpose of the law to prevent harm (*dar' al-mafasid*), and on the legal maxim which stated that preventing harms (*dar' al-mafasid*) had preference over achieving benefits (*jalb al-masalih*). A major difference between *maslaha* and *sadd al-dhara'i'* was that the latter did not target what was "beneficial"; it targeted what was "harmful" or led to harm (*darar*). While employing *sadd al-dhara'i'*, jurisprudents differentiated between three frequencies of harm: recurrent, infrequent or rare, and imminent.[39]

I translate *maslaha* as public interest "when it referred to the permissibility of the political authorities to issue rulings that concur with the public good within the sphere of . . . politics. When, however, a jurist . . . gives a legal opinion on the grounds of *maslaha*, this [has] little to do with public well-being but was usually based on considerations of a single private case."[40] I highlight the fact that the boom in printing press use in the twentieth century blurred the distinction between the "private" and the "public": that is, once a jurist published a legal opinion based on *maslaha*, in a private case, the circulation of the legal opinion via the printing press makes it step from the private into the public domain. This makes the opinion more authoritative regardless of the ruler's position from it. The printing press thus gave the 'ulama' a greater voice in the context of modernization.[41] They used the press to show that Islamic law is not an obstacle to social reform; rather, it maintains a rational frame of reference that is compatible with modern reform projects and that can accommodate modern inventions. Thus, the authority of the 'ulama' increased as the guardians and transmitters of knowledge in both public and private lives.[42] Their new power allowed the political authorities to activate *maslaha* so as to issue rulings in accord with their instrumental value of public interest within the intersecting spheres of religion and politics, perceived in Egypt at that time as a more secular domain.

2. The *Maslaha* of Figural Representation (*Taswir*)

Rashid Rida limited the use of *maslaha* in Islamic jurisprudence to cases of necessity and need. Although he gave *maslaha* priority over contradictory textual rulings, he excluded acts of worship from *maslaha*, "which does not override evidence from the Qur'an, Sunna, or consensus."[43] Therefore, Rida does not begin his argument by directly stating that *taswir* is a *maslaha*, despite the fact that he considers it a matter of common sense (*amr badihi*). Instead, he begins his argument by highlighting the contradiction in the textual sources on the prohibition of *taswir*. In what follows, I will analyze how Rida used *maslaha* to break down the previous consensus on the prohibition of *taswir* in the case of a "living being with a soul". Next, I will discuss his view that photography is a form of *maslaha*.

In 1918, Rida wrote about *taswir* in the journal *al-Manar*. He framed his view as a fatwa, pointing out that he approached the question of *taswir* in response to a letter from an anonymous reader who resided in Singapore. The reader asked about the legal status of images made of gypsum, metal, pencils, or pens, or by means of a camera (*alat habs al-zill*, lit. machine that captures a shadow).[44] Rida replies that historical accounts (*athar*)[45] seemed more tolerant on this subject than Hadith. For example, some historical accounts report that certain narrators, on whose authority the hadiths that prohibit *taswir* were transmitted, owned images themselves. Other accounts mention that the narrator Zayd b. Khalid (d. 655) owned curtains with images, despite reporting the hadith that angels do not enter a house that has representational images. Al-Qasim b. Muhammad b. Abi Bakr (d. 656), a famous authority from the generation of the Successors, reportedly owned a hopping game (*hajla*)[46] that had images of a beaver (*al-qundus*) and a phoenix (*al-'anqa'*), even though he was the narrator of a hadith that discouraged the ownership of curtains embroidered with images. Yasar b. Numayr,[47] a client and personal accountant of Caliph 'Umar b. al-Khattab, owned unspecified images. Some reports state that images or pictures used to be made in the house of Marwan b. al-Hakam (d.685) and Sa'id b. al-'As (d. 679), both of whom were appointed governors of Medina. As for the reports claiming that angels abstain from entering houses with images, Rida argued that this referred only to the Angels of Mercy and to the Prophet's house.[48]

In his fatwa, Rida also cites hadiths supporting the permissibility of *taswir* based on *maslaha*. He refers to a hadith recorded in *Sahih al-Bukhari* and narrated on the authority of the Prophet's wife 'A'isha, who said, "I used to play with dolls (*banat*)[49] at the Prophet's house, and I had girlfriends who used to play with me." He cites another hadith to explain that the term *banat* refers to dolls. This hadith was narrated on the authority of Abu 'Awana (d. 928), who reported that 'A'isha said, "I used to play with *banat*, that is to say, with dolls."[50] Rida supports his argument by citing the legal opinions of jurisprudents such as al-Qadi 'Iyad (1083–1149), Ibn Hajar al-'Asqalani (1371–1448), and al-Qurtubi (1214–73), all of whom permitted full-form statues of living beings with a soul. For example, al-Qadi 'Iyad mentioned that dolls could be used to train girls in how to run a household and raise children. According to Ibn Hajar, the permissibility of dolls for girls was a matter of explicit consensus. Al-Qurtubi permitted sugar statues (*halwa*) because they were perishable.[51]

To further argue for the permissibility of *taswir* as a *maslaha*, Rida contested the use of the legal concept of "blocking the legal means" to prohibit the creation of images. He argued that *taswir* is less likely to be a pretext for idol-worship than building a mosque over the grave of a righteous person, circumambulating such a grave, or asking the dead to provide good and drive away evil. According to Rida, the Prophet's Companions did not demolish any of the images in the palace of Khosrow Anushirvan, although the shrines built over the graves of righteous Muslims were demolished. One sound hadith, transmitted on the authority of Abu al-Hayyaj al-Usdi, states that 'Ali b. Abi Talib ordered both the destruction of shrines built over graves and the demolition of statues.[52]

Rida concludes that the consideration of "blocking the legal means" in the case of *taswir* is an exaggerated argument (*ghuluww*) that is abrogated by the necessity of producing images under special circumstances. For him, the need to produce a preeminent benefit (*maslaha rajiha*) abrogated the prohibition of a thing that is prohibited in itself (*al-muharram li-dhatih*). For example, eating pork and carrion is permissible for Muslims in case of necessity, for example for survival. By the same token, a physician may look at the private parts of a woman, on the basis of the legal principle that believers are obligated to choose the least harmful option when faced with two undesirable choices (*irtikab akhaff al-dararayyin wajib*).[53] Rida points out that representational images are necessary for illustrating natural history, the history of medicine, the anatomy of humans or animals, the preservation of language, and the many sciences and arts essential for military, administrative, and political activities. He adds that modern innovations in *taswir*, such as photography, are a form of *maslaha* because, in modern warfare, it is necessary to take photographs of locations, roads, army units, and munitions. Photography is also necessary for keeping records of criminal suspects. The prohibition of *taswir* in the past, he points out, made it difficult for contemporary scholars to identify the names of plants and animals in some classical texts. "Had the author bothered to put a picture next to the name, as the Ancient Egyptians used to do, and as civilized nations do nowadays, it would have been the best means to preserve knowledge in Arabic."[54] Rida further advocated the use of photography as a modern invention that could be useful for military and industrial purposes.

While Rida successfully activated *masalaha* to permit photography, the consensus on the absolute prohibition of *taswir* did not cease to exist, and many mainstream Azhari 'ulama' could not overlook it. Some tried to permit photography without reliance on *maslaha* and by reconsidering the authenticity of the textual sources contested by Rashid Rida. Alternatively, the content of the hadith was given more attention than its chain of transmission, thereby shifting the debate to the *matn* of the hadith instead of the *isnad*.

In 1941, Muhammad 'Abd al-Latif al-Fahham, an Egyptian jurisprudent,[55] a personal status law jurist, a chair of al-Azhar *fatwa* committee, and later a rector of al-Azhar,[56] chaired a committee to provide a legal opinion on the lawfulness of *taswir*.[57] He received a question from Hamza Yusuf Mijaj from British Somalia. In his response, al-Fahham acknowledges that not all hadiths on the prohibition of *taswir* are sound. But he emphasizes that some of these hadiths can be reliable because they are popular (*mashhur*), a grade of authenticity in which a tradition has more than two transmitters, some being sound and others not.[58] Al-Fahham supports the consensus on prohibiting full-form *taswir* of animates based on the legal principle of "blocking the legal means." He bases his legal opinion on a particular denotation of *taswir*, which signifies the depiction of full-form statues of animates for the purpose of idol worship. Statues of inanimates, and incomplete statues of animates, flat depictions including photographic images, oil paintings, and depictions on tapestries or frescos, although some of the 'ulama' classify them as despised (*karaha*) and they preferred (*istahsanu*) to avoid them, can be permitted on the basis of two sources of law. The first is a sound hadith, which states that angels do not enter a house that has a dog or a *suwar*. The hadith excludes *suwar* on tapestries. The second is the legal principle of a void *ratio legis* (*intifa' al-'illa*), which refers to a context in which the *ratio legis* of a particular case ceases to exist or becomes invalid. Since no people have been reported historically to worship flat depictions, al-Fahham argues that there is no reason to prohibit photographic images, oil paintings, and depictions on tapestries. He stresses, however, that the principle of void *ratio legis* cannot be applied in the case of full-form statues of animates, because people in the past used statues for the purpose of idol worship, which continues even in the most scientifically progressive stages of human history, including the twentieth century. He contests the possibility of applying the principle of void *ratio legis* on the basis of the intention of the depictor, or the impossibility of finding a person in the twentieth century worshipping a stone, or Muhammad Abdu's argument that all forms of *taswir* should be considered fine art.[59] Instead, al-Fahham contends that human reason is easily influenced by imitation, which often controls the mind, especially when the milieu and the cultural heritage of the believer are suppressive enough to inactivate human will and the ability to distinguish the fake from the true. While al-Fahham acknowledges the noble purpose of making statues to celebrate figures who positively influenced history, he stresses that an act is judged on the basis of its consequences. Since there is a contingency, that is, a possibility that statues can be worshiped in the future, hence threatening the cult of the oneness of God, al-Fahham prohibits *taswir* as full-form statues of animates. He supports his views with a textual source, a hadith narrated on the authority of Ibn 'Abbas. The latter, while talking about the idols that used to be worshiped by the people of the Prophet Noah, reported that Waddun, Suwa'un, Yaghuthu, and Nasrun were names of good persons from the people of Noah.[60] When they passed away, Satan motivated their people to inaugurate statues for them. Initially, the statues were not worshipped, but when traditions were abrogated, people started to worship the statues. Al-Fahham further explains that Islam is not against fine arts, which should not be reduced to the making of full-form statues. He comments on the high cost of the statues made for politicians in Cairo and suggests that a more influential way of celebrating and commemorating the legacy of a historical figure is to spend the cost of the statues on charity projects that carry their name and help the poor. He adds that writing books on the noble deeds and history of those politicians can also be a better alternative to statutes.

In a major departure from the views of al-Fahham, his Azhari peer, 'Abd al-Rahman Muhammad 'Awad al-Jaziri, relies on the principle of void *ratio legis* and on *maslaha* to sanction all forms of *taswir* positively.[61] Al-Jaziri's influence on legal reasoning comes from his membership of Hay'at Kibar al-'Ulma' (Association of Eminent Azhari Scholars). The association used to have a representative from each *madhhab*, and the head of al-Azhar, Shaykh al-Azhar, used to be its elected chair before Nasser dissolved it in 1961.[62] In an article published in *al-Azhar* magazine in 1941, al-Jaziri explains that jurisprudents who stand for the prohibition of *taswir* attempt to advance the use of abrogation to solve what they see as a contradiction between a Qur'anic verse and a hadith. While the Qur'an does not explicitly prohibit painting or other representational arts, the Qur'anic verse 34:13 speaks of statues being made for Solomon. The verse does not elaborate on the context. The Qur'an attributes to Solomon the best of traits, declares him to be an infallible dignified

Messenger, and declares his innocence with regard to the sin of idol worship. Because Solomon could not have been included among those promised "the direst punishment" in the hadiths on *taswir*, some of the 'ulama' tried to solve the contradiction through the theory of abrogation. They argued that *taswir* of human and animate in full form could have been permissible in the law of Solomon, but it became abrogated in Islam. Being an adherent of the Hanafi *madhhab* that gives priority to the Qur'an while deriving legal rulings, al-Jaziri rejects harmonization based on the theory of abrogation. He explains that there is no contradiction between the verse and the hadith. Instead, he points out that there is a misunderstanding with regard to the signification of the word depictors (*musawwrin*), which recurs in the bulk of hadiths on *taswir*. According to al-Jaziri, the word does not signify the makers of statues or images in general. Rather, it specifically signifies the practice of building mosques over graves and introducing full-form statues of animates inside those graves. Al-Jaziri cites a hadith that appears in *Sahih al-Bukhari* under *Kitab al-Salat* (Book of Prayers) and is narrated on the authority of 'A'isha. The hadith reads: "Umm Habiba and Umm Salama[63] talked about a church they saw in Abyssinia and about some *tasawir* they saw inside the church. They mentioned the incident to the Prophet, who said, 'Those were people who, when good men among them die, used to build mosques over their graves in which they made *suwar*. Those would be the evilest in The Day of Judgment.'" On the basis of this hadith, al-Jaziri sees the *ratio legis* behind the prohibition as having to do with *taswir* only in the context of building mosques over graves, a practice which he sees as being in direct violation of the doctrine of the oneness of God. As for the hadiths which state that angels do not enter a house which has a dog or a *sura*, al-Jaziri favors the views of Ibn Hibban (883–965),[64] who explains that the prohibition of *taswir* in those hadiths is among the particulars (i.e. it is limited only to the Prophet and his house). Al-Jaziri finds Ibn Hibban's view plausible, because idol worship at the time of the Prophet was common, and Islam was a new religion; people needed time to forget pre-Islamic practices.

Al-Jaziri concludes that as long as *taswir* is not associated with idol worship, and as long as *suwar* are not highly looked upon or dignified, all forms of *taswir* are *maslaha*, on the basis of the necessity of knowledge (*'ilm*) and ethics (*akhlaq*). He further argues that scientific research intended for the welfare of humanity has become dependent entirely on all forms of *taswir*. Students of medicine, for example, who cannot afford to study an actual human body, must buy full-form statues to learn and study the different organs of the human body and their functions. To tell these students that *taswir* is prohibited, al-Jaziri argues, is a stagnation that is rejected in Islamic law.

The use of *maslaha* and the principle of void *ratio legis* did not, however, solve the question of the lawfulness of *taswir* for good. Many 'ulama' continued to be challenged by the cinematic image. For example, Ahmad al-Sharabasi, a professor in the College of Arabic at al-Azhar and chair of al-Azhar's censorship division that used to provide legal opinions on controversial publications, leaned more toward the Shafi'i view that prohibited all forms of *taswir* on the basis of the *ratio legis* that figural representation is an emulation of the Creator and thus violates the Islamic doctrine of the oneness of God. He took this position despite the fact that he was head of the Hanafi legal school in Egypt, despite being a strong supporter of theater and author of several plays. However, he found a way to sanction photography by arguing that the photographic image did not fall under prohibited forms of *taswir* because the *ratio legis* of emulating the Creator ceases to exist in the case of photography as opposed to painting. He stated that photography relies on capturing shadows on paper (*habs al-zill*) without the intervention of the human hand. That is to say, the photographer does not technically "make" the forms of the objects depicted in a photograph. According to this reasoning, photography is not really an attempt to emulate the Creator. And since photography is a *maslaha*, Muslims should not shy away from making the best use of the new medium.

The use of *maslaha* to sanction *taswir* positively was a major step that permitted the use of photography throughout the Muslim world. It was also a significant step toward sanctioning acting and film production in Egypt. In the following section, I analyze the use of *maslaha* to proscribe acting in theater and cinema.

3. The *Maslaha* of Theater Acting

In 1918, Rashid Rida addressed the lawfulness of acting in *al-Manar*.[65] He framed his argument as a fatwa, which he provided for a reader by the name of Muhammad Muhammad Sa'fan, a student of Islamic jurisprudence.

The latter inquired about the legal rulings for acting as a profession for Muslim women. He also asked about the permissibility of performing the characters of the Prophets, in general, and the Prophet Muhammad, in particular. Sa'fan explained how he had raised these questions among a group of well-read people in a social club. Some of the group members found acting permissible for Muslim women; they did not see a problem with acting in the characters of the Prophets, for they made an analogy between acting and sermons (*wa'z*). Other members prohibited acting absolutely and perceived it as a source of evil that endangered the morals of the Muslims. They further stigmatized acting as a European conspiracy intended to control uneducated Muslims and convince them that acting was imperative for modernization.[66]

Responding to the first question, Rida thought acting was a *maslaha* as long as it did not bring harm or include reprehensible practices (*munkarat*). He found the argument on the importance of women's participation in acting sensible. Still, he denied the absolute permissibility of acting for Muslim women, because he considered it inclusive of a number of reprehensible practices, which Islam required Muslim women to avoid.[67] These reprehensible practices included women appearing unveiled in front of men, hugging scenes between women and men, directly touching the skin of women, love-making scenes, and women dressed like men or vice versa.[68] Rida reasoned that acting was recommended (*mustahabb*) for Muslim women if a Muslim author wrote a story in which Muslim women did not have to show their ornaments (*zina*) or participate in any of the aforementioned reprehensible practices. One example that Rida gave was a story about the legacy of the poet al-Khansa', whom Rida praised as a role model for virtue and perfection. If such a context was created, Muslim women could act. Otherwise, Rida felt that non-Muslim women could satisfy the need for the presence of women on the stage.[69]

Commenting on the lawfulness of acting the characters of the Prophets, Rida prohibited their figural representation absolutely. He based his opinion on three reasons. The first was the *ratio legis* of degradation, which was considered a major sin (*kabira*) and a heresy (*kufr*) if proven. Rida argued that although Islam taught that the Prophets were humans, they had a higher status than other humans. To him, the human forms of Prophets were veils on the eyes of the unbelievers. While Islam did not allow the glorification of Prophets, it encouraged Muslims to dignify them without excess—that is, without violating the Islamic doctrine of the unicity of God. Acting the characters of the Prophets, Rida explained, might lead to their degradation. Examples of degradation included having actors "who belonged to lower social classes"[70] appear on the screen as Prophets. Even if the actor was of a noble origin, Rida feared that some reckless people (*khula'a*) might not shy away from using the name of the Prophet as a nickname for the actor in real life. Those reckless people might also find it funny if the actor committed a sin while acting or in daily life and might comment sarcastically, "Oh Messenger of God, send thy blessings [i.e. sins] our way" (*madad ya rasulallah*). Rida further claimed that degradation also included depicting Prophets in weak situations, such as depicting Joseph among criminals in prison or as a Bedouin being seduced by a woman.[71]

Because of the difficulty of avoiding degradation, the prohibition of figural representation of Prophets became an Islamic common practice or custom (*'urf*). One example that Rida gave of common Islamic practice during his time was a public controversy about a legal case involving a primary school teacher. The latter was accused of attempting to seduce a married woman by explicitly expressing his views on her beauty. The judge found the teacher not guilty because his words indicated nothing but thoughtfulness and courtesy. Rida described the judge as westernized. To Rida, the common Islamic practice, as expressed in newspapers and media, which he considered indicative of the view of the majority of Muslims, condemned the judge's sentence. The head of the Printing Press Administration, which was in charge of censorship, had to interfere in order to suppress criticism of the judge in the newspapers. Another example of common Islamic practice, again provided by Rida, involved rulers who did not allow dramatic representations of themselves because they feared degradation of their status. Since the Prophets were of a higher status than rulers, the prohibition on the figural representation of the Prophets was stricter. Rida cited an incident about a group of Christians in Syria. They wanted to act the story of Joseph.[72] Their news infuriated Muslims, who tried to prevent the performance by force. When the news reached the Ottoman sultan 'Abd al-Hamid al-Thani (r. 1876–8), he banned the acting of similar stories.[73]

Second, Rida prohibited acting in the characters of the Prophets because he saw acting as inclusive of lying. If lying about the Prophets occurred, the authenticity of reports about them might be harmed. Lying about the Prophet also has consequences in the afterlife. While Rida acknowledged that intentionality in lying was a condition for afterlife punishment, he cited other versions of the hadith that did not mention intentionality as a condition for punishment. Thus, the punishment included both intentional and unintentional lying regarding the Prophet. Rida further argued that even if lying was avoidable by means of writing authenticated stories, the authenticated writing could be an excuse for abusing the literature on the Prophet's life.[74] Primarily, it was not possible to represent accurate information on the lives of the Prophets by relying on Islamic sources. The Qur'an did not include complete stories, except those of Joseph and Solomon with Queen Sheba. The only story the Sunna deemed suitable for acting was that of the Prophet Muhammad. According to Rida, nobody among the 'ulama' during his lifetime had ventured to write a story for acting based on Sunna. Rida further warned that allowing that adventure to take place might lead authors who were ignorant of Sunna to forge stories to appeal to the audience, because authors prioritized financial gain and fame above everything else. He denied the possibility of tolerating lying in acting for didactic reasons, such as in Maqamat al-Hariri, in which the author made animals talk.

To Rida, thus, acting stories about Prophets was permissible only by avoiding degradation and lying, as well as abiding by the condition of dignifying the Prophets without violating the Islamic doctrine of the oneness of God. In such cases, only scholars known among Muslims for their conclusive knowledge would deliberate in order to decide if acting was a *maslaha*. Of course, Rida continued to set limitations on the permissibility of acting as a profession for Muslim women—along with the figural representation of Prophets, the Rightly Guided Caliphs, and the Companions. Rida's opinions on sanctioning photography and acting paved the way for what came to be known as Islamic acting.

4. The Rise of Islamic Acting

The term "Islamic acting" refers to the Arabic expression *al-tamthil al-Islami* advocated by the founder of the Society of Muslim Brotherhood, Hasan al-Banna. Al-Banna defined "Islamic acting" as a type of acting that was free from unrealistic romance stories that were detached from everyday life. Three major theater troupes practiced Islamic acting: the Muslim Brotherhood Troupe, the Young Muslim Men's Association (YMMA) Troupe, and the al-Azhar Troupe. The brother of Hasan al-Banna, 'Abd al-Rahman al-Banna, started the Muslim Brotherhood Troupe in the mid-1930s and adopted his brother's views on acting.[75] Al-Banna advocated the idea of acting as an open art (*al-fann al-maftuh*). That is to say; the Muslim Brotherhood Troupe welcomed actors whether or not they were Muslim Brotherhood. He also supported the notion of conservative art (*al-fann al-multazim*), art that does not lead to committing or celebrating prohibited acts. In addition, he employed the principle of "the universality of art," which considered any form of acting "Islamic" if it achieved an "Islamic" goal.[76] To support these views, he drew an analogy between poetry and acting. For example, he used hadith reports mentioning that the Prophet Muhammad did not prohibit poetry composed by non-Muslim poets, so long as the poetry did not encourage sinful desires (*fuhsh*). For instance, the Prophet reportedly commented on the poetry of Ibn al-Salt (630)[77] and stated that the latter's poetry affirmed belief in God, although the poet himself did not believe.[78] The Prophet also reportedly said, "Most truthful were the words of the poet Labid (661),[79] who used to say, 'Everything except God is void.'" Overall, al-Banna favored a tolerant approach to legal reasoning (*al-taysir*) when there was no clear precedent to limit a ruling, if the sources of law were speculative (*zanni*), or if the legal arguments for prohibition or permissibility were of equal validity.[80]

The goal of the Brotherhood Theater Troupe was missionary, that is, it primarily aimed to spread their ideology in rural areas deprived of theaters and cinemas. In the book *al-Ikhwan al-Muslimun: ahdath sana'at al-tarikh* (The Muslim Brotherhood: Events That Made History), Mahmud 'Abd al-Halim describes how, in the rural area of Fuwah, there were no institutions for entertainment such as cinemas or theaters. He saw this gap as an opportunity to spread the Muslim Brotherhood's ideology among the villagers. He wrote a few plays for this purpose, such as a play about the siege of Mecca and another on the battle of al-Qadisiyya (636).[81] These plays were performed in vernacular Arabic at a time when the majority of Egyptians were illiterate. 'Abd al-Halim decided to present his plays in colloquial Egyptian to echo the success of the vernacular theater and the rise of cinema, whose actors also spoke colloquial Egyptian. In particular, his plays addressed the widespread practice in the countryside of borrowing money with excessive interest rates.[82]

The first documented play performed by the Muslim Brotherhood Troupe presented the story of the platonic love between the Umayyad poet Jamil b. 'Abdullah b. Ma'mar b. al-'Adhri al-Quda'i (701) and his beloved Buthayna. When Buthayna's father objected to her marriage with Jamil, the latter composed some of the most famous *ghazal* poetry in Arabic literature. The play was so successful that the Egyptian Ministry of Education—through the Association for the Encouragement of Theater (est. 1934)—produced the play. Many leading Egyptian actors at the time took part in these performances. Chief among them were George Abyad, Ahmad 'Allam, 'Abbas Faris, Hasan al-Barudi, Fattuh Nushati, Mahmud al-Miligi, Fatima Rushdi, and 'Aziza Amir. 'Allam was a theater actor who is best remembered for his role as the Arab poet Qays b. al-Mulawwah in a short operetta sung by 'Abd a-Wahhab in *Yawm Sa'id*/Happy Day, 1939, directed by Muhammad Karim. Another famous role of 'Allam's is his portrayal of the feudal lord in *Rudd Qalbi*/Return My Heart, 1957, directed by 'Izz al-Din Dhu al-Faqqar, whose film remains a milestone in the history of Egyptian cinema. The movie was produced during Nasser's presidency as nationalist anti-feudal propaganda. 'Abbas Faris started his career as a theater actor in the troupe of George Abyad and worked later with Nagib al-Rihani. In cinema, Faris's career began as early as 1929, and he continued to work as a supporting actor in more than sixty films. Chief among his movies is *al-Sarab*/Mirage, 1970, directed by Anwar al-Shinnawi, an adaptation of Naguib Mahfouz's novel that carries the same title. Hasan al-Barudi acted in the troupes of Fatima Rushdi and Nagib al-Rihani. Among his most famous roles is that of the station vendor in *Bab al-Hadid*/Cairo Station, 1952. Al-Barudi also worked in the movie *Khartoum*, 1966, directed by Basil Dearden and Eliot Elisofon. Fattuh Nushati was a theater actor who participated in more than sixty plays. Mahmud al-Miligi is an icon in Egyptian popular culture; he is most famous for representing the face of evil on the screen. Fatima Rushdi is not only recognized as a producer who managed her own theater troupe; she was also celebrated as a successful theater and film actor, and is often compared to Sarah Bernhardt. One of her most famous roles is the portrayal of *al-'Azima*/Perseverance, 1939, directed by Kamal Salim 1939. 'Aziza Amir is one of the six pioneer women filmmakers. With the participation of all those actors in *Jamil Buthayna* (Jamil and Buthayna), it is hard to dismiss the success of the play.

The Muslim Brotherhood Troupe also performed the play *Bint al-Ikhshid* (The Ikhshidid's daughter), a historical play that delivered a message of tolerance between Sunni and Shiʻi Muslims.[83] Another play, *al-Muʻizz li-Dinillah* (Caliph al-Muʻizz), was performed to celebrate the one-thousandth anniversary of al-Azhar University and to commemorate the life and legacy of its founder, the Fatimid Caliph al-Muʻizz li-Dinillah (r. 953–75). The famous actor Sirag Munir directed the play, which was performed at the Royal Opera House in Cairo. Another play produced by the Muslim Brotherhood Troupe was a musical called *Suʻda* (Suʻda), which was performed by the artist Malak at the theater in her casino, known as the Malak Opera and Theater.[84] Malak was famous for demanding that Egyptian casino owners should not force female singers and dancers to sit and drink alcohol with customers.[85] This stance helps explain why a religious association like the Muslim Brotherhood tolerated its theatrical performances in her casino. In addition, the Brotherhood Troupe presented a play on the emigration of the Prophet Muhammad from Mecca to Medina and another play that commemorated the legacy of the Ayyubid Sultan Salah al-Din (Saladin, r. 1174–93).

The overall experience of the Brotherhood theater succeeded in attracting iconic actors such as ʻAbd al-Munʻim Madbuli, Sirag Munir, ʻAbd al-Badiʻ al-ʻArabi, Saʻd Ardash, Hamdi Ghayth (and his brother ʻAbdullah), and the comedian Ibrahim Saʻfan. Some of these actors were established theater and film stars, and many of them became iconic actors in Arabic theater, film, and television production. To mention but a few examples, Hamdi Ghayth's role as Richard I in masterpiece *al-Nasir Salah al-Din*/Saladin, 1963 introduced the latter into Arabic popular culture. Similarly, Gayth's brother ʻAbdullah introduced the character of Hamza, the uncle of the Prophet Muhammad, to the Arabic screen for the first time when Mustafa al-ʻAqqad, the director of *al-Risala*/The Message, 1976, had ʻAbdullah Gayth replace Anthony Quinn as Hamza in the Arabic version of the film.

Sources are unclear as to whether the Brotherhood Troupe continued its performances after al-Banna's assassination in February 1949. However, if we accept that it did, it would not have enjoyed the same level of success as before. This was due to a number of factors, chief of which was the ban on Muslim

Brotherhood activities due to the numerous assassinations that took place in Egypt at that time.[86] A second reason was that the persecution of the Muslim Brotherhood during the Nasser era that suppressed their theatrical activities. A third reason was the elegiac mode that dominated Muslim Brotherhood cultural production after al-Banna. Finally, a more conservative approach to legal reasoning was adopted by the Brotherhood in this period.[87]

Al-Azhar Theater Troupe also adopted the idea of Islamic acting. The troupe was part of Al-Azhar's initiative to reform its curriculum. A number of prominent Azhari 'ulama' used to attend theater performances. For example, the rector of al-Azhar, Mustafa al-Maraghi (1881–1945), used to go to the Opera House; he also attended premiere shows for some Egyptian movies. His successor, Mustafa Abd al-Raziq (1885–1947), was famous for his friendship with the singer and musician Muhammad 'Abd al-Wahhab (d. 1991) and the singer Umm Kulthum (d. 1974). The legal scholar 'Abd al-Jalil 'Isa talked to his students about the importance of the theater. A report in the *al-Ithnayn* magazine, the most popular variety magazine in Egypt at the time, records Azhari students rehearsing a play on the life and legacy of the Prophet's Companion Khalid b. al-Walid (d. 642). The play was performed in the Azbakiyya Garden Theater House during the anniversary of al-Azhar's founding. The students received positive comments from their teachers and professionals in the field of theater. The performance started with Qur'anic recitation. Between acts, students presented popular religious songs (*anashid*). At the end of Act II, one of the students called for the Maghrib (sunset) prayer, after which the performance resumed.[88]

The Young Muslim Men's Association (YMMA) also adopted the idea of Islamic acting. After attending a German theater production on the passion of Christ, the association's manager, Muhammad 'Uthman, was inspired to make similar plays. The chair of the YMMA at that time, former Minister of Defense Salih Harb, welcomed the idea.[89] However, he banned the participation of women in the performances. The first play presented the life story of the Prophet's Companion *Bilal*, and was written by Muhammad Yusuf al-Mahjub. In 1944, the troupe performed at the Royal Opera House in Cairo, starting with a play on the life of Khalid b. al-Walid. This play was written by Ahmad al-Sharabasi, who was then a student at al-Azhar.[90] In 1945, the YMMA performed another play to commemorate the life and legacy of the Umayyad

Figure 3.3 Students of al-Azhar on stage with director Mahmud 'Uthman. Image adapted from al-*Ithnayn* magazine.

Figure 3.4 Students from al-Azhar during rehearsals. Image adapted from *al-Ithnayn* magazine.

Figure 3.5 A student from al-Azhar reminds actors of their lines. Image adapted from *al-Ithnayn* magazine.

نخبة من أعضاء فرقة التمثيل ، يتهيأون للظهور على المسرح
وقد راحوا يراجعون الكلمات والاشارات التي تستلزمها أدوارهم

Figure 3.6 Students getting ready to appear on stage. Image adapted from *al-Ithnayn* magazine.

نخبة من شيوخ كليات الأزهر وأساتذتها ، وقد جلسوا في
«اللواوير» يرمقون طلبتهم في اعجاب وهم يؤدون أدوارهم على المسرح

Figure 3.7 Teachers at al-Azhar University attending rehearsal. Image adapted from *al-Ithnayn* magazine.

PROTECTING THE AMOUR-PROPRE OF ISLAM | 173

Figure 3.8 Students acting in the play *Khalid Ibn al-Walid*. Image adapted from *al-Ithnayn* magazine.

Figure 3.9 An Azhari student trying the piano during rehearsal. Image adapted from *al-Ithnayn* magazine.

Caliph of al-Andalus, 'Abd al-Rahman III al-Nasir (891–961). The troupe performed another play on the legacy of 'Abdullah b. al-Zubayr (d. 692), which was aired by Egyptian Radio.[91] The YMMA Theater Troupe received support from the future Prime Minister Mahmud Fahmi al-Nuqrashi, who was then the Minister of Foreign Affairs and a government consultant on artistic matters. Al-Nuqrashi influenced the association and was able to change its view on the participation of women in performances. The play *'Abd al-Rahman al-Nasir* was the first YMMA production in which women acted, and featured the notorious Zuzu Nabil. The latter, known as the Scheherazade of Egyptian Public Radio, was a theater actor who worked with Yusuf Wahbi in Ramsis Theater Troupe. She is famous for playing the roles of non-conformist female characters. She is best remembered for her role as the divorced wife of Ahmad 'Abd al-Jawwad in Hasan al-Imam's filmic adaptation of Naguib Mahfouz's *Trilogy*. The role is often credited as one of the major depictions of uneducated women challenging patriarchal norms. The YMMA Theater Troupe traveled both inside and outside Egypt; it worked in partnership with the al-Azhar troupe in two plays, *Islam Hiraql* (Heraclius becomes Muslim) and *Khalid b. al-Walid* (Khalid bin al-Walid). The troupe also teamed up with students from Dar al-'Ulum College to perform the play *al-Hadi* (The Guide). A number of YMMA plays were adapted for the cinema, such as *Bayt Allah al-Haram*/The Sacred House of God, 1957, directed by Ahmad al-Tukhi, 1957. By 1961, the total theatrical production of the YMMA numbered fourteen plays, most of which focused on Islamic history.[92]

Despite its popularity, the idea of Islamic acting faced fierce secularist and religious opposition. One example of secular opposition was that of the Egyptian socialist intellectual Salama Musa (1887–1958). Responding to the growing popularity of the Muslim Brotherhood Theater Troupe, Musa wrote an article against Islamic acting and accused the Muslim Brotherhood of promoting regressive ideas. He blamed the government for the lack of action in facing social backwardness. According to Musa, the term "regressive" referred to the Muslim Brotherhood's attempt to mix religion with politics and the association's insistence on reviving forms of governance that prevailed among Muslims in past centuries. He found the concept of "Islamic acting" dangerous because it similarly aimed to resurrect an ideal past in modern form. While he did not deny the Muslim Brotherhood its civil rights and freedom to engage in political activism, Musa saw art as a predominantly secular domain with no room for religion. He thus considered Islamic acting nothing but a propaganda tool for Islamist ideologies. Such propaganda, he argued, could easily agitate sectarian sentiments in Egypt because Coptic Christians might call for the enforcement of the laws of "enlightened Christian Europe."[93]

The following passage illustrates Musa's objection to Islamic acting:

> We read in the published program of Egyptian Radio that at 9:50 p.m., there will be a live broadcast of a play on the life of al-Mu'izz li-Din Allah. The Muslim Brotherhood Troupe will perform the play at the Royal Opera House. This news means that we are facing a governmental policy that contradicts the order of things before 1942, when [Egyptian Prime Minister] al-Nahhas shut down all offices of the Muslim Brotherhood, lest their extremism tears apart our national unity. My pen trembles in my hand at the news that our government supports the troupe. This is a dangerous sign of leniency towards fanaticism. God will punish a homeland that tolerates such fanaticism. Every day there are magazines, plays, and street protests in which Copts are insulted. What do these pessimists (*manakid*), who do not live in the twentieth century, want? I hereby accuse the Egyptian government of supporting regressive fanatics and fighting tolerant secularists.[94]

Such harsh accusations did not pass without a response. *Majallat al-Ikhwan al-Muslimin* (The Muslim Brotherhood Magazine) published a rebuttal of Musa's article. The magazine attributed its response to one honorable citizen (*muwatin sharif*) by the name of Tawfiq Ghali, a Christian merchant and school-uniform contractor. In his response, Ghali claimed to have interacted closely with the Muslim Brotherhood and found no regressive values among them. He denied Musa's claim that the Muslim Brotherhood had insulted Copts and accused him of serving an imperialist agenda.[95]

5. Traditionist Condemnation of Islamic Acting

A more vigilant opposition to Islamic acting came from proponents of traditionist jurisprudence that favored textual sources of law, particularly hadith, over methodological sources.[96] For example, 'Abdullah al-Ghumari relied selectively on the views of Rida to proscribe all forms of acting. Al-Ghumari specialized in hadith criticism.[97] In the treatise *Izalat al-iltibas 'amma waqa'a fihi kathirun min al-nas* (Eliminating the Confusion about What Commonly Occurs among People), he objects to the performance of the play *al-Dhabih* (The Sacrificed), presented by the Muslim Brotherhood Troupe in the city of Damanhur. In it, he proscribes acting and criticizes legal opinions that sanction acting based on analogy and *maslaha*.

Al-Ghumari proscribes acting by classifying it as a reprehensible innovation (*bid'a*), frivolousness (*lahw*), an accursed practice (*la'n*), and a form of lying (*kadhib*). Acting is a form of *bid'a*, according to al-Ghumari, because it is an imported European practice, which, if imitated, might lead to unbelief (*kufr*). For this opinion, he relies on a Hadith account, recorded in *Sunan Abi Dawud* and narrated on the authority of 'Abdullah b. 'Umar b. al-Khattab. The report states that a Muslim who imitates a group of people becomes one of them. Al-Ghumari also cites another hadith in *Sahih Ibn Khuzayma* to the effect that Muslims are obliged to differentiate themselves from non-Muslims. This hadith was narrated on the authority of Umm Salama, the Prophet Muhammad's wife, who reported that the Prophet used to fast on Saturdays and Sundays and reportedly said, "These [i.e. Saturdays and Sundays] are holidays for non-Muslims, and I want to differentiate myself from them."[98] He dismisses the proponents of Islamic acting as "a group of allegedly educated people, [who] claim to have knowledge of jurisprudence, and use the adjective 'Islamic' to elevate the status of reprehensible innovations like acting."[99] He continues, "How dare the Brotherhood present [the Prophets] in the same way that they present Antony and Cleopatra!"[100] He warns that allowing Islamic acting might encourage non-Muslims to act in the role of the Prophet. This might lead to hadith forgery, which can become a universal practice, thus complicating the task of traditionists.[101]

In general, al-Ghumari considers acting to be reprehensible frivolity because it includes music and singing,[102] which are associated with idle talk (*lahw al-hadith*).[103] This, he claims, is prohibited in the Qur'an (cf. Q31:6). According to al-Ghumari, Islam dictates only four proper ways for Muslims to spend their leisure time. He relies here on a hadith of lesser quality in al-Tabrani's collection. The hadith states that activities that do not include the remembrance of God (*dhikr*) are reprehensible forms of leisure, except four: taking a walk between prayer times, riding a horse, spending time with one's family, and learning how to swim.[104] Because acting requires the use of makeup to change gender or to play different roles, al-Ghumari condemns it as an accursed practice (*la'n*) that challenges the original form of creation. Islamic acting, he argues, is even more inclusive of *la'n* because actors have to play female roles to compensate for the prohibited appearance of women on stage. He further stigmatizes acting as a form of lying because he considers the representation of dead people's points of view to be lying about them.[105] Al-Ghumari was also aware that arguments for the permissibility of acting portrayed it as an extension of figural representation or *taswir*. For this reason, he cites the view of the Egyptian-born Maliki jurisprudent Ahmad al-Dardir (d. 1786), who forbids looking at all types of figural representation.

Al-Ghumari also denies the permissibility of acting on the basis of legal analogy and *maslaha*. He invalidates the analogy between acting and the metamorphosis of Gabriel, who reportedly appeared in human form to Mary and the Prophet, because an action decreed by God should not be compared to human action.[106] Al-Ghumari also denies that acting is *maslaha* because it commemorates the legacy of Muslim historical figures. He argues that since these figures did everything for God's sake, they did not expect worldly rewards in return. He suggests that their legacies can be preserved sufficiently by writing books about them. Islamic acting, he argues, is nothing but an excuse to legalize harmful and illegal practices. He compares the adherents of Islamic acting to a person who uses money earned in the lottery to help the poor. The holy purpose of helping the poor (a legal means) does not legitimize the lottery (that being an illegal end). Similarly, commemoration of the legacy of Muslim figures should not be used to support the illegal *end* of acting.[107] Al-Ghumari concludes that acting, whether Islamic or not, is not a form of *maslaha*.

It is evident from al-Ghumari's views on acting that he uses the principle of "blocking the legal means" to argue against the consideration of *maslaha* as a way of sanctioning Islamic acting. His views, however, were opposed by Azhari scholars, who rose in defense of Rida's use of *maslaha* to sanction acting positively. Chief among these was Ahmad al-Sharabasi.

6. Reformist Celebration of Islamic Acting

Ahmad al-Shirbini Jum'a al-Sharabasi was born on November 17, 1918, in the village of Bajillat in the Nile Delta of Egypt. He graduated from al-Azhar with a degree in Arabic and worked as a teacher in the Ministry of Education but soon moved to work for al-Azhar in the cities of Zagazig, Cairo, and Suhaj. In 1945, he earned his Master's degree, which gained him a position as dean of administrative affairs of the Hanafi doctrinal school. He became the chair of the censorship division in al-Azhar in 1958. The division gave legal opinions on publications and media that raised public controversy or disputes. In 1967, Al-Sharabasi defended his doctoral thesis, which he wrote on Rashid Rida and *al-Manar*. In his introduction to the book, based on his dissertation, al-Sharabasi explains that he does not intend to argue for or against Rashid Rida's views as much as he aims to provide an accurate representation of Rida's anti-colonialist stance and legal views that developed in that context. The book focuses on cultural and political transformations that shaped Rida's time, especially the advance of print capitalism. After earning his doctoral degree, al-Sharabasi was appointed an assistant professor in the College of Arabic Language at al-Azhar University. One crisis that had an immense influence on his life was his detention on April 16, 1949, following the assassination of Hasan al-Banna. He was released in September 1949. As is mentioned in his memoirs, he never knew why he was detained, for he was not a member of the Muslim Brotherhood. While detained, he encountered members of the Muslim Brotherhood, including Yusuf Tal'at. Despite the picture of al-Banna shown on the second page of al-Sharabasi's memoirs, it remains unclear whether al-Sharabasi was a member of the Muslim Brotherhood or not; nevertheless, he was clearly a sympathizer. He lamented the prosecution of the Brotherhood, but he refused its offer to give lessons in exegesis and hadith to its members.[108]

Al-Sharabasi chaired the legal opinions committee at al-Azhar and reformed its curriculum by introducing athletic activities and scouting. He produced three collections of legal opinions titled *Yas'lunak fi al-din wa-l-hayat* (Questions on Religion and Life). He also presented a series of radio programs on the proper conduct of youth in an Islamic society and on raising a family, according to Sunna. He wrote a number of plays as well, such as *Mawlid al-Rasul* (The Prophet's Birth), *Muru'at al-Abtal* (The Valor of Champions), *Mashriq al-Nur* (The Dawning of Light), *al-Hakim al-'Adil 'Umar b.' Abd al-'Aziz* (The Just Ruler 'Umar b. Abd al-'Aziz), and *'Aduw al-Salam* (The Enemy of Peace).[109] Some of these plays were adapted for film and television in the 1980s and 1990s. The greater significance of these plays lies in their heavy reliance on the Qur'an. For example, *'Aduw al-Salam* presents the Qur'anic story of creation.[110] In addition, al-Sharabasi collaborated with the scriptwriter 'Abd al-'Aziz Sallam on the movie *Khalid b. al-Walid*, 1958 directed by Husayn Sidqi. His views on acting are best illustrated by his maxim, "The religiosity of the artist and the artistry of the jurisprudent should meet halfway to serve the correct doctrine and the appropriate art."[111]

In 1947 al-Sharabasi published an article refuting al-Ghumari's prohibition of Islamic acting in the magazine of the Muslim Brotherhood, *Majallat al-Ikhwan al-Muslimin*.[112] In this piece, he argues that not every European innovation is reprehensible. Some innovations did not exist in the Prophet's time, but they later became *maslaha* on the basis of either necessity or need. So long as these innovations introduced a benefit or eliminated harm, Muslims should make use of them, regardless of the inventor's identity. And acting is no exception. Al-Sharabasi argued that acting, in general, is better than other harmful and useless sources of entrainment, such as going to casinos or brothels.[113] For example, a professionally-performed play depicting Islamic history can more efficiently deliver the message of Islam than an archaic sermon (*khutba*).[114] To make a contrast between acting and lying, al-Sharabasi draws an analogy between acting and a sermon in which the preacher reenacts the final sermon of the Prophet Muhammad (*khutbat al-wada'*): "Does the preacher lie about the Prophet, because the Prophet recited the sermon in the past, while the preacher is reenacting the same sermon in Egypt or Khartoum?"[115] The proponents of Islamic acting, al-Sharabasi argues, are keen to present only authenticated information about Islamic history. He thus questions the reasonableness of al-Ghumari's claim that only books can be used to commemorate the greatness of Islam. Al-Sharabasi argues that if Muslims are not permitted to use any communications medium to record history other than books, why should they build mosques, practice preaching, or listen to preachers, radio, and lectures?

He further argues that the linguistic reality of Arabic diglossia in Egypt makes it difficult for people to understand books written in standard Arabic. A play, on the other hand, with its audiovisual effects, is more accessible to the public, who understand the colloquial language. A play is thus a more influential communications medium than a book for commemorating the greatness of Islam.[116] The goal of acting out the stories of Muslim leaders, al-Sharabasi explains, is not to boast about their deeds; rather, Islamic acting aims to present these figures as models for Muslims to follow.[117] He denies that acting is an accursed practice and argues that the prohibited change of form, to which the hadith that al-Ghumari cites refers, is not the kind of temporary change required in acting. He explains that the type of change that is subject to cursing relates only to a permanent change in the original form of creation.[118] While the use of *maslaha* enabled al-Sharabasi to contest al-Ghumari's treatise and reestablish Islamic acting, his invocation of *maslaha* was limited only to acting in theatrical performances. This is because he initially considered the filmic medium to be an extension of flat depictions, which involve the emulation of the Creator, thus violating the Islamic doctrine of the oneness of God. Therefore, al-Sharabasi, contrary to Rashid Rida, used the principle of "blocking the legal means" to exclude film from *maslaha*.[119]

7. The *Maslaha* of Film Production

The first official fatwa on the lawfulness of cinema appeared to be issued in 1950, in response to the film *Zuhur al-Islam* (The Dawn of Islam, directed by Ibrahim 'Izz al-Din, 1951).[120] The film director asked about the permissibility of depicting the character of the Prophet Muhammad in a movie commemorating the story of Islam based on Taha Husayn's book *Al-Wa'd al-Haqq* (The True Promise). Reproduced below is a translation of the fatwa given by the Grand Mufti of Egypt, Hasanayn Makhluf:

> Question: What is the legal ruling (*hukm*) regarding the screen adaptation of the book titled *Al-Wa'd al-Haqq*?
> Answer: We have had a chance to investigate a summary of the themes dealt with in the screen adaption of the well-known book, *Al-Wa'd al-Haqq*. We understand that you [i.e. the director] intend to direct the movie without the depiction of the Prophet, his Companions, or the Rightly Guided Caliphs. In other words, there will be no representation of their figures or voices. If this is the case, Islamic law does not prevent the direction of the movie. Rather, producing this film will spread the cause of truth and will raise the awareness [of people] to adhere to truth, especially during these times in which people are in need of Islam. While deliberating to provide this fatwa, I read the book of Professor Taha Husayn, and

Figure 3.10 Poster showing the actor Ahmad Mazhar in the movie *Zuhur al-Islam*. Image adapted from *al-Ithnayn* magazine.

> I found it truly miraculous in its creativity, depiction, style, and expression. I ask God to guide the author in directing other stories to delineate the truth and guide the people. Therefore, we encourage you to produce the movie. May God guide and reward you in what you intend to do.[121]

Makhluf is most famous for his contributions to legal reform with regard to child custody. In 1944, he was appointed vice-president of the Supreme Court of Islamic Law. Two years later, he became the grand mufti of Egypt (1946–50). He wrote over twenty books on exegesis, treatment of animals in Islam, inheritance, and criticism of hadith, among many other topics.[122]

There was no consensus, however, on the permissibility of cinema as *maslaha*. Al-Sharabasi initially made a distinction between acting and cinema. While he was a strong proponent of theater and wrote a number of plays, he initially saw no benefit in cinema as its content was made up mostly of European romance films.[123] Once, when he was asked about the permissibility of cinema, he exclaimed, "No! No! I do not write romance stories. I am a married man, and I have children."¹²⁴ Al-Sharabasi's reaction shows that he understood the term "cinema" mainly as a signifier for obscene stories that were meant to arouse sinful desires and falsify human aspirations. For this reason, he considered cinema to be a reprehensible form of leisure. Yet later he sanctioned cinema in the context of the debate over the permissibility of *taswir*, for the filmic image did not fall under prohibited forms of *taswir* because the *ratio legis* of emulating the Creator ceases to exist in the case of photography as opposed to painting. Al-Sharabasi joined Makhluf in sanctioning cinematic production as a form of *maslaha* on the basis of its usefulness for discussing life problems and contemplating human error.¹²⁵ He argued that film could be used to serve religion, morality, and nationalist causes. He encouraged filmmakers and jurisprudents to communicate with each other in order to increase the quality of cinematic art and emphasize the role of Islamic values and principles in acting, whether in theater or in film.¹²⁶

Without reliance on *maslaha*, more tolerant legal views that permitted acting as a profession for Muslim women existed. Consider, for example, the opinion of Mahmud Abu al-'Uyun in this regard. Abu al-'Uyun graduated from al-Azhar in 1908. He developed an anti-colonialist stance in 1912 in the wake of the Tripolitania war fought between the Ottoman Empire and the Kingdom of Italy. Abu al-'Uyun marched in and led one of al-Azhar's demonstrations during the 1919 revolution and was arrested. As a jurisprudent, he was most famous for leading media campaigns against prostitution. He fought to cancel the decree issued under Cromer by the Ministry of the Interior in 1896 to legalize prostitution. Abu al-'Uyun was known for being outspoken and confrontational with public officials. On one occasion, a police officer did not recognize him and hit his turban so it fell to the ground. He wrote a petition to the Prime Minister announcing that the Azhari turban was more honorable and important than the Prime Minister's tarbush, after which the Prime Minister, by then al-Nuqrashi, apologized to him. In the following interview, Abu al-'Uyun prohibited dancing, especially European forms, but he explicitly permitted singing and acting as professions for Muslim women:

Question: What do you think of the singing of Umm Kulthum?
Answer: She is a modest woman, and there is no harm in listening to her beautiful voice.

Q: Among the singers whose voice do you like?

A: Umm Kulthum comes first. After that comes Layla Murad, who has a very affectionate voice. I also like Asmahan, for her voice is very nostalgic. Among male singers, I like the voice of Salih 'Abd al-Hayy. As for 'Abd al-Wahhab, I do not like his singing, which lacks the valor of manhood.

Q: Why do you fight Western dance?

A: Because it is worse than the local dance, with all its movements and the way hands surround waists or the way bodies touch other bodies. This kind of dance is indeed a step outside the domain of religiosity and modesty. It kills audacity and manhood. A wife can dance with her husband at home.

Q: What do you think of women becoming actors?

A: There is no harm in that as long as the acting is modest and as long as it is intended for education and calls for morality. However, kissing and the likes of these issues should be avoided. These are sinful practices. I came to know that they opened a college for acting in 1931, where gender mixed in classrooms and there were other activities that morality does not tolerate. I visited the college and saw Ma'am Munira Sabri, who teaches dancing. As soon as I objected to the idea, I found that she and her students were in tears because of my views. I then attacked the college in newspapers. The Minister of Education at that time was Murad pasha Sayyid. He was outraged at my views. However, he resigned, and his successor, Hilmi 'Isa pasha, shut down the college.[127]

In the above interview, Abu al-'Uyun did not classify singing as reprehensible leisure, and he explicitly stated that acting was a permissible profession for women. While he put a limitation on some of the content depicted, his statement on acting has remained one of the most explicit and straightforward statements on the lawfulness of acting as a profession for women up until today.

While *maslaha* was used to sanction film, it also placed many limitations on the content depicted. Both the reformist al-Sharabasi and the traditionist al-Ghumari used the legal principle of "blocking the legal means" to limit the use of *maslaha*, thus making it function as a covert form of censorship.

Maslaha also fails to break the consensus against the *taswir* of the Prophets. This limitation led to covert censorship, which resulted in certain cases of self-censorship. For example, it caused Yusuf Wahbi to abandon his dream of acting in the role of the Prophet in 1926. Hasan al-Banna did the same when he suspended the production of the play *al-Dhabih*. In addition to the movie *Zuhur al-Islam*, Egyptian cinema produced numerous movies on the emergence of Islam, chief of which are Fu'ad al-Gajayrli's *Fath Misr*/Conquest of Egypt, 1948,[128] Niyazi Mustafa's *Min 'Udhama'a al-Islam*/Patriots of Islam, 1970, Ahmad al-Tukhi's *Intisar al-Islam*/Islam Triumphs, 1952, Ibrahim 'Imara's *Hijarat al-Rasul*/The Hijra, 1964, and Husam al-Din Mustafa's

Figure 3.11 A scene from the movie *Fath Misr*/Conquest of Egypt, 1948?, directed by Fu'ad al-Gazayirili. Mansi Fahmi appears as al-Muqawqis, who is mentioned in Islamic history as a ruler of Egypt who corresponded with the Prophet. He is often identified with Cyrus, the Patriarch of Alexandria, who administered Egypt on behalf of the Christian Byzantine Empire. Image adapted from *Akhir Sa'a*.

al-Shayma'/Shayma 1972, although the Prophet Muhammad and many of his companions were not the subjects of these films. Even a multinational production film like Musatfa al-'Aqqad's *al-Risala*/The Message, 1976 faced censorship that *maslaha* could not break.

In addition, the concept of *maslaha* did not solve the problem of the permissibility of acting by women. However, Egyptian women became film and theater stars. While some were non-Muslims, many were Muslims, and their participation is still criticized in public media as anti-Islamic even today. The withdrawal of many female stars, including Shadiya and Shams al-Barudi, from acting is a symptom of the unresolved problem of acting as a profession for Muslim women.[129] Limiting the *maslaha* of film production to cases of necessity and social utility falls short of addressing the value of film as an artistic experience. As an art form, it is not possible to subject film to conventional linguistic, ethical, philosophical, or religious standards. Art, like science, improves knowledge by introducing new knowledge.[130] Both art and science involve a continuous process of development that bases itself on transcending current standards by reevaluating them critically and introducing new standards. In both fields, this process demands freedom of creative practice and experimentation, which are closely connected with broader reform efforts that should include big Islamic institutions like al-Azhar. And these efforts should extend beyond the scope of form. Otherwise, covert censorship will continue to persist.

Notes

1. See Yusuf Wahbi, *'Ishtu alf 'am: Mudhakkirat fannan al-sha'b Yusuf Wahbi*, 5 vols. (Cairo: Dar al-Ma'arif, 1973), 3:75.
2. "'Ala masrah al-fann: Fi al-nihaya," *Al-Masrah*, May 27, 1926.
3. 'Abd al-Baqi Surur, "Kayfa yusawwirun al-Nabi?," *Al-Ahram*, May 21, 1926.
4. Ayman al-Hakim, *Al-fann al-haram: Tarikh al-ishtibak bayn al-salafiyyin wa-l-mubdi'in* (Cairo: Dar Kitabat, 2012), 8–29.
5. Wahbi, *'Ishtu alf 'am*, 3:75.
6. Yusuf Wahbi, "Khitab maftuh li-l-'ulama'," *Al-Ahram*, May 24, 1926.
7. See Wahbi, *'Ishtu alf 'am*, 1976, 3:72. The Marcos Film Company had initially nominated many famous actors for the role, including the German actors Emil Janings (1884–1950) and Conrad Vidt (1893–1943), the Canadian actor

Matieson A. Lang (1879–1948), the Italian actor Carlo Ninghi (1896–1974), and the French actor Edouard Alexandre Max, known as De Max (1869–1924). However, the Turkish filmmaker Widad 'Urfi selected Wahbi.

8. "Al-Nabi Muhammad kayf yusawwirunah: Nihayat al-niza'," *Al-Masrah*, May 31, 1926. *Al-Masrah* published three photographs of Wahbi wearing a short beard, a white gown, and a white turban. A caption under one of the photos states that it was taken for casting, as Wahbi was preparing for the role of the Prophet. I compared two of the photos published in *al-Masrah* with an almost identical photo of Wahbi in his memoirs. It appears to me that the two photos published in the magazine are of Wahbi as the Amazigh freedom movement leader 'Abd al-Karim al-Khattabi. Wahbi played the role of al-Khattabi in the anti-imperialist play *al-Isti'bad* (Enslavement), which was performed after the assassination of Sir Lee Stack on November 19, 1924. The play was censored at the end of Sa'd Zaghlul's term as Prime Minister on November 24, 1924. The third photo might be of Wahbi as the Prophet Muhammad. Although Wahbi appears to be wearing the same turban in the four photos, his makeup differs in the third photo published in *al-Masrah*. The makeup artist made his eye makeup appear more intense. It is often reported that the Prophet used kuhl. In addition, the angle of light in the photo renders the face fairer, conferring an aura of holiness.
9. *Al-Ahram*, May 24, 1926.
10. *Al-Ahram*, May 26, 1926.
11. Wahbi, *'Ishtu alf 'am*, 3:76.
12. Art historians argue that the prohibition found in hadith could not have had an impact on the early Muslim community, because canonical hadith collections appear only in the ninth century. The earliest extant evidences of *taswir* in Islam are the images in Qusayr 'Amra (in present-day Jordan), which date to the reign of the Umayyad Caliph Yazid b. 'Abd al-Malik (720–4). Some argue that some Christians prohibited icons during the formative period of Islam, a proscription that influenced the early Muslim community and might explain the lack of evidence concerning *taswir* during the Prophet's lifetime. The famous Christian iconoclastic movement coincided with the rise of Islam. Others argue that *taswir* flourished during the Prophet's lifetime. They rely on a report in *Akhbar Makka*, attributed to the Meccan historian al-Azraqi (d. 864?), stating that when the Prophet entered the Ka'ba after the opening of Mecca (*fath Makka*) he destroyed all the idols inside the Ka'ba except for a picture of Mary and Jesus. Art historians agree that, although an ideologi-

cal reaction against Byzantine doctrinal art grew during the Umayyad period, *taswir* continued to be practiced until the thirteenth century, when al-Qarafi (683/1285) practiced sculpting. For details see: Thomas Arnold, *Painting in Islam: A Study of the Place of Pictorial Art in Muslim Culture* (New York: Dover, 1965); Anna Contadini, *Arab Painting: Text and Image in Illustrated Arabic Manuscripts* (Leiden: Brill, 2007); K. A. Creswell, "The Lawfulness of Painting in Early Islam," *Ars Islamica* 11 (1946):159–66;Top of FormBottom of Form Patricia Crone, "Islam, Judeo-Christianity and Byzantine Iconoclasm," *Jerusalem Studies in Arabic and Islam* 2 (1980): 59–95; Richard Ettinghausen, *Arab Painting* (New York: Rizolli, [1962] 1977); Marshall G. S. Hodgson, "Islam and Image," *History of Religions* 3, no. 2 (1964): 220–60; G. R. D. King, "Islam, Iconoclasm, and the Declaration of Doctrine," *Bulletin of the School of Oriental and African Studies*, University of London 48, no. 2 (1985): 267–77; W. J. T. Mitchell, *Iconology: Image, Text, and Ideology* (Chicago, IL: University of Chicago Press, 1986); Daniel Sahas, *Icon and Logos: Sources in Eighth Century Iconoclasm* (Toronto: University of Toronto Press, 1986); Christian C. Sahner, "The First Iconoclasm in Islam: A New History of the Edict of Yazid II (AH 104/ AD 723)," *Der Islam* 94, no. 1 (2017): 5–56; Edward James Martin, *A History of the Iconoclastic Controversy* (Milan: Mimesis, 2014); Patricia Crone, "Islam Judeo-Christianity and Byzantine Iconoclasm," *From Kavad to al-Ghazalī: Religion, Law and Political Thought in the Near East, c.600–c.1100* (Aldershot: Ashgate), 63; Tharwat 'Ukasha, *Mawsu'at al-taswir al-Islami* (Beirut: Maktabat Lubnan Nashirun, 1999), 1–20.

13. See, for example, Qur'an 3:6, 7:11, 40:64, and 64:3.
14. Rashid Rida, "Fatawa *al-Manar*: Hukm al-taswir wa-ittikhadh al-suwar," *al-Manar*, 20 vols. (Cairo: Matba'at al-Manar, 1918), 5: 220–35.
15. According to G. H. A. Juynboll, *mashhur* is a technical term used in the science of hadith for a well-known tradition transmitted via a minimum of three different chains of transmissions (*isnads*). See *EI2*, s.v. "Mashhur."
16. Muhammad 'Abd al-Latif al-Fahham, "Bab al-as'ila wa-l-fatawa: Al-taswir wa-l-suwar," *Al-Azhar*, ed. Muhammad Farid Wajdi, 29 vols. (Cairo: Matba'at al-Azhar, 1940), 11: 163–5.
17. Ibid. Abu Sulayman al-Khattabi distinguished between the depiction of entities with and without soul (*ruh*). He considered the depiction of an entity with soul to be of the same genus (*jins*) as (i.e. identical with) an idol. On al-Khattabi, see Jalal al-Din 'Abd al-Rahman al-Suyuti and Muhammad Ibrahim, *Bughyat al-wu'at fi tabaqat al-lughawiyyin wa-l-nuhat* (Beirut: Dar al-Fikr, 1979), 546–7.

See also Shams al-Din al-Dhahabi, *Kitab tadhkirat al-huffaz*, 4 vols. (Beirut: Dar al-Kutub al-'ilmiyya, [1955] 1998), 3: 1018–19.
18. 'Abd al-Rahman al-Jaziri, "Al-Sunna: Al-taswir wa-ittkhadh al-masajid 'ala al-qubur fi nazr al-Islam," *Al-Azhar*, ed. Muhammad Farid Wajdi, 29 vols. (Cairo: Matba'at al-Azhar, 1941), 12: 328–38.
19. It is reported that 'Aisha had a curtain with images and that the images prevented angels from entering her house. See Muslim b. al-Hajjaj, *Sahih Muslim bi-sharh al-Nawawi*, 18 vols. (Cairo: al-Matba'a al-Misriyya bi-l-Azhar, 1929), 14: 81–92.
20. Ibid.
21. Rashid Rida, *Tarikh al-ustadh al-imam al-shaykh Muhammad 'Abduh: Wa-fihi tafsil siratihi wa-khulasat sirat munqidh al-sharq al-hakim wa-l-Islam Jamal al-Din al-Afghani*, 2 vols. (Egypt: Matba'at al-Manar, 1906), 2: 498–501.
22. Samir Subhi, "Al-shaykh Wafi awwal rassam fi al-Ahram," *Al-Ahram*, August 13, 2001. Wafi earned a degree from the School of Fine Arts in Cairo, where he studied with famous Egyptian artists including Ahmad Sabri and Husayn Bikar. At *al-Ahram*, Wafi painted many public figures including Salim and Bishara Taqla, the owners and founders of the newspaper. He also painted portraits of the national leader Sa'd Zaghlul, the rector of al-Azhar 'Abd al-Majid Salim, Taha Husayn, and members of the Free Officers movement such as Nasser, Sadat, Kamal al-Din Husayn, 'Abd al-Latif al-Baghdadi, Salah Salim, and Husayn al-Shafi'i. He founded the Art Association of Wikalat al-Ghawriyya or al-Ghawriyya—the Egyptian colloquial form of al-Ghawriyya, referring to al-Sultan al-Ghawri (r. 1501–16). He painted an enormous portrait of the leader of the 'Urabi revolt, Ahmad 'Urabi. The painting is in the Urabi museum in the Sharqiyya governorate in the Nile Delta.
23. For example, in the *al-Bayt Baytuk* [*Baytak*] show—produced by Egyptian National Television and aired on Channel 1 in June 2009—Egypt's grand mufti, 'Ali Jum'a, stressed that 'Abduh's argument on *taswir* should be treated as a personal opinion (*ra'y*), not a fatwa. Jum'a's comments occurred in the context of a heated debate with the Egyptian secularist intellectual and poet Ahmad 'Abd al-Mu'ti Hijazi, who criticized the lax attitude of al-Azhar toward the growing religious fanaticism in Egyptian society.
24. In this case, *ra'y* is used negatively. *Ra'y* had a broadly positive connotation until the mid- or late eighth century CE. After this time, *ra'y* was invoked in the context of adherence to a body of theological doctrine of *ahl al-ra'y* vis-à-vis *ahl al-hadith*, i.e. adherents of reason versus the adherents of textual sources.

Every subsequent *ra'y* is a negative evaluation, namely an opinion that is not based on authoritative textual sources. See Ahmad Hasan, "Early Modes of Ijtihad: *Ra'y*, *Qiyas* and *Istihsan*," *Islamic Studies* 6 (1967): 47–79.

25. It is not clear when "*taswir*" started to denote "photography," but the origin of the *camera obscura* has been traced back to the Basra-born polymath al-Hasan Ibn al-Haytham (965–1040), who identified the laws of refraction and produced accurate anatomical descriptions of the eye. The daguerreotype equipment was introduced in Egypt as early as 1839 at the hands of three French painters, Horace Vernet, his student Fredric Goupil Fequest, and the Swiss-Canadian Pierre-Gustav Joly de Lotbinière. According to Golia, Colonel Muhammad Sadiq bey was the first Egyptian Muslim to practice photography. He studied photography in France, where he received an engineering degree from the Paris École Polytechnique. In 1862, he used a wet-collodion plate camera to record his pilgrimage journey, producing the earliest photographic images on record of Medina. During his first journey he spent five days in Medina, where he photographed the Prophet's mosque and tomb. He also improvised a panorama of the town. His made a second trip to Mecca in September 1880 and photographed the pilgrim camps as well as the circumambulations around the Ka'ba. He befriended 'Umar al-Shaybani, the guardian of the key of the Ka'ba, who sat for a portrait. In the same year, Sadiq attended an assembly of the Khedival Geographic Society, at which he met and described his journey to Richard Burton.

26. See Abdul 'Aziz Bin Sattam, *Shari'a and the Concept of Benefit* (London: I. B. Tauris, 2015), 3.

27. On what is considered a necessity, see Birgit Krawietz, "*Darura* in Modern Islamic Law: The Case of Organ Transplantation," *Islamic Law, Theory and Practice*, ed. R. Gleave and E. Kermeli (London: I. B. Tauris, 1997), 185–93.

28. See Felicitas Opwis, "Islamic Law and Legal Change: The Concept of *Maslaha* in Classical and Contemporary Islamic Legal Theory," *Shari'a: Islamic law in the Contemporary Context*, ed. Abbas Amanat and Frank Griffel (Stanford, CA: Stanford University Press, 2007), 66–7.

29. See Opwis, "Islamic Law and Legal Change," 2007, 68.

30. As a legal term, *dalil* is usually used to refer to types of evidences. The first type is called certain (*qat'i*), which includes textual evidence from the Qur'an, the Sunna transmitted with an uninterrupted chain of transmission, and a definite consensus. The other type is called probable (*zanni*), which includes but is not limited to hadith with interrupted chain of transmission.

31. Ibid.
32. See Opwis, "Islamic Law and Legal Change," 69.
33. See Muhammad Khalid Mas'ud, "Shatibi's Theory of Meaning," *Islamic Studies* 32 (1993): 5–16.
34. See Opwis, "Islamic Law and Legal Change," 69.
35. Ibid.
36. Ibid.
37. Opwis, *Maslaha*, 324.
38. As a legal term *asl* refers to the textual source of law such as the Qur'an and Sunna; it refers to "the base" of a legal analogy and to a legal principle based on necessity.
39. See Noel J. Coulson, *A History of Islamic Law* (Edinburgh: Edinburgh University Press, 1964), 141. See also *Encyclopedia of Islam Second Edition Online*, s.v. "Sadd al-dhara'i'." The third category was based on the intention of the person rather than the possible outcome. Due to the significance of the intention, jurisprudents from the four doctrinal legal schools vary in how often they refer to *sadd al-dhara'i'*, with the Hanbali and Maliki schools referring to it most frequently. This was caused by their different methodology in establishing the intention of a person. While al-Shafi'i was reluctant to formulate a ruling based on showing the circumstances proving intention, the Hanafi, Maliki, and Hanbali schools referred to the circumstances to find the proof.
40. See Felicitas Opwis, "*Maslaha* in Contemporary Legal Theory," *Islamic Law and Society* 12, no. 2 (2005): 182–223.
41. See Opwis, "Islamic Law and Legal Change," 71–2.
42. See Felicitas Opwis, "Changes in Modern Islamic Legal Theory: Reform or Reformation?" *An Islamic Reformation?* ed. Michaelle Browers and Charles Kurzman (Lanham, MD: Lexington Books, 2004), 33–4.
43. See Opwis, "Islamic Law and Legal Change," 68.
44. Rida, "Fatawa *al-Manar*," 5: 220–35.
45. See *EI2*, s.v. "Hadith." *Athar* usually refers to traditions from Companions or Successors, but the word is sometimes used to refer to traditions from the Prophet. *Athar* should not be mistaken for a hadith.
46. This game seems to be similar to the children's game hopscotch. According to traditional rules, images might be drawn in the rectangles.
47. His death date is not known. He narrated on the authority of 'Umar. Ibn Sa'd considers him trustworthy (*thiqa*). See Muhammad b. Sa'd, *Kitab al-Tabaqat al-Kabir*, 11 vols. (Cairo: Maktabat al-Khanji, 2001), 8: 266.

48. Rida here relied on the views of the historian, judge, and scholar of hadith al-Hafiz Ibn Hibban al-Busti (d. 965).
49. The word *banat* refers to dolls. See *Lisan al-'Arab*, s.v. "*b-n-i*."
50. The hadith appears in *Fath al-Bari*, a commentary on *Sahih al-*Bukhari by Ibn Hajar al-'Asqalani (d. 852/1449).
51. Rida, "Fatawa *al-Manar*," 5: 220–35.
52. Ibn Sa'd, *Kitab al-Tabaqat al-Kabir*, 8: 342. Ibn Sa'd mentions that al-Usdi narrated on the authority of 'Ali b. Abi Talib. This hadith gained widespread circulation because of its reference to 'Ali, whose mention in the hadith allows for a fundamental condemnation of the Shi'a practice of commemorating the legacy of 'Ali and his family by building mosques over their graves.
53. Rashid Rida, "Fatawa *al-Manar*: Hukm al-taswir wa-ittikhadh al-suwar," *Al-Manar*, 20 vols. (Cairo: Matba'at al-Manar, 1918), 6: 270–6.
54. Rida, "Fatawa *al-Manar*: Hukm al-taswir wa-ittikhadh al-suwar," 6: 270–6.
55. Al-Fahham attended Azhar High school in Alexandria and was influenced by the reformist views of Mahmud Shaltut (1893–1963). He graduated from al-Azhar in 1922 and was appointed to al-Azhar High School in Alexandria to teach hadith, Arabic linguistics, and mathematics. In 1935, he received a job offer to work in the College of Islamic Law where he taught logic and hermeneutics. While working there, he received a scholarship to earn a PhD at the Sorbonne in France, to which he traveled in 1936. While in France, he studied at Alliance Française School. The outbreak of World War II interrupted his study plans in Paris and forced him to leave Paris for Bordeaux. Two months after the end of World War II, specifically on July 1, 1945, he received his PhD from the Sorbonne with distinction. His thesis was on Arabic lexicography, focusing on compiling an Arabic–French dictionary, which dealt primarily with Arabic linguistic terminology. He returned to Egypt in 1946 to join the College of Islamic Law and College of Arabic Language, where he taught comparative literature, grammar, and morphology. In 1967, he was appointed a rector of al-Azhar, during which time he was able to stabilize the institution following the 1967 *naksa*. His intellectual contribution was primarily in the fields of logic and Arabic grammar.
56. See Khayr al-Din al Zirikli *al-A'lam, Qamus Tarajim li-Ashhar al-Rijal wa-al-Nisa' min al-'Arab wa-al-Musta'ribin wa-al-Mustashriqin*, Vol. 6 (Beirut: Dar al-'Ilm lil-Malayin), 218; 'Alam Mahdi, *al-Majma'iyyun fi Khamsin 'Amn* (Cairo: al-Hay'a al-'Amma li-Shu'un al-Matabi' al-Amiriya, 1986); 'Ali 'Abd al-'Azim, *Mashyakhat al-Azhar Mundhu Insha'iha hatta al-An* (Cairo: al-Hay'a

al-'Ama li-Shi'un al-Matabi' al-Amiriyya, 1978); Muhammad Khafaji, *Al-Azhar fi Alf 'Am*, Vol.1 (Cairo: Maktabat al-Kulliyat al-Azhariyya, 1988), 351.

57. Muhammad 'Abd al-Latif al-Fahham, "Bab al-As'ila wa al-Fatawa: al-Taswir wa al-Suwar," *Majallat al-Azhar*, Vol. 11, Part 2, ed. Muhammad Farid Wajdi (Cairo: Al-Azhar Printing Press, 1940), 163–5.

58. A grade of *hadith* in which a tradition has more than two transmitters, some being *Sahih* and others not. See Robson, *EI2*.

59. Fahham, "Bab," 163–5.

60. See Hisham Ibn al-Kalbi, *The Book of Idols Being a Translation from the Arabic of Kitab al-Asnam*, trans. Nabith Amin Faris (Princeton, NJ: Princeton University Press), 2016.

61. 'Abd al-Rahman al-Jiziri, "*al-Sunna: al-Taswir wa Itkhadh al-Masajid 'ala al-Qubur fi Nazr al-Islam*," ed. Muhammad Farid Wajdi *Majallat al-Azhar*, Vol. 12 (Cairo: Matba 'at al-Azhar, 1941): 328–38.

62. He was born in 1882, the same year that witnessed the British occupation of Egypt. He grew up in Jazirat Shandul, a village near the city of Suhaj in Upper Egypt. He graduated from al-Azhar and specialized in Hanafi *madhahab*. He began his career as supervisor in the division of mosques at the Egyptian Ministry of Waqf. During his time in this post, he accepted responsibility for improving the quality of preaching and the qualifications of preachers. For example, he encouraged preachers to master the art of rhetoric and to discuss topics affecting everyday life instead of focusing on capital punishments. When he retired from this post, he was offered a lectureship at the College of the Fundamentals of Religion. Al-Jaziri's intellectual production focused on the field of *usul al-fiqh*. He co-authored a book titled *Al-Fiqh 'ala al-Madhahib al-Arba'a* and wrote a book on the cult of *tawhid* (the unicity of God) titled *Tawdih al-'Aqa'id*, as well as a book on the proofs of certainty titled *Adillat al-Yaqin*. He wrote systematically in the al-Azhar monthly periodical known as *Mijallat al-Azhar*.

63. Two of the Prophet's wives. For details on their biographies see Muhhammad b.'Asakir and Ghazwah Budayr, *Kitab Al-Arba'in fi Manaqib Ummahat al-Mu'minin* (Dimashq: Dar al-Fikr, 1986).

64. Muhammad b. Hibban b. Ahmad b. Hibban was a transmitter, a compiler, and a critic of hadith. He wrote a book on weak transmitters and a collection of sound hadith known as Sahih Ibn Hibban.

65. Rashid Rida, "Fatawa *al-Manar*: al-tamthil al-'Arabi, ishtighal al-mar'a al-muslima bi-hi wa-tamthil qasas al-anbiya'," *al-Manar*, 20 vols (Cairo: Matba'at al-Manar, 1918) 6: 310–15.

66. Ibid.

67. Ibid.
68. This argument is based on the legal process of *sadd al-dhara'i'*.
69. Rashid Rida, "Fatawa *al-Manar*: al-tamthil," 6: 310–15.
70. Ibid.
71. Ibid.
72. It is not clear to whom he refers.
73. Rashid Rida, "Fatawa *al-Manar*: al-tamthil," 6: 310–15.
74. Ibid.
75. 'Isam Talima, *Hasan al-Banna wa-tajribat al-fann* (Cairo: Maktabat Wahba, 2008), p. 10.
76. Talima, *Hasan*, 67.
77. Bahjat 'Abd al-Ghafur Hadithi, *Umayya b. Abi al-Salt: hayatuh wa-shi'ruh* (Baghdad: Wizarat al-I'lam, 1975).
78. The hadith, narrated on the authority of Ibn 'Abbas, appears in Muhammad b. Ishaq al-Fakihi and 'Abd al-Malik b. 'Abdullah b. Duhaysh, *Akhbar Makka fi qadim al-dahr wa-hadithih* (Beirut: Dar Khiḍr, 1994), 203. See also Ibn Hajar al-'Asqlani, *Kitab al-isaba fi tamyiz al-sahaba* (Cairo: Markaz al-Buhuth wa-l-Dirasat al-Islamiyya, 2008), 251.
79. William Milligan Sloane, *The Poet Labid* (Leipzig: Breitkopf & Haertel, 1877), and Labid b. Rabi'a, *Diwan Labid b. Rabi'a al 'Amri*, trans. Arthur Wormhoudt (Oskaloosa, IA: William Penn College, 1976).
80. Talima, *Hasan*, 10.
81. Al-Qadisiyya was a fortification on the edge of the Syrian Desert. After this battle, Arab Muslims took control of Persia. Salah Abu Sayf depicted the battle in his film *al-Qadisiyya*, released in 1981.
82. Talima, *Hasan*, 12.
83. *Majallat al-nadhir*, no. 18, 1939.
84. *Majallat al-ikhwan al-Muslimin al-nisf shahriyya*, no. 5, October 24, 1942.
85. *Majallat al-dunya al-musawwara*, no. 4, June 12, 1929.
86. Richard P. Mitchell, *The Society of the Muslim Brotherhood* (Oxford: Oxford University Press, 1996), 68–9.
87. Talima, *Hasan*, 12–14.
88. *Al-Ithnayn*, no. 774, April 11, 1951.
89. He was the Egyptian commander-in-chief (1939–40). Muhammad Salih Harb, Ahmad Hasan Muhammad Kinani, and Ahmad Zakariyya al-Shalaq, *Dhikrayat al-liwa' Muhammad Salih Harb* (Cairo: Al-Hay'a al-'Amma li-Qusur al-Thaqafa, 2009).
90. I discuss al-Sharabasi's efforts to sanction acting in more detail below.

91. Talima, *Hasan*, 34.
92. Talima, *Hasan*, 36.
93. Talima, *Hasan*, 36–9.
94. Ibid.
95. *Majallat al-ikhwan al-Muslimin al-nisf shahriyya*, no. 103, May 25, 1945.
96. See Christopher Melchert, "Traditionist-Jurisprudents and the Framing of Islamic Law," *Islamic Law and Society* 8, no. 3 (2001): 383–406.
97. Abu al-Fadl 'Abdullah Muhammad b. al-Siddiq al-Hasani al-Ghumari al-Tanji (1910–93) was born and raised in Morocco. He traveled to Egypt to study at al-Azhar in the 1930s. Chief among al-Ghumari's works are *Bida' al-tafasir* (Reprehensible Innovation in Qur'anic Exegesis) and *al-Rasa'il al-Ghumariyya* (The Ghumari Treatises). His elder brother, Abu al-Fayd Ahmad al-Ghumari, specialized in hadith criticism. Abu al-Fayd traveled to Egypt in 1921 to study at al-Azhar, and again in 1923 to attend the Caliphate Conference in Cairo. Abu al-Fadl is famous for his debates with his fellow hadith traditionist, Muhammad Nasr al-Din al-Albani. Despite Abu al-Fadl's attestation to al-Albani's knowledge of hadith, the debate became personal and involved character attacks. The two brothers wrote tracts on the prohibition of *tamthil*. Abu al-Fadl wrote the first tract, titled *Izalat al-iltibas 'amma waqa' fihi kathirun min al-nas* (Eliminating Confusion about Common Sinful Practices among People). The second tract, *Iqamat al-dalil 'ala hurmat al-tamthil* (Establishing Proof for the Prohibition of Acting), was written by Abu al-Fayd. The brothers posed similar claims and used similar textual and methodological sources to prohibit acting. I focus here on the earliest tract, written by Abu al-Fadl between 1919 and 1952.
98. Ibid., 33–4.
99. Ibid.
100. Ibid.
101. Ibid.
102. Mahmud Shaltut, *Al-Fatawa* (Cairo: Dar al-Shuruq, 1959?), 355–9. The prohibition of music and singing was not predominant during al-Ghumari's time. The rector of al-Azhar, Mahmud Shaltut, allows the listening to and learning of music so long as the practice did not prevent believers from carrying out their religious duty. Shaltut argues that the purpose of the divine law is not to suppress natural desires. Divine law aims to limit extremes to preserve moral consciousness and help people carry out their everyday-life responsibilities. The principle of moderation and the use of intellect (*'aql*) help Muslims reconcile apparent contradictions. God tasks intellect as His agent in His Creation

(*hujja 'ala 'ibaduh*) to discipline nature according to the divine law. The ears are created to be naturally inclined (*majbulin*) to enjoy nice sounds, as the process of discovering the unknown—the sight of green landscape, a pleasant smell, a soft surface—pleases hearts. Because God is the creator of nature, it is not possible that He prohibits music and singing, for His law does not contradict the nature of His creation.

103. See Muhammad Al-Atawneh, "Leisure and Entertainment (*malahi*) in Contemporary Islamic Legal thought: Music and the Audio-Visual Media," *Islamic Law and Society* 194 (2012): 397–415. It is important here to note that the association between reprehensible leisure and music and singing is subject to dispute. This is mainly because the word *lahw* recurs in the Qur'an in disputed contexts. The most common dispute on *lahw* concerns the interpretation of the Qur'anic notion of idle talk (*lahw al-hadith*; e.g. Q31:6) and the activities that falls under that definition. Classical commentaries refer more explicitly to the association between entertainment, music, singing, and the Qur'anic notion of idle talk. According to al-Tabari, *lahw* referred to any activity which diverted a person from the right path (*al-tariq al-mustaqim*) and listed in that category polytheism, playing musical instruments, and singing. Al-Zamakhshari suggested that *lahw* referred to the performance of evil actions, such as ill-joking and laughter, singing, or engaging in musical activities. Fakhr al-Din al-Razi argued that *lahw* meant abandoning wisdom. Authors of treatises on music disagreed on the association between music and idle talk (*lahw al-hadith*). Ibn Abi al-Dunya, the author of *Dhamm al-Malahi*, linked idle talk to music and song, whereas al-Mufaddal b. Salam and Ibn Khurradadhbih wrote a book titled *Kitab al-Malahi* on musical instruments without any negative reference to idle talk. The main association between *lahw* and music appeared more explicitly in the hadith literature. Classical jurisprudents, including Ibn Hazm al-Zahiri, al-Sulami, al-Ghazali, Ibn al-'Arabi, al-Kasani, and Ibn al-Humam, contested the authenticity of those hadiths. Yet the hadith continued to influence the lawfulness of music. While literalists were more in favor of prohibition, Hanafi jurisprudents such as al-Kasani and Ibn al-Humam argued that music was permissible, so long as it positively influenced people. Ibn al-Humam listed a number of conditions for music to qualify as positive. To him, singing should not include descriptions of a living person's beauty and features, the virtues of wine, encouraging wine drinking, the intimate details of private matters, or songs that mock and ridicule others. On the other hand, songs that describe natural landscape such as scenes of flowers and streams, religious hymns, or

songs in praise of relatives, are permissible. He sanctioned the playing of tambourines at weddings and celebrations, even when they were rimmed with bells.

104. Al-Ghumari, *Iqamat al-dalil*, 34.
105. Ibid.
106. Al-Ghumari explains that the *ratio legis* behind the metamorphism of Gabriel is that human nature cannot stand the original form of an angel. Here, al-Ghumari refers to a report describing how Gabriel's original form (he was reported to have had 600 wings that blocked the horizon) made the Prophet faint.
107. Al-Ghumari, *Iqamat al-dalil*, 34.
108. See Muhammad Khafaji, *Al-Azhar fi alf 'am*, 6 vols. (Cairo: Maktabat al-Kulliyya al-Azhariyya, 1988), 3: 466. See Ahmad al-Sharabasi, *Mudhakkirat wa'iz asir* (Cairo: Maṭba'at Dar al-Kitab al-'Arabi, 1952).
109. *Majallat al-kawakib*, no. 2, April 2, 1957.
110. Q2:34.
111. Ahmad al-Sharabasi, *'Aduww al-salam* (Beirut: Dar al-Ra'id al-'Arabi, 1981), 9.
112. *Majallat al-ikhwan al-Muslimin al-nisf shahriyya* no. 140, February 22, 1947.
113. *Majallat al-ikhwan al-Muslimin al-nisf shahriyya* no. 140, February 22, 1947.
114. Al-Sharabasi, *Yas'alunak*, 644–5.
115. Ibid.
116. Ibid.
117. Ibid.
118. Ibid.
119. Ibid.
120. The film was released on Monday, April 9, 1951 in the movie theater of Studio Misr in Cairo and in Cinema Ritz in Alexandria.
121. Hasanayn Makhluf, "'Adam al-ta'arrud li-shakhsiyyat al-rasul fi aflam al-sinima," *Fatawa al-Azhar*, May 7, 1950.
122. For more insights on the legacy of Makhluf, see Ahmad 'Umar Hashim, *Al-muhaddithun fi Misr wa-l-Azhar* (Cairo: Maktabat Gharib, 1993). His fatwa allows production of the film on the *maslaha* on the grounds that it leads to the benefit of spreading the cause of truth. However, he places limitations on the content of what can be depicted. For example, the figures or voices of the Prophet, the Companions, and the Rightly Guided Caliphs cannot be depicted. In accordance with his opinion, the movie *Zuhur al-Islam* was produced without any depictions of the Prophet.

123. Ahmad al-Sharabasi, *Yas'alunak fi al-din wa-l-hayat* (Beirut: Dar al-Jil, 1977), 644–5. This view, as I hope to show in discussing al-Sharabasi's argument for the permissibility of cinema, will change.
124. *Majallat al-kawakib*, no. 2, April 2, 1957.
125. Ibid., 632.
126. Ibid., 644–5.
127. *Akhir Sa'a*, "Sa'a li-qalbak ma'a al-Shaykh Abu al-'Uyun" no. 513, 1946.
128. *Akhir Sa'a*, "Fath Misr," no. 693, 1948; page no. unclear in the source.
129. See Lila Abu-Lughod, "Movie Stars and Islamic Moralism in Egypt," *Social Text* 42 (1995): 53–67.
130. Nasr Hamid Abu Zayd, *Al-Tajdid wa-l-tahrim wa-l-ta'wil* (Beirut: Al-Markaz al-Thaqafi al-'Arabi, 2010), p. 91.

4

Caricaturing Dominant Modernity (*Tafarnug*)

1. Thou Shalt Not Listen to Foreign Music

One of the earliest critiques of dominant modernity (*tafarnug*) appears in Muhammad Karim's *al-Warda al-Bayda'*/The White Rose, 1933, often labeled as the second Egyptian musical. This film can be studied as 'Abd al-Wahhab's film because he played the leading male character and was the producer. But it appears to me that this approach marginalizes the mastermind behind the film, namely, the director. Because all the movies starring 'Abd al-Wahhab constitute the lifework of Karim as a director, I study them here through the lens of their director, not their star.

Muhammad Karim wrote the screenplay of *al-Warda al-Bayda'* in collaboration with Sulayman Nagib and the actor Tawfiq al-Mardinli.[1] It was Karim and writer Fikri Abaza who convinced 'Abd al-Wahhab to make movies. The shooting of the film started on March 12, 1932. The shooting location was mainly Cairo, and the sound was recorded in Studio Topis in Paris as Egypt did not have a sound studio by then. Karim did the makeup for the main actors himself. He finished shooting in Paris on August 1, 1932. It took thirteen days to shoot 165 scenes in fifteen decors. He also made the montage himself and sold the movie to theaters before finalizing the montage. The brother Ra'isi, the owners of Royal and Metropolis movie theaters, visited Karim in Paris to bargain for hosting the premiere in their movie theaters. The movie sold 2000 tickets on the first day, an unprecedented number at that time, especially for Egyptian films. Initially the movie was screened twice a day, and later four times a day.[2]

The collaboration with 'Abd al-Wahhab was initially doubted by Karim, for two main reasons. At one level, Karim had little knowledge of music and singing. He was concerned that singers might have a performance style and facial expressions that could significantly interfere with the facial expressions required for acting. Karim, however, was reassured after watching 'Abd al-Wahhab sing without making any facial expressions.[3] As Karim put it in his memoirs, 'Abd al-Wahhab had little to no interest in the story. His interest in cinema was secondary to his main interest in filming his songs.[4] All that 'Abd al-Wahhab cared about was to work with a director who could successfully empower and magnify 'Abd al-Wahhab's star aura. There is no doubt that Karim succeeded in achieving this end. On another level, it appeared to Karim that 'Abd al-Wahhab's physique could be too weak to tolerate the intense labor of filmmaking. Karim's statement does not necessarily imply, as Armbrust once suggested, that Karim found 'Abd al-Wahhab to be "westernized." In an interview with 'Abd al-Wahhab, he responded to "westernization" as a discourse that every innovator had to face. He recalled that, while studying music, he and his colleagues had smuggled songs of Sayyid Darish like *hashish* because his tutors were more invested in teaching them orthodox standards as practiced by 'Abdu al-Hamuli and Shaykh Abu al-'Ila, who was the early tutor of Umm Kulthum. It was not that 'Abd al-Wahhab was not invested in orthodox standards. He used to listen to Umm Kulthum performing the songs of Shaykh Abu al-'Ila. 'Abd al-Wahhab explained that he had his vision, which was shaped by his experience in the theater. He elaborated on the difference between his school and Umm Kulthum's. While they shared a similar upbringing, the roots of their experimentation were different. His roots were nourished in theaters where challenging dominant culture was the norm; adaptations of world literature and engaging with other cultures were also established norms. Her roots were in the genre of invocations (*ibtihalat*), where the singer had to entertain without reliance even on music. In a way, his experimentation made him open to foreign forms, while her experimentation placed her more in command of the potential of her voice and its variant vibrations; she could always repeat, while every repetition and closure added a new meaning to the song. Here, as an artist, 'Abd al-Wahhab explained the process of innovation as a process of continuity and change. He gave an example of Tawfiq al-Hakim's play *Ahl al-Kahaf* (The People of the Cave) and explained that while the story had its roots in the Qur'an, al-Hakim brought to it a new form, a new content, and a new context.[5] So when Karim described 'Abd al-Wahhab as delicate, he specifically referred to his concern about ʿAbd al-Wahhab's stamina as regards bearing the labor-intensive shooting conditions. Karim's concerns were primarily due to the lack of the latest light technology in Egypt and the need to subject the actor to lights at a very close distance in an unconditioned shooting location. Karim was proven right, for ʿAbd al-Wahhab often complained during the shooting and used to retreat early because of the heat. This was confirmed by ʿAbd al-Wahhab in another interview in which he described how he had initially underestimated the work that cinema required. To use his words, "cinema is a very demanding work" (*alabanda kibira awi*).⁶

Al-Warda al-Bayda' follows the unfulfilled dreams of Muhammad Galal, whose father, a former feudal lord, dies, leaving his family in debt. Galal quits his education as well as his passion for music and singing. He seeks the help of his father's friend, Ismaʿil bey (Sulayman Nagib). Ismaʿil offers Galal a clerical position on Ismaʿil's estate. The relationship between Galal and Ismaʿil takes a sharp turn when the latter discovers that his daughter Ragaʾ (Samira Khulusi) is in love with the new employee. Ismaʿil bey objects to the relationship primarily because he cannot resist the pressure of *tafarnug* exercised on him by his wife (Dawlat Abyad) and her brother, Shafiq (Zaki Rustum), who also wants to marry Ragaʾ. Ismaʿil fires Galal, who decides to pursue his childhood dream of becoming a professional singer. Galal hopes his new career will change Ismaʿil's mind. But the latter's objection to his daughter's relationship with Galal intensifies, primarily because Galal's new profession is a source of social shame and a threat to the amour-propre of Ragaʾ's Cairene-bourgeoisie family.

Karim simultaneously constructs and critiques *tafarnug* in *al-Warda al-Bayda'* through the character of Ismaʿil bey's wife, Fatima. The character was played by Dawlat Qasabgi, known as Dawlat Abyad or Mrs. Abyad. She was born in the city of Assiut in Upper Egypt to a mother of Russian origin and an Egyptian father who worked as a translator at the Egyptian Ministry of War in the Sudan. She attended a Catholic high school in Khartoum. In 1917, the pioneer theater director ʿAziz ʿId discovered her talent and recruited her to his theater troupe before she moved to al-Rihani's theater troupe. In 1923, she met George Abyad and they married. Together they worked at Wahbi's Ramsis troupe when it merged with Abyad's troupe. In 1944, Dawlat Abyad built her theater in Qubba Gardens in Cairo.

In *al-Warda al-Bayda'*, Dawlat Abyad plays the role of a stepmother, a middle-aged woman obsessed with foreign fashion. She first appears on the screen in a distant shot showing her back while she tries on her newly-made dress; this, in a way, creates a psychological distance between her and the audience. She wears her hair in the famous Joan Crawford hairstyle of the 1920s; her new dress looks like Anita Page's sleeveless party dress. In the next scene, she appears looking at her dress in the mirror. It is tempting to interpret the scene as an attempt to reveal the self-centered attitude of the character—a technique that Karim uses in other movies too. But the scene seems to stress the dress as the main point of focalization. The following scene and the dialogue between the stepmother and Isma'il further underscore the same idea. Karim's barely moving camera depicts Isma'il talking to his daughter. When the stepmother appears in the shot, Isma'il praises the dress and asks her to make one for his daughter, Raga'. Karim underscores the character's obsession with European (mainly French) fashion by dedicating four shots to the stepmother's dress. But he also draws attention to the contradiction in her personality.

Figure 4.1 Staging *tafarnug* (1). Dawlat Abyad as Fatima, with her back to the camera as the tailor helps her try on the new dress. *Al-Warda al-Bayda'*, 1933.

Figure 4.2 Staging *tafarnug* (2). Dawlat Abyad as Fatima looking at her new dress in the mirror. *Al-Warda al-Bayda'*, 1933.

Contrary to the stepmother's fascination with European costume, she is not interested in European aesthetics. In the movie's opening scenes, she notices that Raga' is dancing while holding her cat; Raga' appears, enjoying the sound of music on the radio. Annoyed by the music, the stepmother rushes to turn off the radio; she criticizes Raga' for listening to the "Western" piece, which she refers to as *mazzika afrangi*. "Did not we agree earlier that you will not listen to Western music anymore?," says the stepmother.

The contradictory personality of the stepmother is accentuated in the piano scene when she appears to test her recently fixed piano. Of all the notes that she could have played on the piano, she plays oriental notes. What does it mean to depict the villain in the movie as an adherent of *tafarnug* playing oriental notes on a piano (a European musical instrument, after all) while simultaneously discouraging a young woman like Raga' from listening to foreign music? What does it mean to include that scene in a movie primarily about the marginalization of musicians and artists in society? It seems that Karim's stepmother's piano scene is a nascent attempt to show how the Cairene-bourgeoisie appropriates the narrative of the preservation of tradition—represented here through the oriental notes—to exercise a monopoly over local culture and any attempts to innovate it. Adherents of *tafarnug* exercise monopoly in two overlapping ways. First, they monopolize access to "the foreign" and "the modern," as the stepmother does when she reproaches Raga' for listening to foreign music. She dictates which art form may be considered "high" or "low" and what sort of "foreign" practice should be embraced or banned. This explains the contradiction between discouraging Raga' from listening to foreign music and hosting a European instrument like the piano, to tune which the stepmother hires a French pianist.

As an adherent of *tafarnug*, the stepmother is trying to cultivate an amour-propre of being modern while simultaneously dictating what counts as innovation while experiencing the foreign. Here, "westernization" emerges as a discourse of *tafarnug*. Karim was aware of this process. But even 'Abd al-Wahhab, the protagonist in *al-Warda al-Bayda'* and a musician himself, was aware of it; he often dismissed the accusations of "westernization" that followed any attempt to break that monopoly. In one interview, 'Abd al-Wahhab emphasized that the artist (*fannan*)—here being the musician—could not survive without being open to foreign influence, be it Eastern or Western, be it from Latin or from North America. While responding to a question as to whether he discouraged the influence of Western classical music on Arabic music, 'Abd al-Wahhab smiled and denied the possibility that he opposed Western influence. He acknowledged that he had copied some pieces of Beethoven in songs like *Ya ward min yishtirik* (Flower for Sale) and had used pieces from Russian folklore in his song *Ma ahlaha 'ishat al-fallah* (How Beautiful the Peasant's Life Is). While 'Abd al-Wahhab was not proud of having copied somebody else's music, he explained that it had been at a time when he had been more in the artistic phase of imitation than innovation. He added that, when he had copied those pieces, there was no clear-cut line describing fair use versus plagiarism. At the time 'Abd al-Wahhab was being interviewed, the famous song *Strangers in the Night* was a big hit of Frank Sinatra, and the interviewer, Layla Rustum, asked 'Abd al-Wahhab if he had said that its melody was borrowed from his song *La mush ana illi abki*

(No, Not I. I Am Not the One to Cry). 'Abd al-Wahhab smiled and hinted at the similarity, while emphasizing that his song had been written first. He used the opportunity to critique the claims of westernization. Jokingly, he stated that had his song been written after Sinatra's song, the newspaper headlines the next day would have been about the dangerous theft (*sariqa khatira*) and westernization.[7] So the discourse of westernization that Karim depicted through the stepmother character in *al-Warda al-Bayda* was not unfamiliar to filmmakers. And it is therefore not surprising to see Karim showing these claims as a byproduct of *tafarnug*, which he sees as a false consciousness of modernity.

The more complex construction of *tafarnug* in *al-Warda al-Bayda'* appears in the character of Shafiq, the stepmother's brother, played by Zaki Rustum, who was not by then the best Egyptian method actor, which he would become later. Shafiq's character is perhaps the first representation in Egyptian cinema of the print-capitalism *effendi* who works for a government institution which Shafiq refers to as the *diwan*. Karim frames the character as a materialist hypocrite, a wealth hunter who achieves his ends through *tafarnug*. He wants to marry Raga' to control the wealth of Isma'il bey. His *tafarnug* is underscored by both costume and dialogue. Shafiq first appears in the movie talking to Raga' while simultaneously carrying books. He strives to cultivate his amour-propre as an educated modern man who is well-versed in the latest foreign cultural productions and speaks foreign languages. When he first speaks, Shafiq greets Raga' in French by saying: "*Bonjour,*" instead of "*Sa'ida/sabah al-khayr,*" the more common morning greeting in Arabic, particularly among the Cairene-bourgeoisie at that time. Shafiq is always depicted paying attention to the latest trends and costumes. In the morning, he dresses in a white shark-skin suit and a French bow. At night, he spends time with his French friends at Shepherd Hotel, where he dresses in a smoking suit and comes home drunk every night to sleep, again in the same suit. He also tries to cultivate an amour-propre of individualism by emphasizing his independence as a self-made man. Yet, as the movie unfolds, we know he relies on nepotism to be promoted.

Karim's critique of Shafiq's *tafarnug* as a false consciousness of modernity does not explicitly unfold in the movie until his sister visits him in his apartment. She gives him money to buy a proposal ring for Raga'. In a patriarchal society, a man who depends on the wealth of a female family member is not customarily respected. Most of the scenes taken in Shafiq's apartment emphasize his fascination with his amour-propre as a person who masters the modern dress code. He appears dressed in his *robe de chambre*; he is depicted checking his looks (*qiyafa*) in the mirror. In some shots, Karim's stable camera only displays Shafiq's costume. The cadre sometimes conceals Shafiq's head; the dialogue attracts attention to his sister as she sits. Shafiq's head's absence from the cadre (whether intentional or not)[8] amplifies Shafiq's superficial materialist and chauvinist personality. The cadre also reveals Shafiq's view of women as nothing but objects of flirtation. Before his sister arrives, he tries to harass a woman, dressed very fashionably, who is standing on her balcony opposite Shafiq's own balcony.

Similarly, Shafiq considers Raga' nothing but a good retirement plan. Thus, when Shafiq discovers the relationship between Raga' and Galal, he does not blame Raga'. To him, she is a helpless girl with no will. The responsibility falls on the man who must have seduced her. Therefore, Shafiq storms into Isma'il's house, urging him to punish Galal.

The scene of Shafiq telling Isma'il about the relationship between Muhammad and Raga' shows how *tafarnug* eventually blocks the conscience of its adherents. In this scene, Karim resorts to "showing" more than "telling." Instead of using dialogue, Karim depicts Shafiq's back blocking the camera. This shot dramatizes the class pressure which Shafiq exercises on Isma'il. This choice of *mise-en-scène* is meant to represent intimidation and emphasize the dominant nature of *tafarnug* in the life of Isma'il and his class. *Tafarnug* prioritizes cultivating an amour-propre of being modern while suppressing the right of women to choose and fall in love, no matter how educated they are. As Shafiq's body blocks the audience's vision, it also blocks the sight of a tapestry on the wall behind Isma'il. The phrase written on the tapestry reads In God we trust (*tawakkaltu 'ala Allah*). The phrase represents Isma'il's conscience and ability to act according to his better judgment. The idea of *tawakkul* does not denote fatalism and dependency. It is best defined as the taking of risk and the capacity to act in a contingent situation, relying on intellect (*'aql*) as God's agent in humans enabling one to act according to one's better judgment. Its antonym, *tawakul*, which looks very similar, refers to "lack of action due to denial of human will as relevant to action," thus referring to fatalism.[9] It is

Figure 4.3 *Tafarnug* blocks Isma'il's conscience. Zaki Rustum as Shafiq with his back to the camera. Sulayman Nagib as Isma'il, seated right, and Dawalt Abyad as Fatima, seated left. *Al-Warda al-Bayda'*, 1933.

Figure 4.4 Trapped in *tafarnug*. Sulayman Nagib as the bey in the middle being pressured by his in-laws to oppose his daughter's decision to marry Galal. *Al-Warda al-Bayda'*, 1933.

not uncommon in Egyptian colloquial to find *tawakkul* used to denote both meanings. Here the context plays a role in the construction of meaning. By blocking the tapestry, Shafiq's *tafarnug* censors the possibility of Isma'il activating *tawakkul* to support his daughter's right to marry a man of her choice, a basic right in Islam.

The use of Qur'anic verses is directly connected to Karim's perception of himself as a Muslim. In his memoir, he mentioned his discomfort with the marginal position assigned to metaphors representing Islam in foreign films about the "East." This did not make him reactionary by overemphasizing metaphors representing Islam. Instead, he employed the presence and absence of these metaphors for a reason. For example, in the opening scene of *al-Warda al-Bayda'*, the camera follows the heroin Raga' as she dances with her cat and moves from one room to another in Isma'il's house. In all the objects the camera depicts, barely any objects represent an Islamic influence on the decor. The decor dramatically changes when the family moves to the village of Kafr al-Sawalih. It becomes less complex, and tapestries appear on the walls behind characters in almost every scene. Most tapestries depict Qur'anic verses, including verses expressing the glory of God, such as "God is the light of heavens and earth" (*allahu nur al-samawati wa-l-ard*) Q24:35. Other Qur'anic phrases express faith, such as "in God, I trust" (*tawakkaltu 'ala Allah*) Q11: 56.

Islamic metaphors appear in *al-Warda al-Bayda'*, not only through the choice of decor but also in characterization. For example, Shaykh Madbuli is introduced as a pious man (*ragil Salih*). He appears to be offering consolation to the hero, Galal, when the latter is fired. In one scene, Madbuli says, "God shall not abandon you" (*rabbak ma yinsash 'abduh*). But Islam and its metaphors remain on the margin of *tafarnug*. Like the village where he lives, Madbuli is on the margin of Isma'il's Cairene-bourgeoisie life. Karim constructs this marginalization by avoiding depicting Madbuli inside Isma'il's Cairene house. When Madbuli visits Isma'il in Cairo, the camera never shows Madbuli inside the villa.

While the characters of Shafiq and his sister exemplify *tafarnug* as a hegemonic practice, the passiveness of Isma'il bey discloses how *tafarnug* is a dominant culture that cannot be resisted by the bourgeoisie even when they are aware of its falsity. Isma'il admits his awareness of the falsity of *tafarnug* and his entrapment. In the following dialogue, he explicitly comments on *tafarnug* being a backward mindset, which marginalizes the profession of the artist as it did that of the lawyer earlier:

> *Ismaʿil:* [Galal, my son,] no matter how you succeed, I cannot justify this relationship. You will never understand me. I am talking as a father who knows his circumstances, his family's circumstances, and the traditions of his country. However, you are listening to me as a young man who cares only about his passion and love. Is it not so? . . . Who would agree that I should approve of my daughter's marriage to a singer? Thirty years ago, even lawyers had difficulty proposing to a girl from a noble family. That was the situation for the lawyer, who is a mediator for good intentions between rivals and a guide to the judge in fulfilling his mission. Why was that so? It is because the country's mindset was backward.

Yet, throughout the film, Ismaʿil cultivates an amour-propre of a modern, non-conservative and progressive father who promotes equal rights for women. In most of Ismaʿil's scenes, he dresses in a full suit without the tarbush, which is viewed "as an accessory marking the idea of being modern, Eastern, Egyptian and pro-Ottoman."[10] When Ismaʿil visits the village, he does not change the suit and wears a galabiya—the more common dress of a feudal bey or pasha living in the countryside. Ismaʿil appears in a suit or in his *robe de chambre*, which he wears above his shirt, tie, and pants. Ismaʿil believes in the importance of education for men and women equally. He sends his daughter to a French school. At the same time, he denies his daughter her freedom to choose and act on that choice. In the following scene, he tells her that he is sending her to receive a better education, not to do as she wishes but to follow his rules (i.e. the norms of his class):

> *Ismaʿil:* No. You are not in love with him! I do not expect this kind of answer from my daughter. Do you understand? Was I wrong to allow you some freedom? It seems I have given you more space than I should. I am your father. I have more foresight than you have. I know what benefits and what harms you.

Ismaʿil's anger, in the above scenes, is not only caused by his daughter's choice of acting freely, but is also due to his awareness of the social pressure caused by the dominance of *tafarnug*. He is concerned that Raga's attitude will violate the norms of *tafarnug* and that will make her a misfit in her class. He is concerned that the Cairene-bourgeoisie social circles to which his family belongs will not consider her education adequate proof that she is capable of differentiating between benefit (*manfaʿa*) and harm (*darar*), and hence protect her interest. Karim further emphasizes the social pressure caused by the dominance of *tafarnug* in Ismaʿil's life in the *mise-en-scène*. He depicts the father and daughter physically close when Ismaʿil elicits information from his daughter about her reasons for rejecting Shafiq's proposal. When Ragaʾ confesses her feelings, the next frame shows Ismaʿil and Ragaʾ apart. Karim first separates the two characters by Ismaʿil's hand gestures accusing his daughter of betraying him. The distance increases until a marble table separates the two characters. The table symbolizes the stagnancy and rigidity of *tafarnug* with its immense pressure on Ismaʿil and his daughter. This pressure allows women to be modern so long as their modernity is reduced to *tafarnug*, an idea that is more deeply explored in Karim's *Yawm Saʿid*/Happy Day, 1938.

Figure 4.5 Dad's favourite doll. Sulayman Nagib as Ismaʿil comforting his daughter Ragaʾ, played by Samira Khulusi. *Al-Warda al-Baydaʾ*, 1933.

210 | FILMING MODERNITY AND ISLAM IN COLONIAL EGYPT

Figure 4.6 Creating psychological distance. Sulayman Nagib as Isma'il, right, accuses Raga', played by Samira Khulusi, of betraying him. *Al-Warda al-Bayda'*, 1933.

Figure 4.7 The marble-like rigidity of *tafarnug*. On the right, Sulayman Nagib as Isma'il. On the left, Samira Khulusi as Raga'. *Al-Warda al-Bayda'*, 1933.

2. Where Is the *Frak* You Wore Last Night?

Yawm Saʿid/Happy Day, 1938 is a more optimistic version of Karim's *al-Warda al-Bayda'*. Karim wrote the story and initially called it *Gharam* (Passion),[11] but changed the name after collaborating with the theater actor ʿAbd al-Warith ʿAsar in writing the dialogue. Most of the movie's 35 mm boxes were lost to a fire in ʿAbd al-Wahhab's office. The police investigation, which ended inconclusively, revealed that the fire was not an accident. Were it not for a copy stored in Studio Misr, where most of the shooting took place, the movie would have been lost

The story follows the fulfilled dreams of Kamal, an emerging singer and musician who refuses the commodification of his art. For the same reason, Kamal does not make enough money and is often delinquent in paying rent to the owner of his property, Shaykh Mitwalli (Fu'ad Shafiq). Kamal changes his view of the relationship between art and mechanical reproduction when he falls in love with Amina (Samiha Samih), a young woman who works for a vinyl-records shop. Initially, Amina's parents disapprove of her relationship with Kamal. Amina's parents approve of the relationship when Kamal succeeds as a singer. The story gets further complicated when Suhayr, a recently divorced aristocratic woman, has a crush on Kamal. Suhayr threatens Amina's father, ʿAtif *effendi* (ʿAbd al-Warith ʿAsar), saying she will fire him from his job as a manager of Suhayr's estate unless ʿAtif *effendi* opposes his daughter's plan to marry Kamal.

Suhayr is the lead female character in *Yawm Saʿid* and the central representation of *tafarnug* in the movie. Through her character, Karim critiques how the Cairene-bourgeoisie class reduces the modern freedom of women to the practice of *tafarnug*. Karim's memoirs described his first meeting with the actress playing Suhayr. It initially occurred to him that she was not Egyptian because of what Karim referred to as her *tafarnug* (*farnagitha*)[12] until he learnt that her full name was Ilham Husayn al-Raʿi. He recommended her for the role because it occurred to him that he could capitalize on her seeming *tafarnug*, which would come naturally in the movie. But he could not initially hire Ilham Husayn, because she was seventeen years old and the hiring process required the consent of a legal guardian to sign the film contract. To Karim's surprise, Ilham Husayn was customarily married, and her husband was the famous film star and director Anwar Wagdi, who was by then an emerging actor in the Egyptian Theater Troupe, who later married the diva Layla Murad. Karim chose the character's costumes himself. He recalled that the cost of Suhayr's costumes was 600 Egyptian pounds, a massive budget at that time.

Karim constructs a complex duality for the character of Suhayr. On the one hand, she is a Cairene-bourgeoisie, a younger version of the stepmother played by Dawlat Abyad in *al-Warda al-Bayda'*. On the other, she is depicted as a feminist trying to regain her freedom and reinvent herself after a messy divorce. Karim uses different techniques to emphasize this duality. For example, he emphasizes equally and simultaneously the character's vulnerability and arrogance. This is evident in Suhayr's relationship with her employee 'Atif *effendi*, whom she considers a family member and does not shy away from informing that she is in love with the suitor of his daughter, Amina. Yet Suhayr considers 'Atif *effendi* inferior in class. In one scene, Karim depicts the character of Suhayr exercising her feudal power to influence the decision of 'Atif *effendi* while simultaneously begging him to understand that she is in love with Kamal. Karim's construction of such a duality in Suhayr's character preserves the audience's empathy with the character. This empathy further increases when Suhayr gives a self-pitying monologue filmed as one wide shot showing the character's entire body. The distance between the audience and the subject of depiction in this shot is slightly less than the standard distance between the audience and the stage in a theater. This shrinking physical distance diminishes the psychological distance between the audience and the character, thereby gaining the character more empathy. The light angle emphasizes one side of Suhayr's face to convey the good side of Suhayr, who is tormented by her experimentation in search of an understanding of the position of self in society after divorce. The monologue allows Suhayr to ask what went wrong and why she cannot be loved the way she wants, given that she perceives herself as a free and liberated modern woman who forced the decision of divorce on her husband (Sulayman Nagib).

Karim blames Suhayr's sense of failure on *tafarnug* as a delusive amour-propre that reduces modernity to mastery of the European code of apparel and leisure activities. For example, when Suhayr tries to convince 'Atif *effendi*

Figure 4.8 What went wrong? *Yawm Saʿid*, 1938.

to oppose his daughter's plan to marry Kamal, Suhayr celebrates the traits of modern life mastered by the son of Fadil pasha, whom Suhayr perceives as a better suitor for Amina than Kamal. These traits include being a *gentian* man, knowing how to play tennis and bridge, and dancing impressively. Similarly, what attracts Suhayr to Kamal is his ability to master the European code of apparel. Suhayr is impressed by the ability of an Egyptian singer to sing in a tailcoat (*frak*). She first listens to Kamal's singing at a charity party, after which she invites Kamal to her villa. The first question she asks him is, "Where is the *frak* that you wore last night?" (*ummal fayn il-frak illi kunt labsuh imbarih?*). Kamal faces Suhayr's question with a sarcastic smile and says, "In the closet." Suhayr's question is an unusual way of initiating a conversation with a guest who comes to visit her in her villa for the first time. Through this unfamiliar exchange, Karim implies how Suhayr reduces Kamal's success as an emerging singer to his ability to master a foreign dress code. She expects Kamal to be an adherent of *tafarnug* since he does not fit with her stereotypical image of the Egyptian singer wearing a suit and a tarbush, holding a lute, and accompanied by a traditional band (*takht*). She expects Kamal to behave like a foreign *artiste*, whose lifestyle she also stereotypes in the following scene:

Suhayr: Have you been to the horse race?

Kamal: Unfortunately, I have not.

S: That makes sense! After all, what would you do there? You seem to be the type of person who loves parties, night-outings, and dancing. I know all *artistes* belong to that type.

K: Well, I guess I am an exception!

S: This way, you cannot claim you are an *artiste*!

K: If there is no art (*fann*) except in cabaret and dance clubs, then I am not an artist (*fannan*).

S: Where do you compose your art (*fann*)?

K: In my room.

S: Only inside your room! Nothing happens outside of it!

Here Karim revisits the idea of the marginalization of the artist and the reasons why adherents of *tafarnug* do not respect art as a profession. This also seems to ban attempts, on the part of Karim, to break the stereotype of the artist and to promote the idea that being an artist (here specified as a musician) is as noble as any other profession. For this purpose, Karim highlights the difference between Suhayr's and Kamal's word-choice in referring to "artist." While Suhayr uses the French "*artiste*" to describe Kamal's profession, Kamal prefers the Arabic word "*fannan*." The initial implication here is that Kamal uses the word *fannan* to differentiate between his "high" art and "low" art as presented in the cabaret. Yet Kamal's distinction between *artiste* and *fannan* in this context appears more of an attempt to create a space for respect for his emerging art in the Cairene-bourgeoisie culture, that often views foreign art as immoral (*khaliʿ*) and looks down upon local art or at best views it with an Orientalist gaze.[13] Karim emphasizes this Orientalist gaze in Suhayr's reaction to innovation by local artists. To Suhayr, local art is not capable of innovation; local artists are neither capable of mastering European musical instruments such as the piano nor able to master foreign dress codes such as wearing a tailcoat. Karim constructs Suhayr's position in the scene featuring the song *al-Siba wa-l-jamalu milku yadayyki* (Youth and Beauty Lay in Your Palms), written by al-Akhtal al-Saghir (Bishara al-Khuri). As Kamal plays the piano and sings while sitting behind a silk curtain, Suhayr watches him. Suhayr's villa is almost like a *harem* prison; she enjoys the idea that Kamal sings and plays the piano for her alone in her villa; she tries to keep Kamal locked inside her mansion. Every time Kamal visits, Suhayr claims she is holding a party. Kamal arrives to find Suhayr making the illusion of party noise by turning on the radio or playing a record.[14] There is, however, no party and no invitees but Kamal. Suhayr's gaze symbolizes the Cairene-bourgeoisie gaze at the innovative and creative non-bourgeoisie Egyptian belonging to the underprivileged classes. This gaze further intensifies in Kamal Salim's *al-'Azima*/Perseverance, 1939, in which he explores the Cairene-bourgeoisie's preconceived notion of the incompatibility of working-class Egyptians and modernity unless they master *tafarnug* as the only path to becoming modern.

3. I Am Muhammad *Effendi*'s Wife!

The director of *al-'Azima*/Perseverance, 1939, Kamal Salim, was born in 1924 in the popular neighborhood of al-Gammaliyya to a wealthy father, a member of parliament and owner of a silk factory. Having witnessed the struggle of the Egyptian working class during two World Wars, Salim made films revealing the many challenges while struggling to acquire up-to-date knowledge of the world inside and outside Egypt. Chief among those challenges is the Cairene-bourgeoisie's dominant culture of *tafarnug*, which *al-'Azima* depicts as a hegemonic practice among the working class.

Egyptian filmmakers, critics, and film scholars have long categorized *al-'Azima* as the true beginning of realism. It is the first film to depict different professions among working-class Egyptians living in the alley (*hara*).[15] The story follows the challenges facing Muhammad Hanafi (Husayn Sidqi), who graduates from the school of commerce and hopes to be an entrepreneur instead of working for the government or serving in an administrative post to become an *effendi*. He is in love with his uneducated neighbor Fatima (Fatima Rushdi), whose father owns a bakery in the same neighborhood. Initially, Muhammad Hanafi works in partnership with his friend 'Adli (Anwar Wagdi), a son of a pasha who encourages his son to start a small business with Hanafi. Yet 'Adli's *tafarnug* puts an end to that partnership and Hanafi's ambitions. An alluring example of 'Adli's *tafarnug* is the scene depicting the bullying scheme through which 'Adli's friends describe how they think of Muhammad Hanafi:

'Adli: Oh, God! Now we have to face this useless fuss!

Woman friend: What is wrong, 'Adli?

Shawkat: What is bothering you, 'Adli?

A: That guy named Muhammad. I gave him an appointment to meet now, and I completely forgot about it. He came on time to cause me a headache with work-related issues; he came to interrupt my fun. How could he ever imagine I am free for his nonsense!

Sh: Just dismiss him. [Addressing the servant] Tell him the bey is not here. Tell him he is sleeping.

A: No. That would be very rude. He would figure out it is a lie.

Sh: What type of person is he?

A: 'Izzat knows him.

'Izzat: Who are you talking about?

A: Muhammad Hanafi.

'I: Do you mean the commerce school guy? It is an excellent opportunity to make fun of him. Bring him in.

A: No, 'Izzat, please do not do that.

'I: It will be done in a subtle, mischievous way. Folks, do you know what he looks like? He looks like a bundle of carrots dressed in a suit and tarbush.

A: Please do not do that. It is not appropriate to mock him here.

Sh: Do not worry! We will try to appear serious. [Addressing 'Adli's friends] Folks, stop dancing, take the girls inside, take these [drinks] inside, and turn off the radio quickly.

A: But, Shawkat, that is so inappropriate to do.

Sh: Stop worrying! This is going to be fun.

Tafarnug dehumanizes working-class Egyptians, a class to which Muhammad Hanafi belongs. Shawkat refers to Muhammad as a bundle of carrots. The carrot at that time was an inexpensive vegetable sold by street vendors in bundles without cutting the green leaves. That is to say, the carrots are not washed, peeled, and finely sliced: they are sold with the mud sticking to the roots. To 'Adli's Cairene-bourgeoisie friends, Muhammad is similar to that bundle of carrots, and he needs to be reminded that he can never be "refined," "modern," and "equal" to them, for he belongs to a social class that does not experience the luxuries of *tafarnug*.

Tafarnug leaves no option for Muhammad Hanafi but to accept a clerical job so that he can help his father, a barber, pay his debt. The clerical job also allows Hanafi to marry Fatima. The movie takes a sharp turn when a file is lost, and Hanafi is accused of negligence. Having lost his job, he finds no option but to accept a low-paid part-time job at a department store, where he wraps gifts. Muhammad, however, never tells Fatima that he has lost his clerical position. And he chooses to face his financial difficulties alone. When Fatima discovers the truth and appears ashamed of him and his new job, Muhammad realizes that *tafarnug* has infiltrated his house.

The character of Fatima, played by Fatima Rushdi, who was often referred to in the Egyptian press of the time as Sara Bernardt of the East, is a metaphor for how *tafarnug* became a hegemonic practice among working-class Egyptians. Her image forms one of the earliest female faces printed on an Egyptian stamp. Born in 1908 in Alexandria, she, along with her two sisters, Ratiba and Insaf, grew up to find a career in the arts. Her sisters used to sing in the Amin 'Atallah Theater Troupe. In 1923, she met 'Aziz 'Id, who recruited her to Yusuf Wahbi's newly established troupe. She took leading roles and married 'Aziz 'Id, until they separated, and she formed her troupe that presented fifteen plays. Her film career started with Badr Lama in 1928 when she appeared in *Faji'a Fawaqa al-Haram*/Scandal Near the Pyramids. Still, her actual cinematic presence started with *al-'Azima*, which solidified her legacy on the screen and for which she has been most remembered.

The first time Salim hints at Fatima's adherence to *tafarnug* is when she changes her dress code after getting married to Hanafi. Fatima ceased to wear the black wrap (*milaya*) and the colorful embroidered scarf (*mandil bi-quya*), which was part of the traditional dresses of *banat al-balad* at the time. As the movie unfolds, Fatima associates social status and success with *tafarnug*. For example, Salim depicts Fatima reading a letter from her cousin, who has written to congratulate her on getting married to an *effendi*. As Fatima reads the letter aloud, she repeatedly stresses how her cousin is impressed by the new social status of Fatima as a wife of an *effendi* who dresses in a suit and works in an office. To Fatima, marrying an *effendi* is a better opportunity than marrying a worker or an artisan. The sound of the title "respected wife of the employee Muhammad effendi Hanafi" (*haram* Muhammad effendi Hanafi

Figure 4.9 On the right, Fatima Rushdi as Fatima is getting ready to put on her *milaya* to meet Muhammad on the stairs. *Al-'Azima*, 1939.

Figure 4.10 Fatima after changing her apparel. On the right, Husayn Sidqi as Muhammad; on the left, Fatima Rushdi as Fatima. *Al-'Azima*, 1939.

al-muwazzaf) is mind-blowing to Fatima. It allows her to appear modern and feel superior to her fellow *banat al-balad*.

Through the roles played by supporting actors, like Fatima's parents and friends, Salim frames Fatima's *tafarnug* as false consciousness of modernity. In the opening scene, Salim's camera depicts the daily routine of Muhammad Hanafi's father vis-à-vis the daily routine of Fatima's father. As the dawn call to prayer (*adhan al-fajr*) plays in the background, Salim's camera moves to announce the locality as Ma'tuq Street. The camera then follows Muhammad Hanafi's father heading toward the mosque to pray. At the same time, the call to prayer marks the end of the night for Fatima's father, who comes back from the bar as the call to prayer plays in the background. He approaches his bakery shop while simultaneously singing a popular song of the time, *Qamar lahu layali* (The moon has been shining for a few nights). Fatima's father asks his assistant if the latter has covered up for his boss's absence in front of Fatima's mother. As the assistant assures his boss there is no problem, the latter pulls out a bottle of wine and transfers the wine from the bottle to a traditional Egyptian water jar so that he can drink as much as he wants during the day, and it will look as if he drinks water. The implication is not only that the father of Fatima is invested in cultivating an amour-propre of religiosity. Later in the movie, Fatima's father makes a case justifying his excessive drinking by saying "A little amount of alcohol is useful for the stomach" (*Qalilun minhu yusilihu al-ma'ida*), thereby using a legal means (alcohol can sometimes be beneficial) to achieve an illegal end (gerttig drunk). After all, he does not just have a glass or two; he has been drinking from a water jar equal to a liter. Here, Salim critiques the appropriation of Islam among adherents and hegemonic subjects of *tafarnug*. Likewise, Salim critiques Fatima's *tafarnug* through the supporting roles of her girlfriends. They are aware of Fatima's hegemony over *tafarnug*, and her wish to single herself out as superior in social status to *banat al-balad*. They are also mindful of Fatima's gaze of inferiority at the local dress code, such as represented by galabiya and *milaya*, which she considers inferior to the modern dress code such as shown by *chemisier* and *le tailleur*. On one occasion, Fatima's friends convince her that they need her newly acquired chic and fashionable taste to help them buy cloth.

The unannounced intention of Fatima's friends is to see the shock on Fatima's face when she sees her husband wrapping gifts in the same department store as the one where Fatima and her friends go shopping. When she arrives at the store and sees her husband wrapping gifts, Salim depicts Fatima as devastated, not so much by the news that her husband has lost his full-time job or that he has kept this a secret from her, but mainly by his loss of the *effendi* apparel. She cannot bear the fact that her husband is no longer an *effendi* who works with pen and paper and sits at a desk. She is ashamed of his yellow uniform (*al-badla al-safra*), a phrase she frequently repeats when she recalls her shock. That uniform is why Fatima's friends took Fatima to the shop. They want her to see her husband dressed in what Fatima perceives as inferior attire to the *effendi*'s. In this scene, Salim depicts Muhammad Hanafi in a middle shot to convey the disorientation in Fatima's mind. Ironically, Fatima's hegemony to *tafarnug* makes her lose the love of her life. As much as *tafarnug* looks down upon the culture of *awlad al-balad*, it does not think any better of the culture of the peasants. Tugu Mizrahi and Yusuf Wahbi critique the inferiority gaze at the peasants in *Layla Bint al-Rif*/Layla, Daughter of The Countryside, 1941 and *Bint Dhawat*/The Daughter of the Nobles, 1942.

4. Peasantry! What an Elegant Lifestyle!

Layla Bint al-Rif is directed by Tugu Mizrahi, a son of a wealthy Egyptian Jewish mercantile family of Italian origin. The family's trade was primarily in cotton. Mizrahi left a successful career as a merchant and in 1921 traveled to France and Italy to study economics and cinema. Upon returning to Egypt, he established The Egyptian Film Company, for which Mizrahi rented Yusuf Wahbi's Ramsis Studio in Giza. Like many filmmakers of the time, Mizrahi had to go by a fame name, Ahmad Mishriqi. Why he took a Muslim name and later restored his family name is not clear. It seems that his choice was in line with the practice of hiding the family name because a career in filmmaking was not a source of pride at the time. Most of Mizrahi's films dealt with class struggle and income disparity, among many other issues. He is most famous for his trilogy adaptation of the *One Thousand and One Nights* on the screen. Mizrahi directed around thirty-nine films, out of which he wrote the scenario of eighteen films.[16] Perhaps no filmmaker in the 1940s celebrated the aesthetic of the rural woman as Mizrahi did in *Layla Bint al-Rif*, which uses various techniques to construct *tafarnug* and its inferiority gaze at Egyptian peasants.

Layla Bint al-Rif follows the story of Fathi (Yusuf Wahbi), whose birthplace is the village of Kafr al-Shamayila, where his mother is the feudal lady and the head of the family. After earning a degree in medicine from Cambridge, Fathi returns to Cairo and refuses to resume a career as a surgeon. Fathi's relationship with Kafr al-Shamayila is limited to his receiving his mother's financial support, a check of a hundred pounds that the mother sends her son every month. He despises the lifestyle of the village; he looks down on farming communities. Under the pressure of his extravagant lifestyle, he accepts his mother's wish for him to marry his cousin Layla (Layla Murad). While Layla is in love with him, Fathi agrees to the union only so that his mother will not deny him his status as the legal heir of the family's estate. In the following scene, Fathi expresses his contempt for Kafr al-Shamayila as a backward place where aspects of societal modernization have not arrived:

Maid: [She hears the chamber's door open] Is it you, Sir? I did not expect you to come so early. I thought you were taking a walk. The weather is charming outside.

Fathi: A walk! Are you kidding? You mean stumble (*adabbish*) in the darkness and wade in (*akhwwad*) the drainage.

M: I bet you aren't used to the peasantry lifestyle yet.

F: I am not, and I am not planning to get used to it. What an elegant lifestyle! A smoky lamp, a suffocating mosquito net, and on top of that, people won't leave me alone or respect my privacy.

Instead of blaming the delay of societal modernization on the colonial state, which up until 1941 did not extend infrastructure to the countryside, Fathi blames the lag on the peasants. Similarly, Fathi reveals to his mother that he cannot marry Layla, whom he considers a backward peasant woman without any knowledge of the attributes of modern life. Fathi cannot imagine introducing Layla in her traditional village dress (i.e. the galabiya and the long black silk scarf) to his Cairene-bourgeoisie friends. To Fathi, Layla is a source of social shame, for she cannot master the latest foreign dress code and etiquette; she is not even good enough to be hired as a maid in his Cairene house, which French-looking maids run.

Like his dialogue, Mizrahi's camera also constructs *tafarnug* and its gaze of inferiority at the peasants. When Layla arrives at her new home in Cairo,

Mizrahi's *mise-en-scène* and deep shot underscore Layla's inferiority even to the Cairene servants in the house. At the center of the image, Mizrahi positions Fathi. The servant is positioned next to Fathi to the right. Fathi's superiority to the servant is emphasized when the servant greets Fathi and kisses his hand. Layla is positioned behind Fathi and his servant at the back of the shot. Her face appears at a distance. When the servant notices Layla's presence, he summons her to run to the kitchen. The implication is that the servant thinks Layla is a new servant Fathi has brought with him from the village. Fathi's French-looking maid appears shocked at the sight of Layla's braid. Through the maid's gaze at the braid, Mizrahi conveys how the braid is seen as a symbol of a backward non-modern hairstyle, which is inferior to the maid's shorter, styled hair. To the servants in Fathi's Cairene house, Layla is a crazy peasant who comes to disturb the house routine by insisting on waking the entire household every day at 6.00 a.m., when Fathi usually comes back home after having spent the night before at a cabaret.

Mizrahi blames Fathi's *tafarnug* on the inferiority gaze at the peasant woman. Here, supporting roles who condemn Fathi's *tafarnug* help Mizrahi do the job. For example, Mizrahi employs the character of Samira (Zuzu Shakib), a Cairene childhood friend of Layla, to help Layla, her cousin Salwa (Salwa 'Allam), and their uncle (Hasan al-Barudi) become aware of *tafarnug*'s inferiority-gaze at the peasant's sensibilities. Making the object of the inferiority gaze conscious of the gaze is a process that can be described as transferring the gaze to reveal the nature of the ideology behind it. For this purpose, Mizrahi relies on both dialogue and cinematography. In the following scene, Samira explains to Layla why her husband is rude to her. In the process, she transfers and reveals the inferiority gaze to Layla:

> *Samira:* Listen, Layla, I have, to be frank with you, and I hope you will not be offended. Your husband is embarrassed by who you are.
> *Layla's cousin:* How come?
> *Layla's uncle:* How come?
> *S:* Yes, he is. Come over here. [Layla stands up as Samira holds her braid] How can you call this [braid] a hairstyle? [Samira holds Layla's dress] How can you call this a dress? Look at your nails! Sit down. [Layla sits down as Samira pulls up Layla's dress to her knees] How can you call

CARICATURING DOMINANT MODERNITY (*TAFARNUG*) | 223

Figure 4.11 Mizrahi's deep shot. Left: Layla Murad as Layla. Middle: Yusuf Wahbi as Fathi. Right: Muhammad Kamil as the servant. *Layla Bint al-Rif*, 1941.

Figure 4.12 Inferiority gaze at the peasant woman's hairstyle. Left: Bishara Wakim as Fathi's friend. Right: Su'ad 'Abduh as Fathi's maid. *Layla Bint al-Rif*, 1941.

these socks? You need to change all this. You have to hang out outside the home, have fun, wear the latest fashion, become *spore* and *moderne* like your husband.

L: *Moderne* like my husband! What does this mean?

S: Tell me, did we not go to the best schools together? Did you forget French and English? [Samira speaks in French] Did you forget the days of the *Mère de Dieu*?[17]

L: [Answers in French] No, I did not. I do not know what I would have done without you.

S: All right, come with me, then.

L: Where are we going?

S: Do not worry. Just come with me.

LC: Can I come too?

S: Sure, you can come. [Addressing the uncle] And you too can join us.

LU: What do you intend to do?

LC: Let us go, Uncle; they will cut my hair and let us see what they can do to style yours.

Samira, who gives Layla a recipe for *tafarnug*, is a Cairine bourgeoisie woman. She and Layla attended the same French schools. Unlike Layla, Samira resides in Cairo. She mingles in the Cairene-bourgeoisie social circles of Fathi. Samira's list of reasons for why Fathi rejects Layla is similar to the list of the attributes of *tafarnug*, which Suhayr mentions to 'Atif *effendi* in *Yawm Sa'id*. To be modern, as Samira points out, Layla must master a foreign dress code and go to downtown cafes like Groppi—a Swiss coffee shop founded in Cairo by a southern Swiss baker in 1891; it was a breakfast destination for the elites of the time.[18] She has to hold evening tea and dance parties at her house, attend horse races, have male friends, learn how to dance, speak French, and get rid of her village sensibilities. This recipe is supposed to help make Layla aware of the gaze of inferiority and, at the same time, reveal the nature of the ideology of *tafarnug* to the subaltern, this here being the peasant woman and the audience. Mizrahi's camera depicts Samira transferring the gaze by making the objects of the gaze (Layla, her cousin, and their uncle) look at themselves and compare their apparel to Samira's modern apparel.

CARICATURING DOMINANT MODERNITY (*TAFARNUG*) | 225

Figure 4.13 Transferring the inferiority gaze to the subaltern. In the middle, Zuzu Shakib as Samira, holding Layla's braid. On the left, Lyala Murad as Layla. From the right, Hasan al-Barudi as Laylas's uncle, and Salwa 'Allam as Layla's cousin. *Layla Bint al-Rif*, 1941.

Figure 4.14 Subaltern internalization of the inferiority gaze. In the middle, Zuzu Shakib as Samira. On the left, Lyala Murad as Layla. From the right, Hasan al-Barudi as Layla's uncle, and Salwa 'Allam as Layla's cousin. *Layla Bint al-Rif*, 1941.

Figure 4.15 Subaltern realization of the inferiority gaze. On the right, Zuzu Shakib as Samira transferring the inferiority gaze to Layla (Layla Murad), who is depicted gazing at her socks. *Layla Bint al-Rif*, 1941.

Layla's ability to master *tafarnug*, which her husband idolizes, while realizing its falsity, is Mizrahi's third technique for critiquing *tafarnug*. Layla follows Samira's advice. She dresses more fashionably, replacing the scarf with a hat and the galabiya with a *tailleur*. She changes her daily routine and wakes up at noon instead of at 6.00 a.m. Instead of her simple homemade breakfast, she heads downtown to Groppi. But Layla, unlike her husband, is proud of her cultural heritage. In a way, Layla accepts the modern sensibilities of European apparel without having an inferiority gaze at the local culture. Therefore, it is not surprising to see Mizrahi deepening his critique of *tafarnug* by making supporting actors comment sarcastically on European sensibilities idolized by the adherents of *tafarnug*. For example, when Layla attends her first party in modern apparel, her uncle (Hasan al-Barudi) cannot understand the Italian soprano singer. The uncle wonders why people clap their hands feverishly after listening to a woman who sounds like she is mourning a dead person (*bit'addid*). Surprised that the Italian lady is singing, not mourning, Layla's uncle wonders what the guest's reaction would be if they listened to Layla's

CARICATURING DOMINANT MODERNITY (*TAFARNUG*) | 227

Figure 4.16 Mastering *tafarnug* (1). On the right, Layla Murad as Layla having tea at Groppi's café with her friend Samira. *Layla Bint al-Rif*, 1941.

Figure 4.17 Mastering *tafarnug* (2). On the right, Layla Murad as Layla and on the left Zuz Shakib as Samira, at a horse race. *Layla Bint al-Rif*, 1941.

Figure 4.18 Mastering *tafarnug* (3). In the middle, Layla Murad as Layla. *Layla Bint al-Rif*, 1941.

voice singing in Arabic without an orchestra. By comparing Layla's voice as a local form of art to foreign art, Mizrahi, long before Pierre Bourdieu, addresses the social theory of taste.

Mizrahi inserts advertising scenes to empower local culture further and promote local over foreign products. For example, when Layla goes to have her hair styled in a beauty salon, Samira asks the hairdresser if he has the most recent shampoo from Paris. The hairstylist replies that they use Nabulsi Faruq soap, which the hairstylist describes as better than a hundred French shampoos.

Mizrahi takes the critique of *tafarnug* a step further by critiquing the Cairene-bourgeoisie's inferiority gaze at the peasants' lifestyle as something independent of their wealth. In other words, Mizrahi shows how the inferiority gaze at the peasants is not merely a class gaze. Instead, a gaze of racial supremacy disdains the Egyptian peasant, who is considered ethnically inferior. After all, Layla is a feudal lady. And in this sense, Mizrahi adds another layer to the critique of *tafarnug* among Egyptian directors of his time. Yusuf Wahbi further develops this critique in his movie *Bint Dhawat*/The Daughter of the Nobles, 1942, which traces the origin of the inferiority gaze at the peasants to the Orientalist gaze. While Mizrahi reveals the nature of the ideology of *tafarnug* by transferring the gaze, Wahbi chooses confrontation and forces adherents of *tafarnug* to accept the sensibilities of the peasants as equal.

5. *De La Blaj Kafr Al-Matamir* and Ma'am Abu Dishish

Bint Dhawat/The Daughter of the Nobles, 1942, follows the conflicting aspirations of Samiya (Raqiya Ibrahim), who falls in love with Ibrahim (Yusuf Wahbi), the son of hajj Mitwalli, a gardener (*khuli*) in the estate of Samiya's father, Murad pasha Sarhan (Bishra Wakim). Samiya grew up with Ibrahim and his sister (Layla Fawzi) in the village of Abu al-Matamir, located in the northern governorate of al-Bihiyra. She is aware of the class difference between herself and Ibrahim. When Ibrahim proposes to Samiya after getting his degree in engineering from an unnamed school in Europe, she rejects his proposal. She believes in a class hierarchy that cannot be violated through education. She is keen to preserve her father's *tafarnug* in the social circles of the Cairene-bourgeoisie and *Khawagat*. The father, Murad pasha Sarhan, spends extravagantly on parties and gambling on horses; he travels to Europe to spend the summer in Karlsbad, where he can maintain his diet. He is least interested in his thousand acres in the village. Sarhan's interest in the village is limited to four visits in fifteen years. He dehumanizes the peasants and considers the village inferior to the city. On one occasion, Sarhan comments sarcastically on the possibility of spending one summer in his village; he says to the manager of his estate, "Do you want me to spend the summer in the pools of the *de la blaj kafr al-matamir* and watch Ma'am Abu Dishish (a nickname for donkey)—i.e. the wife of the peasant—in her bathing suit." To Sarhan, there is an ontological contradiction between the village and *la blaj*, between the French woman and the Egyptian village woman. To him, French leisure activities and women are superior to Egyptian village activities and village women. This is not so much an appreciation of French beauty as an objectification of the female body.

To Sarhan, peasants are a commodity. In one scene, Sarhan takes the train from the village back to Cairo. His children cry because they have to leave the village, and they will not be able to play with the children of the gardener, whom Sarhan takes with him as if they were two toys bought to entertain his children. Wahbi could have depicted the scene by allowing the gardener's children to get into the train properly, through the door. However, Wahbi emphasizes Sarhan's perception of the peasants as a commodity by showing the children being handed to the pasha through the window, like two baskets or two bottles. In a later scene in which Ibrahim becomes a successful engineer, Wahbi depicts Ibrahim remembering that moment in his childhood to counter-argue the pasha's claim that Ibrahim's success is a direct result of the Cairene upbringing that Ibrahim receives at the pasha's house in Cairo. Ibrahim confronts the pasha and critiques his *tafarnug*, pointing out that the gardener's children were admitted to the pasha's palace for the sole purpose of entertaining the pasha's children. Ibrahim argues that it is primarily through his hard work and dedication that he has been able to secure one scholarship (*al-maganiyya*) after another and become an engineer.

To lampoon Murad pasha's *tafarnug* as a false consciousness of modernity, Wahbi relies mainly on reaction shots. In the opening scene, Murad pasha boards the train from Cairo to the village. The scene depicts him looking out of the train window and chatting with those who come to bid him farewell. At the same time, he looks around for his servant, who goes to fetch him two bottles of wine. The pasha is depicted as anxious that the train may leave without

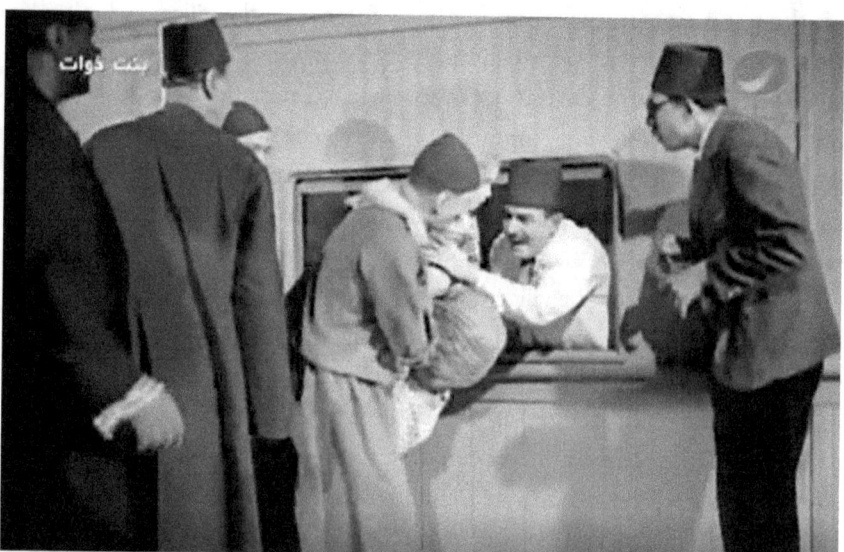

Figure 4.19 The body of the peasant as a commodity. Bishara Wakim as Murad pasha Sarhan receives the gardener's children through the train window. *Bint Dhawat*, 1942.

him having hold of the wine. At the same time, he tries to avoid being judged, not so much for drinking per se as for being so keen on it at the last minute. To preserve his amour-propre as a moral person, the pasha lies to his friends, telling them that his anxiety is because he is afraid his servant will be late buying two bottles of medicine. When the servant arrives, the train starts moving. Accidentally, the servant drops the bottles while passing them to the pasha through the window. The pasha cries over the spilled wine and shouts, "The medicine, the medicine," while the camera moves to reveal that the broken bottles were bottles of wine, not medicine. The image of the damaged bottles is sufficient to frame the pasha's amour-propre as delusive. However, Wahbi adds the voice of a supporting actor who comments sarcastically, "It looks like the pasha's prescription is issued from Yanni's bar." Yanni is a common name among Greeks living in Egypt and is often used in Egyptian cinema to refer to a bartender. The comment further emphasizes the delusive amour-propre of religiosity that the pasha is keen to cultivate. But he had no respect for religion, this here being Islam. And Wahbi reveals this idea in the second train scene.

On the train to Cairo, Murad pasha shares a private compartment with Azhari Shaykh, who appears busy reading a newspaper, not giving attention to his fellow passengers. Murad wants to take a sip from a small bottle of wine, which he keeps in his pocket. It again occurs to Murad that he has to preserve his amour-propre of religiosity in front of the Shaykh, whom Sarhan perceives as an ignorant person who could easily be fooled into thinking that the bottle of wine is a bottle of medicine. Sarhan initiates a conversation while sipping some wine and telling the Shaykh that it is time for him to take his daily dose of medication. When the Shaykh shows sympathy regarding Sarhan's "sickness" and asks about the name of the medicine, Sarhan twists his tongue with words that do not make any sense, but include scientific terms such as "hemoglobin." The Shaykh offers to read the name of the medicine for the pasha, who becomes very confused. Assuming that the Shaykh cannot understand the French letters printed on the bottle, the pasha hands the bottle to the Shaykh, who reads the words on the bottle out loud: "Cognac Tennessee *primaire qualité*." Surprised at the Shaykh's ability to read French, the pasha wonders, "How come you could read French?" The Shaykh replies, "I went to Paris on a scholarship." In this, Wahbi critiques how adherents of *tafarnug* have a preconceived notion of a fundamental contradiction between being

Figure 4.20 Metaphors of Islam ridiculed. Bishara Wakim as the pasha, to the left, lying to the Shaykh about the bottle of wine. *Bint Dhawat*, 1942.

religious and knowing French, often celebrated by proponents of *tafarnug* as the language of modernity and modernization. Wahbi's construction of the ridicule of Islam among the adherents of *tafarnug* is primarily connected with Islam being a component of the culture of the peasants. This correlation unfolds explicitly in the banquet scene.

In the banquet scene, Wahbi critiques *tafarnug* by introducing the Orientalist gaze at the peasants, the gaze of the *Khawagat*, in whose eyes the Cairene-bourgeoisie is keen to cultivate an amour-propre of being modern and civilized. Wahbi dedicates multiple shots to the depiction of unknown characters playing the roles of *Khawagat* invited to a banquet held at Ibrahim's house after he has got married to Samiya, who does not accept marriage to Ibrahim, although she loves him. And when she eventually agrees to the marriage, she does it to save her father from bankruptcy. Ibrahim holds a banquet to celebrate his victory in the parliamentary elections. A separate shot is dedicated to a lady holding up her magnifying glasses to look closely at Ibrahim's parents, who have just arrived at the party. Wahbi's shot shows the character of the *Khawagaya* as if she is examining alien creatures. Embarrassed by the apparel and behavior of her in-laws and feeling sorry about her amour-propre of *tafarnug* in front of her guests, Samiya appears to shrink in her seat. At the same time, Ibrahim's parents congratulate her on her marriage. She then faints out of shame. Simultaneously, the camera shifts to show Murad, pasha, and Sarhan rushing to hide under the table to escape the embarrassment. As the parents take their seats to dine next to their son, the following dialogue occurs:

> *Mother:* What type of dish is this?
>
> *Ibrahim:* Help yourself!
>
> *M:* [Pointing to the servant] Ask this guy to place the dish in front of me.
>
> *I:* [Addressing his servant] Place the dish in front of her, please. [Addressing his parents] Why do you look so confused? Father, show me your guts/courage (*himma*) and start eating.
>
> *Father:* I cannot eat with a fork and knife, son.
>
> *I:* And how about your hands? Are they not clean?
>
> *F:* I performed my ablution, and I prayed too. But I thought eating with your hands might be rude to your guests.
>
> *I:* No, of course not! What is rude about that? Many people do not eat with a fork and knife, and their hands are purer than others who eat with a fork and knife.
>
> *F:* If you say so! OK. [Let me start by taking] the name of God, the most merciful and the most compassionate. [Addressing his wife] Here, Bahana, take this piece [The camera moves to depict Ibrahim's guests laughing at his parents].
>
> *I:* [Ignores his guests' reaction and addresses his mother] Mother, cut a piece for me with your hand.
>
> *M:* Here you go, son [She hands him a piece from the turkey].

The above scene is not a conflict between traditional rituals (eating with washed hands) and modern rituals (eating with knives and forks). The conflict is a class conflict, in which *tafarnug* does not allow room for respecting the peasants and their dining habits, which are shaped partially by the peasants' culture of which Islam is a significant component. Wahbi starts the banquet scene with Ibrahim's parents arriving at their son's party in traditional dress, unlike all the other invitees, who dress in fashionable and expensive Parisian dresses and tuxedos. The father is dressed in a galabiya, a gown, and a turban. The mother is dressed in a black silk galabiya and a black silk scarf; she wears a traditional golden necklace (*libba*). The very announcement of the parents' arrival serves to declare the arrival of the culture, the language, and the tradition of the village. This message is evident in Wahbi's choice of the mother's words as she enters the dining room. Her northern rural accent precedes her physical presence. That is to say, the audience hears her voice before seeing her. She raises her voice, calling endearingly her son "Birahim" instead of using the standard pronunciation of the name Ibrahim. To Ibrahim's Cairene-bourgeoisie guests, the mother's vernacular is less classy than the Cairene vernacular. When the parents notice the luxury of the party and Ibrahim's new house in Cairo, the father chants, "May a stone reside in the eye of the envious, who would not wish to drive away the evil eye by remembering to mention a prayer for the Prophet" (*haswa fi 'ayn illi ma yisalli 'ala al-nabi*). The father's colloquial chant to Ibrahim's guests is also less modern and hence less classy. Ibrahim is depicted as aware of his guests' perception of his parents, and he orchestrates the scene to elicit that same reaction, which he knows is a product of his guest's adherence to *tafarnug*. In other words, the scene is a double-acting scene (i.e. Wahbi acts in the role of Ibrahim, and Ibrahim acts in front of his guests). We know this from Wahbi's employment of the reaction shot in which he depicts Ibrahim's servant smiling secretly at his master's scheme to challenge the *tafar-*

Figure 4.21 Arrival of the peasants at the banquet. On the left, 'Abd al-Migid Shukri as Ibrahim's father. On the right, Latifa Amin plays the mother. *Bint Dhawat*, 1942.

Figure 4.22 The Orientalist gaze; the gaze of the *Khawagat*. An unknown actress playing the role of a *Khawagaya* invited to the banquet. *Bint Dhawat*, 1942.

nug of his guests. By the same token, to Ibrahim's father ablution (*wudu'*) is a marker of purity of both body and soul before prayer (*tahara*). As a man who lives in the countryside, Ibrahim's father is used to eating with his hands; he is not used to eating with a knife and fork. To him, the ablution ritual is a good enough indication of cleanliness. To the adhernts of *tafarnug*, eating with hands signifies hygienic backwardness, and ablution is insignificant in this regard.

By establishing a connection between *tafarnug*'s inferiority gaze at the peasants, metaphors representing Islam, and the Orientalist gaze, Wahbi does not only lampoon the class hierarchy of the 1940 and the supremacy of the *Khawaga*; rather, he presents a harsh critique of the falsity of modernity which the *Khawaga* and the Cairene-bourgoisie wish to enforce. This idea is more explicitly addressed in the dialogue of Wahbi's *Ibn al-Hadad*/The Son of the Blacksmith, 1944, in which he pinpoints how *tafarnug* commodifies the female body.

6. In Which Time Do You Live?

Ibn al-Hadad follows the misfortunes of Taha (Yusuf Wahbi), a son of a blacksmith who invests in his son's education and sends him to earn a doctoral degree in engineering in Europe (again, exact location unnamed, and this was most likely to avoid censorship). Taha's tragedy begins when he marries Zinat (Madiha Yusri), a young Cairene-bourgeoisie woman who, along with her family, has an extravagant lifestyle, which they see as the "good" modern lifestyle. To them, the attributes of "being modern" are the ability to master foreign forms of leisure like attending a *bal masqué* in the Arizona Hotel every week, holding a weekly cocktail party and birthday parties, going on safari trips to enjoy the "Oriental" atmosphere in the desert, gambling, and holding weekly dinner parties. Zinat's parents do not think that Taha's education in Europe can help him become the modern person they expect him to be. They consider Taha a socially inept person whose poor origins and upbringing among working-class Egyptians will prevent him from appreciating the modern Cairene-bourgeoisie lifestyle. Practices and festivals associated with Islam are objects of ridicule among Taha's in-laws. Consider the following scene:

> *Izzat:* We must throw a Christmas party this year.
> *Midhat:* Taha bey, the blacksmith, will not like the idea!
> *'Izzat:* What does this cook fixer (*kanun ni'ammar*) understand? Here comes Mum. Mum, is it true that we won't hold a Christmas party this year in our villa?
> *Taha:* [having entered the living area and the scene] No, 'Izzat bey, this year, we will hold a party to celebrate the anniversary of the Prophet's migration to Medina.
> *M:* [Sarcastically] Great! We will throw a Qur'anic recitation party (*khatma*)!
> *T:* Why not! Every person has religious beliefs. Until now, we never heard of foreigners holding a party for Qur'anic recitations in Ramadan, and neither do they celebrate the birth anniversary (*mawlid*) of Muslim saints like al-Sayyida's [Zaynab or Nafisa].
> *M:* I bet when you were a kid, you carried a lantern and roamed around the streets of your [poor neighborhood] along with kids singing in

CARICATURING DOMINANT MODERNITY (*TAFARNUG*) | 237

Figure 4.23 *Tafarnug* and the ridicule of Islamic festivities. To the left, Yusuf Wahbi as Taha talking to his in-laws about their plans for celebrating the New Year. *Ibn al-Haddad*, 1944.

>   celebration of Ramadan *Wahawi ya wahawi iyyaha* (Come Closer to
>   See the Crescent).
> *T:* That is true; I did. You have not enjoyed the pleasure of that incredible
>   experience because you lived all your life as strangers in your country.
>   You lived intruding on festivals of other peoples.
> *M:* [Responding in French] That is too much, 'Izzat (*alo 'Izzat! Ç'est trop*).

The conflict in the above scene is not because Taha does not like to celebrate Christmas. The conflict is a class conflict. Taha is seen as less modern than his in-laws because he adheres to the practices of *awlad al-balad*, who celebrate Islamic religious festivals such as the Hijra, and the Prophet's birth (*mawlid*), by holding a Qur'anic recitation banquet (*khatma*).

Through Taha's characterization and awareness of the Cairene-bourgeoisie's inferiority gaze at working-class Egyptians, Wahbi critiques *tafarnug*. Not only is Taha depicted as being aware that his in-laws accept him to save them from bankruptcy, but he is also aware that they expect him to be ashamed of his class of origin, a point of weakness that it occurs to them they can use to control his wealth. While Taha does not see himself as inferior and finds Zinat's family's dependency shameful, he does not use it to make the family feel inferior. To Taha, the issue at stake does not just involve a class trying to live above its means. He sees it as a symptom of a deeper societal problem facing modernity in Egypt. Taha accuses Zinat and her family of misunderstanding and misrepresenting the values of modernity, hence setting a deformed example of modernity for others. In the following scene, Taha returns from the factory after reading in the popular *al-Dustur* newspaper that Zinat is lost in the desert, where she went on a safari trip with her friends for a few nights. After checking that Zinat is back home safe and sound, Taha seizes an opportunity to react to what he finds a consistent irresponsible pattern in Zinat's lifestyle:

> *Taha:* What happened was too much to comprehend. From now on, I prevent my wife from mixing with banal (*mubtadhal*) youth . . . I stop you from mingling in that environment.
> *Zinat's Mother:* What nonsense!
> *Zinat's Father:* What kind of time do you live in?
> *T:* We live in the most dangerous time; it is the time of non-gradual transition from exaggerated prohibitions (*hijab*) to the banal expression of liberties (*sufur*); it is the time in which vices overcome virtues. We live in chaos everywhere, a confused father, a blind imitator mother, and a daughter adhering to nothing but *tafarnug*. Yesterday, a girl would be shy to stand behind the window, and today parents celebrate their daughter's presence among a group of drunk people in the middle of the desert. What remained undone is to legalize (*nihallil*) and illegalize (*niharram*) without consideration of honor (*sharaf*) and reputation (*'ard*) . . . [Taha addresses Zinat]. You did not marry me. You put your class on one side of the scale pan and my wealth on the other. This way, we become equal in your eyes. You are nothing but a doll who cares only about ornament and clothes. I have not found any life partner in you, unfortunately.

For the moment, I shall resist the temptation to critique Wahbi's depiction of Taha's views on women's freedom. I shall deal with this point later.

The implication of the above scene is not Taha's objection to Zinat's interest in being an independent woman. It lies instead in her lack of interest in her independence and in reducing the idea of being a free modern woman to the practice of *tafarnug*. In contrast, she remains utterly dependent on others.[19] What Taha's in-laws advocate as freedom for women is primarily an objectification and commodification of the female body. They teach their daughter freedom of choice by teaching her only how to master foreign forms of dance and music and develop a sensibility for enjoying art originating in Egypt, but through an Orientalist gaze, while favoring tango more. They encourage her not to breastfeed her child and to hire a nanny to look after the child even when the child is ill. They encourage the child to detach emotionally from the mother so that Zinat can spend the night partying while her son suffers from fever. They are not interested in modern notions of equity and social justice that support men's and women's education and financial independence. After all, their two sons are as dependent as their daughters. They have no interest in developing human behavior by encouraging innovation. Instead, they value and encourage imitation. On one occasion, Taha returns home carrying a gift for his child. His in-laws fail to understand his reasons for him choosing a toy grinding machine over a more conventional toy, like a wooden horse or a plastic doll. Taha's point is to raise the child's interest and curiosity in creativity rather than buying him a toy, which teaches him passivity, repetition, and imitation. Similarly, Taha's Cairene-bourgeoisie in-laws fail to understand Taha's motives for inviting the workers for dinner at his villa; they fail to see his stance as an expression of gratitude to the workers as business partners. To the adherents of *tafarnug*, Taha is merely an advocate of communist values. In short, they fail to see that he is not anti-modern; he is anti-*tafarnug*.

Kamal Salim takes the critique of *tafarnug* a step forward by representing modes of local resistance in *al-Mazahir*/Appearances, 1945. A new bourgeoisie class that emerged in Egypt at the end of World War II led to that resistance. The emerging bourgeoisie class could not resist *tafarnug* on its own, because the financial interest of the class members was bound by their acceptance in existing Cairene-bourgeoisie social circles and their adherence to *tafarnug*. But that new bourgeoisie class leaned more toward *awlad al-balad* and supported their resistance to *tafarnug*.

7. Stop Behaving Like an *Indigène*!

Al-Mazahir/Appearances, 1945, unlike earlier movies, presents an explicit critique of *tafarnug* in the dialogue and gives voice to the uneducated working-class woman. Earlier films made it a pre-condition for peasants or working-class Egyptians to be educated and to have exposure to European culture (primarily French) in order to be tolerated under the same roof as the adherents of *tafarnug*. In earlier movies, a mediator (an educated subaltern) often spoke for the uneducated subaltern, who had no exposure to Europe. In *al-Mazahir*, the working-class Egyptians have no physical encounters with Europe. To them, if modernity is nothing but *tafarnug*, it is indeed an unjust practice. By allowing the uneducated working class to critique *tafarnug* without resorting to a mediator, Salim empowers the subaltern to claim their space on the screen as a constructed public sphere.

Al-Mazahir follows the story of Mahmud (Yahya Shahin), a mechanic who advocates socialist democratic views among the uneducated working-class Egyptians living in Bab al-Sha'iriyya, a popular neighborhood in Cairo. Mahmud's beloved neighbor, Haniyya, moves out of the neighborhood to live with her uncle, Radwan (Fu'ad Shafiq). The latter made his money during the war and moved to Zamalek, a rich neighborhood in Cairo at that time. In Zamalek, Haniyya is introduced to feudal dependency, which she briefly favors over her life with Mahmud.

Kamal Salim constructs *tafarnug* through the character of Munira ('Ulwiyya Gamil), a Cairene-bourgeoisie woman who lost her wealth and had to marry Radwan, who does not come from an aristocratic family but is rich enough to keep up with Munira's standards of living. The following scene depicts Radwan and his wife Munira in conflict over the cultural code of communication that ought to be used in their daily life:

> *Gizawi:* Please pardon me for interrupting you, Your Excellency.
> *Radwan:* What is it? What is up, Gizawi?
> *Munira:* [Shouting at her husband] Radwan, this is unbearable! When will you stop behaving in an indigenous (*baladi*) way? I told you a thousand times not to call him by the name Gizawi.

R: [Sarcastically] Do you prefer if I import a name for him? [addressing Gizawi] Is not your name Gizawi?

M: [Answering on behalf of Gizawi] Yes, but at my Dad's house, we used to call him Jizi.

G: That is true. The pasha used to call me Jizi, and the noble brothers of the lady also called me Jizi.

M: [Addressing her husband Radwan] Please do not confuse the house's ambiance. Here, we live in Zamalek, not in Bab al-Sha'iriyya.

R: Did Bab al-Sha'iriyya commit a sin (*kafarit*)? Why did you marry a man from Bab al-Sha'iriyya if you grew up in Garden City? But I shall overlook all this nonsensical talk of yours! [Addressing Gizawi] Why did you interrupt us, Mr. Jizi?

G: There is a girl outside. She looks *indigène* and *pauvre*.

R: [addressing his wife] What does *indigène* mean? Ma'am, please translate!

M: [laughs] Jizi meant to say she is an indigenous (*baladi*) girl.

R: An indigenous girl!

J: Yes, your Excellency, and she also said she is your relative!

R: My relative! I do not have any relatives alive.

J: She explained to me that she is your niece.

R: My niece!

J: Her name is Haniyya, your Excellency.

R: Haniyya! That is true. I remember now.

M: Is she the daughter of your brother Mubarak?

R: [addressing Gizawi] Invite her in!

J: Where do you want me to invite her, your Excellency? Indeed, you do not want me to ask her here inside the salon? Her looks . . . [interrupted]

R: That is nonsense! Hurry up and do as I said. Invite her in.

M: [addressing her husband] Radwan, this girl should not know anything about her share of the inheritance.

R: How come? Is that not right? Do you want me to steal her money? Was not my brother my partner in the mills?

M: When he was your partner, the mills were facing foreclosure, and you used to live in dust and mud in the dirty narrow slums.

> *R:* Munira, those dirty narrow slums gave you the money which enabled you to live in the clean houses with those high ceilings.
>
> *M:* Rudi, behave yourself.
>
> *R:* My name is not Rudi. My name is Radwan. Do not make me a *Khawaga*, please.

The above tension between Radwan and Munira is a byproduct of Munira's *tafarnug*. She names everything around her in French; she uses short English forms of names to call her husband and butler. Instead of the Arabic name Radwan, Munira calls her husband "Rudi." Instead of the name "Gizawi," an adjective relating the butler to the Giza governorate, Munira calls her butler "Jizi". Rudi and Jizi are the short forms that follow the same pattern as is used in English to "shorten" the "long" form of James into Jimmy and John into Johnny. Likewise, Munira uses a short form for her name, and her butler calls her "Lady Rudi."

Salim critiques *tafarnug* through the conflict between the butler Jizi (Muhammad al-Dib) and Umm 'Azzuz, a working-class Egyptian woman (*bint balad*) nanny (Fardus Muhammad) who used to work at Radwan's house before he married Munira and moved to Zamalek. Unlike Jizi, Umm 'Azzuz, in the following scene, challenges Munira's enforcement of *tafarnug*:

> *Radwan:* Please listen carefully!
>
> *Umm 'Azzuz:* Yes, master (*si*) Radwan.
>
> *Munira:* My blood boils when I hear you say the word "*si*." Where do you think you live? We do not live in an alley here. He is to be addressed as the "bey." Address him with "Your Excellency."
>
> *U:* I cannot. My tongue is not used to this title. I am used to addressing him as *si* Radwan. That is how it used to be when I lived in his father's house. Even when he becomes a pasha, I will still address him as *si* Radwan.
>
> *R:* [Addressing his wife] Please keep yourself busy with your *Khawaga* Jizi and leave us to our norms (*akhlaqina*). We are *awlad balad*.

The tension in the above scene is not only class tension. Umm 'Azzuz is aware of her status as a servant in Radwan's house, but she also thinks that she is a member of Radwan's family and entitled to an opinion on family affairs. That is how she used to be treated in the house of Radwan's father in the allies of the popular neighborhood of Bab al-Shaʿiriyya. The tension arises because of Munira's interest in suppressing Umm ʿAzzuz's status as a member of Radwan's family. Through her attempt to enforce *tafarnug*, Munira stresses the inferiority of Umm ʿAzzuz, who refuses to be programmed. To Umm ʿAzzuz, accepting behaving like Jizi means accepting to be treated as inferior, which she forcefully refuses as she is used to being respected. She is not, for example, used to being addressed by her first name. The name "Umm ʿAzzuz" is *kunya* used to show respect for her age. She respects her employer Radwan and is used to calling him in Egyptian colloquial *si*, a short form for the colloquial *sidi*, which could be traced to the standard Arabic word *sayyidi* (my master/lord). On many occasions, the word signifies a master–servant relationship. The word can be seen as a symbol of a woman's inferiority to her husband. But on many other occasions, it is used to show respect between wife and husband. The equivalent of the masculine *si* is the feminine *sitti* or *sitt*, which translates literally as lady. The famous singer Umm Kulthum used to be called *al-sitt* to acknowledge her respected status as "the lady" or the *diva* of Egyptian or Arabic singing. The mutual respect between Umm ʿAzzuz and Radwan infuriates Munira,

Figure 4.24 Confronting *tafarnug*. To the left, Muhammad al-Dib plays the butler Jizi. To the left, Fardus Muhammad as Umm ʿAzzuz. *Al-Mazahir*, 1945.

because it challenges her efforts to impose *tafarnug* as the only way to become modern.

In addition to making the subaltern challenge the superiority of *tafarnug* and its adherents, Salim capitalizes on costumes to mark the difference between *tafarnug*, modernity, and counter-modernity. Umm 'Azzuz is mainly dressed in the famous black silk scarf and galabiya, a typical dress for a middle-aged *bint balad*. In all her scenes with Jizi and adherents of *tafarnug*, Umm 'Azzuz is depicted in her traditional attire. Her choice, however, is not necessarily a stance against modern fashion. Umm 'Azzuz functions as a mediator between Radwan's niece, Haniyya, and her new life in Zamalek; she teaches her how to acquire the latest fashion. Umm 'Azzuz also wears a dress and a coat and carries an umbrella. She boldly resists the local prejudices of a tarbush maker (*tarabishi*), who tries to tease her by calling her names like "Ma'am Umbrella" to stigmatize her as a westernized woman because she is not dressed in the more traditional galabiya. Salim frames the character of the tarbush maker ('Abd al-'Aziz Khalil) as a negative representation of tradition. Since the fashion of the tarbush was on the wane, tarbush-makers bullied people into wearing it in the name of tradition and authentic nationalism. Salim uses this character to depict a counter-modern reaction that reduces tradition to a question of the form via which regressive forces thrive and preserve their power and wealth. In recording a confrontation between the *trabishi* and Umm 'Azzuz, Salim underscores the difference between modernity as primarily a question of eliminating social inequality, counter-modernity as a false representation of tradition, and *tafarnug* as a false representation of modernity.

Despite attempts at resistance, it seems that *tafarnug* became more dominant after World War II. By 1945, Fu'ad Shafiq, the same actor who played Radwan, played another role that represented *tafarnug* as a Faustian temptation among uneducated and educated working-class Egyptians. Yusuf Wahbi, in *Safir Gahannam*/The Ambassador of Hell, 1945, introduces *tafarnug* as a product of a new capitalist economy resulting from the United States' growing influence in the region after World War II. The new *tafarnug* intensifies the gap between classes and gives the new Cairene-bourgeoisie class more power and control than it already has. Here Wahbi takes the critique of *tafarnug* a step forward by showing how it shifts from being a delusive amour-propre and false consciousness of modernity to being what later became dubbed neoliberalism backed by the instrumental use of reason.

8. Is Columbus Any Better than de Lesseps?

Safir Gahannam was written and directed by Yusuf Wahbi. The movie is a thriller that presented Satan on the screen for the first time in Egyptian cinema. Wahbi employs the *Thousand and One Nights* frame story. The first narrator is a mother telling her daughter about the newly released film by Yusuf bey Wahbi, thereby underscoring the rising popularity of Wahbi as a filmmaker after World War II. The second narrative frame is a dream. The hero, Ramadan Abd al-Khallaq (Fu'ad Shafiq), is a primary-school teacher; he goes to bed angry after having had a bad day at work and a fight with his wife and children. The influence of the *Nights* on the narration can hardly be grasped from the cinematography. Much of the effect shows in the dialogue, which is written in the form of rhymed colloquial prose, like the *Nights*.

The movie constructs *tafarnug* as a Faustian temptation. Satan first appears to the audience as a deformed human figure. The film characters, however, only get to see Satan in disguise. Of all the possible forms of disguise that Wahbi could have chosen to frame and present Satan, he chooses the character of Bahir 'Irfan, a lawyer from the United States, described in the movie as *bilad al-Amrikan*. Mr. 'Irfan wants to make a deal, or tempt a poor primary-school teacher named Ramadan 'Abd al-Khallaq. The agreement entails that Ramadan betray his conscience by taking a false oath that he has a twin brother who migrated to America a long time ago and died there. In return, Ramadan will inherit the wealth of that alleged brother. After giving up on his prayers, which he finds useless as they do not save him from poverty or cure his sick wife, Ramadan decides to take the false oath, thus accepting the deal and betraying his conscience.

As the journey of Ramadan's temptation unfolds, Wahbi constructs a correlation between Satan and American *tafarnug*, which is not so different from European forms of luxury and is even more hegemonic when it comes to French culture. For example, Satan's two assistants, Samir ('Abd al-Ghani al-Sayyid) and Samira (Layla Fawzi), abide by the French dress code. When Satan transforms his assistants from statues to humans, they greet Ramadan and his wife in French. Similarly, Ramadan is introduced to modernity as

Figure 4.25 Yusuf Wahbi as Satan before metamorphosing. *Safir Gahannam*, 1945

Figure 4.26 The arrival of American *tafarnug*. Yusuf Wahbi as Satan in the disguise of the lawyer Bahir 'Irfan. *Safir Gahannam*, 1945.

an indulgence in American and European forms of luxury through the presence of a tailor who also speaks French and introduces Ramadan to different dress codes. Satan, in disguise, looks like Charles Boyer in *Gaslight*, 1944, dir. George Dewey Cukor, the well-known Hollywood thriller released in Egypt as Wahbi worked on his movie. Satan plays classical music. Of all the notes that Wahbi could have chosen, he makes Satan play one which sounds like an improvisation on the famous motif from Beethoven's Fifth Symphony known as "Fate knocking on the door." This choice, probably supported by the composer of the film's soundtrack, Ibrahim Haggag (1916–87), surely helps Wahbi complement the scene in which Ramadan's son attempts to kill Bahir 'Irfan (or Satan), hence implying that demise knocks on the door of everyone, not just Satan. In a sense, the scene correlates perishing with American *tafarnug*, which, as Satan declares, idolizes money that will enslave nations. Wahbi further correlates American *tafarnug* with societal modernization without cultural modernity. His Satan has a science lab in which he uses machines that aids him in his schemes. When Satan tries to tempt the son of Ramadan, he resorts to cocaine, which then represented a new form of drug addiction. Satan seduces the son and makes him kill his mistress by supplying him with dynamite to blow up the theater as the performance takes place. The scene in which the theater is being blown up seems to be an attempt by Wahbi to correlate American *tafarnug* with massive destruction and even terror (in the context of the film, directed against the performing arts, which is a domain for the public use of reason). This is quite surprising, because the first use in World War II of weapons of mass destruction took place in August 1945, and the film was released in February 1945.

American *tafarnug* acts on both the body and the conscience to reassign values and regulate the imagination of what is a superior body and superior luxury. Ramadan and his wife already have a local schema for the expressions of wealth and luxury. For example, Ramadan's imagining of luxurious dress has to do with silk suits made in Mahalla, famous for its textile industry. Ramadan's wife wants a colorful scarf with crystal beads (*mandil bi-quya*) to look wealther. However, as Satan argues, there is no way of introducing Ramadan and his wife to the Cairene-bourgeoisie community without shaping the body according to the American and European criteria of fitness and beauty. This transformation means that Ramadan and his wife must lose

248 | FILMING MODERNITY AND ISLAM IN COLONIAL EGYPT

Figure 4.27 Correlating American *tafarnug* with demise. Wahbi as Satan playing the piano. *Safir Gahannam*, 1945.

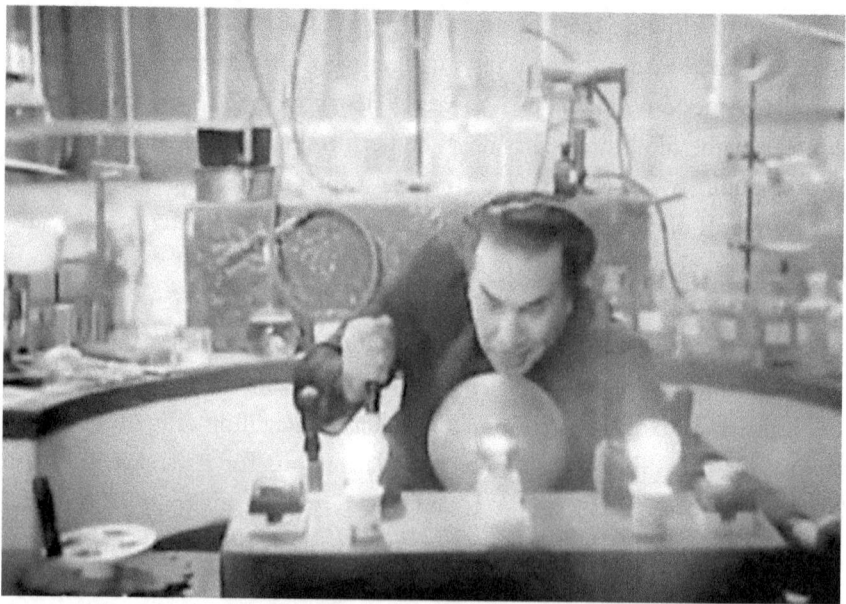

Figure 4.28 Correlating American *tafarnug* with the utilitarian use of technology. Wahbi as Satan in his technologically advanced lab. *Safir Gahannam*, 1945.

CARICATURING DOMINANT MODERNITY (*TAFARNUG*) | 249

Figure 4.29 American *tafarnug* and the spread of weapons of mass destruction. On the right, Wahbi plays Satan, holding dynamite while talking to Ramadan's son (Fakhir Fakhir), to the left. *Safir Gahannam*, 1945.

Figure 4.30 Introducing the subaltern to American *tafarnug*. On the left, Fu'ad Shafiq as Ramadan. In the middle, Yusuf Wahbi as Satan. On the right, Fardus Muhammad, Ramadan's wife, talks to the tailor (standing far right). *Safir Gahannam*, 1945.

Figure 4.31 American *tafarnug* and the false notion of choice. Unknown actress as the costume designer, who introduces Ramadan's wife to her hats options. *Safir Gahannam*, 1945.

weight, receive a massage, and go into an oven, just like cars go into the oven. This process transfers the bodies of working-class Egyptians from human bodies to commodities. Yet what makes American *tafarnug* far more dangerous than European *tafarnug* is how it leads to a systematic erasure of integrity and freedom of conscience in society. Consider the following scene depicting an argument between Ramadan and his superior at school:

> *Headmaster:* So, you failed the student 'Ali Khatir. Why did you give the student seven points in Arabic, two in history, and one in geography?
> *Ramadan:* Sir, the student deserves zero points in every subject.
> *H:* What! Do you want to close the school and shut down my business?
> *R:* God forbid, Sir!
> *H:* Don't you know that the student's father is wealthy? He might think we neglected his son's education, and he might send the child to another school. And all this fuss will happen because you refuse to give a few extra credits. Let us see; you gave the student seven in Arabic. This grade is unfair; his handwriting looks exquisite.
> *R:* What has his handwriting got to do with his knowledge of the language?

H: Well, let me explain the connection in one line. It is because he is the son of Khatir pasha

R: I do not understand!

H: You do not need to understand. Let us add eight credits for his handwriting. This way, he will pass in Arabic. Let us move to his grade in geography. You gave him one. Could you explain why?

R: He said that Paris was the capital of the USA.

H: How do we know he was wrong? Nobody can guarantee the borders of countries these days. He is a foresighted kid. Add ten points for his foresight and another four points for his sense of humor.

R: Points for a sense of humor! How is this even possible?

H: Sense of humor, these days, is one of the main reasons for success. What remains is his grade in history. Did you give him two points? Your grading system is discriminatory!

R: He said that de Lesseps discovered America.

H: So what! Is Christopher Columbus any better than de Lesseps? Are you making exceptions for Columbus and discriminating against de Lesseps? Did you see Columbus while discovering America with your own eyes?

R: And how about his answer to the second question on who built the pyramids?

H: What was his answer?

R: Greta Garbo!

H: [laughs] That kid's sense of humor is hysterical. It is a great advertisement for our monuments because Greta Garbo is more famous than [the pyramids of] Khufu and Manqara'. The kid must pass all subjects. Have a good day, Mr. Ramadan Abd al-Khallaq.

R: But this is a matter of integrity!

H: Get out of here! Idiot!

Through the double standards, hypocrisy, and contradictions in the character of the headmaster, Wahbi simultaneously represents and caricatures the neoliberal economics accompanying American *tafarnug* and the subsequent loss of freedom of conscience. On the one hand, the headmaster names his school Public Integrity School (*madrasit al-dhimma al-ahliyya*); he has a picture on the wall with the word "integrity" framed. On the other hand, the headmaster finds Ramadan's integrity a threat to enrollment among

Figure 4.32 Correlating American *tafarnug* with loss of integrity. On the left, Fu'ad Shafiq as Ramadan 'Ab al-Khallaq. On the right, Muhammad Kamal al-Masri as the school headmaster. *Safir Gahannam*, 1945.

upper-class families who ensure the financial stability of the school, which has become a mere business. Ironically, the scene frames integrity as proportional. To the headmaster, there is a fundamental crisis in integrity around the world and in writing the history of this world. By making the headmaster present the discovery of America by Christopher Columbus and the Suez Canal project initiated by de Lesseps as two faces of the same coin, Wahbi sends up American *tafarnug* as a byproduct of neocolonial projects. More ironically, and as the movie unfolds, Ramadan's American *tafarnug* does not change his deteriorating economic situation. Instead, it makes him fall into more debt. And the film becomes an allegory for the consequences of an American *tafarnug*, another false consciousness of modernity with, potentially, more massive impact and more deteriorating social conditions. *Safir Gahannam*, however, remains one of the earliest and rarest commentaries on the correlation between American *tafarnug* and the threat to the principle of freedom of conscience that makes secularism central to the liberal political philosophy of modernity in Egypt. It is almost an early prediction of the American imperial adventure in the Muslim world, which begins after World War II. Wahbi here suggests that American *tafarnug*'s secular cast reveals itself in its civilizing and disciplinary aspects that contradict its core value of immunizing politics from religion and guaranteeing freedom of religion and religious tolerance by ensuring that faith is practiced without coercion, out of individual choice and personal consent. American *tafarnug* thus violates people's right to religious freedom and hence contradicts a core commitment at the center of modern liberal democratic governance. Instead, American *tafarnug* is a regression that will bring nothing new save further enslavement of peoples and nations whose religions come under fire. It is not surprising, then, to find explicit critiques of how *tafarnug*, be it American or European, leads to the appropriation of Islamic legal tradition to sustain a class hierarchy that thrives on colonization and war. In *Talaq Su'ad Hanim*/Divorce of Su'ad Hanim, 1948 and *al-Zawja al-Sabi'a*/The Seventh Wife, 1950, Anwar Wagdi and Ibrahim 'Imara respectively present a rising trajectory showing the changing images of women's agency in condemning *tafarnug*'s appropriation of Islamic personal law. More importantly, the films share an understanding of the appropriation of Islamic law amidst caricatures of modernity to be the use of "legal means to achieve an illegal end" (sig. *dhari'a* pl. *dhara'i*).[20]

9. Marry, Divorce, Remarry, and Humiliate!

Talaq Su'ad Hanim/Divorce of Su'ad Hanim was directed in 1948 by Anwar Wagdi (1904–54), an Egyptian film star and director born in Syria and who migrated to Egypt during his early teenage years. Wagdi started his acting career in theater. He got his first role in an adaptation of Shakespeare's *Merchant of Venice* performed by Yusuf Wahbi's Ramsis Theatre Troupe. Wagdi's film career started in 1927 when Badr Lama gave him a supporting role in Lama's film *Qubla fi al-Sahra'*/A Kiss in the Desert, 1927. Wagdi left a legacy of over sixty films, of which the most famous are the ones in which he acted with his wife, the *diva* Layla Murad. Wagdi is also credited with introducing young Fayruz, the Egyptian version of Shirley Temple, in his blockbuster musicals *Yasmin*/Jasmin, 1952 and *Dahab*/Dahab, 1953. *Talaq Su'ad Hanim* is Wagdi's fifty-fourth film. He wrote the screenplay in 1940 when he was an actor with the National Theater Troupe, earning only seven Egyptian pounds a month and struggling to make ends meet. On one occasion, he wanted to sell the story to consolidate his debts to the butcher in his neighborhood. When Wagdi met Muhammad Karim around the time the latter was finishing the shooting of *Yawm Sa'id*/Happy Day, 1939, Karim initially refused to read the story because he doubted that Anwar Wagdi was the author, since he did not think highly of Wagdi and was always under the impression that he was a opportunist (*halangi*). Impressed by the screenplay, Karim convinced 'Abd al-Wahhab to buy it for a hundred pounds. Later, Wagdi repurchased the story from 'Abd al-Wahhab, who had kept it in his office for years, hoping to produce it one day.[21]

The plot of *Talaq Su'ad Hanim* follows Su'ad (Bahiga Hafiz) and her husband, Hasan bey (Farid Shawqi). They strive to impress their Cairene-bourgeoisie peers with their ability to master European forms of modern luxury at home and during leisure-time. Su'ad and her husband do not work. They are depicted as feudal brats living off their families' inheritance. They rush into one divorce after another until they find themselves trapped in a situation where they cannot remarry unless Su'ad marries someone else first. In normal circumstances, Islamic law allows the same couple to be divorced twice, and they can remarry a third time. However, if divorce occurs for the third time, the couple cannot remarry unless the wife marries someone else and gets divorced. That is to say, a fourth reunion between the same couple cannot take place unless the wife is given a complete chance to marry and settle with another man. To overcome the dilemma, Su'ad's family resorts to the practice of legitimator (*muhallil*), which translates literally as someone who makes something legal. In practice, the legitimator is the man who marries the divorced wife to authenticate or make permissible some legal process that is otherwise of doubtful legality or prohibited. The unannounced part of the contract is that this temporary marriage's consummation does not occur. The practice of *muhallil* formed part of the mechanisms and procedures subsumed under legal tricks (*hiyal*) used to evade the spirit of the law while technically satisfying its letter.[22] Su'ad and her family find their potential legitimator; a homeless young man named Wahid (Anwar Wagdi). He agrees to marry Su'ad in exchange for a large sum of money. But soon, Wahid regrets his participation in the deal. In the following monologue, Wahid condemns Su'ad's obsession with projecting herself as a modern woman through *tafarnug*, which leads not only to the appropriation of Islamic law but to essentializing a woman's respective share in her own humiliation and suffering in a patriarchal society:

> *Wahid:* You resorted to the *muhallil*, which you thought is a legal practice approved by Islamic law, while it is nothing but deceit (*tahayul*), lies, and hypocrisy (*nifaq*). The Prophet PBUH was reported to have said, "God cursed the *muhallil* and the one who accepts it" (*al-muhallal lahu*). I happened to be that cursed *muhallil*, and your plan was against my will. I participated with you in this conspiracy without being aware of its dishonesty. You are now pressuring me to divorce my wife. But why do you want me to do so? It is just so that Su'ad could return to the matrimony (*'isma*) of Hasan bey so that he could humiliate her again, torture her again and divorce her repeatedly. How is it possible to build a family and give birth to healthy children in this chaos, this cheating, and this hypocrisy? The *muhallil* serves an unjust end. Your participation in all this is a crime. [Addressing Su'ad's

Figure 4.33 *Tafarnug* appropriating Islamic personal law. From the far left: Anwar Wagdi as Wahid, Bishara Wakim as Su 'ad's father, Farid Shawqi as Hasan, and 'Aqila Ratib as Su'ad. In the middle, Fu'ad al-Gazayrli, the clergyman, who has performed the rituals and written the marriage contract. *Talaq Su'ad Hanim*, 1948.

father] You sacrificed your conscience, your honor, and your dignity, and you got your daughter married to an unknown man, a man you found in the street. You do not even know who he is? You tried to outwit (*tahayltum*) religion, people, and law. I am the poor, the homeless crook (*nassab*) who could not afford a piece of bread; I refuse to participate in these crimes at any cost. That does not mean I wish to keep my marriage rights. On the contrary, I do not aspire to that— [Addressing Su'ad] I am a poor man, and you are a rich woman. There are many barriers between us. Rest assured, I would not hesitate to divorce you if it is in your interest.

While Anwar Wagdi uses a male character to present his critique of the appropriation of Islamic personal law, director Ibrahim 'Imara, in *al-Zawaja al-Sabi'a*, takes the critique further by giving a voice and agency to women, the primary victims of the appropriation of Islamic personal law. 'Imara is mainly recognized as a director with a legacy of at least forty films, although he took supporting roles in many of his movies. He started his film career as an assistant director to Niyazi Mustafa in directing Nagib al-Rihani's most celebrated classic, *Si 'Umar*/Mr. 'Umar. In addition to *Al-Zawja al-Sabi'a*, some of 'Imara's most celebrated films include *Musmar Juha*/Juha's Tack, 1952 (an anticolonialist film set in Kufa under Ottoman rule), *Lahn al-Wafa*/A Tune of Loyalty, 1955 (a romance musical featuring Shadiya and 'Abd al-Halim Hafiz), and *Hijrat al-Rasul*/The Migration to Medina, 1964, a representation of the Prophet Muhammad's second migration from Mecca to Medina in AD 622.

Al-Zawja al-Sabi'a follows the story of Wahid (Muhammad Fawzi) and his seventh marriage to Samiha (Mary Quieni), a feminist who believes in and advocates for the modern social roles of women as equal citizens to men. As the movie evolves and Samiha falls in love with Wahid, they decide to get married. But Wahid has kept his past hidden from Samiha. Before Wahid met Samiha, his *tafarnug* made him marry and divorce six times, primarily because none of his wives gave birth to a baby boy. When, eventually, Wahdi's secret is discovered, Samiha decides to teach him a lesson, that a woman is not merely a pot (*ma'un*) carrying a child; she is an equal actor in the universe and is capable of changing the unjust order of things. Through a series of comic schemes, 'Imara depicts Samiha employing every possible trick to prevent the consummation of her marriage so that Wahid would be forced outside his comfort

Figure 4.34 Mary Quini and Muhammad Fawzi. Posters for *al-Zawja al-Sabi'a*, 1950.

zone and become disoriented enough to divorce her according to her own will, not according to his will. When Samiha achieves her goal, the director Ibrahim 'Imara depicts her reciting the following monologue:

> I am glad that I won over you at last. I forced you to divorce me. I made you divorce me against your will; this divorce is not according to your wish and your money. You divorced me before consummating the marriage and before deciding to throw me away like the six women you threw away before me. Can you explain to me what crime those six women committed? Their crime was that they did not give birth to a boy. This, in your view, was their horrible crime. I wanted to be separated from you at any cost because I never

Figure 4.35 *Tafarnug* abusing Islamic personal law. Mary Quini as Samiha reciting Qur'anic verses in *al-Zawja al-Sabi'a*, 1950.

felt my future would be safe. I have always felt threatened with divorce. [Let me remind you] dear bey that children are sustenance (*rizq*) from God just like wealth, and do not forget that God said in the Holy Book, "In God lies the supremacy over heaven and earth. God creates what He wills. He gives whom He wills girls and gives whom He wills boys or both. And He makes barren whom He wills. He is All-knowing and All-Capable."[23]

In this scene, Samiha quotes directly from the Qur'an to critique Wahid's claim to be modern. He does not acknowledge women's new social roles as citizens; instead, he denies women even their traditional rights dictated by Islamic law. Some of these basic rights include sharing with Samiha that he was married before and acknowledging that women are not responsible for the sex of the fetus. By depicting Samiha reciting a verse from the Qur'an, Ibrahim 'Imara forcefully puts forward a textual source of Islamic law to challenge how *tafarnug* preserves patriarchal norms and its appropriation of Islamic law to concentrate wealth and power within male members of the family, even if the cost is to challenge God's omnipotence, a fundamental doctrine in Islamic law.

By 1950, *tafarnug* produces a form-focused counter-*tafarnug* stance in which the female body becomes a battleground for the proponents of *tafarnug* and the advocates of counter-*tafarnug*. Perhaps no film reveals how the counter-*tafarnug* position is a form-focused reaction to *tafarnug* better than the monologue on modernity (*madaniyya*) in Sayyid Ziyada's film *Khadra wa-l-Sindibad al-Qibli*/Khadra and the Upper Egyptian Sindibad, 1951.

10. What Modernity, Your Excellency?

Khadra wa-l-Sindibad al-Qibli/Khadra and the Upper Egyptian Sindibad, 1951 is a light romantic comedy and the second film in a series of movies produced by the brothers Ziyada. They made several films through their newly established film company, the People's Film Company. Unlike previous filmmakers whose works are discussed in this chapter, the brothers Ziyada grew up in rural Egypt near Tanta. Sayyid Ziyada used to work as a journalist in the popular variety magazine *al-Lata'if al-Musawwara*. He was a poet and songwriter. Although not as famous as Karim, Salim, Mizrahi, and Wahbi, Ziyada started producing movies as early as 1935, producing more than sixty features. Many of his films presented a melodramatic imagination of the migration from the country to the city; he focused on the misfortunes that befell non-Cairene women when encountering the norms of a Cairene-bourgeoisie community. He also tackled topics like honor killing and forced marriages. The *Khadra* series was inspired by the release of Richard Wallace's *Sinbad the Sailor*, 1947, which was influenced by *The One Thousand and One Nights*. The influence of the *Nights* on Ziyada's movie appears in his use of rhymed colloquial prose. It can also be traced in the costumes and soundtrack. For example, Ziyada makes Khadra's father dress like Sindbad and uses Rimsky-Korsakov's *Scheherazade* as a soundtrack in some scenes.

In both films, *Mughamarat Khadra*/The Adventures of Khadra, 1950 and *Khadra wa-l-Sindibad al-Qibli*/Khadra and the Upper Egyptian Sindibad, 1951, Ziyada presents a character-based comedy: that is, the comic effect or humor is driven by a persona invented by the performer, and often relies on stereotypes. For example, the persona of Khadra is presented as a stereotype of a young woman from Upper Egypt; she is illiterate, wealthy, and outspoken. Ziyada employs the Cairine-bourgeoisie's oversimplified image of the upper Egyptian woman to caricature *tafarnug*. This ironic power of Ziyada's stereotype in the *Khadra* series takes the critique of *tafarnug* to its utmost by framing adherents of *tafarnug* as a criminal gang using *tafarnug* as a camouflage to control rural bourgeoisie wealth through identity theft. It is imperative to note here that Ziyada's movies are also critical of the rural bourgeoisie, especially regarding the accumulation and transfer of wealth. For instance, Khadra's father is criticized for saving gold instead of investing his money in developing farming communities. Part Two, *Khadra wa-l-Sindibad al-Qibli*, questions the injustice that often befalls the peasants when the court assigns an adherent of *tafarnug* as the custodian of a trust fund. I read the two parts of the *Khadra* series as one unit. In doing so, I consider the thematic unity of the two movies. I by no means intend to overlook the dramatic context of each film and the slight variation in the plot dynamics.[24] I find it imperative to read the two movies as one unit because the construction of the character of Khadra as the main voice which critiques *tafarnug* starts in the first part of the

Figure 4.36 Poster for *Mughamarat Khadra* in *al-Ithnayn* magazine.

series. It is inaccurate to interpret Khadra's counter-*tafarnug* reaction in the modernity monologue—a song sung in the second part of the series—without considering her celebration of Cairo as the land of enlightenment, a song she sings in the first movie.

Mughamarat Khadra is the first part of the series. The film follows the challenges facing Khadra, who wants to protect her inheritance, over which two parties are competing. The first party is depicted as a group of greedy rural bourgeoisie characters. The second group is represented as a group of Cairene-bourgeoisie characters, whom Khadra's father mistakenly identifies as his nephews and nieces. To introduce Khadra, Ziyada utilizes reaction shots of Khadra's father and village men praising Khadra for being smarter (*ansah*) than her brother Faris (Ismaʻil Yasin). We know that village men value and respect Khadra's opinions and often consult her. Khadra first appears in the movie singing about her recently born buffalo that has fallen sick. The buffalo is Khadra's favorite pet, which she considers more of a family member. The scene is familiar and regular in the eyes of the village woman, who milks her buffalo daily and has a bond with it as a source of income. However, the scene is funny to the Cairene-bourgeoisie because it confirms their stereotype of a village woman whose life is tied to the buffalo. The Cairene-bourgeoisie often refer to this stereotype in Egyptian colloquial as "she comes from the buffalo side" (*gaya min wara al-gamusa*). The implication is that the village woman grows up behaving in the same way a buffalo does. That is to say, the village woman is rude and unable to express her thoughts in what the Cairene-bourgeoisie approve of as a "civilized manner," because a village woman spends a lot of her time in non-verbal communication attending to her buffalo's needs.

Khadra's first encounter with *tafarnug* is when her alleged Cairene-bourgeoisie cousins visit the village. When she first meets them, she comments, "I never knew that I have cousins who know how to dress so nicely." The comment implies that she is impressed by their European dress code and that she finds her cousins less conservative than she has imagined them to be. However, Khadra listens to her father's criticism of her views about her cousins. The father sums up her inability to understand their less conservative attitude as her failure to understand the idea of becoming modern, which Khadra's father describes in his vernacular as modernity of Cairo (*al-tumuddun bitaʻ Masr*).

Figure 4.37 Human–animal bond. Durriyya Ahmad as Khadra singing to her buffalo. *Mughamarat Khadra*, 1950.

To Khadra, Cairo becomes the land of light (*nur*), a common metaphor for enlightenment (*tanwir*). When Khadra travels with her alleged cousins to Cairo, she sings celebrating her expected experience of enlightenment in Cairo:

> Here I am; I left my village for the land of light (*bilad al-nur*)
> [Repeat]
> Will I find equity (*atnisif*) and live for months and years?
> Will I go back to the village tormented with sorrow?
> How puzzling are these thoughts!
> If only I could predict the future!

Khadra has many expectations from Cairo, where she hopes to find social justice. While Khadra develops a gaze at her Cairene cousins' adherence to the European dress code and social practices, Ziyada constructs the gaze as a stereotypical reaction of the peasant toward the unfamiliar practices of the city. Chief among the unfamiliar practices that receive Khadra's gaze are the

Figure 4.38 Transferring the inferiority gaze. Kamal al-Shinnawi as Kamal, right, and Durriya Ahmad as Khadra, left.

scenes of women smoking cigarettes, men giving attention to facial grooming in public, and a woman feeling free to take off her stockings in front of men, owning nude pictures in the house, and installing statues inside and outside her house.

A paradigm shift occurs in Khadra's attitude toward the Cairene-bourgeoisie's dress code when she travels with her Cairene-bourgeoisie cousins to Alexandria. On the beach, girls wearing bikinis exercise the inferiority gaze at Khadra because of her dress. When she asks Kamal (Kamal al-Shinnawi), a pianist she meets and falls in love with, why the girls are laughing, he replies, "Did I not tell you that people will find the way you dress funny?"

Just as Mizrahi employs the character of Samira in *Layla Bint al-Rif*, Ziyada uses the character of Kamal to transfer onto Khadra the peasant woman the inferiority gaze of adherents of *tafarnug*. The inferiority gaze that Khadra experiences on the beach produces a counter-*tafarnug* reaction, which focuses primarily on the rejection of the idea of "being modern" as expressed in the practice of *tafarnug*. Ziyada does not depict that rejection explicitly. He shows a process of negotiation of Khadra's amour-propre through a negotiation of her choice of apparel. This idea unfolds in two scenes. The first is Khadra's song, in which she criticizes beach practices.

On the beach, Khadra's initial unfamiliarity gaze at modern forms of dress changes to a reactionary immorality gaze, which could initially be interpreted as the male gaze. But Ziyada gives equal attention to the depiction of both male and female bodies in bathing suits. His choice seems to suggest that the focus of the gaze is the beach practices which Khadra considers degrading to local inhabitants (*ahl al-balad*), who overlook what Khadra describes as propriety (*adab*) and local norms of respectability (*hishma*). A connection between the inferiority gaze that Khadra experiences on the beach and the negotiation of her amour-propre is constructed in her interior monologue:

> *Khadra:* Does he love me as I love him? I do not think so. He is of a higher social status than I am. He looks a modern (*ala franka*) young man. He sees every day hundreds of beautiful Cairene girls who know how to wear modern dresses (*farankawi*); they speak foreign languages (*yurtunu*) and dance. Why cannot I be like them? I must be like them!

Torn between her condemnation of the inferiority gaze and the effect of the gaze on her, Khadra starts daydreaming of herself as a Cairene-bourgeoisie

Figure 4.39 Gazing at the unfamiliar. Durriyya Ahmad as Khadra gazing at beach activities. *Mughamarat Khadra*, 1950.

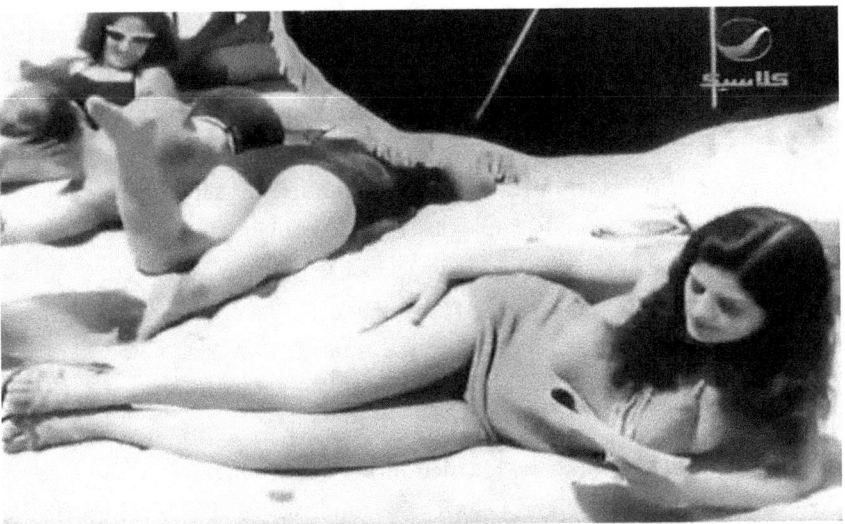

Figure 4.40 Unknown actors as a subject of the peasant gaze at unfamiliar beach activities. *Mughamarat Khadra*, 1950.

woman who has mastered *tafarnug*. Ziyada presents this conflict and its negotiation in Khadra's choice of dress in the dream. On the one hand, the dream scene depicts Khadra's desire to preserve her village dress. Khadra's conscience blames her for mistakenly thinking that she needs to change her dress code to appeal to Kamal, who is not an adherent of *tafarnug*. On the other hand, the scene reveals Khadra's desire to prove that she is equal to the adherents of *tafarnug*; she fancies showing her ability to master the attributes of *tafarnug* by mastering the French language and French fashion. As the story unfolds, Khadra finds nothing of modernity in Cairo but *tafarnug*, of which she becomes more conscious and more ready to fight back against in the second part, *Khadra wa-l-Sindibad al-Qibli*/Khadra and the Upper Egyptian Sindibad, 1951. Here, unlike Mizrahi, Ziyada does not make the peasant woman participate in a scheme to prove her equality through her ability to master *tafarnug*. He directly gives the peasant woman voice, and allows her to critique *tafarnug* as an exclusionist and false consciousness of modernity.

Khadra wa-l-Sindibad al-Qibli/Khadra and the Upper Egyptian Sindibad, 1951 tells the story of Muhsin pasha ('Abbas Faris), who loses his sanity after he learns that Lula, his daughter and heir residing in Brazil, has passed away. His nephew Zaki (Mahmud al-Miligi) and his girlfriend Fifi (Zuzu Shakib) manage to get a court order that makes Zaki the legal guardian of the pasha's estate. The manager of the estate, Fu'ad (Kamal al-Shinnawi), comes to know of the falsity of the news of Lula's death. Fu'ad seeks Lula's help to save her father and his wealth. Lula is scheduled to arrive in Cairo before the court order, but she postpones her trip suddenly. Faced with the delay to Lula's flight and the possibility that Zaki can act on the court order, Fu'ad convinces an Upper Egyptian village girl by the name of Khadra to introduce herself to Zaki and his Cairene-bourgeoisie social circles as Lula. Fu'ad has met Khadra on the train from Bani Suwayif to Cairo. Khadra was taking the train to al-Wasta, a stop between Cairo and Bani Suwayif, to treat her father, a fisherman with a mental disorder. The father (Hasan Fa'iq[Fayi']) lost his mind after watching the Hollywood blockbuster *Sinbad the Sailor*. He identifies with the character of Sindbad to the extent that he dresses and behaves like Sindbad; he also calls himself the southern Sindbad (*al-sindibad al-qibli*). The title serves to differentiate him from the Hollywood Sinbad, whom Khadra's father considers a northerner (*bahari*). The distinction also emphasizes Khadra's identity as southern girl vis-à-vis northern girls (*banat bahari*), who are often stereotyped in the south as less conservative and as leaning more toward *tafarnug*.

Ziyada takes the criticism of *tafarnug* a step ahead by framing it not only as a criminal activity but also as a sham (*fashr*). As a project of modernity, *tafarnug* fails to extend societal modernization to the countryside, for Khadra had to travel from her village to the peripheral city of Bani Suwayf and the center of the state, Cairo, just to find a doctor and treat her father. Moreover, adherents of American *tafarnug* after World War II lacks efficiency even when mastering their *tafarnug*. For example, Zaki doubts that Khadra is lying about her identity as Lula. When Khadra is introduced as Brazilian-Egyptian Lula to the Cairene-bourgeoisie community, Zaki decides to test her Spanish. The only Cairene-bourgeoisie person who knows Spanish turns out to be faking it. On another occasion, the estate manager, Fu'ad, tells Khadra that she can fake *tafarnug* to appear as Lula. Ironically, Khadra assures Fu'ad that she will fake all the etiquette required for *tafarnug*. She cannot pronounce the word "etiquette" correctly and often confuses it with the Arabic word for baby chicken (*katakit*). Somehow she manages the situation by forging a completely new word, namely "*kitikat*," with the last syllable prounced /kate/. The new word of course sounds neither like "baby chicken" nor like "etiquette." But

Khadra's statement "Do not worry, I memorized all the *kitikat* [i.e. etiquette]" (*ma-tikhafishi hafazt al- kitikat kulluh*) became one of the most popular jokes in Egypt, referred to in day-to-day conversations even today. Responding to modernity as a very inefficient version of *tafarnug* operating after World War II, Khadra sings the monologue below, which Ziyada co-authored with the prolific songwriter Fathi Qura:

Galal: What a paradise the era of modernity is!
Compare not the past to how the present is!
The present is a paradise! Indeed it is!
Our life progressed, and we adapted to a new lifestyle
Our daughters went to American schools
We transformed and understood how the world is.
Compare not the past to how the present is!
The present is a paradise! Indeed it is!

Khadra: Cut it short! Forget it. It is a gross failure! Indeed it is.
Pull yourselves together, Messrs. and Mistresses!
What modernity are you talking about, Your Excellency? It is a mess.
[Repeat]
It is over! You have turned modernity into a mess!
[Repeat]
Forget it! It is nothing but a gross failure! Indeed it is.
[Repeat]
[Interruption by young Cairene woman]

Young Cairene woman 1: What is she, and what does "it" want?

Khadra: I want you to cover your arm for our sake! That is what I want!
I want you to live for your man! That is what I want!
I swear that if he were to sell you in the market, you wouldn't trade for a rusted nickel.
That is all that your worth is.
Forget it! It is nothing but a gross failure! Indeed it is
[Repeat]
[Interruption by old Cairene woman]

Old Cairene woman: Oh, No! You became unbearably rude.

Khadra: The rudeness is your behavior. It is no use blaming you.
    It makes no difference in your case.
    For how much are you selling your flesh? I hope you are trading according to the law.
    Forget it! It is nothing but a gross failure!
    [Interruption by another young Cairene woman]

Young Cairene woman 2: Why are you so astonished?
    Do you not have [people dressed like us] in Brazil?

Khadra: In our southern (*qibli*) Brazil, you will be killed if you go dressed like this.
    [Repeat]
    There, if people saw my toe, I would cut it and throw it in the field.
    Forget it! It is nothing but a gross failure!

Cairene man: You are backward and poor.

Khadra: I hope you will be too poor to live! Pull yourself together!
    Are not you ashamed of your [lack of manhood and passion]?
    Put your mustaches to some use!
    [Repeat]
    How could you approve of your wife's dress? Your name must be Jacki, not Jack.
    Forget it! It is nothing but a gross failure! Indeed it is.

Galal (Galal Sadiq) sings the first part of the monologue. His character forms part of the group adhering to *tafarnug* in the movie. His lines celebrate and mark modernity with the passage of time from the past, which Galal refers to as "the year eight," to the present, which he refers to as "the year nineteen hundred." Another marker of modernity as the lines of Galal celebrate it is women's education in American schools; such education teaches women how to understand the world and adapt to new lifestyles. In support of Galal's lines, earlier in the movie, Khadra's lover Fu'ad explains to Khadra that industrialization is a marker of modernity, for the year 1900 is no more the age of reliance on mules and donkeys as the primary means of transportation.

The lines sung by Khadra should not be mistaken for anti-modernity stances. She instead reacts to the reduction of modernity to *tafarnug*. To Khadra, who lives in the underprivileged regions of Upper Egypt, the year 1900 and the year 1951 are still the age of mules and donkeys; the time is still that when people take a mentally-ill person to a quack instead of to a psychiatrist. For example, when Khadra meets Fu'ad on the train, she asks if she can reach the town of al-Wasta to see a quack who can make some protection icon (*hijab*) to cure her father. Suffering from the lack of infrastructure which societal modernization brings to the city without the countryside, in addition to the inferiority gaze at the peasants from the Cairene-bourgeoisie, Khadra reacts to Galal's celebration of modernity. The lines sung by Khadra are thus a reaction of anger-release, known in Egyptian colloquial as *fashsh ghill*, at the practice of *tafarnug*. Ziyada underscores this idea when he depicts Fu'ad blaming Khadra for messing his plans up (*labbakhit al-dunya*) with her song that insults the guests at the party. Khadra replies, "I did not mean to be rude; I just wanted to release my anger" (*fashshayt ghilli wi-khalas*).

The Cairene stereotype of the peasant woman, which Ziyada creates in the character of Khadra to critique *tafarnug*, reveals a dichotomy of *tafarnug* and counter-*tafarnug*, both of which commodify the female body. Modernity that is reduced to *tafarnug* leads to a battle of gazes between the forces of *tafarnug* and those of counter-*tafarnug*. The battle starts with the Cairene-bourgeoisie exercising an inferiority gaze against the peasants, who are stereotyped as ignorant, backward, and poor, for they cannot adhere to *tafarnug*; the peasants counter-react by exercising an immorality gaze at the adherents of *tafarnug*, who become perceived as less moral. To the peasants, thus, education in American schools makes the Cairene-bourgeoisie master nothing of modernity but *tafarnug*. But modern notions of social justice, which Khadra expects to see more among people with access to better social resources, do not exist. And the battle shifts to the female body, which becomes commodified and becomes a battlefield. For example, Khadra perceives women's bodies as flesh for sale. She perceives herself as a mythical creature who will not hesitate to cut her toe, but cannot publicly uncover it. This brutal image objectifies the body of the peasant woman and reduces it to a mere container used to

270 | FILMING MODERNITY AND ISLAM IN COLONIAL EGYPT

Figure 4.41 Counter-modernity and the condemnation of *tafarnug*. Durriyya Ahmad as Khadra criticizing the dress of a Cairene-bourgeoisie woman. *Khadra wa-l-Sindibad al-Qibli*, 1951.

Figure 4.42 The female body as a battlefield. Zuzu Shakib as Fifi receiving Khadra's immorality gaze. *Khadra wa-l-Sindibad al-Qibli*, 1951.

mummify a false consciousness of an imagined ideal tradition. Ziyada uses this image to transfer Khadra's counter-*tafarnug* gaze of immorality at Cairene women adhering to *tafarnug*. For example, when Khadra mentions cutting her toe, the camera shifts to depict Fifi gazing at her own body, covering her shoulders with her arms. These two extremes are meant to make adherents of *tafarnug* aware of the gaze of immorality. The gaze of inferiority at the peasant woman and the gaze of immorality at *tafarnug* thus make the female body a battleground for *tafarnug* and the reactionary counter-*tafarnug*.

Notes

1. While it is true that the idea of *al-Warda al-Bayda'* was sparked by a short story written by Muhammad Mitwali, a relatively unknown writer, the screenplay was significantly different from Mitwali's story.
2. Muhammad Karim, *Mudhakkirat Muhammad Karim*, ed. Madkur Thabit (Cairo: Akadimiyyat al-Funun, 2006), 252–5.
3. Karim, *Mudhakkirat*, 252–5.
4. Ibid.
5. Samir Sabri and Muhammad 'Abd al-Wahhab, "Musiqar al-Ajyal Muhammad 'Abd al-Wahhab fi al-nadi al-dawli ma' Samir Sabri," Maspero Zaman, August 7, 2017, https://www.youtube.com/watch?v=vVJrioMsFqI (last accessed December 12, 2020).
6. Layla Rustum and Muhammad 'Abd al-Wahhab, "Liqa' al-zikrayat," 2 parts, July 17, 2012, https://www.youtube.com/watch?v=ETJwKWFN_CU (last accessed December 12, 2020); see also Layla Rustum and Muhammad 'Abd al-Wahhab, "Najmak al-Mufaddal," *Maspero Zaman*, August 18, 2016, https://www.youtube.com/watch?v=dRRxST5uanI&t=14s (last accessed December 12, 2020), and Layla Rustum and Muhammad 'Abd al-Wahhab, "Nujum 'Ala al-Ard," November 29, 2016, https://www.youtube.com/watch?v=yVT_wAMdKb0 (last accessed December 12, 2020).
7. Layla Rustum and Muhammad 'Abd al-Wahhab, "Nujum 'Ala al-Ard," November 29, 2016, https://www.youtube.com/watch?v=yVT_wAMdKb0 (last accessed December 12, 2020).
8. In some versions of the film the head does not show, but in other versions it does. This might be due to different preservation techniques used over time.
9. See Zafar Ishaq Ansari, "Taftazani's Views on *taklif, jabr* and *qadar*: A Note of the Development of Islamic Theological Doctrines," *Arabica*, 16 (1969): 65–78.

David Arnold Ede, *Mulla Sadra and the Problem of Freedom and Determinism: A Critical Study of the Risala fi al-Qada wa-al-Qdar*. Ph.D. diss., McGill University (Canada), 1978. Antonio Guillaume, "Some Remarks on Free Will and Predestination in Islam Together with a Translation of the *Kitab al-Qadar from Sahih al-Bukhari*," *Journal of the Royal Asiatic Society* (1924): 43–63. Hassan Qasim Murad, "*Jabr* and *Qadar* in Early Islam: Reappraisal of their Political and Religious Implications," *Islamic Studies Presented to Charles J. Adams*, ed. Wael B. Hallaq, Donald P. Little, and Charles Joseph Adams (Leiden: Brill, 1990). Julian Obermann, "Political Theology in Early Islam: al-Hasan Al-Basri's Treatise on Qadar," *Journal of the American Oriental Society* 55, no. 2 (1935): 138–62. Fazulr Rahman, *Major Themes of the Qur'an* (Minneapolis, MN: Bibliotheca Islamica, 1994). Helemer Riggern, *Studies in Arabian Fatalism* (Uppsala: Alqvist & Wiksells, 1955). Montgomery Watt, *Free Will and Predestination in Early Islam* (London: Luzac, 1948). Michael Cook, *Early Muslim Dogma*: A Source-Critical Study (Cambridge: Cambridge University Press, 1981). György Fodor, "Some Aspects of the Qadar-controversy in Early Islam," *The Arabist: Budapest Studies in Arabic* 1 (1988): 57–65. Richard M. Frank, "The Structure of Created Causality According to al-Asʿari," *Studia Islamica* 25 (1966): 13–57.

10. See Wilson Jacob, *Working out Egypt: Effendi Masculinity and Subject Formation in Colonial Modernity, 1870–1940* (Durham, NC: Duke University Press, 2011), 219.
11. Karim, *Mudhakkirat*, 300.
12. Ibid., 307.
13. I will come back to Kamal's perception of art in later chapters on *asala*.
14. It is not clear exactly where the noise is coming from.
15. Muhammad Shusha, *al-Nass al-kamil li-sinariyu film al-ʿAzima* (Cairo: al-Hayʾa al-ʿAma al-Misriyya lil-Kitab, 1975), 7.
16. Baydas, *Abyad wa-aswad*, 2013, 113–22.
17. The name of a French Catholic school.
18. Mr. Groppi started his first bakery in Alexandria in 1890. He founded a company in Cairo in 1891. Then he opened a branch in ʿAdli Street and another in Sulayman Pasha Street. See Sharif ʿIzzat, "Maqahi ʿAtiqa fi al-Qahira . . . Groppi," al-Jazeera documentary, June 25, 2015, https://www.youtube.com/watch?v=Nr01LP0Bx8w (last accessed December 12, 2020).
19. Wahbi's view on the freedom of woman and her individualism in relation to modernity appears best in the movie *Jr. Madiha* (al-Avukatu Madiha, 1950).
20. See Noel J. Coulson, *A History of Islamic Law* (Edinburgh: Edinburgh University

Press, 1964), 141. See also *Encyclopedia of Islam, Second Edition Online*, s.v. "Sadd al- dhara'i'."
21. *Akhir Sa 'a*, no. 710, 1948.
22. See *Encyclopedia of Islam, Second Edition Online*, s.v. "*Muhallil.*"
23. See Q42:49.
24. In both movies, Ziyada kept his entire primary cast unchanged. Even when he replaced some of the cast, the replacement did not affect the characterization.

5

Lampooning Risidual Modernity (*Ta'ssul*)

1. Throw Not a Stone at Every Barking Dog!

Niyazi Mustafa's *Salama fi Khayr*/Salama Is Fine, 1937 is one of the earliest films to depict the critique of *ta'ssul* as a false consciousness of modernity that presents itself as innovation. But *ta'ssul* offers nothing but an egocentric view of individualism adopted by the degree-educated *effendis* who look down upon working-class Egyptians and consider them the main obstacles facing efforts at modernization in Egypt. While the screenplay is an adaptation of Nagib al-Rihani's comedy of errors that carries the same title, *Salama fi Khayr* remains Niyazi Mustafa's film.

Niyazi Mustafa was born in the Upper Egyptian city of Asyut in 1911 to a mother of Turkish origin and a father of Sudanese origin. He studied film in Germany before working in the famous Studio Misr as a *monteur*. He worked as an assistant director to Yusuf Wahbi until he met Wahbi's theater rival, al-Rihani, and directed two of the latter's famous cinematic trilogy of films, *Salama fi Khayr* and *Si 'Umar*/Mr. Omar, 1941. While this beginning seems to have paved the way for Mustafa to specialize in situation comedies, he sometimes rebelled against the comedy frame. For example, he deals with religious themes in films like *Rabi'a al-'Adawiyya*/Rabi of Basra, 1963, which depicts the life of the famous Sufi mystic Rabi'a who lived in Basra between 713 and 801 CE. And his film *'Antr Ibn Shaddad*, 1961 is an epic presenting the struggle of the classical Arabic poet 'Anatar b. Shaddad against racism in pre-Islamic Arabia. Unlike many directors of the same generation, Mustafa never stopped directing. He continued to work until 1987, when he was murdered in his apartment before screening his last film, leaving behind a legacy of around a hundred and fifteen films.

The plotline of *Salama fi Khayr* follows the misfortunes of Salama (Nagib al-Rihani), a middle-aged man living with his wife, Sattuta (played by Fardus Muhammad), and his mother-in-law (Amina Zuhni), in a folk neighborhood ironically named "The Pashas' Alley." Salama shares a three-story apartment complex with Greek *khawaga* Kustin and Bayumi *effendi* Murgan (Muhammad Kamal al-Masri). The latter is depicted as an inconsiderate neighbor who often fights with Salama. Salama works as an office boy (*farrash*) in a textile department store owned by another *khawaga*, Khalil Hindawi (Fu'ad Shafiq). The latter is overly reliant on Salama's assistance but does not spare an opportunity to blame Salama and describes him as a lazy employee who keeps asking for paid vacation leave. Salama finds Hindawi a manipulative employer because he refuses to promote Salama, despite having worked with him since the department store's inauguration in 1912.

The film opens with Hindawi meeting a textile factory representative, a third *khawaga*, Albert (Admun Tuwayma). He carries a black wallet full of clothes samples for marketing purposes. Albert tries to convince Hindawi that the factory offers him the same quality as Prince Kandahar of Bludistand (a fictional country between Indian and Afghanistan), who happens to be visiting Cairo. The meeting ends inconclusively, and Albert leaves with the promise to come back with better samples in a couple of days.

The story takes a sharp turn when Hindawi tasks Salama with depositing a large sum of money in the bank. On his way, Salama is distracted by a street accident when a school bus hits a milk-seller's bike. When Salama identifies one of the passengers as his rival and neighbor Bayumi *effendi* Murgan, he sides with the milk-seller until the police arrive and arrest them all. Released half an hour before the bank's closing time, Salama misses the opportunity to deposit the money in the bank. When he returns to work, he finds the store closed to celebrate the birth of Hindawi's first child. Salama then stops by a barber's shop to phone his boss at home. Yet a talkative customer keeps the phone busy, and Salama kills time by having his beard shaved. Overhearing other customers talking about daily pickpocketing in Cairo, Salama gets paranoid and rushes to his house to keep Hindawi's money safe. No sooner does he arrive at his apartment than he learns that some thieves have broken into his apartment and stolen the copper pots. Realizing that even his bedroom cannot be a safe place to keep his boss's money, Salama seeks the help of a friend, who advises him to keep the money in a hotel safe. Salama then heads to Nefertiti Palace Hotel.

At the hotel, Rustum pasha (Istifan Rusti) and his family extend their stay when they overhear that prince Kandahar of Bludistan will be staying at the same hotel. Rustum's daughter, Jihan (Raqiya Ibrahim), plans to seduce the prince; she phones her maid, Nahid (Rawhiyya Khalid), in Alexandria. She asks her to come to Cairo, bringing party dresses and uniforms suitable for meeting the prince.

In the middle of the desert road connecting Cairo to Alexandria, Nahid's car breaks down. She is rescued by Kandahar, who falls for Nahid and decides to hide his true identity.

As Kandahar's guards await his arrival at the hotel, Salama approaches the reception desk to rent a safe and deposit Hindawi's money. Since only hotel guests can rent a safe and Salama cannot afford to book a room, he is denied service. He is mistreated, belittled, and kicked out of the hotel when Kandahar arrives. Overwhelmed by the news, the hotel manager, who rushes outside to welcome the prince, finds Salama shouting near the front door and mistakes him for the prince. Kandahar seizes the opportunity to continue hiding his identity from Nahid. He then plans to prove to his assistant Gawdat (Mansi Fahmi) that people (especially women) do not respect a prince for his noble character or deeds; they appreciate his wealth and ability to sustain their *tafarnug*. Kandahar invites Salama to his suite and offers him the opportunity to earn five hundred pounds, live in the hotel for a few days, and keep Hindawi's money safe. Initially, Salama suspects the prince, but he soon accepts the deal and presents himself as the prince.

Acting as the prince, Salama visits the school where his neighbor Bayumi Murgan works; the latter doubts his identity and informs Salama's wife, who goes to the hotel to see her husband. When Salama ignores his family and neighbors, Bayumi reports Salama to the police.

Meanwhile, the clothes factory representative, the *khawaga* Albert, arrives at the hotel to meet the prince and convince him to purchase clothes necessary for Bludistan's army uniform. When Albert meets the prince, Albert's wallet, full of fabric samples, gets mixed up with Salama's wallet.

Kandahar carries out his plan to test Nahid; he gifts Nahid a bracelet and Jihan a necklace. Then Kandahar asks Salama to seduce Nahid to test her.

Nahid decides to meet the prince and return the bracelet; she gets angry at Salama's sexual advances and throws the bracelet at his face, leaving the hotel and her job. Kandahar follows her outside the hotel to apologize and tell her the truth.

When the police arrive to investigate Salama for identity theft, he confesses and tells the police about the story of the wallet and his deal with Kandahar. To prove his story, Salama pulls out the wallet to show the money to the police, only to find that the wallet is full of fabric samples. Salama is then arrested and charged with identity theft.

At the department store, Hindawi returns from Alexandria to discover that Salama has disappeared with the money. When Hindawi learns from the newspaper that Salama is accused of identity theft, he suspects he embezzled the money. Salama and the police officer arrive at Hindawi's office to check Salama's identity. Simultaneously, Kandahar comes to save Salama; he offers to compensate Hindawi on condition that Salama is set free. At the same time, Albert arrives to meet Hindawi and resume business negotiation. No sooner does Albert open his wallet than he finds Hindawi's money and realizes that his wallet has been mixed up with Salama's. The police release Salama while the prince and his fiancé, Nahid, reward Salama with seven hundred pounds.

While the construction of *tafarnug* in *Salama fi Khayr* is accomplished through Rustum and his children, the construction of *ta'ssul* is achieved through the character of Salama's neighbor, Bayumi *effendi* Murgan. Depicted as an archetype of the *effendi*'s utilitarian view of modernity, Murgan appears dressed in a full suit and tarbush; he teaches in a government primary school. His education and mastery of standard Arabic make him claim superiority over his poor and uneducated working-class neighbors. Niyazi Mustafa's camera underscores the *effendi*'s claims to superiority by depicting Murgan living on the top floor; he appears at the top of the stairs insulting his neighbors in standard Arabic. Society, for Murgan, is a hierarchy of classes where people forge relationships on the basis of interest. Indeed, Murgan pursues his self-interest at the expense of his neighbors. He thinks logically, spends time scrutinizing evidence to arrive at conclusions, and appears quite articulate in his relationship with the state. Unlike Salama and the third neighbor, the Greek-Egyptian *khawaga* Kustin, Murgan lives alone, and if he is married we never get to see his wife; he appears all throughout the movie as an individual.

Bayumi *effendi* Murgan perceives people like Salama as obstacles facing modernity in Egypt. The only way to move forward is to crush them, just like he minces his meat daily using a traditional pestle, thereby creating outrageous noise but caring less about his neighbor, Salama, who lives downstairs and suffers daily from this noise. When the school bus, which Murgan takes daily to work, crashes into a milk seller's bike, Murgan blames the milk seller and orders the driver to drive over him, along with Salama who happens to be passing by at the same time. Notwithstanding the scene's comic effect, Murgan sees all these uneducated people (milk sellers, office boys like Salama, and the vast majority of the working class) roaming freely in Cairo's modernized streets as being the main cause of the bus accident. They obstruct the state's efforts at modernization, promoting a hierarchy of social rank as the only path to wealth and power. Therefore, when Salama's social status changes because he meets Kandahar, Murgan is infuriated and informs the police. When Salama is found not guilty and is rewarded at the end of the movie, Bayumi rushes to pledge allegiance by reciting lines of classical Arabic poetry by Hassan ibn Thabit,[1] known for writing poetry in praise of the Prophet Muhammad. The lines read:

Wa ahsanu minka lam tara qatt 'ayni
Wa ajmalu minka lam talid al-nisa'u

As lovely a personality as yours, I have not seen anyone.
As beautiful as you, women have not given birth to anyone.

The above lines reveal an extreme paradigm shift in Murgan's attitude toward Salama. At the beginning of the movie, Bayumi refuses to talk to his neighbor. He used to recite a line of poetry that reads "If I were to throw a stone at every barking dog passing by, the stones' price would increase" (*lawu kulu kalbin 'awa alqamtuhu hajaran la'asbaha al-sakhru mithqalan bi-dinari*).[2] Bayumi *effendi* Murgan implies that Salama is not an equal human being; he is as worthless as the many dogs roaming Cairo's streets. By depicting Murgan changing his position radically at the end of the film, the director correlates Murgan's *effendiness* with a utilitarian view of modernity that does not shy away from appropriating metaphors representing Islam.

To frame Murgan's *ta'ssul* as a caricature, Niyazi Mustafa employs the character of *ibn al-balad* Salama, who confronts and resists Murgan's supremacist attitude. It is important here to explain that despite his friends occasionally calling him an *effendi*, Salama is primarily depicted as *ibn al-balad*; his boss never calls him an *effendi*. His identity and social status as *ibn al-balad* are externalized through his dialogues and the character of his wife, Sattuta. Here the title of *effendi* is used to acknowledge that Salama does not wear a galabiya like his friend Rihan, for example, and that he is literate. As *ibn balad*, Salama is depicted as empathetic regarding his neighbors, friends, and customers. At the same time, he is street-smart, not easily fooled, a critical thinker with a sense of humor, and he does not always take things at face value. For example, he meets a beggar at the alley entrance where he lives. He is used to giving him change even though he knows that the man has taken up begging as a profession. When the beggar asks Salama to spare him some change to save his wife, who is giving birth at home, Salama gives him money but sarcastically advises him to change his reasons, for the beggar's wife could not have been in labor for the last nineteen years.

Confronting the supremacist attitude of the *effendi* is further amplified through Salama's insistence on lampooning Murgan. Instead of using his last

Figure 5.1 Confronting *effendiness* (1). On the left, al-Rihani as Salama, and on the right al-Masri as Bayumi *effendi*, in *Salama fi Khayr*, 1937.

Figure 5.2 The hypocrisy of the *effendi* unfolds. On the right, al-Rihani as Salama skeptical about the *effendi*'s paradigm shift, in *Salama fi Khayr*, 1937.

Figure 5.3 Condemning egocentrism as the driving force of the *effendi*'s *ta'ssul*. Al-Rihani and al-Masri in *Salama fi Khayr*, 1937.

name, "Murgan," Salama calls him "Bitingan," the Egyptian colloquial word for "eggplant." The implication is that Bayumi Murgan's head is stuffed with "eggplant" instead of a functioning brain; hence he is insane, and so is his *ta'ssul*. When Salama, acting in the prince's role, meets Murgan at school and attends his math session, he comments sarcastically on Murgan's teaching methods, criticizing his illogical examples for being disconnected from everyday life.

Salama fi Khayr ends with Salama using colloquial rhymed speech to counter the *effendi*'s egocentric utilitarian view of modernity. Salama's poetry reads:

> *idha lam takun li wa-l-zamanu shurum burum fa-la khayra fika wa-l-zamanu taralali*
> If you give me a cold shoulder in my misfortunes, save me your warm welcome in my fortunes.

2. Thou Shalt Drink Migahid's Cocktail

An improvement on the character of Bayumi Murgan is the character of Migahid bey in Muhammad Karim's *Yahya al-Hub*/Long Live Love, 1938. Although he does not carry the title *effendi*, Migahid is the ultimate expression of *effendiness*. He adheres to *ta'ssul* as the only path to becoming modern and expects the same from everybody around him. Migahid does not talk to communicate, he talks to dictate; "to listen," for him, means "to agree with." He presents his ideas as innovations, while they are nothing but a sham.

Muhammad Karim's *Yahya al-Hub*/Long Live Love, 1938 follows the story of Nadiya (Layla Murad), a student of music, who falls in love with her neighbor Muhammad Fathi (Muhammad 'Abd al-Wahhab), a bank clerk who shares with Nadiya her passion for music and singing. Muhammad Fathi was born to a feudal lord, but he refused feudal dependency and decided to live only within his means. The story takes a sharp turn when Nadiya mistakenly thinks Muhammad is having an affair with another woman. The misunderstanding is cleared up when Nadiya realizes that the woman is Muhammad's sister, not his mistress. The following scene depicts Nadiya at the beginning of the movie before falling in love with Muhammad. Nadiya breaks off her engagement with Migahid bey (Amin Wahba), a professor of entomology:

Nadiya: Did you not come to tell me you discovered, after research and investigation, that I am not qualified to be your bride?

Nadiya's Father: Not qualified. How dare he say so?

Migahid: Nadiya!

N: This situation is, indeed, unfortunate. But the breakup is not as sad as our engagement. How did it even happen? A woman who spends her entire day learning music and her evenings going to movies can never be fit to marry a serious man who is a professor of entomology in whatever bloody college!

M: No, Nadiya! Music and cinema are not points of conflict. Indeed, music does not appeal to my ear, but I can't deny its benefits. We often use music to tame insects, whose life cycle I teach. And nobody can make fun of cinema. I teach most of my lectures on the insect's life and anatomy through cinema [Nadiya smiles. Migahid notices her smile]. What is it that you find so funny?

Nadiya: Nothing! You know, sometimes when I want to cry, it looks like I am smiling. But I am happy to hear you say so because [your words] explain many issues my father would ask me about, but I won't have answers for him.

N: Like what?

Nadiya: Like why Migahid drives you crazy!

M: What is it about me that drives you crazy? I lecture in front of three hundred male and female students.

Nadiya's Father: [addressing Migahid] I do not understand why there is even a problem. You proposed to Nadiya, and now she is turning down the proposal.

M: [Addressing Nadiya] Breakup should not be considered my fault. I tried to leave my imprint on your personality. I tried to make you a carbon-copy of myself. I tried to explain that tea contains a poison that could be neutralized by adding more sugar. But you would prefer to drink tea without sugar. Even when it came to colors, I tried to change your view. Who would agree that the red color is less refined than the champagne pink color?

N: I do not understand what point you are trying to make here. Are you trying to prove to me that I am superficial?

M: Nadiya, for your information, I think we should stay apart for some time and think more about our relationship. This is not a breakup.

Through the character of Migahid bey in *Yahya al-Hub*, Muhammad Kaim lampoons *ta'ssul*. Migahid's *ta'ssul* features his desire to establish continuity between an imagined ideal past and a reductionist understanding of a modern present, which Migahid approaches through instrumental rationality. To construct Migahid's *ta'ssul*, Karim depicts Migahid giving attention to the European dress and etiquette code. Migahid dresses in a suit, tarbush, or tailcoat throughout the movie. At the same time, he insists on using standard Arabic in his conversation. In the above scene, for example, he emphasizes the *tanwin* in expressions like "Pardon me" (*ma'dhiratan*), "Well" (*hasanan*), and "Goodbye" (*wada'an*). The *tanwin* is dropped in colloquial Arabic, whereas the standard Arabic expressions which Migahid employs are not commonly used in day-to-day conversation. The colloquial equivalent for *ma'dhiratan* is *ma'alihshi*, and the colloquial version of *hasanan* is *kuwayyis*. Migahid's insertion of standard expressions into his day-to-day conversation with Nadiya shows how he creates an artificial construct; it frames his amour-propre of modernity as artificial.

Figure 5.4 Breaking up with *ta'ssul*. Layla Murad as Nadiya, right, breaks off her engagement to Migahid, seated far left. *Yahya al-Hub*, 1938.

By the same token, Migahid refuses to acknowledge a fundamental conflict between his instrumental view of a modern invention like film and Nadiya's view of film as art. Karim employs Nadiya's reaction to Migahd's idea to caricature it. For example, she sarcastically smiles and says, "You know how sometimes when I cry, it looks like I am smiling." The implication is that if Migahid's doctoral degree cannot help him realize the apparent contradiction between the instrumental use of film and film as art, as a domain for freedom of expression and creativity, he might as well not notice the visible sarcastic smile at Nadiya's face and take it for crying. The problem of Migahid's *ta'ssul* is that it eventually becomes totalitarian, that is, he tries to impose his reductionist understanding of modernity as *ta'ssul* on his fiancée. Migahid cannot accept Nadiya as a modern woman who can think, choose, and act according to her will. To Migahid, Nadiya's modernity means that she has to imitate and follow his choices and his instrumental use of reason. In short, she has to follow *ta'ssul*, or she fails to be modern.

To further caricature *ta'ssul*, Karim depicts Migahid as a hypocrite; that is, there is always a contradiction between Migahid's amour-propre of modernity and his subject position on modern social values, especially those pertaining to the modern social roles of women. For example, they have their first fight soon after Nadiya falls in love with her neighbor Muhammad Fathi. When they meet at one social gathering, Muhammad refuses to sing unless Nadiya leaves the party. Migahid, who is also invited, blames Muhammad for his rude behavior. Migahid says to Muhammad, "How dare you insult a woman like that." To Migahid, denying a woman her equal will to choose and act in society is not insulting, so long as discrimination against women is not done publicly. Migahid's bar scene is another instance in which Karim ridicules Migahid's *ta'ssul* as hypocritical. Here, Migahid is depicted as undecided about whether to drink, for he is concerned about inebriation. While sitting at the bar, Migahid asks the bartender, " If we mix gin, and lemon, with ice and add an egg, what would you call this drink?" The waiter replies, "It would still be called a cocktail." Migahid disagrees and says, "No, it will be called Migahid's cocktail." While the invention of gin is often traced to the mid-seventeenth century, the popular twentieth-century gin and tonic is a modern drink. In tropical British colonies, gin was used to mask quinine's bitter flavor, the only effective anti-malarial compound. Migahid's attempt to spoof gin's effect by calling the drink by his name seems to be an attempt on the part of Karim to show how Migahid's *ta'ssul* makes him unable to accept "the modern" as it is. Migahid has to make his imprint even when it introduces no substantial change. Migahid's *ta'ssul* was not welcomed among the Cairene-bourgeoisie, but it was tolerated. At least that is the case presented by Karim in *Yahya al-Hub*.

3. Thou Shalt Listen to "The Slaughtered Dove"

In *Yawm Sa'id*/Happy Day, 1939, Karim employs the same actor, Amin Wahba, as plays Migahid to play the character of 'Azzuz bey. *Yawm Sa'id* takes the critique of *ta'ssul* a step further by depicting 'Azzuz as a "mediocre" person (*sakhif*) who tries to market and sometimes enforce his *ta'ssul* among *awlad al-balad* who are not very welcoming either.

In this film, the character of 'Azzuz mediates between classes. Through his connections, he introduces the hero Kamal, an emerging singer, to the Cairene-bourgeoisie social circles. In exchange, 'Azzuz wants Kamal to promote 'Azzuz's philosophy of *ta'ssul* in songwriting. Karim depicts this theory as a caricature, or another Migahid cocktail. However, this time, 'Azzuz exercises *ta'ssul* by casting a traditional frame on another product of modernity, namely, the theory of new modernism. For example, to prove he is a new modernist poet, 'Azzuz draws on themes from everyday life practices. But he also wants to present his version of new modernist poetry. Since he is an adherent of *ta'ssul*, his new modernism means abiding by the traditional form of the Arabic poem, that is, he adheres to the pattern (*al-wazn*) and rhyme (*al-qafiya*) instead of free verse. Consider the following example:

> They slaughtered my heart and soul when they slaughtered the dove
> They hung it and let it softly dangle. It looked like "a crescent wrapped in dark blue."[3]
> It was swinging and shaking like the threads of an *effendi*'s tarbush (*zirr al-afandi*)

'Azzuz called the above poem "The Slaughtered Dove" (*Al-hamamatu al-madhbuha*). His poem sketches an image of a typical scene in a souk. The scene depicts a dove slaughtered and hanged, awaiting further processing before being sold. 'Azzuz creates a simile involving the swinging slaughtered

Figure 5.5 *Ta'ssul* rejected by *awlad al-balad*. On the left, Fardus Muhammad, the *bint al-balad* Umm Anisa, listening impatiently to Amin Wahba as 'Azzuz. *Yawm Sa'id*, 1939.

dove and the red threads dangling from an *effendi*'s tarbush, another contemporary scene in the streets of Cairo at that time. As an adherent of *ta'ssul*, 'Azzuz insists on framing contemporary everyday scenes in classical poetic form, applying classical Arabic rhyme to colloquial Egyptian words.

For the same reason, 'Azzuz does not favor French greetings. He creates his own version of greetings. For example, when he visits Kamal and the owner of his property, he greets them using a combination of French and Arabic greetings. He says, *"Bonjour 'alayikum,"* a line that has remained a popular joke among Egyptians to the present day.

To lampoon 'Azzuz's *ta'ssul* as a false consciousness of modernity, Karim resorts to the main characters' reception of 'Azzuz's thoughts and ideas. This depiction applies to both educated and uneducated characters. For example, Karim depicts Kamal and the owner of his property, Shaykh Mustafa, smiling at 'Azzuz's code-switching in greetings. Kamal and Shaykh Mustafa reply, in Arabic only, "Peace and God's mercy be upon you" (*wa-'aliykum al-salam wa-rahmatullah*). They being two educated *awlad al-balad*, their reply implies that they find 'Azzuz's choice of greeting artificial. Similarly, 'Azzuz waits for Kamal at the apartment of his landlady, Umm Anisa. 'Azzuz tries

Figure 5.6 Amin Wahba as 'Azzuz reciting his poetry among his drunk friends. *Yawm Saʿid*, 1939.

to convince Umm Anisa to listen to his poem. Here, Karim depicts Umm Anisa listening impatiently to 'Azzuz, who ignores her obvious boredom and continues reciting the poem. Umm Anisa being an uneducated *bint balad*, her impatience and boredom are primarily due to her inability to understand the standard Arabic in 'Azzuz's poetry. She can only connect to the word pigeons (*hamam*) in the poem as she has been cooking stuffed pigeons for lunch, and the poem reminds her that the food might burn as 'Azzuz urges her to sit in the living room and listen to his poem. Similarly, Kamal refuses to sing 'Azzuz's poem and comments sarcastically, "Where am I supposed to sing this poem, in the theater or at the vegetable market?"[4] The only group depicted celebrating 'Azzuz's *taʾssul* is a group of drunken friends. The scene implies that one must be drunk to promote 'Azzuz's *taʾssul* as innovation.

4. Her Mouth Is Bigger than God's Mercy

While Karim depicts *taʾssul* as a sort of mediocrity (*sakhafa*), in *'Aris min Istanbul*/A Groom from Istanbul, 1941, Yusuf Wahbi capitalizes on *sakhafa* and depicts *taʾssul* as a deformed (*maskh*) understanding of modernity. The film follows the story of Muhsin (Yusuf Wahbi) and Samira (Raqiya Ibrahim), whose Turkish grandfather, Faruq pasha Ertugrul, makes their matrimony a precondition for them keeping their share in the family's trust fund (*waqf*). Muhsin's grandfather turned a hundred thousand acres into a trust fund (*waqf*) and made himself the sole beneficiary and custodian as long as he was alive. Upon his death, his family members will inherit the *waqf*. For the grandfather to allow the normal inheritance process to occur after his death, he insists that Muhsin marries his Egyptian cousin, Samira. Otherwise, the grandfather will leave the trust fund to the state, and all legal heirs will lose their anticipated shares. Since Muhsin is a successful lawyer, the consequences of him refusing his grandfather's unjust condition are not severe. However, Muhsin's refusal will have a negative impact on the female members of the family, whose future financial stability depends on their shares in the *waqf*. Initially, Muhsin objects to the marriage idea. Unable to act according to his better judgment, it occurs to him that he can escape the arranged marriage by exchanging social roles with his driver, Rashid (Mahmud al-Miligi). Muhsin introduces himself to his cousin as the chauffeur, and the driver is introduced as Muhsin, the anticipated groom from Istanbul. Likewise, Samira disapproves of her grandfather's plans, and she introduces herself to Muhsin as the chief maid in the house. Throughout the movie, Samira's existence as Muhsin's cousin and future wife is presented through a picture on the wall. The picture features Badawiyya, Samira's teacher.

Through the character of Badawiyya, played by Ibrahim Husayn, Wahbi constructs *ta'ssul* and critiques it as deformed modernity. As with the characters of Migahid and 'Azzuz, Badawiyya's *ta'ssul* sweeps under the rug any seeming contradictions between products of the present and products of the past. While Migahid and 'Azzuz practice *ta'ssul* by placing a traditional frame on the modern, Badawiyya's *ta'ssul* attempts to resurrect an imagined ideal tradition, be it associated with an Arabic, Islamic (here reduced to Ottoman), or Pharaonic cultural heritage, and place it in a modern frame.

Badawiyya is Samira's Arabic teacher. She lives with her husband Shaykh Baratishi, somewhere between Tanta and Mansoura in the Nile Delta. They come to Cairo to visit Samira and gift her a photograph of Badawiyya. Wahbi depicts Badawiyya and her husband abiding by the modern code of dress. Badawiyya always wears a *tailleur* and a hat, while her husband wears a suit and a tarbush. Both insist on speaking rhymed standard Arabic in day-to-day

Figure 5.7 Raqiya Ibrahim plays Samira disguised as a maid. *'Aris min Istanbul*, 1941.

Figure 5.8 Ibrahim Husayn as Badawiyya. *'Aris min Istanbul*, 1941.

conversation. For example, when Badawiyya expresses how much she misses Samira, she does not say the common Egyptian colloquial phrase "I missed you" (*wahshtini*). Instead, she says, "Hugs, longings, and woe, caused by distance, have torn my heart apart" (*'inaqun wa-ashwaq wa law'atu firaq asabat mararat al-qalbi bi-infitaq*). Badawiyya also applies Arabic inflection rules to foreign words like the English word "pose," to which she adds accusative case ending to make it *"posan."* The implication is that she wants to domesticate the foreign by enforcing a traditional frame. While explaining to Samira how she took her new photograph, Badawiyya says, "No, I did not take the picture in the street. I took it at a studio, where I posed modestly. It came out so lovely that the photo almost spoke" (*la lam akhudhha fi al-shari' bal 'inda al-rassam waqaftu posan fi ghayit al-ihtisham, fa-kharajat suratan natiqa bidun kalam*). Through this combination of modern apparel and adherence to the classic linguistic register, Wahbi constructs Badawiyya's *ta'ssul* as a caricature of modernity, which presents nothing new save casting a traditional frame on anything new, modern, or foreign.

To critique Badawiyya's *ta'ssul* as a deformed and mythical understanding of modernity, Wahbi, like Karim, relies on other characters' reception of the unfamiliar physical form of Badawiyya. For example, Badawiyya's husband, Shaykh Baratishi, constantly complains about his wife's physical condition. He perceives Badawiyya as a mythical figure and describes her as a deaf monkey with a beard (*qirdatun wa-tarsha'*). He imagines her face like a mountain torn down by a continuous flow of volcanic lava (*wa-wajhin yukhriju al-hamama fi kul hin*) from her nose. He makes an analogy between her hands and snakes' heads. To Baratishi, living with such a mythical construct is the worst of divine punishments (*hadha ashaddu anwa' al-bala'*). He complains that he must have been "among the misled and cast away from God's mercy" (*al-maghdub 'alayihim wala al-dalin amin*) and that he is punished by being Badawiyya's husband. When Badawiyya tries to prove to Samira that she has no problem with modern innovations like photography, Baratishi comments on his wife's photograph by saying, "This is what they call the ugly depictions" (*hadhihi hiya al-qaba'ihu al-musawwara*). The comment is an oxymoron about *al-Lata'ifu al-Musawwara*, a famous variety magazine of the period. Wahbi further capitalizes on Baratishi's remarks by having major characters like Muhsin make similar comments. In a scene depicting Muhsin talking to Badawiyya's photograph, Muhsin, who thinks the photo is for his promised bride Samira, says, "Oh! No! Her mouth is bigger than God's mercy."

Another technique that Wahbi uses to frame Badawiyya's *ta'ssul* as deformed modernity is the reliance on other characters' reception of Badawiyya's choice of speaking rhymed standard Arabic in day-to-day conversation. For example, when Badawiyya first arrives at Samira's house in Cairo, the latter's cousin, Tahir (Fakhir Fakhir), comments sarcastically on Badawiyya's use of standard Arabic in day-to-day conversation. Tahir says to Samira, "Here you go, your teacher has arrived, and she will speak to you in the language of Ibn al-Muqqafaʿ. And you will be forced to speak to her in the same language until your throat comes out." The implication is that speaking in standard Arabic in day-to-day conversation is artificial; it requires effort and practice because it is not natural for Egyptians living in the 1940s. For Tahir, it does not make any sense that Badawiyya wants to resurrect a language that may have been spoken in eighth-century Baghdad, where Ibn al-Muqqafaʿ lived and wrote his famous *Kalila and Dimna*.

Wahbi's critique of *ta'ssul* does not apply only to the attempt to resurrect standard Arabic as an attribute of an imagined ideal Arabic culture in Wahbi's contemporary Egypt. The critique of *ta'ssul* equally applies to attempts to resurrect an imagined ideal Pharaonic past. For example, in the climactic scene of *'Aris min Istanbul*, Wahbi brings almost all his characters together in one scene taken in one long shot. The scene starts with all the characters lying on the floor. Each has fainted in previous scenes for various reasons. The camera moves slowly to depict Badawiyya, the first among all the characters to wake up. When she had fainted in an earlier scene, Muhsin's *chauffeur* had carried her body and hid it in what looks like a mummification box (*tabut*). When Badawiyya wakes up, Wahbi depicts her getting out of the same box and repeating, "The ghosts, the spirits, the dead, the pharaohs, ancient Egyptians, Khufu, Khafraʿ, Manqara, Ramsis, Tut Ankh Amun" (*al-ashbah, al-arwah, al-mawta, al-faraʿina, qudmaʿ al-misriyyin, Khufu, Khafra, Manqara, Ramsis, Tut 'Ankh Amun, Tut 'Ankh Amun, Tut 'Ankh Amun*). Badawiyya has been reading a book on ancient Egyptian history, which her student Samira gifted to her a long time back. As the camera shows other characters waking up one after the other, they gradually repeat the last words of Badawiyya by repeating the name of the famous King Tut as a *mantra*. All the characters simultaneously swing their heads round. The depiction makes them look like they are in a Sufi circle (*halqa*) intended to remember God (*dhikr*) and chant words of gratitude (*tasbih bi-l-hamd*). The implied sarcasm consists in the fact that the characters are performing *tasbih* using Tut's name instead of God's. It is important to mention here that the Arabic expression *al-tasbih bi-l-hamd* is not necessarily limited to God. It is often used sarcastically in Egyptian colloquial to criticize hypocrisy. So when, for instance, someone says "X *yusabbih bi-hamid* his work-superior," the speaker implies that X is ready, at any cost, to show the utmost solidarity with and loyalty to his superiors. In this sense, the scene lampoons the idea of holding to the praise of, or hailing, an imagined ideal past as salvation from the challenges faced in the present. For Wahbi, any attempt to do this will be as mythical and false as the character of Badawiyya.

By the same token, attempts to resurrect an imagined ideal Islamic past (here reduced to the Ottoman past) are ridiculed through the character of the grandfather. Wahbi depicts the Ottoman past in the movie through the many pictures of Muhsin's ancestors spread across the villa's walls in Istanbul. To the grandfather, these pictures are the ultimate expression of Ottoman patriarchal power and its guardianship of Islam, a trait that is missing from and must be cultivated in his modern grandson, Muhsin. The latter is less masculine, as he shaves his beard and mustache and refuses to wear a tarbush. Every time the grandfather meets his grandson, he makes him stand in front of their great-grandfather's portrait to acknowledge its grandiose masculinity. The great-grandfather was a man on whose mustaches two hawks could stand and whose nose could produce fire. This mythical construct is very similar to Shaykh Baratishi's image of Badawiyya. To Muhsin, however, his grandfather's attempts are futile, and thus he refuses to listen to his grandfather's commemoration of his ancestors. Muhsin says, "Grandpa, we've heard this record a thousand times." He comments sarcastically on his great grandfather's name, "Kharshufughli." The word, to Muhsin, sounds like a mixture of artichoke (*kharshuf*) and the Turkish surname "Ughlu." There is, of course, the more explicit burlesque of the father of Osman I, Ertugrul, whose name is the same as that of Muhsin's great-grandfather. To further critique the *ta'ssul* of the grandfather, the latter is depicted speaking broken Arabic and using case endings and inflections for colloquial words. More importantly, the grandfather makes unreasonable family connections. Consider, for example, the following lines:

> I swear by the name of Artughul, his father, and the father of the father of his father. I swear by the aunt of the grandmother of the father of Ertugrul, Muhsin must immediately marry. Otherwise, all of you will be denied your shares in the inheritance.

The grandfather's unreasonableness, exaggerated swearing, and attempt to forge impossible connections between family members imply the artificiality of *ta'ssul* as an attempt to resurrect an imagined ideal Ottoman past in Mushin's contemporary Egypt.

However, the conflict between the grandfather and the grandson is not merely a conflict over Muhsin's lack of interest in his grandfather's celebration of the past. Rather, it is about the hegemony of *ta'ssul*, how *ta'ssul* is propagated as public interest (*maslaha*) for future generations, while actually it is nothing but a means (*dhari'a*) of appropriating Islamic trust fund (*waqf*) law

Figure 5.9 *Ta'ssul* as a mythical construct. Bishara Wakim as Muhsin's grandfather, pointing at his imagined ideal past. *'Aris min Istanbul*, 1941.

to preserve the concentration of wealth and power within an uninterrupted patriarchal order.

In Islamic law, *waqf* has its origin in hadith literature. One hadith, which features in canonical collections of hadith, is narrated on Ibn 'Umar's authority. It tells the story of the second Caliph 'Umar Ibn al-Khattab, who acquired land in Khaybar in Medina. 'Umar once consulted the Prophet about the land. The hadith suggested that 'Umar could, if he wished, make the land itself inalienable and give the harvest away as alms. 'Umar gave it away as alms in the sense that the land itself was not to be sold, inherited, or donated. The practice of 'Umar became the most famous type of trust fund in Islamic law. It is commonly referred to as a public or charitable trust (*al-waqf al-khayri*): "This kind of trust is created for religious and/or charitable purposes from the outset. It may be for the welfare of the poor or the establishment or upkeep of a mosque, hospital, cemetery, or other public facilities."[5] The second type of trust is the private trust referred to as a family trust (*al-waqf al-ahli*) and created for "the benefit of the founder and his relatives to provide for their needs during their lifetime . . . After their death, [it is] used for charitable purposes."[6] Under the category of family trust (*al-waqf al-ahli*) falls another type known as the personal trust fund (*al-waqf 'ala al-nafs*), making it possible for the donor to be the sole beneficiary of his trust fund during his lifetime. The donor can also determine specific beneficiaries after his death, thereby interrupting the normal inheritance process.

The category of personal trust fund (*al-waqf 'ala al-nafs*) is subject to dispute among Muslim jurisprudents. Two major positions may be summed up in this regard. The first leans toward the permissibility of a personal trust fund. Abu Hanifa and Abu Yusuf,[7] some of the Shafi'is,[8] some of Ibn Hanbal's companions,[9] and later Ibn Taymiyya, favored permissibility.[10] They relied on the possibility that a person can benefit from his charity (*sadaqa*), and, by analogy, from his trust fund also. The second position leans toward the prohibition of the personal trust fund, which is considered an invalidation of the principle of donating property to charity. Adherents of the second position constituted the majority (*jumhur*) of Shafi'is, who pointed out some exceptional cases in which personal trust funds could be allowed. These included cases such as (a) a trust fund established for students while the donor was himself a student, (b) a trust fund established for the poor, where the donor himself became poor, and (c) a trust fund founded by a person who named the beneficiaries literally as sons of so and so (*abna' fulan*), while the founder was himself one of the specified sons.¹¹ In *'Aris min Istanbul*, Wahbi seems to favor the second position, thereby depicting personal trust fund as *dhari'a* used by the adherents of *ta'ssul* to sustain the concentration of power and wealth within a patriarchal social order.

5. Our Children Are Our Son's Sons

The correlation between *ta'ssul* and appropriation of Islamic law described above is more extensively explored in Ahmad Badrkhan's *Man al-Gani/Who Is the Criminal?*, 1946, which takes the critique of *ta'ssul* a step forward by showing how its appropriation of Islamic legal tradition produces and sustains *tafarnug*. Thereby, the cycle of injustices keeps going.

Figure 5.10 Poster of *Man al-Gani* in *Akhir Sa'a*. The caption below the poster reads, "Scenes from the movie *Man al-Gani*, which caused controversy when screened in movie theaters such as Korsal, in Cairo, and Ledo in Alexandria. It will be screened in Tanta during Eid al-Adha in al-Baldiyya movie theatre." Image from *Akhir Sa'a*.

Man al-Gani/Who Is the Criminal? is directed by Ahmad Badrkhan, who left a legacy of approximately forty-two films. Born into a wealthy family of Albanian origin (his grandfather was Khurshid pasha Tahir, a military general who led Albanian soldiers in the Ottoman Army), Badrkhan attended the Frères French Catholic high school, established by Saint Jean-Baptiste de La Salle. When Zaki Tulaymat inaugurated the Institute for Acting, Badrkhan joined in 1930 and trained with George Abyad. But he could not complete his degree, because the Institute closed down. Badrkhan then entered the American University Cairo and became a member of its acting troupe. He was also a law student and undertook a long-distance course studying cinema in Paris. Simultaneously, he worked as an editor for the cinema section of *al-Sabah* magazine. In 1931, he secured a scholarship to travel to Paris and study film musicals. While in Paris, Badrkhan met Nagib al-Rihani while filming *Yaqut*/Yacout, 1934, and worked as an assistant to the film's director, Willy Rozier. When Badrkhan returned to Egypt, he directed most of Umm Kulthum's musicals, including *Manayyit Shababi*/I had a Dream, 1937 *Dananir*/Dananir, 1939, *'Ayida*/Aida, 1942 and *Fatima*/Fatima, 1947. He also directed films for singers like Farid al-Atrash, Muhammad Fawzi, Nur al-Huda, and 'Abd al-'Aziz Mahmud. Before marrying Salwa 'Allam, with whom he had his son, the director 'Ali Badrkhan, Ahmad Badrkhan married Rawhiyya Khalid and then the singer Asmahan al-Atrash. He died while filming his last movie, *Nadiya*/Nadia, 1969, starring Su'ad Husni. Some of his most famous masterpieces are movies like *Mustafa Kamil*/Mustafa Kamil, 1952, *al-Iman*/Faith, 1952, *Allah Ma'ana*/God Bless Us, 1955, and *Sayyid Darwish*/Sayed Darwish, 1966. Badrkhan is often credited with the Arabic translation of André Bazin's book *What Is Cinema?*

Man al-Gani/Who Is the Criminal?, 1946 is Badrkhan's tenth film. It follows the misfortunes of Lady Fa'iqa [Fay'a] (Amina Rizq), who faces trial for the murder of her son Yunus (Mahmud Isma'il) and her nephew Rashad (Muhmmad Tawfiq). Her other nephew, 'Abbas (Anwar Wagdi), resigns from his job as a prosecutor to defend her. Using a flashback technique, the director employs the character of 'Abbas to narrate how Fay'a ended up behind bars.

The trouble for Fay'a begins when her father-in-law, Mansur al-Barqi [al-Bar'i] pasha ('Abd al-Migid Shukri), decides to limit the inheritance to his sons and his grandsons, leaving out his daughters and granddaughters. The pasha believes that allowing daughters and granddaughters to inherit means wasting the family's wealth. As soon as the pasha passes away, his eldest son, 'Umar al-Bar'i ('Abbas Faris), urges the family members to open the pasha's safe and check his will. His written will reads:

> Mansur al-Barqi b. Hasan b. Mahmud al-Barqi turned his estate (260 acres) in Qaha into a trust fund and made himself the sole beneficiary of the trust fund. Upon his death, the Qaha trust fund belongs to his eldest son 'Umar, and his male descendants until God inherits the land and its inhabitants [i.e. until the Day of Judgment]. Also, al-Barqi pasha turned his estate in al-Badrashin (240 acres) and his house in al-Hilmiyya al-Jadida neighborhood into a trust fund and made himself the sole beneficiary of the trust fund as long as he was alive. After his death, the Badrashin trust fund belongs to his younger son 'Uthman, and his male descendants, without females. The guardianship of each trust fund belongs to the son assigned to inherit each particular trust fund. Also, each son should donate a quarter of a tenth of the interest of the trust fund for charity.

Distressed by his father's unfair will, 'Uthman (Farag al-Nahhas), the youngest son of the pasha and husband of Fay'a, suggests that he and his brother should commit themselves to paying a fixed amount of money to their mother (Thuraya Fakhri) and sister, 'Adila (Nigma Ibrahim). When 'Umar disagrees, 'Uthman suggests giving them the money dedicated to charity in the will. Again 'Umar disagrees, and 'Uthman takes the issue to court. He succeeds in legally forcing himself and his brother to pay a fixed amount of money to support their mother and sister. Besides, 'Uthman legally makes his sister the sole beneficiary of the revenue of forty acres which are part of 'Uthman's share in the *waqf*, so long as he is alive. To celebrate their victory, 'Uthman takes his family to the Mediterranean city of Ras al-Barr, where 'Uthman and his young son, Mansur, suddenly drown. Losing hope of any sign that her husband and son could be alive, Fay'a leaves for Cairo with her young daughter Safiya, her mother-in-law and her sister-in-law. The death of 'Uthman revokes his deal with his sister and automatically shifts the ownership of the entire *waqf* to the oldest living male heir (i.e. 'Umar). As soon as 'Umar learns about his brother and nephew's death, he ends his vacation in Damascus and returns to Cairo to claim guardianship over the entire *waqf*. 'Ali ('Abd al-'Aziz Khalil), a servant at Fay'a's house, suggests that the only way to save 'Uthman's share in the *waqf* is to find a boy and claim he is the son of 'Uthman and Fay'a. According to the will, this plan allows the boy to inherit 'Uthman's share, and Fay'a can be a legal guardian. Otherwise, 'Umar will not hesitate to kick everybody out from the house, and they might find themselves living on the street. When 'Umar returns to claim his inheritance, the news of Fay'a's pregnancy and delivery infuriates him. He accuses Fay'a of forgery, but his sister argues that he has not visited or checked on them for a year and a half; he thus could not have known about the pregnancy. 'Umar decides to take legal action against Fay'a. He goes to a lawyer (Shafiq Nur al-Din), who explains that the case is a lost one, because in such context the legal ruling states that "the child belongs to the bed" (*al-walad lil-firash*). That is to say, any child that Fay'a gives birth to while married to 'Uthman becomes the latter's son automatically. 'Umar, being full of doubt, wants to test the boy's blood. The lawyer explains that there is "no father" whose blood can be compared to the child's. 'Umar loses the case, and Fay'a maintains control over 'Uthman's share in the *waqf*; she is appointed as a legal guardian.

Yunus grows up to be an ill-tempered young man who disrespects women. He harasses girls at the school where his sister Safiyya works. He resents his rejection by women to the extent that, on one occasion, he threatens to throw nitric acid at a girl's face because she refuses to smile back at him. Yunus befriends Rashad, the son of 'Umar; they both become strong adherents of *tafarnug*. Rashad and Yunus do not believe in education or employment for the rich. Yunus impatiently awaits the end of the three months left until the guardianship is lifted so that he can control the *waqf* and sustain his *tafarnug*. He also decides to marry 'Umar's daughter, Fikriyya (Salwa 'Allam). As Yunus cannot pay the dowry before the guardianship is lifted, 'Umar pressures him to steal the *waqf*'s monthly revenue (fifteen hundred pounds). He convinces him that if a mother steals her minor son's money, she is not legally held accountable, and the same applies to the son if he were to steal money from his mother. 'Umar then advises Yunus not to tell his mother that he has sought advice from his uncle, lest his mother sue 'Umar for the deception of a minor.

Meanwhile, Safiyya succeeds in building a career as a teacher. Her cousin 'Abbas ends his mission with the foreign service in Europe and returns to

Egypt. 'Abbas wants to work independently as a lawyer, but he receives an offer from the Ministry of Justice to work as a prosecutor, and he reluctantly accepts the offer. Against the wishes of his father, 'Abbas proposes to Safiyya. 'Umar threatens to deprive 'Abbas of the *waqf* inheritance.

When the guardianship is lifted, Yunus holds a party to celebrate with his friends and cousins. His mother and aunt refuse to attend. Yunus and his cousins feel insulted and the cousins insist that Yunus invite his mother to apologize to the guests. Yunus, his mother, and his aunt argue. Yunus then threatens to kick them all out of the house. Giving up on her hopes that Yunus will come to his senses, Fay'a becomes angry and tells Yunus the truth about his birth. He threatens to kill her and pulls out his gun. While she is defending herself, two bullets are shot; one hits Yunus, and another hits his cousin, Rashad. The two young men die, and Fay'a goes to jail. The camera shifts back to the court scene, in which 'Abbas concludes that the murder is not deliberate and that Fay'a shot in self-defense.

Badrkhan constructs *ta'ssul* in the movie through the character of the pasha's eldest son, 'Umar, who works as a merchant in al-Ghuriyya. The audience first hears about 'Umar before he arrives at Safiyya's birthday party. The dialogue between other characters reveals that 'Umar was married to Fay'a's sister, who passed away, leaving behind a son, 'Abbas. The latter is raised with his mother-in-law (Mary Munib), who marries 'Umar after his first wife's death. 'Umar's character is depicted as representing continuity and change following the father, al-Bar'i pasha. The question here is, continuity of what and change toward what? It seems that Badrkhan constructs a continuity of injustice, and a change toward essentializing injustices in new forms. Badrkhan achieves this continuity in both costume and dialogue. Both father and son wear traditional dress made up of a galabiya and gown. 'Umar, unlike his father, is keen to acquire a more modern look by wearing a tarbush instead of a turban. Like his father, 'Umar believes that a woman's marriage automatically shifts her alliance and loyalty from her birth family to her husband's family. Hence, giving a female family member her share of the inheritance means losing the wealth to a foreign man (*agnabi*), who did not originally work hard to earn that wealth (*ashab al-qulub al-bawarid*). Badrkhan further traces this injustice to a pre-Islamic convention expressed in a line of poetry that 'Umar recites: "Our children are our sons' offsprings, for our daughters' children belong to foreign men" (*banuna banu abna'ina wa banatuna banuhuna abna' al-rijal al-aba'idi*). Badrkhan here questions the concept of *jahiliyya*, but his attempt should not be mistaken for him implying that the meaning of *jahiliyya* is "the time of ignorance," nor should it be read as an echo of the views of Sayyid Quttub on *jahiliyya*.[12]

Badrkhan's argument here is in line with that of Ignác Goldziher, who argued that when the Prophet contrasted the change brought about by his preaching with earlier times, he did not seek to describe those times as times of ignorance, since in that case he would not have opposed ignorance with devotion to God and confidence in God, but with knowledge (*al-'ilm*). He presumably did not intend to express anything else by *jahiliyya* other than the condition which, in the poetic documents of the time preceding him, is described using the verb *jhl*, the substantive *jahl*, and [the active participle] *jahil*. The original meaning is seen in the antithesis between this word group, much more common in the older language, and *hlm*, *hilm* and *halim*. According to their etymological meaning, these words describe firmness, strength, physical integrity, health, moral integrity, the solidity of a moral character, unemotional, calm deliberation, and mildness of manner. A *halim* is what may be called a civilized man.[13] The opposite of all this is the *jahil*, who follows the leadings of unbridled passion, and, I would add, his greed. Goldziher cites evidence from pre-Islamic poetry that reveals the kind of character and manner of action through which 'Amr b. Kulthum wishes to protect himself by threatening revenge by referring to the ways in which *jahiliyya* is usually contrasted with *al-hilm* (i.e. mildness)—and not *al-'ilm*. This is the kind of contrast that Badrkhan makes in his movie by hinting at 'Umar's stance being driven by pre-Islamic *jahiliyya*. For Badrkhan, 'Umar is a *jahil*, to whom modernity is a matter of resurrecting injustices embedded in tradition in a modern form. That is why he encourages the *tafarnug* of Yunus and Rashad. And it is not an exaggeration to consider that Badrakhan impugns *tafarnug* as driven by *jahliyya* (i.e. following one's unrestrained aspiration and greed).

After all, genuine change that addresses social injustices on the level of form and content threatens 'Umar's interest. It is not surprising, thus, that 'Umar stigmatizes elements of reform represented through his son 'Abbas and his brother 'Uthman as "westernized" and less Islamic. But because he cannot challenge their pro-social-justice stance, he criticizes their arguments; he resorts to undermining them by condemning their openness to foreign ideas. For example, in the opening birthday-party scene, part of the celebration consists of wearing masks and hats to cheer up the children. When 'Uthman offers his brother, 'Umar, a cylinder hat to wear, 'Umar refuses to wear a hat and stigmatizes his brother as a westernized person who imitates Parisians. Here again, Badrkhan presents 'Umar's views as being in disagreement with the more inclusive views of Muhammad 'Abdu, who permits Muslims to wear a hat so long as they are not declaring that they are no longer Muslims. While 'Uthman adopts 'Abdu's views, 'Umar perceives Islam as a system of checks and balances; he abides by the letter of the law and does not hesitate to appropriate Islamic textual sources to serve his interests. For example, when the pasha falls sick early on in the movie, 'Umar refuses to spend money on having his father checked by more than one doctor. After his father's death, 'Umar refuses to support his mother and sister financially and asks 'Uthman to sell the furniture of their father's house along with his cart and horses to help their sister and mother. But when 'Umar's son 'Abbas decides to marry Safiyya against 'Umar's wishes, the latter reminds his son that Islam requires believers to obey their parents and treat them gently. When his alleged nephew Yunus grows up, 'Umar welcomes him at his house despite doubting that he is actually 'Uthman's son. Here, 'Umar explains his attitude by arguing that Yunus's presence in 'Umar's life could be tolerated just like the presence of a mameluke or a slave was tolerated in the old days. In a sense, Badrkhan hints at the idea that 'Umar opposes the abolition of slavery and does not mind if it continues in whatever form it may take.

Badrkhan's speech critiques how *ta'ssul* discriminates against women. Consider the following scene at the beginning of the movie:

Pasha: Were it not for 'Uthman's wish, I would not have come to his daughter's birthday party today.

Wife: Well, you hurried to the house of your son 'Umar when his son 'Abbas passed his exam, and you were thrilled to attend the party.

P: 'Abbas will grow up to be a man one day. He will carry and defend the name of the al-Barqi family, and so will his sons and grandsons. But how worthy is this girl, Safiyya?

W: She is also your grandchild.

P: One day, she will marry and live in a strange man's house. And if her father leaves her a fortune, it will go to men who did not work hard to earn it.

W: That is how life has been since God created the world.

P: Well, this is not the right thing to do.

W: And now you think you are the "chosen one" to fix it. This way of thinking is wrong; it is why your daughter has not received any marriage proposals.

Here, Badrkhan not only condemns the injustice befalling the female members of the al-Bar'i family, he gives voice to the subaltern by allowing a female character to challenge patriarchal views explicitly on the screen. This prelude in dialogue paves the way for a larger argument that Badrkhan makes in the film, namely, that Islamic legal tradition favors women's empowerment and that a false consciousness of modernity like *ta'ssul* appropriates Islamic law in order to discriminate against women. To this end, Badrkhan establishes a continuity between 'Uthman and his nephew 'Abbas. Unlike his father, 'Abbas chooses to finish his education and study law like his uncle. Like his uncle, 'Abbas does not think Muslims should reject all European practices and consider them not in harmony with Islam. For example, 'Abbas does not mind wearing a wedding ring and argues that it is a habit invented by Europeans and not a bad habit to imitate. Like his uncle, 'Abbas wears a suit and tarbush that does not, in this context, imply adherence to *effendiness* or affiliation with the Ottoman past; instead, it has the implication of governmental affiliation, 'Uthman being a judge and 'Abbas a prosecutor. 'Abbas mostly appears throughout the film without a tarbush outside his office and the court.

Both 'Uthman and 'Abbas disapprove of using a personal trust fund as a legal means to arrive at the illegal end of depriving female family members of their shares in inheritance to sustain the concentration of power and wealth in a patriarchal line. In one scene, 'Uthman wonders if his father thinks he is more just than God. When 'Uthman asks 'Umar to allocate the money dedicated to charity to their mother and sister, 'Umar refuses. Instead, he abides by the letter of the law, which specifies that charity money applies only to those who are categorized as deprived (*mahrum*), poor (*ba'is*), or traveler (*ibn al-sabil*).

Here 'Uthman counter-argues that charity money can apply in their mother and sister's case, as the unjust will forces them to become poor and deprived. 'Uthman relies on the Qur'anic maxim stated in Q2: 215 that reads, "They ask thee what they should spend. Say, 'Let whatever of your wealth you spend be for parents, kinsfolk, orphans, the indigent, and the traveler. Whatever good you do, truly God knows it.'" Hence, relatives are more worthy of any charity money. 'Umar becomes cynical and argues that if he were to act on this, 'Uthman could sue him and revoke 'Umar's guardianship over his share of the *waqf*. Following in his uncle's footsteps, 'Abbas condemns the stance taken by his grandfather and father. Although one of the murdered is his brother and the defendant is his father, 'Abbas does not hesitate to resign from his governmental position as a prosecutor to defend his aunt. He perceives his resignation as a way of lifting the injustice. He cites the Prophetic tradition that reads, "Whoever amongst you witnessed an injustice, change it with his hand; if he is unable to do so, then with his tongue; and if he is unable to do so, then with his heart; and that is the least that can be done."

'Abbas's stance should not be mistaken as a call for people to act independently without consideration of law and order. Rather, it is an attempt on the part of Badrkhan to underscore cinema as a public sphere where people across social classes, genders, and professions can come together to deliberate and think about the common good. This stance is further emphasized by Badrkhan's choice of dedicating a reaction shot to showing the servant, 'Ali, commenting on the public prosecutor's request to apply Penal Law articles 230, 231, and 232 (i.e. killing for a private purpose deliberately). 'Ali says, "His [i.e. the prosecutor's] claims do not count. Only God knows the truth."

Similarly, Badrkhan employs the character of 'Ali to open a public debate about the meaning of the word prohibition (*haram*) in the context of the film. When 'Adila, sister of 'Uthman and 'Umar, hesitates about the plan to secure a baby boy to save the *waqf*, she asks 'Ali whether or not the plan is *haram*; 'Ali argues that the real *haram* that ought to be prohibited is the miserable social and financial conditions that would befall the women in the family, if 'Umar were to control the entire *waqf*. While 'Adila refers to the word *haram* as "prohibition," 'Ali refers to it as "injustice." And this is why 'Abbas presents 'Ali's plan to the court as a form of resistance to the injustice done by the grandfather, who deliberately went against God's will as expressed in the sources of law. 'Abbas concludes that the criminal is Mansur al-Bar'i pasha, his grandfather, who wants to use the law for his own interest, while the legal system enables him to control land during his life and after his death.

The critique of *ta'ssul* and its appropriation of the *waqf* is a central theme in Ibrahim Hilmy's *Abu Halmus*/Father of Halmus, 1947. Hilmy correlates the continuity of institutional corruption in the *waqf* system with the *effendis*, who are depicted as the backbone and sword of the feudal institution; they place their skills in its service and justify its biased distribution of power and wealth.

6. Thou Shalt Forge Efficiently or Never Forge!

Abu Halmus/Father of Halmus, 1947 is Ibrahim Hilmy's second film. His first film was *Ibn al-Sharq*/The Son of the East, 1945, starring Madiha Yusri. Hilmy started his film career as an assistant director to 'Izz al-Din Dhu al-Faqqar and Tugu Mizrahi. Here the credit goes also to al-Rihani and Badi' Kahyri, who wrote the screenplay.

Abu Halmus follows the story of Shihata *effendi* (Nagib al-Rihani), who works as a record keeper at a chicken shop. Unhappy with the work conditions and aspiring to become an *effendi*, he applies for an accountancy position at the *waqf* of al-Azmirli. Soon his long-awaited job offer comes in the mail, and he leaves for the good modern life to be. As soon as he starts his new job, he discovers that his fellow *effendis*, and the manager of the *waqf*, 'Abd al-Hamid bey Fath al-Bab ('Abbas Faris), mismanage the *waqf* because Fath al-Bab's family adheres to *tafarnug*. They spend extravagantly and are always short of cash. Fath al-Bab's son, Farid (Hasan Fayi'), fails to finish his law degree and is obsessed with his belly dancer girlfriend Ahlam (Hagar Hamdi). The daughter, Kawthar (Zuzu Shakib), is in love with Anis *effendi* (Muhammad Diab), the *waqf*'s assistant manager. As the story unfolds, Farid's girlfriend gives birth to a boy, Halmus, and decides to fool Farid into believing that Halmus is his son. When Fath al-Bab objects to his daughter's plan to marry Anis *effendi*, Kawthar claims Halmus is her son from an affair with Shihata. She finds this scheme suitable enough to spoil her reputation and make her family more accepting of Anis *effendi* as a suitor. Throughout a series of comic situations, Shihata cannot disprove the allegations and goes along with Kawthar's game; he announces that he is the father of the child, Halmus.

The news about Halmus infuriates Fath al-Bab, and the movie takes a sharp turn when word comes from London that the two lottery tickets which he had initially sold to Shihata have won, and so Shihata now possesses sixty thousand pounds. Fath al-Bab decides to hide the news of the lottery from Shihata and plans to control the money. To this end, he pretends that his attitude towards Shihata's wish to marry Kawthar has changed. He invites Shihata to his home and tells him that he does not object to the couple's union any longer. He makes one condition, however, namely, that Shihata has to sign a number of checks accounting for forty thousand pounds as dowry and gifts to the bride and her family. Supposedly penniless and unaware of the lottery winnings, Shihata at first refuses, but he soon agrees when Fath al-Bab assures him that the checks will not be cashed: Shihata has to sign them only in order to provide some proof that Fath al-Bab's decision to marry his daughter to a poor man like him will not jeopardise his daughter's happiness. This way, Fath al-Baba can save face in front of his Cairene-bourgeoisie friends and family members, who will surely be shocked at the news of this marriage.

Meanwhile, Kawthar learns about the lottery and tells Anis *effendi* that they must confess to everybody that Shihata is innocent. To her surprise, Anis suggests that Kawthar should marry Shihata so they can benefit from the money, and she can always stay in an extramarital affair with Anis. Shocked at her lover's intentions, Kawthar changes her mind about Anis and finds in Shihata a better partner. But when Shihata tells everybody that he has sold the lottery tickets to another person, Ghibriyal *effendi* (Muhammad Kamal al-Masri), the family refuses to finalize the marriage plan and the wedding is cancelled. As Shihata and Kawthar plan to flee, they are stopped by Ghibriyal, who is convinced that the lottery is a sinful practice and wants to sell Shihata the ticket back. Shihata repurchases it, and the movie ends with him winning at both ends.

It is through the externalization of Shihat's *effendiness* that Ibrahim Hilmy critiques *ta'ssul* in *Abu Halmus*. Two characters are employed to serve this end. The first is the character of Anis *effendi*, and the second that of Ghibriyal *effendi*. Shihata escapes the amour-propre of *effendiness*, as depicted in the character of Ghibriyal, for what he sees as the ideal amour-propre of *effendiness* as expressed by Anis. On the one hand, Ghibriyal represents what Shihata could have ended up as had he stayed at the chicken shop. Ghibriyal is a caricature of the *effendi* as a family man sinking in the practice of record keeping. Receipts regulate his relationship with the state; he sounds like a moving archive; he keeps all receipts in his pocket, and when he needs one to prove his right, he can hardly find any. Shihata tries to escape this level of suppression by taking the new job at the *waqf* of al-Azmilri. On the other hand, Anis *effendi*, Shihata's supervisor, represents Shihata's dreams of stability and promotion; he is the ideal modern man who has a decent job and knows how to attract women's attention; Shihata looks forward to becoming Anis.

The falsity of Anis's understanding of modernity is revealed gradually when Shihata discovers that becoming an *effendi* like Anis does not just require him to be appointed as an accountant. He is also expected to serve in the villa of Fath al-Bab, who calls him all the time by the name "Zift," which means "tar." Still, this seems here to connote the English term "useless." Shihata's journey of experimentation with Anis's *effendiness* allows Hilmy, brilliantly and unprecedentedly, to correlate *effendiness* with institutional corruption as governmentality, which, if carefully propagated, maintains the concentration of power and wealth within a centralized feudal system. In one iconic scene, Hilmy depicts Shihata *effendi* explaining the golden recipe for corruption: justify outrageous expenditure and escape audit. He suggests that instead of exaggerating the cost of a single purchase or service, each item should be broken down into smaller transactions, since itemized costs can more reasonably be made up. For example, a charge of ninety-two pounds for a wall painting could be quickly flagged as embezzlement in the 1940s. But three times this amount can be justified by inflating the costs of individual items such as dust removal, dirt removal, trimming, window- or doorframe taping, and wall priming. This scene, known as the scene historicizing bureaucratic corruption in Egypt, is often invoked in contemporary popular culture to comment on political and economic transformations. For example, it gained momentum on social media following the Egyptian Government's decision in May 2018 to increase the ticket price on the subway, the most affordable public transit system in Cairo.[14] On social media platforms, the character of al-Rihani as Shihata *effendi* is employed to criticize policymakers whose amateur decisions

Figure 5.11 Historicization of bureaucratic corruption in Egypt. Right: al-Rihani as Shihata *effendi*. Left: 'Abbas Faris as the corrupt head of the feudal institution. *Abu Halmus*, 1947.

prove they have not learnt the tricks of their trade, these here being governance. The Government should have known this from Shihata in *Abu Halmus*; it should have gradually introduced news of the new policy. First, occasional breakdowns in the subway system should have been announced; this should have been followed by a complete shutdown of one or two lines. Then all lines should have stopped for two or three hours a day. Instead of protesting, people would have begged the Government to fix the subway, and it would even have been possible to increase the ticket price to fifteen pounds instead of the seven pounds currently enforced. The political satire implies that Egypt continues to be governed by the *effendi*'s governmentality, which is driven by a modernity void of social justice even for the *effendi* himself.

Abu Hamlus ends with Shihata getting married to Kawthar and discovering the falsity of *effendiness* and its *ta'ssul*. In making the *effendi* abandon *effendiness* as a false consciousness of modernity, Hilmy's idea is not just to give the audience a happy ending but also to underscore how getting free of *ta'ssul* is a reward as great as winning the lottery.

It was not al-Rihani, however, who mastered the protest against the *effendi*'s *ta'ssul*. His friend and second lead in his films, the famed comedian 'Abd al-Fattah al-Qasri,[15] takes the lead in this regard. His star aura derives from his mastery of the role of the uneducated working-class Egyptian, that challenge the *effendi*'s understanding of modernity. Al-Qasri's peak role performance appears in Henry Barakat's *Ma'alihshi Ya Zahr*/Never Mind, 1950 and Fatin 'Abd al-Wahhab's *al-Ustadha Fatima*/Attorney Fatima, 1952. Both films present him as the uneducated working-class Egyptian whose modernity centers around advancing women's social roles as citizens.

7. But it Is a Matter of Principles

Ma'alihshi Ya Zahr/Never Mind, 1950 is directed by Henry Barakat, who left a hundred and twelve films made over fifty-five years. Born in 1914 in Shubra, the popular Coptic Christian neighborhood of northern Cairo, Barakat grew up going to movies but never dreamt of a career as a filmmaker. He had wanted to study medicine, but followed his father's wish to study law. After he graduated from King Fuad I University (now Cairo University) in 1935, the courts' bureaucracy bored him, and he abandoned law as a profession. With his brother, he started a film company. Barakat's dissatisfaction with revenue and production quality motivated him to travel to Paris to study cinema. There, he learned his trade by attending the shooting of many French films, going to movies, and reading extensively about filmmaking at the library and museum of the Paris Opera known as the Bibliothèque-Musée de l'Opéra National de Paris. The outbreak of World War II forced Barakrat to return to Cairo, where he started working as an assistant director in Asiya Films, owned by Asiya Daghir. Barakat's true beginning as a director started with *Lawu Kunt Ghani*. He cooperated with icons of Egyptian popular culture, including Layla Murad and Fatin Hamama, for whom he directed most of her critically acclaimed films.[16]

Ma'alihshi Ya Zahr was Barakat's thirteenth film and one of three masterpieces he directed in the same year. One of these is Layla Murad's popular musical *Shati' al-Gharam*/Passion Beach, 1950, which was shot in Matruh, located on the Mediterranean Sea a hundred and fifty miles west of Alexandria. The beach hosts a statue to Layla Murad. The movie has turned the city into a tourist destination, and visitors are still today keen to visit the rock on which

Layla Murad sat while singing her epic song *Ya sakini Matruh* (Oh, People of Matruh). The other film is *Amir al-Intiqam*/Revenge, 1950, an adaptation of Alexandre Dumas' *Le Comte de Monte-Cristo*.[17]

Ma'alihshi Ya Zahr was not expected to succeed.[18] It broke with commercial success standards of the time, when directors used to insert illogical scenes of belly dancing, jokes, and songs to break the box office. The film would not have stayed long in theaters. But the producer Asiya Daghir succeeded in convincing Metro Golden Mayer Theater in Cairo to exclusively screen the movie for four consecutive months before other theaters could host it. One promotional poster stated Barakat's motivation for making a realist film about the everyday Egyptian middle-class family crushed under the state's fruitless efforts at modernization. A translation of the text under the ad. reads:

> Do you know this person? You might think he is the film star Zaki Rustum. He is Sabir *effendi*. You meet him daily in the streets of Cairo, the office, or in the coffee shop. He might be your neighbor, your relative, or even you. Sabir *effendi* has a story. It is the story of every one of us. It is a story treated by Barakat, the successful director of the new film *Ma'alihshi Ya Zahr* which will screen very soon in Metro theater.[19]

Ma'alihshi Ya Zahr follows the misfortunes of Sabir *effendi* Abu al-'Izz (Zaki Rustum), a government employee struggling to raise a family in Cairo in the late 1940s. A love relationship develops between Sabir *effendi*'s daughter, Nagafa (Shadiya), and her neighbor Husni (Karim Mahmud), who works with his father, Gum'a ('Abd al-Fattah al-Qasri) in his mini-market. Sabir *effendi* disapproves of his daughter's relationship with Husni because the latter does not have a degree-level education. Sabir hopes to get his daughter married to an *effendi* with a degree, a stable income, and a pension so as to secure her future. At work, Sabir *effendi* has a troubled relationship with his superior, Muhsin *effendi* (Istifan Rusti). The latter does not like Sabir because he, unlike his peers, does not address Muhsin using the title 'bey.' Sabir reasons that since Muhsin does not officially have the title, calling him 'bey' would be hypocritical. On one occasion, the general inspector investigates budget embezzlement at the institution; Muhsin comes under fire, while Sabir is promoted. The story becomes complicated when Sabir receives a legal notice informing him that his apartment has been sold to a new owner,

Figure 5.12 Advertisement for *Ma'alihshi Ya Zahr*. Zaki Rustum as the protagonist Sabir *effendi*. Image adapted from *al-Ithnayn*.

who asks Sabir to pay more rent or vacate. Sabir complains that the apartment has not been renovated for ten years. Zuhayr (Sirag Munir), the new property owner, turns out to be a childhood friend of Sabir's wife, I'tidal (Mimi Shakib), who invites him over for dinner. When Zuhayr arrives at Sabir's apartment, Sabir and his wife discover that Zuhayr is the general inspector at Sabir's institution. Sabir's peers suspect that Sabir's wife has an affair with the inspector. Their suspicions increase when Zuhayr promotes Sabir and fires his superior, Muhsin.

Meanwhile, Sabir's daughter, Nagafa, receives another marriage proposal, from Mahrus *effendi*, a government employee whom Sabir favors over the

Figure 5.13 Poster of *Ma'alihshi Ya Zahr*. Image adapted from *al-Ithnayn*. April 24, 1950, no. 828.

entrepreneur *ibn al-balad*, Husni. In vain, Nagafa tries to convince her father that Husni is a better suitor. Faced with Sabir's stern rejection, Nagafa marries Husni against her father's will. Attempting to get over the news of his daughter's marriage, Sabir seeks refuge in his new promotion. Soon this refuge is disturbed when the corrupt Mushin restores his power in the institution and revokes Sabir's promotion. Sitting at his desk, Sabir questions his worldview and repeats the famous proverb "Never mind" (*ma'alihshi ya zahr*). Lost in his sorrow, Sabir overhears his peers sarcastically suggesting that Sabir should send his wife with a complaint to the general inspector. He fights with them and gets fired.

Barakat blames Sabir *effendi*'s misfortunes on his false consciousness of modernity derived from his idolization of *effendiness* as the only path to leading a modern life. *Effendiness* traps Sabir in contradictory social values that allow him to present himself as modern. For example, the opening scenes introduce the rituals of *effendiness*, including excessive consumption of newspapers, adherence to a strict daily routine, and embrace of European norms regarding festivities. Although he is overworked and underpaid, these rituals are sacred to Sabir *effendi*. He is ready to fall into debt to celebrate birthdays and wedding anniversaries; he has two beds in the bedroom so that he and his wife can sleep separately. These rituals allow Sabir *effendi* to present himself in the eyes of his uneducated working-class neighbors as more modern and civilized; his mastery of standard Arabic enables him to show off his education and exercise class superiority. Despite being keen to present a modern civilized image of himself and his family, Sabir does not acknowledge his daughter's right to choose a partner. When she tells him that she will be miserable if she were to lose Husni, Sabir argues that a modern person has control over their life and happiness. Nagafa responds that her father's claim is only valid when the person has exercised the right to choose in the first place. To Sabir, modernity is rooted in the instrumental rationality of *effendiness*, which leads to certainty, social security, and happiness. In the following scene, Sabir expresses this view while giving his reasons for rejecting Husni's proposal to Nagafa:

> *Sabir:* If Husni were an employee with a secure income, perhaps I would have accepted the proposal.
> *Gum'a:* But he has a job and makes a lot of money, thanks to God.
> *S:* True, but his income is not secure.
> *G:* Are you suggesting that an independent business cannot guarantee a secure income?
> *S:* An independent business has "free" income; it is "free" to come or not to come. But a government employee has secure payment, guaranteed promotions, and a retirement plan.

Barakat shot the above scene on the stairs, implying that Sabir's firm belief in *effendiness* is part of his overall view of the world as a hierarchy of classes similar to institutional ranks. To Sabir, any violation of this order leads to social chaos.

Externalizing Sabir's character through the character of Nagafa's suitor, Mahrus, is another means Barakat uses to lampoon *ta'ssul*. Mahrus is obsessed with social status and his image as a modern and civilized person. He adheres to forms of modern luxury, be it a dress code or a code of communication. Besides the famous suit and tarbush, which marks effendiness, Mahrus always carries a newspaper and a hand fan (*minashsha*) tucked under his arm. While the newspaper frames Mahrus as a consumer of the high culture of print-capitalism produced in standard Arabic, the *minashsha*, which he uses to keep flies away, emphasizes his awareness of modern hygiene. Mahrus treats his marriage proposal as a job application. He visits Sabir *effendi* at home and presents his curriculum vitae and two letters of recommendation. Here, Barakat caricatures the institutional form of communication, which the *effendi* idolizes. The gaze of Sabir's wife, I'tidal, at Mahrus's apparel and behavior transfers the directors' view to the audience, making Mahrus's character appear exaggerated

Figure 5.14 The idolization of *effendiness*. On the left, Zaki Rustum as Sabir *effendi*. On the right 'Abd al-Fattah al-Qasri as *ibn al-balad* Gum'a.

Figure 5.15 Externalization of *effendiness*. Left, the new suitor, Mahrus *effendi*, introduces himself to Sabir *effendi*, right.

and mythical, pretty much like the character of Badawiyya in Yusuf Wahbi's *'Aris Min Istanbul*. Through I'tidal's conversation with Mahrus, the director reveals the superficiality of Mahrus's knowledge and education. He buys newspapers only to read obituaries and locate social functions such as Cairene-bourgeoisie weddings and funerals. There, Mahrus stages himself as an individual and mingles across different social classes according to need. He builds a social network to pursue his self-interest as an *effendi* first and foremost. In a way, caricaturing Mahrus's *effendiness* externalizes Sabir's *effendiness*. Barakat himself refused to be an *effendi*. He studied law, but hated the norms of *effendiness* prevalent among his fellow lawyers in the courts. Cinema offered him a chance to continue exploring the philosophy of law and retain the freedom of entrepreneurship.[20]

Juxtaposition is another technique that Barakat uses to critique *effendiness*, its obsession with form at the expense of meaningful content, and its false hopes of certainty and stability. One example is the character of Sabir's neighbor, *ibn al-balad* Gum'a, who interrogates the *effendi*'s claims of being more modern and superior through his mastery of standard Arabic, the so-called more rational register. Unlike Sabir *effendi*, *ibn al-balad* Gum'a celebrates colloquial culture feverishly; he finds the use of standard Arabic in day-to-day conversation superficial; it makes people sound like the Government's radio broadcast. In a way, Gum'a's rejection of standard Arabic in daily speech is a rejection of the state's authority in everyday life practices. The juxtaposition of the two characters and the two linguistic catalogs reaches its peak at Sabir's marriage anniversary party. To depict both the discourse and the counter-discourse, Barakat relies on a tradition in Arabic poetry known as *jinas*, which has to do with producing words with similar meanings from the same consonantal basis (*ishtiqaq*). There are four common types of *jinas*. When the two terms are identical in the consonantal and vocalic frame and have different meanings, the *jinas* is described as perfect (*tamm*). *Jinas* can be imperfect (*muharraf*) when the difference is in the vowels: pot (*qidr*)/fate (*qadar*). In an incomplete (*naqis*) *jinas*, the difference concerns the number of consonants. One of the two words presents one or two additional consonants: disease (*da'*)/medicine (*dawa'*). This can occur at the beginning, middle, or end of the word. *Jinas* is called flipped (*maqlub*) when the difference lies in variations in the arrangement of consonants: conquest (*fath*)/death (*hatf*).[21] In the following scene, Barakat capitalizes on *jinas* to depict *ibn al-balad* Gum'a making fun of Sabir, who has prepared a speech and asked his son, Wafa, to read it at Sabir's wedding anniversary. Below, Wafa fails to read the speech, which is written in standard Arabic:

> *Wafa:* Mom and Dad, "Slap each other!"
> *Gum'a:* What a hot start for an anniversary speech! Come on, boy, give it another slap—[everybody laughs].
> *Sabir:* He meant to say, "Stand up," not "Slap."
> *W:* [Readdressing his parents and reading correctly this time] "Mom and Dad, stand up, please."
> *S:* Yes, correct. That's my boy! Carry on, please.
> *W:* Mom and Dad, bury your times of happiness!
> *G:* In which grave shall they do that? Is the one who taught you to recite this speech an undertaker? [Everybody laughs. Sabir is embarrassed.]
> *W:* [Continues reading] The party shines in "the fever."
> *I'tidal:* God forbid!

G: Boy! This standard Arabic speech is gravely ill; it needs to see a doctor and rest. [Laughs]

S: [Addressing his son] You mean to say, "in the neighborhood." Carry on.

W: Yes, I meant to say, "in the neighborhood." [He resumes reading] May Wafa always "spit at your face."

S: [Embarrassed by his son's mistakes] Shame on you. [Urging his son to resume] Go ahead, read the line about Mom and Dad.

W: Mom is for Dad like "a pot," and my dad is for my mom like "a dumpster."

S: You confused everything! [Giving up on his son's reading skills in standard Arabic]

W: How do I know? The language is difficult.

I: Who is the idiot who wrote this speech for you to read?

W: Dad!

Here Barakat utilizes different types of *jinas* to caricature Sabir's claims of superiority through mastery of standard Arabic, a legacy he attempts to pass on to his son. The son is depicted betraying this legacy as he confuses meaning by mistaking standard Arabic words for colloquial ones. In line 1, Wafa mispronounces the standard Arabic word *qifa* (stand up) as the colloquial *afa* (back of the neck) due to the famous Egyptian glottal stop.[22] In line 6, Wafa mispronounces the standard Arabic passive voice *turba* (increase) as the colloquial noun *turba* (grave). Similarly, in line 8, he confuses the standard Arabic noun *hima*) (neighborhood) with *humma* (fever), shared between colloquial and standard Arabic. In line 12, he reads the noun *wafa'* (faithfulness) as his name, "Wafa." He reads the emphatic /t/ in the standard Arabic infinitive *taftafa* (to encompass) as a light /t/, thus confusing the standard Arabic verb with the colloquial verb *taftafa* (to spit). In line 14, he blurs the distinction between the standard Arabic noun *hullatun* (suit) and the colloquial *hallatun* (pot), and confuses the standard Arabic *miʿtafun* (new coat) with the colloquial *maʾtafun* (dumpster) which also translates as the English word "basket". The confusion occurs because colloquial speech comes more naturally to Wafa, who recalls his linguistic schema (mostly in colloquial language) and finds the closest possible pronunciation to the standard Arabic script, which he struggles to read. *Jinas* renders Wafa's speech irrational; his mistakes caricature the *effendi's* idolization of standard Arabic as the more rational linguistic register. By depicting the uneducated *ibn al-balad*, Gum'a, making fun of Wafa's standard Arabic skills, Barakat underscores the falsity of the *effendi's* claim to rationality by speaking in standard Arabic.

Barakat further critiques the *effendi's ta'ssul* as being a false consciousness of modernity that undermines a woman's rights to choose and act upon her choices. To this end, he employs juxtaposition to compare the unfair stance taken by the so-called educated *effendi* with the empowering stance taken by the uneducated *ibn al-balad*. Unlike Sabir *effendi*, Gum'a endorses a woman's right to live with a partner of her choice. He encourages the relationship between Nagafa and Husni; he tries to help the young couple, even if the cost is to accommodate Sabir's obsession with *effendiness*. Below, Gum'a creates for his son the *effendi* form, which Sabir idolizes so that the latter approves of the marriage:

> Gum'a: Are you not going to congratulate me? We followed your advice and had Husni employed.
>
> Sabir: Great! Congratulations! Where did you get him employed?
>
> G: Right here, in my shop. I assigned him a desk, a uniform, a log, a monthly salary, and a retirement plan. I think this way: his future becomes more certain and secure against poverty, sickness, and starvation. What do you think?
>
> S: [Laughs] Are you calling this employment?
>
> G: Of course! He comes on time and leaves on time. Starting tomorrow, I will buy him a timer so that we are more precise about his hours. What do you think? We have, I believe, met your standards. Will you accept Husni *effendi's* proposal to Nagafa?
>
> S: Hajj, it is difficult for me to refuse the proposal, but . . .
>
> G: But what? Are you ashamed because I am a shopkeeper? I supply the country with goods.
>
> S: No! Of course not. But it is a matter of principles. I want to get my daughter married to an employee who works for an institution.
>
> G: Pardon me! This is a false principle. Is trade a shame? Why can't you get her married to a merchant? 'Abbud pasha is a merchant; Bank Masr [i.e. Bank Misr] is a merchant; Ford is a merchant.

S: I understand, but I prefer to marry her to an employee who works inside a government institution.

G: Pardon me! This is an illusion. How come you do not consider my shop an institution? Is not Husni now an employee of this institution?

S: I am sorry, hajj, but I have to go.

To *ibn al-balad*, *effendiness* is a sense without sensibility; an *effendi* is a person enslaved by a false consciousness of modernity that reduces the idea of becoming modern to the passive control of uncertainties by restriction of movement and adherence to routine. Since the *effendi*'s livelihood is in the hands of others, he is dependent, and his claims to be modern and liberated appear false. By contrast, the *ibn al-balad* grapples with the contingency in human affairs. He is more inclined toward independent and non-governmental employment. Therefore, the *ibn al-balad* sees himself as more emancipated than the white-collar *effendi*.

Barakat ends his movie with Sabir *effendi* discovering the illusion of *effendiness*. But instead of depicting Sabir in a state of Durkheimian normlessness, where Sabir would have committed suicide, Barakat finds an exit through colloquial culture represented in the proverb "Never mind" (*ma'alihshi ya zahr*), which is also the title of the movie. Sabir repeats the saying to comfort himself, but it signals a paradigm shift; it marks Sabir's realization of the falsity of *effendiness*. Therefore, even though the corruption claims against Sabir are dismissed and he is reappointed with a higher rank, the idea of being an *effendi* loses its glamour in Sabir's eyes. Instead, he starts a company in partnership with his neighbor, *ibn al-balad* Gum'a. Together they earn more than Sabir *effendi*'s monthly income as a government employee. Sabir then recognizes that his daughter's decision to marry a Husni is right, and he welcomes her and her new family back. In the last scene, the narrator's voice states that the most outstanding achievement of Sabir lies in his understanding of when to say the phrase "Never mind" (*ma'alihshi ya zahr*)—that is to say, when to embrace modernity as an attitude of risk-taking that aims at a continuous and gradual critique of oneself in the present moment, in order to compel oneself to have the courage to use reason and face the task of producing and reproducing oneself. It is this attitude, as Barakat's narrator recommends, that should be taught to Sabir's grandson, a symbol of the future of modernity in Egypt.

Figure 5.16 Accommodating *effendiness*. Left, Karim Mahmud as Husni after dressing like an *effendi*.

But Barakat's solution did not bring reconciliation between the *effendi* and the *ibn al-balad*. Degree education and literacy in standard Arabic, the vehicle of the *effendi*'s so-called high modernist culture, continued to irritate the relationship between the *effendi* and the *ibn al-balad*. And this is the central theme of Fatin 'Abd al-Wahhab's movie *al-Ustadha Fatima*/Attorney Fatima, 1952. This time, the uneducated *ibn al-balad* undertakes to advance women's rights to education and the pursuit of a successful career.

8. If Only You Were Educated!

Al-Ustadha Fatima/Attorney Fatima, 1952 is directed by Fatin 'Abd al-Wahhab, whose filmography exceeds sixty-five features made over thirty-three years. Born in Damietta in 1913, Fatin 'Abd al-Wahhab was the youngest son of a manager in the Ministry of Education. His eldest brother is the renowned actor Sirag Munir, whose roles as the Egyptian feudal lord in almost all his hundred and thirty-nine films lampooned Egyptian aristocracy. Unlike his eldest brother, who went to Austria to study medicine but changed his focus to filmmaking, Fatin 'Abd al-Wahhab joined the Military Academy, graduating in 1939. But soon, he followed in his brother's footsteps and worked as an assistant director in Studio Misr. His first film, *Nadiya*/Nadia, 1948, starred 'Aziza Amir. His collaboration with Egypt's most famous comedian, Isma'il Yasin, resulted in a number of police-academy-type films. Fatin also excelled in adaptations, of which the most popular is *Isha'at Hub*/Love Rumor, 1959, based on John Emerson's *The Whole Town's Talking*. *Isha'at Hub* was not only one of the films that featured Omar Sherif before he left Cairo for Hollywood, but it also introduced the godfather of Egyptian tragedy, Yusuf Wahbi, to character comedy. Because of his role in *Isha'at Hub*, Wahbi ventured into another character comedy in *Miramar*/Miramar, 1969, by Kamal al-Shaykh, based on Naguib Mahfouz's novel.[23] Fatin teamed up with the singer Shadiya in eight musicals. Although he married the diva Layla Murad, they never collaborated.

Most of Fatin Abd al-Wahhab's comedies presented satirical commentaries on autocracy and despotism. For example, *Ard al-Nifaq*/The Land of Hypocrisy, 1968 and *Al-Fanus al-Sihri*/The Magical Lantern, 1960 address the entrenched power structure in a deep bureaucratic state that continues to thrive in post-1952 Egypt, thereby carrying a corrupt network of interest to the new era, supposedly void of feudal privileges. *Hukm Qaraqush*/The Rule of Qaraqush, 1953 invokes the autocratic rule of Baha' al-Din Qaraqush, the delegate of Saladin in Egypt, thereby hinting at the fading hopes of constitutional democracy after the army took over in 1952. *Al-'Ataba al-Khadra'*/'Ataba Square, 1959 remains one of the few films that critique the rural bourgeoisie, who are depicted celebrating the convenience of dependency and who are both the first victim and the backbone of the deep state. Movies like *al-Anisa Hanafi*/Miss Hanafi, 1954, *Mirati Mudir 'Am*/My Wife is the General Manager, 1966, and *Karamat Zawjati*/My Wife's Dignity, 1967 condemn social norms that suppress women's modern social roles as citizens who are capable of leading and governing. If it were not for Fatin's *'Arus al-Nil*/Bride of the Nile, 1963, Egyptian cinema would have continued to fall short of presenting popular films capitalizing on ancient Egyptian themes.

Al-Ustadha Fatima is 'Abd al-Wahhab's eleventh film; it tells the story of Fatima (Fatin Hamama), a student of Law at Fu'ad I University and the only child of 'Abd al-'Aziz al-Sharqawi ('Abd al-Fattah al-Qasri), an *ibn balad* who owns a mini-market and spends generously on his daughter's education. Fatima falls in love with her classmate and neighbor 'Adil (Kamal al-Shinnawi). Fatima's father disapproves of the relationship because 'Adil's father, Kamil *effendi*, does not spare an opportunity to remind al-Sharqawi of his illiteracy. Al-Sharqawi decides to build a wall between his house and Kamil's, but the latter contests the project. The dispute between the *effendi* and the *ibn al-balad* takes them to court, which declares the project illegal and causes the *ibn al-balad* to lose face in front of the *effendi*. The father's troubled relationship foreshadows the relationship between 'Adil and Fatima, who graduate from law school and compete to attract customers. When Fatima's new office does not receive as many cases as 'Adil's, Fatima discovers that 'Adil's assistant, Amin *effendi* (Sa'id Abu Bakr), is telling customers that Fatima, being a woman, is not qualified to defend them. Rivalry increases between the two lovers when 'Adil voices his concern that Fatima might not succeed as a lawyer, for law is too logical and dangerous a profession to be undertaken by women. The story takes a sharp turn when 'Adil meets his childhood friend, Kamil. The latter, who is paralyzed, decides to donate the bulk of his wealth to a charity organization. The decision infuriates his wife, Kawthar (Lula Sidqi), who seeks her banker boyfriend's help to kill her husband and accuse 'Adil of murder. To that end, she steals 'Adil's mail opener and uses it to kill her husband. When 'Adil is charged with murder, he asks Fatima to defend him.

The construction of *ta'ssul* in *al-Ustadha Fatima* centers on the *effendi*'s interest in regulating woman's modern social roles as equal citizens. The movie opens with 'Adil and Fatima meeting after class; they pass by a group of children, the majority of whom are girls. 'Adil's gaze at the girls questions whether the investment in women's education will bear fruit and whether women are capable, by temperament, of pursuing successful careers like men. As the film unfolds with Fatima outsmarting 'Adil in college, the question becomes who supports women's right in education and the pursuit of a successful career: is it the uneducated *ibn al-balad* or the *effendi*?

Like Barakat, Fatin Abd al-Wahhab depicted *effendiness* as a false consciousness of modernity. But unlike Barakat, Fatin 'Abd al-Wahhab presents various archetypes of *effendiness* through Kamil *effendi*, the banker Yusuf,

'Adil, and his assistant Amin. These characters have in common a degree-level education and reductionist views of women's modern social roles. Yusuf presents the extreme dependency and materialism of an *effendiness* that views women as objects of desire and a source of income. Amin represents the stereotype of the *effendi* confined to his career and invested in intrigues that here fuel tensions between Kamil *effendi* and *ibn al-balad* al-Sharqawi. 'Adil and his father represent the civilized, law-abiding good *effendis*, who value education and seem ready to accept women as equals. Their position, however, remains contradictory, for Kamil *effendi* values education but spares no opportunity to ridicule *ibn al-balad* al-Sharqawi's late attempt to overcome his illiteracy. He stigmatizes al-Sharqawi as ignorant, irrational, and chaotic because the latter lacks a degree. He does not shy away from publicly stating that the reason for the failure to reach reconciliation over the wall is that Fatima's father is an uneducated, ignorant man (*ragil gahil*). Like his father, 'Adil favors women's education, but not employment, unless they need to earn a living. He claims that women are soft by temperament, which will not help them stand their ground in a court of law.

Fatin critiques *effendiness* as a false consciousness of modernity through the reception of the *effendi* by the character of al-Sharqawi, Fatima's father. Initially, the character could represent a stereotype of the uneducated person with an inferiority complex. He compensates by showing off his mastery of the modern dress code and reading and speaking in standard Arabic. However, a closer look shows that this character serves the same purpose as that of Mahrus in Barakat's *Ma'alihshi Ya Zahr*. Al-Sharqawi's character externalizes Kamil's, making the latter look like a caricature, not as educated, modern, and superior as he presents himself. This is evident in the scenes depicting al-Sharqawi overdoing his mastery of *effendi* apparel. To al-Sharqawi, becoming an *effendi* is not rocket science. Anyone could be an *effendi*. It only takes wearing a suit and tarbush, enrolling at a night school to overcome illiteracy, and carrying a newspaper around to brag about one's consumption of modernist culture produced in standard Arabic and carrying a hand fan around to brag of one's awareness of modern hygiene. This satirical staging of *effendiness* functions as a protest against the *effendi*'s gaze of inferiority at uneducated working-class Egyptians. Consider the following scene, in which al-Sharqawi confronts Kamil *effendi* in the street:

Kamil: Could you please calm down so that we can negotiate?

Al-Sharqawi: No negotiation before evacuation!

K: Hajj, you have no right to build this wall.

Sh: Nonsense! The land is my land; I am the owner; I bought the construction material with my money. Why can't I build the wall?

K: The land is a shared property between us. By building the wall, you will block air and sunlight.

Sh: How come! Do not you always say that education is like light? Let your education light up your house!

Neighbor: There is a court case. Let us wait for the court to decide.

Sh: What is the need for the court? I studied the case closely, and I have not started building except after investigation and roasting (*tahmis*) [He confuses the word "scrutinize" (*tamhis*) with the word "roasting" (*tahmis*)]

K: Your persistence will force me to call the police.

Sh: I am never afraid or terrified or moved by the police.

K: You have always been arrogant!

Sh: And you have never had any insight into things!

K: What can I say?

Neighbor: [Addressing Kamil *effendi*] No, please do not say that word.

Sh: [Holding his temper and grumbling] Let him dare to say it. I want to hear it.

K: If you were an educated man, you would not have behaved like this, but you are ignorant.

Sh: Are you calling me ignorant? You are the one who lacks culture and information.

K: And you lack civility.

While the incoherent argument of the *ibn al-balad* sounds funny, the scene sends up *effendiness* as a travesty of modernity and an agent of colonialism. Al-Sharqawi's reliance on newspaper lines and political slogans such as "No negotiations before evacuation" allows him to show off the fact that he is well-informed about current events, just like any *effendi*. The statement, however, is loaded with political satire. It refers to a political slogan raised by the Watani Party, founded by the nationalist leader Mustafa Kamil. The party adopted a policy against any negotiations with the British authorities. In 1936, the al-Wafd party, led by Mustafa al-Nahhas, perceived the slogan as illogical and participated, along with other parties, in the negotiations leading to the famous Anglo-Egyptian treaty of 1936. Putting this slogan on the tongue of an uneducated working-class Egyptian in 1952 echoes the al-Wafd government's decision, led again by al-Nahhas, to abrogate the treaty unilaterally in 1951 and invoke the pre-1936 slogan. In the movie context, the statement frames Kamil *effendi* as equal to the British colonizer. Thus, the *effendi* is framed as a byproduct of the colonizer's false consciousness of modernity that fails to improve the human condition. It promotes dependency on the state and a heavy reliance on courts, indicating the absence of common sense. This idea unfolds more explicitly in the court scene below, when the court invites al-Sharqawi to speak and defend himself:

> *Al-Sharqawi:* Your Honor, our case today is the case of the struggle between truth and falsity. Truth has revealed itself to us, while falsity "got bored."[24] The defendant standing behind the iron cage is a guilty criminal and a vicious murderer. He attacked honor and virtue, which and "who"[25] are both protected by law. He assassinated human rights, which the Security Council protects. He murdered personal and public freedom. He murdered ethics. He killed honor. He killed modernization and urbanization. He intentionally killed all of these and all of those. For this purpose and the crimes above, I request that the court sentences him to death.

As incoherent as it sounds, most of the expressions that *ibn al-balad* al-Sharqawi uses in the above defense are quoted from newspapers. Through this satirical defense, however, the director allows *ibn al-balad* to lampoon the *effendi*'s understanding of modernity, which idolizes the rule of law over common sense, violating personal and public freedom, thereby destroying the very same values as it advocates. As al-Sharqawi puts it, human rights violations continue to exist despite the Security Council's protection of human rights. And he blames this on the *effendi*'s *ta'ssul*, that seeks to achieve justice through instrumental rationality at the cost of reason, thereby sacrificing the gradual internalization of modern notions of equality, equity, and social justice for all women and men, be they educated or uneducated.

Unlike the many *effendis* in the movie, al-Sharqawi believes in his daughter's potential to pursue a successful career. He spares no opportunity

Figure 5.17 Confronting *effendiness* (2). Left, 'Abd al-Warith 'Asar as Kamil *effendi* fighting with *ibn al-balad* al-Sharqawi ('Abd al-Fattah al-Qasri), right.

to encourage her to outsmart 'Adil in college. He holds a more extrvagant party than 'Adil's when she passes her bar exam. The two party scenes juxtapose the *effendi*'s retrenched, compartmentalized, and exclusionary modernity with the more inclusive staging of modernity advocated by *ibn al-balad*. On the *effendi*'s side, the singer appears obsessed with tuning his instruments and organizing his band, and in the end does not sing anything. On the *ibn al-balad*'s side, the singer sings in the streets among people, allowing them to occupy the public sphere and express their joy and celebration of a woman who has earned a degree with distinction from law school.

Similarly, Kamil *effendi* has no clue as to how to save his son. In contrast, the common sense of the illiterate *ibn al-balad* saves the *effendi*'s university-educated son from a death sentence. For example, al-Sharqawi suggests that the only way to prove to the court the relationship between Kawthar and her boyfriend is to trouble their relationship. He reasons through the standard Arabic proverb "If two thieves dispute, the stolen goods are found" (*idha ikhtalafa al-lissan zahara al-masruq*). And he requests Amin *effendi* to use his intrigues to create doubt between Kawthar and Yusuf just as Amin used

Figure 5.18 Modernity trapped between *tafarnug* and *ta'ssul*. Left, Fatin Hamam as Fatima. Middle, Lula Sidqi as Kawthar. Right, Kamal al-Shinnawi as 'Adil.

to provoke fights between Kamil and al-Sharqawi. Capitalizing on the *ibn al-balad*'s common sense, his daughter Fatima traps Kawthar and her boyfriend. By making Fatima hold Kawthar accountable for her crimes, the director does not merely prove that women are equal to men. Winning over Kawthar is a metaphor for triumph over the idea of dependency being the normative path for women. Kawthar confesses to Fatima, on one occasion, that a woman who pursues a career loses her sense of the feminine. That is why Fatin, until the last scene, emphasizes the feminine side of Fatima's character even when she cries in court. While Kawthar's dependency leads her to crime, Fatima's independence helps her save lives and improve the human condition without sacrificing her femininity. The underlying premise in this context is that a woman should not be forced to step into the domain of masculinity[26] to achieve sovereignty over body and mind.

Reconciliation between the *effendi* and modernity occurs only after 'Adil admits that women could outsmart men, and that he will happily stay home and be a stay-at-home dad. The director ends the movie by empowering his female protagonist, who states that she will gladly do the same thing. The underlying premise here is that accepting women's modern social roles does not mean belittling women's roles inside the household. It is a pro-choice stance. Nevertheless, the *effendi*'s obsession with *effendiness*, its claims of rationality and superiority, persisted. Husayn Sidqi's *al-Shaykh Hasan*/Sheikh Hasan, 1952 takes the critique of *ta'ssul* a step further by questioning the *effendi*'s attempt to rationalize faith.

9. No, Not I, My Faith Is Not Weak!

Al-Shaykh Hasan/Sheikh Hasan, 1952 is directed by Husayn Sidqi. He was born to a Turkish mother and an Egyptian father who died when he was five years old. Unlike many of his peers, Husayn Sidqi studied acting in Egypt and trained with theater giants like George Abyad, Fatima Rushdi, and Zaki Tulaymat. He took leading roles in thirty-nine films. Some of his most notable roles were in movies like *al-'Azima*/Perseverance, 1939, *Shati' al-Gharam*/Passion Beach, 1950, *al-Masri Afandi*/Mr. Masri, 1949, *Tariq al-Shawk*/The Thorny Path, 1950, *Adam wa Hawa*/Adam and Eve, 1951, *Yasqut al-Isti'mar*/Down with Imperialism, 1952, *al-Shaykh Hasan*/Sheikh Hasan, 1954, *Khalid Ibn al-Walid*/Khalid b. al-Walid, 1958, and *Ana al-'Adala*/I Am Justice, 1961.

Sidqi directed and produced sixteen films through his production company, Films of Modern Egypt. Many of these films discussed income disparity and the deteriorating social and economic status of the middle class after World War II, in addition to anti-colonialist themes post the 1948 Arab–Israeli war known in Arabic as the *nakba*.

Some critics label Sidqi as a preacher filmmaker because he built a mosque named after himself. The label was further propagated by the rumor that he wished that all his films be burnt before he died, save *Khalid b. al-Walid*. This does not necessarily indicate that Sidqi condemns his legacy as an actor. His decision to quit acting and directing in the 1960s was not unusual, given his age and the state's monopoly over the film industry at the time. The new work conditions proved impractical for many independent filmmakers. Muhammad Karim, for example, stopped directing around the same time. Even though Sidqi was once a member of parliament under Sadat and proposed a draft law requesting limitation of the alcohol trade, it is unlikely that Sidqi advocated an Islamist political agenda in the contemporary sense of expression. However, he

Figure 5.19 Al-Shaykh Hasan, promotional photograph (1). This was taken before it changed its name from *Laylayt al-Qadr* to *al-Shaykh Hasan*.

was occupied with the philosophical question of human will, predestination, and the struggle to cope with contingency. One example is his film *al-Masri Afandi*, in which he explores themes like the crisis of faith and resenting God during harsh economic conditions. Likewise, *al-Shaykh Hasan* deals with the polemics of Islam as faith and ideology. This is very clear from its original title being *Laylat al-Qadr*/The Night of Power or Decree, which refers to the night of Ramadan when the Prophet Muhammad received the revelation. The film was banned until 1952. It was released in 1954 with the new title *Shaykh Hasan*.

Al-Shaykh Hasan follows the challenges facing Hasan (Husayn Sidqi), a student of Islamic law living with his uneducated parents in a working-class

LAMPOONING RESIDUAL MODERNITY (*TA'SSUL*) | 329

Figure 5.20 Al-Shaykh Hasan, promotional photograph (2).

Cairene neighborhood. Hasan's relationship with his father ('Abd al-Warith 'Asar) is troubled, because the father consumes alcohol and drugs. Hasan's neighbor Nabawiyya (Huda Sultan) is in love with him and hopes they will get married one day. But Hasan does not show interest in her. Nabawiyya's dreams further shatter when Hasan receives a part-time job teaching Arabic to George's son (Istifan Rusti), a chocolate factory owner, whose daughter, Louisa (Layla Fawzi), falls in love with him.

The film takes a sharp turn when one night Hasan comes home to find his father and his friends smoking hashish. He becomes angry and physically attacks them. Insulted by his son's attitude, the father orders Hasan to move out of the family house. The news affects the health of Hasan's mother, who dies. When Hasan's father asks Hasan to come back, he agrees on condition that the father stops smoking *hashish* and drinking alcohol.

Meanwhile, Louisa's parents notice her interest in Hasan and object to the relationship. But as soon as Hasan graduates and starts his practice as a lawyer, he marries Louisa against her parents' will. Louisa then converts to Islam. Shocked at the news, the family contacts the police claiming that Hasan kidnapped Louisa. Because Louisa is not a minor, the police dismiss the claim. Unable to control her daughter's life, Louisa's mother falls sick. When Louisa tries to visit her mother, the father agrees on the condition that she gets a divorce. Hasan divorces Louisa temporarily, with the understanding that they will remarry when the mother's health improves.

After the divorce, Louisa ceases communication with Hasan for three months. Her father arranges her marriage to his friend, Armand, but Louisa's pregnancy interrupts his plans. Despite Louisa being five months pregnant, George insists that she abort the child. To bring the news about Louisa to Hasan, Nabawiyya volunteers to visit her in disguise as her friend. When Nabawiyya arrives, she finds Louisa in labor. Hasan rushes to see Louisa at the villa, where the father refuses to receive him. Overhearing the noise, and despite her childbirth complications, Louisa leaves her bed to see Hasan, and dies soon afterwards.

One immediate interpretation of this film is to read it as a proselytizing film, or propaganda against foreigners living in Egypt, and this is perhaps why the state has banned the movie up until today. However, a closer look at the dialogue and characterization reveals that the film condemns *ta'ssul*

LAMPOONING RESIDUAL MODERNITY (*TA'SSUL*) | 331

as a reactionary counter-stance that strives to present itself as a new alternative through condemning *tafarnug* and rationalizing Islamic rituals and practices.

The construction of *tafarnug* as a supremacist ideology in *al-Shaykh Hasan* is achieved through the character of Louisa's father, George. His rejection of Hasan is not merely motivated by class conflict. George sees Hasan as inferior both culturally and racially. This stance is evident in his decision to force his daughter to abort her child. Louisa's conversion to Islam does not anger George as much as Louisa's betrayal of her people and family. George, after all, does not think highly of religion. He does not treat his brother-in-law, the priest (Anwar Mansi), for example, with due respect. George's *tafarnug* also shapes Louisa's initial view of Hasan. Consider the following scene, depicting Hasan meeting Louisa and her friend for the first time:

Louisa's Friend: [Talking about a friend] She doesn't know how to dress. What kind of dress was that?

Louisa: [Talking to her friend before she notices Hasan in the room] She claims it's the latest fashion from Paris.

F: She is a liar. She didn't even go to Paris this year [Looks toward the salon room]. What is this? It looks like you have a shaykh in the salon.

L: Oh, he doesn't look like Shaykh 'Abd al-'Aziz. Let's go check him out!

F: Yeah, let's check him out. *Regardez, il prie.*

L: [French] I don't like those who pray [for] all. What is this?

F: [French] Maybe it helps them look authentic and be able to deceive people

L: Oui! Oui!

H: [Ending his prayer] May God's peace and mercy befall you [He looks to left and repeats].

L: Peace to you.

F: Peace to you.

H: I am not greeting you.

L: Are you talking to yourself then?

H: I am greeting creatures created from light (*makhluqat nuraniyya*), whose nature you do not understand.

F: Are you the one who summons spirits?

H: Why? Does it look like I called you?

L: [Laughs] He knows how to tell jokes too.

H: I know how to tell jokes, that is true. But I do not know how to cheat and fool people with my prayers.

L: Do you understand French?

H: And English too.

F: Huh! A shaykh who knows French and English! He must be modern.

L: And does the modern person overlook courtesy and pray in other people's house? Should he not wait until he goes home?

H: It looks like you do not come on time when you have an appointment with someone.

L: Who said so? The most important thing for me is to keep my appointments with my friends.

H: And the most important thing for me is to keep my appointment with my God.

L: Huh, is prayer timed in your faith?

H: Prayer has a designated time and should be performed on time.

L: And do you always keep your prayer *rendezvous*?

H: Like you keep your dance *rendezvous*.

L: Dance is a good sport for the body.

H: Prayer is a good sport for the body and the soul (*ruh*).

L: What soul? Is there anything called "soul"?

F: Does he mean the smell (*ruh*) of ammonia? [Louisa and her friend laugh out loud]

H: I was right about my first impression of you both. When my eye fell on you, I knew you were bodies without souls.

L: Who the hell are you? And why did you come here?

H: And who are you, and in what position are you speaking to me?

F: What is this? Did you hear him, Louisa? He is rude.

H: Louisa! I see now that you are the daughter of Monsieur George. If her brother also has the same mentality, I will not be able to tutor him.

F: Now, I know who he is. He is the teacher coming to teach Joseph.

L: You cannot be a teacher at all.

LAMPOONING RESIDUAL MODERNITY (TA'SSUL) | 333

H: Of course, I cannot be a teacher for those who do not have souls like you.

L: Are you insulting us?

H: I am stating a fact. You are the one who insulted me.

L: That was just a statement.

H: Humans are worth as much as the statements they speak.

L: And you are not worthy of any statements.

H: Now you won me over, because when the Mademoiselle uses swear words, one cannot do anything except withdraw. [Louisa and her friend laugh as Hasan leaves the room]

The above scene depicts Hasan's arrival at the house of George for the first time. Before coming, Hasan has been impressed by George, who invests in teaching his kids Arabic. He praises him as a good example of foreigners living in Egypt. When the servant brings Hasan a rug to pray on, a Muslim prayer

Figure 5.21 Ridiculing Muslim prayer. In the middle, Husayn Sidqi as Shaykh Hasan. On the left, Layla Fawzi as Louisa. On the right, Nagwa Salim as Louisa's friend. *Al-Shaykh Hasan*, 1951.

rug at a Christian's house further impresses Hasan. But when Hasan meets Louisa, his initial impressions change. George's domain is hostile, because it is dominated by *tafarnug* which is anti-religion. Louisa and her friends also direct an Orientalist gaze at Hasan, whom they perceive as an undereducated clergyman who lacks knowledge of modern European languages and merely uses religion to gain power and status in society. As a person who believes in the absolute separation between the physical and the metaphysical, Louisa does not think highly of rituals.

While Hasan condemns Louisa's *tafarnug*, his amour-propre of modernity continues to be regulated by it. In other words, Hasan responds to everything around him with Louisa's *tafarnug* in mind. Relying on instrumental rationality, he justifies his views of Islamic rituals and practices to prove to Louisa that Islam is a rationalist religion. As a result, Hasan adopts radical positions that label Muslims who do not share Hasan's views as non-Muslims or, at best, living with an incomplete Islam.

For example, when Hasan's mother dies, Sidqi depicts him objecting to the expression of mourning during the funeral. Hasan describes women mourners as nonsensical; their way increases pain and is resentful toward God's will, an act of unbelief (*kufr*), and is against Islam. Instead, he advises them to pray for the dead silently and read the Qur'an for her soul. When Hasan's father interferes and asks Hasan to leave the women alone to their social norms and standard practices, Hasan argues that his father's reasons are similar to the reasons of those infidels who opposed the Prophet Muhammad saying "This is what we grew up witnessing our parents doing" (*hadha ma wajdna 'alyihi aba'ana*). Similarly, when Louisa wonders why Hasan is not dressed in black after his mother has died, he says that all these practices are false expressions of sorrow. Black affects the nervous system and increases sorrow; plus, dressing in black is a practice that dates back to a pre-Islamic time, which Hasan refers to as the time of ignorance (*jahiliyya*). Instead people should be patient, which is why God made the reward of the patient very great in the afterlife.

Likewise, in the following scene, Hasan explains to Louisa his position on polygamy:

Hasan: One of the foundations (*adab*) of our religion is to believe that we always need knowledge. The Prophet encouraged us to seek knowledge from birth to death.

Louisa: What about the polygamy issue? You marry as you wish, two and sometimes three...

H: Yes, and even four times, for that matter. Why are you objecting?

L: Where I come from, a man marries only one woman, and the woman is assured that there is no other woman in his life.

H: Yes. But as you know, some men have extramarital affairs, and marriage does not prevent this from happening.

L: Yes. But this is not the norm. It is an exception.

H: The wisdom of Islam necessitates that these relationships be regulated instead of humiliating their offspring that committed no crime. [Louisa's brother Joseph cheers Hasan]

L: [Objecting to Joseph's reaction] What is so reasonable about what Hasan says? Where I come from, it is against religion to have an extramarital affair.

H: Yes. In Islam, a person who marries more than one woman without a reason is considered as going against religion. God conditioned the second marriage by justice.

L: Can you give me an example?

H: Many contexts make polygamy inevitable. Sometimes the couple do not have a child. Instead of a man living with his wife with resentment, he can marry another woman to have children.

L: Why can't he divorce her and marry another one?

H: It is unfair to divorce her. God discouraged divorce even when a man hates his wife, as mentioned in the Quranic verse Q4:19, which reads, "And consort with them in a kind and honorable way; for if you dislike them, it may be that you dislike a thing in which God has placed much good."[27]

Joseph: So basically, in Islam, a man should not divorce without reason and should not practice polygamy without cause.

H: Yes. Is not this a better option than a lifelong marriage that leaves them vulnerable to extramarital affairs?

J: Yes. This is why we also have the divorce option.

Hasan's views favoring polygamy as an institution are driven by his instrumental rationality and objectification of the female body. For example, he objects to Louisa's tennis shorts and asks her to wear more modest dress while playing. He then argues that if wearing such dress is inevitable, women and men should not mix while playing tennis. Here, Louisa objects and asks, "Why is your religion so suffocating when it comes to women's dress?" Hasan responds that this is to save men from being seduced. Louisa argued that men should be guided by ethical conduct that prevents seduction, and as time passes women's tennis dress will come to appear quite ordinary. Hasan claims that sexual desires are necessary for society. When Louisa finds his position contradictory, Hasan explains that he does not want absolute suppression of sexual desires; he only wants willingness to be regulated through marriage. To him, the covering of the female body is more romantic because classical poets, for example, used to write poetry praising the beloved's fingers, which happened to show unintentionally behind a curtain. Still, no modern poet cared to describe Alexandria's famous Stanely Beach. Similarly, when one client hires Hasan to arrange her divorce as her husband prevents her from visiting her mother, Hasan encourages her to obey her husband. Islam requires her to protect her, not to make her life difficult. He requests to see her husband in the hope of mending the relationship. When the client explains that her husband is a hopeless case, Hasan insists on talking to the husband first before representing her.

Correspondingly, Hasan argues that Islam did not spread with coercion, because the Qur'anic verse Q 2: 256 states, "There is no coercion in religion,"[28] and Islamic rulings do not force non-Muslim wives of Muslim men to convert. He argues that the most crucial thing that helped Islam spread is the principle of equality before God. When Louisa asks Hasan why, if Islam is so good, Muslim societies suffer from inequality and poverty, Hasan responds that Muslims do not follow Islam properly. But poverty will be eradicated if every Muslim pays the assigned share of alms. And this, he argues, makes Islam a better option than socialism.

In order to frame Hasan's *ta'ssul* as a reactionary sociopolitical stance that seeks shelter in religion to exercise moral superiority in response to *tafarnug*, the director reveals Hasan's anxiety over his social class. For Hasan, living among mostly uneducated working-class Egyptians, education undoubtedly changed his social class. However, he is neither an *ibn balad* nor an *effendi*. His identity becomes tied to his education and social status as an Azhari student who carries the Prometheus burden of educating people about what he sees as "true" and "authentic" Islam. Sidqi underscores Hasan's self-proclaimed prophecy when he depicts Hasan's picture hanging right above his desk instead of the more typical depiction of Qur'anic verses as displayed throughout Hasan's house. For example, there is a picture in the living room that asserts God's eternal justice. The verses, Q99:7–8, read, "So whosoever does a mote's weight of good shall see it. And whosoever does a mote's weight of evil shall see it."[29]

For the same reason, supporting characters are used early in the film to juxtapose Hasan's self-perception with his neighbor's views of him. Some neighbors think highly of Hasan and hope he will become a judge. Others think he will achieve nothing. His most significant accomplishment will be to become a marriage record keeper (*ma'zun*), that is, a state employee authorized by the state to write the marriage-contract and lead prayers.

Hasan's class anxiety further shows in his relationship with his father. When he fights with his father over alcoholism, Hasan says, "You send me to receive education at a prestigious religious institution like al-Azhar to guide people, while you sit here and smoke *hashish* in Ramadan." He then threatens to report his father to the police and goes as far as telling his father he is not a real man, for he consumes drugs secretly, and a real man does not hide in fear. When the tension escalates and Hasan leaves the house, Sidqi depicts him reflecting on his actions in the following self-monologue:

> What have I got to do with all this? I should have left God's creation to God and kept myself busy with my issues. But I could not ignore it. I did the duty dictated by religion, which teaches that whoever sees an injustice (*munkar*) should first try their best to change it with their own hands. What else could I have done, deny it in my heart, and accept resorting to the weakest expression of faith? It is not possible. No, not I. My belief is not weak. Now, I should bear the consequences of my action bravely and patiently.

While the monologue reflects Hasan's occupation with social change, it is dramatically centered around his obsession with his amour-propre. As an Islamic law student, he is aware of the views that encourage believers to mind their own business when it comes to other people's sins or, as Hasan put it to himself in Egyptian colloquial, "leave God's creatures to God." But his obsession, as both religious and rational social reformer, with his amour-propre urges him to justify his actions through the prophetic tradition that reads, "Whoever amongst you witnessed an injustice, change it with his hand; if he is unable to do so, then with his tongue; and if he is unable to do so, then with his heart; and that is the least that can be done." Unlike 'Abbas, in *Man al-Gani*, Hasan's instrumental rationality makes him appropriate the tradition and overlook the Qur'anic verse that reads "Call unto the way of thy Lord with wisdom and goodly exhortation. And dispute with them in the most virtuous manner. Surely thy Lord is He Who knows best those who stray from His way, and He knows best the rightly guided."[30]

Class anxiety in relation to Hasan's *ta'ssul* also appears in Hasan's dress code. After fighting with his father, Hasan gives up on his Azhari uniform and favors wearing a suit. When Louisa notices his change of clothing, she praises it. When Nabawiyya comments on his new and unfamiliar apparel, he laughs and says, "Are you wondering about the suit? I changed. Don't I look better now?" This change is not merely openness to the new or the foreign. In a way, Sidqi underscores Hasan's perception of the suit as superior to his Azhari uniform; he asserts Hasan's interest in acquiring the form of an *effendi*. Here Sidqi employs a reaction shot showing Nabawiyya's dissatisfaction with Hasan's change of apparel, which, to her, is an indication that Hasan, contrary to what he preaches, is under the control of Louisa and her *tafarnug*. Her hopes of getting married to him are completely shattered.

Likewise, when Lousia proposes to Hasan, he hesitates and asks her to seek her parents' permission, which is necessary. Louisa then jokingly says that she will follow his obsession with error-correction (*istidrak*) and argue that their consent is unnecessary, for they will disagree. She further contends that their disagreement is against God's will, for God is the one who made her love Hasan. Hasan makes another *istidrak*, arguing for the need for their consent because Louisa may be unable to replace her luxurious life with his harsh and poor life.

Because of this class anxiety, Hasan applies double standards when dealing with Louisa and his father. When Hasan fights with Louisa, who blames Hasan for dehumanizing her, Hasan says that God asks Muslims to forgive and forget mistreatment. He adds that nobody is naturally evil, and evil can be subdued. But at the same time, he is not as tolerant toward his father, who is not as evil as Hasan thinks. To this end, Sidqi invests in a scene showing the father getting drunk and walking with one of his friends. While the scene serves the plot line by revealing how Hasan's father did not keep his promise to his son and continued to drink, the dialogue between the two drunk characters shows that they are not as evil as Hasan imagines; they also love God. As they wander and cannot control their movement, they fancy visiting the mosque of Imam Shafi'i and eating some pastries near the mosque of Sayyida. Despite Hasan's repeated attempts to convince his father that alcoholism is a sin, the father does not follow Hasan's advice. He only stops drinking when he witnesses firsthand how alcoholism caused his friend's death.

To distinguish Islam as a faith from Islam as an ideology, Sidqi invests in the character of Nabawiyya, whose name is a nisba adjective that translates as "prophetic," thereby emphasizing her spirituality. Because Nabawiyya is in love with Hasan, she refuses many proposals as she waits for him to finish his education and propose to her. Early in the film, her parents make a scene in front of Hasan's family and complain that Nabawiyya must meet her suitors. They want to test whether Hasan intends to marry Nabawiyya. Hasan's mother tells Nabawiyya's mother that Hasan will propose after he graduates. While Hasan likes Nabawiyya, he does not see her as a suitable life partner, for she is uneducated and superstitious.

In one scene, Nabawiyya supplicates and prays to God that she will marry Hasan. When she finishes praying, she looks at the sky and notices a light aura, from which she infers that her prayers have been answered. Her understanding is rooted in popular oral culture, which imagines that those who supplicate on the last ten nights of Ramadan can be blessed by seeing an aura of light (*taqita al-qadr*), a sign of blessing. When Nabawiyya rushes downstairs to share her joy with her neighbors, Hasan meets her on the stairs. He explains that there is nothing called *taqat al-qadr*; she should not be irrational, because she sees only reflections of lights resulting from the movements of the stars. When Nabawiyya objects and says if there is no such thing—what is the Qadr Night which God promises believers?—Hasan responds that while the Prophetic traditions describe it as one of the last ten nights in Ramadan, the Prophet was not reported to have specified a night; the hadith means to encourage people to worship more during these nights. Nabawiyya objects and says that she has prayed wholeheartedly and that God has answered her prayers. The significance of this exchange lies in how it sheds light on Nabawiyya's understanding of faith. Faith is a private stance in which she contemplates the position of the self in the present moment, away from the gaze of authority. Consider her supplication below:

> God, if my love is a sin, I cannot repent it
> I ask Thee to forgive and approve of my love
> With Thy mercy, decree that those who love are loved back
> Bring the lovers together
> Make the two hearts happy
> Let them cherish the blessing of love
> God, if my love is a sin, I cannot repent it
> I ask Thee to forgive and approve of my love
> You are the One who makes hearts melt with the fire of love
> Love is your decree
> If there is a fault, it is not mine
> How can I control a heart taken by love and tortured by doubts?
> If my love is a sin, I cannot repent it
> I ask Thee to forgive and approve of my love
> God, on this Qadr night, let my moonlight face partner love me back
> I shall entrust him with my life and remain faithful to him forever
> God, even the cruel hope for Thy mercy,
> God, if my love is a sin, I cannot repent it
> I ask Thee to forgive and approve of my love

Nabawiyya expresses her feelings about God by addressing a sacred silence whose main attribute is mercy; God is all-Knowing and all-Capable; God decrees and changes what is decreed. Her view creates an infinite domain of possibilities that rebuffs hopelessness and inspires her throughout the film to love even when she loses Hasan to Louisa. Multiple scenes are dedicated to showing that Hasan's father cannot understand Nabawiyya's tolerance and how she helps Louisa adapt to her new lifestyle after marriage. Nabawiyya delivers Louisa's letters to Hasan. It is Nabawiyya who encourages Hasan to go and visit Louisa when communication stops for three months after the divorce.

Figure 5.22 Islam as a faith. Huda Sultan as Nabawiyya making supplication in *al-Shaykh Hasan*, 1951.

Without Nabawiyya's help, Hasan would not have known about his newborn child. When Louisa dies at the end of the film and Nabawiyya offers to take care of the child, it is inferred that Hasan will be united with Nabawiyya, the only one whose prayers, somehow, are answered at the end of the story. This ending shows that Nabawiyya's faith wins over Hasan's instrumental rationality and ideological view of religion.

To further critique Hasan's heavy reliance on instrumental rationality, Siqdi employs the character of Louisa's uncle, the priest. The uncle understands Hasan's internal conflict and obsession with rationalization and logical thinking. Therefore, the priest offers Hasan the rationale of seeing his divorce from Louisa as the best way of serving his interest. The priest argues that if Louisa's mother dies because of her shock at her daughter's marriage and conversion, Louisa will not forget that her relationship with Hasan had led to her mother's death. Soon, her love for Hasan will turn into hate. The priest asserts that he does not speak as a clergyman; he speaks from a humanitarian perspective and as an older and more experienced man. This argument resonates well with Hasan, as he blames his mother's death on his father, whose insistence on separating Hasan from his mother led to the latter's death. Here Hasan again tries to find an exit by rationalizing his choice; he argues that Islam is great and does not leave any problem without a solution. This allows him to divorce his wife momentarily and restore her to matrimony later (*talaq raj'i*). When Hasan visits Louisa and George refuses to host him, Hasan urges the priest to grant him his right to see his wife. Again, the priest recognizes Hasan's obsession with rationality and tells him that while Hasan has a right, George has absolute freedom in his house; he is free to host or dismiss Hasan. Hasan blames George and questions his humanitarianism. When Hasan blames the priest, the priest shows empathy and says that he has divorced Louisa and accepted that she should stay with her mother. The dialogue here shows how Hasan's obsession with rationalizing his faith and rights eventually traps him. It does not help him achieve his ends. In the end, he, like the adherents of *tafarnug*, finds himself in a situation where humanitarianism is the only exit.

Therefore, the final scene further emphasizes humanitarianism as an exit. On her deathbed, Louisa trusts only the priest. She entrusts him with respecting her wish to have a Muslim burial and entrusts him to give the child to Hasan. While she asserts that she is a Muslim, not a Christian, she equally says that her religion is rooted in love. When Hasan holds the child and all the characters gather around them, Hasan's final speech implies that if they all lost their humanitarianism in their modernist quest to attain happiness, maybe their sorrow will remind them how to regain it.

Notes

1. Jennifer Hill, *Hassan Ibn Thabit, a True Mukhadram: A Study of the Ghassanid odes of Hassan ibn Thabit*. Doctoral diss., Georgetown University, 2009.
2. While it is not known who the poet is, this line of poetry is often attributed to al-Mutanabbi.
3. The reference is to the word "lazawardiyy," which means the color of the lapis lazuli gemstone. Apart from the confused meaning and metaphors of the lines of poetry, it seems a simile is made involving a slaughtered dove wrapped in red blood and a crescent wrapped in dark-blue color (presumably of the sky): that is, the dove is wrapped in red as much as the crescent is wrapped in blue. A better translation might actually be "a crescent wrapped in red." But I stick here to the

LAMPOONING RESIDUAL MODERNITY (TA'SSUL) | 343

more literalist translation to convey the inaccurate meanings proposed by the character.
4. In the second section of this chapter, I discuss Kamal's statement in relation to his understanding of the "high" and the "low" forms of singing.
5. Raj Bhala, *Understanding Islamic Law: Shari'a* (Boston: LexisNexis, 2011), 1031.
6. Ibid.
7. See Muhammad Ibn 'Abidin, *Radd al-Muhtar 'ala al-Dur al-Mukhtar Hashiyat Ibn 'Abidin*, 13 vols. (Riyadh: 'Alm al-Kitab, 2003), 4:423 and Kamal al-Din al-Hanafi, *Fath al-Qadir*, ed. 'Abd al-Raziq Ghalib al-Mahdi (Beirut: Dar al-Kutub al-'Ilmiyya, 2003), 216–25.
8. See Shams al-Din al-Shirbini, *Mughni al-Muhtaj* (Beirut: Dar al-Kutub al-'Ilmiyya, 2000), 3:540–52 and Yahya Abu Zakariyya, *Rawdat al-Taibin wa 'Umdat al-Muftin*, 12 vols., ed. Zuhayr al-Shawish (Beirut: al-Maktab al-Islami, 1991), 5:318.
9. See Al-Mardawi, 'Ala' al-Din. *Al-Insaf fi Ma'rifat al-Rajih min al-Khilaf*, 12 vols. (Cairo?: Maktabat al-Sunna al-Muhamadiyya, 1955), 7:3–80; Mansur al-Bahuti, *Kashshaf al-Qina'*, 6 vols. (Beirut: 'Alm al-Kitab, 1983), 4:240–97; al-Maqdisi, *al-Furu'*, 1122; Mansur al-Bahuti, *Sharh Muntaha al-Iradat*, ed. 'Abdullah al-Turki (Riyadh?: Al-Risala Nashirun, 2000), 4:329–66; Hasan al-Shatti, *Matalib Uli al-Nuha*, 6 vols. ([Dimashq]: Manshurat al-Maktab al-Islami bi-Dimashq, 1961), 4:–270367.
10. See Taqiyy al-Din Ibn Taymiyya, *Al-Fatawa al-Kubra*, 6 vols., ed. Muhammad 'Abd al-Qadir 'Ata (Beirut: Dar al-Kutub al-'Ilmiyya, 1987), 5:425–33.
11. Al-Shafi'i, *Mughni al-Muhtaj*, 2:308; Abu Zakariyya, *Rawdat al-Talibin*, 6:315.
12. Ignác Goldziher, *Muslim Studies*, Vol. 2, trans. C. R. Barber and S. M. Stern (London: George Allen, 1971), 202.
13. Ibid.
14. Sky News Arabiyya, "misr . . . raf' si'r tadhakir al-mitru," YouTube, May 12, 2018, https://www.youtube.com/watch?v=Zj63ojM2x4k (last accessed December 12, 2020).
15. Born in 1905 to a merchant of gold, he attended a French high school. But he grew up in the Cairene folk quarter of al-Gammaliyya, where he absorbed the aesthetics and sensibilities of *awlad al-balad*. While he began his career in theater as early as 1930, it was not until 1940 that he collaborated with al-Rihani and co-starred with him in the classic comedy *Si 'Umar*. This role gained al-Qasri true momentum on screen and made al-Rihani jealous, to the extent that the

latter insisted on cutting some of al-Qasri's scenes. The possible competition between a famed comedian like al-Rihani and an emerging comedian like al-Qasri might have disqualified the latter for lead roles, but al-Qasri's being cross-eyed also played a role. His career ended tragically when he lost his eyesight on stage. He died in 1965 at al-Dimirdash hospital in Cairo, leaving behind more than a hundred celebrated classics such as *Lawu Kunt Ghani*/If I Were Rich, 1942 by Henry Barakat, *al-Suq al-Sawda'*/The Black Market, 1945 by Kamil al-Tilmisani, *Fatima*/Fatima, 1947 by Ahmad Badrkhan, *Hasan Wa Murqus Wa Kuhain*/ Hassan, Marcus and Cohen, 1954 by Fu'ad al-Gazayrli, and *Bayn Idayk*/In Your Arms, 1960 by Youssef Chahine.

16. Henry Barakat, interview by Amina Sa, *Hadith al-Zikrayat*, Sawt al-'Arab, 1996, https://www.youtube.com/watch?v=hNMAMiOekpA&feature=youtube (last accessed December 12, 2020); Adel Darwish, "Obituary: Henri Barakat," *The Independent*, May 29, 1997, https://www.independent.co.uk/news/people/obituary-henri-barakat-1264170.html (last accessed December 12, 2020).

17. Adel Darwish, "Obituary: Henri Barakat," *The Independent*, May 29, 1997, https://www.independent.co.uk/news/people/obituary-henribarakat-1264170.html).

18. Ibid.

19. *Al-Ithnayn*, April 10, 1950, no. 826.

20. Barakat, Interview by Amina Sabri.

21. Lidia Bettini, "Jinas," *Encyclopedia of Arabic Language and Linguistics*, ed. Lutz Edzard and Rudolf de Jong, Brill Online, 2013. Reference. Georgetown University. September 14, 2013, http://referenceworks.brillonline.com.proxy.library.georgetown.edu/entries/encyclopedia-of-arabic-language-and-linguistics/jinas-SIM_vol2_0041 (last accessed December 12, 2020).

22. In Egyptian colloquial, the standard Arabic sound /q/ is pronounced /a/.

23. There is, of course, Shadi 'Abd al-Salam's *al-Mumiya'*/The Mummy, 1975, which is a luminous picture and critically acclaimed, but not so popular. See Elliott Colla, "Miramar and Postcolonial Melancholia," in Susan Muaddi-Darraj and Waïl Hassan, eds., *Approaches to Teaching the Works of Naguib Mahfouz* (New York: Modern Language Association of America, 2011), 71–183.

24. The character confuses the standard Arabic word *zahiqa* ("defeated") with the colloquial word for "got bored" (*zihi'*), as he uses the Egyptian glottal stop instead of the standard /q/.

25. The character confuses the demonstrative pronouns in standard Arabic. He uses the feminine demonstrative pronoun before the masculine word "honor."

I use "which" and "who" to underscore the script's emphasis on redundancy as a means of faking eloquence in standard Arabic.
26. At the time the film was screened, the domains of masculine and feminine were sharply defined, at least in public.
27. Seyyed Hossein Nasr, Caner K. Dagli, Maria Massi Dakake, Joseph E. B. Lumbard, and Mohammed Rustom, *The Study Quran* (Sydney: HarperOne, 2015), 548, Kindle edition.
28. Ibid., 125.
29. Ibid., 406.
30. Ibid., 1740–1.

6

Celebrating Emergent Modernity (*Asala*)

1. She Is Brought Up in European Schools

In my earlier discussion of Muhammad Karim's *al-Warda al-Bayda'* I focused on the director's use of supporting roles to critique dominant modernity (*tafarnug*). As I revisit the film in this chapter, I shift focus to the movie's celebration of emergent modernity (*asala*) as presented through the female lead character, Raga' (Samira Khulusi). Initially, another emerging actress, Nagla' 'Abduh Tanuys, was nominated to play the role. But a typhoid infection kept her in bed for almost four months, and the production was compelled to find a replacement. Dawlat Abyad nominated Samira Khulusi, who was a minor and could not be hired without the consent of her legal guardian. Khulusi's French mother, who supported her daughter's career, did not object, but she could not sign on Samira's behalf because her father was the legal guardian. To Karim's surprise, Khulusi's Egyptian father did not object. A public controversy arose when the promotional photograph of *al-Warda al-Bayda'* featured a kiss between the two heroes, Samira Khulusi and Muhammad Abd al-Wahhab. The controversy was not so much over the kiss as about the fact that 'Abd al-Wahhab had kissed her while wearing "the" tarbush, seen by some readers as a national symbol of Egypt. Like many controversies Karim faced, this one passed and benefited the film's publicity.

The character of Raga in *al-Warda al-Bayda'* is marked by a sense of entrapment, which is not uncommon among young Cairene-bourgeoisie women in 1930s Egypt. A daughter of a feudal bey, Raga' graduates from French high school, after which she stays at home awaiting a good marriage proposal. Her life is confined to the house of her upper-class family. Her sense

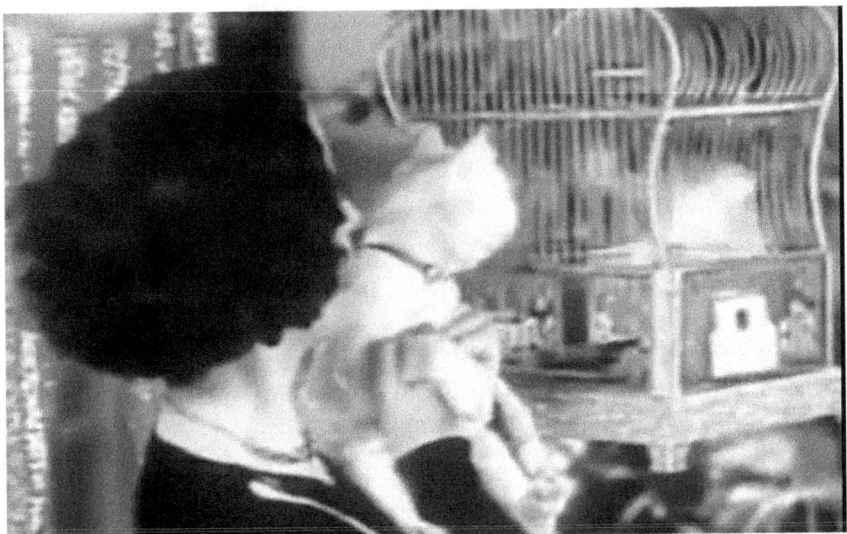

Figure 6.1 Caged modernity. Samira Khulusi as Raga'. *Al-Warda al-Bayda'*, 1933.

of captivity appears in an early scene showing the character holding her cat and looking at a sparrow inside a cage. The cat and the sparrow are allegories of Raga's feeling of captivity within her Cairene-bourgeoisie norms that deny a woman sovereignty over her body and mind. Raga', for example, does not choose her clothes; her sensibilities and aesthetics are regulated by the *tafarnug* of her stepmother, who wants to control her personality and potential inheritance. Because of *tafarnug*, Raga' is stuck in a set of contradictory social standards. On the one hand, her family sends her to French schools, but her stepmother constantly reminds her not to speak French. The family hosts and celebrates a "Western" (here referred to as *afrangi* music) musical instrument like the piano, but Raga's stepmother objects every time she plays Western tunes. Raga's father claims to believe in entrepreneurship. But he insists on getting Raga' married to an *effendi* who works for a governmental institution. The most unjust contradiction is when Raga' discovers that her father, despite the progressive aura he projects, denies her the right to marry a man of her choice.

Raga's understanding of modernity is interrogated in the following scene by the educated middle class, represented in the film by the two managers of Isma'il's estate, Khalil *effendi* (Muhammad 'Abd al-Quddus) and Shaykh Madbuli (Tawfiq al-Mardinli),

> *Khalil:* Have you met with the bey yet?
> *Madbuli:* I met him. The young lady came to greet me. But I honestly could not recognize her.
> *Kh:* What else did you expect? She is brought up in European schools.
> *M:* But thank God, she still knows how to speak Arabic.

While the exchange between Madbuli and Khalil appears a commentary on social anxieties rising around "European" education as a tool that leads to *tafarnug*, the scene simultaneously offers the audience two viewpoints on Raga's modernity. On the one hand, there is the optimistic view of Madbuli, who dresses in a traditional Azhari uniform and represents the rural educated middle class. Madbuli is depicted as more empathetic throughout the film. On the other hand, there is the pessimistic and judgmental view of Khalil *effendi*, who wears the typical *effendi* uniform and represents the urban-educated middle class. Khalil sees Raga' as a child lost to *tafarnug*, whereas Madbuli praises Raga's ability to master Arabic, despite her French education. Here, the tone of Madbuli makes all the difference. It is not a sarcastic tone like Khalil's. And Karim seems to favor Madbuli's empathy toward Raga' over Khalil's judgmental attitude. In his memoirs, Karim recalled how he created Khalil's character to serve as a caricature of *effendiness*. And this seems evident in Karim's choice of lampooning the character of Khalil throughout the film by depicting him as a tedious employee adhering to a routine. He micromanages tasks assigned to his assistant, Galal, to the extent that Khalil tells Galal where and how to walk while running an errand in the city.

As the movie unfolds, the dialogue reveals the third view of Raga's modernity, which does not simply materialize through her choice of emphasizing love as the foundation of marriage. Here Karim constructs *asala* through Raga's choice of standing up for a marginalized segment of Egyptian society in the 1930s, namely, musicians and singers. And this is why Karim and Sulayman Nagib, the screenplay writer, are invested in the following dialogue:

> *Raga':* It seems you know a lot about music!
> *Galal:* I know a little bit.

CELEBRATING EMERGENT MODERNITY (*ASALA*) | 349

R: Do you play the piano?

G: I play the lute.

R: Lute! That is fantastic. And when did you learn to play it?

G: It has been my hobby since childhood. I used to seize every opportunity when my dad was not around to play the lute and sing for hours.

R: And why would you "cease the opportunity"?

G: Because my father disapproved of music. He used to say, "That kind of stuff would distract you from studying." He thought it was useless.

R: Useless! How strange!

G: Actually, he used to say more harsh comments than that. He used to say, "How dare you even think of leaving school and working as a singer." I used to hear a lot of that sort of reproach— [Interruption in French by a pianist who comes to tune the piano. The pianist finishes his task and is about to leave. Galal also is about to leave]

R: [Addressing Galal] Why are you in a hurry?

G: I want to inform Khalil *effendi* that the piano is fixed so he can pay the bill.

R: Why not stay a little longer? Please, have a seat. My father talked a lot about you. Both of us are orphans. As people say, orphans are relatives.

G: True.

R: Since you play the piano and sing, I bet your voice must be beautiful. I like beautiful voices.

G: Ma'am, music is a very beautiful art. It embodies feelings and passions. Unfortunately, its appreciation is very limited in our country.

R: I would love to listen to you sing sometime.

Sitting today on our comfortable couches while watching Netflix's original production, we might think the above dialogue a cliché. But in the 1930s, singers, musicians, actors, and dancers were perceived as reckless and unreliable people who were not to be trusted, and even sub-human and not qualified to testify in a court of law. With this context in mind, the above scene needs to be understood. This scene is the first long one between the two main characters. The director could have situated this meeting in a more romantic setting, and the conversation did not have to be about Galal's suppressed ambition to be a singer. This choice gradually reveals Raga's understanding of modernity by introducing the impossibility that she is about to make possible, namely, forcing her Cairene-bourgeoisie class to accept singing in Egypt in the 1930s as a profession no less honorable than doctor or engineer. Echoes of Galal's marginalization appear in the memoir of Muhammad Abd al-Wahhab, who plays the character of Galal. For example, in 1917, while working with the al-Gazayirli brothers at the Egyptian Club Theater, 'Abd al-Wahhab used to sing the poems of Shaykh Salama Higazi between play acts. Some of 'Abd al-Wahhab's neighbors in the al-Sha'rani area of Cairo happened one night to be among the audience. They reported 'Abd al-Wahhab's performance to his brother Shaykh Hasan, an al-Azhar student. According to 'Abd al-Wahhab, his neighbors twisted their tongues with words lamenting how 'Abd al-Wahhab had lost his morals by becoming a singer, and had strayed from the path of religion and brought shame on the family. One night, while on stage, 'Abd al-Wahhab was struck by a hand pulling his arm and toppling him down the stage. Abd al-Wahhab's brother, Hasan, tied him up with a robe and dragged him for three miles from the al-Husayn neighborhood to al-Sha'rani street, where they lived.[1] 'Abd al-Wahhab did not comment on his brother's belief in the prohibition on or the permissibility of singing from a religious standpoint. However, Karim's memories reveal that Hasan became 'Abd al-Wahhab's closest ally as a singer and actor. Karim also recalled that Hasan used to pray when Karim and 'Abd al-Wahhab signed film contracts. Therefore, this incident in 'Abd al-Wahhab's childhood does not only reveal a religious hostility toward singing, because 'Abd al-Wahhab's family were Sufis after all, and such hatred appears quite paradoxical. However, it shows that the hostility was primarily driven by a culture of shame that suppresses, excludes, and marginalizes those who choose non-religious singing, theater, or acting as a profession.

Raga's stance against this culture of shame marks her *asala* in the film. Yet it remains suppressed in 1933 Egypt. Her Cairene-bourgeoisie family employs every possible scheme so that the hegemony of *tafarnug* can be sustained. Harassment is used to enforce a patriarchal gaze on Raga' and her choices, undermining her agency in her own eyes. The patriarchal gaze differs from the male gaze, in that the latter is invested in female sexuality and how it is implicitly perpetuated and internalized by the female subject so she abides by what the male defines as normal female sexual behavior. That is to say; the male regulates how the female deals with and sees her body. The gaze of patriarchy is invested in regulating the female perception of the body and the mind. An example of the gaze of patriarchy in al-*Warda al-Bayda'* appears in the harassment scenes when Raga's suitor, Shafiq, hires an *effendi* to follow Raga' on her way to Galal's apartment. The gaze implies that it is not safe for a young woman living in Egypt in the 1930s to act in the public sphere. And if she were to act, her morality would be in question. Karim depicts Raga's awareness of this problem when the camera shows her exercising superiority over her harasser. The rumors that Galal is an adherent of *tafarnug* who objectifies and abuses women further demonizes the "idea of modern man" (i.e. the possibility of a man standing up for women as equal citizens) in the eyes of Raga'. And the message of Raga's Cairene-bourgeoisie class is clear: a woman's attempt to be sovereign over her body and mind will eventually lead to her social framing as a slut. A final scheme is to ensure the isolation of "modern man" so that he would not act in favor of the social liberty of women. Karim depicts Galal's isolation when he depicts the Cairene-bourgeoisie's reluctance to accept Galal as an equal, even when he tries to fit in. Nothing, perhaps, represents Galal's

Figure 6.2 Resisting harassment. Samira Khulusi as Raga' looking down on her harasser in *al-Warda al-Bayda'*, 1932.

352 | FILMING MODERNITY AND ISLAM IN COLONIAL EGYPT

Figure 6.3 Modern woman subjected to the gaze of patriarchy. On the right, Samira Khulusi as Raga' in *al-Warda al-Bayda'*, 1933.

Figure 6.4 The mission of subjugation accomplished. Samira Khulusi as Raga', depicted as ashamed of her choices and suppressed by patriarchy in *al-Warda al-Bayda'*, 1933.

attempt to fit in more than the moments of silence, during which his character is expected to speak and maintain a dialogue in defense of its position. When Isma'il, for instance, blames Galal for being in love with Raga', Galal is depicted as silent, looking down at the floor, and his body language is shown as submissive, his shoulders leaning forward. When Shaykh Madbuli asks Galal what went wrong between him and Isma'il bey, he is also depicted as silent, with the same submissive body language.

Although *asala* remains caged in *al-Warda al-Bayda'*, the film successfully drew attention to the centrality of women's sovereignty over body and mind to the question of modernity in Egypt. In a way, it amplifies post-1919 views championed by different feminist movements and disseminated in standard Arabic writings but made accessible in popular culture of the vernacular. The film equally gives voice to the performing arts as a domain for creativity and a catalyst for social change that is equally central to the question of modernity. It is not surprising, therefore, to see the same idea more deeply explored again in the dialogue of Karim's *Yawm Sa'id*.

2. Dad, I Am Confident in My Choices

An improvement on *al-Warda al-Bayda'*, Karim's *Yawm Sa'id* presents a middle-class story. The film uniquely captures the coronation and wedding of young King Farouq and Queen Farida, a sign of hope that seems to have encouraged Karim to depict *asala* being tolerated this time. Whereas the character of the first female lead, played by Ilham Husayn, was the center of earlier discussions of *Yawm Sa'id*, I examine here the construction of *asala* in the character of the second female lead Amina, played by Samiha Samih. Samih was of Greek origin and spoke Arabic with a rural non-Cairene accent. Karim met her while watching the premiere of one of his films in the Delta city of Mansoura and offered her the role of Amina in *Yawm Sa'id*. Unlike her peers, Samih did not have a chance to build a star aura, for she died—was murdered—at a young age after acting in three films, including *Sarkha fi al-Layl*/A Cry at Night, 1940 directed by Badr Lama and *al-'Aris al-Khamis*/The Fifth Groom, 1942, directed by Ahmad Galal and Henry Barakat.

In *Yawm Sa'id*, the patriarchal gaze questions the successful presence of Amina, a middle-class, educated Cairene working woman, in the public sphere. Karim uses different techniques to mark the difference between the male and patriarchal gaze. In the opening scene, the camera zooms out, showing the office boy (Saʿid Abu Bakr) rolling his eyes, before it shifts to show female sales representatives. The actor, whose eyeballs happen to be naturally protruberant, seems a successful choice on Karim's part for constructing the male gaze. His eyes are depicted following Amina and her colleagues as they leave the workspace; he then greets them and says, "Goodbye, young ladies!" Another shot shows the office boy flirting with a female sales representative, who air-kisses him as she leaves the store. Yet this feverish cheerfulness and joy among young working women, depicted as confident enough in their bodies that they could blow a kiss to an office boy, underscores their ability to survive the male gaze. Karim then extends the male gaze beyond the workspace to the streets of Cairo. He depicts Amina walking in downtown Cairo with her friends. She then takes the bus to go home. She meets Kamal (ʿAbd al-Wahhab) on the bus, and he follows her home to apologize for having broken her vinyl record. The scene of Kamal following Amina in the street implies that a working woman in the public space is a target for the male gaze. When Amina comes home and tells her mother about Kamal, Amina says, "An *effendi* followed me while I was coming home." The mother is not depicted as concerned or worried. For her, a male gaze does not seem unusual and is

Figure 6.5 Working women and the male gaze. On the right, Amina and her colleagues going home at the end of the day in *Yawm Saʿid*, 1939.

not a reason to worry. What worries the mother, however, is Amina's wish to challenge the patriarchal gaze.

Different signifiers used by different characters to describe Amina help Karim to construct the patriarchal gaze. To her parents and the adherents of *tafarnug*, Amina is referred to as daughter of 'Atif *effendi*. Her identity is annexed to her father's identity. To her peers, she is a successful salesperson, and her success is rather unusual for she achieves more than the daily average target in music record sales. To her lover, Amina is an individual who does not let society dictate her choices. For example, when Kamal invites Amina to his apartment, he knows that his invitation is unusual in Cairo in the 1930s. But Kamal wants Amina to break the norm. And that is why Karim depicts the dialogue via a series of 'yes' and 'no' responses until Amina finally says 'yes' and goes to his apartment. Similarly, Kamal annexes Amina's father to her identity. He does not use the expression 'the daughter of 'Atif *effendi*' to describe Amina. Instead, he refers to 'Atif *effendi* as 'Amina's father' (*walid al-anisa Amina*). To Umm Anisa, *bint al-balad* in the movie, Amina is a mademoiselle. When Umm Anisa "caught" Amina visiting Kamal, she looked at Amina suspiciously and asked, "What are you doing at Kamal's apartment?" Announcing her dissatisfaction with the behavior of the new generation of women, Umm Anisa is depicted scolding her young daughter (Fatin Hamama) and saying, "God only knows how you will behave when you grow up!" The implication is that working women in 1930s Cairo violate the dominant societal norms, so their morality becomes questionable. Later, Umm Anisa tells her husband that Amina has brought shame on her father, 'Atif *effendi*, who deserves that shame since he wants to raise his daughter to be a working woman, and a mademoiselle. Umm Anisa's use of the French title "Mademoiselle" also conveys the fact that she is envious of Amina, whose education and work mark her superiority in terms of social class.

In *Yawm Sa'id*, Karim marks his female protagonist's *asala* through her choice of refusing the social exclusion of singers and, more importantly, her consciousness of the patriarchal gaze and her resistance to its discourse. Karim tries to achieve this in both his *mise-en-scène* and his dialogue. One example is the scene depicting Amina meeting Umm Anisa on the stairs after visiting Kamal. When Umm Anisa looks at Amina suspiciously, Amina does not accept the accusation. She answers confidently, "I was just visiting

Figure 6.6 Choosing vulnerability. Amina visits Kamal in his apartment for the first time. *Yawm Saʿid,* 1939.

Kamal." The subtlety of Karim's depiction here shows in Amina's response. Amina, who appears fashionably dressed and confident on the screen, is aware that her behavior is not an approved norm within the realm of her social circles. She is also depicted as choosing a vulnerable position. Amina's awareness of the vulnerability of her position shows in her conversation with her mother in a later scene. When Amina comes home from her visit to Kamal, the mother, who has the same patriarchal gaze at her daughter, tries to learn the details of Amina's relationship with Kamal. When the mother is sure that Amina has spent time at Kamal's apartment, the first thing she asks her daughter is, "Did anybody see you?" The implication is that all that matters to Amina's mother is the amour-propre of the family in the neighborhood. The mother becomes paranoid when she knows that Umm Anisa saw Amina. She fears Umm Anisa will talk in the neighborhood and disparage Amina's reputation. Amina responds to her mother's anger with silence. In that silence, Karim depicts Amina's awareness of taking a vulnerable position by visiting Kamal. Her awareness is further emphasized when she says, "Please, do not tell father about it." When Amina's parents confront her with their anger, they question if it was right to send Amina to school in the first place:

Father: Did they teach you to fall in love and have relationships at school?

Amina: Father, it is an innocent friendship.

F: I cannot acknowledge an innocent friendship between a young man and a woman of your age. How long have you known him?

A: A week.

F: Do you think a week is enough time to judge his integrity? You met the man only twice and the third time you went to his house! Have you lost your mind?

A: I am confident I am in charge of my choices, Dad. And if it makes you feel any better, I will not visit Kamal at his place again.

F: Can't you see the consequences of your confidence? Can you imagine the scandal if your mother did not visit Umm Anisa and lied to her about Kamal's proposal to you?

The true merit of the above dialogue is the emphasis on the paradox between modern women's social status as advocated by modern educational institutions and the degree to which this advocacy is achievable on the ground. At school and work, Amina behaves as a citizen who has sovereignty over body and mind. But her social circles have not accepted that attitude, which

Figure 6.7 Enforcement of the patriarchal gaze. 'Ulwiyya Gamil as Amina's mother interrogating her daughter. *Yawm Sa'id*, 1939.

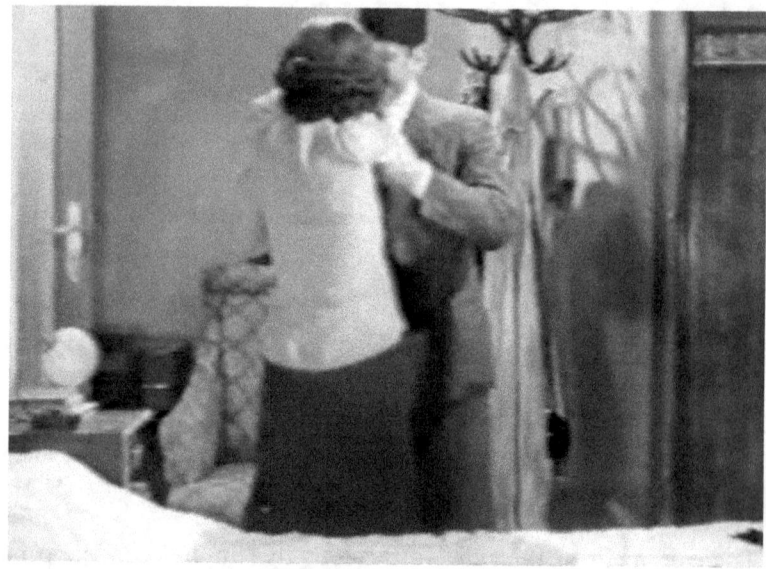

Figure 6.8 Patriarchy and the restoration of sovereignty. ʿAbd al-Warith ʿAsar as Amina's father in *Yawm Saʿid*, 1939.

Amina expresses boldly when she faces her father and says, "Dad, I am confident I am in charge of my choices. And if it makes you feel any better, I will not visit Kamal at his place again." Failing to control her mind, the father is shocked at Amina's stance and attempts to restore sovereignty over her mind and body by holding her and pushing her toward the bed. Karim does not depict Amina fighting her war further. He still acknowledges the presence and dominance of the patriarchal gaze. Therefore, in *Yawm Saʿid*, patriarchy still conditions Amina's *asala*, which becomes collective emergent culture only when patriarchy, represented through the character of the father and the lover, resolves their dispute and stands up for Amina's choices. The key here is *Yawm Saʿid*'s characterization of the male protagonist, which I discuss in the following section.

3. Oriental Music Cares Less about Your Ears

A more optimistic version of the character of Galal in *al-Warda al-Baydaʾ* is that of Kamal in *Yawm Saʿid*. Both characters (Muhammad ʿAbd al-Wahhab) are metaphors for the artist's struggle against a bourgeoisie social order that reduces modernity to *tafarnug* and hence celebrates foreign forms of art while marginalizing and belittling local art forms. While silence is used in *al-Warda al-Bayda'* to mark the artist's attempt to negotiate and fit in, the artist in *Yawm Sa'id* does not even try to fit in. Despite lacking a fair chance to present his innovation in the public sphere, the character of Kamal is constructed as a more confident portrait of the local artist who is aware of *tafarnug* and its suppression of local artists. Therefore, this time Karim gives a voice to the subaltern who resists and condemns the marginalization of local art and its audience, that is, *awlad al-balad* and the peasants.

Through the local artist's quest for the recognition of his art and its audience, Karim depicts *asala* as emergent modernity in *Yawm Sa'id*. Initially, the artist adapts to social marginalization; he distances himself from the social circles of *tafarnug* and *ta'ssul*. On the margin, survival is attained by appealing to a subjunctive or an idealist understanding of art that resists its reification by *tafarnug* and *ta'ssul*. For example, Kamal refuses to sing the poetry of adherents of *ta'ssul* like 'Azuz. Kamal also does not think highly of mechanical reproduction. This initial stance, however, is depicted as hypocritical, a delusive amour-propre of modernity that accepts and essentializes the exclusion of local art. This materializes in the storyline by, for example, Kamal being shown as delinquent in paying rent, and his meals are an act of charity by his landlady, Umm Anisa. Two paradigm shifts, however, take place in Kamal's character. The first has to do with bringing Kamal face to face with the idea of mechanical reproduction to challenge his idealist view of art. For example, the garden scene depicts Kamal meeting Amina and her friend. The two women work in a vinyl record shop; their characterization allegorizes mechanical reproduction. The three characters question how art can represent love and the definition of love itself in the 1930s. On the one hand, Kamal holds the view that love only exists in the metaphysical realm, which he signifies as a spiritual connection/bond (*ittisal ruhayn*). He argues that such a metaphysical understanding of love exists only among the people of the past (*ahl zaman*) regardless of West–East polarization. He gives the examples of Romeo and Juliet, Jamil and Buthayna, Qays and Layla. To Kamal, love is a pastoral dream that exists only in an ideal past, be it local or foreign. That past has an ideal natural environment, free from the 1930s social reality shaped by industrialization and its subsequent pollution and negative effect on climate change. To Kamal, adhering only to societal modernization without cultural modernity forces love into the domain of *tafarnug*. Love becomes a contract between two people who agree to a set of materialist practices to express their love. Kamal lists these practices as flirtation over the phone, having a rendezvous in cinemas and salons, holding parties, and exchanging gifts and compliments. On the other hand, Amina and her friend argue for societal modernization as an emancipatory reality that helps women gain new social roles. Amina sees 1930s industrialization as a positive contribution to human experience, in which science is a machinery of progress and evolution. Amina and her friend cannot understand Kamal's pastoral dream and idealism. In response to Kamal's argument against societal modernization and its commodification of love by turning hearts into steel, Amina's friend argues that science made the steel talk and walk. That is to say, societal modernization brings about cultural modernity, aiming to emancipate people and make them speak their minds. Her argument implies that Kamal's idealism expresses a totality that does not exist in reality. When Kamal argues that a heart cannot accommodate his pastoral dream and societal modernization, she comments sarcastically, "For the Prophet's sake, these days the heart can accommodate two, three, and four." The implication is not that a man can marry four women or that young people have more access to relationships. Rather, the sentence implies that one can imagine what one wants to imagine; that is to say, societal modernization brings about an array of possibilities and potentials. While Kamal admits that industrial reality has not completely diminished his pastoral dream and that people are still capable of falling in love with the same passion as in the past, he still argues that it is rare and that the "rare" occurrence does not dictate the rule. Amina suggests that the solution lies in experimentation. Therefore, Karim ends the scene with Amina and Kamal shaking hands while looking into each other's eyes. This shot does not only signal the beginning of their love story. More importantly, it signals the beginning of the artist's journey of experimentation and his step outside his idealist position. Therefore, the garden scene is not simply a representation of a sentimental love story to construct love as the foundation of marriage. Karim uses the scene as an allegory for a paradigm shift in the artist's view of art; it is a shift that makes Kamal take a vulnerable position by stepping outside that pastoral dream to resist his position on the margin of society and claim a central place in the public sphere from which to present his innovation. But such a shift is easier said than done. Instead of stepping outside the pastoral dream, Kamal initially tries to bring the industrial reality to his pastoral dream. The scenes of Amina's visit to Kamal objectify this idea. The camera zooms out, and the scene is cut to present a one-act play depicting the love story of the famous Layla and Qays. It is not until Kamal faces patriarchy, represented through Amina's father, that Kamal is forced to step outside his pastoral dream.

The character of the father, played by ʿAbd al-Warith ʿAsar, further builds pressure on the artist to step outside his pastoral dream. The father represents the educated middle class ready to support local art but not ready to accept its marginal position and imprisonment inside an idealist view of art. For example, the father objects to the relationship between Kamal and Amina. He accuses Kamal of ignoring social custom (*ʿurf*), which does not refer only to the discouragement of pre-marital relationships. It also indicates the father's views of Kamal's dependency, which makes the father think of Kamal as an adherent of *tafarnug*. When Kamal admits that the father has a point, he finds an exit by temporarily allying with adherents of *taʾṣṣul* to access the public sphere until he presents his innovation and sings his songs. Kamal, for example, makes a deal with ʿAzuzu to sing the latter's poem "The Slaughtered Dove,"[2] but when he goes to the party he sings his own song, namely *Ya ward min yishtirik* (Flowers for Sale), instead.

Nevertheless, *tafarnug* remains the artist's major challenge. It is the dominant culture blamed for the marginalization of local art. A confrontation with *tafarnug* thus seems inevitable. In the following scene, the tension between Kamal and the adherents of *tafarnug* represented by Raʾuf and Suhayr is underscored by Karim:

Kamal: My name is Muhammad Kamal. I am a musician.

Raʾuf: Musician. How nice!

K: And your good name, sir?

R: There is no need for you to know my name.

Ilham: [Addressing Kamal] Mr. Kamal, let me introduce you to Raʾuf bey Fawzi. He is a friend of mine.

K: It is a pleasure to meet you!

R: And what do you exactly play in the music? Do you know how to sing *Aman ya lalalli*.[3]

Kamal: Not at all. I know how to sing *Ta'alili ya batta* (Hi, Hot Chick, Come My Way) [Ilham laughs].

R: In all honesty, my ear does not digest this oriental music.

Kamal: I do not think that oriental music cares a lot about your ear.

R: Suhyar, I was insulted at your house.

K: Suhyar, I beg your pardon; I have to leave.

S: Of course, Mr. Kamal.

The scene depicts Ra'uf bey disrespectful of what he defines as "Oriental" music; he considers it stagnant and incapable of introducing any innovation. To Ra'uf, local artists in 1930s Egypt could not produce anything new, for they were stuck in "traditional" Turkish roles like singing *Aman ya lalalli*. While responding to Ra'uf's contempt for local art, Kamal is not depicted as reactionary. The director depicts a sarcastic tone. This time Karim positions the artist at the center of the shot. Kamal appears in a middle shot; he is alone, calm, and steady to fight back. When Kamal says, "I sing *Ta'alili ya batta*" (Hi, Hot Chick, Come My Way) the implication is that Ra'uf's *tafarnug* can neither appreciate a classic work of art like a classic Turkish song nor imagine any innovation in local culture beyond a song that falls under the category of low art (*isfaf*), as in the case of the song "Hi, Hot Chick." Kamal's answer condemns *tafarnug* and considers it solely responsible for the spread of "low art" and the suppression of the innovative (*asil*) local art which Kamal represents. Here it is important to explain that "Hi, Hot Chick" does not fall into the category of "low art" because it is sung in colloquial, if we accept the high/low binary of standard and colloquial. After all, the majority of the songs sung in *Yawm Sa'id* are sung in colloquial, as are the majority of what Egyptians have perceived up until today as "classics." *Ta'alili ya batta* (Hi, Hot Chick, Come My Way) is used as an example of "low art" because of its sexual connotations, which objectify the female body. This song is often referred to in movies depicting the 1930s. The song gains in popularity for its flirtatious dialogue between a man chasing a woman in the street. The man starts by saying, "Hi, hot chick, come my way," and the woman responds, "No, not this time." The implication is that women *say* no to sex, but they *mean* yes (*yatamanna'una wa-hunna al-raghibatu*), an argument that, in its extreme form, can be used by rapists to justify their crimes. It is because of this connotation that the song falls under the category of "low art," and it is employed by Kamal to comment sarcastically on Ra'uf's reductionist understanding of innovation in local art.

Innovative (*asil*) local art can be understood as a call for an understanding of art as a secular interdependent human experience, in which local cultures influence the foreign and vice versa. This understanding is strongly emphasized by Karim when he depicts Kamal equally celebrating the piano and the lute. Here, it is important to notice that differences are highlighted; they are not suppressed. While innovative art establishes continuity with the past, this continuity is not necessarily an attempt to reinstall an imagined ideal of art in a modern form. Continuity lies in the continuity of experimentation and in acknowledging the innovations of the past, no matter how humble they may seem in the present. This understanding of continuity has its roots in the Egyptian proverb "An *asil* is the one who is not ashamed of the origin no matter how humble that origin is" (*al-asil huwa illi ma yista'arrish min asluh*). In that sense, innovative art is an art that is not ashamed of its origin, be it colloquial or standard, local or foreign. It is thus not surprising to see in *Yawm Sa'id* songs sung in standard and colloquial. Sometimes both linguistic codes exist in the same song, such as in the song *Ya ward min yishtirik* (Flowers for Sale). And it is for the same reason that Karim depicts Kamal as fascinated with rural folk art. For example, when Suhayr executes her plan to abduct Kamal in the countryside and show him what *tafarnug* could offer him as a singer, Karim depicts him as impressed by the folk dance and the singing of the peasants on Suhayr's estate. After a long day working in the field, the peasants gather to listen to music and watch dance. As he recalled in his diaries, Karim is charmed by the Egyptian countryside of the 1930s, a time before the high dam reduced the fertility of the agricultural soil. This fascination appears in almost all his movies. *Yawm Sa'id* depicts different aspects of village life and landscape. For example, many shots are dedicated to village women in local dress fetching water carrying the famous Egyptian clay jars on their heads, waterwheels, and palm trees reflected in the Nile.

Similarly, Karim depicts different aesthetics of folk dance and music. For example, while shooting the scene featuring the song *Ma ahlaha 'ishat al-fallah* (How Wonderful Peasant Life Is), Karim dedicates close-ups of men and women watching dance and listening to music. Karim also attempts to show

Figure 6.9 Celebrating the Egyptian countryside and its environs. *Yawm Saʿid*, 1938.

Figure 6.10 The depiction of folk-dancing scenes. *Yawm Saʿid*, 1938.

CELEBRATING EMERGENT MODERNITY (ASALA) | 365

Figure 6.11 Celebration of peasant aesthetics. A group of farmers coming together to watch dance and listen to music in *Yawm Saʿid*, 1939.

Figure 6.12 Folk music tools. Depiction of the production of music using coffee cups in *Yawm Saʿid*, 1939.

the creativeness of the peasants, who produce music with their traditional instruments, even with household items such as coffee cups. Some of the peasants are depicted shaking coffee cups against their saucers to produce music. The implication is that the peasants can produce music by natural instinct, and their folk music can compete with "high" music, be it foreign or local.

Islam occupies a central position in Kamal's *asala*. The character of Shaykh Mustafa is an improvement on that of Shaykh Madbuli in *al-Warda al-Bayda'*. Shaykh Mustafa symbolizes the possibility that the religious domain can be a host domain for art. As the owner of Kamal's property, Shaykh Mustafa enjoys listening to Kamal's music; he supports Kamal in his pursuit of a professional career as a singer; he refuses to send Kamal an evacuation notice despite Kamal's delinquency in paying rent. Every time the wife of Shaykh Mustafa, Umm Anisa, urges her husband to collect rent from Kamal, Karim depicts Shaykh Mustafa as hesitant to knock on the door. As a symbol of Islam in *Yawm Sa'id*, Shaykh Mustafa is depicted as an understanding husband. His wife often decides on the rules of the household. This does not mean Shaykh Mustafa is depicted as a person with a weak personality. Rather, this is an early depiction of the revisionist views regarding the Qur'anic concept of *qawama* referred to in the Qur'anic verse Q4:34 in reference to women's rights. Here the film extends beyond the literalist interpretation of *qawama* as favoring men over women to the meaning of *qawama* as attending to women's needs. Pioneering Egyptian feminist activists of the late nineteenth century like 'A'isha al-Taymuriyya championed these views, which the film amplifies and present to the uneducated viewer by depicting Shaykh Mustafa doing his share of the housework like cooking and cleaning. When Shaykh Mustafa learns about Kamal and Amina's love story, he celebrates it and functions as a mediator between Kamal and 'Atif *effendi*. Shaykh Mustafa also hosts a gramophone in his house. He does not consider a wedding to be a celebration without dancing. When Shaykh Mustafa is told that there will be no dancers at Kamal's wedding, he says, "Why no dancers? A wedding cannot be one without dancers." Anisa, the daughter of Shaykh Mustafa, further emphasizes the hospitality of the religious domain to the artist. The character of Anisa represents the first introduction of the famed Fatin Hamama in cinema. Her scenes are mostly reaction shots used to convey Shaykh Mustafa's impressions about Kamal's art and his vulnerability as an artist. While it is not rare to use a child to externalize the emotions of a character, it is rare to externalize the character of a male lead through that of a young girl. It is also through the voice of Anisa that Kamal's success as a singer is announced. After Kamal's successful performance in the Opera, Anisa reads the newspaper's headlines aloud: "A great success for a new musician."

Another central metaphor that represents Islam in *Yawm Saʿid* is the notion of *tawakkul* (i.e. taking a risk or acting in a contingent situation by means of relying on intellect (*ʿaql*) as God's agent in human beings, and according to one's better judgment. The opposite of *tawakkul* is *tawakul* (i.e. lack of action due to denial of relative human agency to action), which helps ʿAtif *effendi* overcome his fears about losing his livelihood by losing his job at Suhayr's estate if he were to approve of his daughter's marriage. In one scene, Karim depicts ʿAtif *effendi* awake at dawn to pray. As the call for prayer is heard in the background, ʿAtif *effendi* tells his wife that it is unfair to jeopardize his daughter's future because of his fear of the feudal system. When his wife reminds him of the consequences of being jobless and homeless, he says, "I do not care," and recites the verse Q9:51, "Nothing shall befall us except what God wills; God is the Sustainer. And in the Sustainer, the believers shall trust." The implication here is that ʿAtif *effendi* dismisses his subjugation to any power (other than God) that proclaims it will impact his life. This realization is liberating for ʿAtif *effendi*. By activating *tawakkul*, ʿAtif *effendi* resists the Cairene-bourgeoisie and their *tafarnug* and thus enables *asala* to become

Figure 6.13 The religious domain as a host domain for art. Fu'ad Shafiq, as Shaykh Mustafa, helps his wife prepare the dining table. A gramophone features in the background. *Yawm Saʿid*, 1939.

Figure 6.14 Beyond literalist interpretation of *qawama*. Fu'ad Shafiq as Shaykh Mustafa helping his wife in the kitchen. *Yawm Sa'id*, 1939.

Figure 6.15 Fu'ad Shafiq as Shaykh Mustafa listening patiently to his angry wife. *Yawm Sa'id*, 1939.

CELEBRATING EMERGENT MODERNITY (ASALA) | 369

Figure 6.16 Celebration of Azhari dress. On the right, Fu'ad Shafiq as Shaykh Mustafa, showing Kamal the new dress that he has bought specially for the wedding. *Yawm Sa'id*, 1939.

Figure 6.17 Azharis attending Kamal's wedding. On the right, Shaykh Mustafa receives his colleagues, who have come to attend Kamal's wedding. *Yawm Sa'id*, 1939.

Figure 6.18 Externalization of the artist's conscience. On the left, Muhammad 'Abd al-Wahhab as Kamal. On the right, Fatin Hamama as Anisa. *Yawm Sa'id*, 1939.

an emergent culture, an idea that is further emphasized in Kamal Salim's *al-'Azima*.

4. It Is My Right to Live the Way I Want To

In Kamal Salim's *al-'Azima*, different modes of resistance to social injustices and the quest for equal access to fair competition over opportunities and resources present *asala* as emergent modernity in late 1930s Cairo. The leading male character of Muhammad Hanafi (Husayn Sidqi) is the only son of Usta Hanfi ('Umar Wasfi), an uneducated barber who believes in education as a vehicle for social change and thus invests all his savings, and often borrows money, to support his son. Hanafi and his wife (Thuraya Fakhri) await their son's graduation impatiently. They hope that he will secure a job and help with their debt payments. But Muhammad, who is about to graduate from the school of commerce at Fu'ad I University (now Cairo University), does not believe in clerical jobs; he finds independent business to be a better career path. As the movie unfolds, earning a university degree proves to be only the beginning of Muhammad's challenges. A key to how Muhammad conquers these challenges is the word *'azima* (perseverance), which is the title of the film. Kamal Salim initially wanted to name the film *al-Hara*/The Alley. It was feared, however, that the title would deliver an explicit message that the film offers a generalized depiction of working-class life in Egypt. Salim's decision to name the film *al-'Azima*, which I translate as "perseverance" instead of the more literal translation of "determination," or "will power," saved him from possible tension with the Palace. But more importantly, the word is a better indicator of *asala* because it signifies "determination" or "perseverance" which is driven by the activation of *tawakkul* in moments of contingency. Here *'azima* is not depicted as a birthmark; it is a learned social skill that is earned through a series of experimentations backed by the support system of *awlad al-balad*, who are mostly inspired by their religious tradition, here Islam.

Resistance to local regressive traditional forces exemplified in the character of the local butcher 'Itr ('Abd al-'Aziz Khalil), who thinks education is a fantasy sold to the poor, and who creates doubts about Muhammad's life choices, also marks Muhammad's *asala*. 'Itr tries to enforce a patriarchal social order rooted in material power and wealth. In this social order, women are treated like slaves and objects of desire. 'Itr also appropriates metaphors representing Islam to serve his ends. For example, he has his eye on Muhammad's beloved Fatima. The opening scenes depict him harassing Fatima, who stands on her balcony while he is in his shop. He looks up toward her balcony and says, "Peace be upon the Prophet as we see the local meat" (*al-nabi ahasn 'ala al-baladi ya baladi*). The expression is a pun; while it sounds as if 'Itr is referring to the meat in his shop, his body language conveys his reference to Fatima as "fresh and young meat." Invoking the name of the Prophet is a permissible means to arrive at the sinful end of harassment. His objectification and mistreatment of women in general is emphasized in another scene, where he insults a *khawagaya* cashier and mistakenly accuses her of fooling him. The cashier boldly objects to his language. 'Itr's utilitarian view of Islam makes him bribe Shaykh Idris (al-Sayyid Budayr [Bidir]). He delivers fresh meat free to the latter's house so that he takes his side when the time comes. 'Itr tells Idris, "You are monumental, Shaykh Idris," a phrase used to mock the Shaykh undoubtedly, but more importantly hinting at an alliance between despotic ideologies and religion. 'Itr hopes to rely on Idris to forge legal solutions in accordance with Islamic teachings to serve his greed. For the same reason, he disrespects working-class people living in the alley.

One of his neighbors works as an undertaker and is known by the name Ruhi (Mukhtar 'Uthman). The name means "spiritual," but 'Itr ridicules Ruhi's craft by calling him Mr. Azrael in reference to the angel of death. In one scene, 'Itr urges Usta Hanfi to allow him to help with the debt. But 'Itr offers help only to brag about himself as a savior. He spreads rumors in the neighborhood that Usta Hanfi begged for help. 'Itr's attitude makes his neighbors call him a nouveau riche (*muhadath*). His character is thus almost the opposite of that of Muhammad, who is depicted as more courteous and more respectful of others.

Kamal Salim surely depicts education as a driving force behind Muhammad's *asala*. Education, for example, fortifies his mental resilience, which enables him to turn a deaf ear to 'Itr's belittling remarks. For example, when Muhammad learns about the confiscation of his father's shop, he does not panic; he tells Fatima that he will solve the problem. When Fatima tells Muhammad that the butcher keeps spreading rumors in the neighborhood about the uselessness of Muhammad's education, he tells Fatima that the butcher's words should never be taken seriously.

But the real empowerment of Muhammad's *asala* comes from his social network, which is highly inclusive in the sense that Muhammad befriends people from different social classes and irrespective of class diffidence and respects them both equally. When Muhammad Hanafi first appears in the film, he appears to be getting ready to go to school and check the results of his final exam. As he leaves his house, almost all the artisans in the neighborhood greet him cheerfully. They think of him and his father as role models; their success marks the success of an entire class. One of the neighbors insists on giving Muhammad a ride to acknowledge his father's integrity and helpfulness in the neighborhood. When Muhammad first meets Nazih pasha, Salim presents a middle shot. In the background to the shot, the stairs allude to the superiority of Nazih in terms of social status. But the *mise-en-scène* emphasizes that they both are equal, thereby implying that Muhammad has the potential to climb the social ladder and stand on an equal footing with Nazih, who is ready to welcome him. The character of Nazih, whose name means a person with integrity, presents Kamal Salim's Kantian vision of the enlightened few who believe in education as a vehicle for social change. Nazih supports Muhammad and praises his attitude toward risk-taking. For the same reason, Nazih does

Figure 6.19 Celebration of *asala*. On the right, Zaki Rustum as Nazih pasha congratulates Muhammad Hanafi on his graduation. *Al-'Azima*, 1939.

not approve of his son's *tafarnug* and hopes his son will follow Muhammad's path. Nazih thus does not hesitate to accept Muhammad's offer of partnership. Nevertheless, the domain of Nazih remains one dominated by *tafarnug*.

Therefore, an ardent condemnation of *tafarnug* further marks Muhammad's *asala*. His schoolmates are mostly Cairene-bourgeoisie, and they dehumanize working-class Egyptians. They spare no opportunity to remind Muhammad that they can only accept him as a "modern" and "equal" unless he adheres to *tafarnug*. Otherwise, Muhammad should become like his father, a barber, and thus should dress like his father in a galabiya, not a suit. He should also remain uneducated, for education should only be accessible to the rich. In the following scene, for example, Muhammad visits the son of Nazih pasha, with whom he plans to open a new accounting agency. Unable to resist peer pressure, 'Adli allows his Cairene-bourgeoisie friends to bully Muhammad:

Shawkat: Look who is here! It is Muhammad.
M: How are you, Mr. Izzat?

'Izzat: [Addressing 'Adli] Would you mind if we join your business meeting? Is it a secret?

'Adli: No, we do not mind at all. There are no secrets. Please have a seat [They all sit down, and 'Adli addresses Muhammad]. What brought you in, Muhammad?

M: I finalized everything, and before we go to the bank . . . [Interrupted by 'Adli]

'A: Are we going to the bank today?

M: Of course, we have to deposit the insurance.

'A: First, could you show me what you have in that file you are holding?

M: There is also the issue of the wood price. The price we proposed was accepted [Handing a file].

'A: That sounds good!

M: And we are lucky that the shipping cost would not be so different from the cost in Sweden.

Sh: Are you importing wood from Sweden?

'A: Of course we are. It is a serious business. Didn't I tell you?

'I: How is that possible? Does Sweden export wood these days?

Sh: This is very strange!

M: What is so strange about that?

F1: Did they not say [in the news] that Hitler captured Sweden?

F2: It was Sudeten, not Sweden.

'I: They are so close to each other.

'A: No, they were very far from each other. What else have you got on file, Muhammad?

M: The textile issue. You know all about it.

'A: Yes, we finalized that issue.

M: What needs much work today and what requires much effort is the leather issue, because those people had a stronghold on the market. We first have to play it cool with them until we figure out what their take on the issue is. As you know, we cannot afford to avoid leather.

Sh: May I ask you a question?

M: Sure!

Sh: Are you going to open a shoemaker's shop?

I: We will all tailor our shoes at your shop.

F2: And we will pay in cash.

F1: I even started hating my current shoemaker.

T: Folks, calm down. The country is full of shoemakers [Addressing Muhammad]. Why do you not open a barber's shop, Muhammad?

The above scene is a staging of a bullying plan orchestrated in a previous scene. The dialogue apparently critiques the adherents of *tafarnug* by underscoring their ignorance, for they cannot figure out the difference between Sweden and Sudetenland despite constantly bragging that they visit Europe. But more importantly, the scene shows how the presence of *ibn al-balad* Muhammad resembles that of a mirror in which the adherents of *tafarnug* are forced to see their failure to succeed despite their monopoly over resources. Their insecurities drive their urge to dehumanize Muhammad, who, despite his impoverished social conditions, is the only one among his peers to finish school and earn a degree. The gravest injustice is depicted when adherence to *tafarnug* risks putting Muhammad behind bars. 'Adli, spend the sum of money allocated for his partnership with Muhammad on a new belly dancer. He later accuses Muhammad of budget embezzlement. Therefore, Salim's dialogue forcefully condemns *tafarnug* as an unethical and inhuman practice. When Muhammad realizes the bullying plan orchestrated by his Cairene-bourgeoisie schoolmates, he says:

> I am so sorry that life circumstances have shown me such unethical conduct. If only you had feelings, you would have been considerate of other people's feelings. What is more painful [than your desire to humiliate others] is that you live in this world without a conscience. If you can find pleasure in belittling people and humiliating them, know that by doing so, you are actually belittling yourselves. People work hard and struggle to build a life, and you are enslaved by your desires. I wonder what greater wrong your parents did in life that they ended up having you as a stigma in their life.

Rejecting the world of *effendiness* is another indicator of Muhammad's *asala*. Muhammad's experience with clerical positions lampoons the world of *effendis* as a world of nepotism resulting from the herd numbers of unemployed university graduates in Egypt in 1939. When he cannot become an entrepreneur, Muhammad looks for a clerical job, which he does not like but finds

Figure 6.20 Resisting *tafarnug*. On the right, Husayn Sidqi as Muhammad Hanafi. *Al-'Azima*, 1939.

himself forced to explore so as to help his parents financially and marry Fatima. Here, the director Kamal Salim presents a harsh critique of government plans, which forged an interwar middle class of degree-educated *effendis* who hoped to both govern and boost the economy. The plan ironically caused nothing but rising unemployment. Salim's references to newspaper headlines seem quite relevant even today. Some of these headlines include *al-Ahram*'s headline that reads "No vacancies available" and "Armies of unemployed people." These lines send up the government's celebration of its recent commerce graduates. The pro-government newspaper *al-Dustur* celebrates the Minister's speech on graduation day. The pro-British *al-Muqattam* newspaper has headlines that project ironic objectivity; the headline reads, "Unemployment in Egypt, its reasons, its consequences, and its cure." Another headline, which reveals how 500 university graduates 180 of whom are commerce graduates, apply for a collector's job that pays four pounds a month, mocks the previous headline. After all, unemployment makes employers raise the bar when hiring. One example is the newspaper ad that requires an office boy to be fluent in foreign languages. Meanwhile, *al-Sabah* magazine shows off how someone is spending hundreds of thousands on belly dancers, while another headline declares how a man committed suicide after shooting his wife and children because he gave up on finding a job. Amidst these high waves, Nazih pasha helps Muhammad reach the shores of stability, which *effendiness* promises, and Muhammad secures an accountancy position with one of the many companies that had previously shut their doors to him. In the world of the *effendis*, those who work hard are punished, while those who do not work are less likely to make mistakes, and hence get celebrated. The scenes shot inside the office show Muhammad's fellow *effendis* spending most of their time chit-chatting while smoking cigarettes. In one scene, the manager ('Abbas Faris) passes by to check on them. As soon as the *effendis* notice the manager, they put out their cigarettes, run to their desks, and claim the cigarette butts belong to customers with whom the company is trying to seal deals. Some *effendis* spend most of their work hours sleeping, while others take as many trips as possible to drink water. Many do not hesitate to waste more time by spending almost half an hour getting ready before signing out. The *effendis* do not hesitate to pile files on Muhammad's desk and borrow some files from him when the manager passes by, just to show they are busy. Their negligent behavior causes a file to disappear, and Muhammad, who finds himself accused of negligence, has to choose between going to jail and losing his job.

Muhammad's celebration of his class of origin without rejecting new ideas is another marker of his *asala*. As much as Muhammad enjoys playing billiards with Nazih pasha (Zaki Rustum) at the latter's palace, he cherishes *awlad al-balad*, who represent a more reliable and sustainable support system in Muhammad's life. The fact that he is educated while they are not does not make him distance himself from them. He hangs out with them at the coffee shop; he, like them, celebrates Islamic holidays such as the Prophet's Birthday (*mawlid*) and Ramadan. He endearingly calls his mother Madam Hanafi. The implication is that she is no less important than any French "Ma'am" who lived in Egypt in the late 1930s and deserved not only to be treated with respect but also to be celebrated. Even during harsh times, he does not forget to kiss her goodbye before leaving the house in the morning. His choice of affiliating himself with *awlad al-balad* also materializes through his decision to marry Fatima. When Fatima discovers that Muhammad lost his job as an *effendi* and accepted a low-paid part-time manual job, she says to him, "Aren't you ashamed of yourself?" Muhammad replies, "What is there to be ashamed of?

Earning a living is not a source of shame." This scene is shot in the bakery, where, simultaneously, a baker appears to prepare the bread dough in the background. The choice of *mise-en-scène* empowers the working class and further emphasizes Muhammad's choice of affiliating himself with *awlad al-balad*.

Forging an alliance based on education like that between 'Adli and Muhammad is the peak of depicting *asala* as an emergent culture of modernity. When Muhammad and 'Adli meet, they have both accepted their class of origin but have moved beyond its hegemony. 'Adli, who is let down by his Cairene-bourgeoisie friends after his father has cut all financial support, reconsiders the credibility of *tafarnug* as an expression of modernity. 'Adli takes a clerical job with the same company Muhammad used to work for, and stumbles upon the file that Muhammad was accused of losing. The company phones Muhammad one day to apologize and compensate him for forcing him to leave his job. When they offer to rehire him at a higher salary, he refuses because his return to *effeniness* will feed the hegemony of *tafarnug* among the working class just like it did with his wife, Fatima. Therefore, the dialogue accentuates Muhammad's *asala* when he says, "It is enough! I lived earlier the way others wanted me to live. Now, I think it is my right to live the way I want to live." Instead, he and 'Adli start their independent business.

Metaphors representing Islam are heavily emphasized in *al-'Azima*. The movie starts with the call for prayer. The month of Ramadan marks the period of the film's events. Wide shots are dedicated to the alley where Muhammad lives. The camera shows children playing and singing the famous Ramadan children's song *Wahawi ya wahawi iyyaha* (Come Closer to See the Crescent). The mosque at night appears decorated with lightbulbs, which is still a common practice today. Some shots are dedicated to the flags at Sufi parades. Early in the film, Muhammad's father appears, saying, "'*afwak wa ridak al-satr ya karim*" (Oh Wise One, [we start our day] by asking you to shelter us with your grace (or pardon) and mercy (or satisfaction)).

Salim's celebration of Islamic practices as an integral part of the public sphere is not unique to *al-'Azima*. He opens his movie *Layla Bint al-Fuqara'*/ Layla Daughter of the Poor, 1946 with the depiction of a celebration parade in the *mawlid* of al-Sayyida Zaynab. The parade is supplemented with a short supplication (*inshad*) performed by Shaykh Zakariyya Ahmad, the famous composer and one of Umm Kulthum's teachers. He has composed some of the most celebrated early songs by Umm Kulthum, including songs like *Ahl al-hawa* (Followers of Love). Layla Murad, who sings in praise of Sayyida Zaynab, complements the voice of Zakariyya Ahmad in *Layla Bint al-Fuqara'*. This public display of Islamic festivities, however, started with *al-'Azima*.

In *al-'Azima*, Islam appears as a substratum of daily life in the alley for the people to whom Muhammad belongs. Islam is not a system of checks and balances. It features a support system and a driving force for improving the human condition, especially in moments of contingency. Muhammad, unlike his father, is not depicted praying or going to the mosque. He meets Fatima on the rooftop and kisses her. When Muhammad stops by his father's shop very early in the film, he meets some neighbors, including the undertaker Ruhi. The latter tells Muhammad that he has seen a vision involving him. Ruhi saw Muhammad standing by a seashore while throwing a net into the sea; when he pulled it back, he found a big fish. The neighbors interpret the vision as the fish standing for the degree that Muhammad anticipates. A fish is usually interpreted as sustenance after hard work. Here, Kamal Salim accentuates the practice of dream interpretation as a daily practice. It is an integral body of Islamic literature. The major work on dream and vision interpretations by the Basraian mystic Abu Bakr Muhammad b. Sirin (653–728), of course, comes to mind. The idea here is not to depict dream interpretation as a superstitious idea or to give Ruhi authority over his neighbors. Rather, the introduction of the practice of vision or dream interpretations emphasizes the prophetic tradition of optimism that encourages believers to hope for/or imagine the good to find it (*tafa'alu bi-l-khayr tajiduh*), which echoes the law of attraction in New Thought Philosophy, namely, that positive or negative thoughts bring positive or negative experiences into a person's life. The practice of visual interpretation is the way *awlad al-balad* adopts of wishing Muhammad good luck and supporting him as he heads to school to check the result of his final exam. When Muhammad is let down by his potential business partner's *tafarnug*, Muhammad's father tells him, "Remain strong. I pray to God for things to work out in your favor with the blessings of this holy month of Ramadan." Here, the uneducated father does not give up on or even doubt his son's potential as Nazih pasha often doubts his son, 'Adli. Muhammad's father inculcates in his son the practice of patience (*sabr*), which here means refraining from both panic and complaining when facing difficulties (*man' al-nafs 'an al-jaz' wa habs al-lisan 'an al-shakwa*). This is evident in a scene in which Muhammad's father is urged by the butcher to share his worries. The father says that he would rather not complain, because betrothing one's worries in life to anyone but God can be humiliating (*al-shakwa li-ghayr Allah madhalla*). Therefore, *sabr* here is not a call for dependency and silence but rather a driving force behind perseverance. Here, the role models being invoked are prophets whose patience drove their perseverance (*ulu al-'azm min al-rusul*) and who in Islamic tradition include Nuh, Ibrahim, Musa, 'Isa, and Muhammad. Likewise, *sabr* is a call for non-violent resistance and refraining from acting while angry. For example, when the butcher blames Muhammad for aspiring to education beyond his means and thus makes his father fall into debt, the butcher implies westernization as a discourse of exclusion. He aims to silence Muhammad and suppress all the possibilities of change that Muhammad's existence in the alley represents. Again the father stands up for his son and says, "[Muhammad, do not argue with him,] we seek shelter and refuge in God. One cannot expect honey to pour out of a pot full of salty cheese" (*Hasbi Allah wa ni'ma al-wakil. Ma'un al-mish ma-yandahshi 'asal*). The last sentence is a proverb, which implies that a greedy and envious person can only give a lemon. That is to say, the hope for any help coming from the butcher is a false one. When the barber's shop, the main source of Muhammad's family income, receives a confiscation note from a *Khawaga*, the undertaker Ruhi, who wants to help Muhammad, prays to God to get customers. He blames his bad business on doctors and the progress in medicine, which reduces death rates. Muhammad finds Ruhi's attitude funny and wonders how Ruhi prays to God to solve his problems at the expense of other people's lives. Ruhi says, "It is God's order." When next day, Ruhi gets a customer and helps Muhammad stop the confiscation of his father's shop, the latter tells Muhammad, "The One who helped us with the confiscation note will help you find a job. For the Prophet's sake, all will be well in the end, and you shall remember my words, Muhammad." Ruhi's words imply that despite rapid modernization with its constant quest for ensuring human control over nature, there is an order of cause and effect. This order is beyond human control, and hope exists in this domain of contingency even when, logically, things appear otherwise. Again, the idea of *tawakkul* is further invoked. In this context, it seems to derive from the Qur'anic story of Mary's labor. The following are very popular classic lines

of poetry that appear in *Bahjat al-Majalis wa Uns al-Majalis* by the famous eleventh-century Arab Maliki judge and scholar in Lisbon, Ibn ʿAbd al-Barr (d. 1071):

> *Tawakkal ʿala al-Rahman fi al-amri kulihi*
> *Wala targhaban fi al-ʿajzi yawman ʿan al-talbi*
> *Alam tara anna Allah qala li-Maryami*
> *Wa huzzi ilyaki al-jizʿ yassaqat al-rutab*
> *Wa-law shaʾ an tajnihi min ghayr hazzihi*
> *janathu wa-lakin kullu shayʾin lahu sabab*

> Have faith in the Merciful in all thy making
> And favor not "balk" over "undertaking."
> To Mary, God says, "Shake thee the tree to see the dates falling."
> Could not have the dates fallen without shaking!
> But every effect has a cause preceding.

Forgiveness is another metaphor representing Islam in *al-ʿAzima*. When Muhammad discovers that *tafarnug* rules over Fatima and she asks for a divorce, Muhammad says that he knows that the Islamic legal system supports him in this situation, but he does not abuse a right, and he will abide by her wish to have the divorce as soon as possible. When Fatima realizes that she has made a mistake by asking for a divorce, she visits Muhammad at the office at the end of the movie. Here Salim does not depict Muhammad as absolutely good. Muhammad does not hesitate to be indifferent to Fatima's pain. He is not depicted as moved by her tears or argument that she is a human and God forgives sins, so why cannot Muhammad forgive her mistake? ʿAdli encourages him to forgive her, for she did not harm him as much as ʿAdli's *tafarnug* did, and yet Muhammad forgave ʿAdli. The latter also reminds Muhammad that it is not fair not to forgive Fatima, because she is not as educated as they are, and a comparison between her uninformed stances in life and theirs is not fair. Here what is being invoked is that one should pardon when one is able not to, following the Qurʾanic example of the Prophet Joseph, who, according to verse Q 12: 92, pardoned his brothers.

Islamic personal law also features as a metaphor representing Islam in *al-ʿAzima*. The news of Fatima's forced wedding to the butcher infuriates

Muhammad. According to Islamic personal law, it is not possible for a divorcee to marry immediately. She has to wait for three consecutive menstrual cycles (*'idda*) to pass before she can marry again. During this time, the former husband has priority to remarry his divorcee over anybody else by reclaiming the bond of marriage. Any marriage contract written before the completion of the time dedicated to *'idda* becomes void. Since Fatima's new wedding day is the last day of her *'idda*, Muhammad prevents her new forced marriage and reclaims the old bond of marriage, hence the happy ending of the movie. While Salim constructs the emergence of *asala* among *awlad al-balad*, Tugu Mizrahi constructs it among the peasants in his most celebrated film *Layla Bint al-Rif*/Layla, Daughter of the Countryside.

5. That Peasant Raised You Up and Funded Your Education

Mizrahi's *Layla Bint al-Rif*/Layla, Daughter of the Countryside, is an allegory for a message sent from the countryside to the city in 1940s Egypt. Namely, the village is neither a pastoral dream nor a backyard for the city; it is an independent, self-sustaining domain that is not disconnected from the city; the village cherishes its own aesthetics; it accepts the foreign and the new but is not ready to be swept away by it. The film's very early scenes open with Layla singing in the fields while dressed in a silk galabiya, scarf, and embroidered head-kerchief. Her song, *al-Hub ruh al-amal fi al-haya* (Love Is the Essence of Hope in Life), surely announces the film's love story. But more importantly, Mizrahi's decision to film the song through a variety of distant, middle, and head shots emphasizes his investment in amplifying the message of the village. The scenes shot inside the village house further celebrate peasant life. We hear the voice of a woman saying that she has brought fresh milk and fresh flowers. Mizrahi then juxtaposes the two localities, the country and the city, while simultaneously bridging the gap between the two through his decision to shift swiftly between Layla's house and Fathi's, using music as a soundtrack to create continuity. When Fathi arrives with his friends, all dressed in their latest fashion, Mizrahi does not depict the peasants questioning their choices. Mizrahi's village sees Fathi as an insider; he is the son of the landlady who sent him abroad to become a doctor, and somehow he is a sign of hope for the village and a marker of its investment in modernity. Islam does not feature here as strongly as it does in other films. It is barely noticed in both the country and the city except for the emphasis on Layla's uncle's beads and the background conversations over marriage procedures taking place in accordance with Islamic practice. It seems that Mizrahi's main concern was to emphasize how the tension between the city and the countryside is not only class-based. Rather, it is rooted in the supremacist ideology of *tafarnug* that dehumanizes peasants, drains the wealth of the village, and objectifies women. Therefore, Mirzahi's village is not ready to step into a modernity that does not promote equal opportunities and dignity for all. And it has to resist both the dominance and hegemony of *tafarnug* while simultaneously promoting human welfare as imperatives for *asala* to become an emergent culture of modernity.

Mizrahi's construction of *asala* materializes through his positive depiction of matriarchal resistance to *tafarnug*. Here Mizrahi's village women are not like Karim's *Zaynab*. They are wealthy, matriarchal, and fully back

Figure 6.21 Celebrating the aesthetics of peasant women: main roles. Layla Murad as Layla in the village before she moves to Cairo. *Layla Bint al-Rif*, 1941.

Figure 6.22 Celebrating the aesthetics of peasant women: minor roles. An unknown actress plays a maid resident in the village. *Layla Bint al-Rif,* 1941.

women's choices in life. Fathi's mother (Fardus Muhammad) is the head of the household and the lady of the estate. Her authority is frequently underlined in the *mise-en-scène*. The camera depicts her in a higher position than other characters. For example, she appears to be sitting on her bed while her elder brother talks to her as he sits on the floor next to her bed. In the following scene, Fathi's mother discusses with her son his marriage plan:

> *Mother:* Son, I need to talk to you about an important issue.
> *Fathi:* Me too.
> *M:* Have a seat. I hope your stay in the village made you notice how nice, pleasant, and adorable your cousin Layla is.
> *F:* Yes, She is nice, and that is why I wanted to tell you that . . . [The mother interrupts her son].
> *M:* Yes, I know what you want to say.
> *F:* I wanted to tell you that I am bored here, and I am going back to Cairo.
> *M:* I suggest you sign the marriage contract and take your bride with you to Cairo.

F: Did I just hear you mention the words "contract" and "bride"? Who are you talking about?

M: I meant Layla, your cousin.

F: You want me to marry that . . . [Silence]. Mother, how could you allow your mind to even think about that? You want me to marry that peasant. It is impossible!

M: What is wrong with being a peasant?

F: Nothing! But I cannot marry her. People in Cairo will make fun of me if I do that. I won't even hire her as a maid in my house.

M: You are on the wrong side here, Fathi. Those views do not become you, my son. What happened to your sanity? This is your cousin. You both share the same blood. And who is your mother? Are not you the son of the peasant? Is not that peasant the one who raised you up and made you who you are now? If you grew some feathers and you can fly now, do not forget that your current social status came from the hard work of the peasant. And you must marry Layla.

F: Must! Who would force me to do that?

M: I will. I will force you to marry her. One day you will realize the advice of your peasant mother. I do not understand what exactly is wrong with being a peasant! Nonsense!

The mother's plan to keep the wealth within the family is surely a typical feudal goal. And it initially seems unjust. But a shot of Egypt in 1941, where an uneducated peasant woman forces a Cambridge graduate to act against his will, empowers the peasant on the screen. The subtext here is not concentration of power through wealth so much as the preservation of rural wealth against the supremacist ideology of *tafarnug*. But this counter-dominance exercised by the matriarch does not solve the problem, because *tafarnug* is a dominant culture. To the uneducated mother, *tafarnug* is a venomous snake, and cutting off this snake's head does not entirely guarantee eliminating the traces of its poison.

Therefore, mirroring becomes Mirzahi's tool for constructing *asala* through counter-hegemony exercised by Layla's character. Layla is a rural bourgeoisie who went to a French boarding school. After finishing her education she returns to her village, where she lives with her maternal aunt

386 | FILMING MODERNITY AND ISLAM IN COLONIAL EGYPT

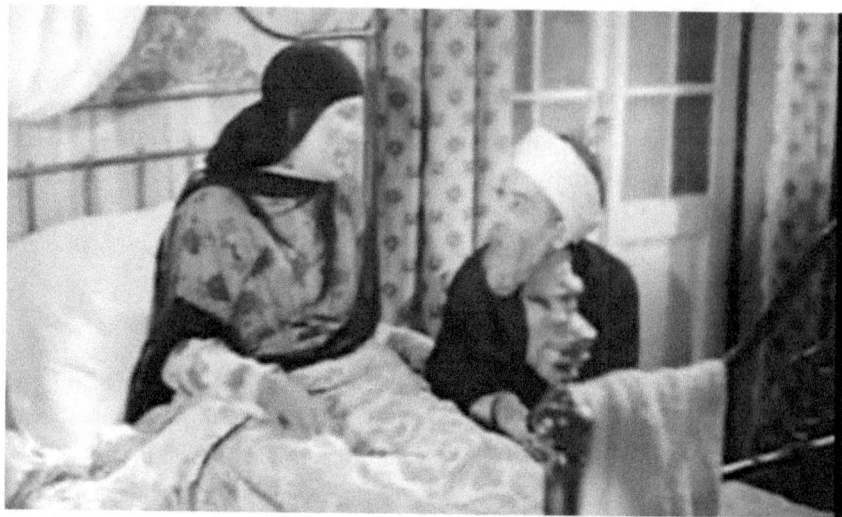

Figure 6.23 Mizrahi's empowerment of the village woman through a character's positioning. Fardus Muhammad as head of the family. *Layla Bint al-Rif*, 1941.

Figure 6.24 Mizrahi's subaltern speaking. To the left, Yusuf Wahbi as Fathi talking to his mother, played by Fardus Muhammad. *Layla Bint al-Rif*, 1941.

in a joint family house. Her uncle and cousins also live in the same house. Layla's cousin Ibrahim (Fakhir Fakir) is in love with her, but she has her eye on her other cousin, the Cambridge graduate Fathi. Her aunt (and mother of Fathi) decides to help her fulfill her dream. After marriage, Layla is faced with *tafarnug*'s hegemony over her husband's life; she finds herself forced to step into the domain of *tafarnug*. Yet she does not embrace it. This is evident in her song *Imta yihun kul da* (When Will All This Pass?). Here, mirroring becomes a conscious imitation of the gesture, speech pattern, and attitude of the hegemonic subject, Fathi. Mizrahi dedicates a number of scenes and headshots to building mirroring and revealing the autocracy of Fathi's modernity in his own eyes; Fathi's modernity is nothing but the resurrection of a patriarchal order that objectifies women. When Layla overhears Fathi saying that she is a peasant whose family forced him to marry her and that he does not think her any better than a servant, she confronts him. And he says, "I am free to behave as I wish and you too. This is a done deal." When she masters *tafarnug* and meets Fathi for the first time at a party, he says, "I was not expecting you to change like that. I thought you are . . ." She completes his sentence and says, "I understand; you thought I am a peasant." He says, "I did not know that you like modern life. You speak French fluently and dance nicely like a fully modern woman." She says, "Understandable. You must be so busy with your life and have no time to use your brain or notice people other than, you know, your patients and hospital. Your career." Resorting to patriarchal power to claim authority over Layla, Fathi wants her to leave the party as he is not feeling well, and it is getting late. To this she says, "No. I like the party. I am neither tired nor do I have headaches. Take an aspirin and sleep tight. Besides, I thought life in the city starts at midnight, modern life, doesn't it?" When, on another occasion, Fathi comes home and objects to one of Layla's parties, he asks her to dismiss people, for she did not tell him before inviting them. Layla repeats the exact words he said to her earlier. She says, "These people are my friends. Is it necessary to tell you? Am I not free in my choices like you are? Should I not invite whoever I like to? Should I not go out and stay up late at night to dance? You have your apartment. You can rest in it. Doesn't everyone has his place? Was not this a done deal?" Here again, mirroring allows Mizrahi to send up Fathi's egocentric view of modernity and reveal its falsity.

However, mirroring alone does not dismantle the hegemony of *tafarnug*. It is only when Fathi sees modernity as a humanitarian project that aims at improving the human condition that a paradigm shift takes place. Layla's role as an enabler is explicitly stated in the dialogue when she blames Fathi for not practicing medicine and says to him, "You have a duty towards humanity, and you must fulfill it." Here, reaction shots help Mizrahi further underscore Layla's *asala* as a practical consciousness of modernity, and Fathi is depicted as impressed by her words. Yet Fathi could not tolerate the fact that a Cambridge graduate like himself could be rejected or silenced by what he describes as a brazen village woman who forces her choices on him. This is why Mizrahi depicts Fathi's initial regaining of interest in his profession as an attempt to win Layla just as he wins an apple. And in that sense, Fathi's attitude toward Layla is not any better than that of his friend 'Izzat (Anwar Wagdi), an adherent of *tafarnug* and a fortune hunter who schemes to seduce Layla and control her wealth. 'Izzat eventually tries to assault Layla and schemes to prove that there was a consensual relationship between the two. This subplot serves Mizrahi by allowing him to show that Fathi's second phase of interest in his profession is nothing but an escape mechanism to blame others for his failures. It is only when Fathi learns to set prejudice aside and sees even his worst of enemies (namely 'Izzat) as human that Fathi gets the message of the village: justice for all and resources for all. Here it was important for Mizrahi to end with Fathi going back to the village to see Layla and marry her again while she is dressed in her peasant dress. The dialogue had to state that Fathi is no longer ashamed of his peasant origin. This idea of correlating *asala* with not being ashamed of one's roots, here involving the people whose free movement in the public sphere is what makes history, is further explored by Yusuf Wahbi in *Ibn al-Haddad*.

6. My Fellow *Awlad al-Balad*, the Unpolluted-by-*Tafarnug*

In Wahbi's *Ibn al-Haddad*, social justice is rooted in a fair-share economy that drives the interpretation of *asala* in this film. The lead male character, Taha (Yusuf Wahbi), is shown as a role model for the Egyptian worker and hope of the working class. Here, the film director does not present hope through the industrialist, nationalist and religious ideal of *effendi* Islam, which reduces modernity to a reactionary stance that utilizes reductionist views of an imagined Islamic idealist past to distinguish the *effendi* from the aristocrat, whose modernity is "bad" modernity characterized by westernization.[4] Hope lies not in holding political views that favor a return to a previous political state of society that possessed positive characteristics absent in contemporary society. Wahbi does not construct Taha's modernity as torn between the superstitious past and the advance in the scientific and rational understanding of reality. It is not a conflict over who owns modernity, the *effendi* or the aristocrat.

Taha's modernity is marked by a rejection of *effendiness* and an investment in a fair-share economy as a vehicle for social change both from below and above. Indeed, Islam informs Taha's modernity, but Wahbi does so not so much by emphasizing metaphors representing Islam as by critiquing *tafarnug* as a supremacist ideology that objectifies women and looks down upon the religion of *awlad al-balad* and the *fellahin*.

For example, Wahbi's Taha, unlike Mizrahi's Fathi, is not ashamed of his social class of origin. When he returns to Egypt after earning a degree in Engineering, his fellow *awlad al-balad* raise their concern that he must have forgotten about them after having spent many years in Europe, and he, like many of the Cairene-bourgeoisie, must have become an adherent of *tafarnug*. Taha replies, "I am not rootless; I am not the kind of person who forgets about origins" (*ma-yinsash asluh illa ibn haram*). While the standard use of the expression *ibn haram* relates to the English "bastard," it has, in Egyptian colloquial, many denotations depending on context. It can denote "naughty/disobedient boy" or "unjust," for example. In this context, it implies that Taha has no reason to stop affiliating himself with his class of origin because he sees nothing shameful in that origin. When Taha says "I am a son of a blacksmith and shall remain as such," Wahbi's dialogue does not call for a return to origins or an imagined authentic ideal past. While he emphasizes class struggle, he simultaneously breaks away from its determinism through a capitalist society where an alliance takes place between the enlightened few and those seeking enlightenment among the peasants and the majority of the urban working class, whose hard labor is the root that needs to be celebrated and respected by the Cairene-bourgeoisie. This is why the life of the working class is not depicted as an absolute good. Cruelty is critiqued by depicting the mistreatment of children, which Taha blames on the lack of resources and lack of access to education.

For the same reason, Taha goes against his father's wish and refuses to become an *effendi*; he turns down a government position that pays twelve pounds a month. The father tells his son that he sent him abroad only to brag about how his son will become an *effendi*, how he will go to the *diwan* every day. Here the father's fascination with *effendiness* is almost like that of Fatima in Kamal Salim's *al-'Azima*. To him, rejecting a clerical position will make the family a laughing-stock in the neighborhood. On the other hand, Taha believes in a fair-share economy; he wants to start an independent business where he can share his expertise and education with the workers whom he wants to be recognized and celebrated. He thus expands the business of his father and turns the blacksmith's shop into a factory. Here, Wahbi is cautious not to be framed as a promoter of a communist agenda in monarchical Egypt. Therefore, in another scene, Taha explains his views to his father. He wants to make money and increase his wealth, no doubt, but he does not want to be a war profiteer. In one scene, Taha tells his father that he has proposed a government project that will not bring great revenue, but that he has learned "to earn a sufficient amount honorably, for the best of all earnings is that which comes with the love of the people." Taha's statement is not only a marker of modesty. It echoes the prophetic tradition, which teaches minimalism by emphasizing the need for earning while simultaneously reminding the believer that earning a sufficient income is better than acquiring the surplus income that promotes indulgence; this also teaches the reasonable spending of earnings and discourages parsimoniousness. And this explains the next scenes dedicated to news headlines. When the price of iron increases as England declares war on Germany, Wahbi's camera shows the news headlines announcing that 'Adawi Factories owned by Taha and his father is seizing an opportunity not to earn more money but to employ 3000 more workers. What is being argued for here is a biologically grounded approach to social justice based on the articulation of a new ideological paradigm that is often referred to as "Fair Shares." This paradigm consists of three complementary normative principles. First, goods and services should be distributed to each according to his or her basic needs. Second, surpluses beyond the provisioning of our basic needs should be distributed according to merit. And third, each citizen is obliged in return to contribute to the "collective survival enterprise" in accordance with his or her ability. Though none of these three principles is new, in combination, they provide a biologically informed middle way between capitalism and socialism.[5]

While Taha's quest to own an independent business stands as an allegory for the possibilities of social change from below, his marriage to the Cairene-bourgeois Zinat is an allegory for the possibilities of change from above. For example, initially, Taha objects to the idea of marrying Zinat. He voices his concerns that the dominant culture of *tafarnug* among the Cairene-bourgeoisie might not bring a happy married life. When he is proven right after marriage, Taha chooses to counter the hegemony of *tafarnug*. As he puts it, *tafarnug* is an epidemic of modernity that swept through society, and the burden of "disinfection" falls on those who have more access to education and resources. Here Wahbi simply suggests that for *asala* to be an emergent culture, it is not enough to allow the working class a fair share of the resources; the falsehood of *tafarnug* had to be acknowledged, and local aesthetics and the sensibilities of the working class and peasants should be respected and celebrated by the Cairene-bourgeoisie. Therefore, reconciliation does not take place in the movie only through allowing *awlad al-balad* access to the same luxuries and resources. Taha schemes to convince his wife that her best friend's understanding of modernity is void of ethical commitments, because it does not prevent her from betraying Zinat and accepting having an affair with Taha. By the same token, Zinat's so-called ultra-modern man-friend spreads rumors that she is having an affair with him, but he lets her down as soon as she seeks his help. For the same reason, Taha announces that he is bankrupt and needs Zinat's help to be able to make ends meet. Here, depicting Zinat realizing the falsity of *tafarnug* while dressed as a working-class woman is not simply a call for women to stay at home. It is a presentation of the division of labor as a solution in her particular situation as a woman who does not have the qualifications to work and earn her living and who should not be forced to roam the streets of Cairo to look for a job like her male siblings. For the same reason, the pasha says, "I will stay in the village with the peasants to farm and harvest with them and wake up at dawn to pray with them." This line, positioned at the end of the movie, is meant to tell the audience that renouncing *tafarnug* and embracing the local sensibilities of *awlad al-balad* and the peasants are categorical imperatives for becoming modern. By making Taha, at the end of the film, gift the pasha his villa back and announce that he has not lost his wealth, Wahbi plays it safe instead of foisting political solutions that see an exit only in punishing the bourgeoisie by stripping them of their wealth. Certainly, had he gone in that direction, the film might have been censored. While the educated Taha speaks for the working class in *Ibn al-Haddad*, Kamal Salim gives the lead to the uneducated working class in *al-Mazahir*.

7. I Won't Wear a Tarbush, I Am Free

Kamal Salim's *al-Mazahir* is an improvement on his more popular film *al-'Azima*. This time, however, education is not represented as the only hope for the working class, whose understanding of modernity is shaped by their interest in a fair-share economy where the worker gains his voice through organized unions and strikes. These are the topics of discussion during the popular practice of *a'da* that takes place in the neighborhood coffee shop, where people get together to talk about life (*ahwal al-dunya*). Conversations are spontaneous and unplanned; they may include day-to-day occurrences, current events, historical topics, medical knowledge, or any trending political, economic or social issues. The space for *a'da* is a secular space that is not anti-religion; while there is room for agreements and disagreement, there is a keenness to avoid exclusionist ideas and silencing. Folk art can sometimes inaugurate the gathering, as is the case with the following monologue sung by Isma'il Yasin, who was an emerging actor at that time:

> Cheer *awlad al-balad*, the reliable men.
> Who dares to compete with our determination and number?
> Some fights we lose, some fights we win,
> For ourselves and our friends, we always stand up.
> We never hesitate to help or share all the money we have
> Have you ever seen us in al-Qanatir Park on one of those breezy mornings?
> Have you ever wondered about our carts and how beautiful they look?
> Aren't our carts much nicer than the Packard car?
> The Packard is speedy and smoky
> Our cart looks cute and is more comfortable.
> Let alone our music, our dance, and our women
> Oh, how beautiful our women look in their red roses
> How wonderful it is when we pass our time eating nuts

Have you ever tasted our beans with caramelized onion?
Our beans taste like honey
Nothing compares to our lightheartedness
Nothing compares to our pure hearts
Helping others is our temperament
Heavy-heartedness is our enemy
Roses and jasmine grow for us all year long
Cheer *awlad al-balad*, the reliable men
Who dares to compete with us in our determination and number?

The celebration of *awlad a-balad*'s local food, aesthetics, ethical code of conduct and even means of transport, and the promotion of the superiority of local over foreign products and practices, should not be mistaken for a reactionary counter-modern stance. *Al-Mazahir* is a film that celebrates societal modernization so long as it promotes cultural modernity that secures social justice. For example, the leading male character, Mahmud (Yahya Shahin), is a mechanic who is proud of his profession, and he owns a car. He first appears in the film while driving into the alley, an introduction that marks not just modernization but, more importantly, the arrival of recourses for *awlad al-balad*. Some of them, like Radwan, the owner of the mill, became war profiteers; he shifted alliance by moving to Zamalek and succumbing to dominant cultures of modernity enforced by his Cairene-bourgeoisie wife, Lady Rudi. As a war profiteer, Radwan only hopes to be tolerated as a newcomer to Cairo's elite circles. While Radwan's constant complaints to his wife about his rejection of *tafarnug* could be seen as a reactionary counter-modern stance, Kamal Salim creates an alternative path for the working class. Consider the following depiction of *a'da* at the very beginning of the film:

> *Mahmud:* [Addressing his friends] Folks, I have an idea! Why do we not join the local sports club? It will be a place to get together to talk and play sports.
>
> *Worker:* What for? We get together in this coffee shop.
>
> *M:* The coffee shop is a different kind of leisure. I am talking about a sports club where we can exercise to strengthen our bodies and improve our health. Healthy mind, healthy body.

Worker 1: You are right.
Worker 2: That is true.
Worker 3: This is a good idea.
W: I spent six months training at Abu Kalil club.
W3: I spent some time in Tirsana club.
M: Is it not a waste to stop exercising?
W2: I know other people in this neighborhood. They might be interested.
W1: Ibrahim al-Kishayn, Isma'il Baraka, and Sayyid Qidra.
W3: And many others too.
W1: [Addressing the cafe owner] 'Abd al-Nabi, we agreed with Mahmud's suggestions to join the sports club.
Cafe Owner: A sports club!
W1: Come over to join the conversation.
Tarbush Seller: What nonsense are you talking about? [He addresses the café owner] Those people are harming your business . . . It is a scam!
CO: Scam!
TS: Mahmud is going to take your customers away if they join that club.
CO: And what is wrong with that?
TS: Who is ever going to spend time here? They will all go to the club and sit there, they will drink coffee there, and you will be staying here with nothing but flies around (*tinishsh*).
CO: Nobody takes the sustenance (*rizq*) of someone else; sustenance comes from *tawakkul*. And the sports club is not a bad idea—just because it is foreign. I heard someone say that a British man can be eighty years old, but he continues to have the energy to play golf. I will also play golf in that club.

The practice of *a'da* in the above scene is not centered on forging a new masculine identity under British colonial rule. Primarily, the discussion interrogates what it means to become modern, whether to accept foreign ideas or not, and what to do if these ideas are introduced by the colonizer. Like the café owner (Hasan Kamil), some workers lean toward accepting foreign ideas, which they see beneficial even when introduced by a colonial power. As *awlad al-balad* join the sports club, Salim depicts a change in their code of dress; most of them appear in sportswear except the café owner, who dresses in a galabiya. One

Figure 6.25 *Awlad al-balad* practicing *a'da* in the coffee shop. *Al-Mazahir*, 1941.

scene depicts him trying to exercise in his galabiya. Kamal Salim's choice of costume here suggests that "becoming modern" is not a practice of consumption of "form" so much as an evaluation and critique of the self in the present moment, as well as an experimenting with new ideas so as to understand the rationale behind them and the need for them both individually and collectively. Surely, new ideas could bring new business models that could threaten existing ones. But here, Salim invokes the notion of *tawakkul* to argue for an open market and a fair-share economy where people have equal access to information and resources that sets a context of fair competition and tolerates difference, thereby allowing for the organic growth of both knowledge and resources.

Because *awlad al-balad* in *al-Mazahir* do not reject foreign and new ideas, however, they oppose reducing modernity to *tafarnug*; all through the film, there is a constant condemnation of *tafarnug* and an attempt to imagine alternatives. The main example, of course, is the characterization of the leading male character, Mahmud. Mahmud is a unionist; he believes that workers must have a legal body to represent them. The union fund should come from the workers to ensure that it serves their interests. To that end,

Mahmud organizes different activities like boxing matches. He then uses the revenue to fund the union. *Tafarnug*, however, stands against Mahmud's efforts of reform. He falls in love with Haniyya, who is lured by the luxuries at her uncle's house in Zamalek, where she has moved after her mother's death. Being a partner to her uncle in the mills, Haniyya is targeted by the manager of the mills, Nabih (Istifan Rusti), whose adherence to *tafarnug* leads to corruption in the mills due to high production and low sales rates. Nabih smuggles the grain and sells it for his own interest to fund his *tafarnug*. This policy leaves the workers in miserable work conditions. The machines are never maintained; workers fear that they will break down one day and cost somebody their life; supervisors steal from overtime money and do not pay the workers; the management does not buy original oil for the machines, so as to cut expenses. Nabih's character is, in short, juxtaposed against that of Mahmud; it is the path to modernity that Mahmud resents the most. When Nabih is exposed and the owner of the mills, Radwan, offers Mahmud the post of new manager, the latter refuses and says he likes to work independently at his mechanic's shop. Here again, Salim presents the same idea as presented in *Ibn al-Haddad*, namely, a sufficient income is favored over a surplus income. When Radwan's wife, Lady Rudi, mocks Mahmud's attitude, Mahmud says, "I was created with dignity (*karama*); why should I lose it?" The notion of *karama* here derives from the Qur'anic notion of the dignifying of the human over every other form of creation, as expressed in Surat al-Isra' (Q17:70). The signification here is that by accepting Radwan's offer, Mahmud risks subjugating himself and the workers to Lady Rudi's dominant culture of modernity, which is simply dehumanizing. Mahmud thus refuses to marry Haniyya, for, as he puts it, he does not want to be another Radwan who has wasted his life pleading to be tolerated. The dialogue emphasizes these ideas further when Mahmud says:

> I do not want to be in-laws with you. I do not want to host another Lady Rudi under my roof; I cannot accept being in-laws with people who are dependent ... a bunch of unemployed people who have nothing else to do but make themselves and others objects of scorn and mockery.

It is only when Radwan rebels against *tafarnug* that reconciliation takes place.

Inasmuch as resisting *tafarnug* becomes central to Mahmud's *asala*, resisting local monopoly in the alley (*hara*) represented through the tarbush-seller, Madbuli, is another marker of *asala*. Madbuli bullies his neighbors for not wearing a tarbush; he does not pay for services on time and tries to achieve the greatest gains with the least effort. He is indeed meant to be a metaphor for local monopoly and greed; he requires new businesses to pay him money before starting so that he can protect them. To gain legitimacy in the alley, Madbuli claims he is acting in the name of "tradition." He stigmatizes anyone who refuses to follow this practice as "westernized." And it is precisely against this claim that Mahmud rebels; he rejects the continuity of injustice in the name of "tradition." When, in one scene, a confrontation takes place between them, Mahmud says, "I am free to wear what I want; nobody can control me." In another scene, Haniyya goes to collect rent from Madbuli; he drops the topic and starts harassing her. When she resists him and insists on taking what is rightfully hers, he pushes her to the ground. Mahmud and other neighbors intervene. One of the neighbors says that Haniyya should have treated Madbuli better as respect (*adab*) is required. The word *adab* is shared between Persian, Arabic, Urdu, and various forms of Turkish spoken in Anatolia and Central Asia. As in Persian, *adab* in Arabic is not only used in reference to manners or etiquette. It also refers to the proper aesthetic or social form of social conduct, especially in public. *Adab* here is not the type of *adab* acquired through education, but through adherence to the normative social practice in a particular social context. In the film's context, the neighbors want Haniyya to respect Madbuli, first for being a man and second for being older than she is, and third because she should not scream and raise her voice in the street. And it is this particular inference of *adab* that Mahmud questions when he says, "Does *adab* mean not to demand what is rightfully ours? Does *adab* mean to objectify women and tolerate violence against them?" The implication is that using *adab* as a discourse to silence people and as a narrative of exclusion to frame anyone who opposes local injustices as an outsider with a foreign agenda or an enemy of the people will not fly. Ironically, almost eighty years after the release of *al-Mazahir*, Madbuli's claims were the very same claims that were made against protesters in Tahrir Square on February 18, 2011. The famous status-quo Prime Minister Ahmad Shafiq at that time used to say that it was not *adab* to ask Mubarak to leave and it was rude on the part of protestors to boldly insist by using the slogan "Leave now."

Figure 6.26 Emergent modernity resisting local monopoly. To the left, Yahaya Shahin as Mahmud. *Al-Mazahir*, 1941.

Kamal Salim maintains a fine line between workers' right to protest and the appropriation of these rights to serve personal and partisan interests. For example, Madbuli creates doubt about Mahmud's reliability and devotion to the union. He encourages the workers to act against their own interests by going to the factory and attacking the corrupt manager. On the other hand, Mahmoud wants them to start by following the legal path and file complaints through the union. Madbuli creates doubt regarding the legal process and the credibility of unions; he believes that connections and word of mouth are the best routes. Law, for Madbuli, is a waste of time, or as he puts it, why waste time sending papers and waiting for papers to come back while workers can take their matters into their own hands by asking Mahmud, if he really cares about them, to talk to his beloved Haniyya and ask her to speak with her uncle, the owner of the mills. Mahmud does not see it as appropriate for the workers to hide in fear behind Haniyya while they can claim their rights themselves. The workers receive his objection negatively, and Madbuli finds an opportunity to add more fuel to the fire by encouraging them to act on their anger even at the cost of their lives. Mahmud calms them down and reminds them of the

Qur'anic verse Q41: 34, which reads, "The good deed and the evil deed are not equal. Repel by that which is better; then behold, the one between whom and thee there is enmity shall be as if he were a loyal, protecting friend."[6] Here again, metaphors representing Islam are invoked not to dissuade workers from asking for their rights, but to prevent them from losing their rights if they let their anger lead their rebellion. When the workers insist, Mahmud listens to the view of the majority and speaks with Haniyya to solve their problems. However, as expected, the corrupt manager, Nabih, overhears the conversation and decides to fire the workers who complain. In a third coffee-shop scene, Madbuli provokes the workers against Mahmud and convinces them that Mahmud has collaborated against them, and the man whom they thought of as Moses turns out to be the Pharaoh who oppressed Moses. Madbuli's efforts, however, are wasted when the workers become aware of Madbuli's propaganda machine, which they describe using the colloquial expression "Buzzing is as effective as magic when it comes to changing someone's minds" (*al-dhann 'ala al-widan amr min al-sihr*). While Kamal Salim tries to construct *asala* by questioning what *adab* is and how to rebel against its appropriation, Muhammad Karim does so by questioning modernity in relation to the Qur'anic notion of justice when defining morality in his 1946 film *Dunya*.

8. It Is Not My Fault, Nor Is it Society's Fault

Like his first film, *Zaynab*, Karim's *Dunya* is both an adaptation and a woman-centered film. Adapted from a German novel titled *Alexandra*, *Dunya* is narrated by its protagonist, an educated middle-class Cairene woman by the name of Dunya (Raqiya Ibrahim). Her successful career at a litigation firm is interrupted when she falls in love with Muhammad (Ahmad Salim). The latter, an adherent of *tafarnug*, abandons Dunya while pregnant, leaving her to face the shame of having a child out of wedlock. Overcome by her self-blame, Dunya cannot provide for herself and her child, who dies. She is then convicted of reckless behavior that has led to the child's death and is sentenced to five years in prison. She comes out of jail determined to avenge herself against Muhammad, with whom she reconnects and who she convinces to marry her. Her goal is to keep the jail sentence a secret and cast on Muhammad's feudal family the shame of having a daughter-in-law who is an ex-convict. In vain, Dunya's lawyer, Fathi bey (Sulayman

Nagib), tries to dissuade her from carrying out her revenge plans and starting a new life.

As the movie unfolds, Dunya meets Muhammad's mother and sister. The mother (Dawlat Abyad) listens to Dunya explaining how she met Muhammad. This story, which Karim has Dunya narrate through a flashback technique, reveals a part of the plot that is kept hidden from the audience, namely, how Dunya perceives herself as a victim of sexual assault, a view that it was very challenging to discuss in 1940s Egypt. The flashback shows Dunya looking younger and walking in the streets of Cairo. As she goes window-shopping, Muhammad follows her to her office, calls her at home, waits for her every day after she finishes her working day, and showers her with gifts and flowers. One day, Muhammad invites Dunya out on his birthday. Instead of driving her back home as planned, he takes advantage of her inebriation and escorts her to his boathouse, where he rapes her, a scene that could not be depicted in the 1940s because of censorship, of course. Only then, Dunya's state of constant distress and her insistence that she has a just cause and that she demands justice starts to make sense, as it is revealed how some parts of her relationship with Muhammad were non-consensual and unwelcomed. After listening to her story, the mother becomes torn between her sense of justice, her rejection of Dunya, and her son's insistence on marriage. She decides to host Dunya for a while at her estate to test the seriousness of the relationship between Dunya and Muhammad. The mother also hopes that the relationship will not stand the test of time. After a series of heated confrontations between the mother and Dunya, the former eventually approves of the marriage. The movie takes a sharp turn when the mother comes to know about Dunya's jail sentence and changes her mind. To the mother, the news of Dunya's jail sentence will affect not only Muhammad's reputation but also the marriage of his sister, whose father-in-law cannot accept an ex-convict in his extended family. Faced with the pressure of rejection, Dunya chooses to follow her lawyer's initial advice, namely, to leave everything behind and move on.

Dunya is not merely a film about the degree of tolerance shown toward premarital affairs in a majority Muslim society or a story about sin. From the very early scenes, Karim's camera announces that justice is a central theme in his film. The decision to start the film at Qara Maydan serves as an establishing shot that draws attention to how justice as a process of retribution, as opposed to rehabilitation and deterrence, continued to dominate the public sphere in Egypt in the 1940s.[7] Qara Maydan, or the Rumayla square, which dates back to the time of Saladin, witnessed many public displays of justice, especially during Mameluke times. When the Mameluke Sultan Hasan built his mosque, the square became more defined and gained the name *qara*, which means black in Turkish. During Napoleon's Egyptian campaign, the famous governor of Alexandria, Muhammad Kurayyim, who led anti-French resistance, was executed in the same square in 1798. The square is also famous for witnessing the parade for the cover for the Ka'aba (*kiswa*) that used to be sent from Cairo to Mecca. In 1898, under British colonial rule, the first centralized prison was built in the square, and it was completed in 1900. The retribution-based justice implied through the depiction of Qara Maydan is juxtaposed with a rehabilitation-based justice by invoking the Qur'anic notion of pardon (*'afw*). Pardon is introduced in the shots dedicated to Dunya's arrival at the hotel. When she enters her room, classical music dominates the soundtrack until she changes the radio station and hears the voice of the radio presenter (who sounds like the actor 'Abd al-Warith 'Asar) talking about pardon and tolerance as among the most beautiful humanitarian experiences; how nothing compares to the feeling of forgiving those who hurt us. *'Afw*, however, should not be mistakenly understood here as an invitation to pardon Muhammad. Rather, a pardon is sought from Dunya toward herself first, and from the unsympathetic audience toward Dunya. This is evident in Karim's constant attempt to construct empathy toward his protagonist.

The key to understanding how Karim constructs empathy toward Dunya is the character of Dunya's lawyer, Fathi bey (Sulayman Nagib). Their exchange in the hotel at the very beginning of the film help neutralize the unsympathetic audience and simultaneously invites viewers to see Dunya's story through the eyes of her lawyer. Fathi's character conveys the tone of the director. The character is a metaphor for hope and for Dunya's acceptance by society. It was the lawyer who arranged for her pickup from jail and her stay at the hotel. He discourages her obsession with retribution and reminds her how her self-blame and decision to confess to a crime that she did not commit left the judge no option but to give her a jail sentence. But had she told the story of how she was sexually assaulted, she would have been acquitted, because she is a victim of a society dominated by *tafarnug* and its objectification of women. Fathi encourages Dunya to put what happened behind her and look forward to a successful life, which she can endure through her education and career. He tries to convince Dunya that revenge will not make the feudal class confess its discrimination against women and its false consciousness of modernity. He proposes to Dunya to prove to her that she is socially qualified to marry a man of a better status than Muhammad. When she refuses, he suspects that she might still be in love with Muhammad. When she dismisses the idea of love and expresses her feelings of hate toward Muhammad, the lawyer says, "There is a very fine line between love and hate." Here, Karim is experimenting with psychoanalysis, a route that he is to explore later in his movie *Junun al-Hub*/Madness of Love, 1954. The lawyer's statement in *Dunya* underscores how Dunya's mind is cluttered; her decisions and judgments are still shaped by her trauma.

However, Dunya sees Fathi's empathetic position as an exception in society. She holds the view that redemption is not possible for women in 1940s Egypt. Her views are amplified through scenes depicting the hotel maids outside her door gossiping about her prison experience, and the hotel manager, presumably a Greek Egyptian, who comes to ask Dunya to leave for she cannot be served. This rejection and discrimination make Dunya determined to carry out her revenge plan. As she tells the audience, revenge is a duty that she will fulfill in the name of so many other girls who have been dehumanized because they trusted that a society dominated by *tafarnug* could actually guarantee them sovereignty over body and mind. Karim thus employs revenge as a metaphor for restoring Dunya's lost sense of humanity. This idea gets amplified through Dunya's response to her lawyer when he reminds her that retribution will inflict pain, not only on the aggressors but on other innocent people like Muhammad's mother, who has a righteous origin (*karimat al-asl*), implying not only her noble birth but also her noble deeds and actions in her community. Dunya asks, "Am I not a *karimat al-asl*, was not my mother *karimat al-asl* when she died out of shock? I was punished, and why was he not punished? I lost my social status; he must lose his. My name was tarnished; his name must be tarnished too. This is justice." Because Fathi's character serves the purpose of reminding the audience that Dunya's story is not a story about sin, it is a story about justice; he discourages Dunya's attempt to hide the information about her jail sentence. He then gives Dunya three days to find a way to reveal her secret. But Dunya could not keep her promise to the lawyer. She suffers a nervous breakdown due to her constant state of distress, which is typical of assault victims. A song and several shots inside Dunya's bedroom externalize Dunya's consciousness. On the one hand, she sees herself as a victim. On the other hand, she blames herself for what happened. Yet her moral awareness cannot tolerate her lies about the jail sentence. At this point, Karim pushes for transparency as a categorical imperative of justice, and the lawyer visits the mother, confirms Dunya's story of sexual assault, and reveals the news of the jail sentence. And more importantly, Fathi criticizes the mother's hypocrisy when she changes her position toward Dunya.

Asala in *Dunya* materializes at best through the protagonist's revenge plan. The very early scenes of *Dunya* bear resemblance to the beginning of Naguib Mahfouz's famous novel *Chased by the Dogs*, although Mahfouz's novel came out in the 1960s, almost fifteen years after Karim's film. The theme of revenge helps Mahfouz interrogate the hypocrisy of the 1960s Egyptian intellectual elite to critique how their political ambition and self-interest are sugar-coated, with slogans of social justice appropriated to fuel populism. Likewise, revenge is a frame that Karim uses to interrogate a number of questions with regard to 1940s public discussions about civil liberties for women in relation to modernity and justice. These questions include: (a) to what extent are the discussions about a woman's liberty inclusive of the liberty to experiment and the possibilities of success and failure?; (b) will the possibility of failure be accepted as much as the possibility of success, or will women, unlike men, remain governed by the conditions of success and perfection (i.e. if a woman wants to be educated and have full sovereignty over body and mind she must succeed or else she will be excluded as subhuman)?; and (c) will society recognize that falling in love with someone does not mean welcoming sexual conduct even when the woman voluntarily accepts a date? The film does not answer any of these questions.

Instead, Karim gives voice to his young educated middle-class protagonist, who became a victim of sexual assault, to question her subjugation to a contradictory and inapplicable moral theory of justice shaped by *tafarnug* (represented in the film through the character of Muhammad) and *ta'ssul* (represented through the character of Muhammad's mother). On the one hand, Muhammad is a feudal brat. He is always well-dressed, sometimes in a suit, sometimes in a *frak* jacket, and sometimes in a hunting suit. He looks pretty much like a British lord. It is not clear what he does for a living. The film does not tell us. But presumably, he runs his father's estate. His daily schedule is planned around meeting friends, and family, holding parties, spending lots of time at elite clubs, and spending nights at reception parties or casinos. When he meets Dunya again, we see a man who wants to redeem himself after hearing about Dunya's miscarriage. He regrets what happened and finds that marriage can heal Dunya and gives him an opportunity to redeem himself. At the same time, Dunya lampoons his longing for redemption and his attitude that continues to reduce a woman's honor and integrity to her sexuality. When Muhammad asks Dunya if she had other affairs, she looks at the camera and smiles sarcastically while assuring him that she did not. She adds, "This is how the customs are. A man will not marry a woman unless she has a 'clean past.'" The underlying sarcasm here is that if women continue to be targeted in the public sphere because no matter how modern and educated they are they will always be seen as nothing but objects of sexual desire, no women with a "pure/clean past" will be left for the likes of Muhammad to marry. Muhammad's attitude is further caricatured through the character of his sister's father-in-law, who wants his daughter-in-law to live in a villa surrounded by a wall that is nine meters in height so that the neighbors who live fifty meters away will not see her. On the other hand, Muhammad's mother is depicted presenting herself as just, righteous and religious. When she first appears on the screen, she appears to be listening to Qur'anic verse Q5:8, which reads, "O you who believe! Be steadfast for God, bearing witness to justice, and let not hatred for a people lead you to be unjust. Be just; that is nearer to reverence. And reverence God. Surely God is Aware of whatsoever you do." The mother cultivates an amour-propre of being rational, broad-minded, and just; she appears keen on social justice by helping, respecting, and celebrating the peasants on her estate. For example, she holds banquets for them and serves the food herself. When she knows about Dunya's story, she acknowledges the injustice that befalls Dunya. She further announces her intention to accept Dunya as a daughter-in-law. But soon, the mother's ideals of justice became overshadowed by her desire to co-opt Dunya's plans. The mother shows empathy toward Dunya so that the latter will feel morally inferior and leave Muhammad. These contradictions being constantly highlighted in the characterization of Muhammad and his mother show how a rehabilitation process in a society dominated by

CELEBRATING EMERGENT MODERNITY (*ASALA*) | 405

Figure 6.27 Advertisement for *Dunya* in *Ruza al-Yusuf* magazine, 1946 (no. 920, January 31).

tafarnug and *ta'ssul* is not possible, because the primal sense of justice, which derives from Islamic textual sources such as the Qur'an, remains overshadowed by a false consciousness of modernity that is prioritized over the commitment to justice. The story of Dunya's acceptance by Muhammad and his mother is thus constructed to critique the hypocrisy of the Cairene-bourgeoisie, who, even in their attempt to be tolerant, continue to care more about their amour-propre of tolerance than for the needs of the victim subjugated to their tyranny.

As Dunya succeeds in carrying out her plan, she sees some sense in the possibilities of compassion. But Dunya still fails to make Muhammad's mother admit that she is being unfair, because the mother is predisposed against her. Therefore, the final scene depicts Dunya leaving her wedding behind and walking aimlessly outside the house. In his memoirs, Karim explains that his ending is a realistic one, for Egyptian society in the 1940s did not accept a Dunya, and it would be delusive to tell women in the 1940s that they could act upon their desires and society would still accept them. However, Karim condemns the suppression of Dunya's *asala* via a monologue spoken by Muhammad to his mother at the end of the movie:

> *Mother:* This marriage shall never take place.
>
> *Son:* I have always believed that you are just, and that is why I allowed you to have a say in my choices. But it never occurred to me that you are merciless and you would be unfair to a poor girl like [Dunya]. Are you not the one who keeps saying that the best thing in life is to make others happy? Where is your sense of justice? Everything that happened was caused by my aggression. I am the one who caused all these miseries. Do I not deserve a second chance in life to redeem myself and fix my mistakes? If not, shall I not pay back for my crimes? If my father, whom you always speak of as a good example, were alive today, what would his judgment be? I shall marry Dunya and make her happy. Do you think I am so keen on the luxury I live in? Do you think I am happy to be a rich brat? No, Ma'am! You are wrong. I do not want anything from you; I will work and earn money and make my wife happy. I will heal her, and I hope God will help me make her forgive me.

A similar monologue is rare in Egyptian cinema in this period. On the one hand, it reflects the interest of Karim and his scriptwriter Sulayman Nagib in holding patriarchy responsible for its actions. On the other, it shows how the feudal system in Egypt in the 1940s promotes patriarchal dependency. Muhammad could not marry Dunya even if he were in love with her, because his feudal class does not allow him to exercise any aspect of modern social liberties save his exercise of *tafarnug*. This question of the civil liberties of women in relation to justice and female sexual desire is further explored in relation to the issue of polygamy in Ahmad Kamil Mursi's *al-Bayt al-Kabir/The Foremost House*, 1949.

9. Don't I Have Desire Like You?

Al-Bayt al-Kabir/The Foremost House, 1949, is directed by Ahamd Kamil Mursi, who began his film career in 1937 with what was, at that time, the unprecedented project of dubbing foreign films into Arabic. One example is the dubbing of *Mr. Deeds Goes to Town*, directed by Frank Capra. Mursi studied acting at the newly established Egyptian Institute for Acting and worked as a film critic in the famous *Ruza al-Yusuf* magazine before he moved to directing radio shows and presenting a weekly program that reported and advertised films screened in Cairo. He also wrote books on cinematic idioms and the history of cinema. Mursi worked as an assistant director to Tugu Mizrahi and Yusuf Wahbi in films like *Layla Bint al-Rif* and *'Aris min Istanbul*. In 1939, Mursi directed his first film, titled *al-'Awda ila al-Rif*/A Return to the Countryside. To date, he remains most celebrated for his movies *al-'Amil*/The Worker, 1943, *Al-Na'ib al-'Am*/The Public Prosecutor, 1946, and *al-Bayt al-Kabir*.[8]

Figure 6.28 Advertisement for *al-Bayt al-Kabir* in *al-Ithnayn* magazine (1).

Figure 6.29 Advertisement for *al-Bayt al-Kabir* in *al-Ithnayn* magazine (2).

The plotline of *al-Bayt al-Kabir* follows the life-changing events facing the Cairene-bourgeoisie family of Amina (Amina Rizq) and her husband Mahmud Fu'ad bey (Sulayman Nagib), who have been happily married for twenty-six years. In addition to owning 2000 acres of land, Fu'ad bey is a successful surgeon who heads his own hospital. Amina and Fu'ad have two sons. The eldest is Jalal [Galal] ('Imad Hamdi), who is a doctor and assists his father in the management of the hospital. The youngest is Kamal, who is a student of law at Fu'ad I University. The stability of family life gets threatened when Galal's fiancée Nadiya (Nadiya Sultan) invites the family to the Bint al-Nil Society's charity party, where a belly dancer, Latifa (Tahiyya Kariyuka), notices Fu'ad bey and plans to seduce him. Being a fortune hunter who masters *tafarnug*, Latifa starts stalking Fu'ad. She visits him repeatedly at the hospital and asks for his medical help at her house. Eventually, Fu'ad falls for Latifa, and their relationship becomes the gossip of the city both in public gatherings and on the front pages of major newspapers. When Amina confronts Fu'ad about his affair, she asks for a divorce. Their younger son, Kamal, supports his mother's decision, while the elder son, Galal, hopes the tension will ease between his parents. Fu'ad leaves his house and marries Latifa. Initially, his new marriage feels rejuvenating, but gradually he realizes how his age—he is twice the age of Latifa—does not help him cope with her lifestyle. His repeated attempts to meet her expectations start to affect his health and his work. On one occasion, a Parisian surgeon, Pierre, visits Egypt for ten days, during which his expertise will help many patients and junior doctors. Fu'ad fails to host Pierre properly because Latifa has parties scheduled for twenty consecutive days. Soon, the quality of medical service at Fu'ad's hospital starts to deteriorate as his schedule is jammed with the needs of *tafarnug*, including dance lessons, sauna, and massage sessions. The film takes a sharp turn when Fu'ad's servant, 'Abd al-Rahim ('Abd al-Warith 'Asar), visits him at his new villa to remind him of his duty as a surgeon. 'Abd al-Rahim says, "I come here to remind you, in the name of our long life together, that you are free to do what you wish at a personal level, but professionally you have a commitment towards your patients." When Fu'ad goes back to the hospital and almost loses the life of a patient because he did not have enough sleep the night before, he realizes that he made a mistake in marrying Latifa. Fu'ad gradually withdraws from Latifa's loud lifestyle and pays more attention to his work. His attitude upsets Latifa, who becomes indifferent. One night, she storms into his room and accuses him of insulting and humiliating her in front of her guests for refusing to greet them and preferring his books over their company. She screams at him saying, "If you cannot handle my lifestyle, why did you marry me? I cannot waste my life with an old man." Shocked at her attitude, Fu'ad leaves the house and returns to his former house, where his servant endearingly hosts him. He then complains to his former wife, Amina, that he cannot continue with Latifa and that he wants to divorce her and remarry her. He remains hesitant, however, because he will have to pay Latifa 20000 pounds as per the marriage contract. While the sum is not an issue for a rich man like Fu'ad, he hates the feeling of being used to fund Latifa's *tafarnug*. Amina, who refuses Fu'ad's offer to remarry, shares with him the news of her plan to marry her maternal cousin Tawfiq (Mukhtar 'Uthman). Meanwhile, Latifa starts eyeing another wealthy man while simultaneously having an affair with a singer. Having had enough, Fu'ad decides to pay Latifa the money and divorce her to save himself a bigger scandal.

Ahmad Kamil Mursi constructs *asala* in al-*Bayt al-Kabir*, through the character of Amina's younger son Kamal. Depicted as a cheerful young man, Kamal is a metaphor for an emergent egalitarian culture that calls for social welfare based on citizenship rights. He, like many of his fellow law students, is among "the masters of social protest," as his father likes to call them. Kamal helps people get free medical services at his father's hospital. He considers his father to be a role model who is keen on social justice and equal opportunities for all. Being highly invested in legal reform, Kamal, in the following scene, debates the issue of polygamy with his professor and colleagues at the university:

Student 1: This view is nonsense!
Student 2: You are the one who does not understand anything.
Hasan: Boy, he was sleeping during the lecture, and he did not understand what the professor said.
S1: That is not true. I understand the lecture better than anyone among you.
S3: If you understood the lecture, you would not argue that Islamic law does not favor polygamy.

CELEBRATING EMERGENT MODERNITY (ASALA) | 411

H: There is a condition for marrying more than one woman. It is as explicit as the sun in the textual sources of law. That condition is justice, which means a man must be able to support the two women equally.

S2: Yes. The sources of the law state that the condition of justice is too difficult to be achieved. For example, it is unlikely that one can spend an equal amount of time with each wife.

S4: Does any of you remember the hadith which the professor talked about last Wednesday?

S1: Yes, I remember it!

H: What was it?

S1: I had it in mind. [But I forgot it.]

H: [It reads] "Whoever had two wives..." [Interrupted]

S5: No. Please, Hasan, do not confuse the hadith of the Prophet (PBUH). [He opens a book to locate the hadith] Listen, please. The hadith reads, "He who has two wives, and he leans more towards one without the other, one side of his body shall come on the Day of Judgement leaning (*aʿwaj*)."

Students: That is it! Correct!

H: What is more [explicit] than the noble verse that reads, "And if you fear not to be just, then [marry] one [woman]. And you will not be just."

Kamal: Folks, do you care for an accurate answer? I think Islamic law prohibits polygamy.

S1: How can you use the word "prohibit," Kamal?

K: Is not the permissibility of marrying two women conditioned by the achievement of justice between the two women?

Students: Of course it is!

K: So, if achieving justice is impossible, it follows that marrying more than one woman is not possible. Therefore, the actual obligation (*wajib*) stated in verse is to marry only one woman.

S1: [Addressing Kamal] No! Mr. Philosopher. You stretched the interpretation excessively. Do you want to dictate something different from personal law?

K: The personal law must be amended.

Professor: What is going on here? Who is that person who wants to amend the law before even graduating? Is it you, Kamal? I agree with that. But won't you be a little bit more patient and have some mercy on scholars and intellectuals? Give them at least some time so that they can defend their views.

K: Sir, I am just saying that the spirit (*ruh*) of Islamic law prohibits polygamy. Therefore, the law has to regulate how marriage takes place so that people will not stray away from the spirit of the law.

Professor: No, Kamal, Islam is a religion that respects personal freedom and works on empowering it. This means that not all laws can be put in the hands of the rulers. Religion dictates respect for private life. At the same time, Islam wants the person to be held responsible for his action in front of God. What Kamal is suggesting is very far from the essence of democracy, which, as I always explain to you, is in the spirit of Islam.

K: So, do you agree that Islam does not permit polygamy absolutely?

P: Islam allows polygamy but restricts it through the condition of justice.

S1: So, the better [solution] is that man should divorce and marry again if marrying again is inevitable.

P: Why did you forget the hadith, which I always repeat to you? The hadith reads, "For God, divorce is the most hated permissibility." And now what! You want me to hold a lecture in class and outside it too. No, you will not fool me. Peace be upon you. [The professor exits the scene]

Students: Peace be upon you.

H: [Addressing S1] I hope now you are convinced.

S1: I still believe that in some circumstances, a second marriage is necessary.

K: How is it so? Are the destruction of the family and the misery of the first wife and children necessary?

S1: What would a man do if he falls for a woman other than his wife?

S2: Why would he do that?

S1: Well, one man did. Newspapers and magazines are talking and publishing their pictures. [He hands Kamal the magazine with his father's pictures] Here you go, Kamal, read this.

Kamal: What does this mean? What do you mean?

S1: It means your father better marry [his mistress] so people would say, "She is his wife," better than saying, "She is his mistress."

K: Shut up, rascal!

Figure 6.30 Contesting polygamy. Fakhir Fakhir as Kamal explaining his views on polygamy in *al-Bayt al-Kabir*, 1949.

The above dialogue poses several questions that interrogate the practice of polygamy in Islam in relation to questions of both justice and modernity. On one level, Kamal's friend, Hasan (Sa'id Khalil), champions the first, and advocates orthodox interpretations of the scriptures that favor polygamy as an absolute birthright for a Muslim male. The underlying premise here is, of course, male supremacy over women. Arguments for male supremacy include: God gave men greater physical strength and capacity; men are more rational, less emotional, and endowed with greater intellectual power; men were the exclusive recipient of divine favors, for God has sent only male prophets, not prophetesses; God first created man, then created woman for his comfort; the Qur'an sanctions that the testimony of two women was equal to that of one man and that a daughter's share was only half that of a son in the inheritance of property; because men may have as many as four wives at once, God gave them more powers. On another level, the law professor is against polygamy but is equally against the idea of "prohibition," which remains today the more dominant view in Egypt. This view is basically against the standardization of Islamic law through state interference in religion, and though it appears somehow pro-choice it still gives scholars more authority and dominance. On a third level, Kamal pushes the boundaries of the authority of the scholars and their consensus to create room for the long-standing tradition of *ijtihad*, through which Kamal prohibits polygamy. His views echo late nineteenth-century responses to colonialist polemics with regard to the institution of polygamy in Islam. Most famous in this regard, of course, are the modernist writings of many Muslim intellectuals (mainly from Egypt and India) like Qasim Amin, Sayyid Ahmad Khan, Chiragh Ali, Amir Ali, Shibli Nuʿmani, and Mumtaz Ali, who refutes polygamy and male supremacy. Their views on polygamy capitalize on Muhammad ʿAbdu's argument for the impossibility of achieving the condition of justice[9] to render polygamy practically illegal and un-Islamic. Most of these views rely on the Qurʾanic verse Q4:3, which reads, "If you fear that you will not deal fairly with the orphans, then marry such women as seem good to you, two, three, or four; but if you fear that you will not deal justly, then only one, or those whom your right hands possess. Thus, it is more likely that you will not commit injustice."[10] Verse Q4:129 further accentuates the impossibility of justice. It reads, "You will not be able to deal fairly between women, even if it is your ardent desire, but do not turn away from one altogether so that you leave her as if suspended. If you come to an accord and are reverent, truly God is Forgiving, Merciful."[11] To these intellectuals, these verses reveal that the Qurʾan prohibits polygamy because love is a condition for justice in a man–woman relationship, and a man is emotionally incapable of loving more than one woman equally at any given time. Chiragh Ali argued that reducing the unlimited polygamy practiced in Arabia was a preliminary measure toward its abolition. "But the final and effectual step taken by . . . [Muhammad] towards the abolition of this leading vice of the Arab community was his declaring in the Qurʾan that nobody could fulfill the condition of dealing equitably with more than one woman."[12] Mumtaz ʿAli went a step further by refuting all orthodox claims of male supremacy in his treatise *Women's Rights*. For example, he held that physical strength could not be considered a criterion for establishing the superiority of men over women. An animal like a donkey can carry more weight than a man, but that does not mean that it is superior to a man. Nor would physical strength establish the right to rule, even though in the dark ages it was "might makes right." However, with the advance of civilization and the emergence of modern institutions of government, the ruler must have understanding and compassion in order to gain the confidence of the ruled. It was not physical strength but wisdom that would determine the right to rule. Further, history shows that when women have been called upon to rule, they have ruled with great skill, wisdom, and justice. Mumtaz Ali also rejected the argument for men's greater intellectual capacity, holding that men and women are of the same species and there is no necessary connection between physical strength and the ability to reason. He reinterpreted the much-quoted verse from the Qur'an that was considered the basis for the justification of men's authority over women. According to the Qur'an, "Men are the managers of the affairs of women for that God has preferred in bounty one of them over another, and for that, they have expended of their property. Righteous women are, therefore, obedient."[13] For him, this verse only dealt with areas of activity like business transactions, where men had greater knowledge than women did, but it did not declare that women should be subordinate to men in all spheres of activity. In the case of court witnesses stating that the testimonies of two women were equal to that of one man, Mumtaz Ali argued that the Qur'an referred specifically to business matters, in which women might be less experienced than men. This lack of experience, however, was the result of social conditions, not an inherent defect in women's character. The Qur'an, however, did not make a distinction between the testimony of men and women in areas such as marriage, divorce, adultery, and so forth, where the sexes were equally experienced.[14]

It is with these views in mind that Kamal, in the above scene, argues for the prohibition of polygamy in Islam, even when polygamy becomes a suitable exit mechanism to preserve the family's social status. Here Kamal's *asala* further materializes as he stands up for his position despite the shame and the stigma he faces at school because of his father's affair. He then encourages his mother to refuse her humiliation and to insist on divorce. Kamal's stance in the Islamic context is often referred to as "avoiding the appropriation of the law to serve a personal interest" (*'adam ittiba' al-hawa*). Here Kamal refuses to use polygamy as a legal means to sugar-coat his social image and overcome his social defamation after the news of his father's extramarital affair.

Kamal's views are more practically put to the test through the position of Amina, which boldly refutes the orthodox argument in favor of polygamy.

Her character is juxtaposed with that of Latifa, whose *tafarnug* essentializes an Orientalist image of "Eastern" women as part of the harem, which is emphasized in the harem dance that Latifa performs at the charity party. Amina, on the other hand, is an active member of Cairene civil society in the 1940s. She is educated and has a passion for reading and watching films. She has raised two successful sons, and she has a unique relationship with both. She befriends them, respects them, and values their opinion, regardless of whether she agrees with them or not. She is also presented as a matriarch; she is invested in the unity and protection of her family. But simultaneously, she expresses a sense of herself as sovereign over her body and her mind. This is fascinatingly depicted in the way the actress Amina Rizq carries her body as she moves in the scenes. This role almost represents a rupture in her career, for it is the exact opposite of most of the roles that shaped her star aura. Her fame is built around playing tragedy roles; she appears mostly as an uneducated wife or a stay-at-home mother who, most of the time, does not have a say in her life. Her role in Henry Barakat's *Urid Hallan*/I Demand a Solution is iconic and representative of her star aura. But in *al-Bayt al-Kabir*, we see a completely different performance by Amina Rizq; she is a strong woman, calm, fashionably dressed, and very well-groomed. Unlike her very similar role in Mizrahi's *al-Tariq al-Mustaqim*/The Righteous Path, 1943, in *al-Bayt al-Kabir*, she confidently asks for a divorce and forces it on her husband. But as a matriarch, she cannot easily accept defeat. She sees her triumph not in getting a divorce but in treating the root of the problem, which is basically a male sense of supremacy and refusal to acknowledge female sexual desire. As the viewer looks forward to knowing how Amina would act, the director explores a number of possibilities based on different viewpoints expressed in the dialogues of different characters. There is the position of the elder son Galal and his wife Nadiya, who encourage Amina to be reunited with Fu'ad. To Nadiya and Galal, it is a problem of human weakness, and the rift in married life should be treated as a responsibility of the couple who need to work on healing their relationship. Galal blames his mother for giving up a lifelong partnership without a fight. For him, his social image will not be saved by divorce. As he put it, the social image became worse, because earlier, the gossip was that the father was *befriending* a woman with a bad reputation, but after his marriage, the gossip became that the father was *married* to a woman with a bad reputation. Amina respects her son's view that a couple's life is too valuable to be lost because of mistakes. But she disagrees with him because of the gender bias implied in his argument, for if the same mistake were committed by the wife, as opposed to the husband, public opinion would not be so tolerant. To her, Galal and Nadiya speak, of course, from the point of view of a young couple who are on their honeymoon and have not yet gone through twenty-six years of the ups and downs of a relationship. Another position is expressed through the Qur'anic verse which the radio airs. The verse is Q 2: 216, which reads, "Fighting has been prescribed for you, though it is hateful to you. But it may be that you hate a thing though it be good for you, and it may be that you love a thing though it be evil for you. God knows, and you know not."[15] The radio reinterprets this to mean that the idea of "fighting," mentioned in the verse, does not refer to not "waging war," but to not giving up without a fight, even when this choice appears difficult and less desirable. A difficult option might appear not good, but it might actually bring goodness, whereas an easy option that appears good might bring lots of misery. Hence the radio recommends that a wife should not give up on her husband, and she should not rush for divorce, because it makes her lonely and she loses a significant social capital. And sometimes, what appears to be an end can be a seed for a new and more powerful beginning. Amina does not like the radio commentary and turns it off. Her position is firmly centered around her sexuality. When Fu'ad comes back and asks for forgiveness, he talks about how he wants to retire in the village and go with Amina to enjoy life away from the city, and the following dialogue takes place:

> *Amina:* Are you asking me to come back to your life, or are you asking about how beautiful life in the countryside is? Now you are thinking of a quiet life because you are coming back to me, but when you were with Latifa, you were having all the fun. No. I am more beautiful than her and have more energy than her to live life fully. When you hated her the most, you bought her a bracelet for fifteen hundred pounds. If I asked you for a diamond necklace, what would you say? This is the truth. Why are you upset about the truth? Did you forget that after twenty-six years of marriage, you simply and without hesitation shelved me like a book? To thine own self be true. If Latifa were to come back now and ask for

forgiveness, what would you do? You would, of course, forgive her and get reunited with her.

Fu'ad: No. I cannot forget or forgive.

A: If you cannot, how can you expect me to forget and forgive just like that and simply reunite with you? You are asking me as if you are asking your tailor to make you a suit.

F: I have faith in your mercy and forgiveness.

A: No way.

F: And you dared to invite me to your wedding!

A: If you cannot come, do not.

The most compelling aspect of the above dialogue is Ahmad Kamil Mursi's investment in asserting Amina's sense of self as sovereign over her body and mind by emphasizing her sexual desire. For example, she does not allow Fu'ad to kiss her hand. Kissing someone's hand is a symbol for asking for their blessing, and she refuses to give him her blessings because she is shocked to realize that Fu'ad sees her as a mere object, a book that he can shelve until he feels an urge to read it again. It hurts her to find out that a woman is not seen as an

Figure 6.31 Asserting female sexual desire. Amina Rizq as Amina confronting her husband in *al-Bayt al-Kabir*, 1949.

equal human being who has sexual desire just like a man and that she is capable of being unfaithful to Fu'ad. That is why, when Fu'ad questions her intent to marry, her answer becomes "Why not, do not I have a desire like you?"(*wa ana malish nifs walla eih*). What she wants him to understand is that the only reason she does not follow her sexual desire is her ethical commitment to the relationship. The director further invests in emphasizing Amina's assertion of her sexual desire as a norm and a right when she is depicted refusing Fu'ad's proposal to retire to the countryside and says, "No. I have more youthful blood than her, and I am more beautiful than her. I want not just to live but thrive." By the same token, she plans to marry her cousin Tawfiq. The latter had proposed to her back in the days when she was young, but she favored Fu'ad over him. It is Tawfiq who helps Amina reveal and defeat Latifa's trap. When Latifa travels to Alexandria to attend the Red Crescent party, she spends the night in a hotel with another man. They fill out the registration with fake names such as Sayyid *bey* 'Abd al-Gawwad and his wife. Tawfiq notices her at the hotel reception and follows her around. He asks a photographer to take pictures of her. When Amina comes to know about her infidelity, she asks Tawfiq to make sure, because his claims are serious accusations. Here, the director is emphasizing Amina's ethical conduct, which derives from the Qur'anic maxim that discourages believers from making accusations of adultery without evidence. When Latifa comes to meet Amina and asks for the twenty thousand, Amina tests Tawfiq's claims and doubts by speaking to Latifa using punning; she tells the story of a woman who after the Red Crescent Association party took her lover to a hotel; Amina then tells Latifa the number of the room where she stayed. She shows her the pictures that were taken of her and her lover and threatens to share them with a lawyer who can sue her for infidelity. When Latifa falls for the trap set by Tawfiq and Amina, the former gives up on the twenty thousand pounds required for the divorce. It is Tawfiq also whom the director employs to depict Fua'd's readiness to admit Amina's sexual desire. Tawfiq visits Fu'ad at the hospital and challenges him to accept his defeat as Tawfiq had done twenty-six years previously. Reconciliation occurs, but only after Fuad accepts that Amina, like him, also has sexual desire, and hence we see the movie's happy ending. While Kamil Mursi's film associates *asala* with Islamic legal reform and male acknowledgment of female sexual desire, Yusuf Wahbi in *Bayumi Afandi*/Mr. Bayumi, 1949 engages with similar issues, focusing primarily on the reinterpretation of the Islamic notion of unbelief (*kufr*).

10. May Man Perish! How Ungrateful He Is!

Bayumi Afandi/Mr. Bayumi, 1949 tells the story of Bayumi Mustafa (Yusuf Wahbi), a middle-aged Cairene man who owns a small kiosk for fixing watches and clocks in the popular neighborhood of al-Hamzawi at al-Gamaliyya in Cairo. Bayumi likes his neighbor Zubayda (Mimi Shakib), who refuses his repeated marriage proposals because Bayumi's income is not enough to meet her standard of living, which is shaped mainly by *tafarnug*. In his neighborhood, Bayumi is known for his efficiency, hard work, and empathy; he does not overcharge his customers and sometimes fixes their clocks for free. People call him *effendi* as he does not dress in a galabiya and because he is literate, but he favors the local title efficient craftsman (*usta*) as he takes pride in his profession. He runs his business without receipts or checks; he relies on integrity and word of mouth. Bayumi's profession is crushed under *Khawaga* Hernan's big business, even though the latter's watches and craftsmanship are not of high quality. Hernan does not hire locals; he discriminates against his customers and favors only Egyptians of European ancestry. Bayumi's life changes dramatically when he meets another watchmaker, a *khawaga* by the name of Monsieur Gerard. His watch, a Zone brand that he has worked hard to develop, has suddenly stopped working. Monsieur Gerard's friend (Amin Wahba) arranges a meeting between Bayumi and Gerard to have the latter's watch fixed. Bayumi assures them that the watch does not have any industry errors. It is only a matter of not considering the climate in Egypt while making the watch; Egypt's weather is hotter, and owing to sweat and dust the watch malfunctioned. Bayumi marks a difference between Gerard and Hernan by calling the former our *khawaga* (*khawagitna*), implying that Gerard represents the idea of a fair-share economy, of business adventure and of investment that is driven by partnership, growing the local economy, opening job opportunities for locals and allowing people like Bayumi to create a name for themselves both in Egypt and Sudan. The partnership between Gerard and Bayumi results in several projects, starting with the purchase of Hernan's shop and eventually leading to the opening a local factory that manufactures Zone watches, creating many employment opportunities for locals.

When Bayumi becomes rich, he marries Zubayda, who finds in this marriage an opportunity to cover up for her pregnancy after having an affair with her employer, Shawkat bey (Farid Shawqi). Zubayda gives birth to two children. The eldest is Nabil (Fakhir Fakhir), and the youngest is Zinat (Fatin Hamam). Bayumi's life takes a sharp turn when Shawkat bey decides on his death-bed to repent. He invites Bayumi to tell him that Nabil is not Bayumi's son. Shocked at the news, Bayumi has to decide between getting a divorce and losing custody of his daughter or living with his family without revealing that he knows about his wife's infidelity. Taking the second choice, Bayumi raises the two children equally and tolerates his ill-treatment at the hands of his wife and her son, Nabil. They are both ashamed of Bayumi for not being as modern as they expect him to be. Meanwhile, Bayumi's daughter Zinat falls in love with a young doctor named Kamal (Kamal Husayn), whose siblings file a paternity case against him to deprive him of his inheritance. Nabil, his fiancée Ulfat (Ivun Madi), his mother, and his father-in-law, Shukri pasha (Sirag Munir), oppose Zinat's marriage to Kamal. At the same time, Bayumi stands with the young couple and supports them. Vainly trying to convince his wife and son that Kamal should not be blamed for his partner's choices, Bayumi reveals to Nabil that he is not Bayumi's son. When Nabil suffers a nervous breakdown, Bayumi regrets that he cannot control his anger and reveals his life secret. Nabil breaks off his engagement with Ulfat and supports his sister's choices in life. The movie ends with Kamal and Zinat getting married, Ulfat returning to Nabil, and Bayumi continuing to live with Zubayda, who now realizes how generous her husband is and renounces her *tafarnug*.

Bayumi Afandi, like many of the films discussed in this book, marks its character's *asala* by its harsh critique of *tafarnug*. For example, Bayumi does not like wearing a collar with a shirt and tells his wife, who insists that he wears one: "Cannot we imitate Europeans in things better than this dog collar?" (*ya'ni ma niqallidishi il-afrang illa fi tawq[tuq] il-kilab da*). He further suggests that using a collar with a shirt should have been canceled along with the 1936 Treaty. It is a statement that sees *tafarnug* as a byproduct of colonialist modernity enforced by the reality of the British occupation, which it was hoped would end, along with the 1936 treaty, after World War II. In another scene, Zubayda finds Bayumi oiling the clocks around the house. She says,

Figure 6.32 Advertisement for *Bayumi Afandi*. Promotional scenes depicting Yusuf Wahbi, Mimi Shakib, Fakhir Fakhir, and Fatin Hamama in *Bayumi Afandi*. Image from *Al-Ithnayn*.

CELEBRATING EMERGENT MODERNITY (*ASALA*) | 423

Figure 6.33 Report on *Bayumi Afandi* in *al-Ithnayn* magazine. Ministers of Social Affairs exchanging views while watching the premiere of *Bayumi Afandi*, 1949.

Figure 6.34 Yusuf Wahbi greeting the audience. Premiere of *Bayumi Afandi*, 1949. Image from *Al-Ithnayn*.

"Man, are not you ever going to learn how to become modern (*hatitmaddin*); send some worker from your factory to fix it." To Zubyada, being modern means embracing *tafarnug* as a supremacist ideology. Like Lady Rudy in Kamal Salim's *al-Mazahir*, Zubayda does not want Bayumi to call himself a watch-man (*sa'ati*). Instead, she wants him to call himself a jewelry seller (*gawahrigi*). And to this Bayumi responds, "I am a watch-man, and I am not a jewelry seller. It is like someone is a cart driver (*'arbagi*) and they call him chauffeur. It is all driving." For the same reason, she bans cooking the popular Egyptian dish *bisara*, which Bayumi likes, and enforces a French menu in the house. When Bayumi's daughter brings him a collar to wear along with his shirt so he can meet and greet guests, Bayumi questions why his wife insists that he looks like a mannequin in a department store. Here, Wahbi presents how *tafarnug* regulates the amour-propre of its subjects and turns them into theatrical stages instead of them *staging and restaging modernity* (i.e. performing and reperforming it). Wahbi is equally invested in critiquing *tafarnug*'s ridicule and appropriation of metaphors representing Islam. For example, Bayumi's wife wants to force her daughter, Zinat, to marry an older man who has been awarded the social title "bey." Bayumi, who stands up for his daughter, comments that his daughter is free to choose her partner and can reject anybody even if he has the title "bey." Bayumi says, "So what if he is a 'bey,' he is not PBUH." Here Wahbi lampoons the fact that his wife's *tafarnug* makes her speak of the suitor as if he is more perfect than the Prophet Muhammad. If the Prophet can be rejected as a suitor, so can Zubayda's candidate. And the implication is that the norm in Islam is to challenge authority, for no authority is holy, dignified, or above being questioned. Here Wahbi brings up the saying attributed to Imam Malik: "Except for the one who lies in this grave [i.e. the Prophet], everybody's arguments are to be questioned and debated."

Yet condemning *tafarnug* is not the only marker of *asala* in this film. Underscoring inclusion and social justice as core values of modernity is another, more important indicator. This is evident in the position of Bayumi and his daughter Zinat regarding her fiancé's paternity case. Kamal is raised and educated in London, but his British education does not make him ashamed of his life situation, namely, being born out of wedlock. When he defends himself in the personal law court, he emphasizes that he is not ashamed of his birth, even if society looks down upon it. He says to the judge that even if his father is not his father, he is not responsible for that. When the court dismisses the case for lack of evidence and Kamal remains disheartened by the scandal and how public opinion continuously condemns him, Bayumi reminds Kamal that all that matters is man's willpower and perseverance, which enables him to resist unkindness. When Nabil objects to Bayumi's empathy toward Kamal and invites Bayumi to see the difference between kindness and foolishness, Bayumi, who does not describe Kamal as illegitimate, tells Nabil, "Do not be harsh on a child of happenstance (*ibn al-sudfa*)," for, after all, Kamal is but a creature among God's many creatures that need to be treated humanely and mercifully. To Bayumi, what matters is man's ability to be self-made; as the Arabic proverb goes, "*la taqul asli wa fasli abdan innma asul al-fata man qal ha ana dha*" (Thou shall not make a name for thyself by relying on the deeds of your ancestors, let thy deeds make thy name). He tells Kamal that by becoming a doctor, whose job is to heal mankind, eliminate pain and save lives, Kamal has fulfilled this condition and thus is worthy to marry Bayumi's daughter.

From the early scenes of this film, Wahbi both shows and tells his audience that Bayumi's *asala* is a host domain for metaphors representing Islam. Bayumi is a devout Muslim. For example, Bayumi hangs a phrase invoking the notion of *tawakkul* on his kiosk; he hears the call to prayer on Friday and answers it by leaving his kiosk and heading to the mosque to pray; we see him praying inside the mosque and talking to his spiritual guide Shaykh Darwish ('Abd al-Warith 'Asar). Bayumi also prays at dawn after a long night spent awake fixing clocks and watches on time. When he marries Zubayda, Bayumi's spiritual guide Shaykh Dariwh administers the marriage. This reminds Bayumi that mercy and affection are the foundation of marriage, as per the Qur'anic verse Q 30: 21, which reads, "And among His signs is that He created mates for you from among yourselves, that you might find rest in them, and He established affection and mercy between you. Truly in that are signs for a people who reflect."[16] When Zubayda gives birth to her children, we see Bayumi praying in the hallway of his apartment and remembering members of the Prophet's household (*ahl al-bayt*) such as al-Sayyida Nafisa and Imam al-Husayn. And he also remembers his spiritual guide, Shaykh Darwish. Rituals are not the only metaphors representing Islam in *Bayumi Afandi*; Wahbi weaves in two Qur'anic notions in this film. The first is the concept of pardon (*'afw*), and the second is the concept of unbelief (*kufr*), which he reinterprets as ingratitude to further construct inclusion as a marker of *asala* and a catalyst for social change.

Wahbi ties Bayumi's *asala* to the Qur'anic notion of pardon (*'afw*) as soon as Bayumi discovers his wife's infidelity. In one scene, Bayumi rushes to his villa and goes straight to the room of his alleged child, Nabil. As he holds the boy in his arms and is about to throw him from the balcony, Shaykh Darwish's shadow appears to him to externalize his conscience and remind him that, as a believer, he should beware God and not commit an injustice, for the child is innocent and bears no responsibility. Shaykh Darwish then reminds Bayumi of the Qur'anic maxim that reads "None shall bear the burden of another," which appears in many Quranic verses, including the following:

> Say, "Shall I seek a lord other than God, while He is Lord of all things? No soul does evil save itself, and *none shall bear the burden of another*. Then unto your Lord is your return, and He will inform you of that wherein you differed." Q6:164[17]

> Whosoever is rightly guided is only rightly guided for the sake of his own soul, and whosoever is astray is only astray to its detriment. *None shall bear the burden of another*. And never do We punish till We have sent a messenger. Q17:15[18]

> *And none shall bear the burden of another*. And though a burdened soul should call for its burden to be borne, naught of it will be borne, even if it be kin. Thou warnest only those who fear their Lord unseen and perform the prayer. And whosoever purifies himself purifies himself only for his own soul. And unto God is the journey's end. Q35:18[19]

> If you do not believe, surely God is beyond needing you. He is not pleased with disbelief for His servants. And if you are grateful, He is pleased therewith for you; *and none shall bear the burden of another*. Then unto your Lord is your return, and He shall inform you of that which you used to do. Truly He knows what lies within breasts. Q39:7[20]

> *That none shall bear the burden of another*. Q53:38[21]

This maxim motivates Bayumi to choose to pardon, and thus when he enters his room after leaving Nabil's room he finds solace in the Qur'anic emphasis

Figure 6.35 Externalizing Bayumi's conscience. On the left 'Abd al-Warith 'Asar, as Shaykh Darwish's shadow, appears to Bayumi, played by Yusuf Wahbi, right. *Bayumi Afandi*, 1949.

on God being the Most Forgiving and Merciful. The frame holding verse Q5:39 on Bayumi's wall further amplifies pardon, forgiveness, and mercy as the better path for remedying his situation. When we then see Bayumi for the first time after the children have grown up, the same meanings are echoed through another verse, Q25:70, which Bayumi reads while sitting next to the bed of his daughter, who is sick. The verse reads, "Save for those who repent, believe, and perform righteous deeds. For them, God will replace their evil deeds with good deeds, and God is Forgiving, Merciful."[22] The verses help Wahbi fill the time gap between the two scenes, transition, and establish unity and continuity.

Both scenes emphasize that Bayumi as a believer, instead of responding to injustice by committing another injustice, chooses to follow the Qur'anic notion of *'afw*; here, the toleration of sin happens in the hope that the sinner can one day redeem herself through repentance, faith, and doing good deeds.

Asala also features in this film through the correlation between *tafarnug* and the Qur'anic notion of *kufr*, which is commonly translated as "disbelief,"

Figure 6.36 Qur'an used to transition between scenes (1). Q5:39. *Bayumi Afandi*, 1949.

Figure 6.37 Qur'an used to transition between scenes (2). Yusuf Wahbi as Bayumi Afandi, left, reading Q25:70. In the middle, Mimi Shakib as Zubayda, and on the right Fatin Hamama as Zinat. *Bayumi Afandi*, 1949.

or "unbelief" or "infidelity." But here, Wahbi foregrounds the interpretation of *kufr* as "ingratitude." For example, when the doctor comes to check on Zinat, Bayumi enters the room with a incense holder to read the Qur'an near his daughter in the hope of lifting the evil eye of envy (*hasad*) that has befallen his daughter's health. Bayumi then explains himself and says, "I know you will say I am old-fashioned, but envy is mentioned in the Qur'an." When Nabil's *tafarnug* makes him ridicule his father's practices and describe his father as a joke, Bayumi responds by reading verse Q26:6: "Truly it is the same for the disbelievers whether thou warnest them or warnest them not; they do not believe."[23] When Wahbi makes Bayumi use this verse to comment on his son's attitude, he is not referring to the son as a non-Muslim or unbeliever. Rather, Wahbi signifies Nabil's *tafarnug*, which makes him supremacist, arrogant, self-centered, and constantly *ungrateful*. After all, Bayumi did not have to raise Nabil. Instead of "disbelievers" and "disbelief," Wahbi thus foregrounds the meaning of *kufr* in the verse as "ingratitude." Frank Griffel's masterpiece on the treatment of apostates in Islam sheds much light on the meaning of *kufr* and the treatment of apostates in Islam.[24] He argues that the Muslim judgment against apostates has in recent years been applied in cases of publicly expressed conviction that contradict the generally accepted foundations of the history of Islam. Up until the fifth/eleventh century, theological debates could not have applied the judgment of apostasy (*irtidad*), which could not have been used against Muslims who voiced opinions that were regarded as unbelief. The rules for this earlier period were written down by al-Shafi'i in his *Kitab al-Umm*. His interpretation of the legal institution of *istitaba* leads to the acknowledgment that the judgment of *irtidad* is applicable only in a minimal number of cases. Al-Shafi'i's guidelines, based on earlier judgments within the Kufan tradition, gained widespread acceptance in the Hanafi, Hanbali, and Shafi'i schools of law. A first change can be noted in the middle of the fifth/eleventh century, when authors such as al-Mawardi and Abu Ya'la argued for a less generous application of the *istitaba*. Two generations later, al-Ghazali (d. 1111) and his contemporaries, such as Ibn 'Aqil (d. 1119), did not restrict the judgment of *irtidad* to cases of openly declared apostasy. Al-Ghazali develops reasoning, fully aware of the change in law and the deviation from long-established principles. His condemnation of three key statements of the philosophers (*falasifa*), expressed in his

Tahafut al-falasifa, would be impossible without his identification of *kufr* with *irtidad* in earlier works. However, looking back on the formative period of Islam, Marilyn Robinson Waldman in her classic study on the development of the concept of *kufr* in the Qur'an sheds a great deal of light on the shifting meaning of the Arabic word *kufr* by tracing how between the first Meccan period and the end of revelation (the end of the Qur'an), the meaning of *kufr* gradually moves away from "ingratitude" and comes closer to "disbelief" and "unbelief."[25] During the first and second Meccan periods, *kufr* refers to human "ingratitude" by denying the many bounties that come from God and how humans feel themselves to be self-sufficient and, for this reason, become niggardly. This aspect of *kufr* as ingratitude is sharpened by the frequent presence of the root used as its opposite, to give thanks (*shukr*) or to be grateful. By denying God's blessings and refusing to be grateful, and believing in one's own self-sufficiency, a human becomes *kafir*. These meanings appear most clearly in the debate between God and Iblis in Q7:11–18 below:

> And We have indeed established you upon the earth and placed means of livelihood for you therein. Little do you give thanks! 11 Indeed, We created you, then We formed you, then We said unto the angels, "Prostrate yourselves before Adam." And they all prostrated, save Iblis; he was not among those who prostrated. 12 He said, "What prevented thee from prostrating when I commanded thee?" He said, "I am better than him. Thou hast created me from fire, while Thou hast created him from clay." 13 He said, "Get down from it! It is not for thee to wax arrogant here. So go forth! Thou art surely among those who are humbled." 14 He said, "Grant me respite till the Day they are resurrected." 15 He said, "Truly thou art among those granted respite." 16 He said, "Because Thou hast caused me to err, I shall surely lie in wait for them on Thy straight path. 17 Then I shall come upon them from in front of them and from behind them, and from their right and from their left. And Thou wilt not find most of them *thankful*."[26]

Not being *thankful* and grateful becomes the fundamental challenge of temptation in the Qur'an's creation story. In other words, Adam's most significant challenge on earth is not not to sin, but to constantly remain *grateful* and *thankful*.

Wahbi's correlation of *tafarnug* with *kufr* as "ingratitude" is further emphasized in Zinat's choice of marrying Kamal, despite the paternity case. When the news of Zinat's decision to marry Kamal spreads and Nabil's fiancé, Ulfat, comes to know that Zinat insists on the marriage despite the case against Kamal, the following dialogue takes place:

Ulfat: Listen, Zinat, allow me to tell you that I do not accept your marriage to Dr. Kamal

Zinat: Did I ever ask for your permission?

U: Think a little bit. Do you think you are in love with him? Your feelings are mere sympathy. This feeling is not love. It is not worth it to sacrifice yourself.

Z: You are wrong, Ulfat. I know Kamal's morals well, and I respect him.

U: That is all fine. But still, how can you handle this shameful case raised against him?

Z: This is precisely why I insist on marrying him.

U: But people do not understand this position, Zinat.

Z: I do not want to know people who do not have empathy.

U: When you marry him, all your upper-class friends (*ashabik il-kuwayyisin*) will scorn you, and nobody will visit you.

Z: I am fine with that too.

U: Is that so? I see. Alright, you know how much your brother and I love one another, don't you?

Z: Yes, and [my choice should not] prevent you from marrying my brother.

U: Your persistence in following your views will prevent me. I will have to break up with your brother. Do not forget I am the daughter of Shukri pasha Murad. Neither my father nor I can accept this stigma in our family.

Z: Confess then that your pride drives your views. Where is your human empathy?

U: Forget about this empty talk. The likes of Kamal are doomed to be socially inferior.

Z: This is the view passed on by selfish people like you.

U: Are you insulting me? Did you forget I am the daughter of Shukri pasha Murad?

> *Z:* I am the daughter of the self-made man Bayumi Mustaf, the watch fixer who started from below zero.
> *U:* [Sarcastically] Obviously, there is a huge difference between the two names.
> *Z:* Obviously, there is a huge difference between arrogance (*ghatrasa*) and humbleness (*tawadu'*); between mercy (*rahma*) and evil (*sharr*). "May man perish! How ungrateful is he!" [Q80:7].[27]

In the above scene, Zinat's understanding of modernity inspires her belief that equality between genders includes a woman's ability to stand up for her choices and, in this context, not to refrain from healing her partner; as she tells her mother, "I am educated enough to understand that a woman can share her man's pains." She does not admire Kamal for his wealth and British education, but for his ability to overcome the social stigma caused by the paternity case. But Ulfat's understanding of modernity is shaped by *tafarnug*. She admires Nabil for his wealth, ability to master British and French leisure activities, and mastery of foreign languages. When Nabil suffers a nervous breakdown, all that matters to Ulfat is that the newspaper headlines talk about how a young man had a nervous breakdown after Ulfat Murad broke up with him. When Zinat describes Ulfat's attitude as *kufr*, she underscores how *tafarnug* sustains "ingratitude" and promotes a culture of greed that nurtures the supremacy of the colonizer, lack of social injustice, and social exclusion. Similarly, when Shukri pasha on one occasion comments that they live in such "speedy" times, for the 1940s are the age of speed and Egyptians should forget about the proverb that reads "safety is slowing down" (*fi al-t'anni al-salama*), Bayumi smiles, because Shukri (who is an adherent of *tafarnug* and whose estate will soon be confiscated to pay his debt, and who thus sees his daughter's marriage to Bayumi's son as an exit) completely misses the meaning of the proverb. To Bayumi, the proverb does not refer to "slowing down" to discourage action. It rather discourages "action without thorough reasoning," which is necessary to assess risks and avoid rushed decisions. To Bayumi, Nabil and his father-in-law neither reason nor slow down; they merely adhere to *tafarnug* to nourish a sense of supremacy that is discouraged in the Qur'an in Q17:37. The verse reads, "And walk not . . . [vaingloriously and arrogantly] upon the earth; surely thou shalt not penetrate the earth, nor reach the mountains in height."[28]

Bayumi's problem with *tafarnug* is thus not its fascination with foreign everyday life practices, or speaking French and English in everyday speech. Zinat, for example, sometimes speaks French, but unlike Nabil, she does not use her skill to claim that she is superior to others. Bayumi despises Nabil's *tafarnug* as it encourages the ill-treatment of his father, which, he repeatedly reminds his son, is discouraged in the Q17:23, which reads, "Thy Lord decrees that you worship none but Him and be virtuous to parents. Whether one or both of them reaches old age, say not to them 'Uff!' nor chide them, but speak unto them a noble word."[29]

Yusuf Wahbi's repeated reference to Islamic sources should not be mistaken for an interest in promoting an Islamist agenda in today's more contemporary sense of the word "Islamist." To Wahbi and his generation of filmmakers, the screen functioned as a supplemental secular public sphere that can accentuate the crucial difference between Islam as a faith, Islam as an ideology, and Islam as a man-made body of legal knowledge that has the "vital semantic potentials" to be translated into secular idioms, in a "universally accessible language." Wahbi simply calls attention to the importance of decoding the ethical intuitions of religious traditions, which could be incorporated into a post-secular stance that finds an ally in religious sources of meaning in challenging the forces of colonialist projects of domination. More importantly, his films, including *Bayumi Afandi*, show that such a task falls not only to experts (these here being the 'ulama'/theologians) and religious citizens, but also to all citizens—both religious and secular—who wish to engage in the public use of reason. Wahbi and his generation of filmmakers are what Charles Taylor describes as Islam's internal critics; their films were attempts to create a space for religion to exist among predominantly secular efforts of modernization while simultaneously safeguarding the screen as a secular domain that aims primarily at revealing the ideology of the powerful (here, the dominant, and exclusionist modernity).

Notes

1. Muhammad 'Abd al-Wahhab, *Mudhakkirat Musiqar al-Jil* (Beirut: Dar al-Thaqafa, 1969), 1–12.
2. See Chapter 4.
3. A popular Egyptian song of Turkish origin.

4. Lucie Ryzova, *The Age of the Efendiyya: Passages to Modernity in National-Colonial Egypt* (Oxford: Oxford University Press, 2014), 74.
5. Peter A. Corning, "Fair Shares: Beyond Capitalism and Socialism, or the Biological Basis of Social Justice," *Politics and the Life Sciences* 22, no. 2 (2003): 12–32, http://www.jstor.org/stable/4236707 (last accessed December 12, 2020).
6. Seyyed Hossein Nasr, Caner K. Dagli, Maria Massi Dakake, Joseph E. B. Lumbard, and Mohammed Rustom, *The Study Quran* (Sydney: HarperOne, 2015), 3082, Kindle edition.
7. Rudolph Peters, "Egypt and the Age of the Triumphant Prison," *Shariʿa, Justice and Legal Order* (Leiden: Brill, 2020), 238–77.
8. "Ahmad Kamil Mursi al-Sira al-Dhatiyya," *Kunuz Maspero*, https://www.maspero.eg/ (last accessed December 12, 2020).
9. Rashid Rida, *Tarikh al-Ustadh al-Imam al-Shaykh Muhammad ʿAbduh: Wa-Fihi Tafsil Siratihi wa-Khulasat Sirat Munqidh al-Sharq al-Hakim wa-l-Islam Jamal al-Din al-Afghani*, 2 vols. (Egypt: Maṭbaʿat al-Manar, 1906), 113–19.
10. Nasr, *The Study Quran*, 545.
11. Nasr, *The Study Quran*, 562.
12. Mansoor Moaddel, "Religion and Women: Islamic Modernism versus Fundamentalism," *Journal for the Scientific Study of Religion* 37, no. 1 (1998): 108–30.
13. Ibid.
14. Ibid.
15. Nasr, *The Study Quran*, 18.
16. Nasr, *The Study Quran*, 2615.
17. Ibid., 934.
18. Ibid., 1827.
19. Ibid., 2798.
20. Ibid., 2973.
21. Ibid., 3425.
22. Ibid., 2350.
23. Ibid., 93.
24. Frank Griffel, "Toleration and Exclusion: Al-Shafi'i and al-Ghazali on the Treatment of Apostates," *Bulletin of the School of Oriental and African Studies, University of London* 64, no. 3 (2001): 339–54.

25. Marilyn Robinson Waldman, "The Development of the Concept of Kufr in the Qur'an," *Journal of the American Oriental Society* 88, no. 3 (1968): 442–55.
26. Nasr, *The Study Quran*, 1078.
27. Ibid., 3903.
28. Ibid., 1829.
29. Ibid., 1828.

Bibliography

Archival and Unpublished Sources

Great Britain, Public Records Office, Kew Gardens
FO141   English Education and Culture Reviews
FO 371   Limiting French Culture in Egypt after the War
P News 2388 Report on the Distribution of Films in Egypt
FO 395   Films/Film Library for Egyptian Ministry of Education
FO 371   Publicity in Egypt for Her Majesty's Government's Rearmament Programs
CO 323   British Cultural Propaganda
P 553   Concerns about the Representation of British Officers

Arabic Periodicals

All periodicals are printed in Cairo.

Akhir Sa'a
Al-Ahram
Al-Ahram al-Masa'i
Al-Azhar
Al-Basir
Al-Dunya al-Musawwara
Al-Hilal
Al-Ikhwan al-Muslimin al-Nisff Shahriyya
Al-Jarida
Al-Kawakib
Al-Liwa'
Al-Manar
Al-Mahrusa

Al-Masrah
Al-Minbar
Al-Muqattam
Al-Nadhir
Al-Waqa'i' al-Misriyya
Ruza al-Yusuf

Published Diaries and Memoirs

Karim, Muhammad, *Mudhakkirat Muhammad Karim*. Ed. Madkur Thabit. Cairo: Akadimiyyat al-Funun, 2006.

Mumtaz, I'itdal, *Mudhakkirat Raqibat Sinima*. Cairo: al-Hay'a al-'Ama al-Misriyya lil-Kitab, 1985.

Wahbi, Yusuf, *'Ishtu alf 'am: mudhakkirat fannan al-sha'b Yusuf Wahbi*. 5 vols. Cairo: Dar al-Ma'arif, 1973.

Films

Abu Halmus. Directed by Ibrahim Hilmy. Cairo: Nihas Film, 1947.

Al-'Azima. Directed by Kamal Salim. Cairo: Sharikat Misr lil-Tamthil wa-l-Sinima, 1939.

Al-Bayt al-Kabir. Directed by Ahmad Kamil Mursi. Cairo: Studio Misr, 1949.

Al-Mazahir. Directed by Kamal Salim. Cairo: Film al-Qawmiyya lil-Tawzi' wa-l-Tijara, 1945.

Al-Warda al-Bayda'. Directed by Muhammad Karim. Cairo: 'Abd al-Wahhab Film, 1933.

Al-Zawja al-Sabi'a. Directed by Ibrahim 'Imara. Cairo: Bahna Film and Studio Galal, 1950.

Al-Zawaja al-Thaniya. Directed by Salah Abu Sayf. Cairo: Sharikat al-Qahira lil-Intaj al-Sinima'i, 1967.

'Aris min Istanbul. Directed by Yusuf Wahbi. Cairo: Nihas Film, 1941.

Bayumi Afandi. Directed by Yusuf Wahbi. Cairo: Studio Misr, 1949.

Bint Dhawat. Directed by Yusuf Wahbi. Cairo: Nihas Film, 1942.

Dunya. Directed by Muhammad Karim. Cairo: Nihas Film, 1946.

Ibn al-Haddad. Directed by Yusuf Wahbi. Cairo: Nihas Film, 1944.

Khadra wa-l-Sindibad al-Qibli. Directed by al-Sayyid Ziyada. Cairo: Sharikat Aflam al-Sha'ab, 1951.

Layla Bint al-Rif. Directed by Tugu Mizrahi. Cairo: Sharikat al-Aflam al-Misriyya, 1941.

Mamnu' al-Hub. Directed by Muhammad Karim. Cairo: 'Abd al-Wahhab Film, 1938.

Man al-Gani. Directed by Ahmad Badrkhan. Cairo: Nihas Film, 1944.

Mughamarat Khadra. Directed by al-Sayyid Ziyada. Cairo: Sharikat Aflam al-Sha'ab, 1950.

Safir Jahannam. Directed by Yusuf Wahbi. Cairo: Nihas Film, 1945.

Salama fi Kahyr. Directed by Niyazi Mustafa. Cairo: Studio Misr, 1937.

Shaykh Hasan. Directed Husayn Sidqi. Cairo: Aflam Misr al-Haditha, 1951.

Talaq Su 'ad Hanim. Directed by Anwar Wagdi. Cairo: Anwar Wagdi, 1948.

Yahya al-Hub. Directed by Muhammad Karim. Cairo: 'Abd al-Wahhab Film, 1939.

Yawm Sa'id. Directed by Muhammad Karim. Cairo: 'Abd al-Wahhab Film, 1939.

Zaynab. Directed by Muhammad Karim. Cairo: Nihas Film, 1952.

Secondary Sources

Abdelfattah, Heba Arafa. "The *Maslaha* of Film Production in Pre-Revolutionary Egypt, 1896–1952: A Sanctioning Apparatus or Covert Censorship." *Journal of Islamic and Muslim Studies 2*, no. 2 (2017): 1–37.

'Abd al-Wahhab, Muhammad. *Mudhakkirat Musiqar al-Jil*. Beirut: Dar al-Thaqafa, 1969.

Abi-Mershed, Osama. *Apostles of Modernity: Saint-Simonians and the Civilizing Mission in Algeria*. Stanford, CA: Stanford University Press, 2010.

Abul-Magd, Zeinab. *Imagined Empires: A History of Revolt in Egypt*. Berkeley: University of California Press, 2013.

Abu Shadi, 'Ali. *Al-sinima wa-l-siyasa*. Dimashq: Dar al-Mada lil-Thaqafa wa-l-Nashr, 2000.

Abu Zayd, Nasr Hamid. *Al-tajdid wa-l-tahrim w-l-ta'wil*. Beirut: al-Markaz al-Thaqafi al-'Arabi, 2010.

Abu Zakariyya, Yahya. *Rawdat al-talibin wa-'umdat al-muftin*. 12 vols. Ed. Zuhayr al-Shawish. Beirut: al-Maktab al-Islami, 1991.

Abu Zuhra, Muhammad. *Ibn Hanbal*. Cairo: Dar al-Fikr al-'Arabi, 1965.

Adams, Charles. *Islam and Modernism in Egypt: A Study of the Modern Reform Movement Inaugurated by Muhammad 'Abduh*. New York: Russell & Russell, 1968.

Adorno, Theodor and Max Horkheimer. "The Culture Industry: Enlightenment as Mass Deception." In *Dialectic of Enlightenment*, 94–137. Ed. Gunzelin Schmid Noerr. Trans. Edmund Jephcott. Stanford, CA: Stanford University Press, 2002.

Ahmad, Aijaz. "Orientalism and After: Ambivalence and Cosmopolitan Location in the Work of Edward Said." *Economic and Political Weekly* 27, no. 30 (1992): 98–116.

Al-Albani, Muhammad Nasir al-Din. *Silsilat al-ahadith al-da'ifa wa-l-mawdu'a wa atharuha al-sayyi' fi al-umma*. Dimashq: al-Maktab al-Islami, 1965.

Al-'Alim, Mahmud Amin. *Al-wa'yy wa-l-wa'yy al-za'if*. Cairo: Dar al-Thaqafa al-Jadida, 1986.

Al-'Arabi, Muhammad, and Muhammad Bakr Isma'il. *Ahkam al-Qur'an*. 2 vols. Cairo: Dar al-Manar lil-Tab' wa-l-Nashr wa-l-Tawzi', 2002.

Al-'Asqlani, Ibn Hajar. *Kitab al-isaba fi tamyyiz al-sahaba*. Ed. Muhammad Turki and A. Yamama. Cairo: Markaz al-Buhuth wa-l-Dirasat al-Islamiyya, 2008.

Al-Atawneh, Muhammad. "Leisure and Entertainment (*malahi*) in Contemporary Islamic Legal Thought: Music and the Audio-Visual Media," *Islamic Law and Society* 19, no. 4 (2012): 397–415.

Al-'Awwa, Muhammad Salim. *Al-nizam al-siyasi lil-dawla al-islamiyya*. Cairo: al-Maktab al-Misri al-Hadith, 1983.

Al-Bahuti, Mansur. *Kashaf al-Qina'*. 6 vols. Beirut: 'Alm al-Kitab, 1983.

Al-Bahuti, Mansur. *Sharh Muntaha al-Iradat*. Ed. 'Abdullah al-Turki. Riyadh?: al-Risala Nashirun, 2000.

Al-Baji, Abu al-Walid and 'Abd al-Majid Turki. *Ihkam al-fusul fi ahkam al-usul*. Beirut: Dar al-Gharb al-Islami, 1986.

Al-Dusuqi, Ibrahim, Sami Hilmi and Muhammad al-Qalyubi. *Al-sinima al-Misriyya al-samita al-watha'iqiyya al-tasjjiliyya*, 1897–1930. Cairo: al-Majlis al-A'la lil-Thaqafa, 2010.

Al-Fakihi, Muhammad ibn Ishaq. *Akhbar Makka fi qadim al-dahr wa-hadithih*. Ed. 'Abd al-Malik ibn 'Abdullah ibn Duhaysh. Beirut: Dar Khidr, 1994.

Al-Ghumari, 'Abdullah. *Kitab bida' al-tafasir*. Cairo: Maktabat al-Qahira, 1965.

Al-Ghumari, 'Abdullah. *Al-rasa'il al-Ghumariyya*. [Beirut]: Dar al-Janan, 1991.

Al-Ghumari, 'Abdullah. *Iqamat al-dalil 'ala hurmat al-tamthil*. Cairo: Maktabat al-Qahira, 2004.

Al-Hajajji, Ahmad Anas. *Ruh wa-rayhan min hayat da'in wa-da'wa*. Cairo: Dar Ihya' al-Kutub al-'Arabiyya, 1945.

Al-Hakim, Ayman. *Al-fann al-haram: tarikh al-ishtibak bayn al-salafiyyin wa-l-mubdi'in*. Cairo: Dar Kitabat, 2012.

Al-Hanafi, Kamal al-Din. *Fath al-Qadir*. Ed. 'Abd al-Raziq Ghalib al-Mahdi. Beirut: Dar al-Kutub al-'Ilmiyya, 2003.

Al-Khatib, Lina, "Nationalism and Otherness: The Representation of Islamic Fundamentalism in Egyptian Cinema." *European Journal of Cultural Studies* 9, no. 1 (2006): 65–80.

Al-Khozai, Mohamed. *The Development of Early Arabic Drama, 1847–1900*. London: Longman, 1984.

Al-Makhzumi, Mahdi. *Madrasat al-Kufa wa-manhajuha fi dirasat al-lugha wa-l-nahw*. Cairo: Mustafa al-Babi al-Halabi, 1958.

Al-Maqdisi, Shams al-Din. *Al-furuʿ*. ʿAmman: Bayt al-Afkar al-Dawliyya, 2004.

Al-Maraghi, Muhammad. *Al-fath al-mubin fi tabaqat al-usuliyyin*. 2 vols. Cairo: Muhammad ʿAli ʿUthman, 1947.

Al-Maraghi, Muhammad. *Al-ijtihad fi al-Islam*. Ed. Muhammad Hamid Ghadban and Saʿd al-Din Hilali. Cairo: Maktabat Jazirat al-Ward, 2010.

Al-Mardawi, ʿAlaʾ al-Din. *Al-insaf fi maʿrifat al-rajih min al-khilaf*. 12 vols. Cairo?: Maktabat al-Sunna al-Muhamadiyya, 1955.

Al-Messiri, Sawsan. *Ibn al-Balad: A Concept of Egyptian Identity*. Leiden: Brill, 1978.

Al-Nowaihi, Magda. "The Middle East?" Or . . ./Arabic Literature and Postcolonial Predicament." In *A Companion to Postcolonial Studies*, 282–304. Ed. Henry Schwarz and Sangeeta Ray. Malden, MA: Blackwell, 2000.

Al-Qushayri, Muslim. *Sahih Muslim bi-sharh al-Nawwawi*. 18 vols. Cairo: al-Matbaʿa al-Misriyya bi-l-Azhar, 1929.

Al-Sayyid-Marsot, Afaf. *Egypt's Liberal Experiment: 1922–1936*. Berkeley: University of California Press, 1977.

Al-Sharabasi, Ahmad. *Mudhakkirat waʿiz asir*. Cairo: Matbaʿat Dar al-Kitab al-ʿArabi, 1952.

Al-Sharabasi, Ahmad. *Yasʾalunak fi al-din wa-l-haya*. Beirut: Dar al-Jil, 1977.

Al-Sharabasi, Ahmad. *ʿAduww al-salam*. Beirut: Dar al-Raʾid al-ʿArabi, 1981.

Al-Sharuni, Subhi, *Bikar*. Cairo: Dar al-Shuruq, 2002.

Al-Shatti, Hasan. *Matalib uli al-nuha*. 6 vols. [Dimashq]: Manshurat al-Maktab al-Islami bi-Dimashq, 1961.

Al-Shirbini, Shams al-Din. *Mughni al-muhtaj*. Ed. Muhammad Bakr Ismaʿil. Beirut: Dar al-Kutub al-ʿIlmiyya, 2000.

Al-Zirikli, Khayr al-Din. *Al-aʿlam, qamus tarajim li-ashhar al-rijal wa-l-nisaʾ min al-ʿArab wa-l-mustaʿribin wa-l-mustashriqin*. 8 vols. Beirut: Dar al-ʿIlm lil-Malayin, 1990.

ʿAli, Mahmud. *Dirasat fi tarikh al-sinima al-Misriyya*. Cairo: al-Hayʾah al-ʿAmma li-Qusur al-Thaqafa, 2012.

ʿAli, Mahmud. *Fajr al-sinima fi Misr*. Cairo: Wizarat al-Thaqafa, 2008.

'Ali, Mahmud. "Al-judhur al-tarikhiyya lil-raqaba wa-masadiriha." *Al-raqaba 'ala al-sinima al-quyud wa-l-hudud*. Ed. Husayn Bayumi. Cairo: Maktabat al-'Usra, 2012.

Allen, Roger. *The Arabic Novel: A Historical and Critical Introduction*. Syracuse, NY: Syracuse University Press, 1982.

Allen, Terry. *Five Essays on Islamic Art*. Manchester: Solipsist Press, 1988.

Amin, Samir. *Eurocentrism: Modernity Religion and Democracy: A Critique of Eurocentrism and Culturalism*. New York: Monthly Review, 2009.

Amin, Samir. *Global History: A View from the South*. Chicago: Pambazuka Press, 2010.

Anderson, Benedict, *Imagined Communities: Reflections on the Origin and Spread of Nationalism*. London: Verso, 1991.

An-Naìm, Abdullahi. *Islam and the Secular State: Negotiating the Future of Shariá*. Cambridge, MA: Harvard University Press, 2010.

Arabi, Afif. "The History of Lebanese Cinema, 1929–1979: An Analytical Study of the Evolution and the Development of Lebanese Cinema." PhD diss., Ohio State University, 1996.

Armbrust, Walter. *Mass Culture and Modernism in Egypt*. Cambridge: Cambridge University Press, 1996.

Armbrust, Walter. "The Formation of National Culture in Egypt in the Interwar Period: Cultural Trajectories." *History Compass* 7, no. 1 (2009): 155–80.

Arnold, David, "Mulla Sadra and the Problem of Freedom and Determinism: A Critical Study of the Risala fi al-Qada' wa-l-Qadar." PhD diss., McGill University, 1978.

Arnold, Thomas Walker. *Painting in Islam: A Study of the Place of Pictorial Art in Muslim Culture*. New York: Dover, 1965.

Asad, Talal. *Formations of the Secular: Christianity, Islam, Modernity*. Stanford, CA: Stanford University Press, 2003.

Askari, Kaveh, and Marc S. Bernstein. "Locating Muslim Cinema(s)." *Journal of Religion and Popular Culture* 33, no. 3 (2021): 123–5.

'Awad, Ramsis. *Al-itijahat siyasiyya fi al-masrah qabl 1919*. Cairo: al-Hay'a al-Misriyya lil-Kitab, 1979.

Badawi, Muhammad Mustafa. *A Short History of Modern Arabic Literature*. Oxford: Clarendon Press, 1993.

Bahgat, Ahmad Ra'fat. *Al-Yahud wa-l-sinima fi misr*. Cairo: Sharikat al-Qasr, 2005.

Bassiouney, Reem. *Functions of Code-Switching in Egypt: Evidence from Monologues*. Leiden: Brill, 2006.

Baudelaire, Charles. *The Painter of Modern Life: And Other Essays*. Trans. Jonathan Mayne. London: Phaidon, 1964.

Baydas, Ashraf. *Abyad wa-aswad*. Cairo: Sama, 2013.

Bazin, André. *What Is Cinema?* Berkeley: University of California Press, 1967.

Benjamin, Walter. *Understanding Brecht*. Trans. Anna Bostock. London: Verso, 1998.

Bhabha, Homi. "The Other Question: Difference, Discrimination and the Discourse of Colonialism." In *The Politics of Theory, Proceedings of Essex Sociology of Literature Conference*, 18–36. Ed. Francis Barker. Colchester: University of Essex Press, 1983.

Bhabha, Homi. *The Location of Culture*. London: Routledge, 1994.

Bhaskar, Roy. *A Realist Theory of Science*. London: Routledge Taylor & Francis, 2015.

Biltereyst, Daniel. *Cinema Audiences and Modernity: An Introduction*. New York: Routledge, 2012.

Bin Sattam, Abdul Aziz. *Shari'a and the Concept of Benefit*. London: I. B. Tauris, 2015.

Boraïe, Sherif, Mustafa Darwish, Rafik al-Saban, and Yasser Alwan. *The Golden Years of Egyptian Cinema*. Cairo: The American University in Cairo Press, 2008.

Botman, Selma. *Egypt from Independence to Revolution 1919–1952*. Syracuse, NY: Syracuse University Press, 1991.

Braudy, Leo, and Marshall Cohen. *Film Theory and Criticism: Introductory Readings*. New York: Oxford University Press. 2004.

Bryan S. Turner. *Weber and Islam: A Critical Study*. London, Boston: Routledge & Kegan Paul, 1978.

Burns, James. *Flickering Shadows: Cinema and Identity in Colonial Zimbabwe*. Ohio: Ohio University Center for International Studies Ohio University Press, 2002.

Calder, Norman. *Studies in Early Muslim Jurisprudence*. Oxford: Clarendon Press, 1993.

Chakrabarty, Dipesh. "Add, Calcutta: Dwelling in Modernity." *Alternative Modernities*. Ed. Dilip Gaonkar. Durham, NC: Duke University Press, 2001.

Chatterjee, Partha, *The Nation, and Its Fragments: Colonial and Postcolonial Histories*. Princeton, NJ: Princeton University Press, 1993.

Clark, Toby. *Art and Propaganda in the Twentieth Century: the Political Image in the Age of Mass Culture*. New York: Harry N. Abrams, 1997.

Clifford, James. "On Orientalism." *The Predicament of Culture*. Cambridge, MA: Harvard University Press, 1988.

Coates, Paul. *Cinema, Religion, and the Romantic Legacy: Through a Glass Darkly*. Burlington, VT: Ashgate, 2003.

Cohn, Bernard. *Colonialism and Its Forms of Knowledge*. Princeton, NJ: Princeton University Press, 1996.

Colla, Elliott, *Conflicted Antiquities: Egyptology, Egyptomania, Egyptian Modernity.* Durham, NC: Duke University Press, 2007.

Colla, Elliott, "How Zaynab Became the First Egyptian Novel," *History Compass* 7, no. 1 (2009): 214–25.

Colman, Felicity. *Deleuze and Cinema: The Film Concepts.* Oxford: New York, Berg. 2011.

Confino, Alon. *The Nation as a Local Metaphor: Wurttemberg, Imperial Germany, and National Memory, 1871-1918.* Chapel Hill, NC: University of North Carolina Press, 1997.

Contadini, Anna. *Arab Painting: Text and Image in Illustrated Arabic Manuscripts.* Leiden, Boston: Brill 2007.

Coulson, Noel J. *A History of Islamic law.* Edinburgh: Edinburgh University Press 1964.

Dallal, Ahmad. "Appropriating the Past: Twentieth-Century Reconstruction of Pre-Modern Islamic Thought." *Islamic Law and Society* 7, no. 3 (2000): 325–58.

Davis, Diana K. *Resurrecting the Granary of Rome: Environmental History and French Colonial Expansion in North Africa.* Athens, OH: Ohio University Press, 2007.

Davis, Eric. *Challenging Colonialism: Bank Misr and Egyptian Industrialization, 1920-1941.* Princeton, NJ: Princeton University Press. 1983.

Dayif, Shawqi. *Al-madaris al-nahawiyya.* Cairo: Dar al-Mʿarif, 1992.

Deacy, Christopher, and Gaye Williams Ortiz. *Theology and Film: Challenging the Sacred/Secular Divide.* Malden: Blackwell, 2008.

De Certeau, Michel. *The Practice of Everyday Life.* Berkeley: University of California Press, 1984.

De Grazia, Victoria. "Mass Culture and Sovereignty: the American Challenge to European Cinemas, 1920–1960." *Journal of Modern History* 61, no. 1 (March 1989): 53–87.

Delabar, Walter and Walter Fähnders, *Heinrich Mann 1871—1950.* Berlin: Weidler, 2005.

Dickinson, Eerik. "Ahmad ibn al-Salt and His Biography of Abu Hanifa." *Journal of the American Oriental Society* 116 (1996): 406–17.

Dutton, Yasin. *The Origins of Islamic law: the Qurʾan, the Muwattaʾ, and Madinan ʿAmal.* Surrey: Curzon, 1999.

Eagleton, Terry. *Marxism and Literary Criticism.* Berkeley: University of California Press, 1976.

El Khachab Chihab. *Making Film in Egypt: How Labor Technology and Mediation Shape the Industry.* Cairo: American University in Cairo Press, 2021.

Encyclopedia of Islam Second Edition Online. s.v. "Al-Shafi'i'."
Encyclopedia of Islam Second Edition Online. s.v. "Al-Azraqi."
Encyclopedia of Islam Second Edition Online. s.v. "Hadith."
Encyclopedia of Islam Second Edition Online. s.v. "Hisba."
Encyclopedia of Islam Second Edition Online. s.v. "Muhallil."
Encyclopedia of Islam Second Edition Online. s.v. "Sadd al- dhara'i'."
Encyclopedia of Islam Second Edition Online. s.v. "tamthil."
Encyclopedia of Islam Second Edition Online. s.v. "taswir."
Fahmy, Khaled. *All the Pasha's Men: Mehmed Ali, His Army, and the Making of Modern Egypt.* Cambridge: Cambridge University Press, 1997.
Fahmy, Ziad. *Ordinary Egyptians: Creating the Modern Nation through Popular Culture.* Stanford, CA: Stanford University Press, 2011.
Farhun, Ibrahim, and Ahmad ibn Ahmad Baba. *Kitab al-dibaj al-mudhahhab fi ma'rifat a'yan 'ulama' al-madhhab.* Cairo: 'Abbas ibn 'Abd al-Salam ibn Shaqrun, 1932.
Farid, Samir. *Tarikh al-raqaba 'ala al-sinima fi Misr.* Cairo: al-Maktb al-Dawli li-Tawzi' al Matbu'at, 2001.
Foucault, Michel. *The History of Sexuality.* New York: Pantheon, 1978.
Foucault, Michel. "What is Enlightenment?" *The Foucault Reader*, ed. Paul Rabinow. New York: Pantheon, 1984.
Foucault, Michel. *The Foucault Reader.* Ed. Paul Rabinow. New York: Pantheon, 1984.
Gaonkar, Dilip, *Alternative Modernities.* Durham, NC: Duke University Press, 2001.
Gershoni, Israel, and James Jankowski. *Egypt, Islam, and the Arabs: The Search for Egyptian Nationhood, 1900–1930.* New York: Oxford University Press, 1986.
Gordon, Joel. *Nasser's Blessed Movement: Egypt's Free Officers and the July Revolution.* New York: Oxford University Press, 1992.
Graham, William. "Traditionalism in Islam: An Essay in Interpretation," *The Journal of Interdisciplinary History* 23, no. 3 (1993): 495–522.
Griffel, Frank. "Toleration and Exclusion: Al-Shafi'i and al-Ghazali on the Treatment of Apostates." *Bulletin of the School of Oriental and African Studies*, University of London, 64, no. 3 (2001): 339–54. http://www.jstor.org/stable/3657603.
Gross, David. *The Writer and Society: Heinrich Mann and Literary Politics in Germany, 1890–1940.* New Jersey: Humanities Press, 1980.
Guillaume, Antione. "Some Remarks on Free Will and Predestination in Islam Together with a Translation of the Kitab al-Qadar from Sahih al-Bukhari." *Journal of the Royal Asiatic Society* (1924): 43–63.

Günther, Sebastian. "Fictional Narration and Imagination within an Authoritative Framework: Toward a New Understanding of *Hadith*." *Story-Telling in the Framework of Non-Fictional Arabic Literature*. Wiesbaden: Harrassowitz, 1998.

Golia, Maria. *Photography, and Egypt*. London: Reaktion Books, 2010.

Goldziher, Ignác. *Muslim Studies*. 2 vols. Trans. C. R. Barber and S. M. Stern. London: George Allen, 1971.

Gomery, Douglas. *The Coming of Sound: a History*. New York: Routledge, 2005.

Grabar, Oleg. *The Formation of Islamic Art*. New Haven, CT: Yale University Press. 1987.

Guo, Li. *The Performing Arts in Medieval Islam Shadow Play and Popular Poetry in Ibn Daniyal's Mamluk Cairo*. Leiden: Brill, 2011.

Habermas, Jürgen. "Modernity—An Incomplete Project." *The Anti-Aesthetic: Essays on Postmodern Culture*. Ed. Hal Foster. Port Townsend, WA: Bay Press, 1983.

Habermas, Jürgen. *The Structural Transformation of the Public Sphere: An Inquiry into a Category of Bourgeoisie Society*. Cambridge, MA: MIT Press, 1991.

Habermas, Jürgen. "Myth and Ritual." *The Berkley Center Lectures*, Georgetown University, 2011.

Hadari, Ahmad. *Tarikh al-sinima fi Misr*. Cairo: Nadi al-Sinima, 1989.

Hadari, Ahmad. *Maswuʿat Tarikh al-Sinima fi Misr*, 3 vols. Cairo: al-Hayʾa al-ʿAma al-Misriyya lil-Kitab, 2019.

Hadithi, Bahjat. ʿAbd al-Ghafur. *Umayya Ibn Abi al-Salt: hayatuh wa-shiʿruh*. Baghdad: Wizarat al-Iʿlam, 1975.

Haikal, Mohammed Hussein. *Mohammed Hussein Haikal's Zainab: The First Egyptian Novel*. Trans. John Mohammed Grinsted. London: Darf, 1989.

Hallaq, Wael. "Was the Gate of *Ijtihad* Closed?" *International Journal of Middle East Studies* 16, no. 1 (1984): 3–41.

Hallaq, Wael. "From Fatwas to Furuʿ: Growth and Change in Islamic Substantive Law," *Islamic Law and Society* 1 (1994): 29–65.

Hallaq, Wael. *A History of Islamic Legal Theories: An Introduction to Sunni Usul al-Fiqh*. Cambridge: Cambridge University Press, 1997.

Hallaq, Wael. "The Authenticity of Prophetic Hadith: a Pseudo-Problem." *Studia Islamica* 89 (1999): 75–90.

Hallaq, Wael. *The Origins and Evolution of Islamic Law*. Cambridge: Cambridge University Press, 2005.

Hamid, Shadi. *Temptations of Power: Islamists and Illiberal Democracy in a New Middle East*. New York: Oxford University Press, 2014.

Hammad, Hanan. *Unknown History: Layla Murad the Jewish Muslim Star of Egypt*. Stanford, CA: Stanford University Press, 2022.

Harb, Muhammad Salih, Ahmad Hasan Muhammad Kinani, and Ahmad Zakariyya Shalaq, *Dhikrayat al-liwa' Muhammad Salih Harb*. Cairo: al-Hay'a al-'Amma li-Qusur al-Thaqafa, 2009.

Harrison, Robert T. "Alexandria, British Occupation of (1807)." *Historical Dictionary of the British Empire*. Ed. James Stuart Olson and Robert Shadle. London: Greenwood, 1996.

Hasan, Ahmad. "Early Modes of *Ijtihad*: *Ra'y*, *Qiyas* and *Istihsan*." *Islamic Studies* 6 (1967): 47–79.

Hashim, Ahmad 'Umar. *Al-muhaddithun fi Misr wa-l-Azhar*. Cairo: Maktabat Gharib, 1993.

Heyworth-Dunne, James. *An Introduction to the History of Education in Modern Egypt*. London: Frank Cass, 1968.

Hill, John. "UK Film Policy, Cultural Capital, and Social Exclusion." *Cultural Trends* 13.2, no. 50 (June 2004): 32.

Hindi, Inas. *Bikar: ma'zufat al-kalima wa-l-furshat*. Cairo: al-Majlis al-A'la lil-Thaqafa, 2009.

Hinds, Harold E., Marilyn Motz, and Angela Nelson. *Popular Culture Theory and Methodology: A Basic Introduction*. Madison, WI: University of Wisconsin Press, 2006.

Ibbi, Andrew Ali. "Hollywood, the American Image and the Global Film Industry." *Cinema Journal* 3, no. 1 (2013): 96–106.

Ibn 'Abidin, Muhammad. *Radd al-muhatar 'ala al-durr al-mukhtar hashiyat b. 'Abidin*. 13 vols. Al-Riyad: 'Alm al-Kitab, 2003.

Ibn al-Kalbi, Hisham. *The Book of Idols: Being a Translation from the Arabic of Kitab al-Asnam*. Trans. Nabith Amin Faris (Princeton, NJ: Princeton University Press), 2016.

Ibn Rushd, Muhammad. *Al-muqaddamat al-mumahhadat li-bayan ma iqtadathu rusum al-mudawwana min al-ahkam al-shar'iyyat wa-l-tahssilat al-muhkimat li-ummahat masa'iliha al-mushkilat*. Ed. Muhammad Hajji. Beirut: Dar al-Gharb al-Islami, 1988.

Ibn Taymiyya, Taqiyy al-Din. *Al-fatawa al-kubra*. 6 vols. Ed. Muhammad 'Abd al-Qadir 'Ata. Beirut: Dar al-Kutub al-'Ilmiyya, 1987.

Jacob, Wilson. *Working Out Egypt: Effendi Masculinity and Subject Formation in Colonial Modernity, 1870–1940*. Durham, NC: Duke University Press, 2011.

Jameson, Fredric. *A Singular Modernity: Essay on the Ontology of the Present*. London: Verso, 2002.

Johnston, Robert K. *Reframing Theology, and Film: New Focus for an Emerging Discipline*. Grand Rapids, MI: Baker Academic, 2007.

Kamali, Mohammad. *Principles of Islamic Jurisprudence*. Cambridge: Islamic Text Society, 1991.

Kant, Immanuel. "An Answer to the Question: What Is Enlightenment?" *Practical Philosophy*, 11–23. Trans. and ed. Mary J. Gregor. Cambridge: Cambridge University Press, 1996.

Karnouk, Liliane. *Modern Egyptian Art, 1910–2003*. Cairo: American University in Cairo Press, 2005.

Khafaji, Muhammad. *Al-Azhar fi alf 'am*. 6 vols. Cairo: Maktabat al-Kulliyya al-Azhariyya, 1988.

Klepper, Robert K. *Silent Films, 1877–1996: A Critical Guide to 646 Movies*. Jefferson, NC: McFarland, 1999.

Krawietz, Birgit, "*Darura* in Modern Islamic Law: The Case of Organ Transplantation." *Islamic Law, Theory, and Practice*. Ed. R. Gleave and E. Kermeli. London: I. B. Tauris, 1997.

Kunin, Seth D., and with Jonathan Miles-Watson. *Theories of Religion: A Reader*. New Brunswick, NJ: Rutgers University Press, 2006.

Landau, Jacob. *Studies in the Arab Theater and Cinema*. Philadelphia, PA: University of Pennsylvania Press, 1958.

Landau, Jacob. "Popular Arabic Plays, 1909." *Journal of Arabic Literature* 17 (1986): 120–5.

Lane, Edward William. *An Account of the Manners and Customs of the Modern Egyptians: Written in Egypt during the Years 1833–1835*. London: East–West, 1978.

Lerner, Daniel. *The Passing of Traditional Society: Modernizing the Middle East*. New York: Free Press, 1964.

Levine, George. *Aesthetics and Ideology*. New Brunswick, NJ: Rutgers University Press, 1994.

Lockman, Zachary. "Imagining the Working Class: Culture, Nationalism, and Class Formation in Egypt, 1899–1914." *Poetics Today* 15, no. 2 (1994): 157–91.

Lockman, Zachary. "Exploring the Field: Lost Voices and Emerging Practices in Egypt, 1882–1914." *Histories of the Modern Middle East: New Directions*. Ed. Israel Gershoni, Hakan Erdem, and Ursula Wokock. London: Lynne Rienner, 2002.

Lombardi, Clark B. *State Law as Islamic Law in Modern Egypt: The Incorporation of the Shari'a into Egyptian Constitutional Law*. Leiden, Boston: Brill, 2006.

Loomba, Ania. *Colonialism/Postcolonialism*. London: Routledge, 1998.

Lyden, John C. *Film as Religion: Myths, Morals, and Rituals*. New York: New York University Press, 2003.

Maghraoui, Abdeslam. *Liberalism Without Democracy: Nationhood and Citizenship in Egypt, 1922–1936*. Durham: Duke University Press, 2006.

Marlowe, John. *Cromer in Egypt*. London: Elek, 1970.

Marshik, Celia. *British Modernism and Censorship*. New York: Cambridge University Press, 2006.

Marshik, Celia. *The Cambridge Companion to Modernist Culture*. New York: Cambridge University Press. 2015.

Martin, Thomas M. *Images, and the Imageless: A Study in Religious Consciousness and Film*. Ed. Lewisburg, PA. London: Bucknell University Press: Associated University Presses, 1991.

Masud, Muhammad Khalid, "Shatibi's Theory of Meaning," *Islamic Studies* 32 (1993): 5–16.

Mauthner, Martin. *German Writers in French Exile, 1933–1940*. London: Vallentine Mitchell in association with the European Jewish Publication Society, 2007.

Mehrez, Samia. *Egypt's Culture Wars: Politics and Practice*. London: Routledge, 2011.

Mendieta, Eduardo, and Jonathan Vanantwerpen. *The Power of Religion in the Public Sphere*. New York: Columbia University Press, 2011.

Mitchell, Richard P. *The Society of the Muslim Brothers*. New York: Oxford University Press, 1969.

Mitchell, Timothy. *Colonizing Egypt*. New York: New York University, 1991.

Mitchell, Timothy. *Questions of Modernity*. Minneapolis, MN: University of Minnesota Press, 2000.

Mitchell, Timothy. *Rules of Experts: Egypt, Techno-Politics, Modernity*. Berkeley: University of California Press, 2002.

Mitchell, W. J. T. *Iconology. Image, Text, Ideology*. Chicago, IL: University of Chicago Press: 1986.

Mitchell, W. J. T. *Picture Theory: Essays on Verbal and Visual Representation*. Chicago, IL: University of Chicago Press, 1994.

Moosa, Matti. *The Origins of Modern Arabic Fiction*. Washington, DC: Three Continents Press, 1983.

Morier, James Justinian. *A Second Journey through Persia, Armenia, and Asia Minor to Constantinople between the Years 1810 and 1816 with a Journal of the Voyage by the Brazils and Bombay to the Persian Gulf, Together with an Account of the Proceedings of His Majesty's Embassy under His Excellency Sir Gore Ouseley.* London: J. G. Barnard & A. Strahan, 1812.

Motzki, Harald, "The *Musannaf* of 'Abd al-Razzaq al-San'ani as a Source of Authentic Ahadith of the First Century A.H." *Journal of Near Eastern Studies* 50, no. 1 (1991): 1–21.

Mumtaz, I'itdal. *Mudhakkirat Raqibat Sinima.* Cairo: al-Hay'a al-'Ama al-Misriyya lil-Kitab, 1985.

Nieuwkerk, Karin Van. *Muslim Rap, Halal Soaps, and Revolutionary Theater: Artistic Developments in the Muslim World.* Austin: University of Texas Press, 2011.

Obermann, Julian. "Political Theology in Early Islam: al-Hasan al-Basri's Treatise on Qadar," *Journal of the American Oriental Society* 55 (1935): 138–62.

Obermann, Julian. "Changes in Modern Islamic Legal Theory: Reform or Reformation?" In *An Islamic Reformation?* Ed. Michaelle Browers and Charles Kurzman. Lanham, MD: Lexington Books, 2004.

Opwis, Felicitas. "Maslaha in Contemporary Legal Theory," *Islamic Law and Society* 12, no. 2 (2005): 182–223.

Opwis, Felicitas. "Islamic Law and Legal Change: The Concept of Maslaha in Classical and Contemporary Islamic Legal Theory." In *Shari'a: Islamic Law in the Contemporary Context.* Ed. Amanat Abbas, and Frank Griffel. Stanford, CA: Stanford University Press, 2007.

Opwis, Felicitas. *Maslaha and the Purpose of the Law: Islamic Discourse on Legal Change from the 4th/10th to 8th/14th Century.* Leiden: Brill, 2010.

Orr, John and Olga Taxidou. *Post-war Cinema and Modernity: A Film Reader.* New York: New York University Press, 2001.

Pak-Shiraz Nacim. "The Qur'anic Epic in Iranian Cinema," *Journal of Religion & Film* 20 (2016): 1–25.

Pak-Shiraz Nacim. *Shi'i Islam in Iranian Cinema Religion and Spirituality in Film.* London: I. B. Tauris, 2018.

Parker, Holt. "Toward a Definition of Popular Culture." *History and Theory* 50 (May 2011): 147–70.

Perkins, V. F. *Film as Film: Understanding and Judging Movies.* New York: Penguin, 1986.

Petersen, Kristian. *New Approaches to Islam in Film.* Abingdon: Routledge, 2021.

Petersen, Kristian. *Muslims in the Movies: A Global Anthology.* Boston: Harvard University Press, 2021.

Philipp, Thomas. *Gurgi Zaidan His Life and Thought*. Beirut: Orient Institute, 1979.

Pollard, Lisa. "The Family Politics of Colonizing and Liberating Egypt, 1882–1919." *Social Politics* 7, no. 1 (2000): 47–79.

Pollard, Lisa. "The Habits and Customs of Modernity: Egyptians in Europe and the Geography of Nineteenth-Century Nationalism." *Arab Studies Journal* 7, no. 2–8(1) (fall 1999–spring 2000): 52–74.

Porter, Denis. "Orientalism and Its Problems." *Colonial Discourse and Post-Colonial Theory*, 151–61. Ed. Patrick Williams and Laura Chrisman. New York: Columbia University Press, 1993.

Porter, Vincent, "The Robert Clark Account: Films Released in Britain by Associated British Pictures, British Lion, MGM, and Warner Bros., 1946–1957," *Historical Journal of Film, Radio & Television* 20, no. 4 (October 2000): 469–511.

Potter, Rachel. *Obscene Modernism: Literary Censorship and Experiment, 1900–1940*. Oxford: Oxford University Press, 2013.

Rahman, Fazulr. *Major Themes of the Qur'an*. Minneapolis, MN: Bibliotheca Islamica, 1994.

Ramadan, Tariq. "*Ijtihad* and *Maslaha*: The Foundations of Governance." In *Islamic Democratic Discourse: Theory, Debates, and Philosophical Perspectives*. Ed. M. A. Muqtedar Khan. Lanham, MD: Lexington Books, 2006.

Reid, Donald Malcolm. *Cairo University and the Making of Modern Egypt*. New York: Cambridge University Press, 1990.

Reid, Donald Malcolm. *Whose Pharaohs? Archaeology, Museums, and Egyptian National Identity from Napoleon to World War I*. Berkeley: University of California Press, 2002.

Richardson, H. W. "The Economic Significance of the Depression in Britain," *Journal of Contemporary History* 4, no. 4 (1969): 3–19.

Rida, Rashid. *Tarikh al-ustadh al-imam al-Shaykh Muhammad 'Abduh: wa-fihi tafsil siratuhu wa-khulasat sirat munqiz al-sharq al-hakim wa-l-Islam Jamal al-Din al-Afghani*. 3 vols. Egypt: Matba'at al-Manar, 1906.

Russell, Mona. *Creating the New Egyptian Woman: Consumerism, Education, and National Identity, 1863–1922*. New York: Palgrave Macmillan, 2004.

Ryzova, Lucie. "Egyptianizing Modernity through the 'New Effendiya': Social and Cultural Constructions of the Middle Class in Egypt under the Monarchy." In *Re-envisioning Egypt, 1919–1952*. Ed. Arthur Goldschmidt, Amy Johnson, and Barak Salamoni, 124–63. Cairo: American University in Cairo Press, 2005.

Ryzova, Lucie. *The Age of the Efendiyya: Passages to Modernity in National-Colonial Egypt*. Oxford: Oxford University Press 2014.
Said, Edward. *Orientalism*. New York, Vintage, 1979.
Said, Edward. *The World, the Text, and the Critic*. Cambridge, MA: Harvard University Press, 1983.
Said, Edward. *Culture and Imperialism*. New York: Vintage, 1993.
Said, Edward. "The Clash of Ignorance." *The Nation*, October 22, 2001, 11–14.
Said, Edward. Humanism and Democratic Criticism. New York: Columbia University Press, 2004.
Said, Edward and Jacqueline Rose. *Freud and the Non-European*. London: Verso, 2003.
Salah al-Din, Muhammad. *Al-din wa-l-'aqida fi al-sinima al-Misriyya*. Maktabat Madbuli, 1998.
Schacht, Joseph. *An Introduction to Islamic Law*. Oxford: Clarendon Press, 1964.
Schaub, Mark. "English in the Arab Republic of Egypt." *World Englishes* 19, no. 2 (2000): 225–38.
Scott, James C. *Seeing Like a State: How Certain Schemes to Improve the Human Condition Have Failed*. New Haven, CT: Yale University Press, 1998.
Sedra, Paul. *From Mission to Modernity Evangelicals, Reformers, and Education in Nineteenth-Century Egypt*. London: I. B. Tauris, 2011.
Sethe, Kurt. *Die Alta Egyptischen Pyramidentexte*. Leipzig: Hinrichs, 1908.
Shafik, Viola. *Popular Egyptian Cinema: Gender, Class, and Nation*. Cairo: American University in Cairo Press, 2007.
Shakry, Omnia. *The Great Social Laboratory: Subjects of Knowledge in Colonial and Postcolonial Egypt*. Stanford, CA: Stanford University Press, 2007.
Shraybom-Shivtiel, Shlomit. "Language and Political Change in Modern Egypt." *International Journal of the Sociology of Language* 137 (1999): 131–40.
Shusha, Muhammad. *Al-nass al-kamil li-sinariyu film al-'Azima*. Cairo: al-Hay'a al-'Amma al-Misriyya lil-Kitab, 1975.
Sislian, Jack. "Missionary Works in Egypt during the Nineteenth Century." *Educational Policy and the Mission Schools: Case Studies from the British Empire*. Ed. Brian Holmes. London: Routledge & Kegan Paul, 1968.
Sloane, William Milligan. *The Poet Labid*. Leipzig: Breitkopf & Haertel, 1877.
Soueif, Ahdaf. *Cairo: My City, Our Revolution*. New York: Pantheon, 2013.
Speight, Marston. "The Creation of Hadith as Commentary on the Quran." *Approaches to the History of the Interpretation of the Qur'an*. Ed. Andrew Rippin. Oxford: Oxford University Press, 1988.

Stam Robert, Louise Spence. "*Colonialism, Racism and Representation.*" Screen 24, no. 2 (1983): 2–20.

Starr, Deborah A. *Togo Mizrahi and the Making of Egyptian Cinema* (Berkeley: University of California Press, 2020).

Street, Sarah. *British National Cinema*. London, New York: Routledge, 1997.

Talimah, 'Isam. *Hasan al-Banna wa-tajribat al-fann*. Cairo: Maktabat Wahba, 2008.

Taylor, Charles. "Two Modernities." *Alternative Modernities*. Ed. Dilip Gaonkar. Durham, NC: Duke University Press, 2001.

Thapar, Romila. "What Secularism Is and Where It Needs to be Headed." *The Wire*, October 18, 2015. http://thewire.in/2015/10/18/what-secularism-is-and-where-it-needs-to-be-headed-12539/

Thapar, Romila. "The Nation and History: Then and Now." *Stand with JNU*, March 6, 2016. https://www.youtube.com/watch?v=UmlfokUvOiw

Tignor, Robert L. *Modernization and British Colonial Rule in Egypt, 1882–1914*. Princeton, NJ: Princeton University Press, 1966.

'Ukasha, Tharwat. *Mawsu'at al-taswir al-Islami*. Beirut: Maktabat Lubnan Nashirun, 1999.

Ulff-Moller, Jens. "The Origins of French Quota Policy Controlling the Import of American Films 1920–1939." *Historical Journal of Film Radio and Television* 18, no. 2 (1998): 167–82.

Vatikiotis, P. J. *The History of Modern Egypt: From Muhammad Ali to Mubarak*. Baltimore, MD: Johns Hopkins University Press, 1991.

Versteegh, Kees. *Greek Elements in Arabic Linguistic Thinking*. Leiden: Brill, 1977.

Vitalis, Robert. *When Capitalists Collide: Business Conflict and the End of Empire in Egypt*. Berkeley: University of California Press, 1995.

Vitalis, Robert. "Hollywood and Revolution on the Nile." *Mass Media New Approaches to Popular Culture*. Ed. Walter Armbrust. Berkeley: University of California Press, 2000.

Vogt, Guntram, and Mitarbeit Philipp Sanke. *Die Stadt im Film: Deutsche Spielfilme 1900–2000*. Marburg: Scharen, 2001.

Watkins, Gregory J. 2008. *Teaching Religion and Film*. Oxford: Oxford University Press.

Watt, Montgomery. *Free Will and Predestination in Early Islam*. London: Luzac, 1948.

Weiss, Bernhard. *The Search for God's Law: Islamic Jurisprudence in the Writings of Sayf al-Din al-Amidi*. Salt Lake City: University of Utah Press, 1992.

Wierzbicki, James. *Music, Sound, and Filmmakers: Sonic Style in Cinema*. New York: Routledge. 2012.
Williams, Alan. *Film and Nationalism*. New Brunswick, NJ: Rutgers University Press, 2002.
Williams, Raymond. *The Long Revolution*. New York: Columbia University Press, 1967.
Williams, Raymond. *Marxism and Literature*. Oxford: Oxford University Press, 1977.
Williams, Raymond. "British History New Perspectives." *British Cinema History*. Ed. James Curran and Vincent Porter. Totowa: Barnes & Noble, 1983.
Youssef, Mervat, and Anup Kumar. "Egyptian Uprising: Redefining Egyptian Political Community and Reclaiming the Public Space." *Cyber Orient* 6, no. 1 (2012). http://www.cyberorient.net/article.do?articleId=7766
Zebiri, Kate. *Mahmud Shaltut and Islamic Modernism*. Oxford: Clarendon Press, 1993.
Zuhur, Sherifa. *Images of Enchantment: Visual and Performing Arts of the Middle East*. Cairo: American University in Cairo Press, 1998.
Zuhur, Sherifa. *Colors of Enchantment: Theater, Dance, Music, and the Visual Arts of the Middle East*. Cairo: American University in Cairo Press, 2001.

Index

'Abbas I, 81
Abaza, Fikri, 115, 116, 117, 198
Abd al-Aziz, Brigadier Ahmad, 123
'Abd al-Hamid al-Thani, 164
'Abd al-Raziq, Mustafa, 169
'Abd al-Wahhab, Fatin, 320, 321
'Abd al-Wahhab, Muhammad, 23, 28, 29, 31, 44, 45, 198, 199, 200, 203, 254, 346, 350, 354, 358, 370
'Abd al-Warith, 'Asar, 10, 30, 38, 211, 325, 330, 361, 401, 425, 427
'Abidin, 13, 108
'Abduh, Muhammad, 153
'Abduh, Raga', 12
Abu al-'Abbas, al-Morsi, 10
Abu al-'Uyun, Mahmud, 62, 182
Abu Bakr, Sa'id, 321, 354
Abu Halmus, 67, 304–7
Abu Sayf, Salah, 32–5, 44
Abu Ya'la, 429
Abyad, Dawlat, 12, 200–2, 212, 364, 400
Abyad, George, 9, 167, 200, 296, 327
a'da, 56–8, 392–5
adda, 56–7
Ahmad, Durriyya, 262, 246, 270
'afw, 401, 426–7
al-Ahram Studio, 123
al-'Aqqad, 'Mustafa, 168, 185
al-'Asqalani, Ibn Hajar, 157

al-Atrash, Farid, 125, 296
al-'Azima, 327, 370–82
al-Banna, Hasan, 165–6, 178, 184
al-Bayt al-Kabir, 406–19
al-Dahaya, 22
al-darurat, 153
al-dhawq al-'am, 131
Alexandria 120, 123, 184, 217, 263, 276, 277, 295, 308, 336, 401, 419
al-Fahham, Muhammad 'Abd al-Latif, 159–60
al-Farabi, 60, 61
al-Ghazali, Abu Hamid, 7, 60, 61, 153, 154
al-Ghumari, 'Abdullah, 66, 157–77, 179, 180, 183
al-hajiyyat, 153
al-Hubb al-Khalid, 22
al-Imam, Hasan, 9, 174
al-Jaziri, Abd al-Rahman, 160–2
al-Jurjani, 7
al-Kassar, 'Ali, 7, 10, 63
al-Khawarizmi, 60
al-Kindi, 60, 62
Ali, Muhammad, 8, 50, 51, 81, 101
'Ali, Mumtaz, 414–15
'Allam, Ahmad, 167
'Allam, Salwa, 225
al-Mardinli, Tawfiq, 198, 348

INDEX | 455

al-Masri, Muhammad Kamal, 22, 252, 275, 279, 280, 305
al-Mawardi, 429
al-Mazahir, 57, 67, 68, 239, 240, 243, 392, 393, 395, 397, 398, 424
al-Miligi, Mahmud, 167, 265, 288
al-Munira (Cairene neighborhood), 14
al-Nahhas, Mustafa, 28, 83, 84, 85, 89, 109, 122, 123, 132, 137, 175, 297, 324
al-Nasir, 'Abd al-Rahman III, 174
al-Nasir Salah al-Din, 168
al-Nuqrashi, Mahmoud Fahmi, 89, 123, 174, 182
alternative modernity, 50
al-Qadi 'Iyad, 157
al-Qalyubi, Muhammad Kamil, 1, 10
al-Qarafi, Shihab al-Din, 154
al-Razi, Abu Bakr, 60
al-Razi, Fakhr al-Din, 54
al-Sharabasi, Ahmad, 66, 162, 169, 177–83
al-Shatibi, Abu Ishaq, 154
al-Shinnawi, Anwar, 167
al-Shinnawi, Kamal, 62, 263, 266, 321, 326
al-tahsinat, 153
al-Tufi, Najm al-Din, 154
al-Ustadha Fatima, 67, 308, 319–21
al-walad lil-firash, 298
al-waqf 'ala al-nafs, 249
al-Warda al-Bayda', 66, 68, 198, 200–11, 345, 346, 347, 351, 352, 353, 358, 366
al-Zahrawi, 60
al-Zawja al-Thaniya, 32, 33–7
al-Zawja al-Sabi'a, 67, 256–8
A Matter of Life and Death, 135
Amir, 'Aziza, 4, 5, 62, 93, 167, 320
amour-propre, xvi, xvii, 52, 53, 56, 64, 65, 80, 81, 103, 105, 107, 108, 111, 113, 114, 115, 120, 137, 147, 203, 204, 208, 219, 231, 232, 244, 263, 264, 283, 284, 305, 306, 344, 338, 356, 359, 404, 424

Anglo-Egyptian Treaty, 50, 80, 81, 126, 130, 135, 324
Anglo-Egyptian Union, 87, 90, 94
Arabic Acting House, 101
apostasy, 45, 429
apparel, 3, 18, 55, 212, 213, 218, 220, 224, 226, 232, 264, 290, 313, 322, 338
appropriation, 9, 42, 46, 51, 52, 60, 67, 219, 253, 254, 256, 258, 295, 304, 398, 399, 415, 424
asala, 51–2, 56–8, 68–9, 346, 348, 350, 353, 355, 357, 358, 359, 361, 363, 366, 367, 370, 371, 372, 373, 375, 377, 378, 382, 383, 385, 388, 391, 397, 399, 403, 406, 410, 415, 419, 421, 423, 424, 425, 426, 427
asil, 362, 363
Austria, 3, 10, 319
autocracy, 35, 320, 387
awlad al-balad, 3
Awlad al-Dhawat, 26, 27, 28, 44

Badrkhan, Ahmad, 44, 62, 67, 93, 109, 120, 121, 217, 253, 259, 296, 299, 300, 301, 300–3
Bahlawi, Muhammad Rida, 12
Bank De Rome 10, 17
Barton, Charles, 134
Barsum Yabhath 'an Wazifa, 21, 35
Bayumi Afandi, 69, 124, 419, 421, 422, 423, 425, 427, 428, 433.
Bayumi, Muhammad, 10, 18, 21, 22, 35, 93
Baudelaire, Charles, 48
Bazin, André, 7, 31, 296
Behna Film, 22
Bender Lee, 'Aziz, 10
Berlin, 3, 12, 20, 21, 22, 23, 96

Capitol Theater, 129–35
Capitulations, 1, 11, 85, 91

censorship, 12, 15, 16, 17, 24, 25, 26, 28, 31, 44–7, 50, 53, 64, 65, 66, 67, 80, 95, 96, 99, 100, 101, 102, 104–11, 115–23, 150, 153, 162, 164, 178, 184, 185, 236, 400
Chaplin, Charlie, 18, 22
Cinematograph Trade, 95–6
citizenship, 148, 410, 1, 2, 7, 32, 61
Clot, Antoine Barthelemy, 99
Columbus, Christopher, 245, 251, 252
counter-modernity, 66, 67, 244, 270
counter-*tafarnug*, 258, 259, 269, 271
critical realism, 29, 31, 32, 34, 35, 39, 41, 44, 45, 47

Dahaya al-Jahl, 101, 103
Daghir, Asiya, 308, 309
Dalton, Charles, 91
darar 79, 155, 158, 209
dar' al-mafasid, 155
Darwish, Sayyid, 5, 9, 296
De Certeau, Michel, 46
DeMille, Cecil B., 22, 119
despotism, 33, 109, 320
Dinshuway, 100, 121
Dixon, Sir Pierson, 126
Doris, Umberto, 10
Downing Street (London), 126
dominant modernity, 52, 198
Dumas, Alexandre, 14, 307
Dumu' al-Hub, 28
Dunya, 68, 399–406

effendi, 50–1, 54–6, 67–8, 92, 204, 215–17, 220, 274–81, 285–6, 302–27, 337–8, 347–8, 351, 354
emergent modernity, 68, 346, 359, 370, 398
Emerson, John, 320
European Administration, 99

Fahmi, 'Abd al-Rahman, 11
Fa'iq [Fayi'], Hasan, 266
Fakhir Fakhir, 62, 249, 291, 413, 421, 422
Fakhri, Thuraya, 12, 297, 370
false consciousness, xvii, 12, 15, 18, 49, 51, 53, 66, 67, 68, 204, 219, 230, 245, 252, 265, 271, 274, 286, 302, 307, 312, 317, 318, 322, 324, 402, 405
Farah, Iskandar, 101
Fawzi, Layla, 12, 62, 63, 229, 245, 330, 333
Federation of British Film Industries, 95, 96
Fi Sabil al-Istiqlal, 101
fisq, 113
Ford, 317
Foucault, Michel, xviii, 47–9
Four Feathers, 106–8
fujur, 113

Ga'far Brothers, 123–38
Galal Studio, 123
Gamil, 'Ulwiyya, 12, 357
Gamil, Sana', 34
Gaslight, 247
Ghazal al-Banat, 124
governmentality, 49, 306, 307
Greg, Sir Robert, 87–91

Habermas, Jürgen, xviii, 18, 48, 49
Hafiz, Bahiga, 12, 254, 62, 93
Hanbalis, 79, 152
Hart, William, 14
High Institute of Cinema, xv
hiyal, 254
Hukum Qaraqush, 320
Husayn, Ilham, 12
Husayn, Taha, 89
Husni, Su'ad, 32, 36, 37, 296

Ibn 'Abd al-Barr, 381
Ibn Abi Bakr, al-Qasim b. Muhammad, 157

ibn al-balad, 2, 3, 278, 279, 311, 313, 315, 317, 318, 319, 321, 322, 324, 325, 326, 375
Ibn al-Haddad, 67, 68, 237, 388, 392, 396
Ibn al-Hayathm, 60
Ibn al-Khattab, 'Umar, 157
Ibn al-Muqqafa, 291
Ibn 'Arabi, 60
Ibn Danyal, 61
Ibn Ishaq, Hunayn, 60
Ibn Khalid, Zayd, 157
Ibn Numayr, Yasar, 157
Ibn Rushd, 60
Ibn Sina, 60
Ibn Thabit, Hassan, 278
Ibn Tufayl, 60
Ibn Yaqzan, Hayy, 66
Ibrahim, 'Abd al-Mun'im, 33
Ibrahim, Raqiya, 2, 39, 41, 42, 62, 63, 64, 127, 229, 276, 288, 289, 399
'idda, 382
ijma', 153
ijtihad, 154, 414
indigène, 240
instrumental rationality, 283, 312, 325, 334, 336, 338, 341
irtidad, 429
isfaf, 362
Isha'it Hub, 320
ishtiqaq, 315
Islamic acting, 165
Islamic law, 69, 150, 156, 162, 180, 181, 253, 254, 255, 258, 294, 295, 302, 328, 338, 410, 411, 414
Islamic personal law, 253, 255, 256, 258, 381, 382
istitaba, 429
'Izz al-Din, Ibrahim, 180

Jaffa, 10
jahiliyya, 300
jalb al-masalih, 79
jinas, 315, 226

Kalila and Dimna, 291
Kamal, Prince Yusuf, 90
Kamil, Hasan, 394
Kant, Immanuel, 48, 372
Karim, Muhammad, xv, 3, 10, 13, 15, 16, 23, 29, 31, 44, 62, 63, 66, 67, 93, 167, 198, 254, 281, 328, 399
Kariyuka, Tahiyya, 12, 409
Kazan, Elia, 117
Khadra wa-l-Sindibad al-Qibli, 67, 259
khala'a, 148
khali', 113, 214
Khalid, Rawhiya, 12
Khalil, 'Abd al-'Aziz, 244, 298
Khartoum, 10
Khawaga, 2, 5, 11, 12, 13, 16, 17, 18, 21, 23, 25, 26, 27, 28, 56, 88, 115, 121, 229, 232, 235, 242, 380
khawaga, 1, 2, 5, 6, 7, 10, 11, 13, 17, 28, 105, 275, 276, 277, 278, 371, 420
Khedive Isma'il, 1, 8
Khulusi, Samira, 12, 13, 62, 68, 200, 209, 210, 364, 347, 351, 352, 407
King Farouk, 44, 91, 122, 135
Korsakov, Rimsky, Nikolai, 259
kufr, 69, 163, 176, 334, 420, 426, 427, 428, 429, 430, 431, 432

Lama, Badr, 217
Lama Studio, 123
Lampson, Miles, 58, 108, 85, 86, 108
Lashin, 109
Lausanne Conference, 2
Layla Bint al-Rif, 68, 220–8, 263, 382–4, 386
Lean, David, 134
Le Comte de Monte-Cristo, 309

Lloyd, George, 82, 83, 87, 90
Lumière Brothers, 1, 80

Ma'alihshi Ya Zahr, 67, 308
Macdonald, David, 134
madaniyya, 259
makruh, 152
Mahfouz, Naguib, 167
Makhluf, Hasanayn, 66
male gaze, 264
Malikis, 79, 152
Ma'luf, Yusuf, 40
Man al-Gani, 67, 295–304, 338
Mann, Heinrich, 109
Mansur, Salah, 33, 36
Maqar, 23
maqasid al-shari'a, 153
Marconi, 86
Mar'i, Hasan, 100–1
mariq, 44, 148
Marun al-Naqqash, 8
maslaha, 66, 79, 147, 153–62, 165, 176, 177, 179, 180–5
maslaha mursala, 79, 155
Matruh, 308
Mecca, 154, 166, 168, 256, 401, 430
Medina, 154, 157, 168, 236, 256, 294
Metro Golden Mayer Theater, 309
Metropolis, 20
Min Fat Qadimuh, 109
Misr Studio, 123
Mitchel, Timothy, xviii
Mizrahi, Tugu, 13, 22, 29, 31, 62, 63, 67, 68, 93, 220–9, 259, 263, 265, 304, 382–9, 407, 416
modernity, xviii, xix, 1, 12, 13, 15, 18, 29, 45–69, 122, 204, 209, 212, 215, 219, 230, 232, 235, 238, 240, 244, 245,, 252, 253, 259, 261, 265–270, 274, 277, 278, 281, 283, 284, 285, 286, 287, 288, 290, 291, 300, 302, 306, 307, 308, 312, 317, 318, 319, 322, 324, 325, 326, 327, 334, 346, 347, 348, 349, 353, 358, 359, 360, 370, 371, 378, 382, 383, 387, 388, 389, 391–9, 402, 403, 405, 413, 421, 424, 432, 433
Morsi, Muhammad, xiv
Mughamarat Khadra, 67, 259, 260–5
muhallil, 254, 255
Muhammad, Fardus, 6, 10, 22, 62, 127, 242, 243, 249, 275, 286, 284, 386
Mumtaz, I'tidal, 105, 106, 119, 120, 122
Munib, Mary, 10, 62, 63, 299
Murad, Layla, 12, 31, 62, 63, 64, 183, 212, 221, 223, 226–8, 253, 281, 283, 308, 309, 320, 379, 383
Mursi, Ahmad Kamil, 29, 62, 68, 93, 115, 406, 410, 418
Musa, Salama, 174–5
Muslim Brotherhood, 123, 165, 166, 167–9, 174–9
Mustafa, Niyazi, 5, 6, 31, 44, 63, 93, 184, 256, 274, 277, 278, 438

Najib, Muhammad, 10
nakba, 110, 123, 327
naksa, 32
Nasiban Studio, 123
Nasser, Gamal Abdel, 32, 44, 51, 160, 167, 169
naqs, 152
Nefertiti, 88, 267
Nihas, Jibra'il, 123, 124
Nihas Studio, 125–8

Odeon, 128–36
One Thousand and One Nights, 61, 220, 259
Orfanelli, Elvisi, 10
Ottoman Empire, 2, 7, 100, 182
Overseas, 128–34

painting, 150, 151, 159, 160, 162, 182
Palache Committee, 136
patriarchal gaze, 350–8
Pinky, 177
Port Said, 87
Printing Press Administration, 99, 105, 119, 122, 164
Prince Talal, 132, 133, 137
public culture, xiv, 1
public sphere, xiv, xv, xvii, xviii,, 13, 15, 28, 45, 46, 51, 52, 56, 57, 60, 64, 92, 240, 303, 325, 351, 353, 359, 360, 361, 378, 388, 401, 404, 433

Qura, Fathi, 267

Rami, Ahmad, 109
Rank, J. Arthur, 126–38
Rashid, Mahmud Khalil, 93
residual modernity, 52, 67
Rida, Rashid, 66, 156, 158, 162, 178, 180
Rivoli cinema, 122, 123, 126, 129–36
Riyad, Husayn, 10, 62, 120
Rizq, Amina, 10, 12, 22, 62, 63, 296, 409, 416, 418
Rushdi, Fatima, 12, 62, 63, 93, 104, 167, 215, 217, 218, 327
Rusti, Istifan, 2, 3, 4, 5, 10, 62, 63, 93, 276, 309, 330, 396
Ruza al-Yusuf, 23

sadd al-dhara'i', 2, 66, 79, 154, 155
Safir Gahannam, 67, 244–53
Salama fi Khayr, 247–81
Salim al-Naqqash, 8
Sannu', Ya'qub, 8, 9
Sarhan, Shukri, 33, 35
sculpting, 150
sequestration, 130, 137
Shafi'is, 79, 152, 294

Shafiq, Fu'ad, 367–9
Shakib, Mimi, 10, 12, 62, 63, 313, 420, 422, 428
Shakib, Zuzu, 10, 12, 62, 222, 225, 226, 266, 270, 304
Shakespeare, William, 14, 253
Shawqi, Farid, 39, 254, 255, 421
shirk, 152
Show Life, 95
Shubra Studio, 123
Sidqi, Husayn, 10, 13, 29, 62, 63, 68, 111, 115, 118, 120, 121, 179, 215, 218, 327, 333, 370, 376
Sidqi, Isma'il, 12, 81, 84
Sirag Munir, 10, 17, 32, 39, 51, 52, 56, 61, 62, 168, 310, 319, 421, 404, 410, 424
social justice, 239, 262, 269, 301, 307, 324, 388, 390, 393, 403
Suez Canal, 252, 112
Suez Crisis, 5
supremacist, xvi, 278, 279, 331, 383, 385, 389, 424, 429

tafarnug, 52–6
Talaq Su'ad Hanim, 67, 253–65
Tal'at Harb, 11, 22, 23, 24
tarbush, 277
ta'ssul, 53–6
taswir, 151–3, 156–62, 177, 182, 184
tawakul, 205, 367
tawkkul, 68, 205, 207, 367, 371, 380, 381 394, 395
Taylor, Charles, xviii, 433
The Diadem of Stars, 91
The Merchant of Venice, 253
The Red Shoes, 134, 135
Three Musketeers, 121, 122
Tommy Atkins, 95
Tugu Studio, 123
Tuwayma, Admun, 275

Umm Kulthum, 12, 62, 63, 109, 135, 169, 183, 199, 243, 296, 378

Wahbi, Yusuf, 7, 11, 13, 25, 27, 29, 38, 43, 62, 63, 67, 69, 93, 115, 116, 117, 118, 120, 123, 124, 147, 174, 184, 185, 220, 221, 221, 228, 229, 236, 237, 244, 246, 249, 253, 274, 288, 314, 320, 386, 388, 407, 419, 420, 422, 423, 427, 428, 433
Wagdi, Anwar, 10, 13, 29, 31, 62, 63, 67, 115, 116, 117, 124, 212, 215, 253, 254, 255, 256, 296, 388
Wafi, 'Abd al-Majid, 153, 155
westernization, xv, 13, 23, 61, 199, 203, 204, 380, 389
Wilhelm II, 20

Williams, Raymond, xviii, 46
World War II, 28, 55, 64, 65, 80, 85, 88, 106, 108, 122, 123, 132, 137, 239, 244, 245, 247, 253, 266, 267, 308, 227, 421

Yahya al-Hub, 281–5
Yasin, Isma'il, 10, 261, 392
Yasqut al-Isti'mar, 121
Yawm Sa'id, 211–15, 285–95, 353–8

Zaghlul, Sa'd, 5, 11, 14, 16, 28, 81, 82, 83, 84
Zaghlul, Safiyya, 28
Zanuck, Darryl F., 117
Zaydan, Jurji, 8
Zoltan Korda, 106
Zuhur al-Islam, 180, 181, 184

EU representative:
Easy Access System Europe
Mustamäe tee 50, 10621 Tallinn, Estonia
Gpsr.requests@easproject.com